FLUID MECHANICS HYDRAULICS AND ENVIRONMENTAL ENGINEERING

The Essential User Friendly Books Including Over 350 Solved Examples

Book One for First and Second Year Undergraduate and Diploma Students and a reference for Practising Engineers

Companion Book for Third and Fourth Year Students
APPLIED HYDRAULICS, HYDROLOGY AND ENVIRONMENTAL ENGINEERING
Published Separately

Professor S K Al Naib
BSc (Eng) PhD (Lond) ACGI DIC CEng FICE FIMGT
Professor of Civil Engineering and Head of Department
University of East London
Great Britain

Contents and Preface

PREFACE

Dear Reader - This book has been written in order to share with you my knowledge of the specialist subject of fluids which I have taught for many years. I have set up the book to take you through a course, just as I would if you came to me and attended some of my classes. If you complete the exercises progressively as they appear, by the time you have finished you will have covered a comprehensive course. For maximum benefit I suggest you read through the theory and exercises of each chapter once. Then slowly read it again, only this time do each example of your choice in depth. If you can, work through the exercises with a colleague or friend.

Each chapter commences with a concise theory which will provide an invaluable reference when you are working on that area of your study. The solved examples have been selected to demonstrate to you the various engineering aspects of design and construction. The ***miniature encyclopaedia*** has been arranged to help you work through practical and theoretical exercises in fluids in order to provide solutions to 'real' problems.

ISBN 1 8745 36 058
First Printing October 1997

Internationally Acknowledged Books by the Author

"Fluid Mechanics, Hydraulics and Envir. Eng."	**ISBN 1 8745 36 066**
"Applied Hydraulics, Hydrology and Envir. Eng."	**ISBN 1 8745 36 058**
"Jet Mechanics and Hydraulic Structures"	**ISBN 0 9019 87 832**
"London Dockland Guide" Heritage Panorama	**ISBN 1 8745 36 031**
"London Illustrated" History, Current & Future	**ISBN 1 8745 36 015**
"Discover London Docklands" A to Z Guide	**ISBN 1 8745 36 007**
"London Docklands" Past, Present and Future	**ISBN 1 8745 36 023**
"European Docklands"Past, Present & Future	**ISBN 0 9019 87 824**
"Dockland" Historical Survey	**ISBN 0 9089 87 800**

The author is Professor of Civil Engineering and Head of Department at the University of East London, England.
(Tel: 0181 590 7000/7722 ext 2478/2531, Fax: 0181 849 3423)

Please Order through: Research Books, P. O. Box 82, Romford, Essex RM6 5BY, Great Britain.

Printed by KPC Group, London & Ashford, Kent.

PART I

BASIC FLUID MECHANICS AND HYDRAULICS

Book One - Theory and Solution Manual

This book is student centred and contains a basic and intermediate treatment of Fluid Mechanics and Hydraulics, intended to serve first and second year degree and diploma students and their lecturers. Whilst written mainly with the needs of students in mind, the book should prove of value to professional engineers who are actively engaged in the practice of Hydraulic and Environmental Engineering.

Each chapter contains a concise theory, extensive worked out examples and problems enhancing understanding of theory. Diagrams have been inserted in all sections to make them self-contained. In the book, computer applications and examples are briefly given as a method in the solution of engineering design problems. The fourteen chapters cover more material than that required for the usual first and second years course. The book is a complete and expert source of problems and solutions. Any type of example pertinent to the student's understanding of the subject is included.

Chapter One - Fluid Properties

Definitions of the quantities of density, specific gravity, specific volume, pressure, viscosity and surface tension. Ideal fluid theory. SI units and dimensions. Useful data on properties. Measurement of viscosity. Solved examples and problems. (p4 - p6)

Chapter Two - Fluid Statics

Relationship between pressure and elevation for a fluid. Absolute and gauge pressure. Pressure measurement and examples. Magnitude and line of action of pressure forces on plane and curved surfaces immersed in fluids of uniform density, metacentre and height. Solved examples and problems. (p7 - p16)

Compressible Fluids

Laws of a perfect fluid. Stability of the atmosphere. International standards. Solved examples and problems. (p17 - p18)

Chapter Three - Kinematics and Dynamics of Fluids

Definitions of steady, unsteady, uniform and non-uniform flow. Streamlines and tubes. Equation of continuity. Flow net. Euler's equation. Bernoulli's equation. Momentum principle and application to impact of jets. Velocity and discharge measurements. Pitot and Pitot-static tubes. Applications of total head equation to nozzles, pipe bends and orifices. Solved examples and problems. (p19 - p28)

Chapter Four - Fluid Friction

Laminar and turbulent flows. Relation between head loss and velocity. Derivation of Poiseuille's equation. Turbulent flow in pipes. Reynolds number and friction factor. Secondary losses in pipes. Analysis of pipelines. Pipes in parallel and in series. Uniform flow in open channels. Solved examples and problems on pipes and channels. (p29 - p46)

Chapter Five - Dimensional Analysis

General theorem of dimensional analysis. Applications to wholly and partially submerged bodies. Reynolds and Froude numbers as examples of flow criteria. Lift and drag forces and coefficients. Solved examples and problems. (p47 - p51)

Chapter Six - Unsteady Flow

Quasi-steady analysis of time of emptying a container. Applications to tanks and reservoirs with orifices and notches. Solved examples and problems. (p52 - p56).

CHAPTER ONE

FLUID PROPERTIES

Introduction

Fluid Mechanics is the special branch of general mechanics that applies its fundamental principles to fluids. These principles are Newton's laws of motion, the conservation of energy, and the indestructibility of matter. The word "fluid" comes from the Latin "fluidus" which means a substance having particles that change their relative positions. Fluid refers, therefore, to both gases and liquids, as opposed to solids. A liquid has a volume and mass but it lacks shape, i.e. it has little resistance to distortion. A gas lacks volume and shape but it has mass and is very compressible.

Fluid Properties

A fluid is characterised by its ability to flow. Unlike a solid, a fluid will deform under shear stress no matter how small that shear stress is provided that sufficient time is allowed for deformation to take place. Hence a fluid is shapeless, and will take the form of the vessel containing it.

Density: The density of a fluid is its mass per unit volume; it is designated by the symbol ρ. The units are kg/m^3 (ML^{-3}). For water ρ is 1000kg/m^3 at 4°C. There is a slight decrease in density with increasing temperature, but in practice this is not significant and is usually ignored.

Specific gravity (Relative Density): The specific gravity of a fluid is the ratio of its density to that of water. It is designated by the letters *SG* and being a ratio is dimensionless.

Specific weight: This is the weight force of a fluid in a unit volume, for water $w = \rho g = 9.81 \times 1000 = 9.81 kN/m^3$.

Specific volume: This is the volume of fluid contained in a unit mass, that is the reciprocal of density $(1/\rho)$.

Pressure intensity: The pressure on a surface is the force per unit area. It is denoted by the letter p and typical units are kN/m^2 (ML^{-1} T^{-2}).

Viscosity: This is the property of fluids which produces resistance to rate of change of shape. If we have two solid parallel plates at a small distance y apart, the lower one at rest and the upper one is moving with a velocity v, the intervening space being occupied by a fluid, a thin film of fluid will adhere to each plate and the rest of the fluid will shear in thin layers, Fig.1.1.

The velocity of each layer depends on its distance from the lower plate. This velocity distribution may often be assumed to be linear between the two plates. At a given temperature it has been found experimentally that the resistance offered by most fluids to the motion of the upper plate is given by $P = \mu A\,(dv/dy)$ (1.1)

where A denotes the area of the upper plate and μ is a constant, called the coefficient of viscosity. The intensity of viscous shear or viscous shear stress for this type of fluid is

$$\tau = P/A = \mu\,(dv/dy) \qquad (1.2)$$

Coefficient of Viscosity μ is measured in Ns/m^2 (ML^{-1} T^{-1}).

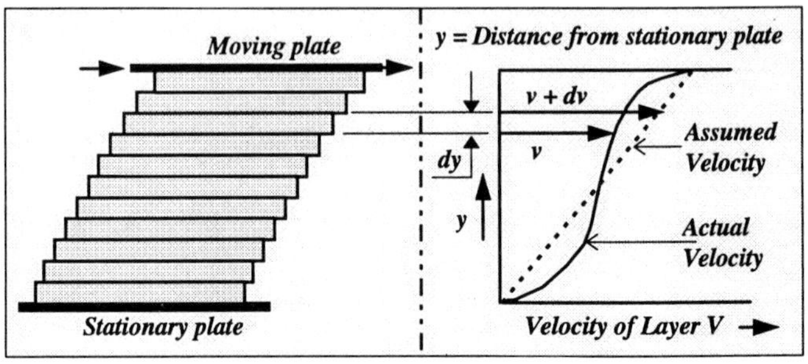

Fig.1.1- Viscous shear between two parallel plates.

Kinematic Viscosity: This is an alternative way of describing viscosity denoted by the symbol $\nu = \mu/\rho$; it is used as a convenient way of expressing viscosity in equations where the density ρ of the fluid occurs. The units are m^2/s (L^{2}T^{-1}).

Compressibility of Fluids: Application of a force F, Fig.1.2, to the piston will increase the pressure p in the fluid and cause the volume to decrease from V_1 to V_2. Plotting p against V_2/V_1 produces the volumetric stress - strain diagram giving the **Bulk Modulus, K,**

$$K = \text{Pressure stress} / \text{Volumetric Strain} = -dp/(dV/V_1) \qquad (1.3)$$

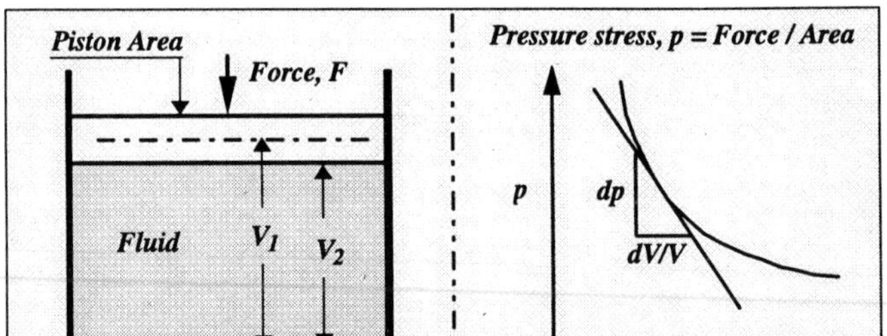

Fig.1.2- Compressibility of a fluid.

Surface Tension: Liquids have properties such as cohesion and adhesion, both of which are forms of molecular attraction. Cohesion enables a liquid to resist tensile stress, while adhesion enables it to adhere to another body. Surface tension is due to cohesion between particles at the surface of a liquid. Capillarity is due to both cohesion and adhesion.

When the former is of less effect than the latter, the liquid will wet a solid surface with which it is in contact and rise by h at the point of contact. If cohesion predominates the liquid surface will be depressed at the point of contact. Thus capillarity causes water to rise in a glass tube while mercury is depressed below the true level, Fig. 1.3.

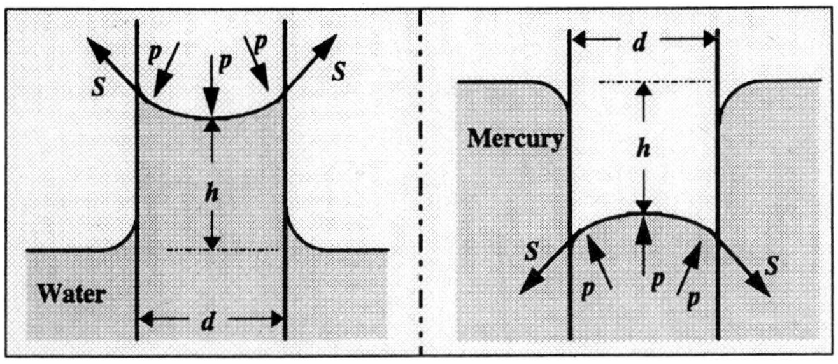

Fig.1.3- Capillarity effect in tubes.

Surface tension is the property which allows a vessel to be filled slightly above the brim and yet not spill, and which allows a needle to float on the surface of a liquid. The effect is similar to the surface acting as a uniformly stressed elastic membrane. The surface tension forces acting across a line on the surface of a liquid is proportional to the length of the line and acts in a direction at right angles to the line. Hence, surface tension per unit length (σ) is measured in N/m (MT^{-2}).

Ideal Fluid Theory

The preceding paragraphs have reviewed the principal physical properties of fluids. It is however, rare to take into account all the properties involved in a specific engineering problem, for the mathematics soon become too complicated and a simplification is necessary. The simplification is usually done by assuming that the fluid is ideal. That is to say it complies with the definition of a fluid but its coefficient of viscosity is zero, so that a velocity gradient cannot cause any shear stresses. Further, the ideal fluid is compressible, has no surface tension and does not vaporise. Many problems of fluid motion can thus be solved.

SI Units and Dimensions

SI is the abbreviation in all languages for the Systéme International d'Unités which is a coherent system having six basic units. In this system the product or quotient of any two unit quantities is the unit of the resultant quantity, e.g. a unit force results from multiplying unit mass by unit acceleration. Hence a force of 1 Newton applied to a mass of 1 kilogram will result in an acceleration of 1 metre per second squared. The basic units applicable to fluid mechanics are:

Quantity	Name	Symbol	Dimensions
Mass	kilogram	kg	M
Length	metre	m	L
Time	second	s	T
Temperature	Celsius	°C	-
Derived physical quantities are:			
Force	Newton	N	MLT^{-2}
Work, energy	joule	J = Nm	ML^2T^{-2}
Power	watt	W = J/s = Nm/s	ML^2T^{-3}
Pressure	Pascal	N/m²	$ML^{-1}T^{-2}$

Useful Data on Fluid Properties

Density of Air	**1.2 kg/m³**
Dynamic Viscosity of Air	1.8×10^{-5} **Ns/m²**
Kinematic Viscosity of Air	1.5×10^{-5} **m²/s**
Density of Water	**1000 kg/m³**
Dynamic Viscosity of Water	1.1×10^{-3} **Ns/m²**
Kinematic Viscosity of Water	1.1×10^{-6} **m²/s**
Surface Tension of Water	7.35×10^{-2} **N/m**
Bulk Modulus of Water	21×10^{5} **kN/m²**
Specific Weight of Water	**9810 N/m³**
Kinematic Viscosity of Petrol	8.2×10^{-4} **m²/s**
Specific Gravity of Petrol	**0.82**
Fluid pressure units: 1 Pascal = 1 Pa = 1 N/m² and 1bar = 10^5 N/m²	

Note multiples used: $\times 10^9$ (giga G), $\times 10^6$ (mega M), $\times 10^3$ (kilo k), $\times 10^{-3}$ (milli m). For example, for measurement of atmospheric pressure 1 millibar = 10^{-3}N/m².

Measurement of Viscosity

The coefficient of viscosity of a liquid can be found experimentally by measurement of time t of fall of a steel ball in the liquid between two reference marks L apart. Consider a sphere of diameter d and density ρ_s falling through a fluid of density ρ_l and viscosity μ. When the sphere is falling with a uniform velocity U, the downward weight force must equal the viscous drag on the sphere. By a complex mathematical process, Stokes derived that the drag force to be $3\pi\mu dU$.

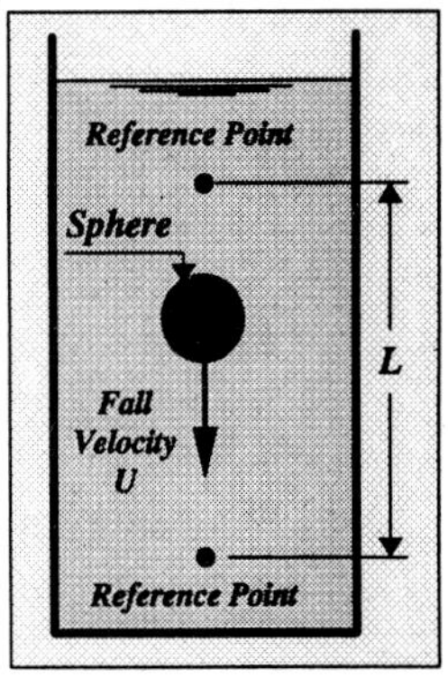

Equating these forces:

$$\frac{(\rho_s - \rho_l) \times \pi g d^3}{6} = 3\pi \mu dU \quad (1.4)$$

Hence ***coefficient of viscosity,***

$$\mu = \frac{(\rho_s - \rho_l) \times g d^2}{18U} \quad (1.5)$$

Since velocity of fall, $U = L/t$, then

$$\mu = \frac{(\rho_s - \rho_l) \times g d^2 t}{18L} \quad (1.6)$$

Advantage of Lubrication

Consider a flat rectangular plate 2m × 3m and of mass 7000kg, which slides over a level surface with a steady velocity 0.5m/s. Calculate the force required to overcome friction when: (a) there is no lubricant fluid between the plate and the surface and the coefficient of solid friction is $\eta = 0.2$, and (b) there is a film of lubricant, 1mm thick, of kinematic viscosity $v = 0.001 m^2/s$ and specific gravity $SG = 0.7$.

(a) With no lubricant the force, $F_a = \eta \times \text{Weight of plate}$

$F_a = 0.2 \times 9.81 \times 7000 = 13{,}734N$.

(b) With lubricant the force, $F_b = A\mu \times \frac{dV}{dy}$, ***(A = area of plate)***

$\mu = \rho_l v_l = SG \times \rho_W v = 0.7 \times 1000 \times 0.001 = 0.7 Ns/m^2$.

The force, $F_b = 3 \times 2 \times 0.7 \times \frac{0.5}{0.001} = 2100N$. $\therefore F_b << F_a$.

Examples on Fluid Properties

Units and Dimensions

(1) The density of water ρ_w is 1000kg/m^3. What are its specific weight *w* and its specific volume?

Specific weight, $w = \rho_w g = 1000 \times 9.81 = 9810\ N/m^3$.

Specific volume, $SV = 1/\rho_w = 1/1000 = 0.001\ m^3/kg$.

(2) What is the density of glycerine if its specific gravity is SG = 1.26?

$\rho_g = 1.26 \times \rho_w = 1.26 \times 1000 = 1260 kg/m^3$.

(3) If 5m^3 of oil weighs 43,000N, calculate: its specific weight, its specific gravity and its density. Assume the acceleration due to gravity 9.0m/s^2.

$$\textit{Specific weight} = \frac{43,000}{5} = 8,600 N/m^3.$$

$$\textit{Specific gravity} = \frac{8600}{9 \times 1000} = 0.956.$$

Density (relative) $= 0.956 \times 1000 = 956 kg/m^3$.

(4) A liquid decreases in volume by 6% when subjected to a pressure of 35 × 10^6 N/m^2. Calculate its **Bulk Modulus of Elasticity (*K*).**

$$K = \frac{\text{Pressure stress}}{\text{Volumetric strain}} = \frac{35 \times 10^6}{0.06} = 5.83 \times 10^8\ N/m^2.$$

Shaft Rotating in a Bearing

A shaft of diameter 74.9mm rotates in a bearing of diameter 76.1mm and of length 75mm. The annular space between the shaft and the bearing is filled with oil having a coefficient of viscosity 9.25×10^{-1}Ns/m^2. Determine the power used in overcoming viscous resistance in this bearing at 1400 rpm.

Shear stress, $\tau = \mu\,(dv/dy)$.

For small thickness t, $\tau = \mu\,(v/t)$

Viscous force on shaft $\tau = \mu\,(v/t) \times \pi DL$

Power absorbed by friction, P,

P = Viscous force × Peripheral velocity $= \mu \times (v^2/t) \times \pi DL$

$$v = \frac{\pi D \times 1400}{60} = \frac{\pi \times 0.075 \times 1400}{60} = 5.495 m/s.$$

$$t = \frac{76.1 - 74.9}{2} = 0.6 mm.$$

$$\textit{Power absorbed, } P = \frac{0.925 \times 5.495^2 \times \pi \times 0.075^2}{0.0006} = 822W.$$

Force on Shaft Moving Inside a Cylinder

Define "Coefficient of Viscosity" and derive an expression for its dimensions in terms of Mass, Length and Time. A smooth cylinder 50.1mm inside diameter and 100mm. long is placed with its axis vertical. If the clearance space is entirely filled with oil of viscosity 2.58 Ns/m^2, calculate the force to push a shaft of 50mm diameter through the cylinder with a velocity of 0.6m/s.

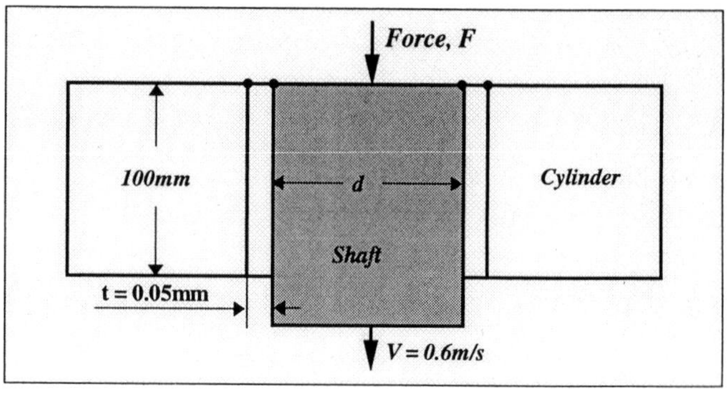

In laminar flow, the cohesion of fluid creates the property of viscosity which gives rise to viscous shear stresses between layers when they have different speeds. At a given temperature, the ratio of the shear stress, τ, to the velocity gradient is found experimentally to be constant, i.e. $\mu = \tau / (dv/dy)$, where μ = constant and known as the coefficient of viscosity. The dimensions of viscosity are seen to be:

$ML^{-1}T^{-2}\,(LT^{-1}/L) = ML^{-1}T^{-1}\,(M/LT)$

Shear stress, $\tau = \mu\,(dv/dy)$. We assume that the clearance between the cylinder and the side is so small that $\tau = \mu\,(v/t)$.

$$\text{But the shear stress, } \tau = \frac{\textit{Force}}{\textit{Surface area}} = \frac{F}{\pi\, dl} = \frac{\mu v}{t}$$

Force required to push shaft,

$$F = \frac{\mu v \times \pi\, dl}{t} = \frac{2.58 \times 0.6 \times \pi \times 0.05 \times 0.1}{0.00005} = 486N.$$

Problems on Fluid Properties

[1] A piston 119.6mm diameter and 140mm long works in a cylinder 120mm diameter. If the lubricating oil which fills the space between them has a viscosity of 0.65Ns/m^2, calculate the speed with which the piston will move through the cylinder when an axial load of 0.86 kg is applied.
(0.493m/s)

[2] A 250mm diameter piston 200mm long is concentric with a cylinder of 253mm bore and the space between the piston and the cylinder is filled with oil of viscosity 8.42 × 10^{-2} Ns/m^2. Calculate the power dissipated in overcoming viscous resistance when the piston is moved at a uniform velocity 0.5m/s. (4.42 watts)

CHAPTER TWO

FLUID STATICS

Introduction

Fluid statics is concerned with fluids at rest and treated in two parts : the study of pressure and its variation throughout a fluid and the study of pressure forces on finite surfaces. Since there is no motion of a fluid layer relative to an adjacent layer, there are no shear stresses in the fluid. Hence, all free bodies in fluid statics have only normal pressure forces on them.

Unit Pressure

The unit pressure, which is the intensity of pressure at any point, is the amount of pressure per unit area. If the unit pressure is the same at every point on any area, A, on which the total pressure force is P,

Pressure intensity, $p = P/A$ (2.1)

If, however, the unit pressure is different at different points, the unit pressure at any point is equal to the total pressure on a small differential area surrounding the point divided by the differential area, or

$p = dP/dA$ (2.2)

Pressure Variation in Vertical Direction

Consider a free body of fluid (Fig.2.1a) consisting of a cylinder of fluid of area A, with axis vertical and height dz. The base is at elevation z from an arbitrary datum.

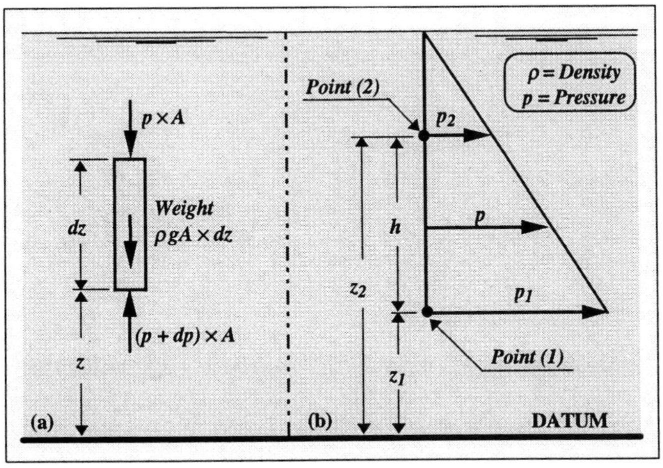

Fig.2.1- Hydrostatic pressure.

Since no shear forces exist, the two pressure forces and weight shown must be in equilibrium, so

$$pA-(p+dp)\times A+\rho gA\times dz=0 \tag{2.3}$$

In the limit as the volume reduces to a point,

$$dp = -\rho g \times dz \tag{2.4}$$

Consider two points 1 and 2 in a liquid of constant density ρ.

Integrating equation (2.4), $\int_1^2 dp = -\int_1^2 \rho g\, dz$. Therefore,

$p_2 - p_1 = -\rho g \times (z_2 - z_1) = -\rho g h$, or

Pressure head, $h = (p_1 - p_2)/\rho g$ (2.5)

If point *(2)* is at the liquid surface where the pressure is atmospheric (zero gauge) then $h = p_1/\rho g$ or in general

Head, $h = p/\rho g$. i.e. ***Pressure at a point,*** $p = \rho g h$ (2.6)

Therefore, the pressure at a point depends on local acceleration g and its position below the liquid surface. For constant density ρ and g, the pressure p varies linearly with the head h below the liquid surface.

Absolute and Gauge Pressure

Most pressures measured in fluid mechanics are relative pressures and above atmospheric pressure. It is usual therefore to regard atmospheric pressure as datum and quote pressures as being so much above atmospheric. Such pressures are referred to as gauge pressures when above atmospheric and vacuum pressures when below it. If, however, true zero is taken as datum, pressures are quoted as absolute. Standard atmospheric pressure is the mean pressure at sea level, 0.76 metres of mercury or approximately 10 metres head of water.

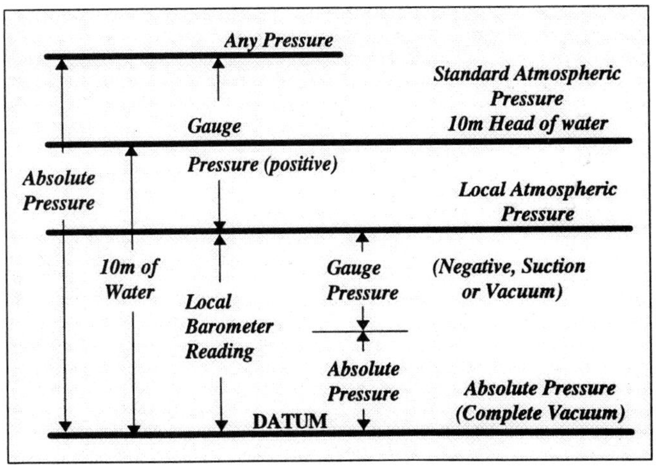

Fig.2.2- Units and scales for pressure measurement.

Pressure Measurement

There are three principal methods of measuring pressure.

1- Gauges Measuring Absolute Pressure

Mercury Barometer: The barometer is used for measuring the atmospheric pressure. It consists of a tube 0.9m long filled with mercury with top end closed and the bottom immersed in a vessel containing mercury. The height of the mercury column in the tube above the level of mercury in the vessel is equivalent to the atmospheric head which is normally 0.76m of mercury and is equivalent to 10m of water.

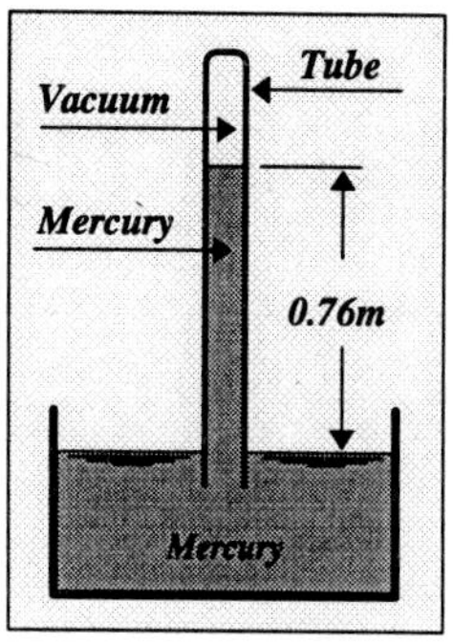

2- Gauges Measuring Relative to Atmospheric Pressure

(i) Bourdon Gauge: The pressure element (Fig.2.3) is a hollow, curved flat metallic tube, closed at one end and connected to the fluid whose pressure is to be measured at the other end. The fluid pressure acts on the interior of the tube, tending to straighten it, and so, by means of a linkage, moving the pointer over the scale. When the inside and the outside of the tubes are at the same pressure the dial reads zero.

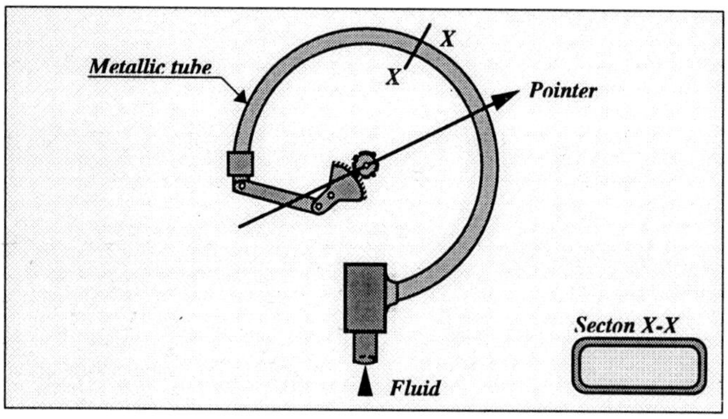

Fig.2.3- Bourdon gauge used for commercial pressure measurement in a pipeline

(ii) Manometers: The simplest type of manometer, known as the piezometer, is the straight vertical tube shown in Figure 2.4a. The manometers shown in Figures 2.4a and 2.4b use the fluid whose pressure is being measured. For the manometer in Fig.2.4a the pressure at $A = \rho g h_1$, where ρ is the density of the fluid. For the manometer shown in Fig.2.4b the pressure at $A = -\rho g h_2$, i.e. the pressure at A is less than atmospheric.

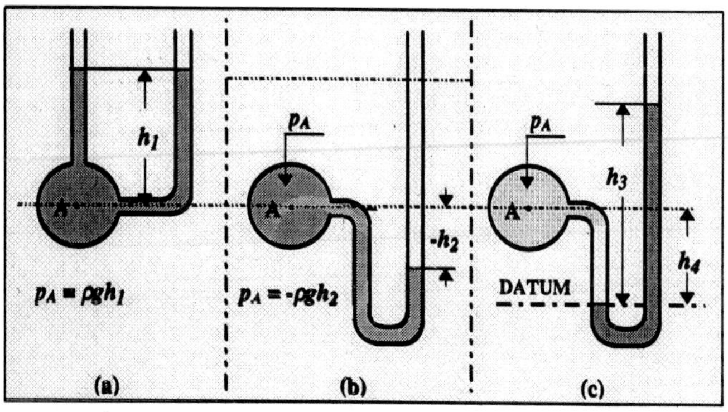

Fig.2.4- Examples on simple manometers.

The U-tube manometer shown in Fig.2.4c is useful when the fluid being measured is a gas which would escape or when the pressure to be measured would produce too large a head in the other types of manometer. If the density of the fluid being measured is ρ and the density of the manometer fluid is ρ_m then the pressure at point A in Fig.2.4c is

$$p_A + \rho g h_4 = \rho_m g h_3 \qquad (2.7)$$

$$p_A = \rho_m g h_3 - \rho g h_4 \qquad (2.8)$$

or the equivalent head is, $h_A = (\rho_m \times h_3 / \rho) - h_4$ (2.9)

(iii) Differential Manometer: Differential manometers can only measure the difference in pressure between two points, the pressure difference cannot be related to actual pressure.

Consider the equilibrium condition at datum level in Fig.2.5a.

$$p_A + \rho_1 g h_1 = p_B + \rho_2 g h_2 + \rho_3 g h_3 \qquad (2.10)$$

$$p_A - p_B = \rho_2 g h_2 + \rho_3 g h_3 - \rho_1 g h_1 \qquad (2.11)$$

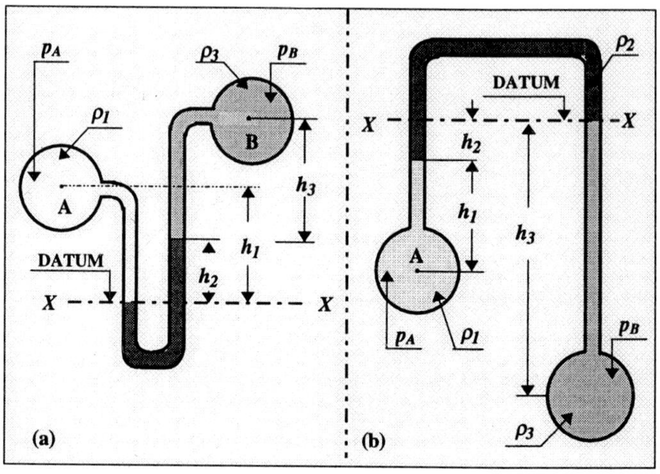

Fig.2.5- Differential manometers.

Similarly for the inverted manometer shown in Figure 2.5b

$$p_A - \rho_1 g h_1 - \rho_2 g h_2 = p_B - \rho_3 g h_3 \qquad (2.12)$$

$$p_A - p_B = \rho_1 g h_1 + \rho_2 g h_2 - \rho_3 g h_3 \qquad (2.13)$$

Applications of Manometers

(1) Determine the value of h_1 in Fig.2.4a when the pressure in the water pipe is $35kN/m^2$ gauge.

$p_A = \rho g h_1$, or

$$h_1 = \frac{p_A}{\rho g} = \frac{35 \times 10^3}{10^3 \times 9.81} = 3.57m \text{ of water}.$$

(2) Determine the value of the pressure in the water pipe when the manometer head is $h_2 = -0.9m$ (Fig.2.4b).

$p_A = -\rho g h_2 = -10^3 \times 9.81 \times 0.9 = -8.829kN/m^2$ *(gauge).*

(3) Determine the value of h_3 in Fig 2.4c if the pressure in the pipe p_A *is* $400kN/m^2$ gauge, and $h_4 = 1.8m$. The pipe carries water while the manometer fluid is mercury of SG = 13.6.

$$h_3 = \frac{p_A - \rho g h_4}{\rho_m g} = \frac{400 \times 10^3 - 10^3 \times 9.81 \times 1.8}{13.6 \times 10^3 \times 9.81} = 2.866m.$$

Examples on Pressure Measurement

Pressure Measurement in a Vertical Pipe

Oil of specific gravity 0.86 flows in a vertical pipe as shown in diagram below. Calculate the pressure p_x of the Bourdon gauge.

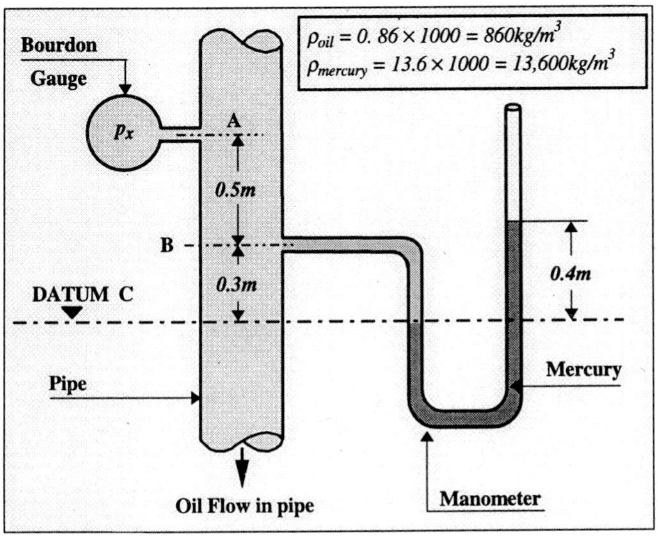

Pressure at level *C*, $p = \rho g\, h$.

$p = 13.6 \times 1000 \times 9.81 \times 0.4 = 53{,}367 N/m^2$.

Pressure at level A is less by 0.8m of oil, i.e.

$\Delta p = 0.86 \times 1000 \times 9.81 \times 0.8 = 6750 N/m^2$.

Pressure in pipe, $p_x = 53{,}367 - 6750 = 46.62 kN/m^2$.

Pressure by a Differential Manometer

The pressure difference between two pipes, both carrying water, is to be measured by means of the system of inverted U-tubes shown in the sketch below. Calculate the pressure difference between the pipes.

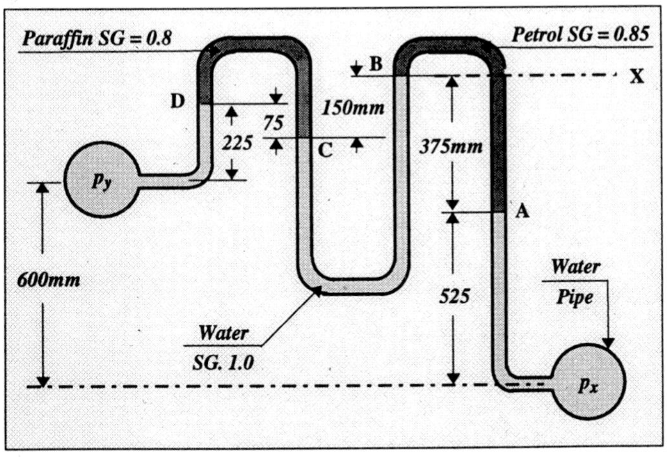

$$p_B = p_x - 1000 \times 9.81 \times 0.525 - 850 \times 9.81 \times 0.375$$

$$p_B = p_y - 1000 \times 9.81 \times 0.225 + 800 \times 9.81 \times 0.075 - 1000 \times 9.81 \times 0.15$$

$$p_x - p_y = 1000 \times 9.81 \times (0.525 + 0.85 \times 0.375 - 0.225 + 0.8 \times 0.075 - 0.15)$$

$$= 1000 \times 9.81 \times 0.5287$$

Pressure difference, $p_x - p_y = 5.187 kN/m^2$.

Pressure Difference Between Two Pipes

In the differential manometer shown below the specific gravity (relative density) of manometer liquid 1 is 0.7 and that of the liquid in the two pipes is 0.9. If the pressure in pipe B is 40 kN/m^3 , calculate the pressure in pipe A. State clearly where you take your datum. *(Take $g = 10m/s^2$).*

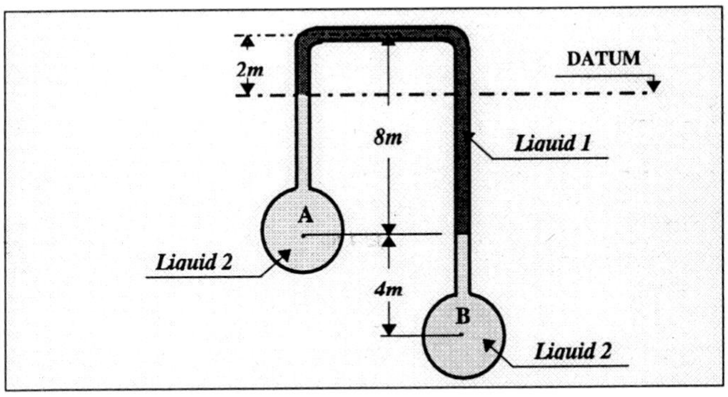

Take the datum at liquid interface in left-hand limb of the manometer. Equating pressures at this datum.

$p_A - 0.9 \times 1000 \times 10\,(8 - 2) =$

$40000 - 0.9 \times 1000 \times 10 \times 4 - 0.7 \times 1000 \times 10 \times (8\text{-}2)$.

$p_A - 54{,}000 = 40{,}000 - 36{,}000 - 42{,}000 = 38{,}000$.

Pressure in pipe A, $p_A = 16000 N/m^2 = 16 kN/m^2$.

Tank with Two Liquids

An open tank contains 0.6m of water covered with 0.3m of oil of specific gravity 0.83. Find the pressure at the interface and at the bottom of the tank.

At the interface, $p_1 = \rho g h$

$p_1 = 0.83 \times 1000 \times 9.81 \times 0.3 = 2.442 kN/m^2$.

At the bottom of the tank, the pressure is that at the interface plus that of the water, i.e.

$p_2 = 2.442 \times 1000 + 1000 \times 9.81 \times 0.6 = 8.328 kN/m^2$.

Pressure Forces on Surfaces

Pressure Forces on Plane Surfaces

The location and magnitude of the resultant pressure force on a plane submerged surface may be determined by reference to Fig.2.6. The lamina *LM* represents a submerged surface which when extended cuts the water surface at *O* at angle θ.

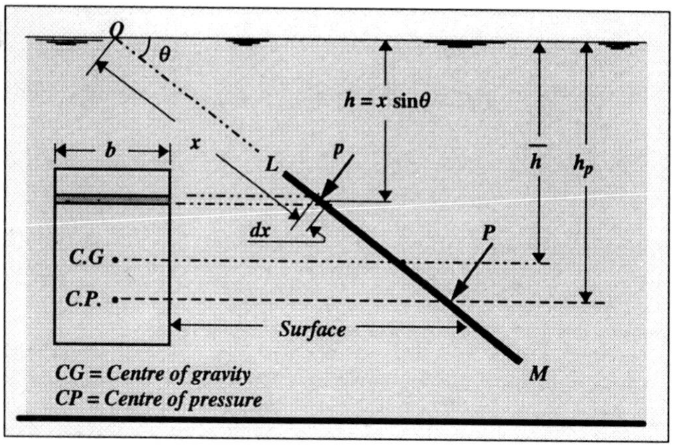

Fig.2.6- Pressure force on a plane surface.

The notation is as follows:

$\bar{h}$ = depth of centre of gravity,
x = distance to point of incremental pressure,
dA, A = incremental area and area of submerged surface,
θ = angle of inclination of plane,
p, P = pressure intensity and resultant pressure force,
h_p = depth of centre of pressure.

For an elementary horizontal strip at a distance x from O, the pressure is $p = \rho g x \sin\theta$.

Area of strip, $dA = bdx$

Force on strip $= p \times bdx = \rho gx \times \sin\theta \times b\, dx$

Total force on surface, $P = \rho g \times \sin\theta \times \int b \times x\, dx$

But $\int b \times dx \,.\, x$ = *1st moment of area about O* $= A\bar{h}/\sin\theta$.

Therefore, ***Resultant force,*** $P = \rho g A \bar{h}$ (2.14)

Centre of Pressure

The centre of pressure on a plane surface is the point on the immersed surface through which the resultant force may be considered to act. If h_p is the depth of centre of pressure below the surface of the liquid, taking moments about O.

Moment of thrust on strip $= (\rho gx \times \sin\theta \times bdx) \times x$

Sum of moments of forces on strip $= \rho g \times \sin\theta \times \int bdx \times x^2$.

But $\int bd \times x^2$ = *2nd moment of area of surface about O* $= I_o$.

Therefore, ***total moment*** $= \rho g \times \sin\theta \times I_o$.

Equating this moment to the moment of the resultant P, we get:

$$\frac{P \times h_p}{\sin\theta} = \rho g \times \sin\theta \times I_o \;.\; \therefore\; h_p = \frac{\rho g \times \sin^2\theta}{P} \times I_o \qquad (2.15)$$

Substituting from equation (2.14) for P.

$$h_p = \frac{\rho g \times \sin^2\theta}{\rho g A\bar{h}} \times I_o \text{ or } h_p = \frac{\sin^2\theta}{A\bar{h}} \times I_o \qquad (2.16)$$

$$\text{But, } I_o = I_G + A \times \frac{\bar{h}^2}{\sin^2\theta} \qquad (2.17)$$

where I_G = *2nd moment of area about the C.G.*

If this is substituted in equation (2.15)

$$h_p = \bar{h} + \frac{\sin^2\theta}{A\bar{h}} \times I_G \qquad (2.18)$$

If k is the radius of gyration about an axis through the *C.G.* parallel to *O*, then $I_G = Ak^2$. Therefore

$$\textit{Depth of centre of pressure, } h_p = \bar{h} + \frac{k^2}{\bar{h}} \times \sin^2\theta \qquad (2.19)$$

For the case of a vertical plane, that is $\theta = 90^0$, $\sin\theta = 1$ and equation (2.19) becomes,

$$h_p = \bar{h} + \frac{k^2}{\bar{h}} \qquad (2.20)$$

Values of the radius of gyration k^2 for different shapes are given below in Fig.2.7.

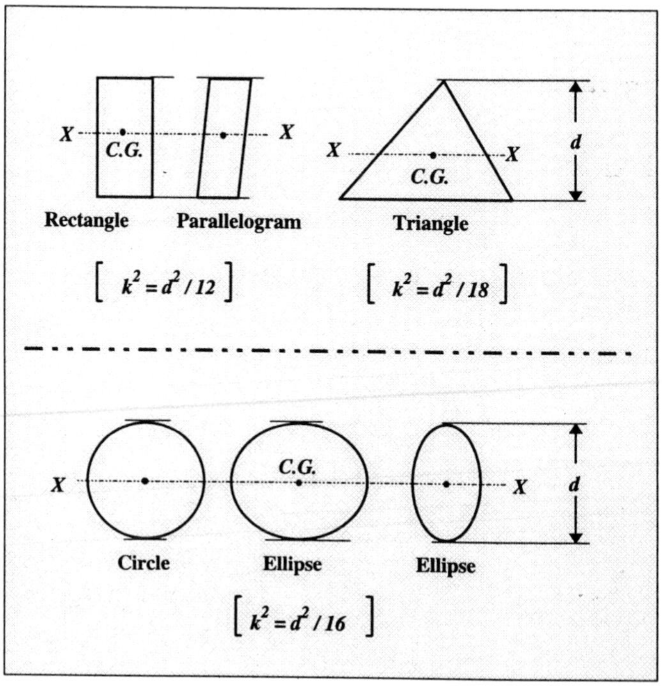

Fig.2.7- Values of the radius of gyration k^2 about axis X-X.

Forces on Curved Surfaces

Consider the horizontal and vertical components of the pressure force F separately on a curved surface of length L (Fig.2.8).

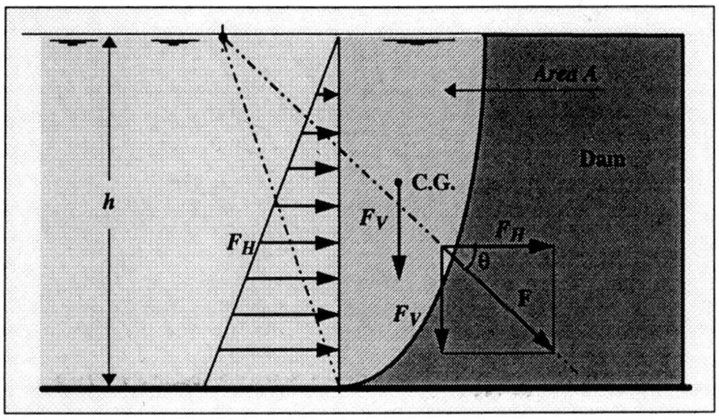

Fig.2.8- Pressure distribution on a curved surface.

The horizontal component of the pressure force on the curved surface is equal and acts at the same point as the force on a vertical plane surface formed by projecting the curved surface horizontally. That is

Horizontal component, $F_H = \rho g A \bar{h} = \dfrac{\rho g h^2}{2} \times L$ (2.21)

The vertical component of the force on the curved surface is equal to the weight of the fluid above the surface and acts at its centre of gravity. Thus:

Vertical component, $F_V = \rho\, g A \times L$ (2.22)

where A = area of fluid under consideration and L the length of the surface.

Resultant force, $F = \sqrt{F_H^2 + F_V^2}$ (2.23)

acting at $\theta = tan^{-1}(F_V/F_H)$ (2.24)

Buoyancy and Archimedes Principle

Archimedes principle states that the upthrust U on an immersed body is equal to the weight of liquid which it displaces. Hence a submerged body will float if the weight of the body is less than the weight of the liquid displaced. The centre of gravity of the displaced liquid is known as the **centre of buoyancy,** and a body will orientate itself so that its centre of gravity is located vertically above its centre of buoyancy (Fig.2.9).

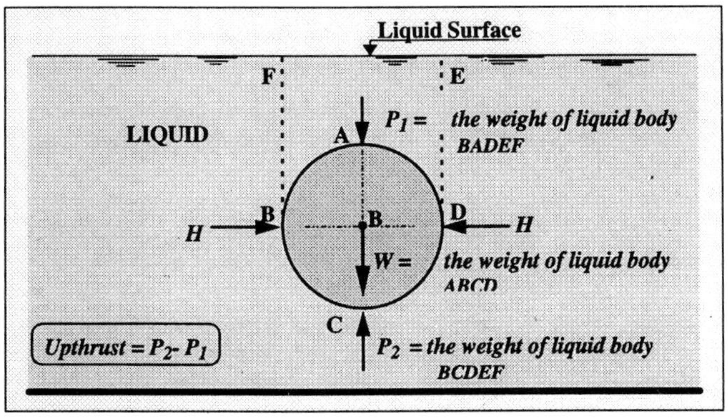

Fig.2.9- Forces acting on submerged bodies.

The weight W equals $(P_2 - P_1)$ which is called the buoyant force or upthrust (U) and equals the weight of liquid displaced. This force acts through the centre of buoyancy (B) - the centre of gravity of the displaced liquid.

Metacentre and Metacentric Height

To determine the stability of a floating vessel we consider the forces acting on it when it is displaced through a small angle from the position of equilibrium. Figure 2.10 shows a vessel in equilibrium.

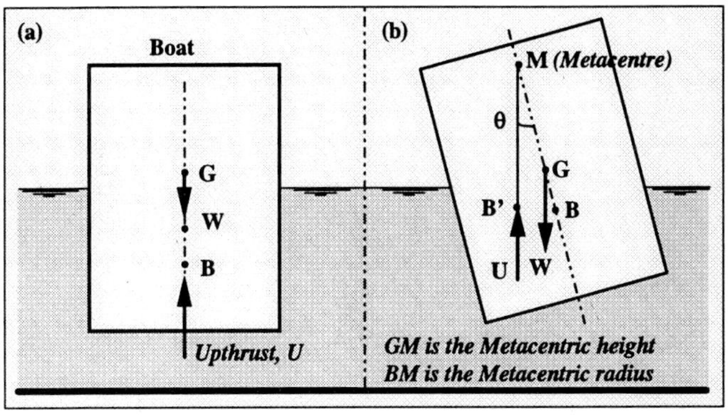

Fig.2.10- Stability of a boat.

When the body is in equilibrium W and U are in same vertical line (Fig.2.10a). For small angles of tilt the centre of buoyancy B moves to B' and the vertical through B' meets original neutral axis in M. GM is known as the metacentric height.

Restoring couple $= W \times GM \times \sin\theta$ (2.25)

Thus when M is above G the body is stable, and when M is at G body is stable in neutral equilibrium. From a consideration of the wedge of liquid displaced it can be shown that (see Chapter 7),

$BM = I/V$ (2.26)

where I is the second moment of area of body at water level through G, and V is the volume of liquid displaced.

Metacentric height, $GM = BM - BG$ (2.27)

Metacentric Height when Cargo Moves on Deck

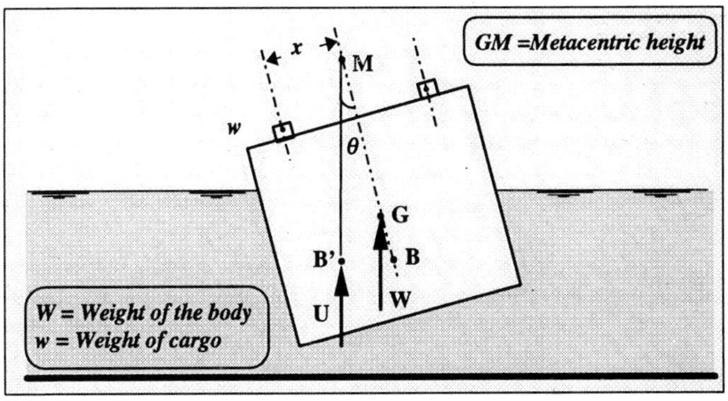

Fig.2.11- Determination of metacentric height.

Consider a load of weight w to be moveable horizontally across the deck of a boat of weight W (Fig.2.11). For small angles of heel θ, taking moments about M:

$w \times x = W \times GM \times \theta$ $\quad (sin\theta \cong \theta)$ (2.28)

$GM = \dfrac{w \times x}{W\theta}$ (2.29)

The angle of heel θ is measured usually by suspending a plumb bob from a known height above a scale over which the point of bob moves. This equation is used for field determination of metacentric height GM.

Examples on Fluid Statics

Moment on Pivoted Gate

A circular sluice, 0.9m diameter, is pivoted about its horizontal axis and covers an opening in the vertical face of a water reservoir. The back of the sluice is entirely at atmospheric pressure. Show that providing the sluice is completely below water level, the turning moment tending to rotate the sluice about its pivot is independent of the depth of water in the reservoir. Calculate the value of the moment in this case.

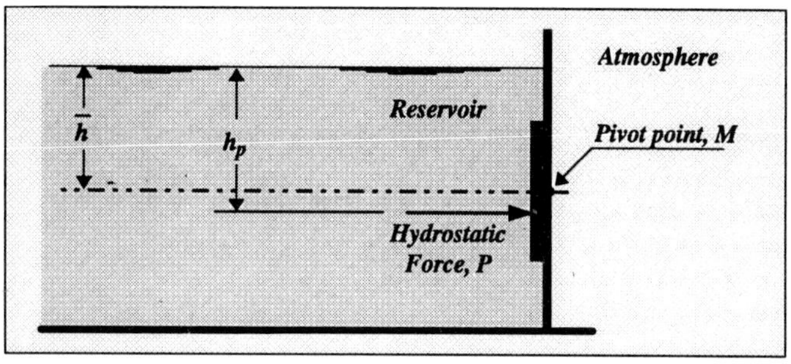

Let P be the hydrostatic force.

Moment about pivot, $M = P \times (h_p - \bar{h})$. But

$$P = \rho g A \bar{h} \text{ and } h_p = \bar{h} + \frac{d^2}{16\bar{h}}.$$

$$M = \rho g \bar{h} \times \left(\frac{\pi d^2}{4} \right) \times \left(\bar{h} + \frac{d^2}{16\bar{h}} - \bar{h} \right) = \rho g \times \frac{\pi d^4}{64}$$

$\therefore$ M is constant and independent of h.

$$M = \frac{\pi \times 0.9^4 \times 1000 \times 9.81}{64} = 315.78Nm .$$

Stability of a Floating Cylinder

a) Define the centre of buoyancy of a floating vessel.

b) Quote a theoretical expression for the metacentric height of a floating vessel GM in terms of BM and BG where M is the metacentre, G the centre of gravity of the vessel and B the centre of buoyancy.

c) Quote an expression for determining BM, defining all symbols used.

d) Show that a cylinder 2m diameter, 2.5m in height and weighing 31.4kN is unstable floating in water with its axis vertical. *(Take $g = 10m/s^2$).*

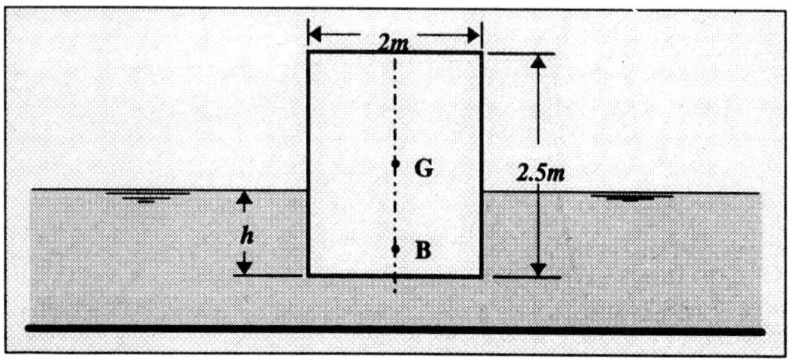

a) Centre of buoyancy of a floating vessel is the centre of gravity of the displaced fluid.

b) $GM = BM - BG$.

c) $BM = I/V$

where I = second moment of area of waterline plane about axis of rotation and V = volume of fluid displaced by vessel.

$$\textit{Volume of water displaced} = \frac{31.4 \times 1000}{1000 \times 10} = 3.14m^3 .$$

If h is depth of floatation, $\pi \times 1^2 \times h = 3.14$. $\therefore h = 1m$.

$$BG = \frac{2.5}{2} - \frac{h}{2} = 1.25 - 0.5 = 0.75m .$$

$$BM = \left(\frac{I}{V} \right) = \left(\frac{\pi \times 1^4}{4} \Big/ \pi \right) = 0.25m .$$

GM** = 0.25 - 0.75 = -0.5m **(is negative).** $\therefore$ **Cylinder unstable.

Force on a Gate Bolt

Write down expressions for (i) the total pressure and (ii) the vertical distance from the surface to the centre of pressure for a lamina wholly submerged in a fluid and inclined at an angle θ to the surface. There is a square gate 2m × 2m in the vertical side of a tank containing water density 1000kg/m^3. It is hinged along the top edge and secured by a bolt in the centre of the bottom edge. What is the force on the bolt when the water level is 2m above the top of the gate? *(Take $g = 10m/s^2$).*

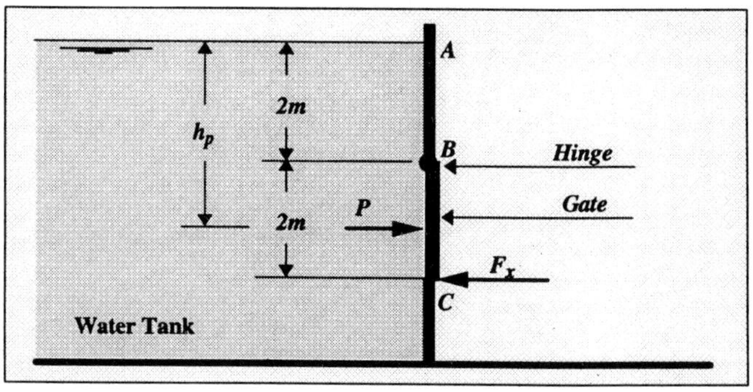

Total pressure $= \rho g A \bar{h}$.

Depth to centre of pressure, $h_p = \bar{h} + \frac{k^2}{\bar{h}} \times \sin^2\theta$

Let F_x = Force on bolt. In this example θ = 90, thus $\sin^2\theta = 1$.

Total Pressure, $P = 1000 \times 10 \times 2 \times 2 \times 3 = 120$ *kN.*

$$h_p = 3 + \left(\frac{2 \times 2}{12} \Big/ 3 \right) \times \left(k^2 \textit{ from } I = \frac{bd^3}{12} = Ak^2 \right) = \frac{28}{9} m .$$

To find x, take moments about B: $120{,}000 \times [(28/9)-2] = F_x \times 2$.

$$\textbf{Force, } F_x = \left(120{,}000 \times \frac{10}{9} \Big/ 2 \right) = 66.67kN .$$

Pressure on a Vertical Gate

Derive an expression for the depth of centre of pressure of a vertical plane area subjected to water pressure on one side. A vertical gate 6.1m wide has water to a depth of 5.49m on the upstream side and to a depth of 3.66m on the downstream side. Determine the magnitude and line of action of the resultant force on the gate.

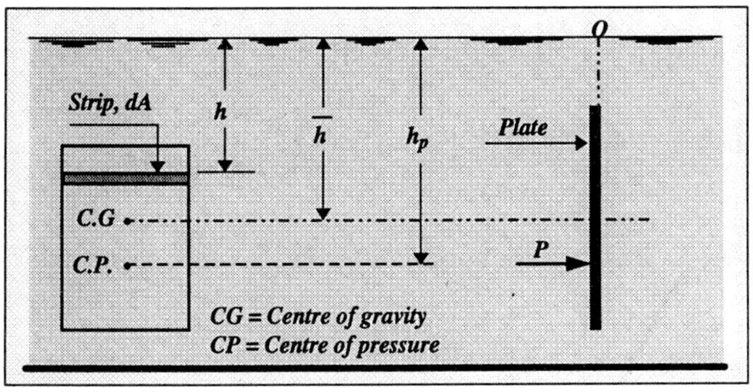

Force on strip area dA $= Pressure \times Area = \rho gh\ dA$

Total pressure force, $P = \int \rho ghdA = \rho g\bar{h}A$

Taking moments about a line through O in water surface:

Moment of strip $= \rho gh\ dAh, \quad \rho g\int dA\, h^2 = \rho g\bar{h} \times A \times h_p$

$\therefore\ h_p = \int dA\, h^2 / A\,\bar{h} = I/A\,\bar{h}$.

where I = 2nd moment of area about line O in water surface.

For a rectangle with the upper edge in the water surface, $h_p = 2h/3$, where h = depth of rectangle.
The breadth of the gate b is 6.1m.

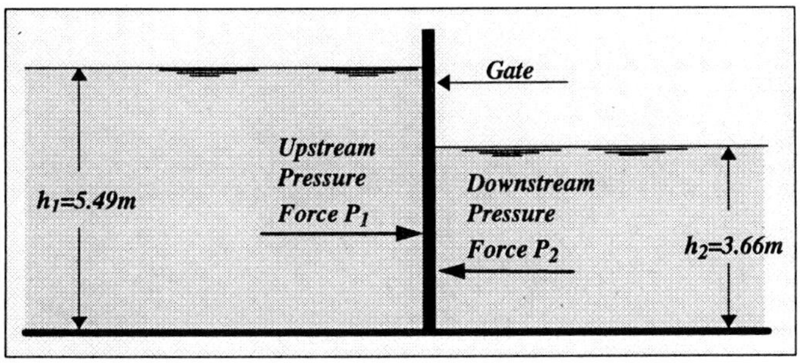

$$P_1 = \frac{\rho gb\, h_1^2}{2} = \frac{1000 \times 9.81 \times 6.1 \times\ 5.49^2}{2} = 901.8kN / m^2$$

$$P_2 = \frac{\rho gb\, h_2^2}{2} = \frac{1000 \times 9.81 \times 6.1 \times\ 3.66^2}{2} = 400.8kN / m^2$$

Resultant force $= 901.8 - 400.8 = 501kN/m^2$.

P for each side will act at $h/3$ from the bottom. Let the resultant act at a distance h_p from the bottom. Taking moments about the bottom edge, $501 \times h_p = 901.8 \times 1.83 - 400.8 \times 1.22$.

$$h_p = \frac{1650.3 - 488.98.}{501} = 2.32m\ from\ bottom\,.$$

Pressure on a Circular Lamina

A circular lamina 1.2m in diameter is immersed in water so that the distance of its perimeter measured vertically below the water surface varies between 0.6m and 1.5m. Find the total force due to the water acting on one side of the lamina, and the vertical distance of the centre of pressure below the surface.

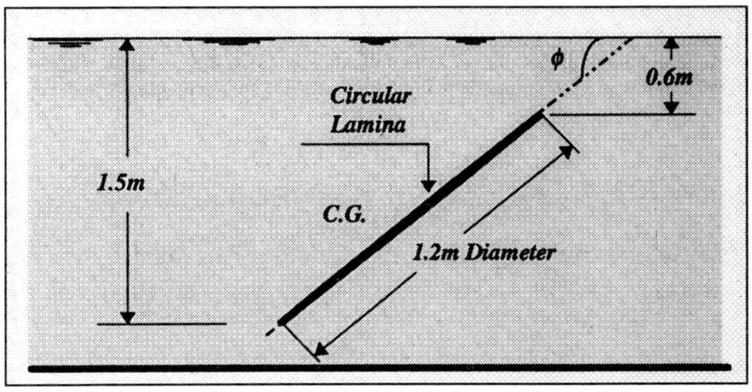

Area of plate, $A = \pi \times 1.2^2/4 = 1.13m^2$.

Depth of C.G., $\bar{h} = (0.6 + 1.5)/2 = 1.05m$

Resultant pressure force, $P = \rho g\,\bar{h}\,A$

$P = 1000 \times 9.81 \times 1.05 \times 1.13 = 11.64kN$

For a circular lamina, $k^2 = \frac{d^2}{16} = \frac{1.44}{16} = 0.09m^2$

$$\sin\phi = \frac{1.5\text{-}0.6}{1.2} = \frac{3}{4}$$

Vertical depth of centre of pressure, $h_P = \bar{h} + \frac{k^2}{\bar{h}} \times \sin^2\phi$

$$h_P = 1.05 + \frac{0.09}{1.05} \times \left(\frac{3}{4}\right)^2 = 1.10m.$$

Thrust on an Arch Bridge

A 6m wide stream is spanned by a bridge with a parabolic arch, the crown of which is 2.4m above the springings which are 7.2m apart. Calculate the upthrust on the bridge when the water level is 0.6m below the crown .

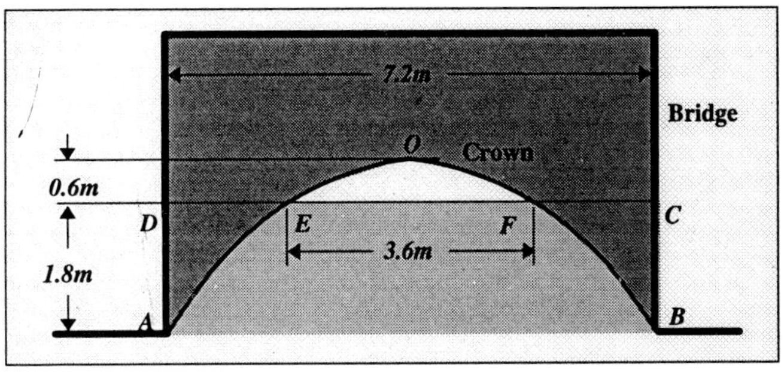

Upthrust of water $=$ *Weight of water displaced*
$=$ *Weight of volume (ADE+BCF)*

Area of parabola EFO $= (2/3) \times 3.6 \times 0.6 = 1.44m^2$

Area of parabola AOB $= (2/3) \times 7.2 \times 2.4 = 11.52m^2$

Area of AEFB $= 11.52 - 1.44 = 10.08m^2$

Area of (ADE+BCF) $= 1.80 \times 7.2 - 10.08 = 2.88m^2$

Volume of water displaced $= 2.88 \times 6 = 17.28m^3$

Upthrust $= 1000 \times 9.81 \times 17.28 = 169.52kN$.

(Note that horizontal forces on the bridge balance each other, and their resultant is therefore zero.)

Hydrostatic Forces on a Parabolic Dam

The profile of a dam is parabolic, as shown below. The dam retains water to a depth of 30m. Calculate the resultant thrust per metre run of the dam, its inclination to the horizontal, and the point where it cuts the horizontal base line.

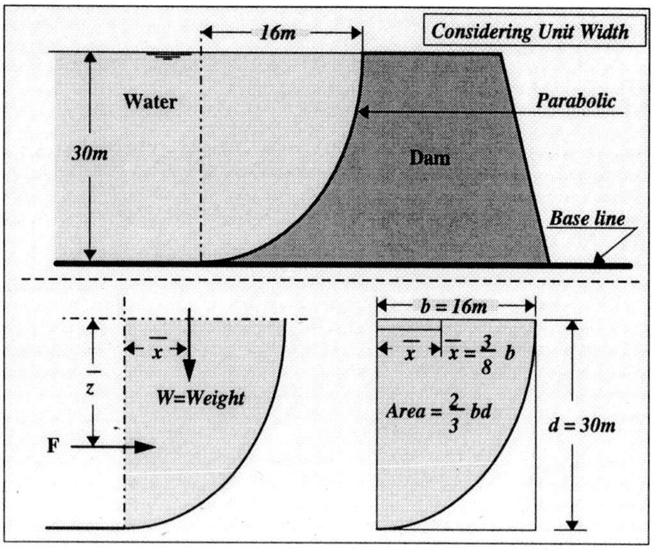

$$F = \rho g A\bar{h} = \rho g \times \frac{30}{2} \times 1 \times 30 = 450\rho g .$$

$$\bar{z} = \frac{\Sigma y^2 \delta A}{\Sigma y \delta A} = \frac{bd^3/3}{bd^2/2} = \frac{2d}{3} = 20m , \quad \bar{x} = \frac{3 \times 16}{8} = 6m .$$

$$W = \rho g \,(Volume\ of\ liquid) = \rho g \times \frac{2}{3}\,(16 \times 30 \times 1) = 320\rho g .$$

Resultant Force, R $= 100\,\rho g \times [4.5^2 + 3.2^2]^{1/2} = 552.2\rho g.$

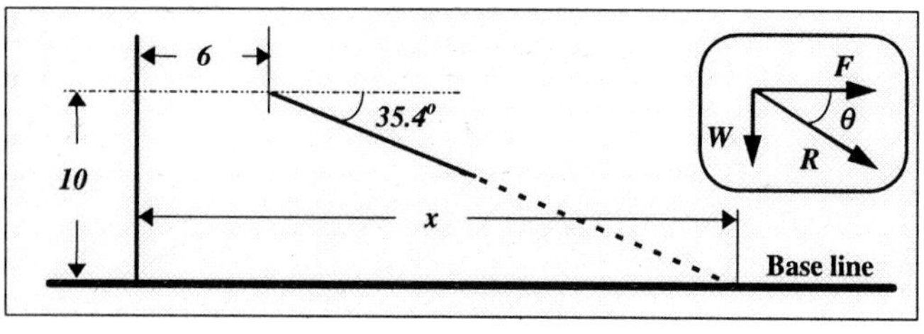

i.e. $R = 552.2 \times 1000 \times 9.81 = 5417kN.$

Inclination angle, $\theta = \tan^{-1}\frac{W}{F} = \tan^{-1}\frac{320}{450} = 35.4^o ,$

Distance, $x = 6 + (10/\tan 35.4^o) = 20.1m .$

Flap Gate for a Tank

A 1m diameter circular flap gate is used to control the water level in a tank. The gate is hinged at top and held closed (in a vertical position) by a 1 tonne counterbalance weight as indicated in the diagram below. Calculate the depth of water *'H'* above the top of the gate at which the gate will begin to open. Derive any formula used by considering Fig.2.6.

$$dP = \rho g x \sin\theta \times dA . \therefore P = \int_A \rho g x \sin\theta \times dA = \rho g \sin\theta \int_A x dA .$$

$$\int_A x dA = A\bar{h} . \quad \therefore P = \rho g h \times \sin\theta \times A = p_{centroid} \times A .$$

$$P = \rho\, g \times (H + 0.5) \times \frac{\pi}{4} , \quad h_p - \bar{h} = \frac{I_G}{A\bar{h}} = \frac{0.0625}{(H + 0.5)} .$$

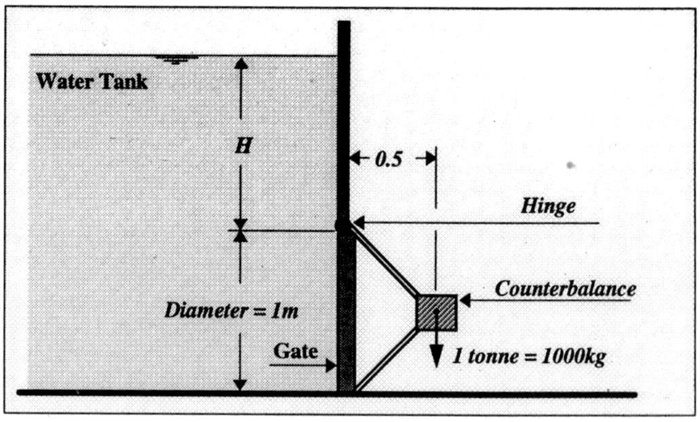

Taking the moment about the hinge gives:

$$1000 \times 9.81 \times 0.5 = 1000 \times 9.81 \times (H + 0.5) \times \frac{\pi}{4}\left(0.5 + \frac{0.0625}{H + 0.5}\right)$$

Depth of water $H = 2 \times \left(\frac{2}{\pi} - 0.3125\right) = 0.648m .$

Hydrostatic Forces on a Circular Dam

A 24m high dam with its upstream face in the shape of a circular arc of 30m radius is shown below. With the upstream water level just coincident with the crest of the dam, calculate: (i) the resultant force per horizontal metre run on the curved upstream face; (ii) the inclination of this force to the horizontal. Indicate the line of action of this force.

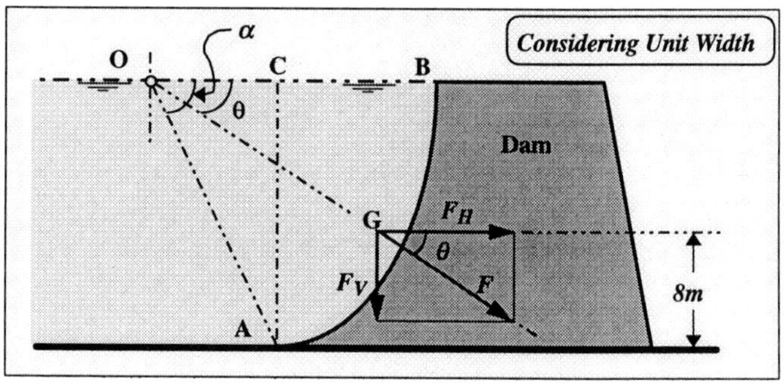

$OA = OB = radius = 30m, \ \therefore Height\ of\ dam,\ AC = 24m.$

$OC^2 = OA^2 - AC^2 = 30^2 - 24^2 = 324m, \ \therefore OC = 18m.$

$CB = OB - OC = 30 - 18 = 12m.$

$$\cos\alpha = \frac{OC}{OA} = \frac{18}{30} = 0.6 \ \ hence\ \alpha = 53^o.$$

Horizontal force per metre run, F_H, is the force on the projection of curved portion AB on the vertical which is AC.

$$F_H = \rho g A\bar{h} = 1000 \times 9.81 \times 24 \times \frac{24}{2} = 2825{,}280N = 2825kN .$$

This component acts at centre of pressure of AC which is $h/3 = 24/3 = 8m$ up from base of dam.

Vertical force F_V is weight of water contained in area ACB which acts through the centre area of this section.

Area ACB = Area OABC - Area triangle OAC.

Area of secant OABC = $(\alpha/360) \times \pi r^2 = (53/360) \times 3.142 \times 30^2$
$= 416.3m^2.$

Area of triangle OAC = $1/2 \times 18 \times 24 = 216.0m^2.$

Hence, *area ACB* = $200.3m^2$.

$F_V = 200.3 \times 1000 \times 9.81 = 1964{,}943\ N = 1965kN$.

Resultant force, F, is given by:

$F^2 = F_V^2 + F_H^2 = (1965^2 + 2825^2) = 3861{,}225 + 7980{,}625$
$= 11841850$.

Hence, $F = 3441kN$.

$\tan\theta = F_V / F_H = 1965/2825 = 0.6958$.

Inclination angle of resultant force F, $\theta = 35^o$.

Line of Action: F acts through a point 8m up from base of dam and on line with the centre of area of ACB - also line of action passes through the centre of the circle O.

Float Operated Flap Gate

The water level in a tank is controlled by a float operated flap gate. The gate is square with a side of 0.75m and hinged along its top edge. It is set at an angle of 45° to the horizontal. The control float is attached to the bottom edge of the gate by a vertical cable as indicated in the diagram below.

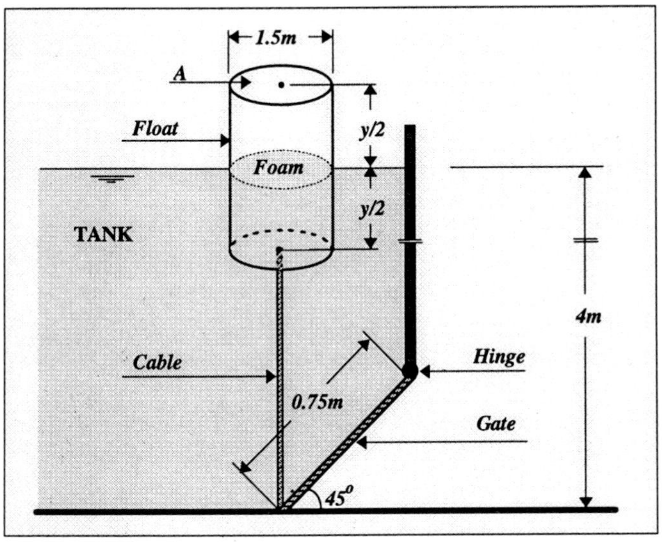

The control float is cylindrical in shape 1.5m in diameter and floats with its circular faces horizontal. It is made of a foam plastic which has a specific weight of 1.58kN/m³. When the depth of water in the tank is 4m and the gate is just opening it was noted that the float was submerged to half its volume. Calculate the length of the float. *(Ignore cable weight).*

Pressure Force, $F = \rho \times 9.81 \times \left(4 - \dfrac{0.75}{2\sqrt{2}}\right) \times 0.75^2 = 20.61kN$.

Taking moments about the hinge, with *T* the tension in the cable,

gives: $T \times 0.75\cos 45^o = F \times \left(\dfrac{0.75}{2} + \dfrac{h_p - \bar{h}}{\cos 45^o}\right)$.

$$\bar{h} = 4 - \frac{0.75 \times \sin 45^o}{2} = 3.735m.$$

$$h_p - \bar{h} = \frac{I_G \times \sin^2\theta}{A \times \bar{h}} = \frac{0.75^4}{12} \times \frac{0.5}{0.75^2 \times 3.735} = 6.28 \times 10^{-3}\ m$$

Tension in the cable, $T = \dfrac{20.61 \times (0.375 + 0.009)}{0.530} = 14.92kN$.

Area of Float, $A = (\pi \times 1.5^2)/4 = 1.767m^2$.

Weight of Water displayed by float = Weight of Float + T

$$\rho_w g \times 1.767 \times \frac{y}{2} = \rho_f g \times 1.767y + 14.92 \times 1000$$

$$\left(\frac{9.81}{2} - 1.58\right) \times y = \frac{14.92}{1.767}.$$

Height of Float, y = 2.54m.

Forces on a Canal Bulkhead

A short length of canal is to be sealed off and pumped dry. The bottom and walls of the canal must not be damaged in any way. The canal is sealed by a plate inclined at 45° to the horizontal as shown in diagram below, propped by a row of struts.

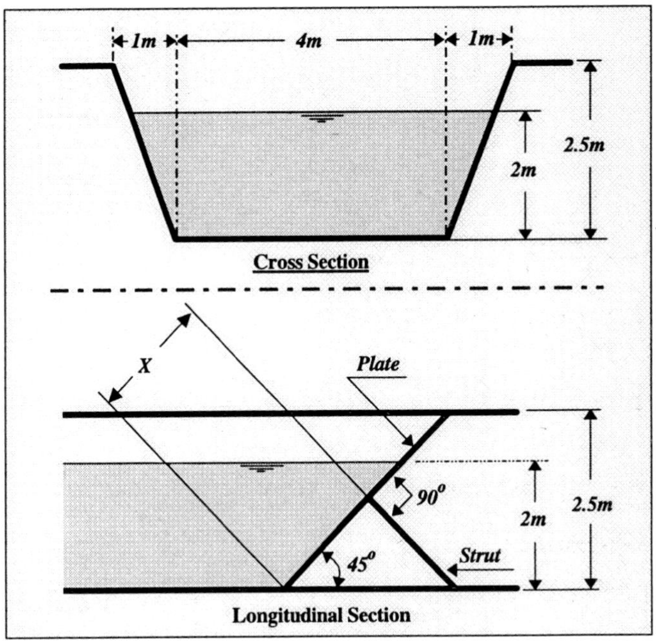

Calculate the distance X to place the struts in line with the resultant hydrostatic force on the plate. How many struts will be needed if each strut can safely carry 45.0kN?

Width of bulkhead at water level $= 4 + [(2/2.5) \times 2] = 5.6m$.

Slope length $= 2\sqrt{2} = 2.83m$.

$$b = 5.6 - \frac{y}{2.83} \times 1.6,\quad \delta A = b \times \delta y = \left(5.6 - \frac{y \times 1.6}{2.83}\right) \times \delta y$$

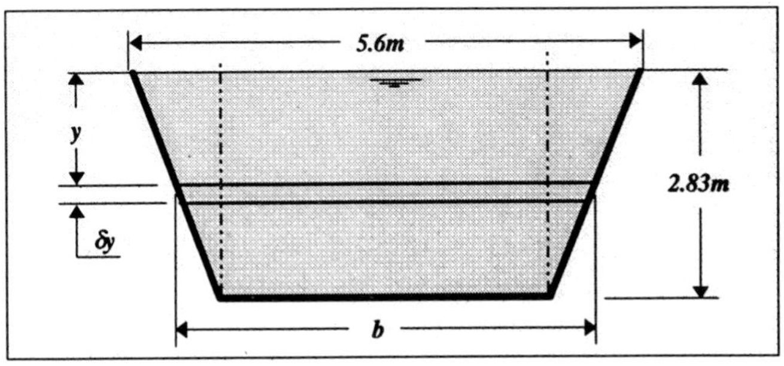

$$\delta M_1 = \delta A y = by \times \delta y = (5.6y - 0.565\,y^2) \times \delta y.$$

$$A = \int_0^{2.83} b\,dy = \left[5.6 \times y - 0.283 \times y^2\right]_0^{2.83} = 13.55$$

$$M_1 = \int_0^{2.83} by\,dy = \left[2.8 \times y^2 - 0.188 \times y^3\right]_0^{2.83} = 18.16.$$

Properties of bulkhead plane, $\bar{y} = \dfrac{M_1}{A} = \dfrac{18.16}{13.55} = 1.33m$.

$$\delta M_2 = by^2 \times \delta y = (5.6y^2 - 0.565\,y^3) \times \delta y$$

$$M_2 = \int_o^{2.83} by^2\,dy = \left[1.87 \times y^3 - 0.141 \times y^4\right]_o^{2.83} = 33.5.$$

$$k^2 = \frac{M_2}{A} - \bar{y}^2 = \frac{33.5}{13.55} - 1.77 = 0.69$$

Hydrostatics Depth to C of A,

$\bar{h} = \bar{y}/\sqrt{2} = 0.94\ m.$

Hydrostatics Depth to C of P,

$h_p = \bar{h} + (k^2 \times \sin^2\theta/\bar{h})$

$h_p = 0.94 + \dfrac{0.69 \times 0.5}{0.94} = 1.31m.$

$x = (2 - h_p) \times \sqrt{2} = 0.975m.$

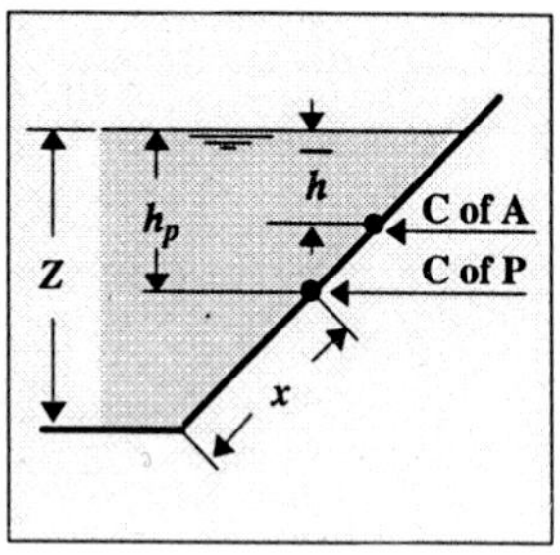

Total thrust on bulkhead, F $= \rho g A \bar{h} = 9.81 \times 0.94 \times 13.6$

$F = 125\ kN.$

Number of struts needed = *F/permissible load = 125/45.*

∴ ***Use three struts.***

Equilibrium of a Floating Cylinder

State the conditions for stable equilibrium of a body floating partially immersed in a liquid. A cylinder of circular section of diameter *d*, made of material of $S.G. = S_1$, floats in a liquid of $S.G. = S_2$. Find the maximum length of cylinder if equilibrium is to be stable with the cylinder axis vertical.

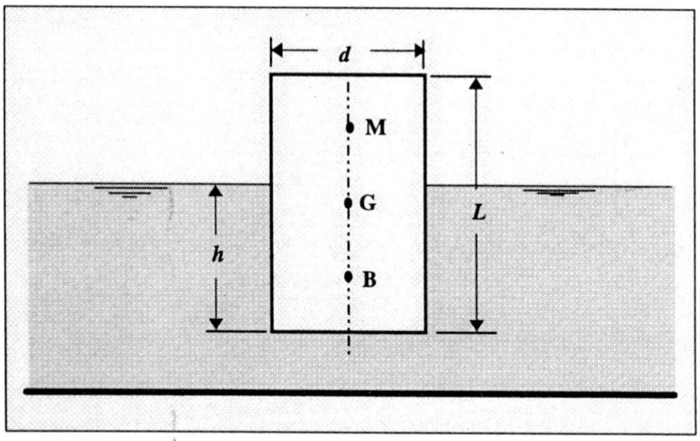

The conditions for stable equilibrium are:

(i) the resultant horizontal hydrostatic force must be 0.

(ii) the resultant vertical hydrostatic force i.e. the buoyancy must balance the weight of the body. Furthermore the centre of buoyancy *B* and the centre of gravity of the body *G* must lie on the same vertical line.

(iii) when the body is disturbed the unbalanced couple produced must be such that it tends to right the position of the body. This can only occur if the Metacentre is above the *C.G.*, and the limiting position for *M*, for stability will be coincident with *G*, i.e. when *BM = BG*.

$\dfrac{S_2}{S_1} = \dfrac{L}{h}$, i.e. $h = \dfrac{S_1}{S_2} \times L$

$\therefore\ BG = \dfrac{L}{2} - \dfrac{h}{2} = \dfrac{L}{2} - \dfrac{S_1 \times L}{2S_2} = \dfrac{L}{2} \times \dfrac{(S_2 - S_1)}{S_2}$, and

$$BM = \frac{I}{V} = \frac{\pi \times d^4}{64} \times \frac{4}{\pi \times d^2 h} = \frac{d^2}{16h} = \frac{d^2}{16} \times \frac{S_2}{S_1 \times L}.$$

For equilibrium of cylinder BM>BG.

$\therefore\ \dfrac{d^2}{16} \times \dfrac{S_2}{S_1 L} > \dfrac{L}{2} \times \dfrac{(S_2 - S_1)}{S_2}$, and

$$L^2 < \frac{d^2 \times S_2^2}{8S_1 \times (S_2 - S_1)}$$

Maximum length, $L = \dfrac{d \times S_2}{\sqrt{8S_1 \times (S_2 - S_1)}}.$

Problems on Fluid Statics

[1] Calculate the magnitude and location of the total hydrostatic force on one side of a circular plate of 0.6m radius, situated with its geometric centre 1.2m vertically below the water surface, when (a) the plate is vertical and (b) the plate is inclined at 30 degrees to the horizontal.
((a) 13.3 kN. 1.275m, (b) 13.3 kN. 1.220m)

[2] A tank containing water has a rectangular opening 0.6m by 0.47m in one of its vertical sides, the longer side being horizontal. The opening is covered by a plate carried on a horizontal hinge located 0.023m above the upper edge of the opening. Two coil springs, each exerting a force of 890N placed 0.05m above the lower edge of the opening. hold the plate against the outer side of the tank wall. Find the level of water above the upper edge of the opening when the plate begins to move. (0.78m)

[3] If the pressure 10 metres below the free surface of a liquid is 3 bars, calculate its specific weight and specific gravity. Express the specific weight in N/m^3. ($3 \times 10^4 N/m^3$, 3.06)

[4] A closed rectangular tank 1.25m high by 2.5m long by 1.5m wide is completely filled with water and the pressure on the top of the water is raised to $138kN/m^2$. Calculate the pressures along the four edges perpendicular to motion when the tank is accelerated horizontally along the direction of its length at $4.5m/s^2$. (138, 149.3, 150.3, 161.6 kN/m^2)

[5] A tank with vertical sides is square in plan, the sides being 1.22m long. It contains water to a depth of 0.61m and on top of the water there is a depth of 0.915 of oil of SG = 0.9. Find (a) the total pressure on each side of the tank and (b) the height of the centre of pressure above the base of the tank.
(12.68kN, 0.5m)

[6] A stream is spanned by a bridge which is a single mass concrete arch in the form of a circular arc of 4.878m radius, the crown being 2.43m above the springings. Measured in the direction of the stream, the overall width of the bridge is 6.1m. During a flood the water level rises to crown level. Calculate the force tending to lift bridge from the foundations. (35.9kN).

Compressible Fluids

Laws of a Perfect Gas

Problems dealing with the pressure and flow of gases are more complex than those applied to liquids. As a gas is easily compressible, in comparison with a liquid, the variation in its density is considerable. It is this variation in density which complicates the calculations on gas flow. The behaviour of gases under changes of temperature, pressure and volume is governed by several well-known laws, all of which have been verified experimentally. They are briefly discussed below.

Boyle's Law which states that if a gas is expanded or compressed at constant temperature the product of its pressure, p, and volume, *V*, at any instant is a constant, or

$$p \times V = a\ constant, \quad or \quad p \propto 1/V. \tag{2.30}$$

Then, $p_1 V_1 = p_2 V_2$ (2.31)

Charles's Law which states that if a gas is expanded or compressed at constant pressure then

$$V/T = a\ constant, \quad \text{or } V \propto T \quad (T = 273^oK\ at\ 0^oC) \tag{2.32}$$

where T is the absolute temperature of the gas. If the change takes place at constant volume then

$$p/T = a\ constant,\ or\ p \propto T \tag{2.33}$$

By combining the **laws of Boyle and Charles** the characteristic equation of a gas is obtained:

$$pV = mRT, \quad and \quad p_1V_1 = m_1RT_1\ ,\ p_2V_2 = m_2RT_2 \tag{2.34}$$

where V is the volume of mass m of the gas at pressure p and absolute temperature, T. The symbol R is known as the gas constant. The density of the perfect gases may be obtained from the above equation of state,

$$\textbf{Density,}\ \rho = \frac{p}{RT}, \text{ and } \rho_1 = \frac{p_1}{RT_1}\ ,\ \rho_2 = \frac{p_2}{RT_2} \tag{2.35}$$

Application of Avogadro's law, ***"all gases at the same pressure and temperature have the same number of molecules per unit of volume"*** allows the calculation of the universal gas constant R. Consider two gases having constants R_1 and R_2, densities ρ_1 and ρ_2 and existing at the same pressure and temperature, p and T. Dividing their equations of state,

$$\left[\frac{p}{\rho_1 T}\right] \Big/ \left[\frac{p}{\rho_2 T}\right] = \frac{R_1}{R_2} \quad (T^oK = {}^oC + 273) \tag{2.36}$$

$$\frac{p_1}{P_2} = \frac{R_1}{R_2} \quad or \quad m_1 R_1 = m_2 R_2 \tag{2.37}$$

in which m_1 and m_2 are the respective molecular weights of the gases. In other words, the product of molecular weight and gas constant is the same for all gases.

Stability of the Atmosphere

The **atmosphere** consists essentially of two layers, the lower being the **troposphere** and the upper the **stratosphere**. The two layers merge in a zone called the **tropopause**, whose altitude varies considerably with latitude, being about *11km* in temperate regions such as Western Europe. In the troposphere there are changes and the temperature falls at an approximately constant rate with increase of altitude. This temperature gradient is usually referred to as the **lapse rate,** $\beta = -dT/dh$. For a constant lapse rate β, the fall in temperature due to an increase in altitude h is βh. Hence the absolute temperature at an altitude h above sea level is,

$$T = T_o - \beta h \quad (T_o\ temperature\ at\ sea\ level) \tag{2.38}$$

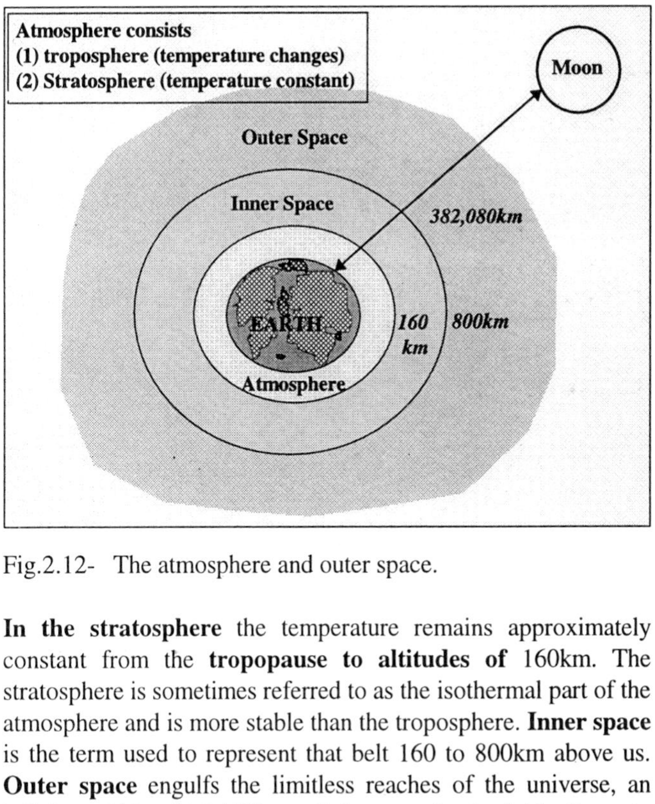

Fig.2.12- The atmosphere and outer space.

In the stratosphere the temperature remains approximately constant from the **tropopause to altitudes of** 160km. The stratosphere is sometimes referred to as the isothermal part of the atmosphere and is more stable than the troposphere. **Inner space** is the term used to represent that belt 160 to 800km above us. **Outer space** engulfs the limitless reaches of the universe, an infinite void in which billions of planets and celestial bodies spin rhythmically. In this outer space the surface of the moon is 382,080km from the surface of the earth.

International Standard Atmosphere

The performance of an aircraft depends on the physical properties of the atmosphere which vary with time and place. In order that estimated and actual performance figures can be compared, a **standard atmosphere** has been adopted by international agreement. This represents the average conditions in Western Europe and performance figures are reduced or corrected to these conditions. The **standard atmosphere** has a sea level temperature of 15°C = 15 + 273 = 288°K (absolute).

Pipeline Carrying Compressible Air

A pipeline is carrying 0.227kg/s of air. At section 1, where the diameter is 150mm, the pressure $p_1 = 27.59 \times 10^4 N/m^2$ and temperature $T_1 = 33.33^oC$, and at section 2, where the diameter is 2.03m, the pressure $p_2 = 20.69 \times 10^4 N/m^2$ and $T_2 = 44.44^oC$. Find the velocity at each section. Take gas constant R as 282.

Density at Section 1, $\rho_1 = \dfrac{p_1}{RT_1}$

$$\rho_1 = \frac{27.59 \times 10^4}{282 \times (288 + 33.33)} = 3.05 kg/m^3$$

Density at Section 2, $\rho_2 = \dfrac{p_2}{RT_2}$

$$\rho_2 = \frac{20.69 \times 10^4}{282 \times (288 + 44.44)} = 2.20 kg/m^3$$

Velocity at Section 1, $V_1 = \dfrac{\dot{m}}{\rho_1 A_1}$

$$V_1 = \frac{0.227 \times 4}{3.05 \times \pi \times 0.15^2} = 4.21 m/s$$

Velocity at Section 2, $V_2 = \dfrac{\dot{m}}{\rho_2 A_2}$

$$V_2 = \frac{0.227 \times 4}{2.20 \times \pi \times 0.203^2} = 3.19 m/s$$

Variation of Air Density with Altitude

Show that the variation of air density, ρ, with height, h, in the troposphere, is given by:

$$\rho_1 = \rho_o \times \left(\frac{T_o - \beta h}{T_o}\right)^{\left(\frac{g}{R\beta} - 1\right)}$$

where T_o, β, R refer to Absolute Temperature, Lapse Rate and Gas Constant, respectively, and suffix o refers to sea level conditions. An aircraft has a take-off speed of 160km/h, at sea level where the temperature is 15°C. If the lapse rate is 2°C per 300m, calculate the speed for take-off at Dychmygol Airport 4200m above sea level assuming gas constant for air is $282 m^2/s^2\,°C$.

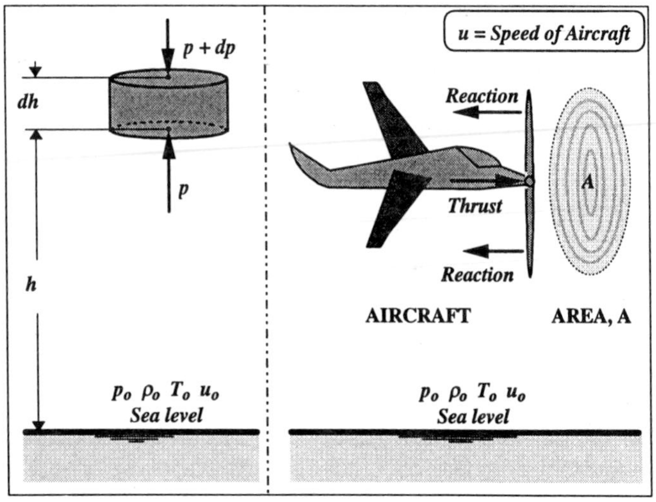

Consider the pressures on an element of fluid at an altitude h above sea level.

$(p - \delta p) \times A - pA + \rho g A \times \delta h = 0 \;\therefore\; dp = \rho g \times dh$

Using, $pV = mRT$, $\therefore\; m/V = p/RT = \rho$, also $T = T_o - \beta h$.

Substituting into the expression for dp, $\dfrac{dp}{p} = -\dfrac{g\,dh}{R \times (T_o - \beta h)}$

Integrating, $\log_e\left(\dfrac{p}{p_o}\right) = -\dfrac{g}{R\beta} \times \log_e(T_o - \beta h) + C$

$p = p_o$ when $h = 0$, $\therefore\; C = (g/R\beta) \times \log_e T_o$.

$$\therefore\; \log_e\left(\frac{p}{p_o}\right) = \frac{g}{R\beta} \times \log_e\left(\frac{T_o - \beta h}{T_o}\right)$$

Hence, $\dfrac{p}{p_o} = \left(\dfrac{T_o - \beta h}{T_o}\right)^{(g/R\beta)}$.

But $\dfrac{p}{p_o} = \dfrac{\rho R T}{\rho_o R T_o} = \rho \times \left(\dfrac{T_o - \beta h}{\rho_o T_o}\right)$.

$$\therefore\; \left(\frac{\rho}{\rho_o}\right) = \left(\frac{T_o - \beta h}{T_o}\right)^{(g/R\beta)} \times \left(\frac{T_o}{T_o - \beta h}\right).$$

$\rho = \rho_o \times \left(\dfrac{T_o - \beta h}{T_o}\right)^{[(g/R\beta) - 1]}$. Using this equation,

$\rho/\rho_o = (288 - 28/288)^{[(9.81 \times 300/282 \times 2) - 1]} = 0.9^{4.22} = 0.643.$

Aircraft thrust is equal and opposite to air reaction

Thrust $= -k\,A\,\rho\,u \times (0 - u)$.

$\therefore$ **For equal thrust,** $\rho u^2 = \rho_o u_o^2$.

$\rho/\rho_o = (u_o/u)^2 = 0.643$. $\therefore\; u = u_o/\sqrt{0.643} = 160/0.802$.

$\therefore$ ***Take-off speed at Dychmygol Airport*** = *199.5km/hour.*

Problems on Compressible Fluids

[1] The International Civil Aviation Organisation specifies that for certain tests the atmosphere shall be deemed to have properties which for moderate altitudes are found from the following table:

Thermodynamic temperature	$T = T_o - (Z/\beta)$
Altitude above sea level	**Z**
A constant	$\beta = 153.85\ m/°K$
Sea level temperature	$T_o = 288.15°K$
Sea level pressure	$P_o = 1$ **Atmosphere** $= 101325 N/m^2$
Specific gas constant	$R = 287.05 J/kg°K = 287.05 Nm/kg\ °K$
Gravitational acceleration	$g = 9.80665 m/s^2$

Determine to 3 significant figures the pressure at an altitude of 10,000m. (0.26 atmosphere)

[2] The pressure and temperature of the atmosphere at ground level are $101.3 kN/m^2$ at 288°K. Find the pressure of the air at a height of 4573m, assuming (a) no density variation and (b) the temperature decreases at a uniform rate of 6.38°C per 1000m of altitude. Take the gas constant R = 286 Nm/kg °K, and $\rho = 1.4 kg/m^3$ for air. ($46.85 kN/m^2$, $57.46 kN/m^2$)

CHAPTER THREE

KINEMATICS AND DYNAMICS OF FLUIDS

Introduction

The science that treats fluids in motion is often divided into kinematics which describes the motion, and dynamics which deals with the forces producing the motion. The quantities which describe the motion of a fluid (kinetic quantities) are those which have dimensions involving length and time, whereas those which include mass in their dimensions are dynamic quantities.

Types of Fluid Motion

Fluid motion is characterised by the speed at which the fluid passes a point of observation and the direction in which it is moving, i.e., by the **velocity vector.** If at this point, the velocity of successive fluid particles remains constant with time, the flow is said to be **steady.** If the velocity at this given point does vary with time, then the flow is said to be **unsteady.** For example, steady flow occurs in a pipe drawing water from a reservoir with the water surface at constant elevation and the valve at a fixed setting. Unsteady flow occurs in the same pipe whenever the valve is being opened or closed.

Uniform flow occurs when the physical dimensions and type of flow is constant between cross sections at different positions along the flow, e.g. the flow in a channel of constant cross section and slope. If the dimensions or type of flow is not the same at different positions along the direction of flow, then the flow is termed **non-uniform**. Examples of non-uniform flow include the case of a stream approaching a dam across a reservoir or river over which the water accelerates from a slow to relatively high velocity at the bottom of the dam spillway.

Stream Lines and Tubes

Visualisation of the pattern of steady motion relative to a given point of observation is conveniently obtained by imagining a family of stream lines drawn through the fluid in such a way as to indicate the direction of motion in various regions of the flow, Fig.3.1.

A streamline is defined as a line which is tangential to the direction of flow at every point along its length. From this definition it is evident that there can be no flow across a stream line, since the velocity vector has no component in this direction. Stream lines are generally curvilinear and either converge or diverge in accordance with the shape of the boundary surface through which or around which the fluid moves. A portion of a fluid, which is bounded by a number of stream lines, is known as a **stream tube.** The space between the streamlines becomes a tube which is theoretically isolated from the adjacent fluid. The elementary rate of flow dQ past any section of the tube is equal to the velocity V times the area of the cross section;

$$dQ = V \times dA \tag{3.1}$$

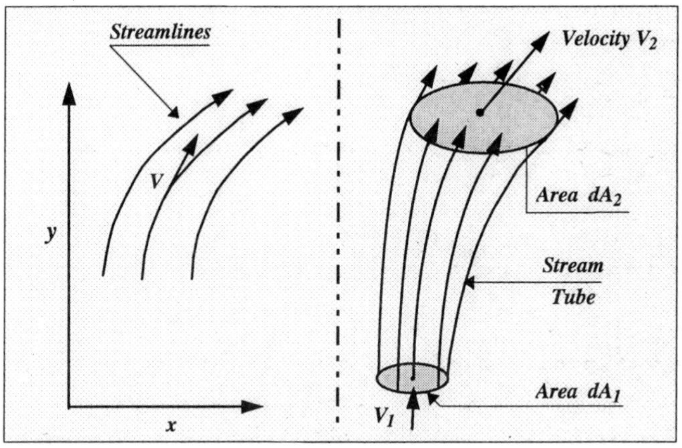

Fig.3.1- Streamlines and stream tubes.

Equation of Continuity

Since the streamtube is bounded by streamlines no fluid can pass through the tube walls. From the law of conservation of mass, the mass crossing one cross-section per unit time must equal simultaneously the mass per unit time passing every other section

$$dm = \rho_1 V_1 dA_1 = \rho_2 V_2 dA_2 \tag{3.2}$$

If the density does not change $\rho_1 = \rho_2$ i.e. if the flow is incompressible

$$dQ = V_1 dA_1 = V_2 dA_2 \tag{3.3}$$

For a series of stream tubes, the equation is integrated to give the discharge,

$$Q = \int_{A_1} V_1 dA_1 = \int_{A_2} V_2 dA_2 \tag{3.4}$$

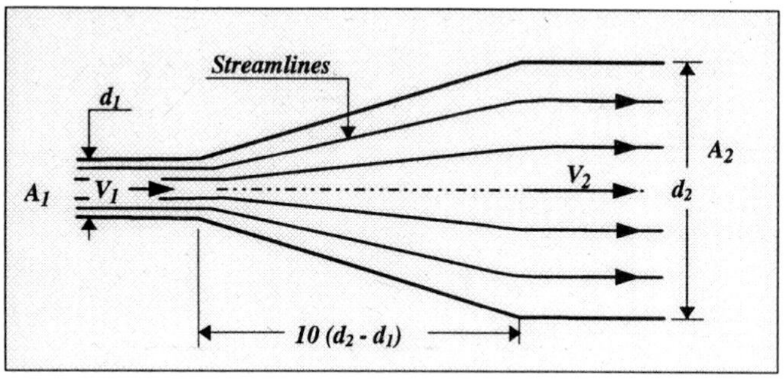

Fig.3.2- Streamlines for a tapered enlargement.

Hence $Q = V_1\, A_1 = V_2\, A_2$ (3.5)

This is the **equation of continuity** of flow.

For example, in a pipe tapered enlargement (varying cross section),

$$V_1 \times \left(\frac{\pi\, d_1^2}{4}\right) = V_2 \times \left(\frac{\pi\, d_2^2}{4}\right) \qquad (3.6)$$

$$\frac{V_1}{V_2} = \left(\frac{d_2}{d_1}\right)^2 \qquad (3.7)$$

Flow Net

To complete the picture of flow visualisation in a given zone, a family of streamlines is drawn in such a way that the unit rate of discharge between each successive pair of streamlines is the same. A glance at the resulting pattern of flow (Fig.3.3) shows both the direction and the relative magnitude of the velocity in every region according to the continuity equation.

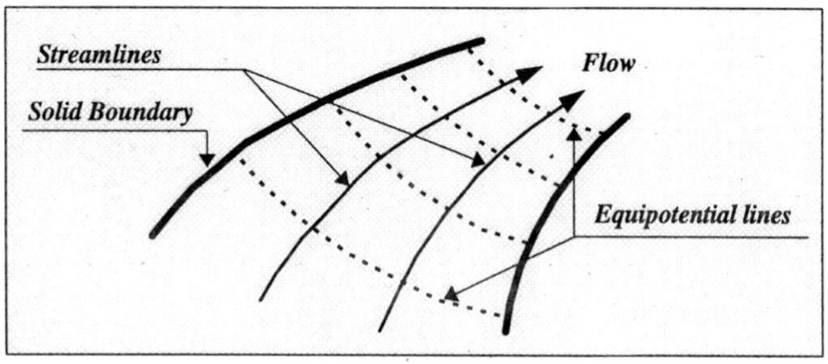

Fig.3.3- A typical flow net for a converging conduit.

A useful guide in drawing the streamlines is found in the fact that in irrotational flow the addition of equipotential lines which are everywhere normal to the streamlines and have the same local spacing, will form a square-meshed grid like that shown in Figure 3.3.

The combination of streamlines and equipotential lines is termed **the flow net.** A trial and error method of plotting the flow net consists of sketching freehand the streamlines and the equipotential according to any plausible ideas and then they are adjusted to fulfil the following conditions:

(1) Each equipotential lines cuts each streamline at right angle.

(2) Each streamtube conveys the same unit of discharge,

(3) The meshes of the flow net are very nearly square.

When liquids percolate through permeable materials, the equipotential lines are in effect lines of equal pressure heads (see Chapter 18).

Euler's Equation

Consider an element of a streamtube as shown in Fig.3.4 applying Newton's Second Law of Motion.

Force = Mass × Acceleration

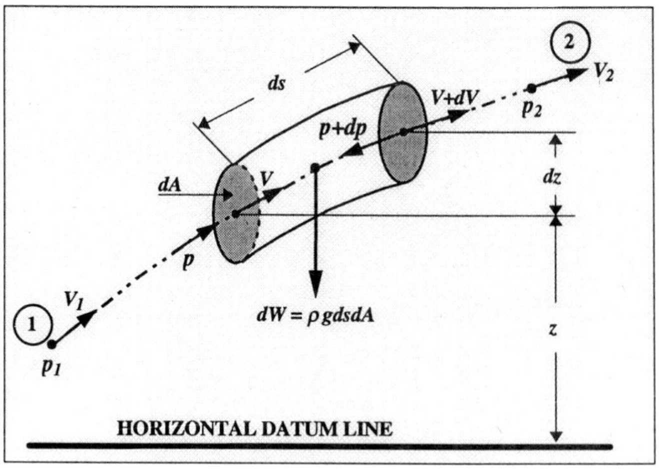

Fig.3.4- Forces on a portion of a streamtube.

The forces acting are the pressure forces on the ends of the element and the component of the weight of the element in the direction of motion, i.e.

$$dF = p dA - (p + dp)\, dA - \rho\, g\, ds\, dA\left(\frac{dz}{ds}\right) \qquad (3.8)$$

which reduces to

$$dF = -dp dA - \rho\, g\, dA\, dz \qquad (3.9)$$

The mass of the element, $dm = \rho ds dA$.

Substituting in Newton's Second Law,

$$-dp dA \;-\rho\, g dA\, dz \;=\; (\,\rho ds dA)\left(\frac{dV}{dt}\right) \qquad (3.10)$$

$$-dp dA \;-\rho\, g dA\, dz \;=\; \rho ds dA\; \times V\;\frac{dV}{ds} \qquad (3.11)$$

Dividing by ρdA the one-dimensional Euler equation results,

$$\frac{dp}{\rho} + V\, dV + g\, dz = 0 \qquad (3.12)$$

For incompressible flow this equation is usually divided by g

$$\frac{dp}{\rho g} + d\left(\frac{V^2}{2g}\right) + dz = constant \qquad (3.13)$$

This is the Euler equation of motion and requires three assumptions:

(i) Motion along a streamline

(ii) Ideal frictionless fluid (i.e. no viscosity)

(iii) Steady flow (i.e. flow conditions are constant with respect to time at a fixed point).

Total Head or Bernoulli's Equation

For incompressible flow, the one-dimensional Euler equation may be integrated (since ρ and g are both constant).

$$\frac{dp}{\rho g} + d\left(\frac{V^2}{2g}\right) + dz = constant \qquad (3.14)$$

This gives the Total Head or Bernoulli equation:

$$\frac{p}{\rho g}+\frac{V^2}{2g}+z=H \qquad (3.15)$$

This equation applies to all points on the streamtube and thus provides a useful relationship between pressure p, velocity V and height above datum z. The term $p/\rho g$ = the pressure head, z = the potential head and $V^2/2g$ is called the velocity head. H is often referred to as the **Total Head** of the streamtube concerned.

Modified Form of Bernoulli's Equation

In the derivation of the Bernoulli's equation the fluid is assumed ideal or inviscid. However, all real fluids have viscosity, and during flow shear stresses result that cause in the flow head losses. The Bernoulli's equation may be applied to a real fluid by adding a term to the equation that accounts for losses. By letting 1 be an upstream point and 2 a downstream point on a stream line, the available total head at 1 equals the available total head at 2 plus all the losses between the two points, $H_1 = H_2 + Losses$. This assumes no fluid machine such as a pump or turbine between the two points. Expanding the above equation,

$$\frac{p_1}{\rho g}+\frac{V_1^2}{2g}+z_1=\frac{p_2}{\rho g}+\frac{V_2^2}{2g}+z_2+Losses \qquad (3.16)$$

When **a pump** adds energy E_p per unit weight between the two points,

$$\frac{p_1}{\rho g}+\frac{V_1^2}{2g}+z_1+E_p=\frac{p_2}{\rho g}+\frac{V_2^2}{2g}+z_2+Losses \qquad (3.17)$$

For a **turbine**, replace E_p by $-E_T$ the energy per unit weight extracted by the turbine. The nature of the losses varies with the application, but experimental data are usually required.

Momentum Principle

There are two distinct methods of approach for determining the interaction of velocities, forces and pressures in fluids in motion. In the Bernoulli's equation approach, the changes of head along a streamline are used to find velocity and pressure changes. When head changes are unknown and only an overall knowledge of the flow is required and mean velocities, we use the momentum principle approach. In mechanics, momentum is defined as the product of the mass of a body and the magnitude of its instantaneous velocity. Both impulse and momentum are necessarily vector quantities. The analysis is applied to the conditions at the boundaries of a fixed control volume, and the changes of momentum arriving and leaving the volume are assessed.

Application of Momentum Equation

Newton's second law of motion may be applied to the conditions of the boundaries of a fixed control volume shown in Fig.3.5. The resultant force on the fluid is equal to the rate of change of momentum in the direction of the force, i.e.:

Force = Mass per second × change in velocity in the direction of force

$$F=\rho Q\times(V_2 - V_1) \qquad (3.18)$$

This is a vector equation in which F is the resultant force and ρQ the mass of fluid per second having its velocity changed from V_1 to V_2.

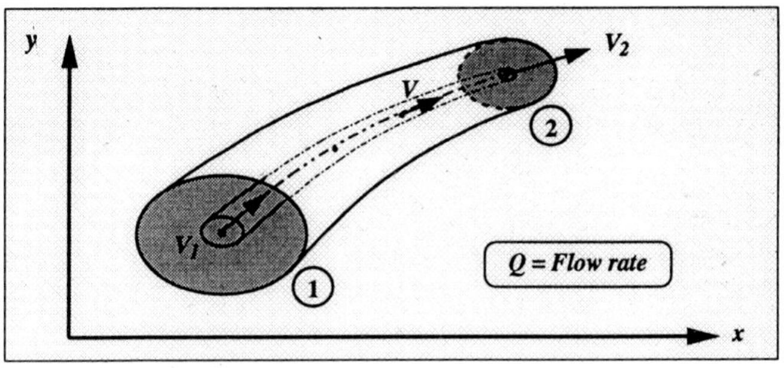

Fig.3.5- Application of momentum equation.

Impact of Water Jets

When a jet of water impinges on a solid surface it forms a thin stream which spreads out along the surface. If the initial and final directions and velocities of the impinging jet are known, the force which it exerts on the surface can be calculated theoretically by using the momentum equation.

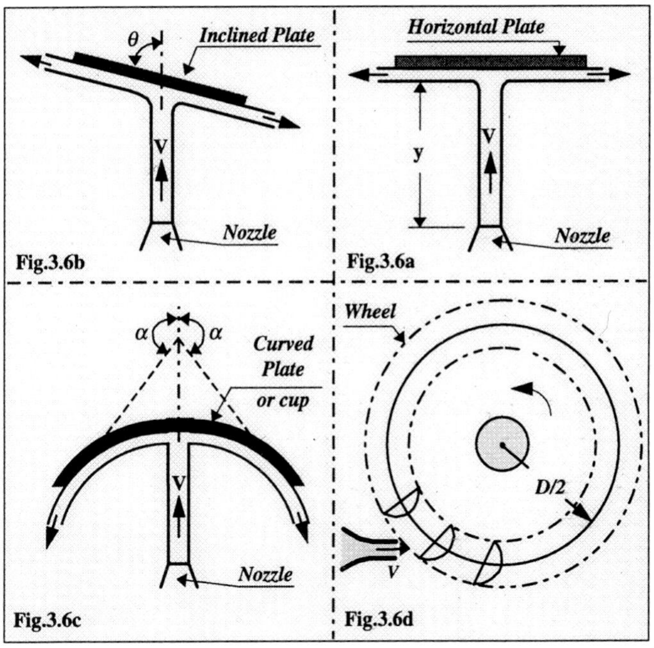

Fig.3.6- Impact of water jets.

Consider a jet strikes normally a flat plate (Fig.3.6a) and leaves it tangentially so that all the momentum in the initial direction of flow is destroyed. The force exerted on plate is:

Force, $F = \rho Q\times(V-0) = \rho QV \qquad (3.19)$

If the plate is inclined by an angle θ to the jet as in Fig.3.6b the jet velocity may be resolved into two components: $V\times\sin\theta$ normal to the plate and $V\times\cos\theta$ parallel to the plate;

Force, $F = \rho Q\times(V\times\sin\theta - 0) = \rho Q\times V\times\sin\theta \qquad (3.20)$

For impact of a jet on a curved surface let α be the angle which the tangents to the curved surface at its edges make with the direction of the jet, Fig 3.6c,

Force, $F = \rho Q\times(V-V\times\cos\alpha) = \rho Q\times V\times(1-\cos\alpha)$

For the case of a hemispherical cup, $\alpha = 180$ degrees so that $\cos\alpha = -1$, and

Force, $F = 2\times\rho QV \qquad (3.21)$

This principle is made use of in the design of impulse water turbines (the Pelton Wheel) for hydro-electric schemes, Fig.3.6d.

Velocity and Discharge Measurements

Measurements of Velocity

The methods can be divided into:

(1) measurements of the velocities at various points of a section of flow which can be integrated into the elementary areas for which each stands and thus the discharge of the whole section may be found and
(2) measurements of discharge from which by dividing by the area of flow the mean velocity can be found. The former are naturally much more laborious, but are necessary if the distribution of the velocity is required.

Measurement of Velocity by Pitot Tube

In its simplest form, the Pitot tube is a pipe with open ends having a right angled head near one end as shown below.

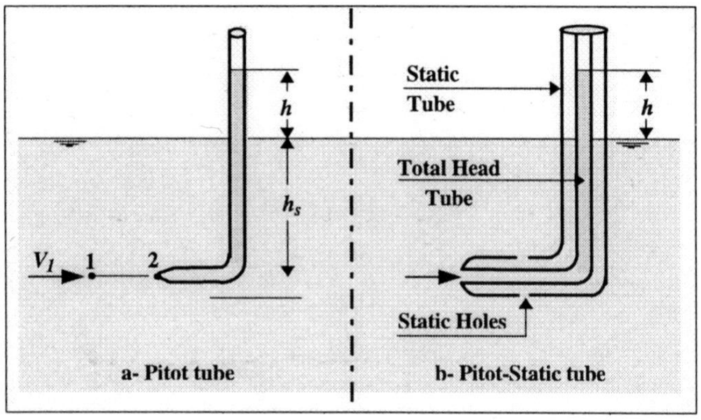

Fig.3.7- Pitot tube and Pitot-static tube.

When it is immersed in a flowing stream with its open end directed against the current, water will rise in the tube to a height h above the water surface. Writing Bernoulli's equation from 1 to 2, neglecting energy losses,

$$\frac{p_1}{\rho g}+\frac{V_1^2}{2g}+z_1=\frac{p_2}{\rho g}+\frac{V_2^2}{2g}+z_2 \qquad (3.22)$$

if the datum plane is taken through points 1 and 2, z_1 and z_2 will be zero. The velocity V_2 is zero because point 2 is the stagnation point where particles of fluid are brought to a complete stop.

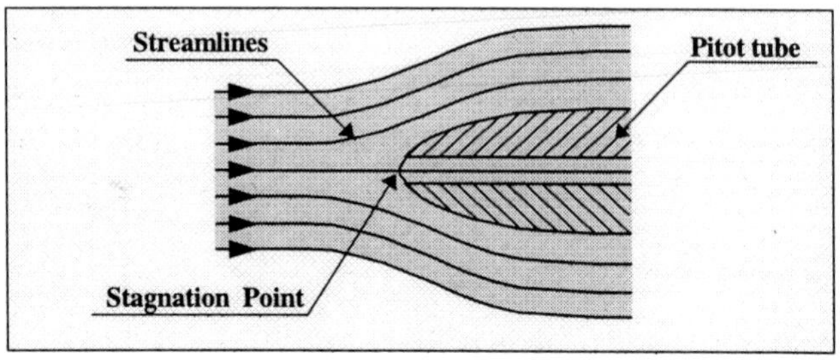

Fig.3.8- Stagnation point at a Pitot tube.

Also $p_1/\rho g$ is equal to h_s and $p_2/\rho g = (h_s + h)$. Therefore,

$$\frac{V_1^2}{2g}+h_s+0=0+(h_s+h)+0 \qquad (3.23)$$

and hence ***Velocity,*** $V_1=\sqrt{2gh}$ (3.24)

which is the required velocity of the stream.

Measurement by Pitot-Static Tube This is an adaptation of the Pitot tube for measuring the velocities of flow in pipes and closed conduits. The inner tube picks up the dynamic pressure, that is the static pressure head plus the velocity head, whilst the outer tube picks up only the static pressure head.

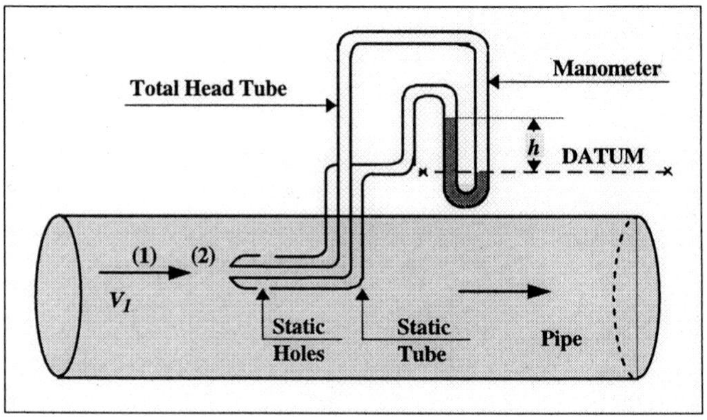

Fig.3.9.- Pitot-static tube with inverted manometer.

Applying the Total Head equation in a similar manner to the Pitot tube, (Fig.3.7),

$$\frac{V_1^2}{2g}+\frac{p_1}{\rho g}=0+\frac{p_2}{\rho g} \qquad (3.25)$$

$$\therefore\ V_1=\sqrt{2\times\frac{(p_2-p_1)}{\rho}}=\sqrt{2gh} \qquad (3.26)$$

For flow in pipe, Fig.3.9, if the density of the liquid in the manometer is ρ_o, then

$p_1-\rho g\times(z+h)+\rho_o gh \ = \ p_2-\rho gz$, or

$$\frac{p_2-p_1}{\rho g}=\left(\frac{\rho_o}{\rho}-1\right)\times h \qquad (3.27)$$

$$\text{But, } V_1=\sqrt{\frac{2g\times(p_2-p_1)}{\rho g}} \qquad (3.28)$$

$$\therefore\ V_1=\sqrt{2gh\times\frac{(\rho_o-\rho)}{\rho}} \qquad (3.29)$$

Volumetric Measurement of Discharge

This is the ultimate or absolute method, viz. to turn the discharge into a large tank, if a liquid, or into a floating gas holder, if a gas, and to measure the increase in volume in a given time. For small quantities of liquid weighing the discharge in a given time is more convenient. ***Discharge, Q = Volume / Time.***

Discharge by Integration of Velocity Profile

The Pitot tube can be used in finding the distribution of velocity in a pipe, as shown in Figure 3.10.

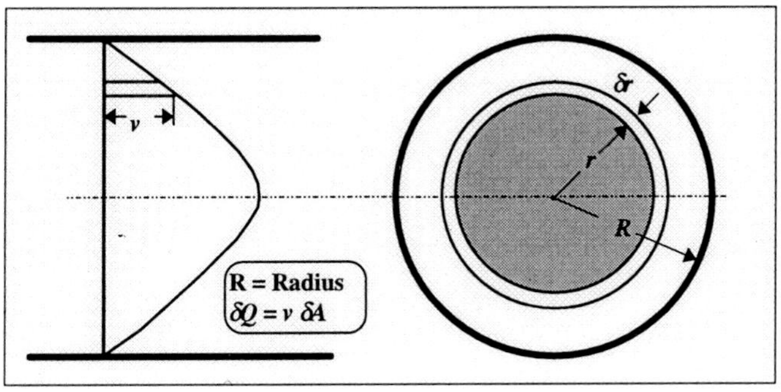

Fig.3.10- Integration of velocity profile in pipe.

The discharge, Q, is found by an integration of the form $Q = \int vdA$ where v is the velocity at right angles to the cross section, and dA is an element of area over which the velocity is constant. The element is a ring of radius r and width dr. Thus the discharge for such a pipe is

$$Q = \int_{o}^{R} 2\pi\, r\, v\, dr \qquad (3.30)$$

The discharge through a pipe or along a river is often expressed by the engineer in terms of the mean velocity V across the section where

$$V = \frac{Discharge}{Area} = \frac{Q}{A} \qquad (3.31)$$

Discharge Measurement by a Venturi Meter

This is an instrument for measuring the quantity of fluid flowing in a pipe. It consists of a short piece of pipe area A_1 followed by a short taper bringing the area down to A_2, which is called the throat. A gradual taper increases the area back to A_1. As the liquid flows through the meter the velocity increases to a maximum at the throat. This increase is velocity results in a decrease in pressure which is measured by piezometers.

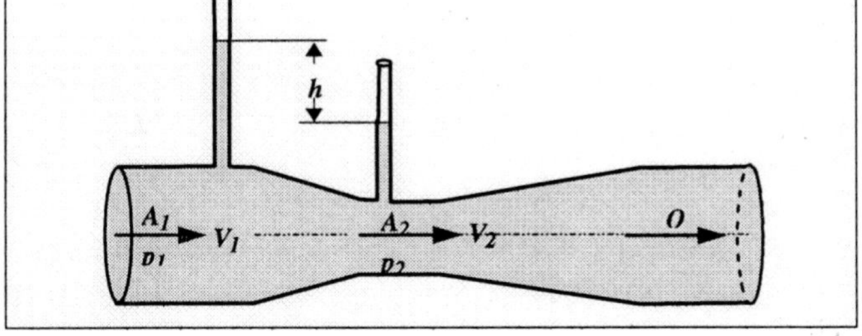

Fig.3.11- Flow through a Venturi meter.

Applying the Total Head equation:

$$\frac{p_1}{\rho g} + \frac{V_1^2}{2g} + z_1 = \frac{p_2}{\rho g} + \frac{V_2^2}{2g} + z_2 \qquad (3.32)$$

If the meter is horizontal $z_1 = z_2$

$$\frac{p_1 - p_2}{\rho g} = \frac{V_2^2 - V_1^2}{2g} \qquad (3.33)$$

From the continuity equation $A_1V_1 = A_2V_2$.

$$V_1 = V_2 \times \frac{A_2}{A_1} \qquad (3.34)$$

Substituting in the above equation,

$$V_2^2 \left[\quad \left(A_2 \right)^2 \right] = h \quad \text{and} \quad V_2 = \sqrt{2gh \Big/ \left[1 - \left(\frac{A_2}{A_1} \right)^2 \right]}$$

$$\frac{2gh}{A_1^2 - A_2^2} \qquad (3.35)$$

.. ..quid flowing, $Q = V_2 A_2$

$$_1A_2 \times \sqrt{\frac{2gh}{A_1^2 - A_2^2}} \qquad (3.36)$$

ıctual discharge is less than this because of head losses due to fluid friction. It is therefore necessary to introduce a coefficient of discharge, C_d (usually 0.96 to 0.99)

$$\text{The discharge is } Q = C_c A_1 A_2 \times \sqrt{\frac{2gh}{A_1^2 - A_2^2}} \qquad (3.37)$$

Discharge Measurement by a Pipe Orifice

These are frequently used for measuring the flow of liquids and gases in pipes and consist of a thin plate fitted into one of the pipe-joints, the plate containing a sharp edged orifice concentric with the pipe. The apparatus is much less costly than a Venturi Meter for a large pipe and takes up much less space as the taper pipes are not required; on the other hand, the net loss of head is much greater.

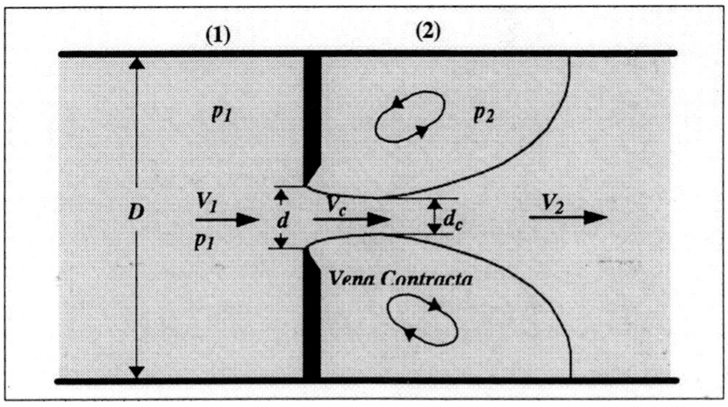

Fig.3.12- Flow through a pipe orifice.

Applying Bernoulli's equation between (1) and (2) we have,

$$\frac{p_1}{\rho g} + \frac{V_1^2}{2g} = \frac{p_2}{\rho g} + \frac{V_2^2}{2g} = \frac{p_2}{\rho g} + \frac{V_c^2}{2g} \qquad (3.38)$$

where p_1 and p_2 the pressures on the two sides of the orifice and V_c is the velocity at the vena contracta. The coefficient of contraction is C_c = *Area of jet at vena contracta / Area of orifice.*

$$\text{But } V_c C_c \times \frac{\pi\, d^2}{4} = V_1 \times \frac{\pi D^2}{4}, \quad \therefore \quad V_1 = V_c C_c \times \frac{d^2}{D^2}.$$

$$\frac{V_c^2}{2g} \times \left(1 - C_c^2 \times \frac{d^4}{D^4} \right) = \frac{p_1 - p_2}{\rho g}$$

$$V_c = \sqrt{2g \times \frac{(p_1 - p_2)}{\rho g} \Big/ \left(1 - C_c^2 \times \frac{d^4}{D^4}\right)} \qquad (3.39)$$

Due to friction the actual velocity is less than the theoretical and so a coefficient of velocity C_v is introduced.

$$Q = C_v C_c \times a \times \sqrt{2g \times \frac{(p_1 - p_2)}{\rho g} \Big/ \left(1 - C_c^2 \times \frac{d^4}{D^4}\right)} \qquad (3.40)$$

where a is the area of orifice. But we can not measure C_c separately as in an orifice discharging into the open air, so it is usual to write,

$$Q = C_d \times a \times \sqrt{2g \times \left(\frac{p_1 - p_2}{\rho g}\right) \Big/ \left(1 - C_c^2 \times \frac{d^4}{D^4}\right)} \qquad (3.41)$$

where C_d is an empirical coefficient of discharge having the value C_d = *actual discharge / theoretical discharge.*

The discharge may be expressed in terms of head,

$$Q = C_d \times a \times \sqrt{2gh \Big/ \left(1 - C_c^2 \times \frac{d^4}{D^4}\right)} \qquad (3.42)$$

The value of C_d is about 0.60.

Pipe Venturi Meter

To measure the flow of water in a system, a venturi meter with an area ratio of 4:1 is installed in a pipe of 100mm diameter. With reference to the diagram shown below, the manometer consists of a large-plan-area reservoir and a small bore gauge tube in which the gauge fluid, a coloured liquid of relative density 1.2, moves against a calibrated scale reading flow-rates directly. Calculate the distance between the zero and 0.001m^3/s scale markings, assuming a coefficient of discharge of 1.0.

$$Q = C_d a_2 \times \sqrt{2g\left(\frac{\rho_a}{\rho} - 1\right)h \Big/ 1 - \left(\frac{a_2}{a_1}\right)^2}$$

$$Q = 1.0 \times \frac{\pi \times 0.05^2}{4} \times \sqrt{\frac{2 \times 9.81 \times 0.2}{1 - 0.062}} \times \sqrt{h} = 4.03 \times 10^{-3} \sqrt{h}$$

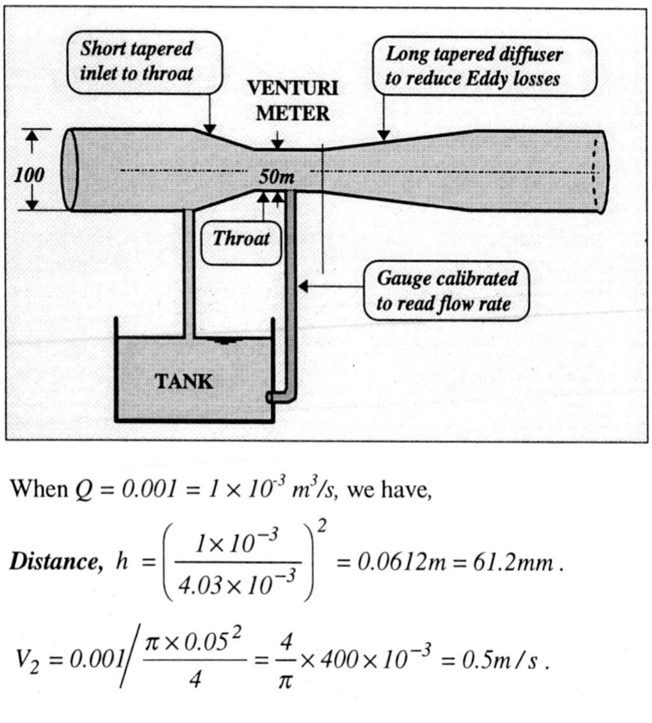

When $Q = 0.001 = 1 \times 10^{-3}\ m^3/s$, we have,

$$\textbf{Distance, } h = \left(\frac{1 \times 10^{-3}}{4.03 \times 10^{-3}}\right)^2 = 0.0612m = 61.2mm.$$

$$V_2 = 0.001 \Big/ \frac{\pi \times 0.05^2}{4} = \frac{4}{\pi} \times 400 \times 10^{-3} = 0.5m/s.$$

Discharge over a V-notch

Show that the discharge of water from a V-notch is given by:

$$Q = \frac{8}{15} \times C_d \sqrt{2g} \times H^{5/2} \times \tan\left(\frac{\theta}{2}\right)$$

where θ is the angle of the notch and H is the head above the vortex. Calculate the discharge of water from a right angled V-notch when the head of water measured above the notch is 1m. The coefficient of discharge C_d for the notch is 0.6. Determine the required accuracy of measuring the head if the error in the estimation of the discharge is not to exceed ± 2%.

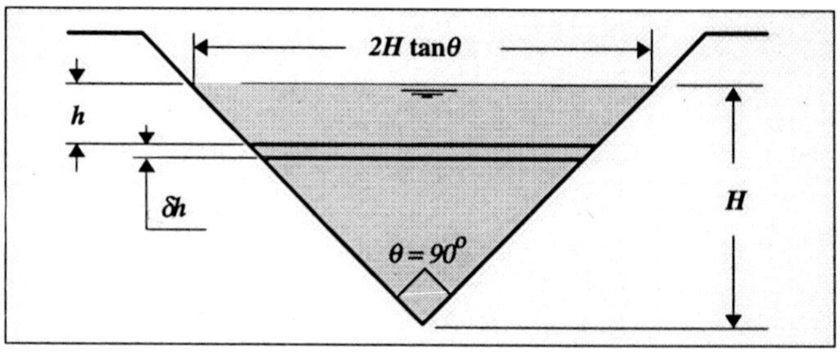

Velocity at depth h, $V = 2\sqrt{2gh}$, neglecting losses.

Flow through elemental strip $\delta Q = Vb \times \delta h$

$$\delta Q = \sqrt{2gh}\ 2\,(H - h)\tan(\theta / 2)\ \delta h$$

$$Q = 2\sqrt{2g} \times \tan\left(\frac{\theta}{2}\right) \times \int_o^H (H - h)\, h^{1/2} dh$$

$$= 2\sqrt{2g} \times \tan\left(\frac{\theta}{2}\right) \times \left[\frac{2H}{3} \times h^{3/2} - \frac{2h^{5/2}}{5}\right]_o^H$$

$$\textit{Theoretical,}\quad Q = \frac{8}{15} \times \sqrt{2g} \times H^{5/2} \times \tan\left(\frac{\theta}{2}\right)$$

$$\textit{Actual,}\quad Q = C_d \times \frac{8}{15} \times \sqrt{2g} \times H^{5/2} \times \tan\left(\frac{\theta}{2}\right)$$

$$Q = 0.6 \times \frac{8}{15} \times \sqrt{2 \times 9.81} \times 1^{5/2} \times \tan 45^o = 1.42\ m^3/s.$$

$$Q = KH^{5/2},\ \therefore\ dQ = \frac{5}{2} \times KH^{3/2} dH.$$

$$\therefore\ \frac{dH}{H} = \pm \frac{2}{5} \times 2\% = \pm\ 0.8\%.$$

Accuracy = 1 ± 0.008m.

British and International Standards

Documents are available which specify nationally and internationally agreed dimensions, procedures and structures for measurements of discharge in pipes and channels. They are called BS or IOS Codes which should be referred to by the engineer when designing or testing flow measuring devices. British Standards and Codes of Practice should be used for pipe fittings and materials. Many commercial fluid meters and recording instruments are available and reference should be made to manufacturer's catalogues for information.

Examples on Fluid Dynamics

Discharge through a Pipe

For turbulent flow through a pipe of radius *r*, the velocity increases as the seventh root of the distance from the wall: $u/U = (y/r)^{1/7}$, where *u* is the velocity at a point *y* from the wall and *U* is the maximum velocity at the axis. In a water main, 1.22m diameter, the velocity at the axis was measured to be 3m/s. Assuming the above velocity distribution, calculate the rate of flow through the pipe and the ratio of the mean to the maximum velocity *U*.

Elemental discharge, $\delta Q = 2\pi\ (r - y)\ u dy$

$$\textbf{Discharge, } Q = 2\pi\ U\int_o^r\left[r\left(\frac{y}{r}\right)^{1/7} - \left(\frac{y^{8/7}}{r^{1/7}}\right)\right]dy \text{ , i.e.}$$

$$Q = 6\pi\left[\frac{r}{r^{1/7}}\times\left(\frac{7}{8}\times y^{8/7}\right) - \frac{1}{r^{1/7}}\times\left(\frac{7}{15}\times y^{15/7}\right)\right]_o^r$$

$$Q = 6\pi\left[\frac{7}{8}\times\frac{r^{15/7}}{r^{1/7}} - \frac{7}{15}\times\frac{r^{15/7}}{r^{1/7}}\right] \text{ and } Q = 2.45\pi r^2 \ .$$

Substituting $r = 0.61m$, $\therefore$ ***Rate of Flow,*** $Q = 2.91m^3/s$.

$$u_{mean} = \frac{2.91}{\pi\times 1.22^2/4} = 2.49 \ m/s, \ \therefore \ \frac{u_{mean}}{U_{max}} = \frac{2.49}{3} = 0.83 \ .$$

Jet Trajectory from a Pipe

Water is discharged from a 150mm diameter pipe flowing full at the outlet, the jet striking the ground at a horizontal distance of 3m and a vertical distance of 1.2m from the end of the pipe. Estimate the rate of flow.

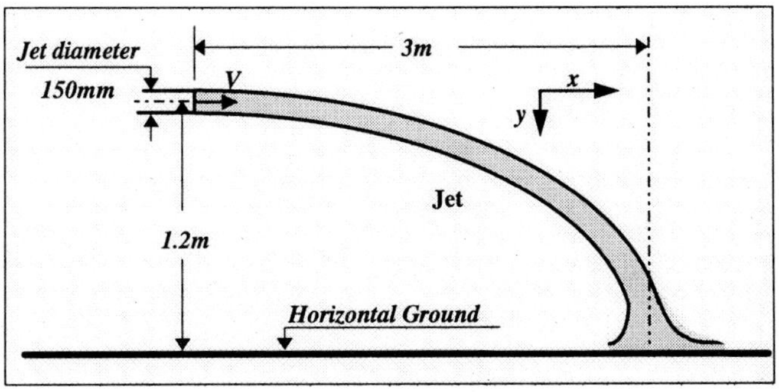

For a time, *t*, the horizontal and vertical distances are given by:

$x = V_1 t$ and $y = -1/2\ gt^2$. *(Vertical velocity at impact is zero).*

Eliminating *t*, the velocity is given by

$$\textbf{Velocity, } V = \frac{x}{\sqrt{-2y/g}} = \frac{3}{\sqrt{-2\times(-1.2)/9.81}} = 6.06m/s \ .$$

$$\textbf{Rate of Flow, } Q = AV = \frac{\pi\times 0.15^2}{4}\times 6.06 = 0.107m^3/s \ .$$

Velocity of an Air Blower

A fan having an efficiency of 65% and driven by a 373W motor, is mounted in a short duct 0.45m diameter with a well-rounded entrance. What is the velocity of air stream as it leaves the duct and what pressure intensity prevails upstream from the fan? Density of air = $1.2kg/m^3$.

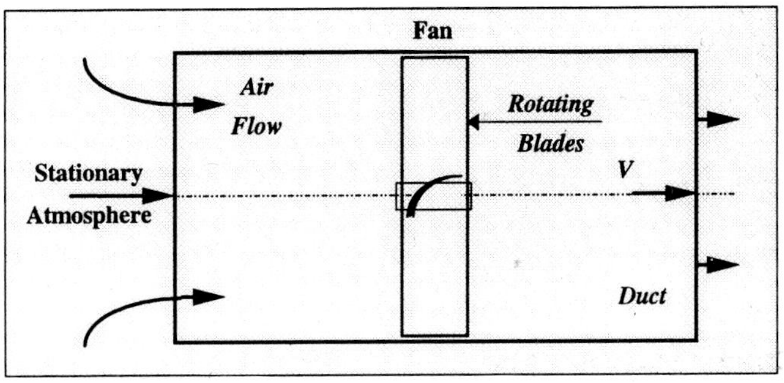

Power = Rate of doing work.
= Rate of flow × Kinetic head/unit volume

$$P = Q\times\left(\frac{\rho V^2}{2}\right) = A\times\frac{\rho V^3}{2}$$

$$\textbf{Velocity, } V = \sqrt[3]{\frac{2P}{\rho A}} = \sqrt[3]{\frac{2\times 0.65\times 373}{1.2\times\pi\times 0.45^2/4}} = 13.65m/s \ .$$

The pressure upstream from the fan is found by applying Bernoulli's equation between a section far from the intake where the air is stationary and one just within the duct.

$$\frac{p_1}{\rho g}+\frac{V_1^2}{2g} = \frac{p_2}{\rho g}+\frac{V_2^2}{2g}, \ \therefore\ 0+0 = \frac{p_2}{\rho g}+\frac{13.65^2}{2g} \ .$$

$$\textbf{Pressure, } p_2 = -\frac{\rho\times V_2^2}{2} = -\frac{1.2\times 13.65^2}{2} = -112N/m^2 \ .$$

Mass Flow Rate in an Air Duct

The table below gives the velocity of air measured along the diameter of a ventilating duct, 1.0m diameter. Estimate the mass flow in kg/s, given that the density of air is $1.2kg/m^3$.

Consider a circular element of width δr with discharge: $\delta Q = 2\pi v\times r\ dr$.

Elemental mass flow rate, $\delta\dot{m} = 2\pi\rho\ v\times r\ dr$. Total mass flow rate $\dot{m} = 2\pi\rho\int_o^R v\times rdr$, where *R* is the radius of the pipe.

Multiply various values of velocity *v* by corresponding values of *r* as shown in the table below.

Radius, *r, (m)*	0	0.10	0.20	0.30	0.40	0.45	0.48
Velocity, *v, (m/s)*	1.81	1.78	1.76	1.77	1.68	1.55	0.90
$v\times r$	0	0.178	0.352	0.531	0.612	0.692	0.432

Plot vr against r.

Area under the graph $\approx 0.5 \times 0.5 \times 0.69$

$\approx 0.1725\ m^3/s.$

Mass flow, $\dot{m} = 2\pi \times 1.2 \times 0.1725 = 1.3 kg/s.$

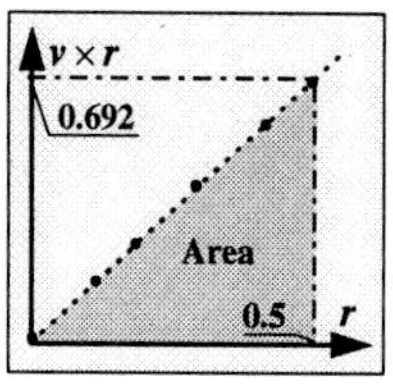

Mercury head in manometer, h, is therefore given by:

$$h = \frac{(p_1 - p_2) - 0.225 \times \rho_p g}{\rho_m g - \rho_p g} = \frac{33900 - (0.225 \times 780 \times 9.81)}{(13{,}600 - 780) \times 9.81}$$

$$\textit{Head,}\ h = \frac{32{,}178}{125{,}764} = 0.256m.$$

Flow Through a Venturi Meter

A venturi meter has its axis vertical. The inlet and throat diameters are 150mm and 75mm respectively. The throat is 225mm above the inlet and the coefficient of discharge for the meter is 0.96. Petrol of specific gravity 0.78 flows upwards through the meter at a rate of $0.0396 m^3/s$. Determine the pressure difference in kN/m^2 between the inlet and throat, the difference of level which would be registered for by a vertical mercury manometer. Take the specific gravity of mercury to be 13.6. Derive any formulae used.

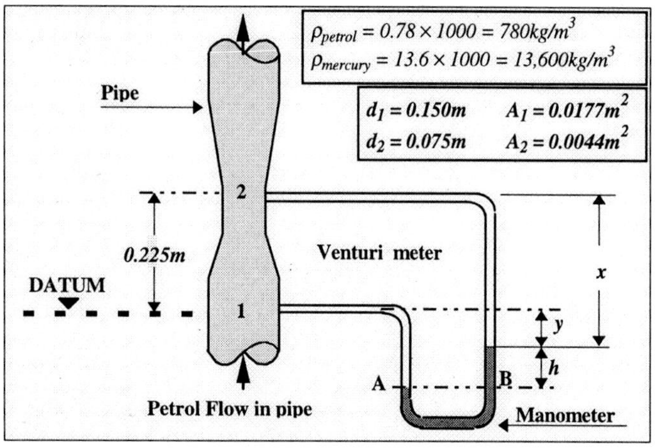

(a) Applying Bernoulli equation between points 1 and 2,

$$\frac{p_1}{\rho_p g} + \frac{V_1^2}{2g} + z_1 = \frac{p_2}{\rho_p g} + \frac{V_2^2}{2g} + z_2$$

Assuming no losses $z_1 = 0$ and $z_2 = 0.225m$.

$$\frac{p_1 - p_2}{\rho_p g} = \frac{V_2^2}{2g} - \frac{V_1^2}{2g} + z_2$$

Rearranging continuity equation:

$Q = Cd\, A_1\, V_1 = Cd\, A_2\, V_2 = 0.0396\ m^3/s.$

$$V_1 = \frac{0.0396}{C_d \times A_1} = \frac{0.0396}{0.96 \times 0.0177} = 2.331 m/s.$$

$$V_2 = \frac{0.0396}{C_d \times A_2} = \frac{0.0396}{0.96 \times 0.0044} = 9.375 m/s.$$

Substituting V_1 and V_2 into above equation, head of petrol is

$$\frac{p_1 - p_2}{\rho_p g} = \frac{9.375^2}{2 \times 9.81} - \frac{2.331^2}{2 \times 9.81} + 0.225 = 4.428m.$$

Therefore, $p_1 - p_2 = 4.428 \times 780 \times 9.81 = 33882\ N/m^2$, or $p_1 - p_2 = 33.9 kN/m^2$.

(b) For Manometer, ***Pressure at A = Pressure at B.***

$p_1 + \rho_p g\,(h+y) = p_2 + \rho_m g h + \rho_p g x,$ or

$p_1 - p_2 = \rho_m\, gh - \rho_p gh + \rho_p g \times (x - y).$

But, $(x-y) = 0.225m.$ $\therefore$ $p_1 - p_2 = h \times (\rho_m g - \rho_p g) + 0.225\, \rho_p g.$

Flow in a 90° Pipe Bend

Water flowing vertically downward in a 300mm diameter pipeline at a rate of $0.1 m^3/s$ is turned through 90° by a bend which is also in a vertical plane. The centre line of the bend at outlet is 1.4m below the inlet and the pressure at the inlet to the bend is $150 kN/m^2$. Assume that the pipe diameter remains constant, that the bend has a volume of $0.2 m^3$ and the bend is held in position solely by the bolts in the flanges at each end. Calculate the stresses in the bolts in the inlet and outlet flanges if each flange has 12-20mm diameter bolts.

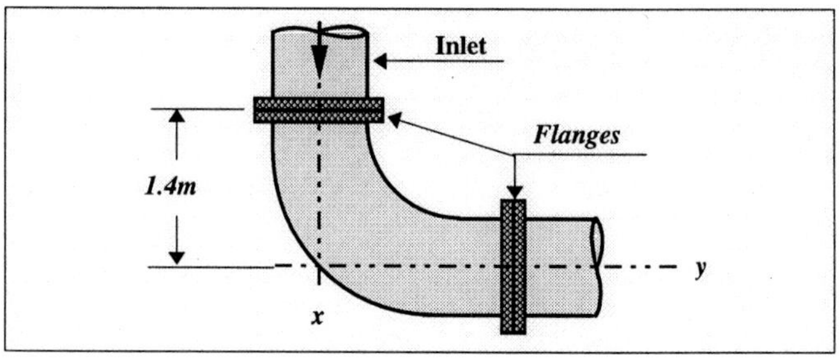

Take axes as shown. Consider forces acting in the x-direction.

(a) pressure force $= p_1 A_1$ acting on inlet.
(b) weight of water in bend, W.
(c) change in momentum of fluid.

$V_1 = 0.1/(\pi/4) \times 0.3^2 = 1.415 m/s.$

Total force, $F_x = p_1 A_1 + W + \rho Q \times (V_1 - V_2)$

$= (150 \times 10^3 \times (\pi/4) \times 0.3^2) + (0.2 \times 1000 \times 9.81) +$

$(1000 \times 0.1 \times (1.415 - 0)) = 12706N$

Area of one bolt, $= (\pi/4) \times 0.02^2 = 3.142 \times 10^{-4} m^2.$

Total area of bolts in flange, $12 \times 3.142 \times 10^{-4} = 3.77 \times 10^{-3}\ m^2.$

Therefore, ***stress in bolts in inlet flange,***

$= 12706 / 3.77 \times 10^{-3} = 3.37 \times 10^6 N/m^2 = 3.37\ N/mm^2.$

Forces acting in y-direction:

(a) pressure force on outlet and (b) change in momentum.

Applying total head equation between inlet and outlet.

$$\frac{p_1}{\rho g} + \frac{V_1^2}{2g} + z_1 = \frac{p_2}{\rho g} + \frac{V_2^2}{2g} + z_2$$

But, $V_1 = V_2$ and $h_1 - h_2 = 1.4m.$ $\therefore$ $\dfrac{p_2}{\rho g} = \dfrac{p_1}{\rho g} + (z_1 - z_2).$

$$p_2 = 9.81 \times 1000 \left(\frac{150 \times 10^3}{9.31 \times 1000} + 1.4 \right) = 163.7 kN/m^2.$$

Total force in y-direction $= F_y = p_2 A_2 - \rho Q \times (V_1 - V_2)$

$= 163.7 \times 10^3 \times (\pi/4) \times 0.3^2 - 1000 \times 0.1 \times (0 - 1.415)$

$\therefore F_y = -11712N.$

Stress in bolt in outlet flange $= 11712 / (3.77 \times 10^{-3})$

$\mathbf{= 3.11 \times 10^6 N/m^2 = 3.11 N/mm^2}.$

Thrust on Vertical Pipe Bend

A horizontal pipe 2.0m diameter is bent downwards through an angle of 45° and tapered to 1.5m diameter. The difference in level between the pipe centre line at entry and outlet is 1.0m and the volume of water in the tapered bend is 7.5m^3. The pressure of the water at the outlet is zero gauge and the discharge is 10 m^3/s. Calculate the thrust on the bend due to the water flow, neglecting all losses.

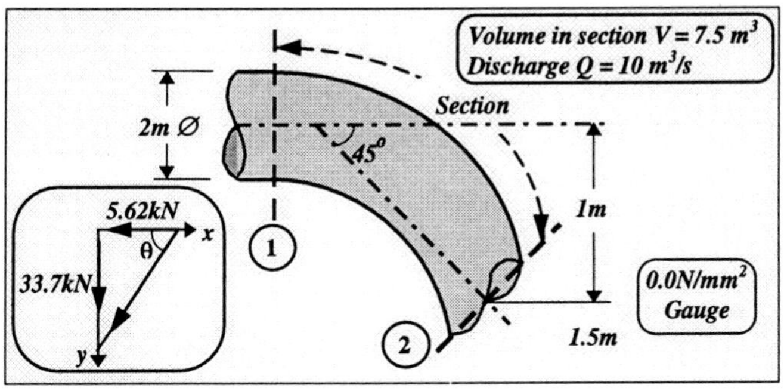

Flow velocity at 1, $= 10/(\pi \times 2^2/4) = 3.18 m/s.$

Flow velocity at 2, $= (2/1.5)^2 \times 3.18 = 5.65 m/s.$

Maximum flow rate, $\rho Q = 10 \times 1 = 10 kg/s.$

Applying Bernoulli's equation between 1 and 2:

$$\frac{p_1}{\rho g} + z_1 + \frac{V_1^2}{2g} = \frac{p_2}{\rho g} + z_2 + \frac{V_2^2}{2g}$$

$$p_1 = p_2 - \rho g\,(z_1 - z_2) + \frac{\rho}{2} \times (V_2^2 - V_1^2).$$

$$= 0 - (9.81 \times 1000) + 0.5 \times 1000 \times (31 - 9.8) = 0.79 kN/m^2.$$

Momentum forces on fluid,
$F_x = \rho Q \times (V_2 \times \cos 45 - V_1) = 10 \times (3.99 - 3.18) = 8.1 kN.$
$F_y = \rho Q \times (V_2 \times \sin 45 - 0) = 10 \times 3.99 = 39.9 kN.$

Pressure forces on fluid, $P_x = (0.79 \times \pi \times 2^2/4) - 0 = 2.48 kN.$
$P_y = 0 - 0 = 0$

Gravity forces on fluid, $W = \rho g V = 9.81 \times 7.5 = 73.6 kN.$

Equivalent forces on fluid, $R_x = F_x - P_x = 8.1 - 2.48 = 5.62 kN.$
$R_y = F_y - W = 39.9 - 73.6 = -33.7 kN.$

Reaction force on bend, $= \sqrt{5.62^2 + 33.7^2} = 34.2 kN.$

$\theta = \cos^{-1}(5.62/34.2) = 80.5^o.$

Force on a Converging Pipe Bend

A converging 60° pipe bend has inlet and outlet diameters of 0.15m and 0.10m respectively. The flow is 0.1m^3/s and the inlet gauge pressure is 0.14N/mm^2. Calculate the magnitude and direction of the resultant force on the pipe bend in the horizontal plane.

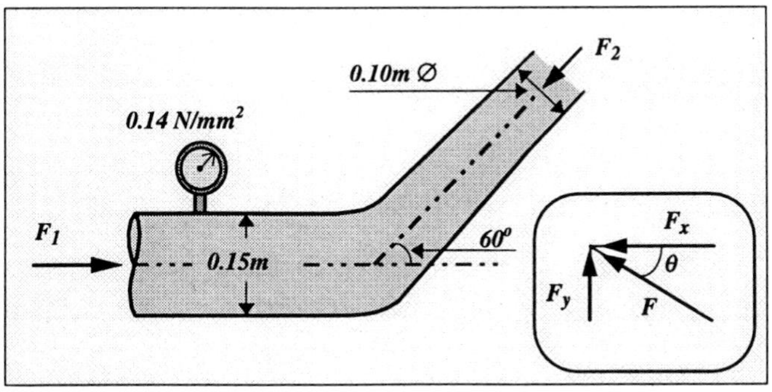

Velocity at inlet, $V_1 = 0.1 \times 4/(\pi \times 0.15^2) = 5.56 m/s.$

Velocity at outlet, $V_2 = 0.1 \times 4/(\pi \times 0.1^2) = 12.8 m/s.$

Total head at inlet $= 140/9.81 + V_1^2/2g$
$= 14.27 + 1.63 = 15.8 m.$

Total head at outlet $= h + V_2^2/2g$
$= h + 8.35 = 15.8 m.$

Pressure head at outlet $= 7.4 m.$
$F_1 = 140 \times 1000 \times 0.15^2 \times \pi/4 = 2475 N.$
$F_2 = 7.4 \times 9.81 \times 1000 \times 0.1^2\ \pi/4 = 570 N.$

Momentum equation in x-direction:
$2475 - 570 \times \cos 60^o - F_x = 0.1 \times 1000 \times [V_2 \times \cos 60^o - V_2]$
$2475 - 285 - F_x = 100\,[\,6.4 - 5.6] = 80.$
$F_x = 2475 - 365 = 2110\ N.$

Momentum equation in y-direction:-
$F_y - 570 \times \sin 60^o = (V_2 \times \sin 60^o)\,\rho Q$
$F_y = 570 \times 0.866 + 12.8 \times 0.866 \times 1000 \times 0.1$
$= 493 + 1107 = 1600 N.$

Resultant force on bend $= \sqrt{2110^2 + 1600^2} = 2640 N.$

$$\tan\theta = \frac{1600}{2110} = 0.76\ .\ \therefore\ \theta = 37^o 24'.$$

Resultant Force acts at 37° 24' to inlet.

Force on a Small Dam

A small control weir built across a 2m wide flume carrying water, as shown in figure below. Assuming a frictionless flow, calculate the horizontal force on the weir due to the given flow.

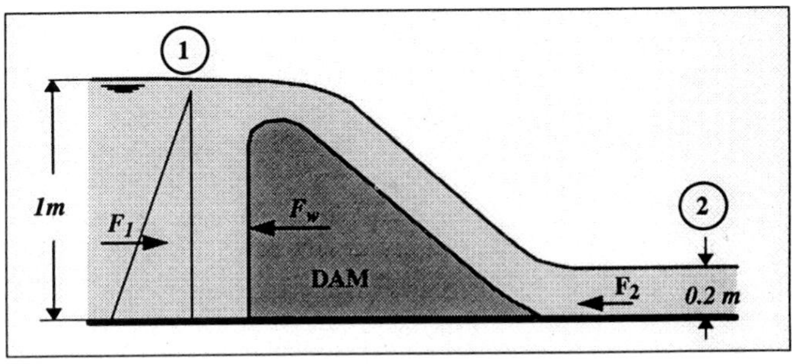

Applying Bernoulli equation between points (1) and (2):

$$1.0 + \frac{V_1^2}{2g} = 0.2 + \frac{V_2^2}{2g}.$$ Hence, $V_1 \times 1.0 = V_2 \times 0.2,\ \therefore\ V_2 = 5V_1$

Substituting, $$1.0 + \frac{V_1^2}{2g} = 0.2 + \frac{25V_1^2}{2g}.$$

$$\frac{24 \times V_1^2}{19.62} = 0.8,\ \therefore\ V_1 = 0.809 m/s.$$

Applied force = Rate of change of momentum
$F_1 - F_2 - F_w = 1.0 \times 0.809 \times 1000 \times (5V_1 - V_1) = 2610 N.$

But, $F_1 = \rho g\, h_1^2/2 = 9.81 \times 1000 \times 1/2 = 4900 N.$
$F_2 = \rho g\, h_2^2/2 = 9.81 \times 1000 \times 0.2^2/2 = 196 N.$
$F_w = 4900 - 196 - 2610 = 2094$ *N/metre width.*

Since there is 2m wide,

Total force on weir is $2 \times 2094 = 4188 N.$

Force on a Horizontal Pipe Bend

A converging 45° pipe bend with a bolted nozzle is shown below. The pipe diameter is 100mm and the velocity at outlet is 4m/s. Calculate: (a) the force of water on the bend, (b) the clamping force for the nozzle and (c) the pressure force on a sealed nozzle.

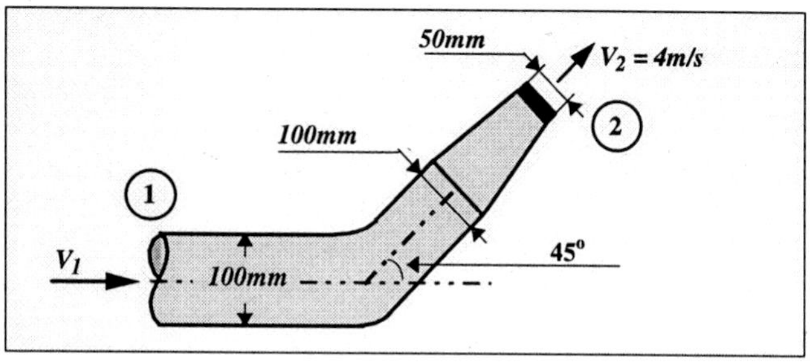

Velocity at outlet, $V_2 = 4m/s$.

Velocity in pipe, $V_1 = 4 \times 50^2/100^2 = 1.0m/s$.

(a) Applying Bernoulli's equation between points 1 and 2 and assuming no losses: $\frac{p_1}{\rho g}+\frac{V_1^2}{2g}=\frac{p_2}{\rho g}+\frac{V_2^2}{2g}$.

$$p_1 = \rho g \times \frac{V_2^2 - V_1^2}{2g} = 9.81 \times 10^3 \times \frac{4^2 - 1^2}{2 \times 9.81} = 7.5kPa.$$

Applying the momentum equation:

$$F_x + 7.5 \times 10^3 \times \frac{0.1^2 \pi}{4} = 10^3 \times 1 \times \frac{0.1^2 \pi}{4} \times (4\cos 45^o - 1).$$

Horizontal force, $F_x = 44.54N$.

Vertical force, $F_y = 10^3 \times 7.85 \times 10^{-3} \times 4 \sin 45^o = 22.21N$.

Resultant force, $F = 49.8N$ *acting at* $26.5°$.

(b) Minimum clamping force, $F - 7.5 \times 7.854 = 7.854 \times (4-1)$

$F = 35.3N.$

(c) Pressure for sealed nozzle, $p = 9.81 \times 10^3 \times (4^2/2g) = 8kPa$.

Minimum clamping force, $F = 8 \times 10^3 \times \left(\frac{0.1^2 \pi}{4} - \frac{0.05^2 \pi}{4}\right)$

$F = 47.2N.$

Impact Force on Pivoted Plate

A uniform plate, 2m square and of mass 2000g, is pivoted along its upper edge which is horizontal. A jet of water, 100mm diameter and moving with a velocity 20m/s, strikes the plate. If the axis of the jet is horizontal and its centre-line is 1.5m vertically below the top of plate, calculate the angle to vertical, θ, at which the plate will be in equilibrium.

To calculate force exerted by jet, define x axis perpendicular to plate as shown below.

Force in x-direction = mass/sec striking plate × change in velocity.

$F_x = \rho a V \times (V\cos\theta - 0) = \rho a V^2 \times \cos\theta$.

Taking moment about pivot

$$2000g \times 1 \times \sin\theta = \rho a V^2 \times \cos\theta \times \frac{1.5}{\cos\theta}.$$

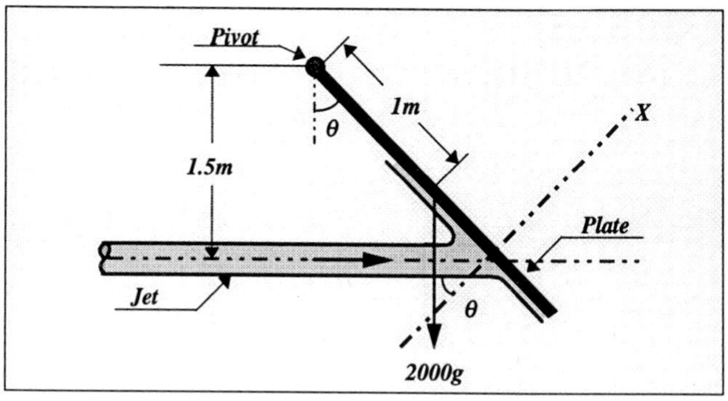

$$\sin\theta = \frac{\rho a V^2 \times 1.5}{2000g} = 1000 \times \frac{\pi}{4} \times \frac{0.1^2 \times 1.5 \times 20^2}{2000g} = 0.24$$

$\therefore$ ***θ = 13.89°.***

Problems on Fluid Dynamics

[1] A venturi meter is employed to measure the flow of liquid of S.G. 1.15. The pipe diameter is 90mm and the throat diameter is 30mm. Calculate the flow when the differential mercury manometer reads 215mm, the liquid being in contact with the mercury. The meter discharge coefficient is 0.95. Specific gravity of mercury = 13.6. ($0.00454m^3/s$)

[2] A horizontal jet of water from a fire hose strikes a vertical wall at an angle of 30° to the normal to the wall with a velocity of 30m/s and a rate of flow of $0.6m^3/min$. Calculate the force exerted by the jet normal to the wall. (260 N)

[3] Calculate the tension force on the flanged connection between a 0.1m diameter pipe and a 0.025m diameter nozzle discharging a water jet to atmosphere at 30m/s. Neglect losses. (3119 N)

[4] Compensation water is to be discharged by two circular orifices under a constant head of 0.75m measured to the centre of the orifice. What diameter will be required to give $13620m^3/day$? Assume $C_c = 0.662$ and $C_v = 0.97$. (0.2085m)

[5] Determine the width of a sharp-crested rectangular weir required to discharge $125{,}000m^3/day$ if the level of the water above the crest must not be more than 0.6m. Assume $C_d = 0.6$. (1.81m)

[6] Calculate the value of the angle θ for a V-notch which is to discharge $0.41m^3/s$ under a head of 0.6m, assuming a coefficient of discharge of 0.6. (91° 24')

CHAPTER FOUR

FLUID FRICTION

Laminar and Turbulent Flows

The effects of viscosity cause the flow of a real fluid to occur under two different conditions: "Laminar" and "Turbulent" flow. In laminar flow each layer of fluid travels parallel to the adjacent layers and the paths of individual particles do not cross. In contrast, in turbulent flow the water particles move in irregular paths. In general, laminar flow occurs at relatively low velocities and turbulent flow at higher velocities.

Experimental Evidence

Observed Behaviour of Liquid Elements

The nature of the two modes of flow was demonstrated by Reynolds in 1883, with an apparatus similar to the one shown below in Fig.4.1.

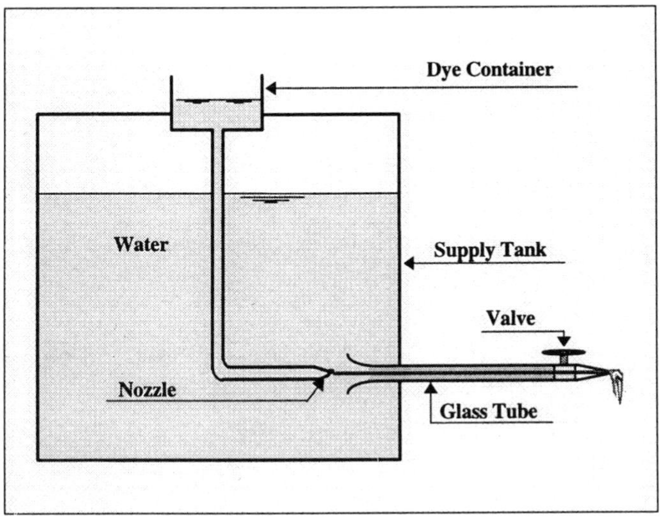

Fig.4.1- Observation of flow in a pipe

Water flows from the tank through a glass pipe, with the rate of flow being controlled by a valve. A fine stream of dye may then be injected through an epidermic tube. When the velocity in the glass tube is low, the dye will be carried through the tube as a **single thread** (Fig.4.2a). As the velocity is increased by opening the valve gradually, the dye **filament wavers** (Fig.4.2b) and then finally breaks up at some intermediate section, beyond which an irregular series of **turbulent eddies** cause the dye to spread over the entire section of the pipe (Fig.4.2c).

Measurements of the change in piezometric head along the tube at different flows, indicates that it remains proportional to the first power of velocity, as long as the flow remains laminar.

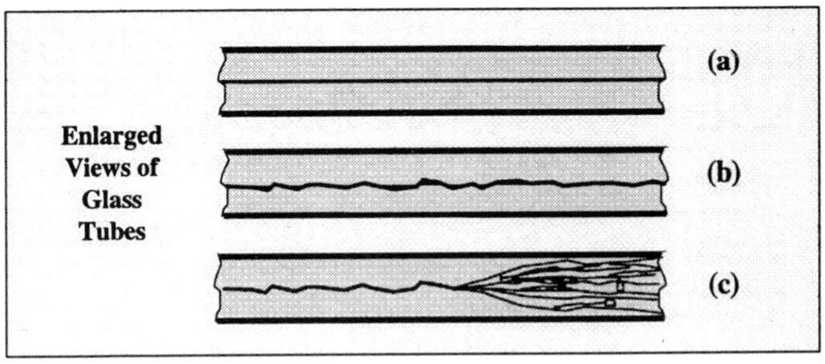

Fig.4.2- Behaviour of the dye filament with increasing velocity.

Relationship between velocity and head loss

With the onset of instability, however, the resistance greatly increases, being almost proportional to the second power of the velocity (Fig.4.3) after the flow becomes fully turbulent.

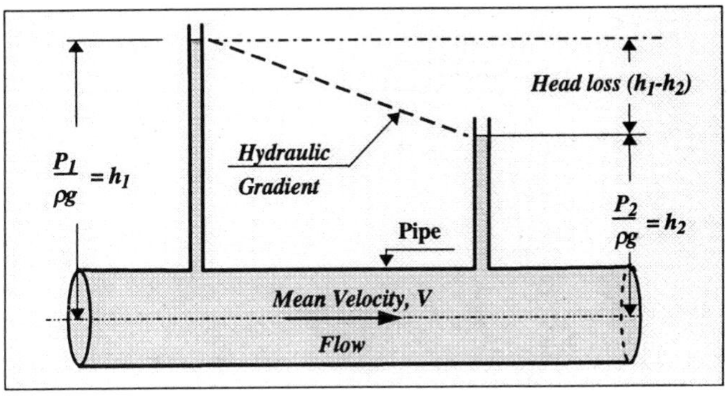

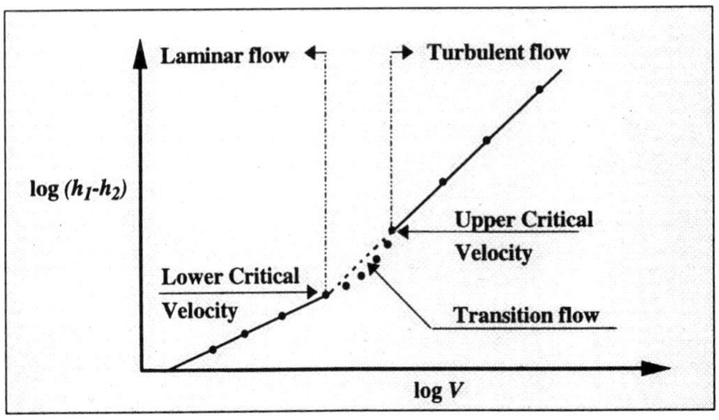

Fig.4.3- Relation between mean velocity and head loss

The departure from laminar conditions thus involves not only a pronounced intermixing between neighbouring zones but also a marked increased in the rate of energy loss.

Laminar and Turbulent Flows

Laminar Flow in Pipes

The law of laminar flow in pipes was determined experimentally, independently by Hagen and Poiseuille and is known by the latter. This law can be developed from fundamental principles as explained below.

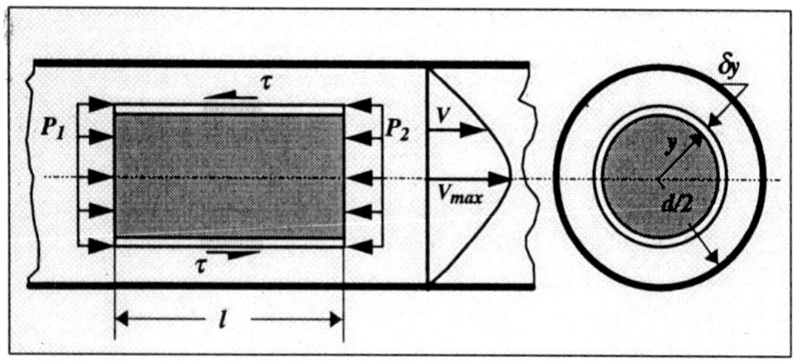

Fig.4.4- Laminar flow in a pipe.

Consider the forces acting on a cylinder of fluid of length l and radius y as shown in Fig.4.4. If steady motion exists, the force caused by the difference in pressures on the ends of the cylinder must be balanced by the force resulting from the shear stress τ on the curved boundaries of the cylinder as expressed by the following,

$$(p_1 - p_2)\pi y^2 = \tau(2\pi y l) \qquad (4.1)$$

Simplifying and introducing the value of τ from the viscosity equation, $\tau = -\mu \dfrac{dv}{dy}$, we have

$$(p_1 - p_2)\, y = -2\,\mu l \frac{dv}{dy} \qquad (4.2)$$

The minus sign being included because increments of v and y are opposite in sign as shown above. Equation (4.2) may be solved for dV as follows:

$$\int_{v=(d/2)}^{v=(y)} dv = -\frac{(p_1 - p_2)}{2\mu l} \times \int_{y}^{d/2} y\, dy \qquad (4.3)$$

Integrating,

$$v = -\frac{(p_1 - p_2)\times y^2}{4\mu l} + C \qquad (4.4)$$

The value of constant C may be obtained from the boundary condition that $y = d/2$ when $v = 0$. Then

$$C = \frac{(p_1 - p_2)\times d^2}{16\mu l} \qquad (4.5)$$

$$v = \frac{(p_1 - p_2)}{4\mu l} \times \left(\frac{d^2}{4} - y^2\right) \qquad (4.6)$$

This is an example of the equation of a parabola: $y^2 = 4\,a\,x$.

This is **Poiseuille's equation** which shows the velocity distribution for laminar flow in circular pipes to be a paraboloid of revolution. The value of the maximum velocity along the centreline may be determined be letting $y = 0$.

Maximum Velocity, $V_{max} = \dfrac{(p_1 - p_2)\times d^2}{16\mu l}$ (4.7)

Since the volume of a paraboloid of revolution is one-half that of the circumscribing cylinder, the mean velocity is one-half the maximum. The mean or average velocity V may be obtained from equation (4.7) by putting by $V = 0.5 \times V_{max}$,

Mean Velocity, $V = \dfrac{(p_1 - p_2)\times d^2}{32\mu l}$ (4.8)

Hence, for laminar flow the maximum velocity is twice the average or mean velocity.

The discharge Q in the pipe is obtained by integration,

$$Q = \int dQ = \int v\, dA = \int_0^{d/2} 2\pi y\, V\, dy \qquad (4.9)$$

Substituting the value of v from equation (4.6),

$$Q = \frac{\pi(p_1 - p_2)}{2\mu l} \times \int_0^{d/2} \left(\frac{y\, d^2}{4} - y^3\right) dy = \frac{\pi(p_1 - p_2)\times d^4}{128 \times \mu l} \qquad (4.10)$$

The expression for the change in piezometric head in a length l may be obtained by solving for $(p_1 - p_2)$ in (4.8),

$$Head\ loss = \frac{(p_1 - p_2)}{\rho g} = h = \frac{32\,\mu l V}{\rho g\, d^2} \qquad (4.11)$$

Introducing a dimensionless parameter called the Reynolds number, $R = \rho V d/\mu$, the above expression becomes:

Head loss due to friction, $h_f = \dfrac{16}{R} \times \dfrac{l}{(d/4)} \times \left(\dfrac{V^2}{2g}\right)$ (4.12)

If in equation (4.12), we write ***f* = 16/*R*,** the expression becomes

Head loss, $h_f = \dfrac{4flV^2}{2gd}$ (4.13)

The straight line shown in Fig.4.6 is a graphical representation of the relation for ***the friction factor*** is,

$f = 16/R$ (4.14)

Turbulent Flow in Pipes

We shall make the assumption that in turbulent flow the liquid is rubbing against the walls of the pipe and that the resistance it experiences is overcome by a gradual fall of pressure in the liquid in the direction of motion. Therefore, the product of the intensity of shear τ_o at the wall and the boundary area in a given length of pipe should equal the product of cross sectional area and the reduction in pressure $(p_1 - p_2)$ in that distance:

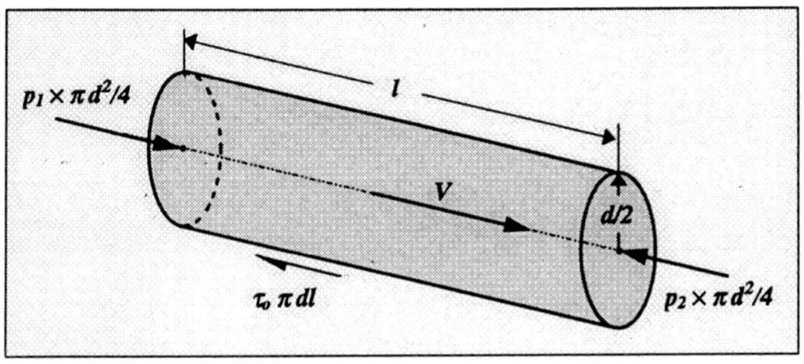

Fig.4.5- Turbulent flow in a pipe.

$$\tau_o \times \pi dl = (p_1 - p_2) \times \pi d^2/4 \qquad (4.15)$$

$$\tau_o = (p_1 - p_2) \times d/4l \qquad (4.16)$$

Divisions of both sides of equation (4.16) by the quantity $\rho V^2/2$ then results a particular number f. That is

$$\frac{\tau_o}{\rho V^2/2} = \frac{(p_1 - p_2)}{\rho V^2/2} \times \frac{d}{4l} = f \qquad (4.17)$$

on dividing by ρg and substituting $\Delta p/\rho g = h_f$, we have

$$\textbf{\textit{Head loss due to friction,}}\ h_f = \frac{4flV^2}{2gd} \qquad (4.18)$$

which is the well known **Darcy-Weisbach** formula for flow in pipes. It still remains for turbulent flow to evaluate the friction coefficient *f* for solving practical problems.

Reynolds Number and Friction Factor

The existence of the two types of flow was described by Hagen in his publications (1839 to 1869) but the law governing transition between laminar and turbulent flow was stated by Reynolds (1883). He observed that the point at which pipe flow changes from laminar to turbulent depends upon the velocity, density, and viscosity of the fluid and upon the diameter of the pipe, arranged in the following dimensionless form, later called the "Reynolds number".

$$R = \frac{\rho V d}{\mu}, \text{ or } R = \frac{Vd}{\upsilon} \qquad (4.19)$$

If the pipe surface is manifestly smooth to the touch, it is found that the friction coefficient, *f*, depends on the Reynolds number. The diagram, Fig.4.6, is a plot of log *f* against log(*R*) for experiments carried out on smooth pipes.

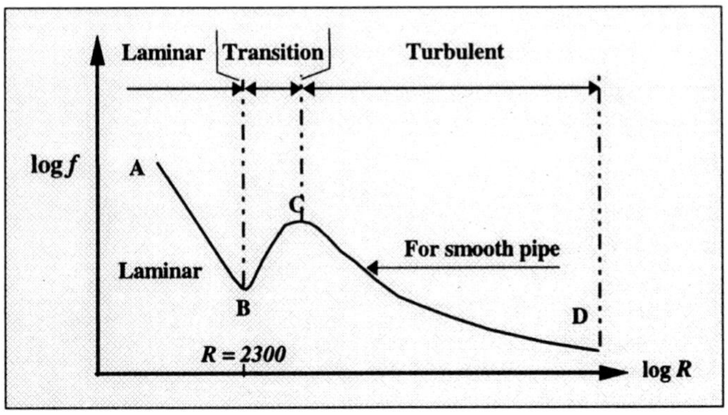

Fig.4.6- Variation of *f* with Reynolds Number, *R*,

The first part AB of the curve is the theoretical line for laminar flow, viz. $f = 16/R$. At B where *R* is about 2300 the curve rises more or less vertically to *C* - this represents the transition stage of flow, at *C* turbulent flow begins.

Within the range of Reynolds number 3000 to 150,000 the relationship,

$$f = 0.08\, R^{-1/4} \qquad (4.20)$$

is adequate. It is important to realise the remarkable range of this simple interconnection between *f* and *R*. It takes into account not only variations of diameter and velocity but also changes in the density and viscosity of the fluid. Not only, therefore, it is valid for water, oil, spirits, but also for gases such as air.

Power Requirements

By definition, power, *P*, is the rate of doing work per unit time. For flow through a pipe, it is dimensionally equivalent to the product of the weight of fluid passing per second and the energy head, *H*, supplied to the fluid by a suitable pump. That is

$$\textbf{\textit{Power,}}\ P = \rho g Q H \text{ (with } H = h_f + \text{secondary losses)} \qquad (4.21)$$

The power required to maintain flow through a horizontal pipe is obtained by substituting the pressure difference $(p_1 - p_2)$ for $\rho g H$,

$$\textbf{\textit{Power,}}\ P = Q \times (p_1 - p_2) \qquad (4.22)$$

Experimental Evidence for Turbulent Flow

A Pitot-Static tube is used to measure the velocity distribution across a 150mm diameter pipe carrying a flow of water. The results of the measurements are given in the table below:

Distance from the centre of the pipe, r *(mm)*	**0**	**20**	**40**	**60**	**70**
Pitot tube head difference of water, h *(mm)*	**157**	**148**	**136**	**113**	**87**

Plot the velocity distribution across the pipe and estimate the mean velocity. Is the flow laminar or turbulent?

Use the velocity equation, $V = (2gh)^{1/2}$ to calculate the values tabulated below.

Distance, r *(mm)*	**0**	**20**	**40**	**60**	**70**
Head difference, h *(mm)*	**0.157**	**0.148**	**0.136**	**0.113**	**0.087**
Velocity, V *(m/s)*	**1.76**	**1.70**	**1.63**	**1.49**	**1.31**

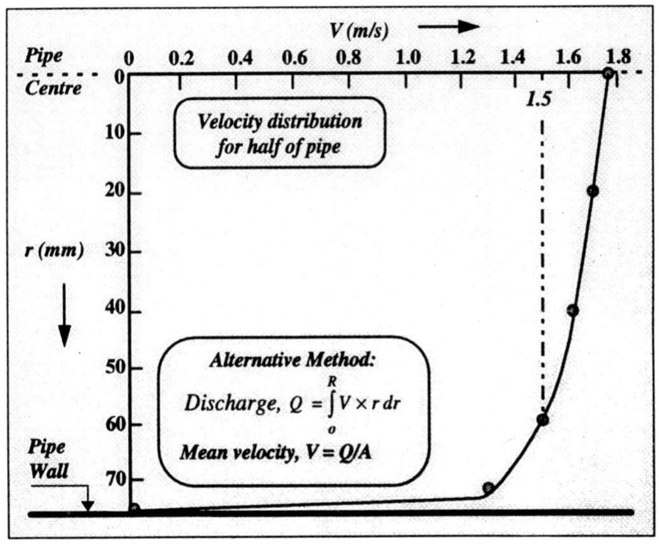

By inspection the average velocity is about 1.5m/s. Assume the kinematic viscosity for water $\nu = 1.141 \times 10^{-6}\ m^2/s$.

$$\textbf{\textit{Reynolds Number,}}\ R = \frac{Vd}{\upsilon} = \frac{1.5 \times 0.15}{1.141 \times 10^{-6}} = 1.972 \times 10^5 .$$

Flow is turbulent since $R > 2300$.

The shape of the velocity distribution also confirms this.

Secondary Losses in Pipes

Introduction

Only rarely is it possible to provide a straight, uniform circular pipe for conveying a liquid from one point to another. On the contrary, the pipe may have to be bent so that it can be carried round the corners, and it may contain junctions and changes of section of various kinds. All such departures from uniformity impose an additional head loss on the flowing fluid which augments the loss due to frictional resistance. In a long pipe (>300m), however, these losses are relatively small compared with frictional losses, for this reason, they are sometimes termed secondary or minor losses.

Sudden Pipe Enlargement

Whenever the cross section of a pipe or channel increases abruptly, the fluid, on passing the enlargement is thrown into a state of unsteady eddying motion with a consequent loss of available energy.

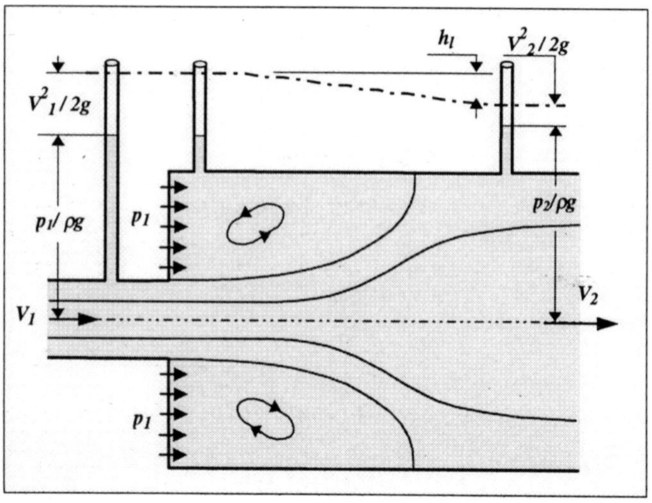

Fig.4.7- Change in head at a sudden pipe expansion.

As indicated in the diagram the fluid emerges into the larger section as a parallel jet, around the periphery of which there exists an intense state of shear between the rapidly moving central fluid and the relatively stagnant surrounding fluid. This becomes a zone of pronounced eddy generation, the eddies cause lateral mixing, and through this mechanism the jet gradually expands to fill the larger section.

The continuity equation between uniform sections upstream and downstream from the expansion is simply

$$Q = A_1 V_1 = V_2 A_2 \tag{4.23}$$

The momentum equation *(if the pressure over the face of the enlargement is assumed the same as that of approaching flow)* takes the form

$$p_1 A_1 + p_1 (A_2 - A_1) - p_2 A_2 = \rho Q (V_2 - V_1) \tag{4.24}$$

The head equation, written to include the loss in head, is

$$\frac{V_1^2}{2g} + \frac{p_1}{w} = \frac{V_2^2}{2g} + \frac{p_2}{w} + h_l \tag{4.25}$$

Simultaneous solution of the above equations then yields an expression for h_l,

$$\textit{Head loss, } h_l = \frac{(V_1 - V_2)^2}{2g} \tag{4.26}$$

Submerged Pipe Outlet

A special case of sudden enlargement occurs at the outlet of a pipe beneath the water surface of a tank or reservoir.

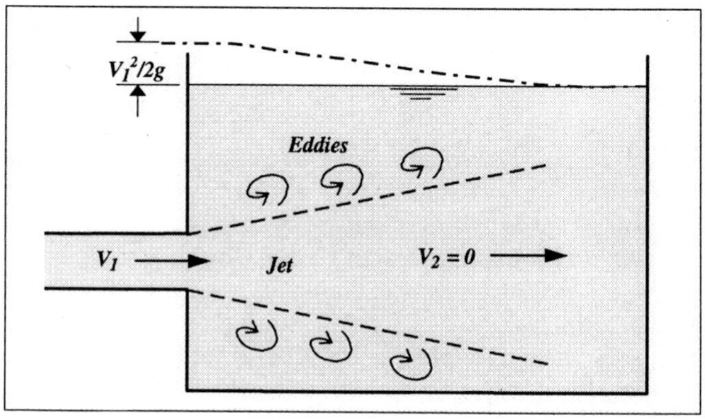

Fig.4.8- Submerged pipe outlet into a tank.

The condition is shown in the above diagram. Due to friction between the jet and the water surrounding it, the jet or stream from the pipe is quickly checked. For this case the value of V_2 is approximately zero and therefore the value of h_l for sudden enlargement equation (4.26) becomes for this case nearly equal to the velocity head in the pipe, i.e. $h_l = V_1^2/2g$.

Tapered Pipe Enlargement

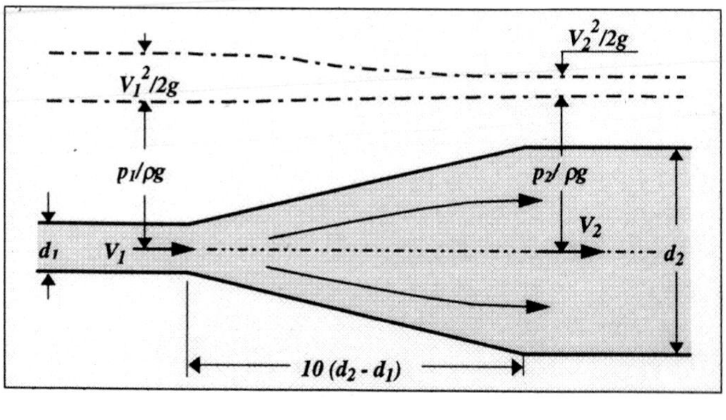

Fig.4.9- Tapered enlargement.

By means of a tapered or gradual enlargement of section, the eddying motion in the larger pipe of the sudden enlargement can to a large extent be suppressed and therefore the head loss is diminished. Minimum loss is secured by making the rate of straight taper

$$\frac{Increase\ of\ diameter}{Increase\ of\ length} = \frac{1}{10} \tag{4.27}$$

whereupon experimentally found.

$$\textbf{Head loss, } h_l = 0.15 \times \frac{(V_1 - V_2)^2}{2g} \tag{4.28}$$

Sudden Pipe Contraction

When water flowing along a channel or through a pipe meets with a sudden contraction of the area as shown in Fig.4.10, we also get a loss of head which is due not directly to the contraction of the stream but to the subsequent enlargement which takes place. On entering the smaller pipe, water contracts, but soon expands to the full width of the pipe. The space surrounding the contracted stream is filled with eddying water.

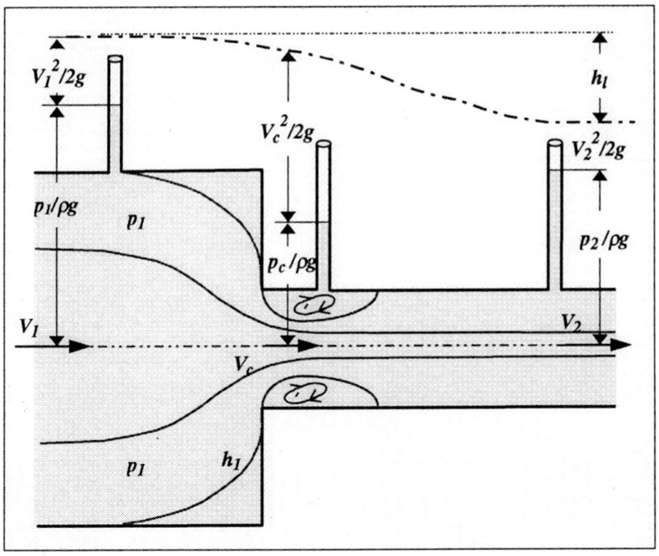

Fig.4.10- Change in head at an abrupt pipe contraction.

The loss is, therefore, due to the sudden enlargement from this contracted section to the diameter of the small pipe.

$$h_l = \frac{(V_c - V_2)^2}{2g}, \quad Q = V_c A_c = V_2 A_2, \quad V_c = \frac{A_2}{A_c} V_2$$

$$h_l = \frac{V_2^2}{2g} \times \left(\frac{A_2}{A_c} - 1 \right)^2 \tag{4.29}$$

Since $A_c/A_2 = C_c$.*(contraction coefficient),* therefore

$$\textbf{Head loss, } h_l = \frac{V_2^2}{2g} \times \left(\frac{1}{C_c} - 1 \right)^2 \tag{4.30}$$

However, application of this equation depends upon evaluation of the contraction coefficient C_c. Values of the contraction coefficient C_c depend on the ratio of the two pipe diameters and can be taken from the table below.

A_c/A_2	0.0	0.1	0.2	0.3	0.4	0.5	0.6	0.7	0.8	0.9	1.0
C_c	0.611	0.612	0.616	0.622	0.631	0.644	0.662	0.687	0.722	0.781	1.000

Table 4.1- Variation of C_c with pipe area ratio.

Abrupt and Rounded Pipe Inlets

Just as the limiting case of the abrupt expansion is outflow from a pipe into a large reservoir, Fig.4.11, the limiting case of sudden contraction is inflow from a vessel or reservoir into a pipe. For this case, the coefficient of contraction C_c is about 0.611 and on substituting this in equation (4.30),

$$h_l = \frac{V_2^2}{2g} \times \left(\frac{1}{C_c} - 1 \right)^2 = \frac{V_2^2}{2g} \times \left(\frac{1}{0.611} - 1 \right)^2, \text{ or}$$

$$\textbf{Head loss, } h_l = 0.41 \times \left(\frac{V_2^2}{2g} \right) \tag{4.31}$$

This is usually taken as $0.5V^2/2g$ where V is the mean velocity in the pipe. If the entrance to the pipe is **rounded or bell-mouthed** the loss of energy incurred is less.

$$\textbf{Head loss, } h_l = 0.10 \times \left(\frac{V^2}{2g} \right) \tag{4.32}$$

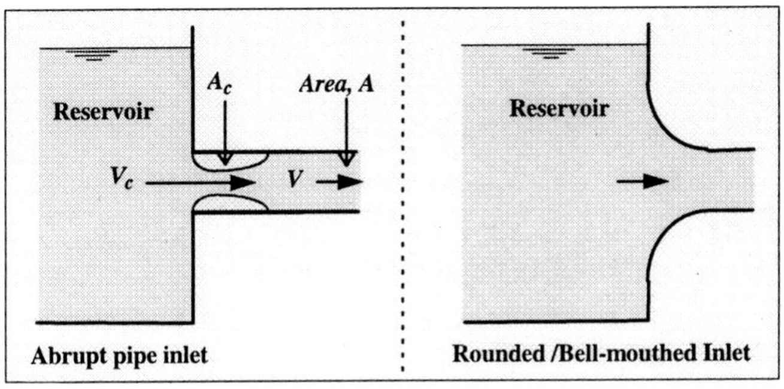

Fig.4.11- Abrupt and rounded pipe inlets from a reservoir.

Losses at Bends and in Valves

Losses due to pipe bends and valves in pipelines in turbulent flow are the results of eddy motion and separation proportional to the velocity head and are given by a loss coefficient K in the form of

$$\textbf{Head loss, } h_l = K \times \frac{V^2}{2g} \tag{4.33}$$

For gate valves, the values of K range from 0.20 fully open to about 6.0 for half open. The appropriate values are normally supplied by manufacturers of these and other types of valves. For pipe drainage fittings it is assumed that K values are 0.9, 0.75 and 0.60 for standard, medium-sweep and long-sweep elbows of 90^0. The values depend on the head loss due to separation of flow at the inside walls and the effects of secondary spiral motion in the bend (see Chapter 8).

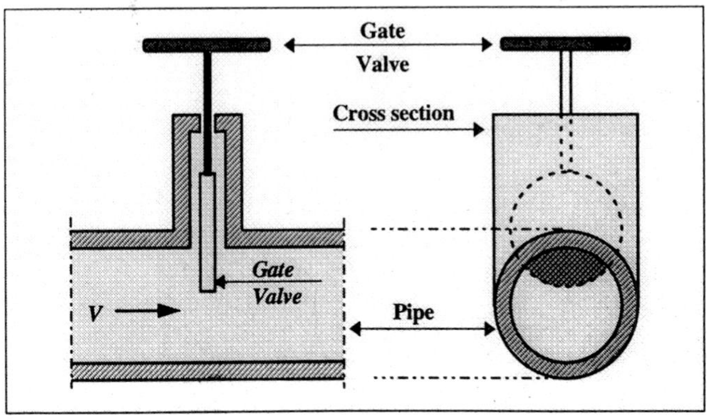

Fig.4.12- Gate valve in a pipe.

Analysis of Pipelines

Gravity Flow Between Two Reservoirs

It is evident that the change in head from the upper reservoir to the lower represents the combination of the entry loss, loss due to pipe friction, and exit loss (Fig.4.13).

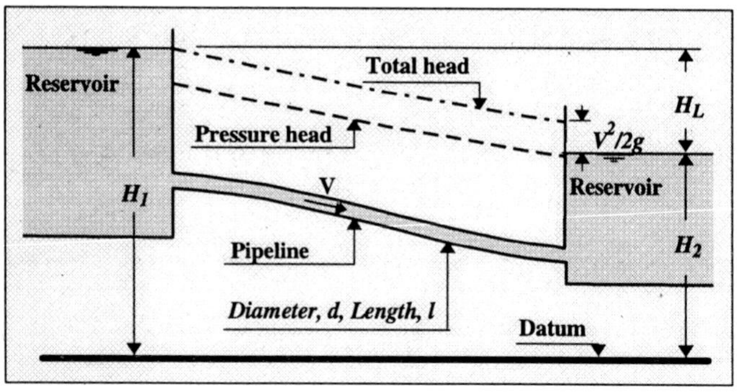

Fig.4.13- Flow between two water reservoirs.

The Bernoulli's energy equation thus takes the specific form

$$H_L = (H_1 - H_2) = \frac{K_1 V^2}{2g} + \frac{4flV^2}{2gd} + \frac{V^2}{2g} \tag{4.34}$$

which through introduction of the discharge relationship $V = Q/A$, becomes

$$H_L = (H_1 - H_2) = \frac{Q^2}{2gA^2} \times \left(K_1 + \frac{4fl}{d} + 1 \right) \tag{4.35}$$

Knowledge of the pipe dimensions, entry loss coefficient K_1 and resistance coefficient f thus permits solution for discharge Q.

Flow by Pumping Between Two Reservoirs

If, instead of flowing by gravity from the upper reservoir to the lower, the water were to be pumped from the lower reservoir to the upper, the variation in head would be as shown in Fig.4.14.

The head equation takes a general form stating that the total head at any section plus any intervening gains in head and minus the intervening losses is equal to the head at any downstream section: $H_1 + H_P - SH_L = H_2$. Herein, the term H_p indicates the gain in head produced by pumping.

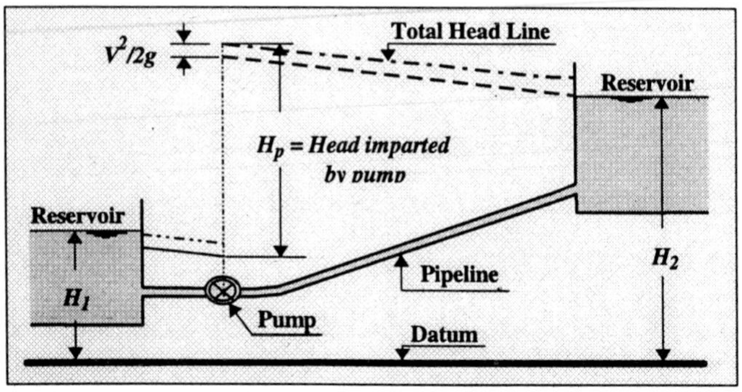

Fig.4.14- Pumping water to a higher reservoir.

Solution of the equation for the head added by the pump indicates that this must be of the increase in surface elevation plus the various losses;

$$H_P = (H_2 - H_1) + \frac{K_1 V^2}{2g} + \frac{4flV^2}{2gd} + \frac{V^2}{2g} \tag{4.36}$$

Upon substituting Q/A for V, we obtain

$$H_P = (H_2 - H_1) + \frac{Q^2}{2gA^2} \times \left(K_1 + \frac{4fl}{d} + 1 \right) \tag{4.37}$$

which through introduction of the entrance coefficient, $K_1 = 0.5$, the equation becomes:

$$H_1 - H_2 = \frac{Q^2}{2gA^2} \times \left(1.5 + \frac{4fl}{d} \right) - H_P \tag{4.38}$$

Knowledge of the pipe dimensions l and d, the resistance coefficient, f, thus permits solution for discharge Q.

Pipes in Parallel

The distribution of flow in the branches shown below (Fig.4.15) must be such that the same head loss occurs in each branch and in the combination of the two; if this were not true there would be more than one energy line for the pipe, above junction 1 and below junction 2 - an obvious impossibility. That is,

$$\textbf{\textit{Head loss, }} h_1 = \frac{4 f_1 l_1 V_1^2}{2gd_1} = \frac{4 f_2 l_2 V_2^2}{2gd_2} \tag{4.39}$$

The second principle applicable to such problems is that the flow rate in the main line is equal to the sum of the flow rates in the branches. That is, $Q = Q_1 + Q_2$,

$$V\left(\frac{\pi d^2}{4}\right) = V_1\left(\frac{\pi d_1^2}{4}\right) + V_2\left(\frac{\pi d_2^2}{4}\right) \tag{4.40}$$

The equations may be solved simultaneously for V_1 and V_2 and allow calculation of the division of a flow Q into two flows Q_1 and Q_2 when pipe characteristics are known.

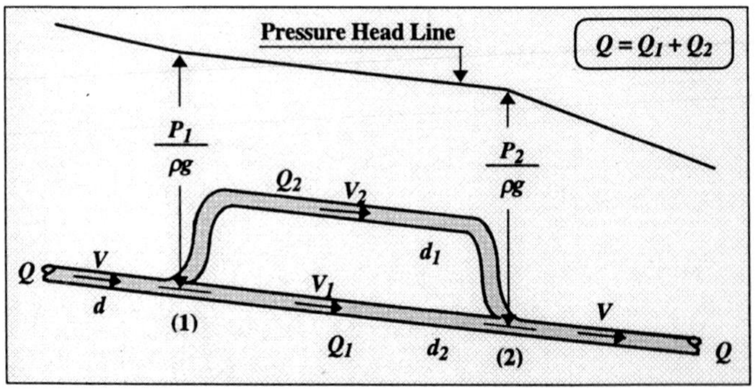

Fig.4.15- Two pipes in parallel.

Two Pipes in Series

If the diameter of a pipe changes from d_1 to d_2 the lengths of the pipe of each diameter being l_1 and l_2 respectively and the discharge, Q, is constant, the total head loss, h,

$$h = h_2 + h_1 = \frac{4 f_1 l_1 V_1^2}{2gd_1} + \frac{4 f_2 l_2 V_2^2}{2gd_2}, \text{ or}$$

Head loss, $$h = \frac{64 Q^2}{2g\pi^2}\left(\frac{f_1 l_1}{d_1^5} + \frac{f_2 l_2}{d_2^5}\right) \quad (4.41)$$

The loss due to the enlargement, or contraction at the junction should of course be added if applicable, compared with frictional loss in both pipes.

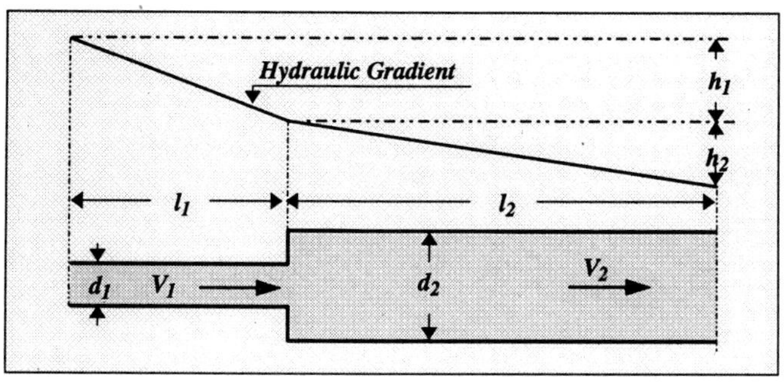

Fig.4.16- Flow in pipes in series.

Partial Doubling of Pipe Lines

A special case of pipe line systems is when a pipeline between two reservoirs is doubled by a parallel pipe for a part, or the whole, of its length. This situation occurs in water supply systems when a city outgrows the capacity of its supply mains and it is desired to increase the flow. The network is shown in the Fig.4.17 below and it is convenient to use the junction pressure z_J as a variable.

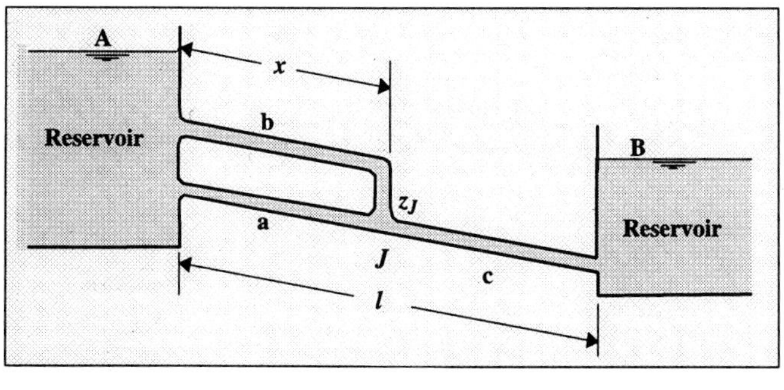

Fig.4.17- Partial doubling pipe lines.

For pipe a, $$h_a = \frac{4f_a l_a}{d_a^5} \times \frac{16 \times Q_a^2}{\pi^2 \times 2g} = z_A - z_J \quad (4.42)$$

For pipe b, $$h_b = \frac{4f_b l_b}{d_b^5} \times \frac{16 \times Q_b^2}{\pi^2 \times 2g} = z_A - z_J \quad (4.43)$$

For pipe c, $$h_b = \frac{4f_c l_c}{d_c^5} \times \frac{16 \times Q_c^2}{\pi^2 \times 2g} = z_J - z_B \quad (4.44)$$

At the junction $Q_a + Q_b = Q_c$, and $l_a = l_b$.

These equations, together with the additional information that the left hand sides of the first two are equal, may be solved directly by the usual methods of subtraction for simultaneous equations.

Siphon Between Two Reservoirs

Where a pipe line is to be laid to connect two reservoirs at different levels over ground which is higher than either water level, the cost of excavation is often so great as to preclude the use of a pipe line which falls below the hydraulic gradient, and in such cases a siphon is commonly used, Fig.4.18.

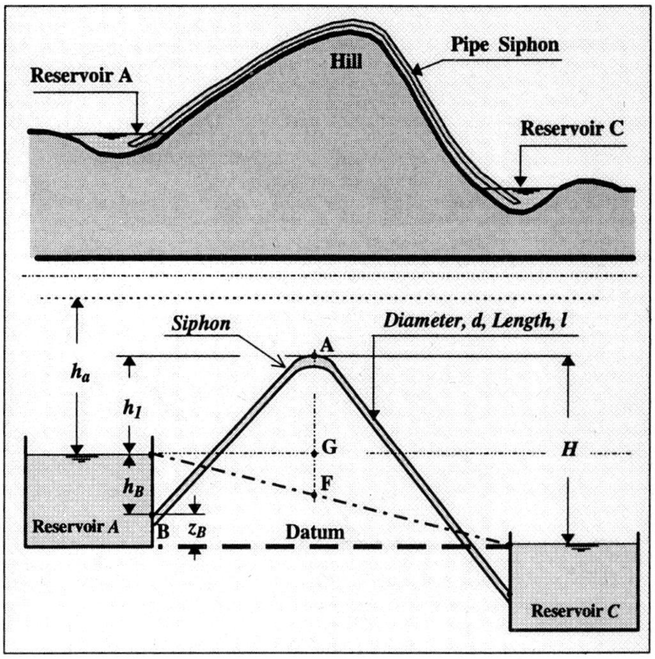

Fig.4.18- Pipe siphon between two reservoirs.

Let h_a= pressure head equivalent to the atmospheric pressure. Let it be assumed that the flow is allowed to take place between the reservoirs A and C, and is regulated so that it is continuous and the velocity is V. Then neglecting the entry and outlet losses, the head loss due to friction is:

Head loss, $h_f = 4flV^2/2gd$, and

Velocity, $V = \sqrt{2g\, d \times h_f / 4fl}$, and $Q = VA$ (4.45)

Theoretically if AF is made greater than h_a, which is about 10.40m, the pressure at A becomes negative and the flow will cease. Practically AF can not be made greater than 8m. To find the maximum velocity possible in the rising limb AB, so that the pressure head at A shall just be zero. Let V_m be this velocity. Let the datum level be the surface of reservoir C.

$h_a + h_B + z_B = (4fl/d) \times (V^2/g) + H + (V^2/2g)$.

But $H = h_B + z_B + h_1$.

$h_a + h_B + z_B = (4fl/d) \times (V^2/2g) + h_B + z_B + h_1 + (V^2/2g)$.

$h_a - h_1 = (V^2/2g) \times [(4fl/d) + 1]$.

Neglecting exit losses, $(V^2/2g) \times (4fl/d) = h_a - h_1$

$$V = \sqrt{2g \times (h_a - h_1) \times d / 4fl} \quad (4.46)$$

If the pressure head is not to be less than 3m of water,

$$V = \sqrt{2g \times (h_a - 3 - h_1) \times d / 4fl} \quad (4.47)$$

If V_m is less than V, the discharge of the siphon will be determined by this limiting velocity, and it will be necessary to throttle the pipe at C by means of a valve, so as to keep the limb AC full and to keep the siphon from being broken.

Examples on Pipe Flow

Laminar Flow in a Pipe

Explain briefly the difference between laminar and turbulent flow. Oil of relative density 0.92 and coefficient of dynamic viscosity 0.3 Ns/m^2 is pumped through a horizontal pipe, 75mm diameter and 50m long, at a rate of 0.01 m^3/s. Show that the flow is laminar and estimate the power required to drive the pump, assuming an efficiency of 65%.

To limit the range of discussion refer to uniform flow only.

Laminar flow - all particles passing a point in the cross section will follow the same path at the same velocity. Paths are sensibly straight and parallel. Based on the mean velocity of flow the Reynolds number is normally less than 2000.

Turbulent flow- every particle passing a point in the cross section follows its own path with varying velocity. Paths are contorted and the velocity of a particle in any position can be represented by the vector sum of the mean velocity of flow and some other velocity, the ratio of the two is an indication of the degree of turbulence. Reynolds number is greater than 2300.

Using the given data, **Reynolds number, *R*** is:

$$R = \frac{\rho V d}{\mu} = 920 \times \left(\frac{4 \times 0.01}{\pi \times 0.075^2} \right) \times 0.075 \Big/ 0.3 = 520 .$$

Since R is < than 2000, the flow is laminar.

Darcy's equation for head loss, $h_f = \dfrac{4flV^2}{2gd}$.

For laminar flow $f = 16/R = 0.031$. Hence

$$h_f = \frac{4 \times 0.031 \times 50}{0.075} \times \left(\frac{4 \times 0.01}{\pi \times 0.075^2} \right)^2 \Big/ 2g = 21.59m .$$

$$\textbf{\textit{Power,}}\ P = \frac{\rho g Q h_f}{\eta} = \frac{920 \times 9.81 \times 0.01 \times 21.59}{0.65} = 2997W .$$

Flow with Half Critical Velocity in a Pipe

Calculate the loss of head in a small pipe 4mm diameter and 10m long, when water flows at half the critical velocity. Assume that critical velocity occurs when Reynolds number $R = 2500$ and the coefficient of viscosity is 0.001 Ns/m^2.

Velocity V occurs when $R = 2500/2 = 1250$.

For laminar flow: $f = \dfrac{16}{R} = \dfrac{16.00}{1250} = 0.0128$.

Also, $R = \dfrac{\rho V d}{\mu}$.

Critical velocity, $V = \dfrac{\mu R}{\rho d} = \dfrac{0.001 \times 1250}{1000 \times 0.004} = 0.3125 m/s$.

Head loss, $h_f = \dfrac{4\, flV^2}{2gd} = \dfrac{4 \times 0.0128 \times 10 \times 0.3125^2}{2 \times 9.81 \times 0.004} = 0.636m$.

Comparison of Laminar and Turbulent Flows

Compare the friction losses in a 0.02m diameter pipe when water flows at a rate of: (a) 7m^3/h and (b) *30m^3/h* given that the friction coefficient $f = 16/R$ for laminar flow and $0.064 \times R^{-0.23}$, for turbulent flow. Coefficient of viscosity for water is 0.001Ns/m^2.

Head loss, $h_f = \dfrac{4fl\,V^2}{2gd}$, *(1 hour = 3600 seconds).*

$$V_a = \frac{Q_a}{A} = \frac{7 \times 4}{3600 \times \pi \times 0.0004} = \frac{7}{0.36\pi} = 6.2\ m/s$$

$$V_b = 6.2 \times \frac{30}{7} = 26.6\ m/s$$

Ratio of head losses is: $\dfrac{h_{fa}}{h_{fb}} = \dfrac{16}{0.064} \times \dfrac{R_b^{0.23}}{R_a} \times \dfrac{V_a^2}{V_b^2}$

$$\frac{h_{fa}}{h_{fb}} = \frac{1}{0.004} \times \left(\frac{\rho d}{\mu} \right)^{-0.77} \times \frac{V_a}{V_b^{1.77}}$$

$$= 250 \times \left(\frac{0.001}{1000 \times 0.02} \right)^{+0.77} \times \frac{V_a}{V_b^{1.77}}$$

$$= 250 \times 0.000488 \times (6.2/330) = 0.00225 .$$

Laminar Flow of Oil

Oil, viscosity 0.1Ns/m^2 and specific gravity 0.88, flows through a horizontal pipe 0.05m diameter. The pressure drop over a length of 300m is 700kN/m^2. Assuming laminar flow so that the velocity distribution is given by $v = V_o (1 - r^2/R^2)$, where V_o is the maximum velocity at centre line, find (a) shear stress in the oil at the pipe wall and (b) the rate of flow of oil in m^3/s. Verify that the flow is laminar.

Velocity distribution, $v = V_o \times \left(1 - \dfrac{r^2}{R^2} \right)$

Shear stress at wall, $\tau_w = \mu \times \left(\dfrac{dv}{dr} \right)_{r=R}$, i.e. $\tau_w = -2 \times \dfrac{V_o \mu}{R}$

For laminar flow: $V_o = 2 \times V$ *(V = mean velocity).*

$$h_f = \frac{4fl\,V^2}{2gd} = \frac{4}{2gd} \times \frac{16lV^2}{R} \quad \text{and} \quad \Delta p = \frac{32lV}{d^2}\mu$$

$$V = \frac{d^2 \times \Delta p}{32\, l\mu} = \frac{0.05^2 \times 700 \times 10^3}{32 \times 300 \times 0.1} = 1.825 m/s .$$

Shear stress at wall, $\tau_w = -2 \times 2 \times \dfrac{1.825 \times 0.1}{0.025} = 29.2 N/m^2$

Rate of flow, $Q = VA = 1.825 \times \dfrac{\pi \times 0.0025}{4} = 0.00359 m^3/s$.

$$R = \frac{\rho V d}{\mu} = \frac{1000 \times 0.88 \times 1.825 \times 0.05}{0.1} = 804.0 < 2300 .$$

Therefore the flow is laminar.

Examples on Pipelines

Flow Between Two Reservoirs

Two reservoirs, having a difference of level of 6.0m are connected by a pipe 0.3m diameter, 981m long and f = 0.005. Calculate the quantity of water flowing, neglect all losses other than pipe friction.

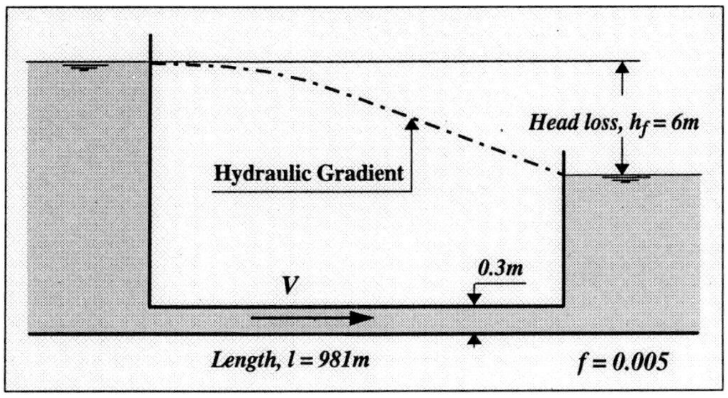

$$\textbf{\textit{Head loss, }} h_f = \frac{4flV^2}{2gd} = 6m.$$

$$\textbf{\textit{Velocity, }} V = \sqrt{\frac{gdh_f}{2fl}} = \sqrt{\frac{9.81\times 0.3\times 6.0}{2\times 0.005\times 981}} = 1.342\ m/s.$$

$$\textbf{\textit{Discharge, }} Q = VA = 1.342\times\frac{\pi\times 0.3^2}{4} = 0.095\ m^3/s.$$

Parallel Pipes Between Reservoirs

Two sharp-ended pipes of 0.05m and 0.1m diameter each 30m long are connected in parallel between two reservoirs whose difference of level is 10m. Find: (a) the flow in m^3/s for each pipe and draw the corresponding hydraulic gradient. (b) the diameter of a single pipe, 30m long, which will give the same flow as the two actual pipes. $f = 0.008$ in each case.

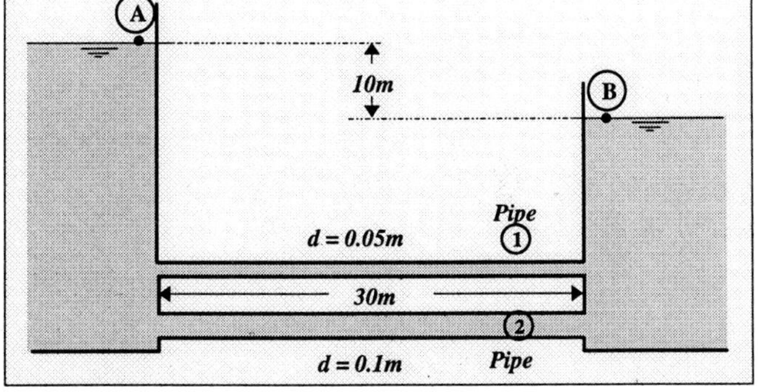

Pipe 1. Applying the total head equation between A and B (note sharp edged pipes)

$$\text{(a)}\ \frac{p_a}{\rho g}+0+10=\frac{p_a}{\rho g}+0+0+\frac{1}{2}\times\frac{V_1^2}{2g}+\frac{4fl_1V_1^2}{2gd}+\frac{V_1^2}{2g}$$

$$10=\frac{V_1^2}{2g}\times\left(1.5+\frac{4fl_1}{d}\right)=\frac{V_1^2}{2\times 9.81}\times\left(1.5+\frac{4\times 0.008\times 30}{0.05}\right)$$

$$\textbf{\textit{Velocity, }} V_1=\sqrt{\frac{20\times 9.81}{20.7}}=3.08m/s.$$

$$Q_1=\frac{3.08\times\pi\times 0.05^2}{4}=0.00605\ m^3/s$$

$$\text{Similarly, } 10=\frac{V_2^2}{2g}\times\left(1.5+\frac{4\times 0.008\times 30}{0.1}\right)=\frac{V_2^2}{2g}\times 11.1$$

$$\textbf{\textit{Velocity, }} V_2=\sqrt{\frac{20\times 9.81}{11.1}}=4.21m/s.$$

Flow, $Q_1 = 0.033m^3/s$, *and the* ***Total flow*** $= 0.039m^3/s$.

(b) Let d = diameter of single pipe. $\therefore V=\frac{0.039\times 4}{\pi\times d^2}=\frac{0.0497}{d^2}\ m/s$

Assume sharp edged pipe, then

$$10=\frac{V^2}{2g}\left(1.5+\frac{4\times 0.008\times 30}{d}\right)=\frac{0.0497^2}{2\times 9.81\times d^4}\left(1.5+\frac{0.96}{d}\right)$$

$$\frac{2\times 9.81\times 10}{0.0497^2}\times d^5=1.5d+0.96$$

i.e. $79400\,d^5 = 1.5\,d + 0.96$, *or* $79400\,d^5 - 1.5d - 0.96 = 0$

Solve equation by trial and error.

1st approximation: $d^5=\frac{0.96}{0.794}\times 10^{-5}=1.21\times 10^{-5}$

$\therefore$ **d ≈ 0.104m.**

2nd approximation: $d^5=\frac{0.96+1.5\times 0.1039}{0.794\times 10^{-5}}=1.405\times 10^{-5}$

$\therefore$ **d = 0.107m.**

3rd approximation: $d^5=\frac{0.96+1.5\times 0.107}{0.794\times 10^{-5}}=1.41\times 10^{-5}$

Diameter of single pipe, d = 0.1071m.

Pumping Through a Pipeline

Water is conveyed at $0.025m^3/s$ through a pipe 0.1m diameter and 200m long from a sump to the atmosphere at a point 10m above the sump water level. The 0.1m diameter delivery from the pump is 0.5m above the sump water level and the gauge pressure in the delivery is 29m of water. Estimate the value of the Darcy friction coefficient f for the pipe. Assuming that the pump efficiency remains the same, estimate the percentage reduction in power required if a similar parallel pipe is connected to the pump delivery and the same discharge is maintained.

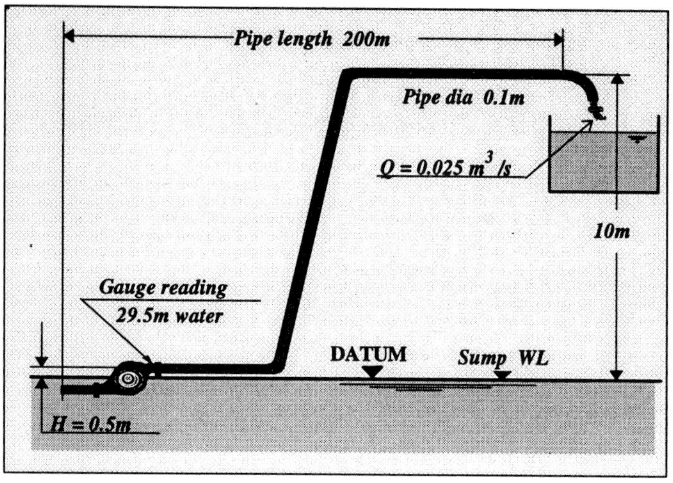

Total head delivery from pump taking water sump as datum: $(29.5 + 0.5 + V^2/2g)$ m.

Total head at discharge to atmosphere: $(0 + 10.0 + V^2/2g)$ m.

$$\therefore\ h_f = 20m = \frac{4flV^2}{2gd},\ V = \frac{Q}{(\pi \times d^2)/4},\ \therefore V^2 = \frac{16Q^2}{\pi^2 d^4}.$$

$$h_f = \frac{4fl}{d} \times \frac{16 \times Q^2}{\pi^2 \times d^4 \times 2g}, \text{ or}$$

$$f = \frac{h_f \times \pi^2 \times d^5 \times g}{32 \times l \times Q^2} = \frac{20 \times \pi^2 \times 0.1^5 \times 9.81}{32 \times 200 \times 0.025^2}$$

$$f = \frac{20}{32} \times \frac{\pi^2}{200} \times \frac{9.81}{10^5} \times 1600 = 0.00485.$$

Kinetic head for velocity $V = V^2/2g = 0.51m$.

If two equal bore pipes are used in parallel $V_1 = V/2$.
Kinetic head for velocity $V_1 = 0.13m$.

Head loss due to friction = $5.0m$.

Total head at delivery = $0.5 + 10 + 0.13 + 5.0 = 15.63m$, compared with $30.51m$.

Power = $\rho g Q H$, thus

$$\textit{Saving in power} = \frac{30.51 - 15.63}{30.51} \times 100 = 48.8\%.$$

Pipes in Parallel between Reservoirs

Two water pipes, 300mm and 150mm diameter, of the same length are coupled in parallel and together are to deliver $0.085m^3/s$. Find the loss of head per kilometre if $f = 0.0075$.

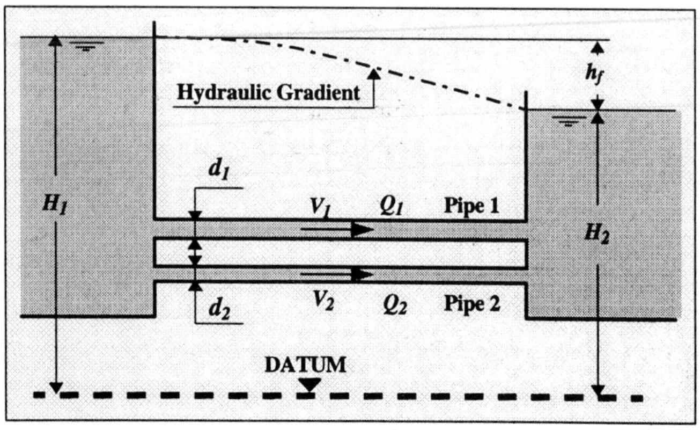

$$\frac{4flV_1^2}{2gd_1} = \frac{4flV_2^2}{2gd_2},\ \therefore \frac{V_1}{V_2} = \left(\frac{d_1}{d_2}\right)^{1/2}.$$

$$\frac{Q_1}{Q_2} = \frac{V_1 A_1}{V_2 A_2} = \left(\frac{d_1}{d_2}\right)^{5/2} = 2^{5/2} = 5.656.\ \therefore\ Q_1 = 5.656\, Q_2.$$

$Q_1 + Q_2 = Q = 0.085.\ \therefore\ Q_2 + 5.656\, Q_2 = 0.085.$ Therefore,

Discharge in pipe 2, $Q_2 = 0.013m^3/s$.

$$\textit{Velocity in pipe 2, } V_2 = \frac{0.013}{(\pi/4) \times 0.15^2} = 0.74\ m/s.$$

$$\textit{Head loss, } h_f = \frac{4fl_2V_2^2}{2g\,d_2} = \frac{4 \times 0.0075 \times 1000 \times 0.74^2}{2 \times 9.81 \times 0.15} = 5.52m.$$

This is the same for both pipes in parallel.

Pipes in Series between Reservoirs

Two reservoirs with a constant level difference of 10m are connected by a pipeline of total length 200m. The portion of pipeline leading from the upper reservoir is of length 75m and diameter 200mm while the remaining portion (of length 125m) is of diameter 300mm. The friction coefficient for the 200mm diameter pipe is 0.0075 while that for the 300mm diameter pipe is 0.01. Determine the discharge between the two reservoirs. Neglect minor losses.

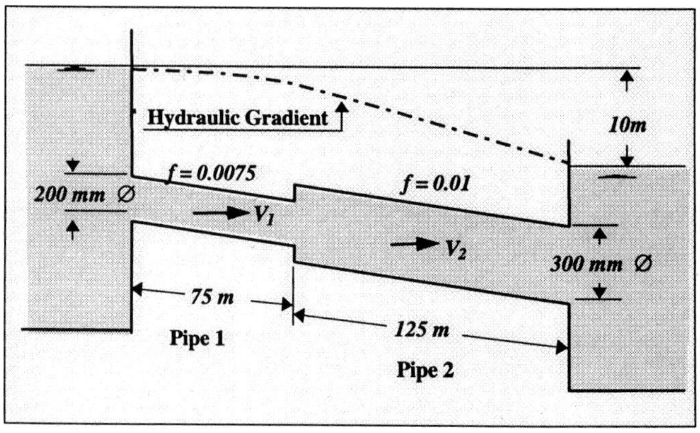

$$\textit{Head loss due to friction, } h_l = \frac{4flV^2}{2gd},$$

$$10 = \frac{4}{2g} \times \left(\frac{0.0075 \times 75 \times V_1^2}{d_1} + \frac{0.01 \times 125 \times V_2^2}{d_2}\right)$$

Substituting $V_1 = \dfrac{4Q}{\pi d_1^2}$ and $V_2 = \dfrac{4Q}{\pi d_2^2}$ in the above, gives,

$$10 = \frac{4 \times 16}{\pi^2 2g} \times \left(\frac{0.0075 \times 75 Q^2}{d_1^5} + \frac{0.01 \times 125 Q^2}{d_2^5}\right)$$

$$Q^2 = \frac{10\pi^2 \times 2g}{4 \times 16} \times \left[1 \Big/ \left(\frac{0.0075 \times 75}{0.2^5} + \frac{0.01 \times 125}{0.3^5}\right)\right]$$

$Q^2 = 0.013315$. Therefore,

Discharge, $Q = 0.1154\ m^3/s$.

Pipe with One Lateral Draw Off

Two reservoirs, having a constant difference in level of 70m, are connected by a 0.23m diameter pipe, 4 km long. The pipe is tapped at a point distance 1.5km from the upper reservoir, and water is drawn off at a rate of 0.04 m^3/s. If $f = 0.009$ determine the rate, in m^3/s at which water enters at the lower reservoir, neglecting all losses except pipe friction. Sketch the hydraulic gradient for the pipe.

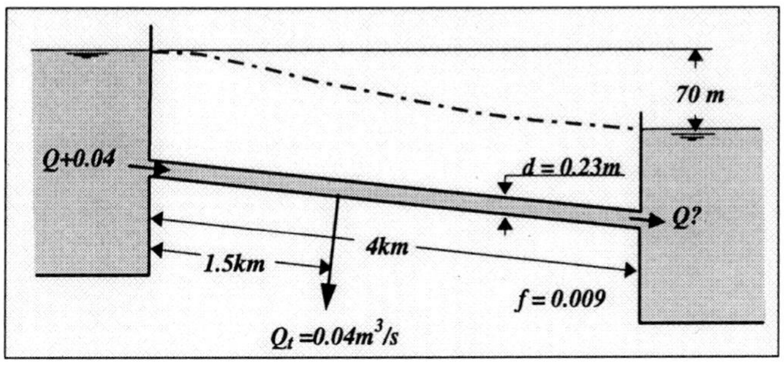

Head loss, $h_f = \dfrac{4flV^2}{2gd}$, and $V = \dfrac{4Q}{\pi d^2}$.

$$70 = \frac{4\times 0.009}{2\times 9.81\times 0.23}\times[1.5\,(Q+0.04)^2+2.5Q^2]\times\frac{16\times 1000}{\pi^2\times 0.23^4}$$

$$\frac{70\times 2\times 9.81\times 0.23^5\times\pi^2}{4\times 0.009\times 16\times 1000} = 1.5(Q^2+0.08Q+0.0016)+2.5\,Q^2$$

$$0.0152 = 4\,Q^2 + 0.12\,Q + 0.0024.$$

$$Q = -\frac{0.12\pm\sqrt{0.0144+0.205}}{8} = \frac{-0.12\pm 0.468}{8} = 0.0435\ m^3/s.$$

$\therefore$ ***Discharge,*** $Q = 0.0435 m^3/s$.

Pipe with Uniform Lateral Flows

A pipe 0.6m diameter and 981m long with $f = 0.008$, connects two reservoirs having a difference in water surface level of 30m. Calculate the flow between the reservoirs and the shear stress at the wall of the pipe. If the upstream half of the pipe is subsequently tapped by several side pipes so that one third of the quantity of water now entering the main pipe is withdrawn over this length, calculate the new rate of discharge to the lower reservoir. Neglect all losses other than those due to pipe friction.

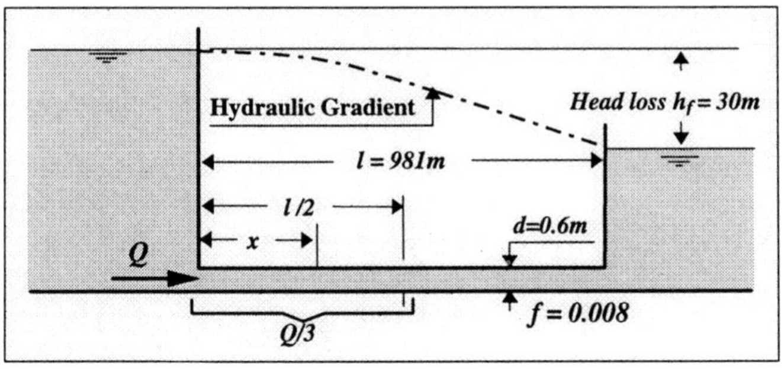

Neglecting all losses other than friction, $h_f = \dfrac{4\,flV^2}{2gd} = 30$.

Velocity, $V = \sqrt{\dfrac{2\times 9.81\times 0.6\times 30}{4\times 0.008\times 981}} = \sqrt{11.25} = 3.35 m/s$.

Flow rate, $Q = VA = 3.35\times\dfrac{\pi\times 0.6^2}{4} = 0.948 m^3/s$.

$$H = h_f = \frac{4f}{2gd}\times\int_o^{l/2} V^2\,dx + \left[\frac{4f}{2gd}\times\frac{l}{2}\times\left(\frac{(2/3)\times 4Q}{\pi d^2}\right)^2\right]$$

Shear at the wall, $\tau = \dfrac{\Delta pd}{4l} = \dfrac{\rho gh\times d}{4l} = \dfrac{1000\times 9.81\times 30\times 0.6}{4\times 981}$.

$\tau = 45 N/m^2$.

$$V^2 = \left(Q - \frac{x}{l}\frac{Q}{3}\Big/\frac{\pi d^2}{4}\right)^2 = \frac{16\,Q^2}{\pi^2 d^4}\times\left[1-\frac{x}{3l}\right]^2$$

$$h_f = \frac{32flQ^2}{g\,d^5\pi^2}\times\int_o^{l/2}\left(1-\frac{2x}{3l}+\frac{x^2}{9l^2}\right)dx + \frac{64flQ^2}{9g\,d^5\pi^2}$$

$$h_f = \frac{flQ^2}{g\,d^5\pi^2}\times\left[32\left(\frac{1}{2}-\frac{1}{12}+\frac{1}{216}\right)+\frac{64}{9}\right] = \frac{20.4\times flQ^2}{g\,d^5\pi^2}$$

$$Q^2 = \frac{9.81\times 30\times 0.6^5\times\pi^2}{20.4\times 0.008\times 981} = 1.41.$$

Rate of discharge, Q =1.182 m^3/s.

Doubling of Pipes Between Reservoirs

Two reservoirs with a constant level difference of 12m are connected by a pipeline 10km long, 0.8m diameter. The friction factor for the pipe is 0.008. Neglecting secondary losses, determine the discharge between the two reservoirs. It is desired to increase the discharge by 50% by installing a new pipe of the same diameter and friction factor, alongside part of the original pipe, joining it at an appropriate point. Determine the new length of the pipe needed.

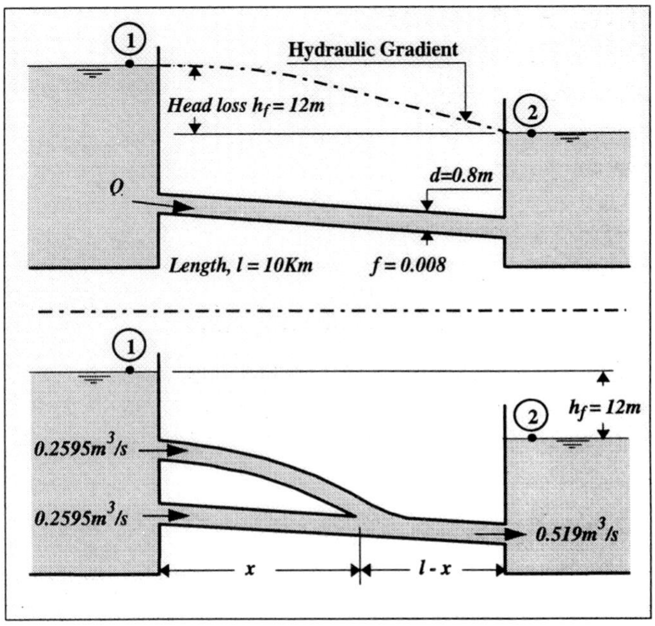

Apply Bernoulli's total head equation with primary losses only:

Head loss due to friction, $h_f = \dfrac{4flV^2}{2gd} = \dfrac{32\,flQ^2}{\pi^2\times gd^5}$. Therefore,

Flow rate, $Q = \dfrac{9.81\times\pi^2\times 0.8^5\times 12}{32\times 0.008\times 10000} = 0.149 m^3/s$.

New discharge, $Q_n = 1.5\times 0.149 = 0.224 m^3/s$.

$$12 = \frac{32fx(Q_n/2)^2}{\pi^2 \times gd^5} + \frac{32f(l-x)}{\pi^2 \times gd^5} \times Q_n^2 .$$

$$\therefore \quad \frac{9.81 \times \pi^2 \times 0.8^5 \times 12}{32 \times 0.008} = \frac{x \times Q_n^2}{4} + (l - x) \times Q_n^2 .$$

$$1487.2 = (10000 - 0.75x) \times 0.224^2.$$

$$x = \left(10000 - \frac{1487.2}{0.224^2}\right) \Big/ 0.75 = 5972m \;\therefore\; x = 5972m.$$

Friction and Secondary Losses in Pipes

A large reservoir discharges through three pipes connected as shown in the diagram below. Pipe AB is 0.15m diameter and pipes BC and CD are 0.25m diameter. Each pipe is 10m long and has a coefficient of friction f = 0.01. All the pipe ends are sharp and there is a valve in pipe CD with a head loss ten times the velocity head in the pipe. The head available is 12m.

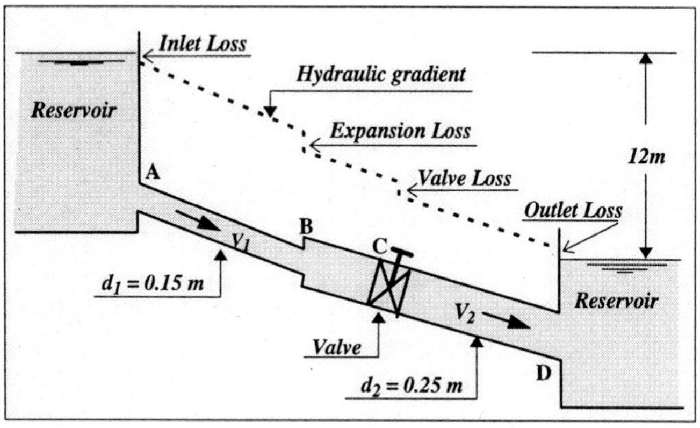

Ratio of velocities in pipes AB and BC

$(V_1/V_2) = (d_2/d_1)^2$, $V_1^2/V_2^2 = (0.25/0.15)^4 \approx 7.72.$

Head losses in pipe AB:

Entry loss $= 0.5 \times (V_1^2/2g) = 3.86 \times (V_2^2/2g)$

$$\textit{Friction loss} = \frac{4flV_1^2}{2gd_1} = \frac{4 \times 0.01 \times 10 \times V_1^2}{2g \times 0.15} = 20.6 \times \frac{V_2^2}{2g}$$

$$\textit{Abrupt expansion loss} = \frac{(V_1 - V_2)^2}{2g} = 3.16 \times \frac{V_2^2}{2g}$$

Head losses in pipe BC:

$$\text{Friction loss} = \frac{4flV_2^2}{2gd_2} = \frac{4 \times 0.01 \times 10 \times V_2^2}{2g \times 0.25} = 1.6 \times \frac{V_2^2}{2g}$$

Valve loss $= 10 \times V_2^2/2g.$

Head losses in pipe CD:

$$\textit{Friction loss} = \frac{4flV_2^2}{2gd_2} = 1.6 \times \frac{V_2^2}{2g}$$

Outlet loss $= V_2^2/2g.$

$$\textit{Total losses for pipes} = H = 41.82 \times \frac{V_2^2}{2g} = 12m$$

$\therefore V_2 = (12 \times 2 \times 9.81/41.82)^{0.5} = 2.372 m/s.$

$$\textit{Discharge, } Q = V_2 A_2 = \frac{2.372 \times \pi \times 0.25^2}{4},$$

$\boldsymbol{Q = 0.116 m^3/s}.$

Pipe Siphon

The siphon shown in figure below is 30m long having its outlet which discharges freely to atmosphere 3.0m below, its highest point 10m above, and its inlet close to the floor of the tank. The pipe diameter is 0.15m. The Darcy friction factor f = 0.01 and the entrance loss is $0.2V^2/2g$. Neglecting bend losses, derive an expression relating the discharge Q with the depth of water D in the tank. When D is 8.0m determine the discharge and the minimum pressure in the pipe. Where will the minimum pressure occur? What is the minimum possible water level in the tank for the siphon to operate?

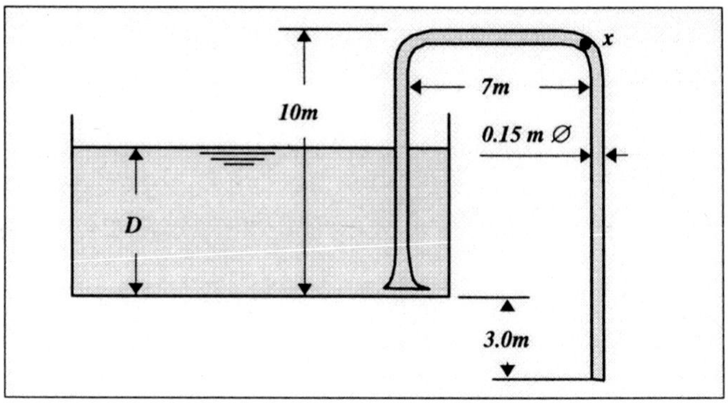

Total head loss, H = Inlet loss + Friction loss + Outlet loss.

$$H = 0.2 \times \frac{V^2}{2g} + \frac{4flV^2}{2g} + 1 \times \frac{V^2}{2g} = (D + 3)\; m$$

$$= \left[0.2 + 1.0 + \frac{4 \times 0.01 \times 30}{0.15}\right] \times \frac{V^2}{2g} = 9.2 \times \frac{V^2}{2g}$$

$$\therefore \quad D + 3 = \frac{9.2}{2g} \times \frac{4^2 \times Q^2}{\pi^2 d^4} = 1500\; Q^2$$

$$\textit{Pressure head at x} = D - 0.2 \times \frac{V^2}{2g} - \frac{4f}{d} \times 17 \times \frac{V^2}{2g} - 10$$

$$D - 0.2 \times \frac{V^2}{2g} - \frac{4 \times 0.01}{0.15} \times 17 \times \frac{V^2}{2g} - 10 = D - 4.73 \times \frac{V^2}{2g} - 10$$

$$(8 + 3) = 11 = 1500 \times Q^2 \text{, i.e. } Q^2 = \frac{11}{1500} = 0.734 \times 10^{-2}$$

$\therefore$ ***Discharge,*** $Q = 8.56 \times 10^{-2}\; m^3/s = 85.6\; l/s.$

Pressure head at (x):

$$H = 8 - 10 - 4.73 \times \frac{V^2}{2g} = -2 - \left[\frac{4.73}{0.15^4 \times 2g} \times \left(\frac{4}{\pi}\right)^2\right] \times Q^2$$

Pressure head = -2 - 772 × 0.734×10^-2^ = - 2 - 5.65 = -7.65m.

Valve Discharge

A pipe, 20m long and 150mm diameter, is supplied with water under a constant total head of 25m of water. It discharges to the atmosphere through a valve for which the coefficient of discharge is $C_d = 0.6 + 0.4k$, where

$$k = \frac{\textit{Area of valve opening}}{\textit{Cross-sectional area of the pipe}}$$

Calculate the ratio *(discharge when k = 0.5) / (discharge when k = 1.0)*, assuming that the value of f in the Darcy equation for loss of head due to pipe friction is constant at 0.005.

Discharge through valve orifice $Q = C_d\ A\ \sqrt{2gH}$

Velocity of flow in pipe $v = Q \Big/ \frac{\pi}{4} \times \left(\frac{150}{1000}\right)^2 = \frac{C_d\ A\ \sqrt{2gH}}{A/k}$

Friction loss $= \frac{4flV^2}{2gd} = \frac{4 \times 0.005 \times 20}{150/1000} \times C_d^2\ k^2 H$.

Effective head at valve , $H = 25 - \frac{400}{150} \times C_d^2\ k^2 H$.

$$H = \frac{25}{1 + 2.67 \times C_d^2\ k^2} .$$

$$Q = C_d \times k \times \frac{\pi}{4} \times \left(\frac{150}{1000}\right)^2 \times \sqrt{2g \times \frac{25}{1 + 2.67\ C_d^2 \times k^2}} .$$

where $C_d = 0.6 + 0.4k$. Hence

$$\frac{Q(k = 0.5)}{Q(k = 1.0)} = \frac{(0.6 + 0.2) \times 0.5 \times \sqrt{1 + 2.67}}{(0.6 + 0.4) \times 1.0 \times \sqrt{1 + 2.67 \times 0.64 \times 0.25}}$$

$$= \frac{0.8}{1.0} \times \frac{0.5}{1.0} \times \frac{1.92}{1.195} = 0.645 .$$

Ratio of discharge = 0.645.

Problems on Pipe Flow

[1] Find the pressure at the highest point in the pipeline shown in the diagram. If $l_1 = 250m$, $l_2 = 500m$, pipe diameter = 1.5m and $f = 0.01$. Ignore secondary losses. (- 5.30m)

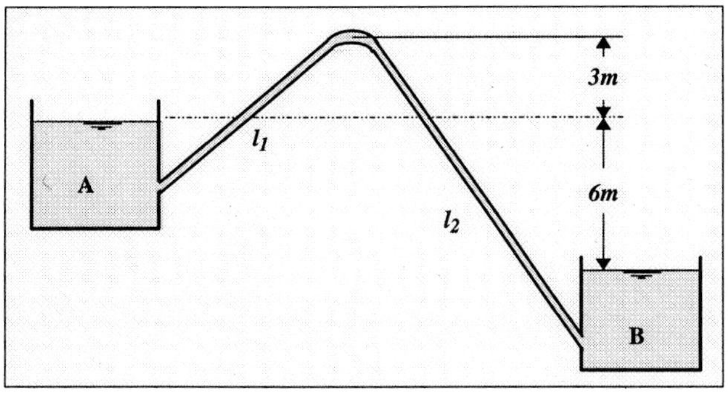

[2] A pipe 3km long and 0.3m diameter, $f = 0.004$ connects two reservoirs whose water levels differ by 6m. It is necessary to increase the flow by 50%. Compare the running costs of an electric pump at ½p per kilowatt hour with the alternative of paying 5% interest on a second pipe 0.3m diameter costing £5 per metre laid, extending for an appropriate distance before joining the original pipe. The efficiency of the pump is 80%. (8.44kW, £369.67, 2226.8m, £556.7)

[3] A pipe 0.6m diameter and 981m long with $f = 0.008$ connects two reservoirs having a difference in water surface level of 20m. Calculate the flow between the reservoirs and the shear stress at the wall of the pipe. If the upstream half of the pipe is subsequently tapped by several side pipes so that one third of the quantity of the water entering the pipe is withdrawn, calculate the new rate of discharge to the lower reservoir. Neglect all losses other than those due to pipe friction. ($0.774m^3/s$, $30N/m^2$, $0.970m^3/s$)

Prandtl's Mixing Length Theory

Prandtl used a theory for fluid turbulence as a scientific basis for the development of a theoretical velocity distribution for flow in pipes (see Chapter 10). Nikuradse carried out experiments on artificially roughened pipes and identified three types of turbulent flows: smooth, transitional and rough. For smooth pipes, the friction f is a function of the Reynolds Number R; passing to transitional flow f is a function of R and k/D where k is the average wall roughness height. In the rough turbulent zone, f is only dependent on k/D. This is shown in the diagram below where f is plotted against R on a logarithmic basis for artificially roughened pipes.

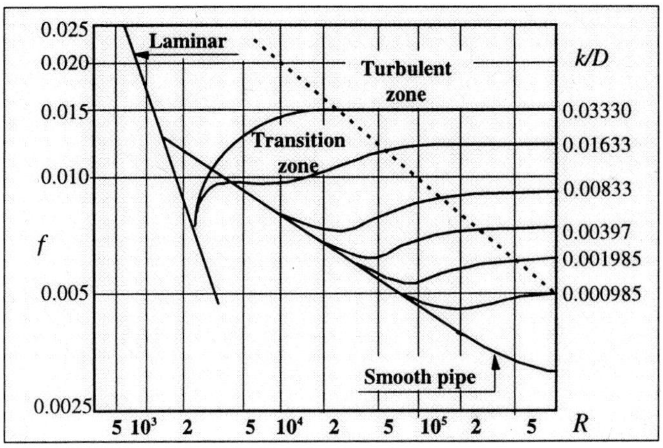

Nikuradse deduced the following equations for smooth and rough flows in pipes:

$$\frac{1}{\sqrt{4f}} = 2 \log_{10}\left(\frac{R \times \sqrt{4f}}{2.5}\right) \qquad (4.48)$$

$$\frac{1}{\sqrt{4f}} = 2 \log_{10}\left(\frac{3.7 \times d}{k}\right) \qquad (4.49)$$

Colebrook and White examined data on commercial pipes and found that the addition of these equations produced a universal equation suitable for use in the three types of turbulent flow in pipes.

$$\frac{1}{\sqrt{4f}} = -2 \log_{10}\left[\left(\frac{k}{3.7d}\right) + \left(\frac{2.51}{R \times \sqrt{4f}}\right)\right] \qquad (4.50)$$

Recommended values of k for different pipe materials are listed below.

Material		Values of k (mm)		
		Good	Normal	Poor
Smooth	Brass, copper, glass, plastic	-	0.003	-
	Cement	-	0.015	-
Metal	Spun bitumen lined	-	0.03	-
	Uncoated Steel	0.015	0.03	0.06
	Coated Steel	0.03	0.06	0.15
	Cast Iron	0.14	0.3	0.6
	Old water mains	0.6	1.5	-
Concrete	Monolithic construction	0.06	0.15	-
	Smooth surface pre-cast	-	0.15	0.3
Clayware	Glazed vitrified clay (depending on size)	0.06	0.15	0.3
Sewers	Slimed sewers	0.6	1.5	3.0
Unlined Rock Tunnel	Granite	60	150	300
Earth Channels	Straight artificial channels	15	60	150
	Straight natural streams	150	300	600

Chart for Pipes and Channels

The Hydraulics Research Station has published "Charts for the Hydraulic Design of Pipes and Channels" which are the graphical solutions of the Darcy Weisbach and other equations *(see Chapter 10).* The plotted variables are discharge Q, diameter D, hydraulic gradient S and velocity V. The sample chart below shows an example with some details omitted from the original and the chart along the lines of two variables the remaining two parameters are read off. Please note the following:

(1) The value of $\lambda = 4f$ in these publications

(2) Secondary losses other than friction have to be calculated separately.

(3) Effective roughness sizes, k, have to be estimated from tables provided in publications.

There exists many empirical formulae of the exponential type and monographs are used to facilitate their solutions. These should only be used within the limited range on which they have been developed.

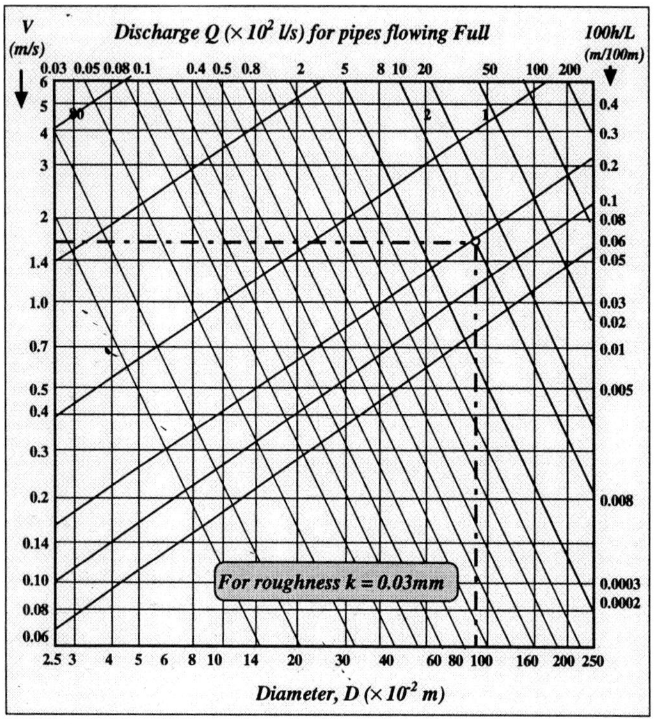

Simplified design chart for flow in pipes.

List of surfaces with roughness k = 0.03mm

Good examples of	Wrought iron. Coated steel. Clayware (glazed or unglazed) with sleeve joints. Sewer rising mains, mean velocity 2m/s.
Normal examples of	Asbestos cement Spun bitumen lined metal pipes. Spun concrete lined metal pipes. Uncoated steel. Clayware (glazed or unglazed) with spigot and socket joints and 'O' ring seals - diameter <150mm. Pitch fibre pipes running part full. uPVC with chemically cemented joints.

Use of Hydraulic Design Charts

A concrete pipe is required to carry storm water discharge of *1000 l/s* when laid at a gradient of 1 in 500. Calculate the pipe diameter and velocity of flow. Take $k = 0.03$ *mm.*

$Q = 1000$ *l/s* and $S = 1/500 = 0.002 = 0.2$ *m per 100m.*

On the design chart for $k = 0.03mm$, read $Q = 1000$ on the top scale and 0.2 on the right hand scale. The intersection of these inclined grids gives: ***Velocity,*** $V = 1.6 m/s$ (left hand scale)
Diameter, D = 0.9 m (bottom scale)

A pipe of 900 mm diameter or near equivalent is required.

Pipeline Between Two Reservoirs

A pipeline 150mm in diameter and 7km long carries water between two reservoirs. The difference in level between the water surfaces in the two reservoirs is 21m. The pipeline is constructed of steel pipes with a roughness height k = 0.03mm. Calculate the flow rate through the pipeline, neglect minor losses. To increase the flow rate to *20l/s* between reservoirs, a length of 300mm diameter steel pipe is connected in parallel to the 150mm diameter pipe. Calculate the required length x of 300mm diameter pipe if the water surface levels in the reservoires remain unaltered. Plot the hydraulic gradient line to the modified pipe line.

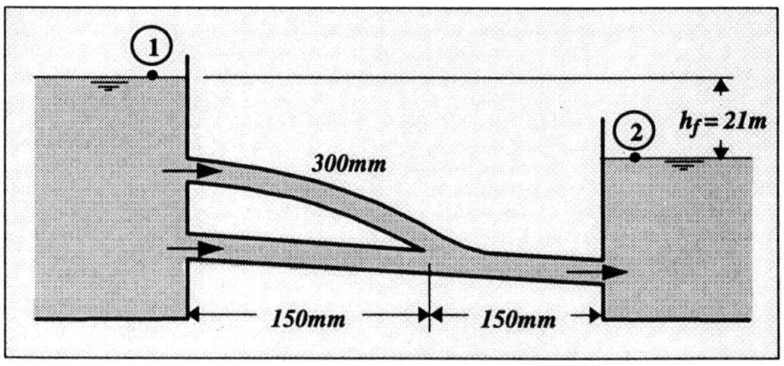

For single pipe, d = 0.15m and k = 0.03mm,

slope $= 100 \times S_1 = 100 \times (21/7000) = 0.3.$

From HRS Chart, $Q = 12$ *l/s.*

For the second pipe assume x to be the required length.
For $Q = 20 l/s$ and D = 0.15 obtained from Chart, therefore,
new gradient $= 100 \times S_2 = 0.78.$

A trial and error procedure is used to find the required length x by assuming different values as shown in the Table below.

$h_{f2} = 0.78 \times (2000 / 100) = 15.6m.$

$h_{f1} = 21 - 15.6 = 5.4m.$

$100 \times S_1 = 5.4 / 5000 = 0.108.$

From Chart, $Q_{150} = 6.8$ *l/s,* and $Q_{300} = 43.2 l/s.$

Similarly, the procedure is repeated for the other two columns in the following table. The length of the 300mm pipe (x) is approximately 4420m.

Trial	(1)	(2)	(3)
x	5000	4500	4420
(7000-x)	2000	2500	2580
h_{f2}	15.6	19.5	20.12
h_{f1}	5.4	1.5	0.876
$100S_1$	0.108	0.033	0.02
Q_{150}	6.8	22.6	3.0
Q_{300}	43.2	(large)	17.0
Q	50 (large)		20

Open Channel Flow

Uniform Flow Through Channels

The fundamental equation for open-channel flow may be derived readily by equating the equal and opposite forces of gravity and resistance and applying some of the fundamental notions of fluid mechanics obtained in the analysis of pipe flow.

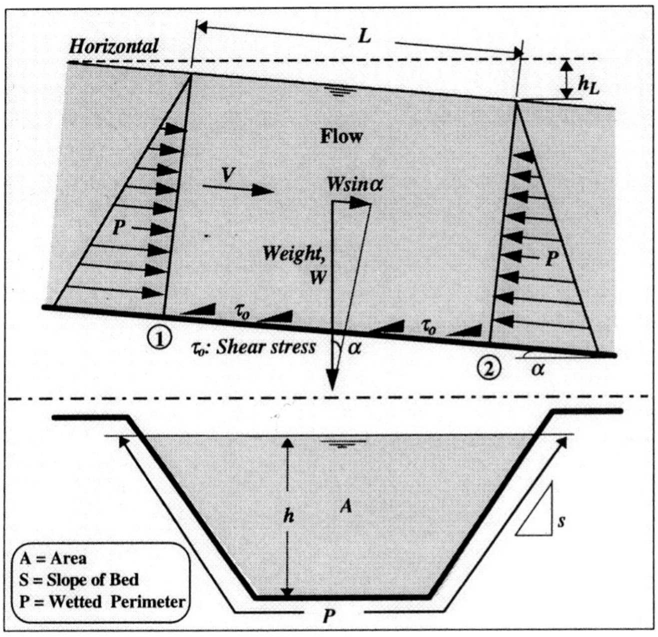

Fig.4.19- Uniform flow in an open channel.

Consider the uniform flow of a liquid between 1 and 2 of the open channel shown above. Force of resistance exerted by the bottom and sides of channel = $\tau_o\ PL$. Component of weight in the direction of flow = $(W \times A_1) \times \sin\alpha$. Since the velocity is constant, the component of the force of gravity parallel to the channel bed must equal the total force resisting the flow. That is

$$\rho g A L \sin\alpha = \tau_o\ PL \tag{4.51}$$

The shear stress at the bed τ_o is assumed to vary as some square power of the velocity so that $\tau_o = FV^2$.

$$\rho g\ \frac{A}{P} \times \sin\alpha = FV^2 \tag{4.52}$$

The slopes of open channels are usually so small that it may be assumed that the slope length equals the horizontal length and

$$\sin\alpha = \tan\alpha = \frac{h_L}{L} = S \tag{4.53}$$

and since $A/P = R$, then $\rho g R S = FV^2$.

Chezy as early as 1775 is reported to have recommended an equation of this form. If $\rho g/F$ is replaced by a coefficient C, the equation reduces to

$$\textit{Velocity,}\ V = C\sqrt{RS} \tag{4.54}$$

which is known as the **Chezy formula,** where R is the hydraulic radius and S the slope of the hydraulic gradient.

It can be shown that **Chezy's formula** is an alternative form of **Darcy-Weisbach formula** for friction resistance through pipes.

$$h_L = \frac{fL}{d/4} \times \frac{V^2}{2g} \tag{4.55}$$

If one assumes that the intensity of boundary shear represents the average value over the wetted perimeter, the quantity $d/4$ in equation (4.55) can be replaced by R, since for a pipe,

$$R = \frac{A}{P} = \frac{\pi \times d^2/4}{\pi \times d} = \frac{d}{4} \tag{4.56}$$

$$h_L = \frac{fL}{R} \times \frac{V^2}{2g} \tag{4.57}$$

where f is a function of Reynolds number. The ratio h_L/L corresponds to the slope of the water surface. Introducing $S = h_L/L$ (often called the hydraulic gradient) followed by solution for V, then yields

$$V = \sqrt{2g/f} \times \sqrt{RS} \tag{4.58}$$

from which it is seen that $C = \sqrt{2g/f}$, and

$$\textbf{Chezy's equation: } V = C\sqrt{RS} \tag{4.59}$$

where C is a coefficient depending on the roughness and cross-sectional shape of the channel, and is most frequently determined by the **Manning equation:** $C = R^{1/6}/n$ (4.60)

Combining the two equations (4.59) and (4.60), gives

$$\textbf{Manning formula: } \textit{Velocity, } V = \frac{1}{n} \times R^{2/3}\, S^{1/2} \tag{4.61}$$

in which n is a **roughness factor** having the values for particular boundaries listed below. This is an empirical discharge equation developed from the analysis of many field measurements and was proposed by an Irish engineer named **Manning** towards the end of the 19th century. Because of its rather simple nature, it is commonly used in practice. Values of coefficient n are also given in Chapter 10.

Manning Roughness Coefficient

The values of Manning's roughness coefficient for various boundary materials are briefly listed below. The values depend on the finish and condition of the channels.

	Values of n	
Material	**Normal**	**Range**
Glass	**0.011**	**0.010 - 0.013**
Concrete	**0.012**	**0.010 - 0.020**
Cast Iron	**0.013**	**0.011 - 0.016**
Clay	**0.013**	**0.012 -0.018**
Brickwork	**0.015**	**0.013 - 0.030**
Earth Channels	**0.022**	**0.020 - 0.050**
Natural Streams	**0.030**	**0.025 - 0.050**
Large Rivers	**0.040**	**0.030 - 0.060**

Table 4.2- Values of Manning's roughness coefficient n.

Channel Section of Greatest Efficiency

The most efficient cross section of an open channel is the one that for given slope and area, has the maximum discharge and therefore the shortest wetted perimeter. This can be seen by considering Chezy's formula,

$$Q = AV = CA\sqrt{RS} = C\sqrt{\frac{A^3}{P}\times S} \tag{4.62}$$

If we can put P in terms of A, we can by differentiation find what value of P will make P a minimum for a given value of A. This will make both the mean velocity and the discharge a maximum for a given value of A, or the area a minimum for given value of Q. This will be the most economical channel to construct and the least likely to silt up, owing to low velocity.

Rectangular Channel

Breadth = b, *Depth* = h, *Area* = bh, $P = b+2h = A/h+2h$.

$$\frac{dP}{dh} = -\frac{A}{h^2}+2 \tag{4.63}$$

Putting $A = bh$ and equation $dP/d(h)$ to zero, we have $b = 2h$.

That is for maximum flow the depth must equal 1/2 the breadth. We then have

$$Q = C\times\sqrt{\frac{A^3}{P}\times S} = C\times\sqrt{\frac{b^3h^3S}{b+2h}} = \frac{C}{4}\times\sqrt{b^5\times S} \tag{4.64}$$

Trapezoidal Channels

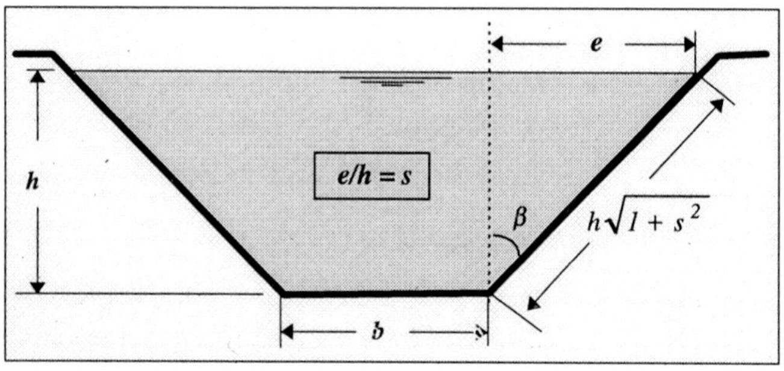

Fig.4.20- Cross-section of a trapezoidal channel.

Properties of trapezoidal sections and methods of determining sections of greatest efficiency are in the following analysis:

$A = bh + sh^2$, from which $b = A/h - sh$. Also,

$$P = b+2h\sqrt{1+s^2} = \frac{A}{h} - sh + 2h\sqrt{1+s^2} \tag{4.65}$$

Assuming A and s constant, and equating to zero the first derivative of P with respect to h,

$$\frac{dP}{dh} = -\frac{A}{h^2} - s + 2\sqrt{1+s^2} = 0 \tag{4.66}$$

Substituting for A from equation (4.65),

$$\frac{bh+sh^2}{h^2} = 2\sqrt{1+s^2} - s \tag{4.67}$$

$$b = 2h\times\sqrt{1+s^2} - 2hs \tag{4.68}$$

from which, the relation between depth of water and bottom width of canal of the most efficient trapezoidal cross section can be obtained for any value of s.

From the above equations:

$$R = \frac{A}{P} = \frac{bh + sh^2}{b+2h\sqrt{1+s^2}} \tag{4.69}$$

Substituting for b and reducing, $R = h/2$ or the trapezoidal cross section of greatest efficiency has a hydraulic radius equal to one half the depth of water.

$$h = \sqrt{A/\left(1-\sqrt{1+s^2}\right) - s} \tag{4.70}$$

Substituting this value in equation (4.65),

$$P = 2\sqrt{A}\times\sqrt{\left(1-\sqrt{1+s^2}\right) - s} \tag{4.71}$$

Equating to zero the first derivative with respect to s and reducing, $s = (1/3)^{1/3} = \tan 30^o$ or $\beta = 30^o$, and the section becomes a half hexagon. Thus, of all the trapezoidal sections (including the rectangle) for a given area, the half hexagon has the smallest perimeter and is therefore the most efficient cross section.

A semicircle having its centre in the middle of the water surface can always be inscribed within a cross section of maximum efficiency.

Friction Factor for Open Channels

The Darcy-Weisbach equation for head loss due to friction in pipes, $h_f = 4fl\,V^2/2gd$, may be used by introducing the hydraulic radius R = *flow area/wetted perimeter,* where R = d/4 and $h_f/l = S$, slope for free surface flow. This yields $S = fV^2/2gR$. The Colebrook-White equation may be modified by replacing d by $4R$:

$$\frac{1}{\sqrt{4f}} = -2\log_{10}\left[\frac{k}{14.8R} + \frac{2.51}{R\times\sqrt{4f}}\right] \tag{4.72}$$

The coefficient C in Chezy's equation $V = C\sqrt{RS}$ is related to f by $C = \sqrt{\frac{2g}{f}}$

In the Manning's formula: $V = 1/n \times R^{2/3}\,S^{1/2}$, n is related to f by,

$$n = \sqrt{\frac{R^{1/3}f}{2g}} \tag{4.73}$$

Channel of Constant Mean Velocity

When a depth of water in a channel may vary with wide limits, it is in general desirable to design this so that the velocity of flow may be as nearly as possible independent of the depth. Otherwise, in any open canal, the velocity may become so great as to damage the sides and bottom by scouring, while in a sewer with low heads, the velocity may become insufficient to produce the necessary flushing.

On the assumption that,

$$V = C\times(RS)^{1/2} \tag{4.74}$$

where C is the constant, the only essential condition to be satisfied for V to be independent of the depth is that the hydraulic mean depth shall also be independent of the depth of water.

Examples on Channels

Discharge of an Irrigation Channel

The cross-section of an irrigation channel is a trapezium with a bottom width B of 3.6m and side slopes of 1 vertical to 2 horizontal. Assuming that C in the Chezy formula is 55, what will be the discharge Q, if the depth of water D is 1.3m and slope S of the bed is 1 in 1600?

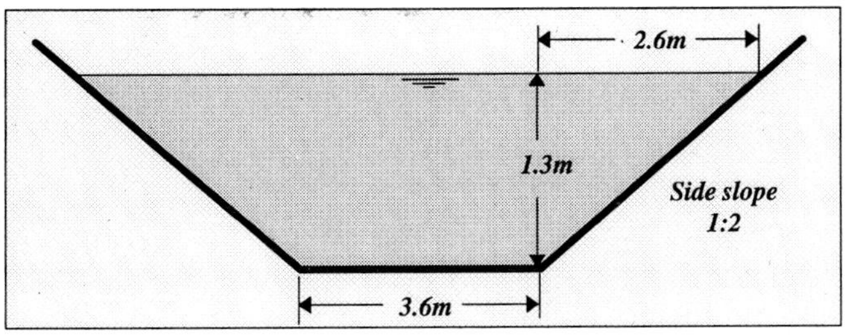

Area of channel, $A = 3.6 \times 1.3 + 2 \times 0.5 \times 1.3 \times 2.6 = 8.06m^2$.

Wetted perimeter, $P = 3.6 \times \sqrt{1.3^2 + 2.6^2} = 9.414m$.

Hydraulic Radius, $R = \frac{A}{P} = \frac{8.06}{9.414} = 0.856m$.

Velocity, $V = C \times \sqrt{RS}$.

Discharge, $Q = AV = AC\sqrt{RS} = 8.06 \times 55\sqrt{\frac{0.856}{1600}} = 10.25m^3/s$.

Channel with Semi Circular Invert

A channel has vertical walls 1.2m apart and a semicircular invert. If the centre line depth is 0.9m and the bed slope is 0.37m per kilometre, what would be the value of C in the Chezy's formula, when the discharge is $0.57m^3/s$?

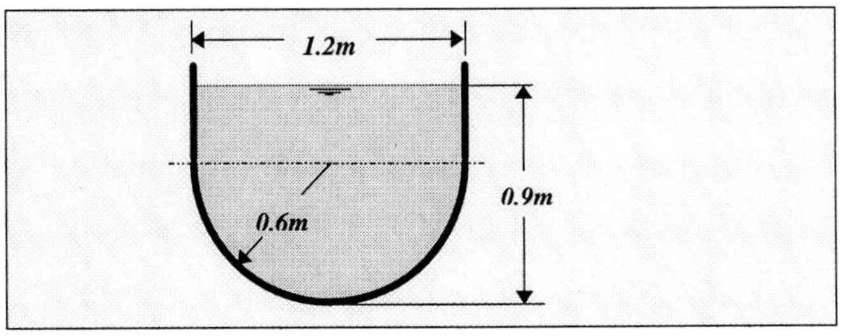

Area of channel, $A = \frac{\pi \times 0.6^2}{2} + 1.2 \times 0.3 = 0.925m^2$

Wetted perimeter, $P = \pi \times 0.6 + 2 \times 0.3 = 2.484m$.

Hydraulic radius, $R = A/P = 0.925/2.484 = 0.372m$.

Bed slope, S $= 0.37/1000 = 0.00037$.

Since the discharge is known, $\boldsymbol{Q = 0.57m^3/s}$.

$Q = AC\sqrt{RS}$, $\therefore\ 0.57 = 0.925 \times C\sqrt{0.372 \times 0.00037}$

Chezy's Coefficient, C = 52.5m $\boldsymbol{C = 52.5m^{1/2}/s}$.

Uniform Flow in a Circular Channel

A channel is of slope 1:1000 and of circular cross section of radius 4m. Uniform flow with a depth of 2m takes place in the channel. Calculate (i) the shear stress on the walls of the channel, and (ii) the discharge in the channel taking Chezy $C = 55\ m^{1/2}/s$.

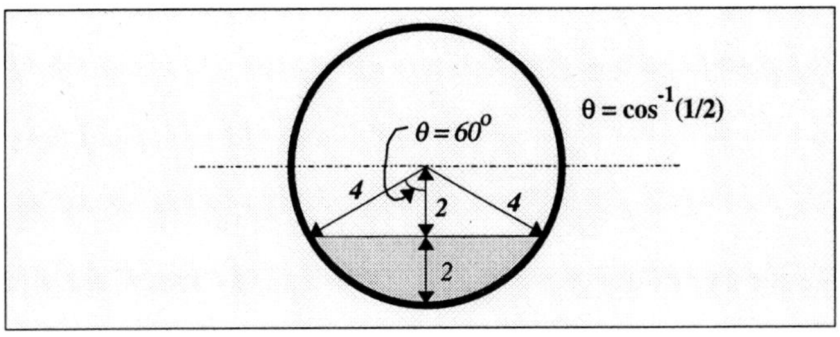

$S = 1:1000$, *Shear stress,* $\tau = \rho g\ RS$, $R = A/P$.

Area, $A = \frac{\pi r^2}{2} \times \frac{2\theta}{180} - 2\sqrt{16-4} = 9.83m^2$.

$P = \frac{\pi r^2}{2} \times \frac{2\theta}{180} = 8.34m$, $R = \frac{A}{P} = \frac{9.83}{8.38} = 1.19m$.

$\tau = \rho g\ RS = 10^3 \times 9.81 \times 1.19 \times 10^{-3} = 11.64N/m^2$.

Velocity, $V = C\sqrt{RS} = 55 \times \sqrt{\frac{1.19}{1000}} = 1.9m/s$.

Discharge, $Q = VA = 1.9 \times 9.83 = 18.7\ m^3/s$.

Flow in a Brick Drain

A brick sewer is 1m diameter and has a fall of 1 in 500. Calculate the discharge of water when the depth of flow at the centre is 0.75m. Take Chezy's coefficient $C = 50\ m^{1/2}/s$.

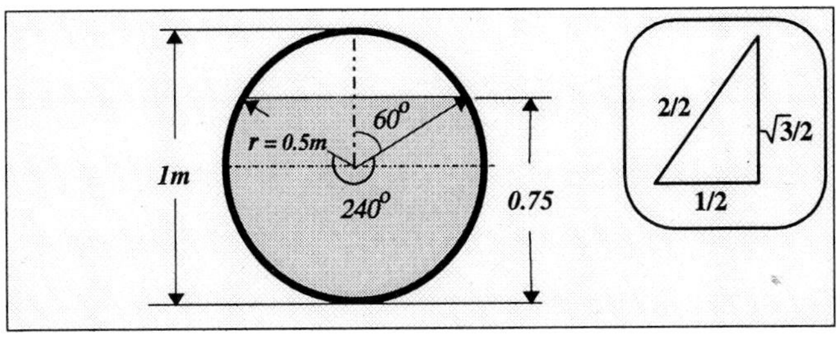

$A = \frac{24}{36} \times \pi r^2 + \frac{r^2}{2} \times \frac{\sqrt{3}}{2} = r^2 \times \left(\frac{2\pi}{3} + \frac{\sqrt{3}}{4}\right) = 2.527 \times r^2$

$\therefore$ ***Area,*** $A = 0.631m^2$

Wetted perimeter, $P = \frac{240 \times \pi D}{360} = \frac{2\pi D}{3} = 2.09m$

Velocity, $V = 50\sqrt{\frac{.631}{2.09} \times \frac{1}{500}} = 1.225\ m/s$.

Discharge, $Q = V \times A = 1.225 \times 0.631 = 0.772\ m^3/s$.

Flow in a Trapezoidal Channel

A trapezoidal channel has a bed slope of 1 in 2000, side slopes of 1 vertical in 2 horizontal and a depth of 1.5m. In the Manning equation $(V = R^{2/3}\ S^{1/2}\ n^{-1})$ the value of n is 0.035 and the discharge is 5.0 m^3/s when running full. Calculate the width of the channel bed required. Comment, without further calculation, on how this section compares with that having the same side slopes and minimum area of cross-section.

Assuming minimum B is associated with maximum depth use the depth of 1.5m for analysis.

Area, $A = \dfrac{(B+2\times(2\times 1.5\,)^2)+B}{2}\times 1.5 = 1.5B+4.5\,.$

Wetted perimeter, $P = B+2\sqrt{5}\times 1.5 = 6.70+B\,.$

Hydraulic radius, $R = \dfrac{A}{P} = \dfrac{1.5B+4.5}{6.7+B}\,.$

$S^{1/2} = \sqrt{\dfrac{1}{2000}} = \dfrac{1}{44.7}$, and $n = 0.035.$

Mean flow velocity, $V = \dfrac{1}{n}\times R^{2/3}\times S^{1/2}$

$$V = \frac{1}{0.035}\times R^{2/3}\times\frac{1}{44.7} = \frac{R^{2/3}}{1.57}\,.$$

Discharge, $Q = V\times A = \dfrac{R^{2/3}}{1.57}\times(1.5B+4.5) = 5m^3/s.$

$$\left(\frac{1.5B+4.5}{6.7+B}\right)^{2/3}\times\frac{(1.5B+4.5)}{1.57} = 5\,.\ \therefore\ B = 2.6m.$$

Further tabulation or plotting the graph yields an acceptable value of B = 2.6m. The channel with minimum cross section area with the specified side slopes would leave sides and bottom tangential to a circle with its diameter at water level.

Flow in a Rectangular Channel

A rectangular concrete channel is 2.5m wide and has a gradient of 1 in 400. Determine the depth of flow when $Q = 10m^3/s$. Take C in Chezy as $50m^{1/2}/s$.

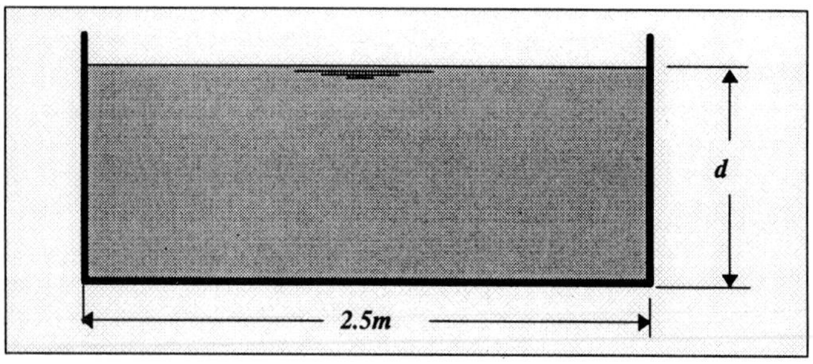

$V = C\sqrt{RS}\,,\quad R = A/P,\,,\quad Q = VA.$

Let d = depth of flow in m. Then $A = 2.5d$ and $P = 2.5 + 2d.$

$Q = 10\ m^3/s,\ C = 50\ m^{1/2}/s,\ S = 1/400.$

$$Q = CA\times\sqrt{RS}\,,\ \therefore\ 10 = 50\times 2.5d\times\sqrt{\frac{2.5d}{2.5+2d}\times\frac{1}{400}}$$

$$\frac{2.5d^3}{2.5+2d} = 2.565\ \therefore\ \frac{2.565}{2.5}\times(2.5+2d) = d^3$$

Therefore, $2.565 + 2.052\,d = d^3$.

Solve the equation by trial and error as tabulated below:

$f(d)$	$= d^3 - 2.05\,d - 2.565$	$= 0$
$f(0.5)$	$= 0.125 - 1.025 - 2.565$	≈ -3.4
$f(0.8)$	$= 0.511 - 1.64 - 2.565$	≈ -3.6
$f(1.5)$	$= 3.375 - 3.08 - 2.565$	≈ -2.0
$f(1.7)$	$= 4.91 - 3.49 - 2.565$	≈ -1.0
$f(1.9)$	$= 6.85 - 3.9 - 2.565$	≈ 0.4
$f(1.82)$	$= 6.05 - 3.75 - 2.565$	≈ 0.2
$f(1.85)$	$= 5.32 - 3.81 - 2.565$	≈ 0.0

Depth of flow = 1.85m.

Problems on Open Channel Flow

[1] An open channel of rectangular section of breadth 1m and slope 2 in 1,000 conveys water at the rate of 3 m^3/sec. What is the depth of uniform flow if C=55? (1.935m)

[2] A channel is of slope 1 in 1,000 and of circular cross-section of radius 4m. Uniform flow with a depth of 2m takes place in the channel. Calculate the shear stress on the walls of the channel. If Chezy C = 55, what is the discharge in the channel? (11.51N/m^2, 18.51m^3/s)

[3] A circular sewer is required to convey 2260m^3 per hour when running at a depth of one quarter of the diameter. The slope is 1 in 2,000 and the Chezy C is 60. Determine the diameter of the sewer. (2.293m)

[4] A trapezoidal channel with side slopes of 60^0 to the horizontal is required to discharge 12m^3/s with a bed slope of 1 in 1200. Calculate the most "economic" dimensions of the cross-section taking the constant n in the Manning formula $V = 1/n\times R^{2/3}\ S^{1/2}$ as 0.0135. (d = 1.848m, b = 2.134m)

[5] Calculate the angle subtended by the wetted perimeter at the centre of a circular sewer (a) when the average velocity of flow is a maximum and (b) when the discharge is a maximum. Use the Chezy formula. Compare the maximum discharge of a circular sewer 1.2m diameter, bed slope 1 in 300, with the discharge when the sewer is running full at atmospheric pressure, assume Chezy $C = 55m^{1/2}/s$. (257°, 308°, 2.066m^3/s, 1.967m^3/s)

[6] An open channel of 'economic' trapezoidal cross-section with sides inclined at 60^0 to the horizontal is required to give a discharge of 10m^3/s when the slope of the bed is 1 in 1600. Calculate the dimensions of the cross-section, taking the constant M in the Manning formula $(V = M\times R^{2/3}\times S^{1/2})$ as $M = 1/n = 74.$ (d = 1.82m, b = 2.11m)

CHAPTER FIVE

DIMENSIONAL ANALYSIS

Introduction

The basis of this method is that all terms of any correct and complete physical equation must have the same dimensions. For example, if one term of an equation is measured in units of a velocity (say m per sec), then all other terms in the equation must be measured in units of velocity. To ensure that this is so, it is necessary to break down all units of measurement into the three primary dimensions, those of **mass M, length L, and time T**. Thus a velocity has the dimensions (length/time) = LT^{-1}.

All the results will fall on one curve which is the graph of the function ϕ. An empirical equation can be found to represent the plotted curve.

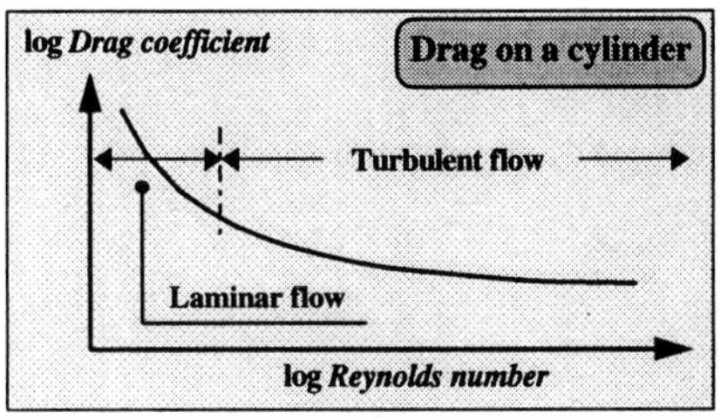

Resistance of Wholly Submerged Bodies

A body in steady motion through a fluid, or at rest in a moving current experiences a resistance whose magnitude depends upon the relative velocity, V, the physical properties of the fluid ρ and μ, the size and form of the body l, and at velocities above the critical, also upon it surface roughness. This will be the case for a deeply submerged submarine, or for an airship. Suppose the frictional resistance F to involve the above quantities in the form

$$F \;\alpha\; l^a V^b \rho^c \mu^d \tag{5.1}$$

Expressing the equation dimensionally gives:

$$MLT^{-2} = [L]^a [LT^{-1}]^b [ML^{-3}]^c [ML^{-1} T^{-1}]^d \tag{5.2}$$

Equating power indices of M T L,

M: $1 = c + d$ $\therefore c = 1 - d$

T: $-2 = -b - d$ $\therefore b = 2 - d$

L: $1 = a + b - 3c - d$ $\therefore a = 2 - d$ so that,

$$F \;\alpha\; l^{2-d} V^{2-d} \rho^{1-d} \mu^d \tag{5.3}$$

$$F \alpha\; l^2 V^2 \rho \left(\frac{\rho V l}{\mu}\right)^{-d} \tag{5.4}$$

Since d is unknown, this may be written as:

$$F = l^2 V^2 \rho \;\phi\left(\frac{\rho V l}{\mu}\right) \tag{5.5}$$

Since the values of both terms in the expression are dependent on V, the form of the function can be determined from experiments on a single body at different speeds in the same medium, and in each one the value of F is measured. The value of the unknown function ϕ may be found by plotting the observed values of $F/\rho V^2 l^2$ against simultaneous values of $\rho Vl/\mu$.

Resistance of Partially Submerged Bodies

When a body is partially submerged, such as a ship, that waves on the surface of the water are produced, part of the resistance to motion is due to this wave upon the distance through which particles of fluid are raised and therefore on the gravitational forces. The influence of gravity and viscosity must therefore be taken into account, and the relation is,

$$F \;\alpha\; l^a V^b \rho^c \mu^d g^e \tag{5.6}$$

Inserting fundamental dimensions,

$$MLT^{-2} = [L]^a [LT^{-1}]^b [ML^{-3}]^c [ML^{-1} T^{-1}]^d [LT^{-2}]^e \tag{5.7}$$

Equating power indices of M T L,

M $1 = c + d$ $\therefore c = 1 - d$

T $-2 = -b - d - 2e$ $b = 2 - d - 2e$

L $1 = a + b - 3c - d + e$ $a = 2 - d + e$, so that,

$$F \;\alpha\; l^{2-d+e} V^{2-d-2e} \rho^{1-d} \mu^d g^e \tag{5.8}$$

$$F \;\alpha\; l^2 V^2 \times \rho \times \left(\frac{\rho V l}{\mu}\right)^{-d} \left(\frac{V^2}{gl}\right)^{-e} \tag{5.9}$$

$$\frac{F}{\rho V^2 l^2} = \phi\left(\frac{\rho V l}{\mu}, \frac{V^2}{gl}\right) = \phi_l\left(\frac{Vl}{v}, \frac{V}{\sqrt{gl}}\right) \tag{5.10}$$

ϕ_l merely meaning another function of ϕ. The resistance or drag of a ship is therefore a function of Vl/v which is known as the **Reynolds number,** and of $V/(gl)^{1/2}$, which is known as the **Froude number.** The first expresses the effect of eddies and surface friction on the drag force; the second expresses the effect of surface waves formation on the drag. In most ship designs the contributions of friction and wave formation to the total drag are of the same order.

Examples on Dimensional Analysis

Pressure Drop in Pipe

Show by dimensional analysis that the pressure drop per unit length of fluid $\Delta p/l$, density ρ, viscosity μ flowing with mean velocity V in a pipe of diameter d is given by

$$\frac{\Delta p}{l} = \frac{\rho V^2}{d} \times \phi\left(\frac{\rho V d}{\mu}\right)$$

Hence, or otherwise, show that the friction factor f in Darcy's equation is a function of Reynold's number.

Darcy's equation for head loss, $h_f = 4flV^2/2gd$

$\Delta p/l = f(\rho, \mu, V, d) = k\,\rho^a, \mu^b, V^c, d^e$

$$\left[\frac{M}{T^2 L^2}\right] = [1].\left[\frac{M}{L^3}\right]^a . \left[\frac{M}{LT}\right]^b . \left[\frac{L}{T}\right]^c . [L]^e$$

Equating powers indices of M L T,

M:	1 = a + b	a = 1 - b
T:	-2 = - b - c	c = 2 - b
L:	-2 = -3 a - b + c + e	e = - 2 + 3 a + b - c= -1 -b

$$\frac{\Delta p}{l} = k\,\rho^{1-b}\,\mu^b\,V^{2-b}\,d^{-1-b} = K\frac{\rho V^2}{d}\left(\frac{\mu}{\rho V d}\right)^b$$

$$\therefore \frac{\Delta p}{l} = \frac{\rho V^2}{d} \times \phi\left(\frac{\rho V d}{\mu}\right), \quad h_f = \frac{4flV^2}{2gd}$$

$$\text{i.e. } \frac{\Delta p}{\rho g} = \frac{\rho V^2 l}{\rho g d} \times \phi\left(\frac{\rho V d}{\mu}\right) = \frac{4fl\,V^2}{2gd}$$

$$\phi\left(\frac{\rho V d}{\mu}\right) = 2f, \text{ i.e. } f = \phi(R).$$

Flow Between Two Tanks

Two tanks are separated by a thin partition in which there is an orifice of diameter d and cross sectional area a. The tanks contain a liquid of density ρ and viscosity μ and when there is a difference of pressure p between the two sides of the orifice the velocity of flow through it is V. Show by dimensional analysis that, if the quantity flow rate Q is expressed by the equation: $Q = C_d\, a\sqrt{2gh}$, where the coefficient of discharge C_d is a function of Reynolds Number R where $R = (\rho V d/\mu)$

Assume Q depends on a and V and dependent on ρ μ and gh.

$Q = K\,a^a\,\rho^b\,\mu^c\,(gh)^d$

Quantity	Dimension	Dimension	LHS	RHS
Q	L^3T^{-1}	M	0	+ b + c
a	L^2	L	3	2a - 3b - c + 2d
ρ	$M\,L^{-3}$	T	-1	- c - 2d
μ	$ML^{-1}T^{-1}$			
gh	$L^2\,T^{-2}$			

Solve in terms of indices of ρ or μ, i.e. in terms of b say.

$c = -b$

$d = 1/2 - c/2 = 1/2 + b/2$

$a = 3/2 + 3/2\,b + c/2 - d = 3/2 + 3/2\,b - b/2 - 1/2 - b/2 = 1 + 1/2\,b$

$$\text{Hence, } Q = K\,a^{(1+1/2\,b)}\,\rho^b\,\mu^{-b}\,gh^{(1/2 + b/2)} = Ka\sqrt{gh}\,\phi\left(\frac{\sqrt{a}\rho\sqrt{gh}}{\mu}\right)$$

Since a α d^2, $a^{1/2}$ α d, $V\,\alpha\sqrt{gh}$,$(gh)^{1/2}$ α V

$\therefore\ \phi = \phi(R)$ and $K\phi R = C_d\sqrt{2}$.

Drag Force on a Sign

Define the coefficient of drag of a solid body immersed in a fluid stream and show that it depends on the Reynolds number, R. A flat sign board 2m × 2m, is subjected to a wind with a velocity 18m/s normal to the surface of the board. Find the force exerted on the sign board, assuming that the coefficient of drag is given by $C_D = 0.5 + 0.3\,R \times 10^{-6}$. The density of air is 1.2kg/m^3 and its coefficient of dynamic viscosity is $1.8\times10^{-5}\text{Ns/m}^2$. If fluid moving at mean general velocity U is brought to rest at a flat normal surface of area A, the kinetic energy of flow is converted to stagnation pressure $0.5 \times \rho U^2$.

Coefficient of drag C_D = *Actual drag* $D / 0.5 \times \rho U^2 A$. A is an area representative of the body and must be specified. Assume that D depends only on μ, ρ, U of the fluid and on some representative length l of the plate. Assume that there is an exponential relationship of the form $D = K\,\mu^a\,\rho^b\,U^c\,l^d$.

In terms of dimensions *(K)*,

$$\left[\frac{ML}{T^2}\right] = \left[\frac{M}{LT}\right]^a \left[\frac{M}{L^3}\right]^b \left[\frac{L}{T}\right]^c [L]^d.$$

Equating power indices:

M:	1 = a + b
L:	1 = - a - 3 b + c + d
T:	-2 = - a - c

Solving in terms of a:

b = 1 - a c = 2 - a d = 1 + a + 3 - 3 a - 2 + a = 2 - a

This gives $D = \rho U^2 l^2 \times \phi(\rho U\, l/\mu)$.

Thus, $C_D = \left(D/0.5 \times \rho U^2 A\right) \times \phi(R)$

Substituting specialised values,

$R = \rho U l/\mu = 1.2 \times 18 \times 2 \times 10^5/1.8 = 2{,}400{,}000.$

$C_D = 0.5 + 0.3\,R \times 10^{-6} = 0.5 + 0.72 = 1.22.$

$D = C_D \times 0.5 \times \rho U^2 A = 1.22 \times 0.5 \times 1.2 \times 18^2 \times 4 = 950N.$

Discharge Through a Triangular Notch

Consider a triangular notch through which water is being discharged under a head H. Let the quantity of flow Q be supposed to depend upon the quantities μ, ρ, g and H, i.e.

$$Q \propto \mu^a \rho^b g^c H^d$$

Inserting fundamental dimensions,

$$[L^3 T^{-1}] = [ML^{-1}T^{-1}]^a [ML^{-3}]^b [LT^{-2}]^c [L]^d$$

Equating power indices of M T L,

M:	0 = a + b	b = - a
T:	-1 = - a - 2 c	c = 1/2 - a/2
L:	3 = - a - 3b + c + d	d = 5/2 - 3a/2

$$Q \propto \mu^a \rho^{-a} g^{(1-a)/2} H^{(5-3a)/2}$$

$$Q = g^{1/2} H^{5/2} \left[\frac{\mu}{\rho g^{1/2} H^{3/2}}\right]^a = g^{1/2} H^{5/2} \phi \left[\frac{\mu}{\rho g^{1/2} H^{3/2}}\right]$$

Taking g as constant and putting

$$C = \phi \left[\frac{\mu}{\rho H^{3/2}}\right], \text{ and } Q = CH^{5/2}$$

C has been found by experiments to be very nearly constant and is equal 1.40. The formula is widely used in practice.

Shear Stress at Pipe Wall

The determination of the loss of head by friction in a pipe resolves itself into determining the frictional force F at the boundary of the pipe in terms of the physical quantities involved.

Let the stress τ_o at the boundary be a function of diameter d, mean velocity V, the density ρ, and viscosity μ, or

$$\tau_o \propto d^a V^b \rho^c \mu^e$$

Inserting fundamental dimensions,

$$ML^{-1} T^{-2} = [L]^a [LT^{-1}]^b [ML^{-3}]^c [ML^{-1} T^{-1}]^e$$

Equating powers indices:

M:	1 = c + e ,	c = 1 - e
T:	-2 = -b -e ,	b = 2 - e
L:	-1 = a + b -3 c - e	a = -e

$$\tau_o = k.d^{-e} \times V^{2-e} \times \rho^{1-e} \times \mu^e$$

The constant k can usually be omitted or placed outside the following bracket.

$$\tau_o = k\rho V^2 \times \left(\frac{\mu}{\rho V d}\right)^e$$

$$\tau_o = \rho V^2 \times \phi \left(\frac{\mu}{\rho V d}\right), \text{ or}$$

$$\tau_o = \rho V^2 \times \phi' \left(\frac{\mu}{\rho V d}\right).$$

Therefore,

$$\frac{\tau_o}{\rho V^2} = \phi' \left(\frac{\rho V d}{\mu}\right) = \phi'(R).$$

Flow Around a Cylinder

Sketch the flow pattern around a circular cylinder placed in a uniform stream indicating the stagnation and breakaway points. Explain briefly why there is a 'form drag' when a real fluid flows past the cylinder.

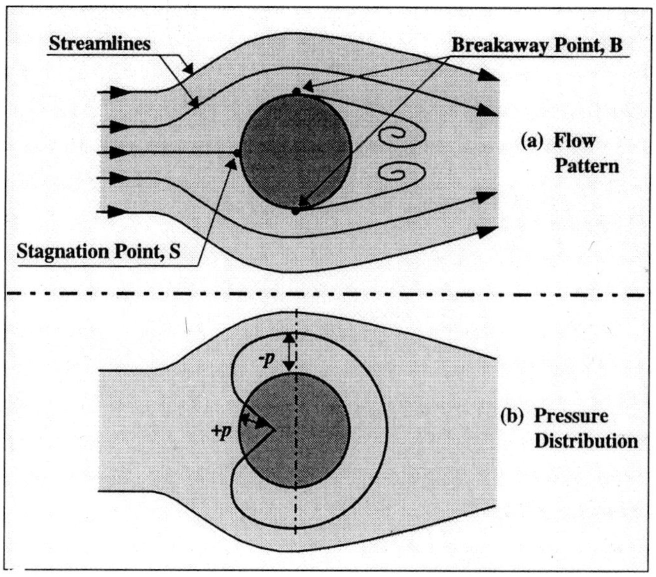

At high Reynolds number the flow of an air stream around a cylinder is turbulent and separates from it at points B, the breakaway points, forming a region of eddying motion on the downstream side where the pressure is less than atmospheric, as the pressure distribution shows above. In consequence of this, there is a net force on the cylinder in the downstream direction known as the 'form drag'.

Besides form drag, there is friction drag on the cylinder due to the boundary layer along the lengths SB, where viscous forces tend to retard the flow. The sum of form and friction drags is the total drag force on the cylinder. When the Reynolds number is low, the flow is laminar and the flow pattern is symmetrical about the cylinder. Here the form drag is zero and only friction drag operates.

Problems on Dimensional Analysis

[1] If the flow rate, Q, through an orifice depends on the diameter of the orifice D, the kinematic viscosity, ν, and the product gH, where H is the head above the orifice and g is the acceleration due to gravity, show by dimensional analysis that $Q = D^2 \times gH \times \phi(D\sqrt{gH}/\nu)$.

[2] If the resistance to motion S of a sphere through a fluid depends on the diameter D and the velocity V of the sphere, and the density ρ and the viscosity μ of the fluid, show that $S = \rho V^2 D^2 \times \phi(R)$. Hence, if by experiment $\phi(R) = 90$, find the steady velocity of fall of a steel sphere 1.6mm diameter through oil of relative density 0.85. The specific gravity of steel is 7.8. (8.64 mm/s)

[3] Show that the resistance to motion S of a ship length l moving with velocity V through a fluid density ρ, viscosity ν in gravitational acceleration g is given by $S = \rho V^2 l^2 \times \phi(R,F)$. R is the Reynolds number and F is the Froude number.

Examples on Lift and Drag

Equations for Lift and Drag Forces

The ability of an aircraft to fly depends to a large extent on its streamlined shape, and in particular its aerofoil wing shape. The wing must be such as to produce a lift force *L*, at least equal to its total weight, whilst at the same time, the drag force *D* should be a minimum. The smaller the drag force is the smaller the propulsive force required.

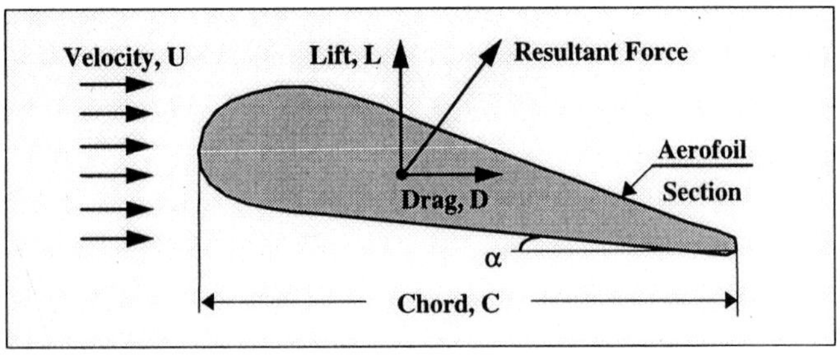

The numerical values of *D* and *L* are computed from the expressions:

$$\text{Drag force } D = \frac{1}{2}\rho U^2 \times A \times C_D \qquad (5.11)$$

$$\text{Lift Force } L = \frac{1}{2}\rho U^2 \times A \times C_L \qquad (5.12)$$

where *D* is the drag on the body, ρ is the density of the fluid, *V* is the velocity, *A* the frontal area, C_D the coefficient of drag, the components of resultant force perpendicular to the direction of flow, and C_L the coefficient of lift. The values of C_L and C_D depend on the shape of the body, surface roughness, the angle of attack and the Reynolds number *R* of flow. In fact is was shown by dimensional analysis that the resistance on a submerged body, Equation 5.4, is a function of *R*.

Drag on a Car Aerial

A car radio aerial consists of a vertical cylinder 10mm diameter and 1m high. What power is required to move the aerial through air at 30m/s? Assume the drag coefficient $C_D = 1.2$.

Drag force, $D = \frac{1}{2}\rho U^2 A C_D$, C_D = Drag coefficient.

Power, $P = DU = \frac{1}{2}\rho U^3 A C_D$, *(Assume* $C_D = 1.2$*).*

$$P = \frac{1}{2}\times 1.23\times 30^3 \times (0.01\times 1)\times 1.2 = 199W .$$

Resistance of a Circular Disc

The drag coefficient of a circular disc placed normal to flow is 1.12. Calculate the resistance to motion of a 0.3m diameter disc at 15m/s, (a) in air, (b) in water.

Drag force, $D = \frac{1}{2}\times \rho V^2 A C_D$, $C_D = \textit{Drag coefficient.}$

Drag in Air, $D = 0.5\times 1.23\times 225\times(\pi/4)\times 0.09\times 1.12 = 10.9\,N$

Drag in Water $D = 10.9\times 1000/1.23 = 8{,}860N = 8.86kN$.

Lift of a Buoy in the Sea

A submarine lying on the sea bed at a depth of 100m releases a 1m diameter buoy having a density 0.4 times that of sea water. The buoy reaches the surface 50s after being released. Calculate its drag coefficient if it travels vertically and at uniform velocity.

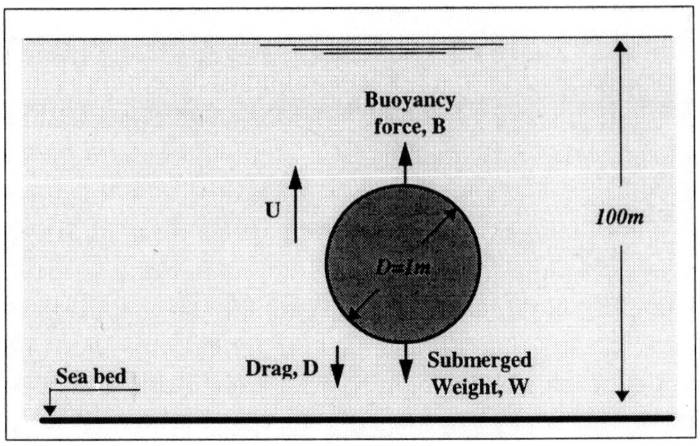

Velocity of Buoy, $U = \frac{100}{50} = 2m/s$, Area $A = \frac{\pi\times 1^2}{4} m^2$.

Drag force, D = B-W, (assuming ascent is uniform)

$$D = \frac{4\pi}{3}\times 0.5^3 \times 9.81\times(\rho_S - \rho_B) ,$$

with $\rho_B = 0.4\ \rho_S$.

$$D = \frac{4\pi}{3}\times 0.5^3 \times 9.81\times 0.6\rho_S = 3.09\rho_S$$

Also Drag force, $D = \frac{1}{2}\rho_S U^2 A C_D$,

$C_D = \textit{Drag coefficient.}$

$$\therefore\ 3.09\rho_S = \frac{1}{2}\times\rho_S\times 2^2\times\frac{\pi}{4}\times C_D$$

Drag coefficient, $C_D = \frac{2\times 3.09}{\pi} = 1.97$.

Lift and Drag on an Aerofoil

An aerofoil of 18m^2 area has lift and drag coefficients of 0.46 and 0.035 respectively. Calculate the lift and drag at 60m/s in air velocity. What power would be required for level flight at this speed?

Lift force, $L = \frac{1}{2}\rho U^2 A C_L$, $C_L = 0.46$

$$L = \frac{1}{2}\times 1.23\times 60^2 \times 18\times 0.46 = 18{,}350N = 18.35kN .$$

Drag force, $D = 18.35\times\frac{0.035}{0.46} = 1.395kN$.

Power, $P = D\times U = 1.395\times 60 = 83.7\ kW.$

Lift and Drag on an Aircraft Wing

An aerofoil wing has a span of 10m and a chord of 1.5m. At 60 m/s the total aerodynamic force on the aerofoil is *20kN*. If under these circumstances the lift/drag ratio is 10, calculate the lift coefficient and the total weight that can be lifted.

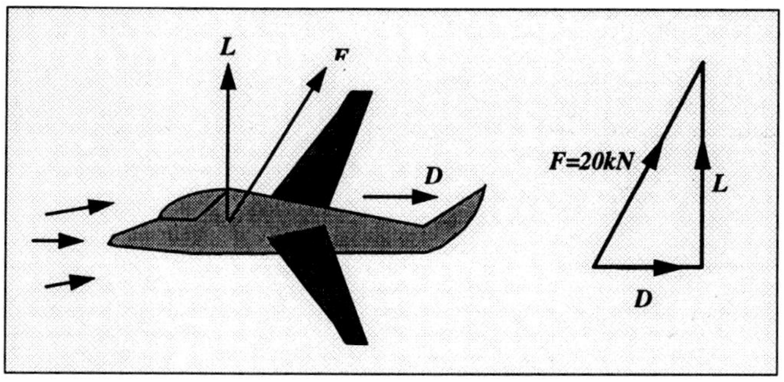

The Lift / Drag ratio, $L/D = 10$ (That is $D = L/10$, $L = 10D$).

$20^2 = L^2 + D^2 = (10D)^2 + D^2 = 101D^2$

Drag force, $D = 20/\sqrt{101} = 1.989kN$.

$20^2 (=400) = L^2 + D^2 = L^2 + (L/10)^2 = L^2 (1 + 1/100)$

Lift force, $L = \sqrt{\dfrac{400}{101/100}} = \sqrt{\dfrac{40000}{101}} = 19.9kN$.

Lift coefficient, $C_L = \dfrac{2L}{\rho U^2 A} = \dfrac{2 \times 19.9 \times 1000}{1.23 \times 60^2 \times 10 \times 1.5} = 0.6$.

Drag of a Towed Submerged Ball

A boat moving at a constant velocity of 3.5m/s tows a submerged 0.3m diameter ball of S.G. 7.2 by means of a short cable. If the cable makes an angle of 45° with the vertical, calculate the power required to pull the ball along and its drag coefficient. Neglect cable weight and its drag.

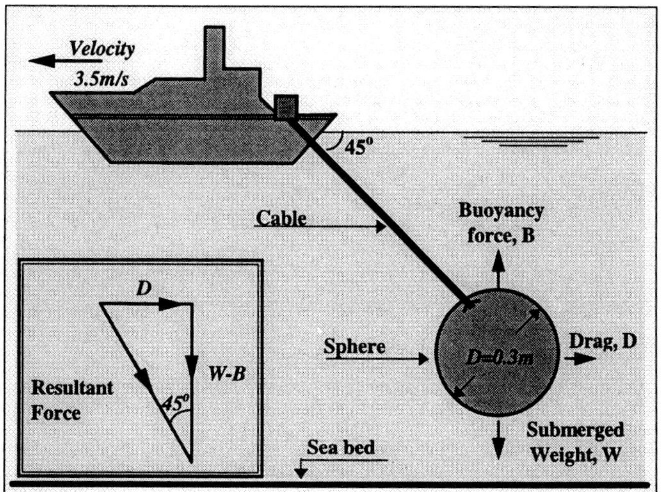

Drag force, $D = W - B = \dfrac{4\pi}{3} \times r^3 \times g \times (\rho_S - \rho_B)$

$$D = \frac{4\pi}{3} \times 0.15^3 \times 9.81 \times (7.2 - 1) \times 1000 = 860N .$$

Power, $P = D \times U = 860 \times 3.5 = 3.01\ kW$.

Drag coefficient, $C_D = \dfrac{2D}{\rho U^2 A} = \dfrac{2 \times 860 \times 4}{1000 \times 3.5^2 \times \pi \times 0.09} = 1.98$.

Drag of an Aircraft

The drag coefficient of an aircraft is given by $C_D = 0.04 + 0.05C_L^2$, and the aircraft has a wing area of 25m^2. If the weight of the aircraft is 40kN, calculate the minimum thrust for level flight and the corresponding aircraft speed.

Lift force, $L = \dfrac{1}{2}\rho U^2 A C_L$, where $C_L = \dfrac{2L}{\rho U^2 A}$

Drag force, $D = \dfrac{1}{2}\rho U^2 A C_D = \dfrac{1}{2}\rho U^2 A \times (0.04 + 0.05 C_L^2)$.

$$D = \frac{1}{2}\rho U^2 A \times \left(0.04 + \frac{0.05 \times 4L^2}{\rho^2 U^4 A^2}\right) = 0.02\rho u^2 A + \frac{0.1 \times L^2}{\rho U^2 A}$$

For minimum thrust,

$\dfrac{dD}{dU} = 0.04\rho UA - \dfrac{0.2L^2}{\rho U^3 A} = 0$. Also,

$$0.04\rho UA = \frac{0.2L^2}{\rho U^3 A}, \quad \therefore U^4 = \frac{0.2 \times L^2}{\rho^2 A^2 \times 0.04} .$$

Velocity, $U = \sqrt[4]{\dfrac{5 \times L^2}{\rho^2 A^2}} = 53.9 m/s$.

Drag force, $D = 0.02 \times 89400 + \dfrac{0.1 \times 40000^2}{89400} = 3580N$.

Problems on Lift and Drag

[1] A hemisphere of radius R is held stationary in a low speed uniform stream of air, with its plane face normal to the stream and the curved surface facing the stream as below. The velocity of air just outside the boundary layer at a point P on the front of the hemisphere is: $(3/2) \times U \times \sin\theta$, where the angle defines the point P, and by reference to the diagram is equal to angle SOP. The pressure on the base is uniform and equal to the pressure at the edge of the base. Derive an expression for the drag acting on the hemisphere in terms of ρ, U and R.. ($9/16\ \rho\ U^2\ \pi R^2$)

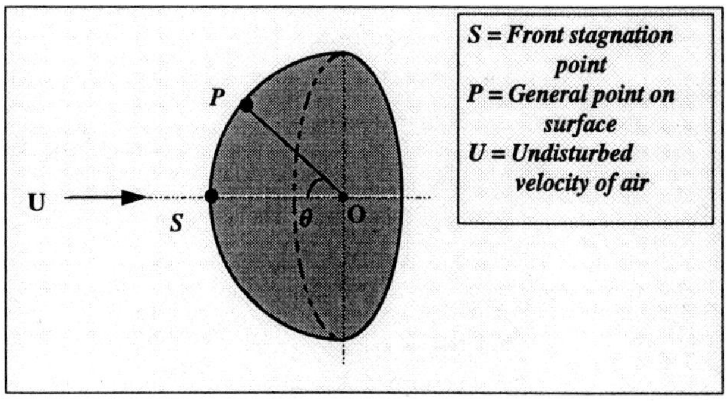

[2] Compute the overturning moment which is exerted by a 96km/hr wind upon a tall chimney having a diameter of 2.44m and a height of 30.49m. Assume a coefficient of drag of 0.35 and density of air = 1.2kg/m^3. (169.4 kNm)

CHAPTER SIX

UNSTEADY FLOW

Introduction

If the head is varying from instant to instant, the rate of discharge is never constant. The usual procedure to be adopted is to consider an instant when the head above some convenient datum is an amount h say. To find the time for the level of the fluid to rise or fall between certain limits it is necessary to integrate the expression for the time mathematically or graphically. The fundamental equation may be obtained as follows.

Flow From Tank Through Orifice

Suppose the surface area A of the vessel to be uniform and large compared with the area a of the orifice. Let V be the velocity of afflux at any instant and h height of free surface above the vena contractor at the same instant.

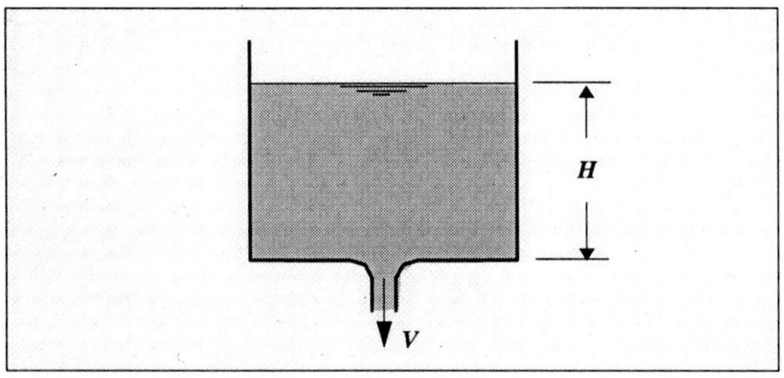

Fig.6.1- Tank orifice.

Assuming that,

$$V = C_V\sqrt{2gh} \tag{6.1}$$

from continuity we have, since

$$\frac{Velocity\ of\ fall\ of\ surface}{Velocity\ of\ afflux} = \frac{C_c a}{A} \tag{6.2}$$

$$Velocity\ of\ surface = -\frac{dh}{dt} = C_d \times \frac{a}{A}\sqrt{2gh} \tag{6.3}$$

$$C_d \times \frac{a}{A}\sqrt{2g}dt = -\frac{dh}{\sqrt{h}} \tag{6.4}$$

Integrating between any two limits of heights h_1 and h_2, we get the time T necessary to lower the surface through the distance h_1 - h_2,

$$\int_T^o \frac{C_d \times a\sqrt{2g}}{A} dt = \int_{h_2}^{h_1} -\frac{1}{\sqrt{h}} dh \tag{6.5}$$

$$T \times \frac{C_d \times a\sqrt{2g}}{A} = 2\,(h_1^{1/2} - h_2^{1/2}) \tag{6.6}$$

$$T = \frac{2A}{C_d \times a\sqrt{2g}} \times (h_1^{1/2} - h_2^{1/2}) \tag{6.7}$$

The time required to empty the vessel is,

$$T_e = \frac{2A\sqrt{H}}{C_d \times a\sqrt{2g}} \tag{6.8}$$

where H is the height of water in the tank. Equation (6.8) shows that T_e is equal to twice the time required for the same volume of water to leave the vessel under a constant head H. That is,

Volume, $V = AH$

$$\textbf{\textit{Discharge,}}\ Q = C_d \times a\sqrt{2gH} \tag{6.9}$$

Time × Discharge = Volume

$$T_c = \frac{AH}{C_d \times a\sqrt{2gH}} = \frac{A\sqrt{H}}{C_d \times a\sqrt{2g}} \tag{6.10}$$

Hence $T_e = 2T_c$.

Time of Lowering the Level in a Reservoir Through a Notch of Weir

A reservoir has a notch length b made in one of its sides and having its sill H metres below the original level of the water in the reservoir. It is required to find the time necessary for the water to fall to a level H_2 above the sill of the weir. It is assumed that the area of the reservoir is so large that the velocity of the water as it approaches the weir may be neglected.

Rectangular Notch: With the usual notation, the volume discharged per second with a head H behind the notch is

$$Q = KbH^{3/2} \tag{6.11}$$

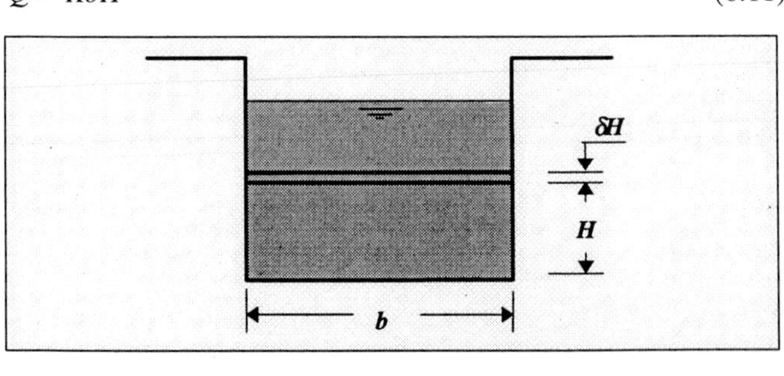

Fig.6.2- Reservoir weir.

Therefore, at any instant we have the velocity of the free surface in the reservoir given by,

$$-\frac{dH}{dt}=\frac{KbH^{3/2}}{A} \qquad (6.12)$$

Integrating this, the time $(T_2 - T_1)$ to lower the level through a distance $(H_1 - H_2)$ is given by,

$$T=\frac{2A}{Kb}\times\left(\frac{1}{H_2^{1/2}}-\frac{1}{H_1^{1/2}}\right) \qquad (6.13)$$

Vee Notch: Similarly the time of lowering the level in Vee notch whose discharge is given below can be found.

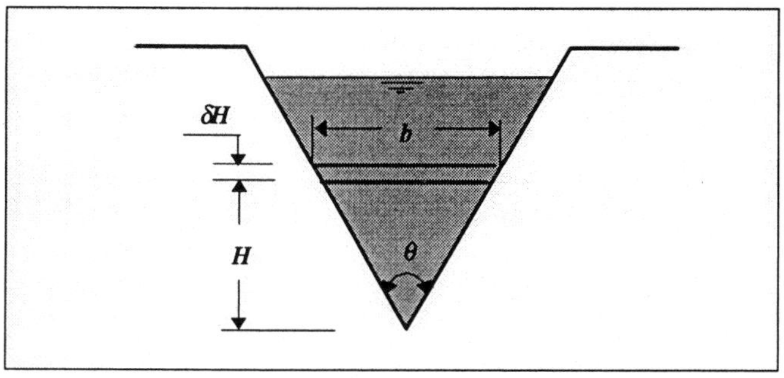

Fig.6.3- Vee notch.

$$Q=\frac{4}{15}\,C\times b\times\sqrt{2g}\times H^{3/2} \qquad (6.14)$$

Put $b/2 = H \tan \theta/2$ where θ is the angle, included between the side of the notch equation (6.14) becomes,

$$Q=\frac{8}{15}C\sqrt{2g}H^{5/2}\times\tan\left(\frac{\theta}{2}\right)=2.36\times CH^{5/2}\times\tan\left(\frac{\theta}{2}\right) \qquad (6.15)$$

As a result of experiments, Thomson estimated the mean value of C for a right-angled notch as 0.593, thus giving a discharge,

$$Q=1.4\times H^{5/2}, \quad -\frac{dH}{dt}=\frac{1.4\times H^{5/2}}{A} \qquad (6.16)$$

$$T=0.476\times A\times\left(\frac{1}{H_2^{3/2}}-\frac{1}{H_1^{3/2}}\right) \qquad (6.17)$$

Time of Emptying a Reservoir of Varying Cross-Section by Small Freely Discharging Orifice

Reservoir with Uniformly Varying Cross-Sectional Area

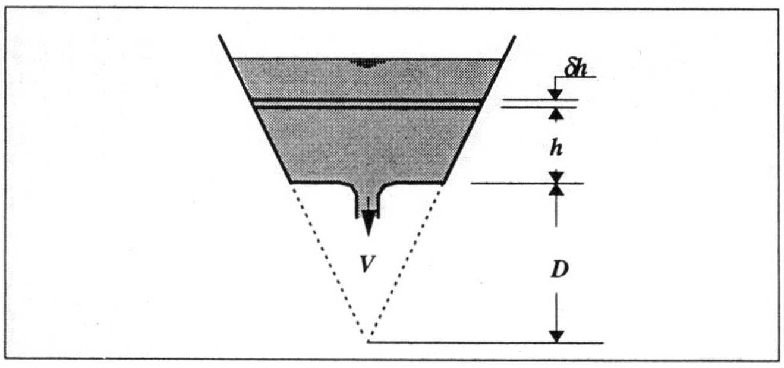

Fig.6.4- Varying cross-section tank.

Let kD = area of reservoir at the orifice. Then $A = k(D+h)$. (A is no longer constant but will be a function h).

$$\text{But,}\quad -\frac{dh}{dt}=\frac{C_d\times a\sqrt{2gh}}{A} \qquad (6.18)$$

and

$$-k\int_{h_2}^{h_1}\left(\frac{D+h}{\sqrt{h}}\right)dh=C_d\int_{h_2}^{h_1}a\sqrt{2g}\,dt \qquad (6.19)$$

$$T_2-T_1=\frac{k}{C}\left(\frac{2D(h_1^{1/2}-h_2^{1/2})+\frac{2}{3}(h_1^{3/2}-h_2^{3/2})}{a\sqrt{2g}}\right) \qquad (6.20)$$

where $C = C_c\, C_v$ = coefficient of discharge.

Hemispherical Bowl Emptied through Hole in the Bottom

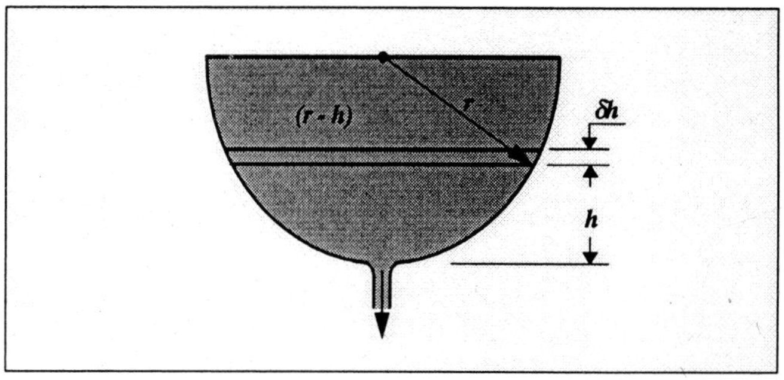

Fig.6.5- Hemispherical Bowl.

$$\text{Here, } A=\pi(r^2-[r-h]^2)=\pi(-h^2+2rh) \qquad (6.21$$

where r is the radius of hemisphere.

$$\text{But,}\quad -\frac{dh}{dt}=\frac{C_d\times a\sqrt{2gh}}{A} \qquad (6.22)$$

$$\int_{h_2}^{h_1}\frac{A}{\sqrt{h}}dh=\pi\int_{h_2}^{h_1}(-h^{3/2}+2rh^{1/2})dh$$

$$=\pi\left(-\frac{2}{5}(h_1^{5/2}-h_2^{5/2})+\frac{4r}{3}(h_1^{3/2}-h_2^{3/2})\right) \qquad (6.23)$$

$$T_2-T_1=\frac{\pi}{C_d}\left(\frac{-\frac{2}{5}(h_1^{5/2}-h_2^{5/2})+\frac{4r}{3}(h_1^{3/2}-h_2^{3/2})}{a\sqrt{2g}}\right) \qquad (6.24)$$

where C_d = coefficient of discharge. When $h_2 = 0$, the time of emptying the vessel is,

$$T_e=\frac{\pi}{C_d\times a\sqrt{2g}}\times\frac{14r^{5/2}}{15} \qquad (6.25)$$

Tank with Constant Inflow, Q_1, and Discharging through an Orifice *a*

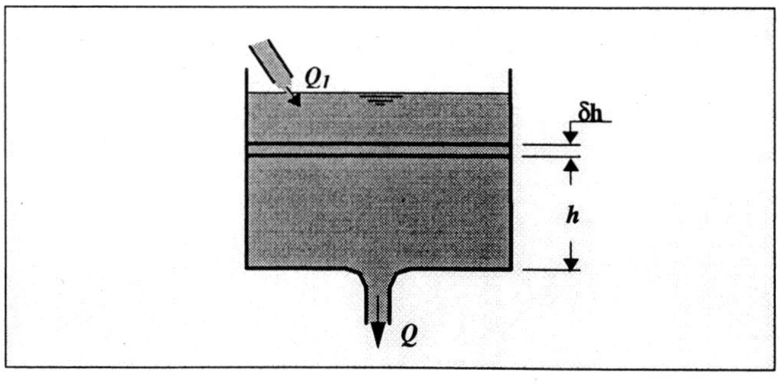

Fig.6.6- Tank with constant inflow.

Here,

$$\frac{dh}{dt}=\frac{Q_1}{A}-\frac{C_d\times a\sqrt{2gh}}{A} \qquad (6.26)$$

Put $\frac{Q_1}{A}=M$, and $\frac{C_d\times a\sqrt{2g}}{A}=N$, then $\frac{dh}{dt}=M-N\sqrt{h}$

$$\int_o^T dt=\int\frac{dh}{(M-N\sqrt{h})} \qquad (6.27)$$

$$\int_o^T dt=\int_{h_1}^{h_2}\frac{dh}{(M-N\sqrt{h})}=\frac{1}{N}\int_{h_1}^{h_2}\frac{dh}{(M/N-\sqrt{h})} \qquad (6.28)$$

$$T=\frac{2}{N}\left[\sqrt{h_1}-\sqrt{h_2}+\frac{M}{N}\log_{10}\frac{M/N-\sqrt{h_1}}{M/N-\sqrt{h_2}}\right] \qquad (6.29)$$

where, $M/N=Q_1/(C_d\times a\sqrt{2g})$

Time of Discharge from a Submerged Orifice

If two vessels whose surface areas are A_1 and A_2 are connected by an orifice of area a, and if at any instant H_1 and H_2 are the heights of their free surfaces above the level of the orifice, we have, neglecting viscosity, and assuming

$$V=\sqrt{2g(H_1-H_2)}=\sqrt{2gh} \qquad (6.30)$$

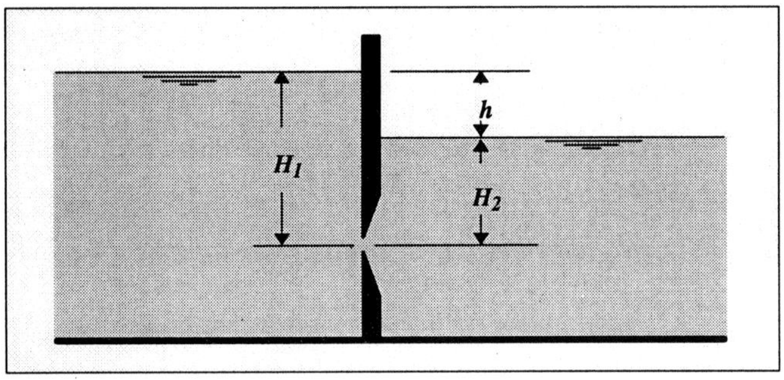

Fig.6.7- Submerged orifice.

***Velocity of surface** A_1, $=Va/A_1$. **Velocity of surface** A_2, $=Va/A_2$*

$$-\frac{dh}{dt}=C_d\times a\sqrt{2gh}\left(\frac{1}{A_1}+\frac{1}{A_2}\right) \qquad (6.31)$$

where C_d = coefficient of discharge. Integrating,

$$T_2-T_1=T=\left[2\Big/C_d a\sqrt{2g}\left(\frac{1}{A_1}+\frac{1}{A_2}\right)\right]\times(h_1^{1/2}-h_2^{1/2}) \qquad (6.32)$$

Time of Emptying a Lock with Vertical Drowned Sluice

This is a special case of the flow between two vessels through an orifice. Where the upper surface remains at the same level we have the state of affairs which holds during the filling of a canal lock through a submerged orifice in the lock gate. The upper surface is in effect now of infinite area, so that putting $A_1=\infty$ in equation (6.32), we get the time of filling the lock.

$$T=\frac{2\,A_2}{C_d\times a\sqrt{2g}}\sqrt{(H_1-H_2)} \qquad (6.33)$$

With submerged orifices the value of C_d is about 0.61, diminishing slightly with an increase in the effective head $(H_1 - H_2)$.

Time of Discharge of a Reservoir Through a Pipe

If we have two reservoirs of surface area, A_1 and A_2 respectively, connected by a pipe of diameter d and length l, then h is the difference of surface level at any instant

$$h=\frac{1}{2}\times\frac{V^2}{2g}+\frac{V^2}{2g}+\frac{4flV^2}{2gd}=\frac{V^2}{2g}\left(1.5+\frac{4fl}{d}\right) \qquad (6.34)$$

$$V=\sqrt{\frac{2gh}{1.5+(4fl/d)}} \quad and \quad Q=a\sqrt{\frac{2gh}{1.5+(4fl/d)}}$$

where a = area of pipe.

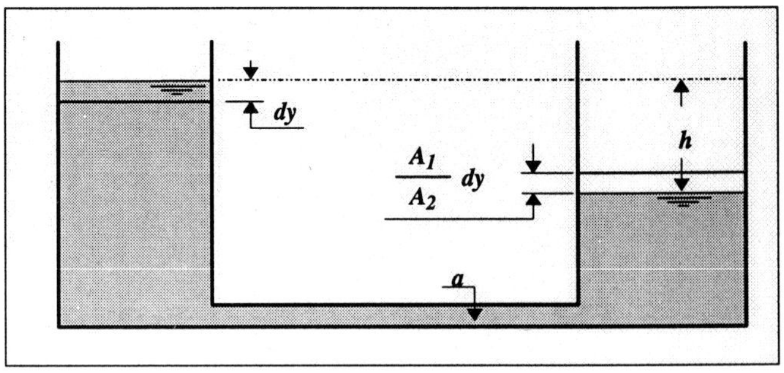

Fig.6.8- Pipe between two reservoirs.

Also, as for the time of discharge through an orifice,

$$-\frac{dh}{dt}=Q\left(\frac{1}{A_1}+\frac{1}{A_2}\right)$$

$$-\frac{dh}{dt}=a\sqrt{\frac{2gh}{1.5+(4fl/d)}}\left(\frac{1}{A_1}+\frac{1}{A_2}\right) \qquad (6.35)$$

Integrating,

$$T=T_2-T_1=\frac{2(h_1^{1/2}-h_2^{1/2})}{a\sqrt{2g/(1.5+(4fl/d))}\times\left(\frac{1}{A_1}+\frac{1}{A_2}\right)} \qquad (6.36)$$

Summary of Analysis

CASE 1: Flow from tank through orifice $Q'\,dt=-A\,dh$ $C_d\times a\sqrt{2gh}\times dt=-A\,dh$	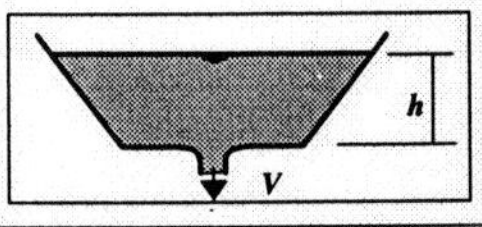
CASE 2: Flow from reservoir over weir. $Q\,dt=-A\,dh$ $C\times h^n\times dt=-A\,dh$	
CASE 3: Flow from tank through pipe $h+Z=(V^2/2g)+h_f+$ *Entry loss* $Q\times dt-Q_1\times dt=-A\,dh$ $aV\times dt-Q_1\times dt=-A\,dh$	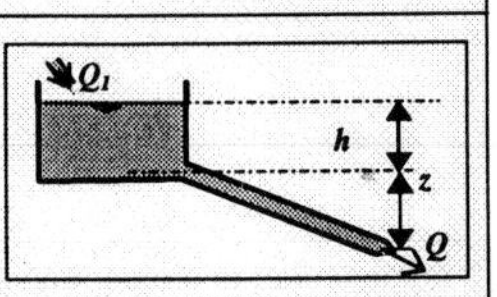
CASE 4: Flow between two tanks. $h_1-h_2=h=(V^2/2g)+h_f+$ *Entry loss* $Q\times dt-Q_1\times dt=-A_1\,dh_1$ $aV\times dt-Q_1\times dt=-A_1\,dh_1$ $A_1\times dh_2-Q_1\times dt=-A_1\,dh_1$	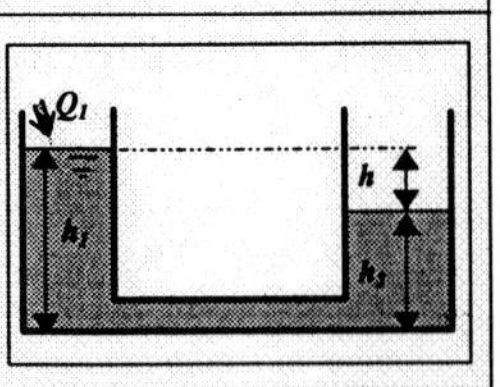

Examples on Unsteady Flow

Unsteady Flow Between Reservoirs

Two pipes each 3000m long, 0.5m diameter and friction coefficient 0.007, are arranged in parallel between two reservoirs. Each reservoir has a constant plan area of 300,000m^2. Find the time taken for the difference in water surface levels in the two reservoirs to decrease from 30m to 25m. Neglect secondary losses.

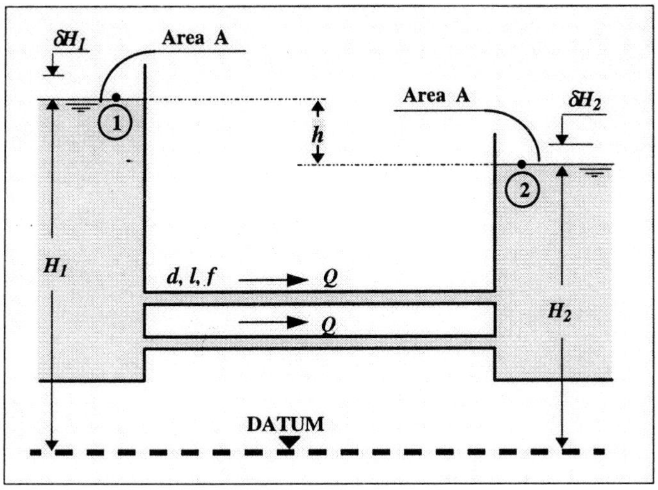

Apply Bernoulli's total head equation between (1) and (2) and neglect secondary losses.

$$\frac{p_a}{\rho g} + 0 + H_1 = \frac{p_a}{\rho g} + 0 + H_2 + \frac{4flV^2}{2gd}.$$

$$\therefore\ H_1 - H_2 = \frac{4flV^2}{2gd} = h_f = friction\ head\ loss.$$

Since $Q = VA$ and $h_f = \dfrac{32flQ^2}{\pi^2 gd^5}$, therefore,

$$Q = \sqrt{\frac{\pi^2 \times 9.81 \times 0.5^5}{32 \times 0.007 \times 3000}} \times \sqrt{h},$$

$$Q = 0.067 \times \sqrt{h}.$$

Total discharge, $2Q = A \times \dfrac{dH_2}{dt}$ *(For two pipes).*

But continuity equation between (1) and (2), $\dfrac{dH_1}{dt} + \dfrac{dH_2}{dt} = 0$.

and $h = H_1 - H_2$, $\therefore\ dh = dH_1 - dH_2$. $\therefore\ dh = -2\,dH_2$.

Hence, $2Q = -\dfrac{A}{2} \times \dfrac{dh}{dt}$, $\therefore\ dt = -\dfrac{A}{4Q} \times dh$.

$$t = -\frac{300{,}000}{4 \times 0.067} \times \int_{h_1}^{h_2} h^{-1/2}\,dh = -\frac{300{,}000}{4 \times 0.067 \times 3600} \times \int_{h_1=25}^{h_2=30} dh$$

Time, $t = 310.94 \times 2 \times (30^{1/2} - 25^{1/2}) = 296.8$ hours.

Unsteady Flow from a Cone

A tank is in the form of a truncated cone 0.9 diameter at the top, 0.3m diameter at the bottom and 1.2m deep. The base has an orifice 25mm diameter with a coefficient of discharge 0.67. The tank contains water to a depth of 1.0m. Calculate the time it takes for the water level to fall by 0.5m.

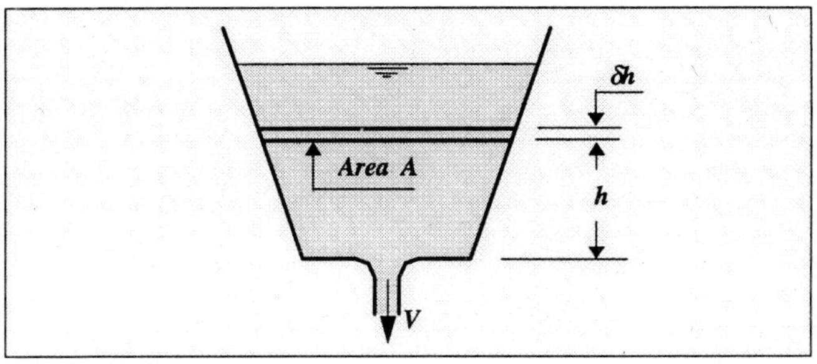

Discharge through orifice, $Q = C_D \times a \times \sqrt{(2gh)}$

Volume through orifice in time δt, $\delta V = C_D \times a \times \sqrt{(2gh)} \times \delta t$

Change of volume in tank, $\delta V = -\pi r^2 \times \delta h$.

Thus, $\delta t = \dfrac{-\pi \times r^2}{C_D \times a\sqrt{2gh}} \times \delta h$

where, $r = 0.15 + (h/1.2) \times (0.45 - 0.15) = 0.15 + 0.25h$.

Hence, $t = \dfrac{-\pi}{C_D \times (\pi d^2/4) \times \sqrt{2g}} \times \displaystyle\int_{h_1}^{h_2} \frac{(0.15 - 0.25h)^2}{h^{1/2}}\,dh$

$$t = \left(\frac{4}{0.67 \times 0.025^2 \times \sqrt{2g}}\right) \times$$

$$\left(0.0225 \times 2h^{1/2} + 0.075 \times \frac{2}{3}h^{3/2} + 0.0625 \times \frac{2}{5}h^{5/2}\right)_{h_2=0.5}^{h_1=1.0}$$

$$t = 2155\,(0.045(1 - 0.25) + 0.05(1 - 0.354) + 0.025(1 - 0.177))$$

Time, t = 198 seconds.

Emptying a Cylindrical Drum

A cylindrical drum is half-full of water and lies with its longitudinal axis horizontal. If the drum is 3m in diameter and 4.5m long, find the time for the drum to empty through a 75mm diameter orifice whose coefficient of discharge is 0.62.

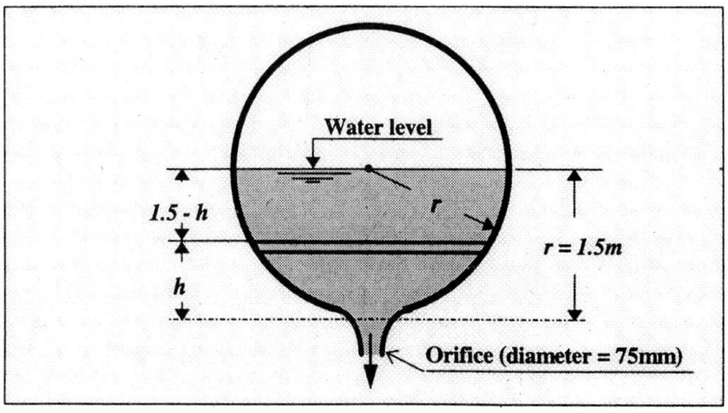

Consider the instant when the head above the orifice is h. By Pythagoras theorem the width of element w is:

$$w = 2\times\sqrt{3h-h^2} \text{ and } A = 9\times\sqrt{3h-h^2}\,.$$

$$Q = C_d A_o\sqrt{2gh} = 0.62\times\frac{\pi\times 0.075^2}{4}\times\sqrt{2gh} = 0.0121\times\sqrt{h}$$

$$Q\,dt = -A\,dh = -9\times\sqrt{3h-h^2}\,dh\,.$$

$$dt = \frac{-9\times\sqrt{3h-h^2}}{0.0121\times\sqrt{h}}\,dh = 743.80\times\sqrt{3-h}\,dh\,.$$

Since, $\int (ax+b)^n\,dx = \frac{(ax+b)^{n+1}}{a}\Big/(n+1)$, therefore,

$$\textit{Time} = 743.80\times\left[\frac{(3-h)^{3/2}}{3/2}\right]_{h=0}^{h=1.5} = \textbf{\textit{27 mins and 46 seconds.}}$$

Tapered Tank with Pipe

A circular tank 2m high is 1m diameter at the base and tapers uniformly to 1.4m diameter at the top. Connected to the base of the tank is a pipe, 200mm diameter and 20m long, whose open end is 3m below the level of the base of the tank. Calculate the time taken for the water level in the tank to fall from 1.8m to 0.5m above the base of the tank. Neglect losses other than pipe friction, and take the friction factor for the pipe as $f = 0.01$.

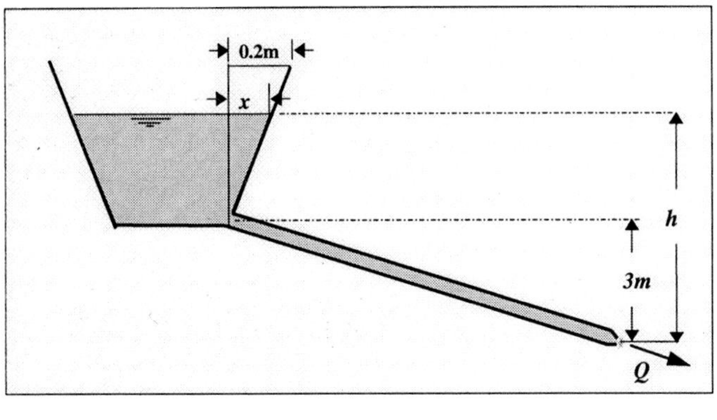

$$h = \frac{V^2}{2g} + h_f + losses\,.$$

$$h = \frac{V^2}{2g} + \frac{4flV^2}{2gd}, \text{ and } V = 1.981\times h^{1/2}.$$

$$\frac{x}{h-3} = \frac{0.2}{2}\,.\ \therefore\ x = \frac{0.2\times(h-3)}{2}\,.$$

$$Q\times dt = -A\times dh, \text{ or } a\times V\times dt = -A\times dh.$$

$$\frac{\pi}{4}\times 0.2^2\times 1.981h^{1/2}dt = -\frac{\pi}{4}\times\left(1+2\times\frac{0.2\times(h-3)}{2}\right)^2 dh\,.$$

$$0.06223\times h^{1/2}\times dt = -\frac{\pi}{4}\times(0.4+0.2h)^2\times dh\,.$$

$$-dt = \frac{2.0193}{h^{1/2}}\times dh + \frac{2.0193}{h^{1/2}}\times hdh + \frac{0.5048}{h^{1/2}}\times h^2dh\,.$$

$$t = -\left[4.0386\times h^{1/2} + 1.3462\times h^{3/2} + 0.2019\times h^{5/2}\right]_{4.8}^{3.5}.$$

Time, t = 33.2 - 21 = 12.2 seconds.

Discharge through a Vee Notch

A tank has a constant water surface area of $5m^2$ at all levels and discharges through a sharp-edged vee notch with a total included angle of 60°. The inflow and outflow are equal when the water level is 100mm above the bottom of the Vee. If the inflow is stopped, how long will it take the water level to drop to 50mm? Assume coefficient of discharge is constant at 0.65. Starting from $V = (2gh)^{1/2}$, derive any formulae used.

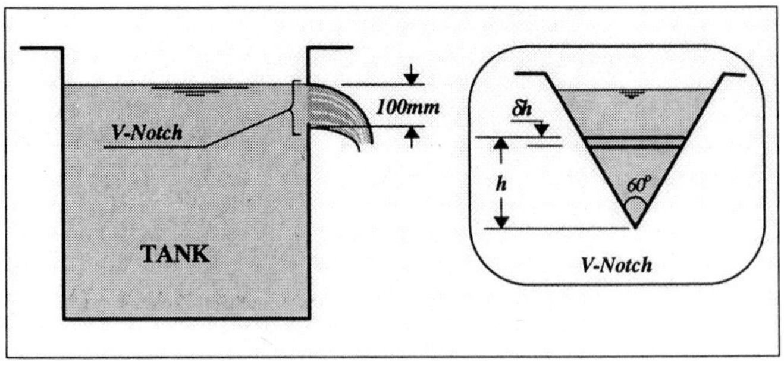

When the water is h above apex the discharge is given by:

$$Q = \frac{8}{15}\times C_d\sqrt{2g}\ h^{5/2}\tan(\theta/2)\,.$$

In time δt, volume passed = $K\times h^{5/2}\times\delta t$, equivalent to a drop in level, and given δt by: $A\times\delta h = K\times h^{5/2}\times\delta t$.

Integration gives $t = -\frac{A}{H}\times\int_{h_1}^{h_2} h^{-5/2}\,dh$

$$A = 5.0,\ K = -0.65\times\frac{8}{15}\times\tan 30\times\sqrt{2g} = 0.885\,.$$

When $h_1 = 0.1m$ and $h_2 = 0.05m$,

$$t = -\frac{5}{0.885}\times\int_{0.05}^{0.10} h^{-5/2}\,dh = -\frac{5}{0.885}\times\left(-\frac{2}{3}\right)\times\left[\frac{1}{h^{3/2}}\right]_{0.05}^{0.10}$$

$$t = 3.7664\times\left(\frac{1}{0.1^{3/2}} - \frac{1}{0.05^{3/2}}\right) = 218 \text{ seconds}\,.$$

Time needed, t = 218 seconds = 3 minutes and 38 seconds.

Problems on Unsteady Flow

[1] A bowl is in the form of a paraboloid with vertical axis, being formed by the rotation of the parabola $y = 4x^2$ about the y axis. If there is initially $1.4m^3$ of water in the bowl, find the time required to empty the bowl through an orifice 50mm diameter with $C_d = 0.6$ in the bottom. (188s)

[2] Two vertical cylindrical tanks, of diameters 2.5m and 1.5m respectively, are connected by a 50mm diameter pipe, 75m long for which f may be assumed constant at 0.01. Both tanks contain water and are open to atmosphere. Initially the level of water in the larger tank is 1m above the smaller tank. Assuming the entry and exit losses for the pipe together amount to 1.5 times the velocity head, calculate the fall of level of the larger tank during 20 minutes. (201.7mm)

PART II

FURTHER FLUID MECHANICS AND HYDRAULICS

CHAPTER SEVEN

HYDROSTATICS OF FLOATING BODIES

Introduction

Floating equipment is often used in the construction of bridges, dams and other engineering projects. The design criteria applied to this equipment is similar to that of boats, ships and dry docks. All these vessels should have sufficient stability in all directions to withstand any outside force or concentrated weight which might be applied or moved across their decks. In case of this stability certain laws of buoyancy and floatation must be satisfied.

Hydrostatic Forces on Immersed Bodies

When a solid body is wholly or partly immersed in a fluid, it is pressed vertically upwards by the fluid with a force equal to the weight of the fluid displaced. This force is called the buoyancy and acts through the centre of buoyancy *(B)* which is the centre of gravity *(G)* of the fluid displaced by the solid.

If the weight W of the body happens to be identical to the buoyant force F, the body will remain at the given level Fig.7.1. If, instead, W is less than F, the body will rise - as in the case of a gas-filled balloon in the atmosphere or a buoy released under water. In the latter, with sufficient portion of its volume still submerged produces a buoyant force equal to its own weight.

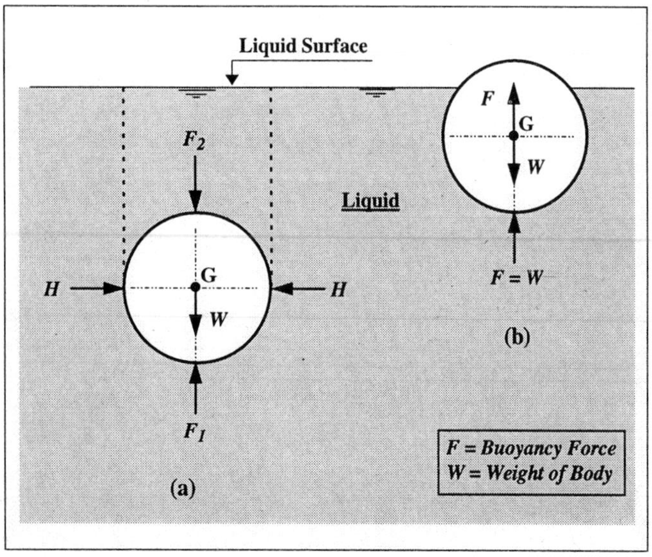

Fig.7.1- Forces acting on submerged bodies.

Stability of Floating Bodies

Consider, for example, a barge having the elementary cross section indicated in Fig.7.2, the loading being such that G lies some distance above B. If the barge is canted through a small angle of heel θ the change in the shape (but not the volume) of displacement region will cause the centre of buoyancy to shift from point B in Fig.7.2a to a point B' in Fig.7.2b.

The intersection of the original vertical line through points B and G with the vertical line through point B' is known as the metacentre M. If the metacentre lies above the centre of gravity for the given angle of heel a restoring couple will be produced and the barge will hence be stable. If M lies below G, as it eventually will if the angle of heel becomes excessive, a condition of instability will prevail and the resulting couple will cause the barge to capsize.

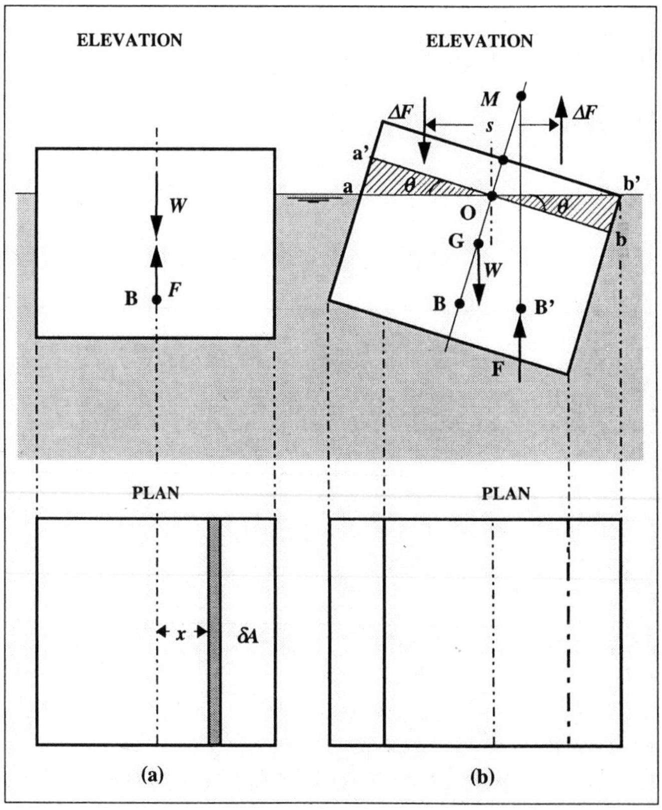

Fig.7.2- Location of the metacentre of a floating body.

General Expression for Metacentric Height

For small angles of heel and known position of the centre of gravity, the metacentric height of a floating body may be found in the following manner. It will be noticed that the effect of heeling is to move an immersed wedge from one side of the barge or ship to the other.

Consider a small prism of the wedge ***bob'*** (Fig.7.2) at a distance x from O having a horizontal cross section δA. For small angles the length of this prism is approximately $x\theta$. The buoyant force reduced by this immersed prism is $\rho g\ x \times \theta dA$ and the righting moment of this force about O is $\rho g\ x^2 \times \theta\ dA$. The sum of all these righting moments over the complete horizontal area at the liquid surface for both wedges is

$$\rho g \theta \times \int_A x^2\ dA = \rho g \theta I \qquad (7.1)$$

since $\int_A x^2\ dA$ represents the moment of inertia I of the area at water line about its longitudinal axis.

The horizontal shift centre of buoyancy r is determined by the change in buoyant forces due to the wedge being submerged, which causes an upward force on the right and by the other wedge decreasing the buoyant force by an equal amount ΔF on the left and the couple formed is

$$Couple = \Delta F \times s \qquad (7.2)$$

This couple must equal the sum of the righting moments for the two wedges derived about O. That is

$$\Delta F \times s = \rho g \times \theta I \qquad (7.3)$$

We can also write down another expression for the righting moment. It is the moment created by the transverse shift of the centre of buoyancy from B to B', then,

$$\Delta F \times s = W \times r = \rho g V \times MB \sin\theta \approx \rho g V \times MB \times \theta \qquad (7.4)$$

in which V is the total volume of liquid displaced. Substituting in equation (7.3), we have

$$\rho g V \times MB \times \theta = \rho g \times \theta I \qquad (7.5)$$

$$MB = I/V \qquad (7.6)$$

(The total restoring moment about B may also be written as the total buoyancy force $\rho g\ V$, multiplied by the lever arm BB').

If the distance BG of the centre of gravity of the vessel above or below the centre of buoyancy is known, we finally arrive at the desired value of **metacentric height** thus

$$GM = \frac{I}{V} \pm BG \qquad (7.7)$$

The minus sign is used if G is above B, the plus sign if G is below B. The righting moment may then be evaluated from the following equation

$$Righting\ Moment = \rho g \theta \left(\frac{I}{V} - BG\right) \qquad (7.8)$$

Evidently, a negative magnitude of the righting moment *(i.e. $BG > I/V$)* indicates a condition of instability.

Floating Body Anchored at Base

Consider a floating body such as a buoy anchored by means of a chain from the centre of its base, Fig.7.3. The tension in the anchor puts an additional downward force on the body causing it to displace a larger volume of water.

Let T be the tension in the anchor cable. Then applying Archimedes' principles,

Total downward force = Weight of displaced water

$$W + T = F = \rho g\ V = \rho g\ A\ d \qquad (7.9)$$

where A is the area of the body in the horizonal plane and d is the draft. Also, $BM = I/V$.

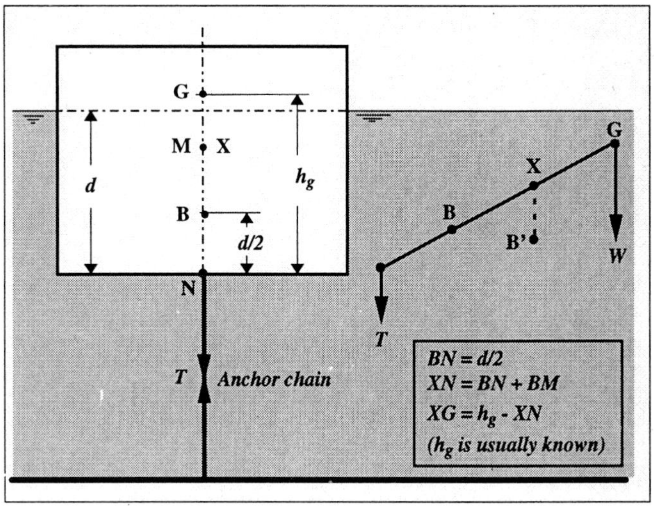

Fig.7.3- Anchored body.

If the body is to just float with its axis vertical, the metacentric height M must coincide with the centre of the force system acting on the body; it is then in neutral equilibrium. Referring to Fig.7.3, let X be the centre of the force system; that is the point of application of the resultant of W and T when the body has small angle of heel. Let N be the point of application of the tension in the anchor chain. When the body has a small angle of heel, as shown to the right of the figure, the moments due to T and W about the point X will balance.

$$\text{Hence,}\quad W \times XG\ sin\theta = T \times XN\ sin\theta \qquad (7.10)$$

from which the value of the tension is calculated. If the system is in neutral equilibrium the upward thrust of the water must pass through X which coincides with N.

Oscillation of a Rolling Ship

When a floating body is given a lateral heel and then the overturning couple is suddenly removed, the body oscillates about the Metacentre M (Fig.7.4) in the same manner as a pendulum oscillates about its point of suspension except that the body does not now oscillate about a fixed axis. The resistance of the water is neglected.

When the overturning couple is removed suddenly, the only force acting on the body is the

$$Righting\ Couple = W \times MG \times \sin\theta = W\ m\ \theta \qquad (7.11)$$

for small angles θ and where m is the metacentric height. It is assumed that the axis of oscillation passes through G; this is approximately correct if m is small.

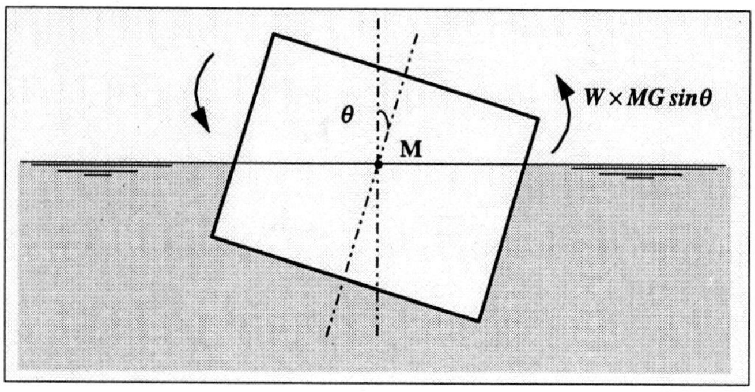

Fig.7.4- Stability of a vessel containing liquid.

Assuming the rate of change of angular momentum is equal to the righting couple, it can be shown that the period of oscillation is given by

$$T = 2\pi \times \sqrt{k^2/mg} \qquad (7.12)$$

where k is the radius of gyration of the body. From this equation the time of oscillation of the floating body can be calculated if m and k are known.

Stability of a Partly Immersed Vessel Containing Liquid

This occurs in oil tank vessels or when water is used as ballast, as in pontoons, where it can be readily pumped in or out to lower or raise the pontoon or again the water may have entered the vessel by accident. As the free surface of the internal liquid tends to lessen the metacentric height it is very important to divide the tanks by partitions, longitudinal and transverse and for safety, to divide all sea-going vessels by watertight **bulkheads**, especially transverse ones, as 'I', for the internal liquid is much greater about a transverse axis than about a longitudinal one: vessels usually sink end on for this reason, the water flowing to the lower end.

The advantages of such sub-division will be shown from the following case where two internal tanks are shown (Fig.7.5). Let,

V_1, V_2 be the volume of liquids of specific weight w_1 in the two tanks and V the displacement of the vessel

I_1, I_2 be the second moments of area of the surface of the liquid, and I the second moment of its water-line area

G be the centre of gravity G of the vessel and its contents,

B be the centre of buoyancy of the vessel.

When the vessel tilts through a small angle θ the centres of gravity of the liquid in the tanks will move

$$\theta \frac{I_1}{V_1} \text{ and } \theta \frac{I_2}{V_2}, \text{ i.e. } G_1G_1' = \theta \frac{I_1}{V_1} \text{ and } G_2G_2' = \theta \frac{I_2}{V_2}.$$

respectively, causing the centre of gravity of the vessel and contents to move to G'.

Weight of vessel + contents = Weight of water displaced = $\rho g V$

Taking moments $$G'G = \frac{W_1\theta(I_1+I_2)}{wV} \qquad (7.13)$$

$$wV \times GG' = \left(w_1 V_1 \times \theta \frac{I_1}{V_1}\right) + \left(w_2 V_2 \times \theta \frac{I_2}{V_2}\right) \qquad (7.14)$$

The vertical through G' intersects the original vertical through G at N where, $GN = GG'/\theta = (w_1/w) \times (I_1+I_2/V)$.

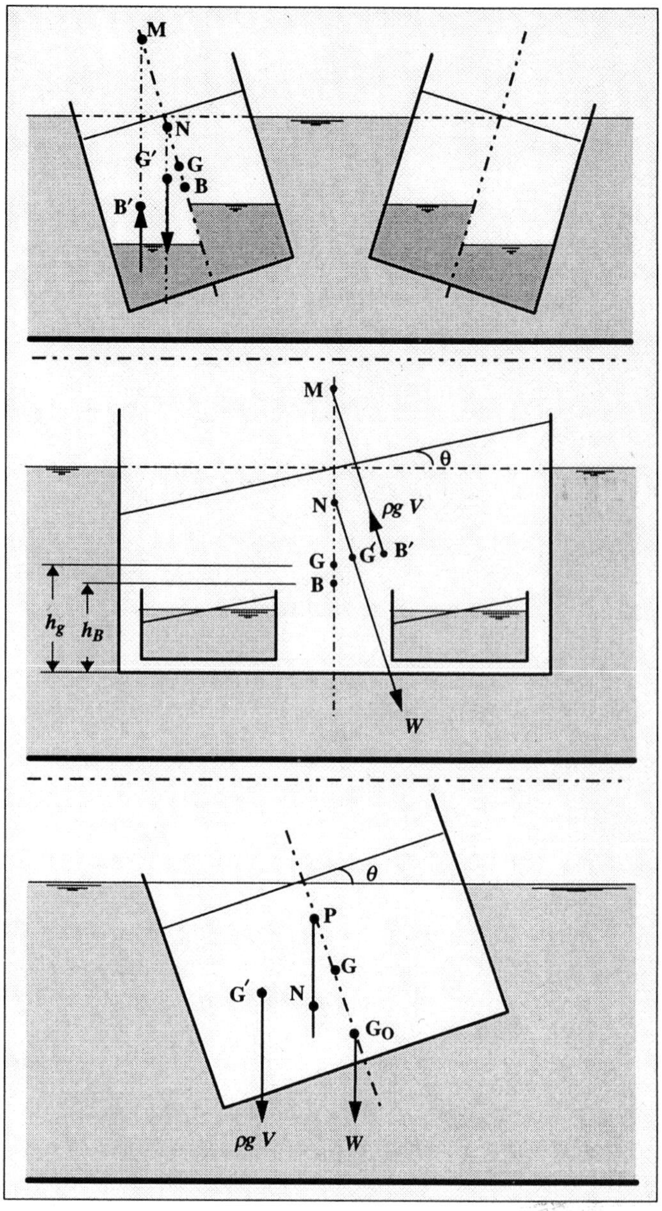

Fig.7.5- Stability of a vessel containing liquid.

The vertical through B', the displaced position of CB cuts GN produced at M where, $BM = I/V$, so that the effective metacentric height is now NM the distance between the positions of N and M for a small value of θ, where

$NM = h_B + BM - (h_g + GN)$
$NM = h_B + I/V - h_g - (w_1/w) \times (I_1+I_2/V)$.

The righting moment for a small angle of heel is now
$R.M. = NM \, Sin\theta \, W$
For water ballast $w_1 = w$ then, $NM = (I - I_1 + I_2)/V - (h_g)$.

Note that the effect of the liquid in the tanks is to reduce the metacentric height and impair stability but this is only the case if there are free surfaces in the tanks so that the CG. of the liquid can move. Sub-division of the tanks improves stability by reducing the sum of the second moments of area of the liquid surfaces.

If a single tank of breadth $2b$ had been used instead of two tanks, each of breadth b, the length of the tanks being l we should have $8lb^3/12$ instead of $2lb^3/12$ for $I_1 + I_2$ in the second term of expression for NM, i.e. the deduction from I would have been four times as large, with a corresponding still further decrease in the metacentric height.

Examples on Floating Bodies

Stability of Cylinder Floating in Oil

A wooden cylinder of circular section and uniform density, specific gravity 0.5, is required to float in oil of specific gravity 0.8. If the diameter of the cylinder is d and its length is l, show that l cannot exceed $\sqrt{8/15} \times d$ for the cylinder to float with its longitudinal axis vertical.

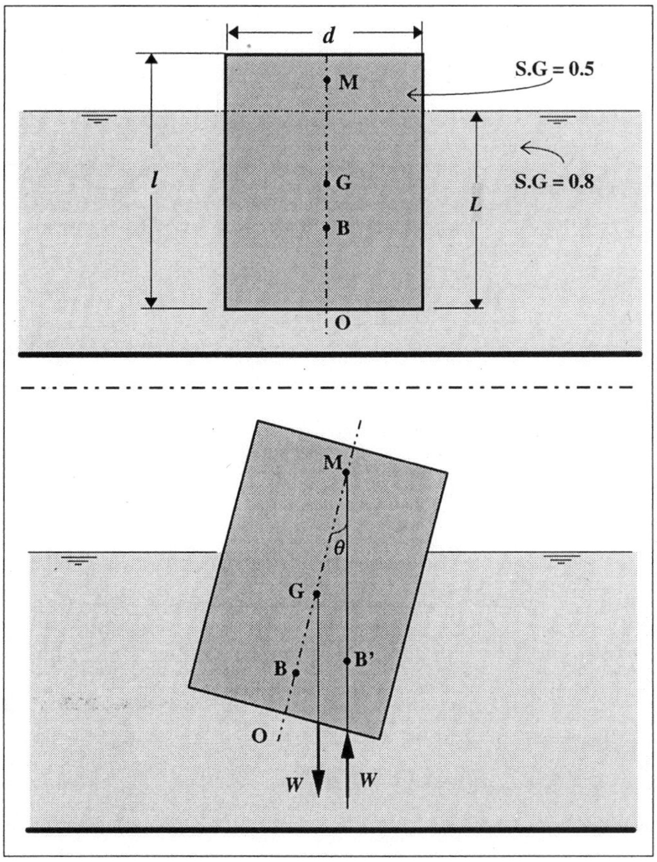

Buoyancy force acts vertically upwards through the centre of buoyancy B' to intercept the L at M. M is called the metacentre when $\theta = 0$, GM is the metacentric height.

For stability, $OB + BM \geq OG$ and $OB + \frac{I}{V} \geq OG$,

i.e. $\frac{L}{2} + \left(\frac{\pi d^4}{64} \Big/ \frac{\pi d^2 \times L}{4} \right) \geq \frac{l}{2}$, $\frac{L}{2} + \frac{d^2}{16L} \geq \frac{l}{2}$.

Relationship between *l* and *L*:

Mass cylinder = Mass of displaced liquid

$$(0.5 \times 1000) \times \frac{\pi d^2 l}{4} = (0.8 \times 1000) \times \frac{\pi d^2 L}{4}. \quad \therefore L = \frac{5}{8} \times l.$$

$$\frac{5l}{16} + \frac{8d^2}{16 \times 5l} \geq \frac{l}{2}. \quad \therefore 3l^2 \leq \frac{8d^2}{5}.$$

Therefore, ***l must not exceed*** $\sqrt{8/15} \times d$ ***for cylinder to remain in vertical position.***

Conical Buoy Floating in Sea Water

State the conditions for the stable equilibrium of a body partially immersed in a liquid. A buoy, floating in sea water of density $1025 kg/m^3$, is conical in shape. The diameter across the top of the buoy is 1.2m and the vertex angle is 60°. Its mass is 300kg and its centre of gravity is 750mm from the vertex. A flashing light of mass 50kg is to be fitted to the top of the buoy. Determine the maximum height of its centre of gravity above the top of the buoy for the whole assembly to remain stable. *(The centre of volume of a cone of height h is at a distance of 3/4h from the vertex).*

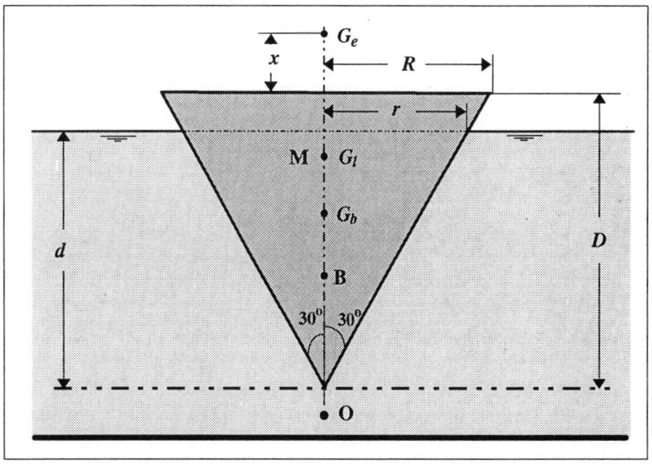

Conditions to be met:

1. Weight of body = Weight of liquid displaced.
2. The metacentric height must be positive.

Mass of buoy = 300kg and Mass of light = 50kg

B = Centre of buoyancy and G_b = its Centre of gravity.

G_e = Centre of gravity of light and G_l = Combined centre of gravity distance x up from top of buoyancy.

$$\tan 30^o = \frac{R}{D} = \frac{0.6}{D} = \frac{1}{\sqrt{3}}. \quad \therefore \quad D = 0.6\sqrt{3}.$$

To determine depth of immersion, *d*:

Weight of buoy + Weight of light = Weight of water displaced

$300 + 50 = \frac{\pi r^2}{3} \times d\rho$. But $r = d/\sqrt{3}$, or $r^2 = d^2/3$.

$$350 = \frac{3.142}{9} \times d^3 \times 1025 \quad \therefore d^3 = 0.978 \text{ and } d = 1.0 \text{ m}.$$

$$OB = \frac{3}{4} \times d = \frac{3}{4} \times 1.0 = 0.75m.$$

At limit of stability points G_c and M coincide i.e. $BM = BG_c$.

Now, $\frac{I}{V_d} = \frac{(1/4) \times \pi r^4}{(1/9) \times \pi d^3} = \frac{9r^4}{4d^3}$, but $r^2 = \frac{d^2}{3}$. Therefore,

$$BM = \frac{9}{4} \times \frac{d^4}{9} \times \frac{1}{d^3} = \frac{d}{4} = \frac{1.0}{4} = 0.25.$$

$OG_c = OB + BG_c = 0.75 + 0.25 = 1.00m.$

Taking moments about vertex O:

$(Mass\ buoy + OG_b) + (Mass\ light \times (D+x)) =$

$(Combined\ Mass \times OG_c)$

$(300 \times 0.75) + (50 \times (1.04 + x)) = 350 \times 1.0$

$225 + 52 + 50x = 350,\ 50\,x = 73,\ \therefore\ x = 1.33\ m.$

Stability of a Buoy in Sea Water

A buoy with plan dimensions of 5m by 4m floats in sea water of density 1025kg/m^3. The buoy is 2m high and has a centre of gravity 0.9m above its base. If the mass of the buoy if 10 tonnes, calculate and indicate on a diagram the position of the centre of buoyancy and that of the metacentre. Is the buoy stable?

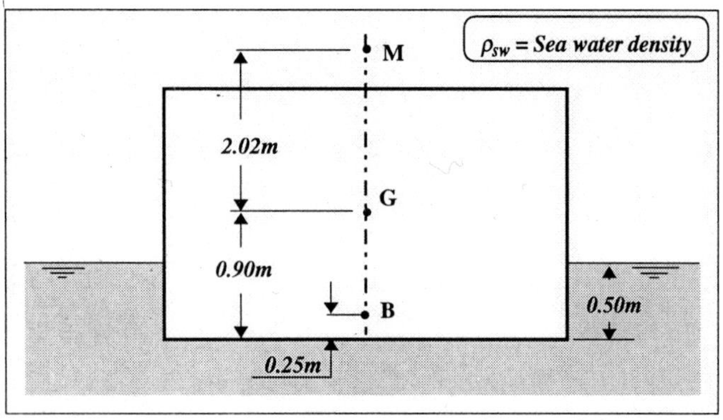

Let d be the depth of floatation. $10\ tonnes = 10^4\ kg$.

Stability equations for small values of θ.

$4 \times 5 \times d \times \rho_{sw} = 10 \times 1000.\ \therefore\ d = 10/(4 \times 5 \times 1.025) = 0.488m.$

$$GM = \frac{I}{V} - BG = \frac{5 \times 4^3}{12} \times \frac{1}{10} - (0.9 - 0.244) = 2.01m.$$

GM is positive, therefore the buoy is stable.

Rectangular Barge with Cargo

Consider a rectangular barge 6m long by 3m wide by 1.5m deep. When unloaded it floats at a depth of 0.25m and has its centre of gravity 0.5m below deck level. When loaded with a cargo of uniform density which completely fills the barge, it floats at a depth of 1m. Calculate the density of the cargo and prove the barge is stable in the loaded condition. Calculate the maximum weight that could be carried at deck level on the barge before it becomes unstable, assuming it carries no cargo other than this deck load.

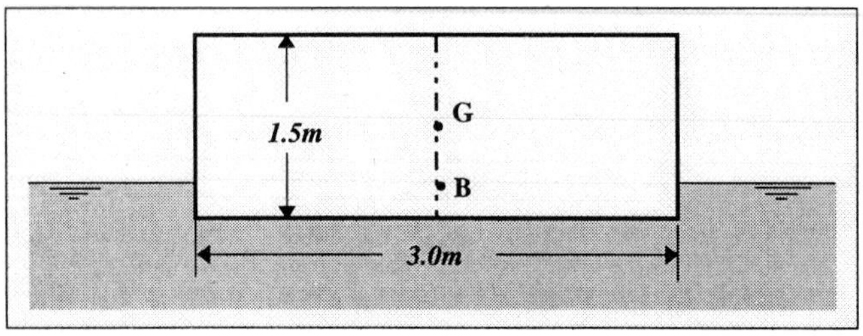

Mass of barge $= 0.25 \times 3 \times 6 \times 1000 = 4500kg = 4.5$ tonnes.

Mass of barge and cargo $= 1 \times 3 \times 6 \times 1000 = 18000kg = 18t.$

Density of cargo $= (18-3.5)/(3 \times 6 \times 1.5) = 0.5t/m^3.$

For stability, $GM = BM - BG = 0.75 - (OG-OB).$

$$OG = \frac{1}{18} \times (1 \times 4.5 + 13.5 \times 0.75),\ \therefore\ OB = 0.8124m,\ \textbf{Stable.}$$

Let the load be X tonnes.

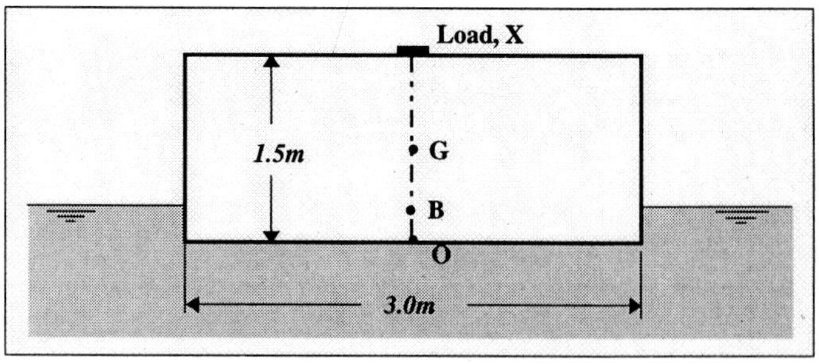

At the point of stability $GM = 0$, i.e. $BM = BG$.

$$\frac{13.5}{X+4.5} = \frac{1}{X+4.5} \times (1 \times 4.5 + 1.5X) - \frac{X+4.5}{2 \times 3 \times 6},\ \text{or}$$

$X^2 + 9X + 20.25 + 486 - 162 - 54X = 0$

$X^2 - 45X + 344.25 = 0.$

$\therefore\ X = 9.77\ tonnes$ or $X = 35.23\ tonnes.$

Check on the depth of floatation $d = 0.543m$ or $d = 1.96m.$

$d = 1.96m$ is too deep. $\therefore$ *Load = 9.77 tonnes = 9.77 $\times$ 10^{3}kg.*

Pontoon with Eccentric Loading

A pontoon, 6m long $\times$ 3m wide $\times$ 1m deep with its centre of mass at its centre of volume, floats with a mean depth of immersion of 0.45m in fresh water. A load of 40kN is placed on the deck of the pontoon with eccentricities as shown in the diagram and with its centre of mass 0.5m above the deck. Calculate the height of the corner A of the pontoon deck above the water level.

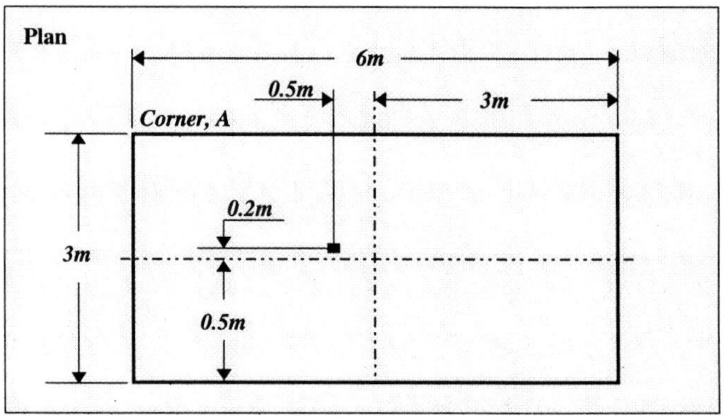

Weight of pontoon, W $= Weight\ of\ displaced\ water$
$= L \times B \times d \times \rho g$
$= 6 \times 3 \times 0.45 \times 9.81 = 79.5kN.$

Weight of load, w $= 40kN.$

Total weight $= 79.5 + 40 = 119.5\ kN.$

Volume displaced loaded , $V = 119.5/9.81 = 12.18m^3.$

Depth of immersion loaded, d $= 12.18/18 = 0.677m.$

Freeboard $= 1 - 0.677 = 0.323m.$

2nd moment of area of water plane area, I.

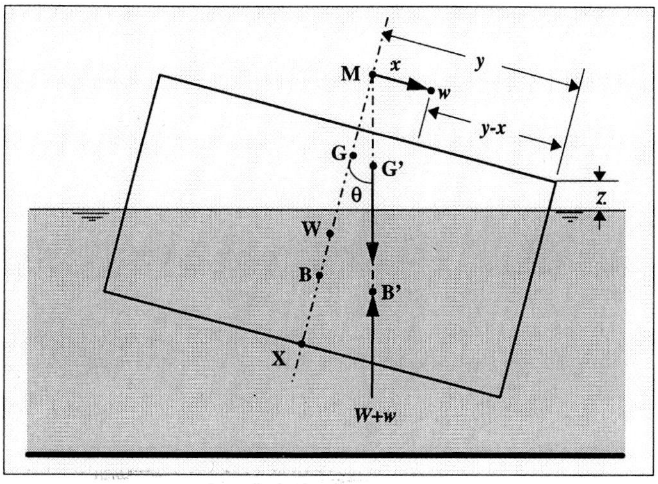

Stability equations for small values of θ:

1. $w \times X = (W + w) \times GG' = (W + w) \times GM \times \theta$, or

$$\theta = \frac{w \times X}{(W+w) \times GM} = \frac{z}{y}.$$

2. $GM = BM - BG$.
3. $BM = I/V$.

Moments about X to locate G:

$$XG = \frac{79.5 \times 0.5 + 40 \times 1.5}{119.5} = \frac{99.5}{119.50} = 0.835\ m.$$

$XB = d/2 = 0.677/2 = 0.339m.$

$BG = 0.835 - 0.339 = 0.496m.$

Rolling, $BM = \frac{6 \times 3^3}{12} \Big/ 12.19 = 1.1m$.

$GM = 1.10 - 0.496 = 0.604\ m.$

Given $x = 0.20\ m$, $\therefore\ y = 1.5m$.

$$\theta = \frac{40 \times 0.2}{119.5 \times 0.604} = 0.118\ rad\ (6.75^o).$$

$z = y \times \theta = 1.5 \times 0.118 = 0.177m.$

Putting, $BM = \frac{3 \times 6^3}{12} \Big/ 12.19 = 4.43m$.

$GM = 4.43 - 0.50 = 3.93m.$

Given $x = 0.5$, $\therefore\ y = 3.0m$.

$$\theta = \frac{40 \times 0.5}{119.5 \times 3.93} = 0.042\ rad\ (7.8^o).$$

$z = y\theta = 3.0 \times 0.042 = 0.126m.$

Total depression of corner A, $E_z = 0.177 + 0.126 = 0.303m.$

Height of A above water level $= 0.323 - 0.303 = 0.020m.$

Bridge on a Pontoon

A rectangular pontoon 5m long × 3m wide × 1m deep weighs 20kN and its centre of mass coincides with its centre of volume. It is required to carry a bridge loading of 80kN at a hinge bearing placed as high as possible above the pontoon deck on a trestle frame, the weight of which may be neglected. Calculate this height, *y*, if the metacentric height must not be less than 0.08m.

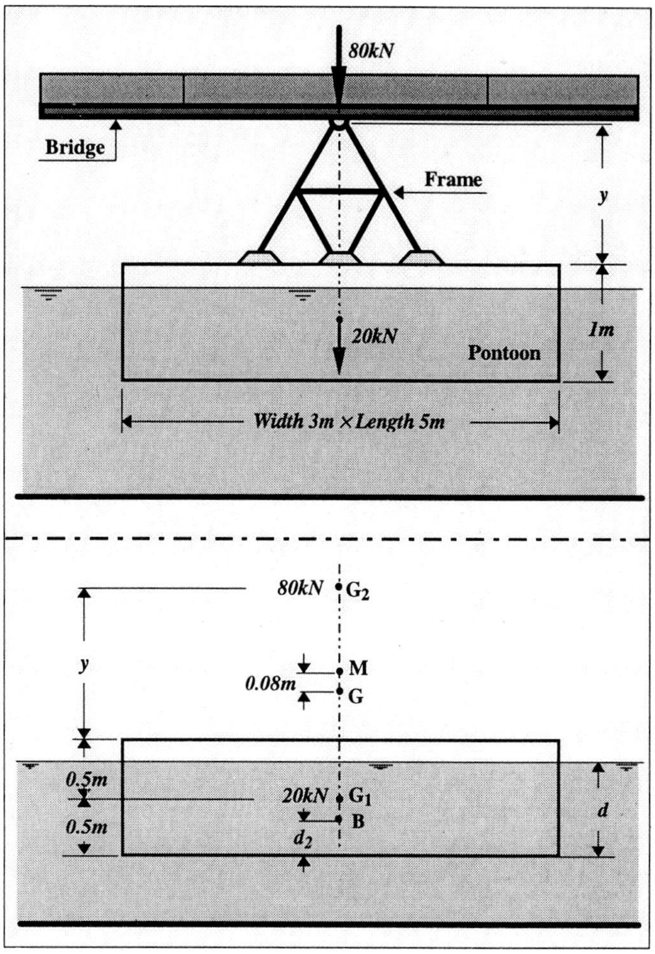

Total weight, $W_T = 20 + 80 = 100kN.$

Volume displaced, $V = 100kN/9.81kN/m^3 = 10.2m^3.$

Depth of Immersion, $d = 10.2/15 = 0.68m.$

2nd moment of water plane area, $I_W = \frac{5 \times 3^3}{12} = 11.25m^4$.

$BM = I/V = 11.25/10.2 = 1.103m.$

$BG = 1.103 - 0.08 = 1.023m.$

Moments about B:

$100\ BG = 80\ BG_2.$

$\therefore\ BG_2 = (100/80)\ 1.023 = 1.28m = y + 1.0 - d/2.$

Height of trestle frame, $y = 0.28 + 0.34 = 0.62m.$

Stability of a Hollow Drum

Discuss with the aid of a sketch the terms centre of buoyancy, metacentre and metacentric height for a freely floating solid body. What are the conditions for such a body to be initially stable? A light hollow drum of thin sheet metal, closed at both ends, is 2m long and 0.6m in diameter and weighs 270N. The drum is half full of water and floats in water with its longitudinal axis vertical. Determine the metacentric height of the half full drum.

The centre of buoyancy *B* of a floating body is the centre of gravity of volume of liquid displaced. When the body heels through a small angle, *B* is shifted to *B'* the vertical through which cuts *yy* at *M* is called the metacentre. *GM* is the metacentric height. $W \times GM \times \sin\theta$ is the righting couple. For initial stability, the buoyancy force must balance the weight of the body and $BM > BG$.

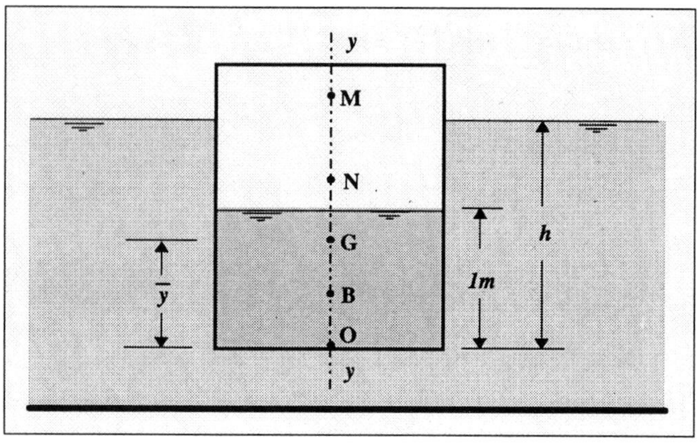

Volume of water in drum $= \dfrac{\pi d^2 \times 1}{4} = \dfrac{\pi \times 0.6^2 \times 1}{4} = 0.283 m^3$.

Weight of water in drum = $1000 \times 9.81 \times 0.283 = 2780N$.

Total weight of body = $270 + 2780 = 3050N$.

Volume displaced $= \dfrac{3050}{9.81 \times 1000} = 0.311 m^3$.

Depth of immersion, $h = 0.311 \Big/ \dfrac{\pi \times 0.6^2}{4} = 1.1m$.

$OB = 0.55m$.

$$I = \frac{\pi \times d^4}{64} = \frac{\pi \times 0.6^4}{64} = 0.00637.$$

$$BM = \frac{I}{V} = \frac{0.00637}{0.311} = 0.0205m.$$

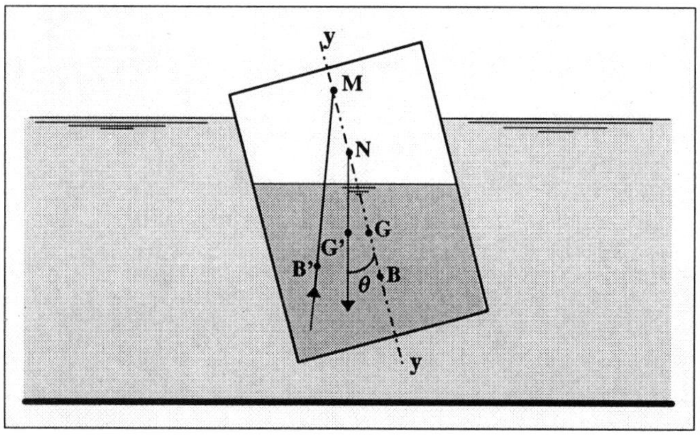

For position of G, the combined centre of gravity,

$$3050 \times \bar{y} = 270 \times 1 + 2780 \times 0.5 \quad \therefore \quad \bar{y} = 0.545m.$$

$GM = BM - BG = 0.0255m$.

$$GN = \frac{I \times w}{W} = \frac{0.00637 \times 100 \times 9.81}{3050} = 0.024m.$$

Metacentric height = $MN = GM - GN = 0.0015m$.

Stability of a Solid Compound Body

A homogeneous solid is formed from a right-circular cylinder and a right-circular cone, each of altitude *h,* on the opposite sides of a circular base of radius *r.* The body floats in a liquid with its longitudinal axis vertical so that the cone and half the cylinder are immersed. Deduce a geometrical criterion for the body to ensure that initial stability prevails. Subsequently, the cone is removed and the same cylinder is allowed to float in the same liquid. Will initial stability now prevail? Justify your answer.

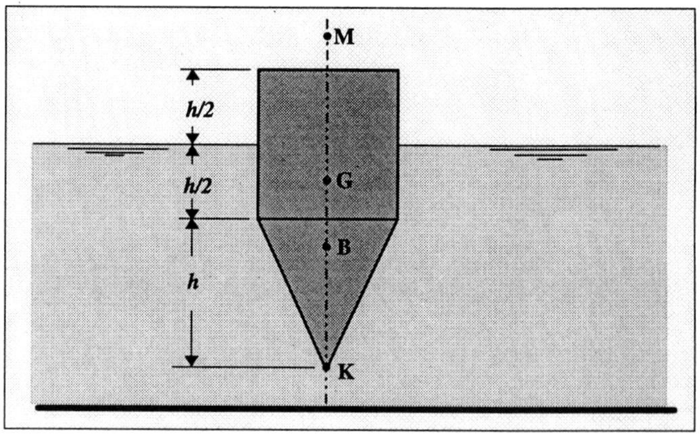

Volume immersed, $\nabla = \dfrac{1}{2}\pi r^2 h + \dfrac{1}{3}\pi r^2 h = \dfrac{5}{6} \times \pi r^2 h$

Total volume of body, $\nabla^* = \pi r^2 h + \dfrac{1}{3}\pi r^2 h = \dfrac{4}{3} \times \pi r^2 h$

Moments about longitudinal axis through G.

$$\nabla^* KG = \frac{3h}{4} \times \frac{1}{3}\pi r^2 h + \left(h + \frac{h}{2}\right) \times \pi r^2 h = \frac{7}{4} \times \pi r^2 h$$

$$\therefore \; KB = \frac{1}{4} \times \pi r^2 h^2 \times \left(1 \Big/ \frac{4}{3} \times \pi r^2 h\right) = \frac{21 \times h}{16}.$$

B is the centre of buoyancy i.e. centroid of immersed volume. Therefore take moments about horizontal axis through K:

$$\Delta\, KB = \frac{3h}{4} \times \frac{1}{3}\pi r^2 h + \left(h + \frac{h}{4}\right), \quad \frac{1}{2}\pi r^2 h = \frac{7}{8}\pi r^2 h.$$

$$\therefore \; KB = \frac{7}{4} \times \pi r^2 h^2 \times \left(1 \Big/ \frac{4}{3} \times \pi r^2 h\right) = \frac{21 \times h}{20}.$$

$$BG = KG - KB = 21h\left(\frac{1}{16} - \frac{1}{20}\right) = \frac{21 \times h}{80}$$

For small angles of heel:

$$\nabla^* KG = \frac{3h}{4} \times \frac{1}{3}\pi r^2 h + \left(h + \frac{h}{4}\right) \times \frac{1}{2} \times \pi r^2 h = \frac{7}{8} \times \pi r^2 h$$

$$BM = \frac{AK^2}{\Delta}(water\ plane) = \frac{1}{4} \times \pi r^2 \times \left(1 \Big/ \frac{6}{5}\pi h\right) = \frac{3r^2}{10h}$$

$$GM = BM - BG = \frac{3r^2}{10h} - \frac{21 \times h}{80} > 0, \text{ for initial stability.}$$

$$\therefore \; \frac{r^2}{h^2} > \frac{7}{8}, \text{ i.e. } \frac{r}{h} > 0.935.$$

If ρ = density of solid; ρ_w = density of water then $\nabla \rho_w = \nabla^* \rho$ for equilibrium.

$$\therefore \; \frac{5}{6} \times \pi r^2 h \times \rho_w = \frac{4}{3}\pi r^2 h \times \rho, \text{ i.e. } \frac{\rho}{\rho_w} = \frac{5}{8}.$$

For cylinder alone, $\pi \times r^2 \times h \times \rho = \pi \times r^2 \times T \times \rho_w$. $\therefore T = 5\,h/8$.

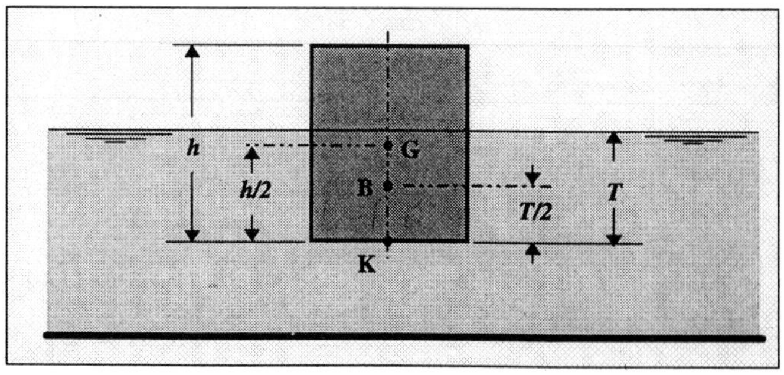

$$KB = \frac{T}{2} \times \frac{5 \times h}{16} l; \quad KG = \frac{h}{2} \quad and \quad BG = \frac{3 \times h}{16}.$$

$$GM = BM - BG = \frac{\pi r^4}{4} \times \left(1 \Big/ \frac{5}{8} \times \pi r^2 h \right) - \frac{3h}{16}$$

$$GM = \frac{2r^2}{5h} - \frac{3h}{16} > 0,$$ for initial stability.

$$\bar{y} \times \frac{r^2}{h^2} > \frac{15}{32}.$$ Therefore, $\bar{y} = \frac{2575}{1960} = 1312m$.

But this condition is already satisfied by the previous r/h> 0.935.

Therefore the cylinder is in stable equilibrium.

Floating Barge with a Cargo

A barge of rectangular cross-section, 5m wide by 20m long floats with its sides vertical in sea water, $\rho = 1026 kg/m^3$. If the centre of gravity is 1.25m above the bottom of the barge, and the depth of immersion is 1.85m, find the metacentric height. Find the new metacentric height if a deck cargo of 100kN, and 2.50m above the bottom of the barge is loaded on the deck centrally.

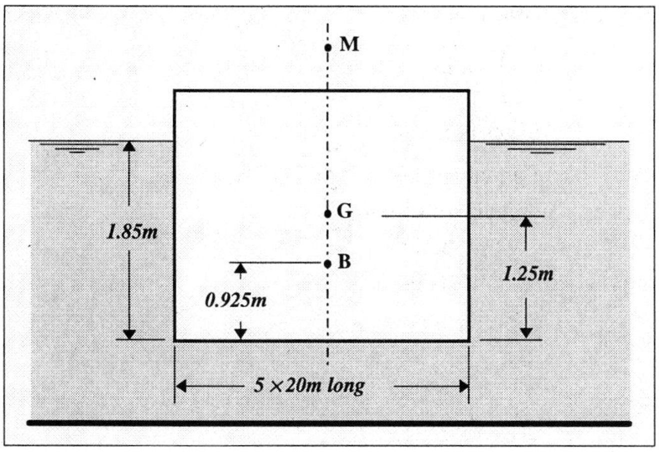

Metacentric height, GM = BM - BG.

$$BG = 1.25 - \frac{1.85}{2} = 0.325m,$$ and

$$BM = \frac{I}{V} = \frac{20 \times 5^3}{12 \times 5 \times 20 \times 1.85} = \frac{25}{22.2} = 1.126m$$

Metacentric height, $GM = BM - BG = 1.126 - 0.325 = 0.801m.$

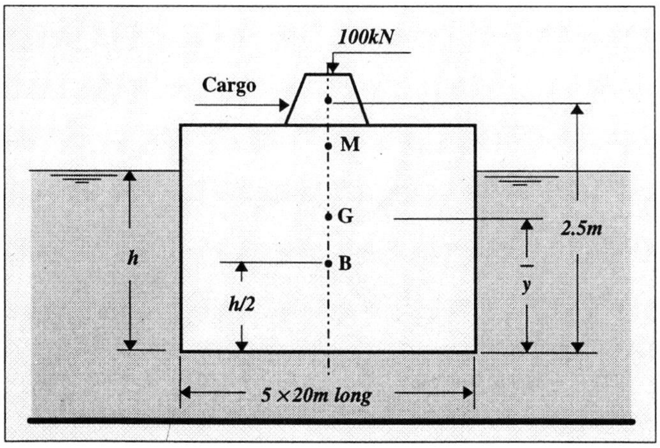

$$W_{barge} = \rho g V = 1026 \times 9.81 \times 5 \times 20 \times 1.85 = 1860kN$$

$$\therefore \; W_{total} = 1862 + 100 = 1962kN.$$

$$V_T = \frac{1962 \times 10^3}{1026 \times 9.81} = 195m^3, \text{ and } h = \frac{195}{5 \times 20} = 1.95m.$$

Depth of immersion, $h = 1.95m.$

$$BM = \frac{I}{V_T} = \frac{20 \times 5^3}{12 \times 195} = 1.07m.$$

To calculate $\bar{y}$, the position of new centre of gravity *G,* take the moments about the base of barge:

$$1962 \times \bar{y} = 1862 \times 1.25 + 100 \times 2.5. \; \therefore \; \bar{y} = 1.312m.$$

$$GM = BM - BG = \frac{I}{V_T} - \bar{y} + \frac{h}{2} = 1.07 - 1.312 + \frac{1.95}{2} = 0.733m$$

The new Metacentric height, $GM = 0.733m.$

Rectangular Pontoon with Ballast Water

A rectangular pontoon 6m wide, 15m long and 2.15m deep weighs 800kN when loaded, but without ballast water. A vertical partition divides the pontoon longitudinally, into two compartments, each 3m wide × 15m long. 200kN of water ballast are admitted to the bottom of each compartment, the water surface being free to move. The centre of gravity of the pontoon without ballast water is 1.5m above the bottom and centrally placed. Calculate (a) the metacentric height of rolling and (b) the angle of heel if 20kN of deck load is shifted laterally 3m across the deck.

G_1 = centre of gravity of pontoon,

G_2 = centre of gravity of ballast

G = centre of gravity of pontoon and ballast,

$\rho_w = 1000 \; kg/m^3.$

Metacentric height = NM = BM - BN = BM - BG - GN

Weight, $W_{pont} = 800kN, \; W_{balast} = 400kN, \; \therefore \; W_{total} = 1200kN.$

$$V_{total} = \frac{1200 \times 10^3}{10^3 \times 9.81} = 122.3m^3 \qquad \therefore \; h = \frac{122.3}{6 \times 15} = 1.36m.$$

$$V_{ballast} = \frac{200 \times 10^3}{10^3 \times 9.81} = 20.4m^3, \; \therefore \; d = \frac{20.4}{3 \times 15} = 0.453m.$$

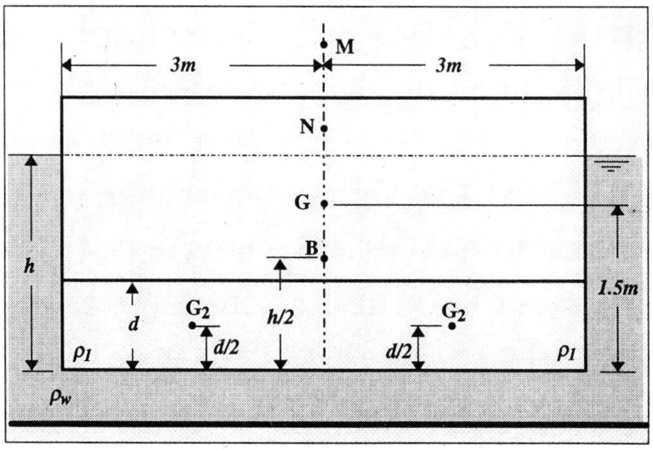

To calculate $\bar{y}$, the position of new centre of gravity G, take the moments about the base:

$$1200\times\bar{y} = 800\times 1.5 + \frac{400\times 0.452}{2}.$$

Height of centre of gravity, $\bar{y} = \dfrac{1291}{1200} = 1.082m$.

Now for small angles of tilt (θ), the centre of gravity of ballast will move $\theta\, I_b/V_b$, where I_b = 2nd moment of area of ballast in each chamber (of its own free surface) V_b = volume of ballast in each chamber, and if density of ballast in chambers are ρ_1, ρ_2, ρ_3... then unit due to total moment of pontoon and ballast driving GG' = moments due to ballast working $\theta\, I_b/V_b$.

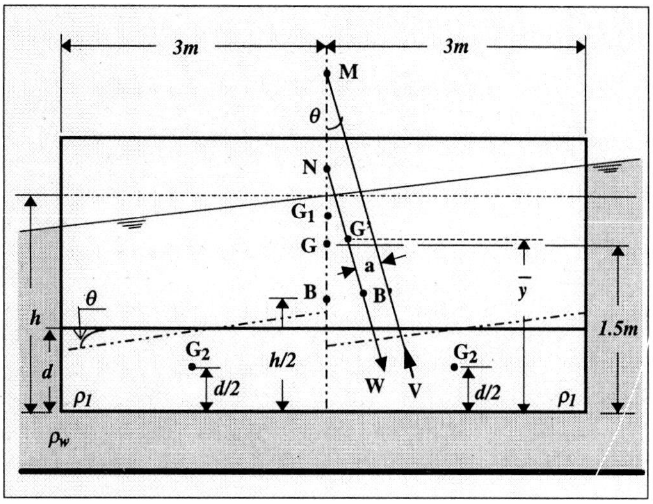

$$W_T GG' = \rho_w g\, V_T GG' = \Sigma\,\theta \frac{I_b}{V_b}\rho_w g V_b$$

$$= \rho_1 g\, V_1 \theta \times \frac{I_1}{V_1} = \rho_2 g\, V_2\theta \times \frac{I_2}{V_2}$$

$$\therefore\ GG' = \theta\,\frac{\Sigma \rho_b I_b}{\rho_w V_T} = \frac{2\theta\, I_b}{V_T}$$

Since as $\rho_1 = \rho_w$ and there are 2 chambers.

$$\therefore\ NM = \frac{I}{V_T} - \bar{y} + \frac{h}{2} - GN \ \ and\ \ GN = \frac{GG'}{\theta} = \frac{2\,I_y}{V_T}$$

$$= \frac{h}{2} - \bar{y} + \frac{I - 2\,I_b}{V_T} = \frac{1.36}{2} - 1.082 + \frac{15\times 6^3 - (15\times 3^2)^2}{12\times 122.3}$$

$= 0.680 - 1.082 + 1.652 = 1.25m.$

When $20kN$ moves 3m on deck, then overturning weight $= 20 \times 3 = 60$kN/m and righting unit = Wg a = W_T NM θ and for equilibrium $60 = W_T \times NM\ \theta$.

Angle $\theta = \dfrac{60}{1200\times 1.25} = 0.04 = 2.29^o$.

Quadrant Body

A long body has the constant section of the quadrant of a circle of 3m radius. The body is made of homogeneous material of relative density 0.5 and floats in fresh water with the vortex of the quadrant upwards. Determine the transverse metacentric height.

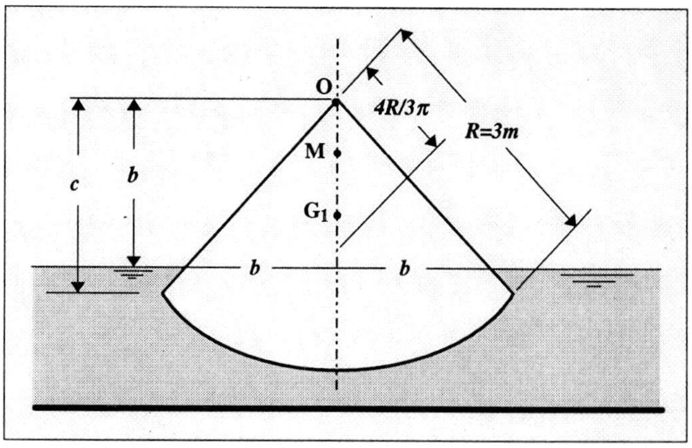

As relative density of body = 0.5, then half of body mass is above water line and half below. As body is homogeneous and of constant cross section, then areas above and below water line are equal.

G = centre of gravity of quadrant.

$$\therefore\ GO = \frac{4R}{3\pi\,\sin\theta} = \frac{4\times 3\sqrt{2}}{3\pi} = 1.80m.$$

Area of quadrant $= \dfrac{\pi R^2}{4} = \dfrac{9\pi}{4} = 7.07\, m^2$.

Assume water line cuts body in the radius, therefore area of triangle above water line is,

$$\frac{7.07}{2} = 2b\times\left(\frac{b}{2}\right).\ \therefore\ b = \sqrt{3.54} = 1.88m \text{ and } c = \frac{3}{\sqrt{2}} = 2.12m$$

The water-line cuts body in radius.

G_1 = centre of gravity of D. ∴ $OG_1 = 2/3 = 0.67m$.

G_2 = centre of gravity of submerged area.

B = centre of gravity of displaced volume and as body is homogeneous B and G_2 coincide.

To find G_2 or B take moments about O.

$$7.07\times OG = 3.54\times OG_1 + 3.54\times OG_2$$

$$\therefore\ OG_2 = \frac{7.08\times 1.82 - 3.54\times 1.25}{3.54} = 2.35m.$$

$$BM = \frac{I}{V} = \frac{l\times(2b)^3}{12\times 3.54\times l},$$ where l = length of body.

$$BM = \frac{8\times 1.88^3}{12\times 3.54} = 1.25m.$$

∴ ***Metacentric height, GM = BM - BG = BM - BO + GO***

= 1.25 - 2.35 + 1.8 = 0.7m.

Floating Steel Caisson

A caisson fabricated from sheet steel is to be floated to its working site in an estuary. It has vertical concentric cylindrical walls 12.5m high, the inner wall being 6m diameter and the outer one 6.75m diameter. Six horizontal plate bulkheads at 2.5m centres from the bottom upwards join the two walls and, at the same time, provide watertight compartments in the annular space between the walls. The caisson weighs 400kN. Would the caisson float stable in sea water ($\rho = 1026 kg/m^3$) with its axis vertical and without any ballast (the sea water being free to rise up within the inner wall)? Show that if the bottom compartment were completely filled with sea water as a ballast, stability would be ensured. Estimate the metacentric height under this condition.

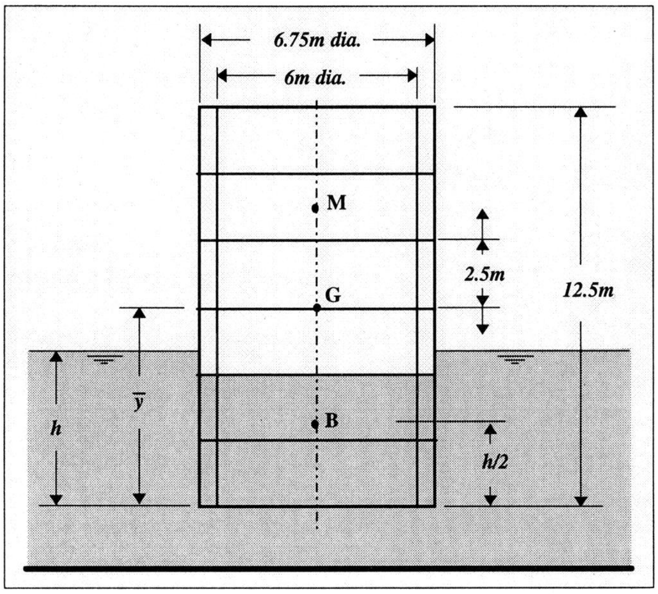

(1) Floating caisson:

Weight of caisson, $W_c = 400kN$.

Volume of caisson, $V_C = \dfrac{400 \times 10^3}{1026 \times 9.81} = 39.7m^3$.

$A = 35.8 - 28.2 = 7.6m^2$, $\quad \therefore\ h = \dfrac{39.7}{7.6} = 5.23m^3$.

$$I = \frac{\pi(D^4 - d^4)}{64} = \frac{\pi(45.5 + 36)(45.5 - 36)}{64} = \frac{\pi(81.5 \times 9.5)}{64}$$

$$BM = \frac{I}{V} = \frac{\pi}{64} \times \frac{81.5 \times 9.5}{39.7} = 0.955m$$

$$GM = BM - BG = \frac{I}{V} - \frac{12.5}{2} + \frac{5.23}{2}$$

$GM = 0.957 - 6.25 + 2.61 < 0\ \therefore$ Unstable $= -2.68 < 0$.

(2) Fill the lowest compartment with seawater:

Therefore caisson sinks a further 2.5m.

Then, $h = 5.23 + 2.5 = 7.73$.

Volume of ballast $= 2.5 \times 7.6 = 19.0m^3$.

Total volume, $V_T = 39.7 + 19.0 = 58.7m^3$

To find $\bar{y}$, the new position of centre of gravity of caisson and ballast, take moments:

$$58.7 \times \rho g \bar{y} = \rho g \times 39.7 \times \frac{12.5}{2} + \rho g \times 19.0 \times \frac{2.5}{2}$$

$\therefore\ \bar{y} = 4.64m$ and $BM = \dfrac{I}{V} = \dfrac{\pi}{64} \times \dfrac{81.5 \times 9.5}{58.7} = 0.643m$

$$GM = BM - \bar{y} + \frac{h}{2} = 0.643 - 4.64 + 3.87$$

$4.51 - 4.64 < 0$. ***Therefore caisson is unstable.***

(3) Fill the second lowest compartment with sea water:

$h = 7.73 + 2.5 = 10.23m$, $\therefore\ V_T = 39.7 + 38.0 = 77.7m^3$.

Therefore, to find $\bar{y}$, take moments:

$$77.7 \times \rho g \times \bar{y} = \rho g \times 39.7 \times 6.25 + \rho g \times 38 \times 2.5$$

$\therefore\ \bar{y} = 4.42m$ and $BM = \dfrac{\pi}{64} \times \dfrac{81.5 \times 9.5}{22.7} = 1.7m$.

$\therefore$ ***Metacentric height, GM = 1.7 - 4.42 + 5.11 = 2.39m.***

Problems on Floating Bodies

[1] State the conditions to be met to ensure the stable equilibrium of a body partly immersed in a liquid. A right solid cone with apex angle equal to 60° is of density α relative to that of the liquid in which it floats with apex downwards. Determine what range of α is compatible with stable equilibrium. (α between (27/64) and 1)

[2] A floating crane is carried by a pontoon 19.51m long, 9.15m wide and 1.83m deep. The crane and pontoon weight 153×10^3kg with the centre of gravity at the centre of the geometry of the pontoon. It is used in fresh water to lift a load of 12.24×10^3kg. Calculate the angle of heel when the centre of gravity of the load is in the plane of the deck of the pontoon at the centre of its length and 6.10m to one side of the centre line. (4.15^o)

[3] A solid buoy, specific gravity 0.6 that for sea water, floats in the sea. The buoy consists of an upright cylinder 1.22m diameter and 1.52m long with a hemisphere 1.22m diameter at the lower end. A chain is attached to the lowest point of the hemisphere. Find the required vertical pull on the chain so that the buoy just floats with the axis of the cylindrical portion vertical. The centre of gravity of the hemisphere is 3/8 radius from the diameter. Sea water density is 1026kg/m^3. (7.876kN)

[4] By assuming the displacement (Δ) of a ship is proportional to $L \times H \times T$, where L and H are the length and breadth of the ship at the water plane and T is the draft, derive expressions for $d\Delta/\Delta$ and $d(BM)/BM$ where BM is the distance between the centre of buoyancy B and the metacentre M of the ship for a rolling motion. State any assumptions you use. It is proposed to design a ship with the following values: $\Delta = 30MN$; $L = 110m$; $H = 13m$; $T = 4m$; the centres of buoyancy and gravity and the metacentre are 2.1m, 5.5m and 6.25m above the bottom of the ship respectively. However, owing to possible operation in restricted waters, it is necessary to examine changes in H and T with Δ and L constant. Determine the limiting values of H and T, consistent with initial stability of the modified ship, assuming the height of the centre of gravity above the keel is proportional to T. ($B_{min} = 12.385$m, $T_{max} = 4.189$m)

CHAPTER EIGHT

CURVED MOTION

Introduction

A mass of rotating fluid is called a vortex. When the fluid is rotating freely without any external forces imposed on it, the motion is referred to as a free vortex. Examples of a free vortex include the flow in a pipe bend and the whirlpool formed in the emptying of a wash basin with a central drain hole. When a fluid is rotated inside a container or casing by a revolving paddle or impeller, the motion is termed a forced vortex. In this flow a centrifugal head is imposed on the fluid. The principles of energy and continuity may be applied to the analysis of both types of motion.

Variation of Total Head

Let AB and CD be two adjacent streamlines in a vertical plane (Fig.8.1) in a fluid having curved motion in two directions.

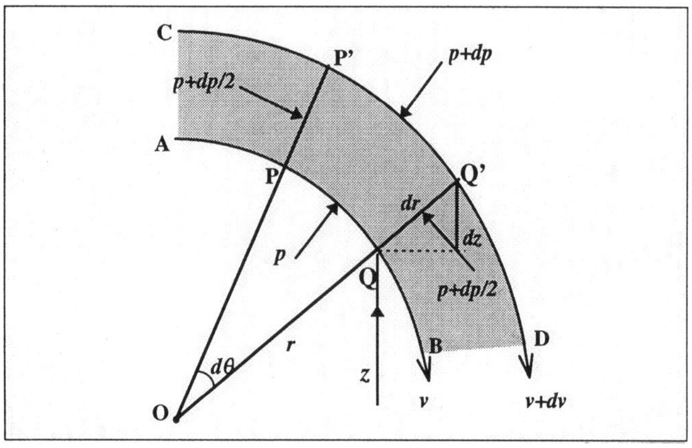

Fig.8.1- Free cylindrical vortex.

Consider the equilibrium of the small trapezium PP'QQ' of unit thickness perpendicular to the paper. Then the mass of trapezium $\rho r d\theta dr$ and the centrifugal force on trapezium

$$= \rho r d\theta dr \times \frac{v^2}{r} \tag{8.1}$$

As the element is in equilibrium, the pressure forces, the centrifugal force and its weight must balance. Hence, resolving radially and writing

$$\sin\left(\frac{d\theta}{2}\right) = \left(\frac{d\theta}{2}\right)$$

$$pr d\theta + 2(p + \frac{dp}{2}) \times dr \frac{d\theta}{2} - (p + dp)(r + dr)d\theta$$

$$-(\rho g r d\theta dr)\frac{dz}{dr} + \frac{(\rho r d\theta dr) \times v^2}{r} = 0 \tag{8.2}$$

On multiplying and ignoring small quantities of the second order, the equation reduces to

$$dp = \frac{\rho dr v^2}{r} - \rho g dz \tag{8.3}$$

from which,

$$\frac{dp}{\rho g} = \frac{dr v^2}{gr} - dz\,. \tag{8.4}$$

Now, applying the Bernoulli's equation to any streamline,

$$H = \frac{p}{\rho g} + \frac{v^2}{2g} + dz \tag{8.5}$$

where H is the total head along the streamline considered.

Differentiating each term for small changes dz, dp and dv over width dr,

$$dH = \frac{dp}{\rho g} + \frac{v dv}{g} + dz \tag{8.6}$$

Substituting for $dp/\rho g$ in above equation,

$$dH = dz + \frac{v dv}{g} - dz + \frac{v^2 dr}{gr}$$

$$\frac{dH}{dr} = \frac{v}{g} \times \left(\frac{dv}{dr} + \frac{v}{r}\right) \tag{8.7}$$

This equation represents the change of total head across any streamline flow in two perpendicular directions. It will be noticed that the z term does not appear in the final equation, which applies to streamlines moving in any plane. Also, assuming one-dimensional flow, we can write

$$\frac{dp}{dr} = \frac{\rho v^2}{r} \tag{8.8}$$

Free Vortex

When a fluid is allowed to rotate freely round a vertical axis the streamlines are concentric circles (Fig.8.2) and there is no variation of the total head with radius:

$$\frac{dH}{dr} = 0,\ \ \frac{dH}{dr} = \frac{v}{g}\left(\frac{v}{r} + \frac{dv}{dr}\right).\ \ \therefore\ \ \frac{dv}{dr} + \frac{v}{r} = 0,\ \ \frac{dv}{V} = -\frac{dr}{r}$$

Integrating, $\log_e v + \log_e r = \log_e vr$ = constant, proving that the law connecting radius and velocity is $vr = C$. Let p_1 and p_2 be the pressures in two concentric streamlines of radii r_1 and r_2 which have velocities v_1 and v_2.

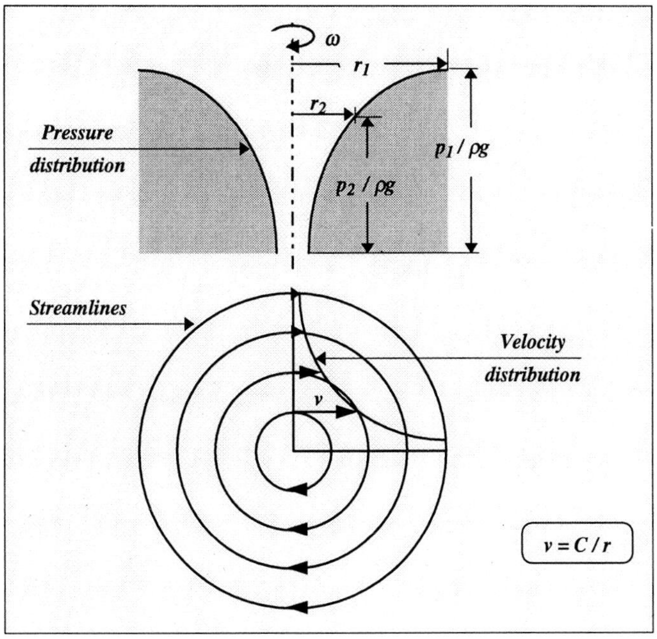

Fig.8.2- Free cylindrical vortex.

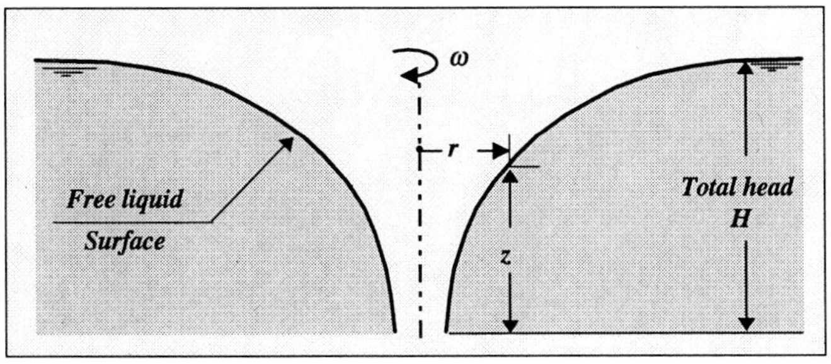

Fig.8.3- Vortex with free liquid surface.

Since there is no change of total head with radius, then for the same horizontal plane

$$\frac{p_1}{\rho g}+\frac{v_1^2}{2g}=\frac{p_2}{\rho g}+\frac{v_2^2}{2g}, \quad \frac{p_1-p_2}{\rho g}=\frac{v_2^2-v_1^2}{2g}$$

$$v_1=\frac{C}{r_1} \text{ and } v_2=\frac{C}{r_2}$$

$$h_1-h_2=\frac{p_1-p_2}{\rho g}=\frac{C^2}{2g}\times\left(\frac{1}{r_2^2}-\frac{1}{r_1^2}\right) \tag{8.9}$$

so that the pressure decreases from the outside. The pressure at the centre *($r = 0$)* would be minus ∞ if the vortex continued to the centre, but this, of course, is impossible. If the vortex is formed with a free surface then since there is no variation of total head.

$$z_1+\frac{p_1}{\rho g}+\frac{v_1^2}{2g}=z_2+\frac{p_2}{\rho g}+\frac{v_2^2}{2g} \tag{8.10}$$

At the free surface $p_1 = p_2$ = atmospheric and so

$$z_1-z_2=\frac{C^2}{2g}\times\left(\frac{1}{r_2^2}-\frac{1}{r_1^2}\right), \text{ and } H=\frac{v^2}{2g}+z, \text{ or}$$

$$H-z=\frac{C^2}{2gr^2} \tag{8.11}$$

The free surface takes the form of a hyperbola asymptotic to the axis of rotation and to the horizontal through $z = H$ as shown in Fig. 8.3.

Forced Vortex

If the fluid is forced to rotate about a vertical axis by revolving paddles, or by the rotation of a revolving casing in which it is contained (Fig.8.4), its angular velocity ω will be constant for all points, the streamlines will be circular and the velocity at any point will be proportional to the radius,

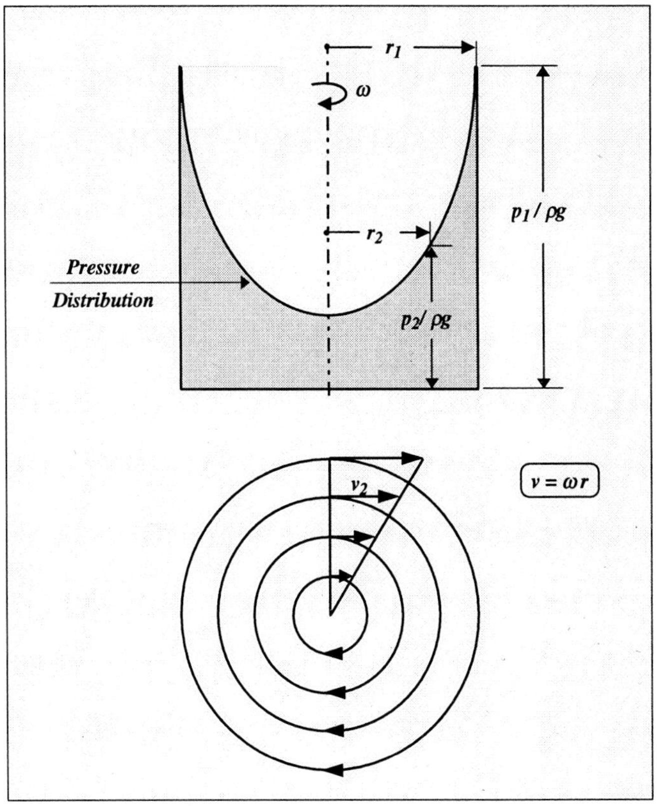

Fig.8.4- Forced vortex.

$$v=\omega r, \quad \frac{v}{r}=\omega \text{ and } \frac{dv}{dr}=\omega \tag{8.12}$$

$$\frac{dH}{dr}=\frac{v}{g}\times\left(\frac{dv}{dr}+\frac{v}{r}\right), \quad \frac{dH}{dr}=\frac{\omega r}{g}\times 2\omega=\frac{2\omega^2 r}{g} \tag{8.13}$$

Integrating, $H=\dfrac{\omega^2 r^2}{g}+B$, B = constant.

$$\text{But the total head } H=\frac{p}{\rho g}+\frac{v^2}{2g}+z=\frac{p}{\rho g}+\frac{\omega^2 r^2}{2g}+z \tag{8.14}$$

$$\text{Thus, } \frac{p}{\rho g}+\frac{\omega^2 r^2}{2g}+z=\frac{\omega^2 r^2}{g}+B, \quad \frac{p}{\rho g}+z=\frac{\omega^2 r^2}{2g}+B \tag{8.15}$$

At the free surface of a forced vortex *$p/\rho g = 0$*. The height z of the surface above datum is given by:

$$z=\frac{\omega^2 r^2}{2g}+B \tag{8.16}$$

Thus the free surface forms a paraboloid. If we integrate between radii r_1 and r_2, we get

$$H_2-H_1=\frac{\omega^2}{g}\times(r_2^2-r_1^2) \tag{8.17}$$

In the forced vortex the total head of each streamline is different, so that although Bernoulli's equation could be applied along each streamline, it cannot be applied to points on different streamlines. The above equation can also be written as:

$$\frac{p_2-p_1}{\rho g}=\frac{\omega^2}{g}\times(r_2^2-r_1^2) \tag{8.18}$$

The pressure, therefore, decreases from the outside towards the centre, as shown in Fig.8.4, and if the vortex is uncovered on the top, this curve will form the free surface. This is the principle of the centrifugal pump; the pressure of the fluid, entering at the centre, and leaving at the circumference, is increased by the forced rotation of the fluid by the pump blades (see Chapter 14).

Combined Vortex

This type of motion is produced when a paddle rotating in a fluid creates a forced vortex within its diameter and a free vortex outside it, Fig.8.5. In both vortices there is a rise of pressure in an outward direction.

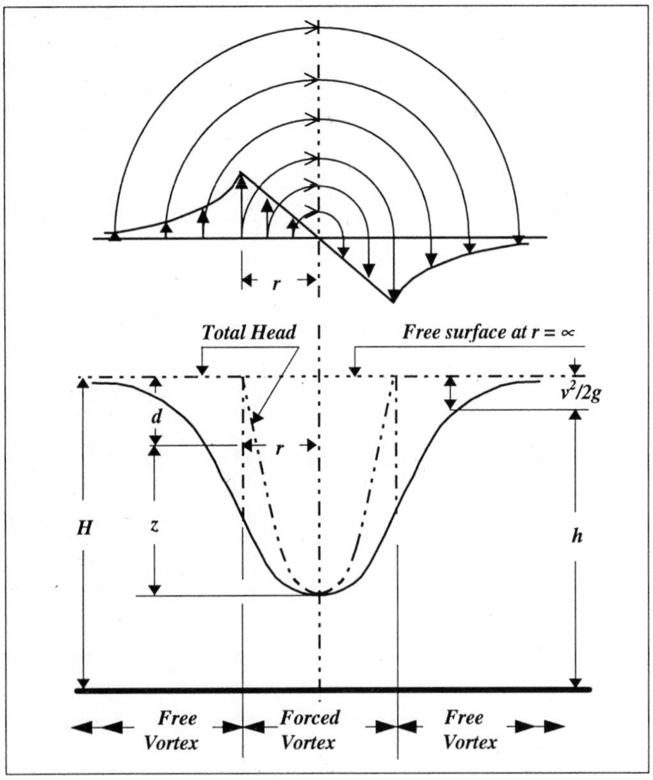

Fig.8.5- Combined vortex.

We have, $\dfrac{dH}{dr} = \dfrac{v}{g} \times \left(\dfrac{dv}{dr} + \dfrac{v}{r} \right)$ (8.19)

For a forced vortex, $v = \omega \times r$, and at any radius r, the height of the surface at infinity is given by:

$$z = \frac{\omega^2 r^2}{2g} \qquad (8.20)$$

For a free vortex $v = C/r$ and the depression of the surface at radius r below the surface at infinity is,

Depression of surface, $d = \dfrac{C^2}{2gr^2} = \dfrac{v^2}{2g}$ (8.21)

Taking r as the common radius of the two vortices,

Total depression $= z + d = \dfrac{\omega^2 r^2}{2g} + \dfrac{v^2}{2g}$ (8.22)

Since at the common radius the velocities of the two vortices are equal, $v = \omega \times r$, so that

Total depression $= z + d = \dfrac{\omega^2 r^2}{g}$ (8.23)

Subcritical Flow in Channel Bends

When the subcritical stream flows around a channel bend, the centrifugal force causes a lateral pressure gradient, with the surface elevation higher on the outside of the bend. This superelevation in water surface can be calculated by assuming the flow in the bend to be a free vortex for which the velocity distribution is $vr = C$, where v is the velocity at radius r.

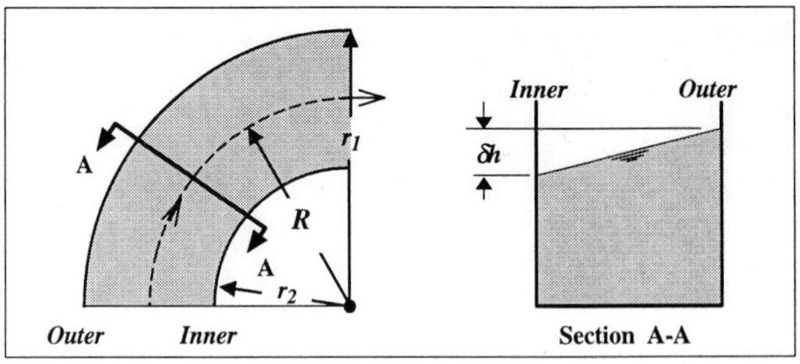

Fig.8.6- Flow in a channel bend.

The corresponding depth of flow at radius r is obtained from the specific energy equation:

$$y = H - \frac{v^2}{2g} \qquad (8.24)$$

The average velocity V_m and average depth y_m are:

$$V_m = \int_{r_1}^{r_2} \left(\frac{C/r}{r_1 - r_2} \right) dr = \frac{C}{r_1 - r_2} \times \ln\left(\frac{r_1}{r_2} \right) \qquad (8.25)$$

$$y_m = \int_{r_1}^{r_2} \left(\frac{ydr}{r_1 - r_2} \right) dr = \int_{r_1}^{r_2} \left(H - \frac{v^2}{2g} \right) dr = H - \frac{C^2}{2g \times r_1 r_2} \qquad (8.26)$$

The discharge is then given by, $Q = V_m \times Area$

$$Q = V_m y_m \times (r_1 - r_2) = C \times \left(H - \frac{C^2}{2g \times r_1 r_2} \right) \times \ln\left(\frac{r_1}{r_2} \right) \qquad (8.27)$$

Since Q, H, r_1 and r_2 are known for a given channel, the constant C is determined from above equation. The superelevation of the water surface is therefore,

$$\Delta h = y_1 - y_2 = \left(H - \frac{C^2}{2g\, r_1^2} \right) - \left(H - \frac{C^2}{2g\, r_2^2} \right)$$

$$\Delta h = \frac{C^2 \times (r_1^2 - r_2^2)}{2g\, r_1^2\, r_2^2} \qquad (8.28)$$

A current is set up by the pressure difference that gives velocities down the outer wall, inwards across the bottom and outwards across the top. This circulation current, together with the main stream gives a spiral combined flow: the dotted lines below show bottom flow.

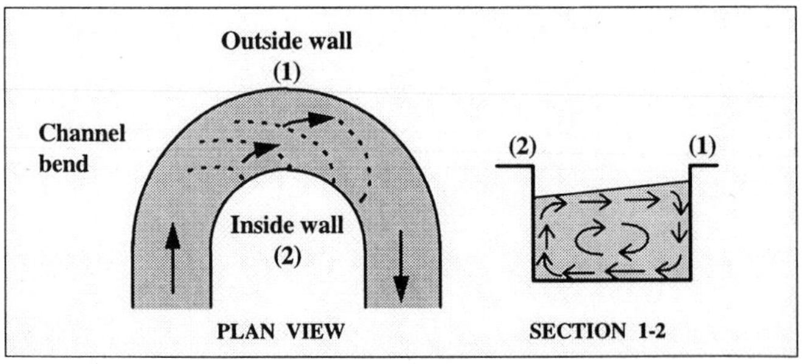

Fig.8.7- Secondary flow in a river bend.

Examples on Curved Motion

Forced Vortex in a Rotating Container

Define a forced vortex and derive an expression for the pressure distribution in it. A closed container in the form of a frustum of a cone has its longitudinal axis vertical and is completely filled with water. The top and bottom are closed with flat ends the diameters of which are 200mm and 350mm respectively. The vessel rotates about its longitudinal axis at a speed of 8 rev/s. Calculate the magnitude of the additional vertical force exerted by the water on the curved surface of the vessel, due to the rotation.

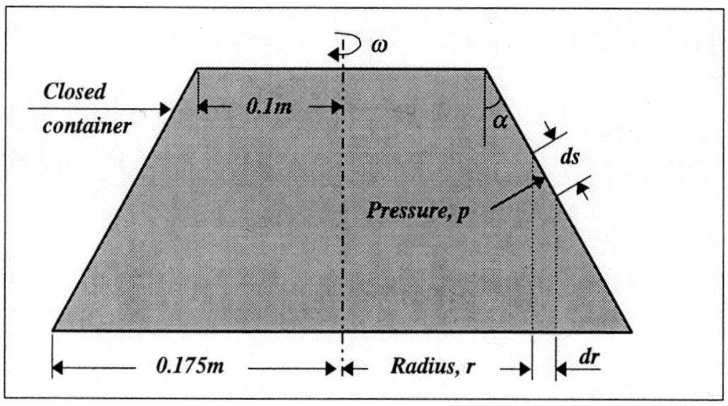

In a forced vortex the fluid is forcibly rotated about a vertical axis, either by paddles or by friction at the walls of the containing vessel. The streamlines are circular and the velocity at any point is proportional to the radius.

$v = \omega \times r.$

Pressure, $p = \rho\, gh = \dfrac{\rho\, \omega^2 r^2}{2}.$

Force on element *ds*, $dF = p\, dA = \dfrac{\rho\, \omega^2 r^2}{2} \times 2\pi\, rds\,.$

Vertical component of force,

$$dF_y = 2\pi\, r \times \frac{p \times dr}{\sin\alpha} \times \sin\alpha = \rho\pi \times \omega^2 r^3 dr\,.$$

Total vertical force, $F_y = \rho\, \pi \times \omega^2 \times \displaystyle\int_{0.1}^{0.175} r^3\, dr$

$$F_y = \frac{1000 \times 3.14 \times (16\pi)^2}{4} \times (0.175^4 - 0.1^4) = 1662\ N\,.$$

Combined Free and Forced Vortices

Distinguish between a free and forced vortex motion. An impeller, 0.3m in diameter, rotates concentrically at 2 rev/s about a vertical axis inside a closed cylindrical casing 1m in diameter. The casing is full of water. Inside the impeller the motion is forced vortex while between the impeller and the side of the casing the motion is free vortex. Calculate the velocity of the water 0.15m and 0.3m from the centre and the increase of pressure head at these radii above the pressure head at the centre.

In a free vortex, the fluid is free to rotate about a vertical axis and *H* is constant for all streamlines. In a forced vortex, the fluid is forcibly rotated, like a solid body, at constant angular velocity, by paddles or by friction at the walls of the containing vessel. In this problem the water within radius of 0.15m has a forced vortex motion while that between radii 0.15m and 0.3m has a free vortex motion.

For forced vortex, $v = \omega \times r$

At $r = 0.15m$, $v = 2\pi \times 2 \times 0.15 = 1.968 m/s.$

For free vortex, $v = C/r$, $C = 1.968 \times 0.15 = 0.295.$

At $r = 0.30m$, $v = 0.295/0.30 = 0.984 m/s.$

In the forced vortex, $dp = \rho\omega^2 r dr = \dfrac{\rho\omega^2 (r_2^2 - r_1^2)}{2}$

Increase of the pressure head, $h_2 - h_1 = \dfrac{\omega^2}{2g} \times (r_2^2 - r_1^2)$

$$h_2 - h_1 = \frac{v_1^2}{2g} = \frac{1.89^2}{2 \times 9.81} = 0.197m \ \ (for\ r_1 = 0).$$

In the free vortex, $dp = p_3 - p_2 = \rho \times \dfrac{v^2}{r} \times dr = \dfrac{\rho C^2}{r^3} \times dr$

$$p_3 - p_2 = \frac{\rho C^2}{2} \times \left(\frac{1}{r_2^2} - \frac{1}{r_3^2} \right)$$

Increase of the pressure head, *(between r = 0.15 to 0.30m).*

$$h_3 - h_2 = \frac{v_3^2 - v_2^2}{2g} = \frac{1.968^2 - 0.984^2}{2 \times 9.81} = 0.148m\,.$$

Pressure head at 0.3m, $h_3 - h_1 = 0.197 + 0.148 = 0.345m.$

Radial velocity for r = 0.3m, $u = \dfrac{0.9 \times 0.15}{0.30} = 0.45\ m/s.$

Resultant velocity, $\sqrt{u^2 + v^2} = \sqrt{0.45^2 + 0.984^2} = 1.082 m/s.$

Inclination to radius, $\theta = \tan^{-1}\left(\dfrac{v}{u}\right) = \tan^{-1}\left(\dfrac{0.984}{0.45}\right)$

$\theta = 65^o 42'.$

Air Flow in a Duct Bend

The cross section of an air duct is a square of a side 1.8m. At one position the duct has a right-angled bend, the radius of curvature of the centre line being 5m. The pressure difference between the inner and outer walls of the bend is 30mm water and inviscid flow may be assumed. Calculate the volume flow rate if the flow throughout the bend is (a) free vortex and (b) forced vortex. Explain why these flow rates are idealised by describing briefly secondary flow and separation in pipe bends and indicate how the design of pipe bends could be improved. *(Note the bend is used as a flow meter).*

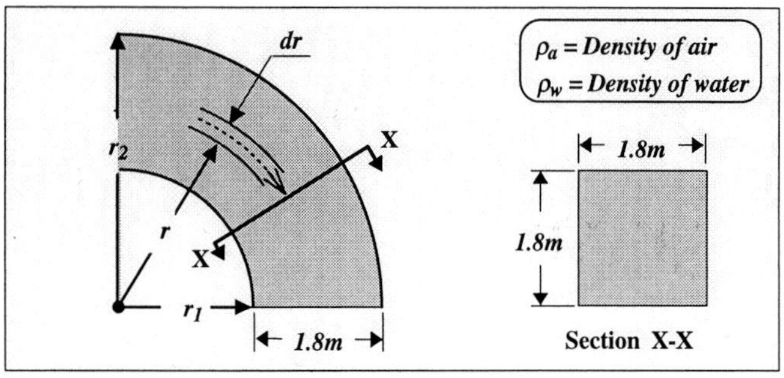

(a) Free vortex flow, $\dfrac{dp}{dr} = \dfrac{\rho v^2}{r}, \quad v = \dfrac{C}{r}$

$$p = \frac{\rho C^2}{r^3} dr, \quad \therefore \quad p_2 - p_1 = \frac{\rho C^2}{2} \times \left(\frac{1}{r_1^2} - \frac{1}{r_2^2} \right), \text{ or}$$

$$\frac{\rho_w}{\rho_a} \times h = \frac{C^2}{2g} \times \left(\frac{r_2^2 - r_1^2}{r_1^2 \, r_2^2} \right), (\rho_a = 1.2 \text{ and } \rho_w = 1000).$$

$$C^2 = 2 \times 9.81 \times \frac{1000}{1.2} \times \frac{30}{1000} \times \frac{4.1^2 \times 5.9^2}{5.9^2 - 4.1^2} = 18769.$$

$\therefore \; C = 126.4.$

Discharge, $Q = b \times \int_{r_1}^{r_2} v dr = 1.8 \times \int_{4.1}^{5.9} \dfrac{126.4}{r} dr$

$$Q = 1.8 \times 126.4 \times 2.305 \times \log_{10} \left(\frac{5.9}{4.1} \right) = 83 m^3 / s.$$

(b) Forced vortex flow, $v = \omega r.$

$$dp = \rho \omega^2 r \, dr, \quad \therefore \quad p_2 - p_1 = \frac{\rho \omega^2}{2} \times (r_2^2 - r_1^2)$$

$$\frac{\rho_w h}{\rho_a} = \frac{\omega^2}{2g} \times (r_2^2 - r_1^2)$$

$$\omega^2 = \frac{2 \times 9.81 \times 10^3 \times 30}{1.2 \times 10^3} \times \frac{1}{5.9^2 - 4.1^2} = 27.25 rad^2 / s^2$$

$\omega = 5.22 \; rad / s$ and ***the discharge***

$$Q = b \times \int_{r_1}^{r_2} \omega \, r \, dr = 1.8 \times 5.22 \times \left(\frac{5.9^2 - 4.1^2}{2} \right) = 84.5 m^3 / s$$

Secondary Flow: Due to friction, the pressure gradient along the centreline is greater than that along the upper and lower walls of duct. This makes the pressure at *B* greater than that at *C* and *E* and the pressure at *A* less than that at *D* and *F*, and hence results secondary flow shown below.

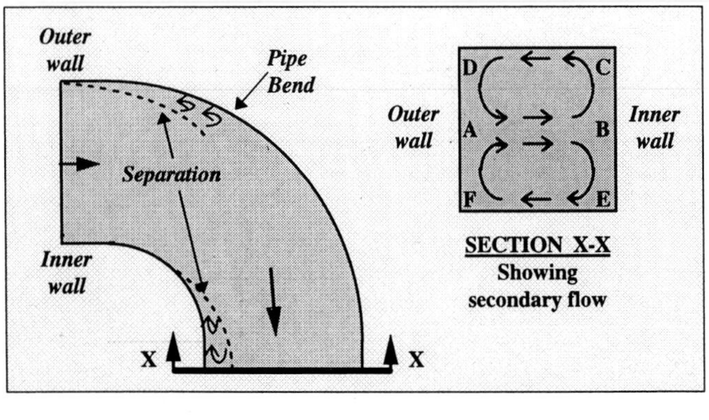

Separation: When the ratio of pipe diameter to the radius of the bend is large, the rapid deceleration of the flow before the midpoint of the bend along the outer wall and past midpoint along the inner wall produces two regions of separation. These effects can be eliminated by fitting curved guide vanes in the bend.

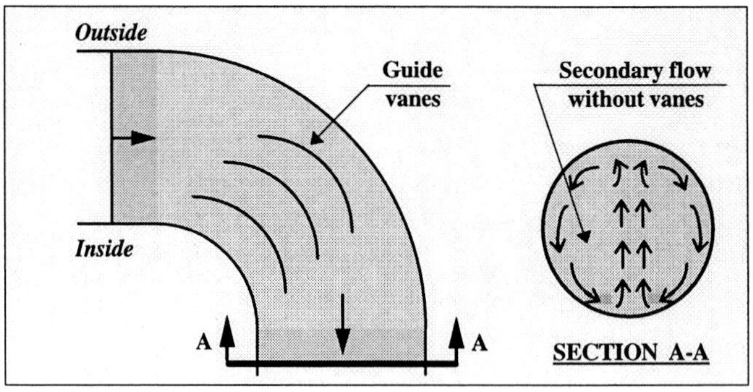

Water Flow in a Pipe Bend

An enclosed horizontal duct 2m square in section has vertical sides. It is running full of water and at one point there is a curved right angled bend, the radius of curvature to the centre line of the duct being 7m. If the flow in the bend is assumed to be frictionless and to have a free vortex distribution, calculate the rate of flow in m^3/s if the difference of pressure head between the inner and outer sides is 0.25m water. (Note the bend is used as flow measurement).

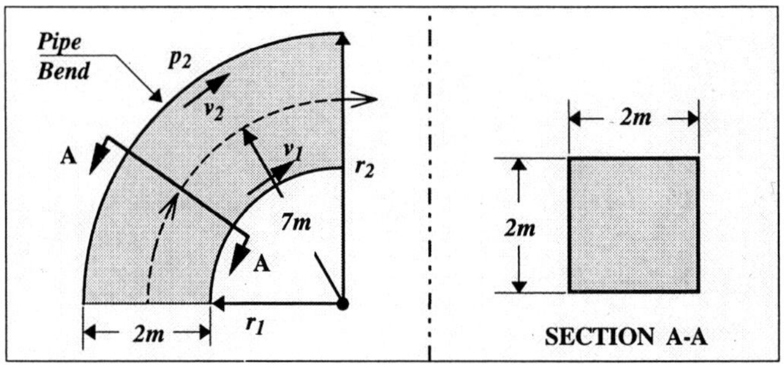

For a free vortex flow, $\dfrac{p_2 - p_1}{\rho g} = \dfrac{C^2}{2g} \times \left(\dfrac{1}{r_1^2} - \dfrac{1}{r_2^2} \right)$

where $v = C/r$, $r_1 = 6m$ and $r_2 = 8m$.

$$\frac{p_1 - p_2}{\rho g} = 0.25 = \frac{C^2}{2g} \times \left(\frac{1}{36} - \frac{1}{64} \right) = \frac{v_2^2 \times 6^2}{2g} \times \left(\frac{1}{36} - \frac{1}{64} \right)$$

$$v_1^2 = \frac{0.5 \times 9.81}{36 \times (0.0278 - 0.0156)} = 11.2 m / s$$

$\therefore \; v_1 = 3.35 m/s.$

$$v_2 = 3.35 \times \frac{6}{8} = 2.51 m / s.$$

$dQ = 2v \, dr$

where $v = C/r = (2.51 \times 8) / r = 20/r.$

Rate of flow, $Q = \int_{r=6}^{r=8} 2v \, dr = 2 \times \int_6^8 \dfrac{20}{r} dr = 40 \; [\log_e r]_6^8$

Discharge, $Q = 40 \, (2.08 - 1.79) = 11.6 \; m^3/s.$

Rotating Cylindrical Tank

A vertical open cylinder 0.2m diameter and 0.8m high contains water to a depth of 0.6m when stationary. Calculate the rotational speed at which (i) the water will just spill over the edge and (ii) a quarter of the original volume of water will spill. If the vessel is now filled with water and a lid of mass 10kg is fitted, calculate the speed at which the lid will theoretically begin to lift.

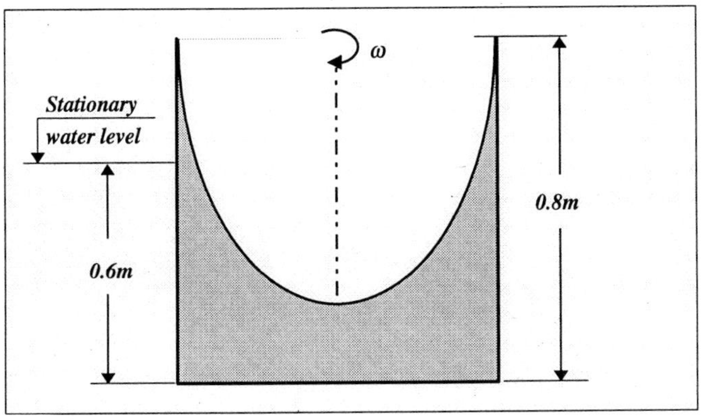

(i) Difference in head, $0.8-\frac{h}{2}=0.6$, $\therefore\ h=0.4m$

$$\frac{p_1-p_2}{\rho g}=\frac{\omega^2}{2g}\times(r_1^2-r_2^2)\ .\ \therefore\ 0.4=\frac{\omega^2}{2\times 9.81}\times(0.1^2-0)\ .$$

$$\omega^2=\frac{19.6\times 0.4}{0.01}=784\ .\ \therefore\ \omega=\sqrt{784}=28rad/s\ .$$

Speed of rotation, $\omega=\frac{28\times 60}{2\pi}=267rev/min.$

(ii) Difference in head, $0.8-\frac{h}{2}=\frac{3}{4}\times 0.6$,

$$\therefore\ \frac{h}{2}=0.8-0.6\times\frac{3}{4}=0.8-0.45=0.7m\ .$$

$$0.7=\frac{\omega^2}{2\times 9.81}\times(0.1^2-0).$$

$$\therefore\ \omega=\sqrt{\frac{19.6\times 0.7}{0.01}}\times\frac{60}{2\pi}=354rev/min\ .$$

Calculation of force and speed.

$$\frac{p}{\rho g}=\frac{v^2}{2g}=\frac{\omega^2 r^2}{2g}\ .\ \therefore\ p=\frac{\rho\,\omega^2 r^2}{2}$$

$$F_r=\int_o^R p\times 2\pi\,rdr=\rho\pi\omega^2\left[\frac{r^4}{4}\right]_o^r=\frac{\rho\,\pi\,\omega^2 R^4}{4}$$

where F_r is the resultant force over the cylinder and equals the force on the lid. Weight of liquid = $10\times g$.

$$10\times 9.81=\frac{10^3\times\pi\times 0.1^4\times\omega^2}{4}$$

$$\therefore\ \omega=\sqrt{\frac{40\times 9.81}{10^3\times\pi\times 0.1^4}}=35.35\ rad/s\ .$$

Speed of rotation, $\omega=\frac{35.5\times 60}{2\pi}=338\ rev/min\ .$

Force on Container Cover

A closed cylindrical container of radius R is full of water which is rotated by paddles of radius a. The axis of rotation of the paddles is the vertical axis of symmetry and their angular velocity is ω. Assuming the pressure at the centre of the top cover is atmospheric, develop an expression for the force exerted by the water on the top cover in terms of a, R, w and the density ρ of the fluid.

Free vortex : $v = C/r$, Bernoulli equations applies along streamlines and H equal for all streamlines, therefore

$$v=\frac{p}{\rho g}+z=H-\frac{v^2}{2g}=H-\frac{C^2}{2gr^2}$$

Forced vortex: $v=\omega\ r=[(\omega^2 r^2)/2g]+C$

Forced vortex in the blade passages, $p=(\rho\omega^2 r^2)/2.$

$$\therefore\ \textit{Total force,}\ F_1=\int_o^a\frac{\rho\,\omega^2 r^2}{2}\times 2\pi rdr=\frac{\pi\rho\,\omega^2 a^4}{4}\ .$$

In free vortex, $v_r r=C,\ \therefore\ v_r\ r=v_a a=\omega\, a\times a.\ \therefore\ v_r=\omega\, a^2/r.$

$$\frac{p_r}{\rho g}=\frac{p_a}{\rho g}+\frac{v_a^2}{2g}-\frac{v_r^2}{2g},\quad p_r=\frac{\rho\,\omega^2 a^2}{2}+\frac{\rho\,\omega^2 a^2}{2}-\frac{\rho\,\omega^2 a^4}{2r^2}$$

i.e. $p_r=(\rho\omega^2 a^2)-(\rho\omega^2 a^4)/2\,r^2.$

Total force due to free vortex, F_2,

$$F_2=\int_a^R\left(\rho\,\omega^2 a^2-\frac{\rho\,\omega^2 a^4}{2r^2}\right)\times 2\pi\,rdr$$

$$=2\pi\ \rho\ \omega^2 a^2\times\left(\frac{r^2}{2}-\frac{a^2}{2}\times\ln r\right)_a^R$$

Total force, $F_2=\pi\,\rho\,\omega^2 a^2\times[R^2-a^2-a^2\times\ln\,(R/a)]\ .$

$$F=F_1+F_2=\pi\,\rho\,\omega^2 a^4\times\left[\left(\frac{R}{a}\right)^2-\left(\frac{3}{4}+\ln\frac{R}{a}\right)\right].$$

Water Spilt from a Tank

When a fluid moves in a circular path the rate of change of Total Head, H, with radius, r, is given by the equation
$dH/dr = v/g \times (v/r + dv/dr)$
Starting with this equation derive an expression which gives the difference in level (h_1-h_2) between two points on the surface of a forced vortex at radius r_1 and r_2. An open topped cylindrical tank 1m diameter and 2m high is located with its longitudinal axis vertical. It contains water which stands to a depth of 1.5m when the tank is stationary. Calculate the speed at which the tank must be rotated about its vertical axis for the water just to touch the top rim of the tank. If the tank is rotated at 2rev/s, calculate the volume of water spilt from the tank. *(ω = angular velocity).*

For forced vortex, $v=\omega\,r$ and $dv/dr=\omega$.

$$\text{i.e.}\ \frac{dH}{dr}=\frac{v}{g}\times\left(\frac{v}{r}+\frac{dv}{dr}\right)=\frac{\omega r}{g}\times\left(\frac{\omega r}{r}+\omega\right),\ \frac{dH}{dr}=\frac{2\omega^2 r}{g}\ .$$

Integrating between r_1 and r_2, $H_1-H_2=\frac{\omega^2}{g}\times(r_1^2-r_2^2)$

$$\left(\frac{p_1}{\rho g}+\frac{v_1^2}{2g}+z_1\right)-\left(\frac{p_2}{\rho g}+\frac{v_2^2}{2g}+z_2\right)=\frac{\omega^2}{g}\times(r_1^2-r_2^2)$$

For points on surface $p_1 = p_2 = 0$.

$z_1 = h_1,\ z_2 = h_2,\ v_1 = \omega r_1,$ and $v_2 = \omega r_2$.

i.e. $$\left(\frac{\omega^2 r_1^2}{2g}+h_1\right)-\left(\frac{\omega^2 r_2^2}{2g}+h_2\right)=\frac{\omega^2}{g}\times(r_1^2-r_2^2)$$

Head difference, $$h_1-h_2=\frac{\omega^2}{2g}\times(r_1^2-r_2^2)$$

Volume of paraboloid = 1/2 × Volume of enclosing cylinder, i.e. forced vortex will be equally distributed about still water level. To touch top rim outer surface must rise by 0.5m, i.e. height of vortex = $1m = h_1 - h_2$, where $r_1 = 0.5m$ and $r_2 = 0$.

$1 = (\omega^2/2g)\times(0.5^2 - 0)$. $\therefore\ \omega = 8.86\ rad/s = 1.4\ rev/s$.

At 2 $rev/s = 12.6\ rad/s$, $h_1 - h_2 = (\omega^2/2g)\times(r_1^2 - r_2^2)$.

$h_1 - h_2 = (12.6^2/2g)\times(0.5^2 - 0) = 2$m. i.e. **Just fills tank.**

Volume of water $= 0.5\times 2\times 3.14\times 0.5^2 = 0.785m^3$.

Original volume of water $= 1.5\times 3.14\times 0.5^2 = 1.18m^3$.

Volume spilled $= 1.18 - 0.785 = 0.395m^3$.

Flow in a Channel Bend

At one station along a concrete drainage channel in a town there is a bend with an average radius of 30.5m. The channel has a width of 10m and carries a flood discharge of $107m^3/s$. The corresponding depth of flow is 2.74m. Calculate the amount of superelevation for the channel bend. Assume a freeboard of 0.4m and design a suitable section for the bend and channel. Discuss the type of secondary flow in the bend.

$Q = 107m^3/s,\ R = 30.5m,\ r_2 = 25.5m,\ r_1 = 35.5m$

$b = 10m,\ y = 2.74m,\ v = 3.9m/s.$

$$Q = C\times\left[H-\frac{C^2}{2g\, r_2\, r_1}\right]\times\ln\left(\frac{r_1}{r_2}\right).$$

$$107 = C\times\left[\left(2.74+\frac{3.9^2}{2\times 9.81}\right)-\left(\frac{C^2}{2\times 9.81\times 25.52\times 35.5}\right)\right]\times\ln\left(\frac{35.5}{25.5}\right)$$

By trial and error, $C = 115.6$.

$$\Delta h=\frac{C^2\times(r_2^2-r_1^2)}{2g\, r_1^2\, r_2^2}=\frac{115.6^2\times(35.5^2-25.5^2)}{2\times 9.81\times 25.5^2\times 35.5^2}=0.54m.$$

Superelevation, $\Delta h = 0.54m$.

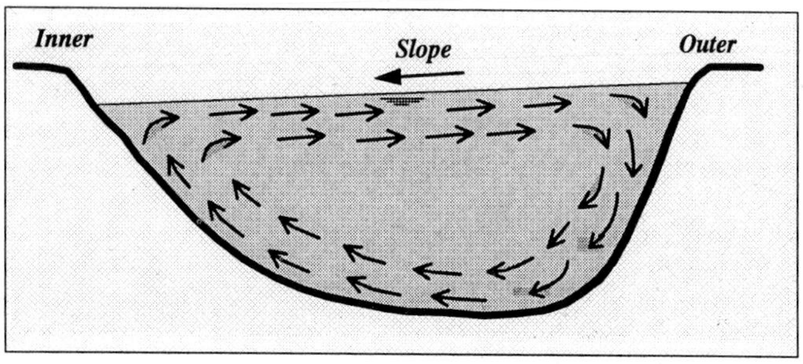

Intake for irrigation canals

The secondary flows in channel bends create problems for the hydraulic engineer in rivers and canals, for the bottom flow will be carrying sand and silt from the outside of bends to the inside; the inside of a bend therefore becomes silted and the outside becomes eroded. This may lead ultimately to the meandering of the river. If the river is to supply water to an irrigation channel or a pipeline, the intake should be placed, if at all possible, on the outside of the bend, where the sand tends to move inward so as to reduce the quantity of sand taken in by the irrigation canal.

Problems on Curved Motion

[1] Water in a large basin runs through a central outlet. At a radius of 175mm it is found that the surface level is 30mm below the free surface level. What is this difference when the radius is 400mm? (6mm)

[2] A vertical cylinder 1200mm diameter and 1600mm high, initially full of water, revolves at 120 rev/min. Find the area of base exposed. ($1.26m^2$)

[3] An impeller, 300mm diameter, rotates about a vertical axis at 120 rev/min in a 1m diameter casing which is full of water. Calculate the velocity of the water at 150mm and 300mm from the centre and the increase in pressure head at these radii above the pressure head at the centre. Assume free vortex motion outside the impeller.

(1.89m/s, 0.9m/s, 0.317m)

[4] Show that a closed vertical cylinder of diameter D(m) is filled with fresh water at atmospheric pressure and rotated about its vertical axis at N (rev/min), the force on the top cover of the cylinder is $0.54N^2D^4$ Newtons.

[5] Two radii, r_1 and r_2 $(r_2 > r_1)$, in the same horizontal plane have the same values in a free vortex and in a forced vortex. The tangential velocity at radius r_1 is the same in both vortices. Determine, in terms of r_1, the radius $2r_2$ at which the pressure difference between r_1 and r_2 in the forced vortex is twice that in the free vortex. ($2\sqrt{r_1}$)

[6] Water at a rate of $2.85m^3/s$ flows inwards between two circular, horizontal parallel plates 2m diameter, 300mm apart, escaping at the centre through two opposite holes, 600mm diameter, in the plates. It enters through a large number of thin vanes, inclined at an angle of 60° to the circumference so as to form a free spiral vortex at a pressure of $70kN/m^2$. Find the velocity and pressure at 300mm radius, and the total force on the upper plate.

(5.8m/s, $55kN/m^2$, 11.5kN).

CHAPTER NINE

BOUNDARY LAYER THEORY

Introduction

When a body is immersed in a fluid flow it is subject to two types of fluid resistance: (i) shear or frictional resistance and (ii) pressure or form resistance. The shear resistance, a tangential stress, is caused by the fluid viscosity and takes place along the boundary of the flow in the general direction of local motion. Pressure resistance, is caused by acceleration of the fluid which results in a decrease in pressure from the upstream side to the downstream side of an object. All fluid resistance can be divided into one or a combination of these two categories.

It has been realised that the whole of the effect of the friction on a solid surface is confined within a thin layer of fluid adjacent to the surface, unless the flow breaks away and leaves a large zone of circulation flow. This relatively thin layer is called the boundary layer. Outside this layer the friction has no effect and any changes in velocity there, are due solely to the distortion of the streamlines by the solid surface (Fig.9.1)

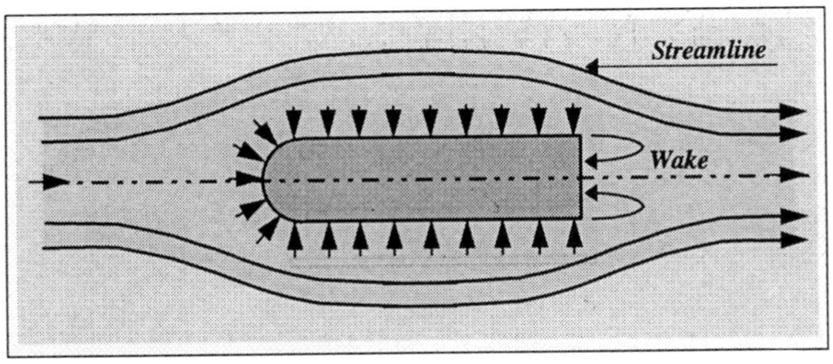

Fig.9.1- Flow past a solid body.

Flow along a Flat Plate

The shear resistance may be analysed simply by considering as a first approximation the development of the boundary along a thin flat plate held parallel to the direction of flow. The resulting velocity distribution is shown in Fig.9.2, the vertical scale being many times enlarged to permit what is actually a very thin zone to be studied in detail. As the fluid first passes the leading edge, the thickness of the viscous action is slight and the velocity gradient du/dy and the intensity of boundary shear are correspondingly high. However, as the fluid travels further along the plate, the shearing forces accomplish the retardation of an expanding portion of the flow and the zone of appreciable deceleration hence grows steadily in thickness.

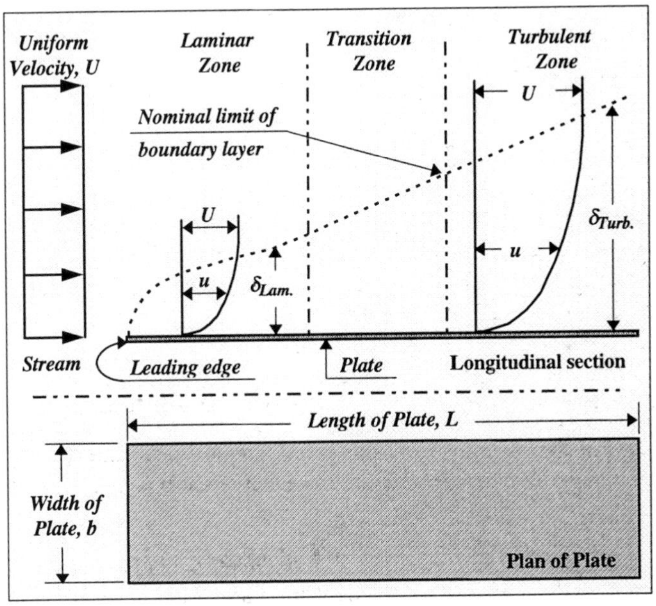

Fig.9.2- Flow along a flat plate.

The boundary layer flow is initially laminar but becomes steadily more susceptible to disturbances and can be expected at some section to break down into turbulence. Once the boundary layer becomes turbulent, the mixing causes the layer to expand more rapidly.

While a knowledge of the **boundary layer thickness** at any distance from the leading edge is often of importance, by far the most pertinent is the magnitude of the resulting **drag force** upon the plate. This is computed by means of the momentum principle, provided that the velocity distribution in the boundary layer is known or assumed. That is, since the effect of the boundary layer is to reduce the velocity of steadily expanding fluid layer, the intensity of shear may be equated to the change of momentum which it accomplishes per unit length of boundary.

Boundary Layer Thickness

For engineering purposes, the thickness of the boundary layer may be defined as the magnitude of the normal distance y at which the velocity u is within one per cent of the undisturbed velocity U, *i.e.* $y = \delta$, when $u = 0.99U$.

This is taken like this because the influence of viscosity in the boundary layer decreases asymptotically. The displacement thickness δ_* is a physically meaningful measure for the boundary layer thickness which is the distance by which the external potential or undisturbed flow is displaced outwards as a consequence of the decrease in velocity in the boundary layer.

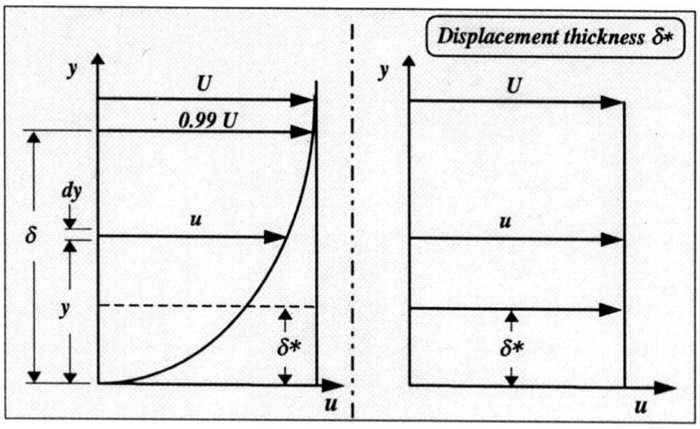

Fig.9.3- Boundary layer and displacement thickness.

The decrease in volume of flow due to the influence of friction is

$$\textbf{Flow deficit} = \int_0^\delta (U-u)\,dy \qquad (9.1)$$

so that for displacement thickness $\delta*$ we have the definition

$$U\delta* = \int_0^\delta (U-u)\,dy\,,\ \text{or}\ \ \delta* = \int_0^\delta \left(1-\frac{u}{U}\right)dy \qquad (9.2)$$

For example, the flow of water at 1.67m/sec on a flat plate 600mm long, $\delta*$ is about 3mm.

Objectives of Boundary Layer Calculations

(1) To calculate skin friction at the boundary. This will enable us to calculate the drag force on the immersed body, e.g. a ship, submarine or bridge pier.

(2) To calculate the boundary layer thickness. When designing pipes and channels, the boundary must be displaced by $\delta*$ to allow for flow deficit.

(3) To find out the physical characteristic of flow along the surface, the separation point of the flow from the surface.

Laminar Boundary Layer

The simplest assumption about the velocity distribution across a section of the boundary layer is that it is linear with y up to the edge of the boundary layer. If we accept this assumption then we can only satisfy the two boundary conditions $y = 0$ for $u = 0$ and $y = \delta$ for $u = U$. This assumption therefore leads to:

$u/U = y/\delta$. Therefore,

$$\textbf{Shear stress},\ \tau_o = \frac{\mu du}{dy} = \frac{\mu U}{\delta}\ \ \text{and}\ \ \delta* = \int_0^\delta \left(1-\frac{y}{\delta}\right)dy \qquad (9.3)$$

The rate of change of momentum = mass flow × change in velocity = drag force *(D)*

$$D = \rho U^2 \times \int_0^\delta \left(\frac{y}{\delta}-\frac{y^2}{\delta^2}\right)dy = \rho U^2 \times \left[\frac{y^2}{2\delta}-\frac{y^3}{3\delta^2}\right]_0^\delta \qquad (9.4)$$

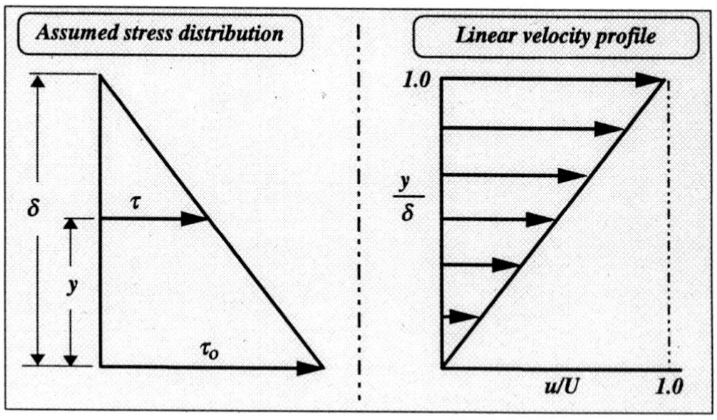

Fig.9.4- Assumptions for boundary layer theory.

$$\text{Also,}\ D = \int_0^\delta \tau_o\,dx = \rho\int_0^\delta u\times(U-u)\,dy = \rho\int_0^\delta \frac{Uy}{\delta}\times\left(U-\frac{Uy}{\delta}\right).$$

$$\textbf{Drag force per unit width},\ D = \rho\frac{U^2\delta}{6} \qquad (9.5)$$

The total drag force of this plate is twice this value. Differentiating with respect to *x*, we get

$$\mu\frac{U}{\delta} = \rho\frac{U^2}{6}\times\frac{d\delta}{dx},\ \int_0^x dx = \int_0^\delta \frac{\rho U}{6\mu}\times\delta\times d\delta$$

$$X = \frac{\rho U}{6\mu}\times\left(\frac{\delta^2}{2}\right),\ \delta^2 = \frac{12\mu X}{\rho U} \qquad (9.6)$$

$$\text{Hence,}\ \frac{\delta}{X} = \frac{\sqrt{12}}{\sqrt{R_x}} = \frac{3.464}{\sqrt{R_x}},\ \text{and}\ R_x = \frac{UX}{\upsilon} \qquad (9.7)$$

Therefore, the local skin friction coefficient defined as

$$C_f = \frac{\tau_o}{0.5\times\rho U^2} = \frac{2\mu U}{\delta\times\rho U^2} = \frac{2\mu}{\rho U\delta} = \frac{2\sqrt{R_x}}{3.464\,R_x}$$

$$C_f = \frac{0.577}{\sqrt{R_x}} \qquad (9.8)$$

where R_x = Reynolds Number.

The overall skin friction coefficient for one surface of a plate is

$$C_f = \frac{2}{6X}\times\frac{3.464X}{\sqrt{R_x}} = \frac{D}{0.5\times\rho U^2\times Area}$$

$$C_f = \rho\frac{U^2\delta}{6}\times\frac{1}{0.5\times\rho U^2\times X} = \frac{1.155}{\sqrt{R_x}} \qquad (9.9)$$

Turbulent Boundary Layer

The turbulent boundary layer extends downstream to an infinite extent on a smooth flat surface if the pressure remains constant. The thickness δ increases also and may eventually be many times greater than that for the laminar boundary layer. For example, the boundary layer at the stern of a 300m long ship travelling at 30 knots (15.5m/s.) is about 1.37m thick if the steel plates are smooth: if they are rough the boundary layer will be still thicker. Because δ is so much greater in the turbulent than in the laminar layer, it is easier to determine the velocity distribution.

Experiments have shown that the velocity distribution can be represented as a power law

$$\frac{u}{U} = \left(\frac{y}{\delta}\right)^n \tag{9.10}$$

n varying from about 1/4 near the transition from laminar flow to 1/7 further downstream.

As in the laminar boundary layer, the drag force D that cause the slowing downing of the fluid is obtained by the use of the momentum principle,

$$D = \rho \int_o^\delta u(U-u)\, dy \tag{9.11}$$

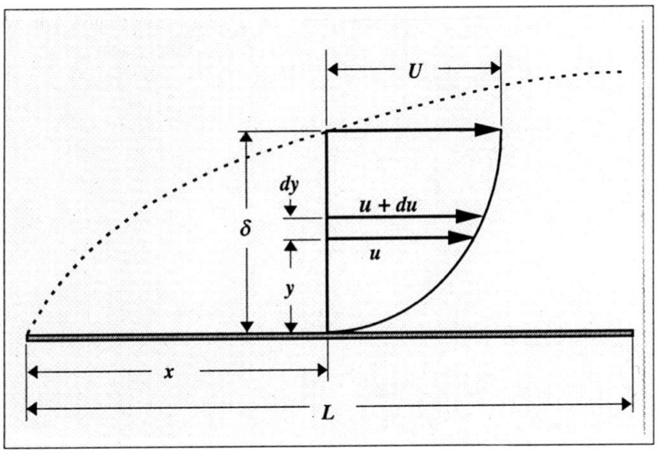

Fig.9.5- Boundary layer and displacement thickness.

Assuming and substituting, $\frac{u}{U} = \left(\frac{y}{\delta}\right)^{1/7}$ (9.12)

$$D = \rho\delta U^2 \int_o^1 \frac{u}{U} \times \left(1 - \frac{u}{U}\right) \times d\left(\frac{y}{\delta}\right)$$

$$= \rho\delta U^2 \int_o^1 \left(\frac{y}{\delta}\right)^{1/7} \times \left[1 - \left(\frac{y}{\delta}\right)^{1/7}\right] \times d\left(\frac{y}{\delta}\right)$$

Drag force per unit with, $D = \frac{7}{72}\rho\delta U^2$ (9.13)

As before, this force also equals the summation of the varying stresses all along the surface from the leading edge. If the surface is long compared with the extent of the laminar layer near its leading edge, then an easy approximation to be made is to ignore the laminar and assume that the turbulent layer occupies the whole surface, so that everywhere is that applicable to a turbulent layer. Thus

$$D = \int_o^x \tau_o dx \tag{9.14}$$

Blasius produced a formula based on experiments for shear stress at the boundary

$$\tau_o = 0.023 \times \rho U^2 \times \left(\frac{\nu}{U\delta}\right)^{1/4} \tag{9.15}$$

Substituting, $\int_o^x 0.023\, \rho U^2 \times \left(\frac{\nu}{U\delta}\right)^{1/4} dx = \frac{7}{72} \times \rho U^2 \delta$

Differentiate with respect to x,

$$0.023 \times \rho U^2 \times \left(\frac{\nu}{U\delta}\right)^{1/4} dx = \frac{7}{72} \times \rho U^2 d\delta \tag{9.16}$$

Integrating this equation,

$$\int_o^x dx = \int_o^x \frac{7}{72 \times 0.023} \left(U\frac{\delta}{\nu}\right)^{1/4} d\delta \tag{9.17}$$

At x the boundary layer thickness is δ.

$$x = \frac{7}{72 \times 0.023} \times \left(\frac{U}{\nu}\right)^{1/4} \times \delta^{5/4} \times \frac{4}{5}$$

$$\frac{\delta}{x} = 0.296 \times R_x^{-1/4}$$

$$\left(\frac{\delta}{x}\right) = C\left(\frac{\nu}{UX}\right)^{1/4} \tag{9.18}$$

Measurements of δ are just as difficult to make in the turbulent layer as they were in the laminar layer. But the foregoing equation for δ/x can be used to determine the resultant coefficient of drag C_f.

$$D = \frac{7}{72} \times \rho\, U^2 \times \frac{0.376X}{\sqrt{R_x}}$$

$$C_f = \frac{D}{\rho\, U^2 X/2} \times \frac{0.075}{\sqrt{R_x}} \tag{9.19}$$

This equation is plotted in Fig.9.6.

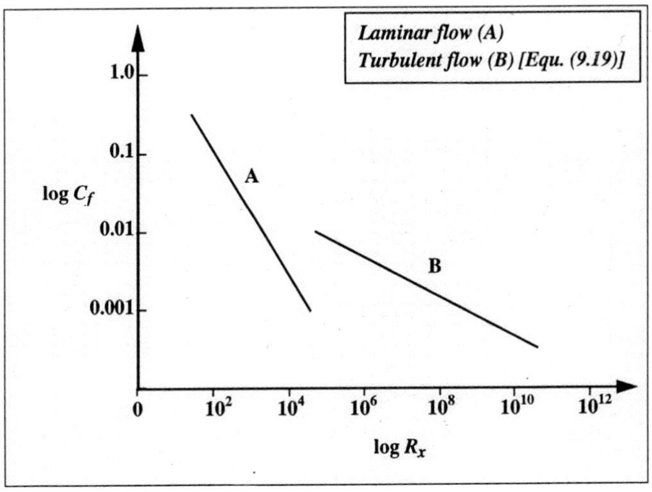

Fig.9.6- Plot of equation (9.19).

Better agreement with the exact solution can be obtained by more plausible assumptions for the velocity distribution satisfying more of the boundary conditions e.g. higher order polynomials, as

$$\frac{u}{U} = \frac{3}{2}\left(\frac{y}{\delta}\right) - \left(\frac{y}{\delta}\right)^3, \text{ or}$$

$$\frac{u}{U} = 2\frac{y}{\delta} - 2\left(\frac{y}{\delta}\right)^3 + \left(\frac{y}{\delta}\right)^4, \text{ or}$$

$$\frac{u}{U} = \sin\frac{\pi}{2}\left(\frac{y}{\delta}\right) \tag{9.20}$$

Examples on Boundary Layer

Drag on an Immersed Plate in Water

Define the displacement thickness of a boundary layer. A thin plate is totally immersed in a water flow and is set at zero incidence angle to the oncoming stream. The plate is 2m wide by 3m long and the thickness of the turbulent boundary layer at the trailing edge is 48mm. The velocity distribution in the boundary layer is given by: $u/U = (y/\delta)^{1/7}$, and the shear stress by: $\tau_o = 0.023 \times \rho U^2 \times (\nu/U\delta)^{1/4}$, where U is the velocity of the stream, u is the velocity at distance y from the surface of the plate, δ is the thickness of the boundary layer, ν and ρ are the kinematic viscosity and density of the water respectively. Calculate the displacement thickness at the trailing edge and the total drag on the plate assuming that the boundary layer is turbulent from the leading edge. Derive any formulae used.

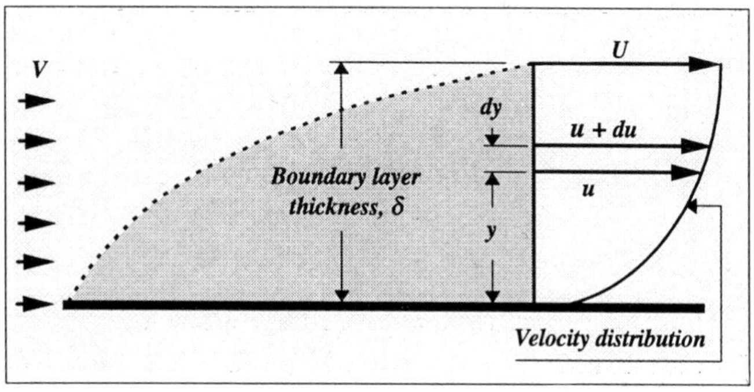

The displacement thickness is that distance by which the external undisturbed flow is displaced outwards as a consequence of the decrease in velocity in the boundary layer.

Drag force per unit with, $D = b\int_o^x \tau_o dx$

$$D = \rho\, b\int_o^\delta u(U-u)\,dy = \rho\, bU^2\delta \times \int_o^1\left[\left(\frac{u}{U}\right) - \left(\frac{u}{U}\right)^2\right] d\left(\frac{y}{\delta}\right)$$

$$= \rho\, bU^2\delta \times \int_o^1\left[\left(\frac{y}{\delta}\right)^{1/7} - \left(\frac{y}{\delta}\right)^{2/7}\right] d\left(\frac{y}{\delta}\right)$$

$$= \rho\, bU^2\delta \times \left[\left(\frac{7}{8}\right)\left(\frac{y}{\delta}\right)^{8/7} - \left(\frac{7}{9}\right)\left(\frac{y}{\delta}\right)^{9/7}\right]_o^1 = \frac{7}{72}\times \rho\, bU^2\delta$$

Also, $b\times\int_o^x 0.023\times\rho\, U^2\times\left(\frac{\nu}{U\delta}\right)^{1/4} dx = \frac{7}{72}\times\rho\, b\, U^2\delta$

$$0.023\times\rho b\, U^2\times\left(\frac{\nu}{U\delta}\right)^{1/4} = \frac{7}{72}\times\rho\, b\, U^2\delta$$

$$\int_o^X dx = \int_o^\delta \frac{7}{72\times 0.023}\times\left(\frac{U}{\nu}\right)^{1/4}\times\delta^{1/4} d\delta$$

$$X = \frac{7\times 4}{72\times 0.023\times 5}\times\left(\frac{U}{\nu}\right)^{1/4}\times\delta^{5/4} \text{ or } \frac{\delta}{X} = 0.377\times\left(\frac{UX}{\nu}\right)^{-1/5}$$

$$U = \left(\frac{0.377\times X}{\delta}\right)^5\times\frac{\nu}{X} = \left(\frac{0.377\times 3}{0.048}\right)^5\times\frac{9.5\times 10^{-7}}{3}.$$

Velocity of the stream, $U = 2.36 m/s.$

$$U\delta^* = \int_o^\delta (U-u)dy = \delta\times\int_o^1 U\times\left[1-\left(\frac{y}{\delta}\right)^{1/7}\right]\frac{dy}{\delta}$$

$$\delta^* = \left[\frac{y}{\delta} - \times\frac{7}{8}\left(\frac{y}{\delta}\right)^{8/7}\right]_o^1 = \frac{\delta}{8} = \frac{0.048}{8}.$$

Drag force, $D = (7/72)\times 1000\times 4\times 2.36^2\times 0.048 = 104N.$

Laminar Boundary Layer on a Plate

The velocity distribution in the laminar boundary layer at a distance x from the leading edge of a thin plate immersed in an air stream is given by: $u/U = [(3/2)\times(y/\delta)] - [(1/2)\times(y/\delta)^3]$, where u is the velocity at a distance y from the plate, δ is the boundary layer thickness and U is the main stream velocity. Develop expressions in terms x and the Reynolds number based on the term x for (a) displacement thickness, (b) boundary thickness, and (c) local skin friction coefficient. At the trailing edge, a distance of 0.5m from the leading edge of the plate, the laminar boundary layer thickness is 40mm when U is 16m/s. Find the local stress at the trailing edge and the total drag on the plate.

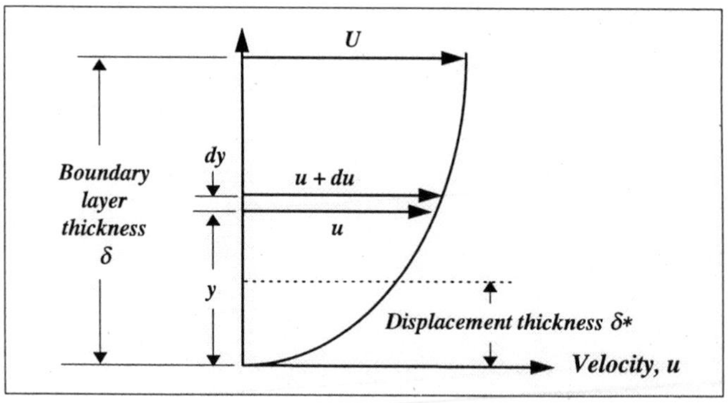

Displacement thickness, $\delta^* = \int_o^\delta\left(1-\frac{u}{U}\right)dy$

$$\delta^* = \int_o^\delta\left(1-\frac{3}{2}\times\frac{y}{\delta}+\frac{1}{2}\times\frac{y^3}{\delta^3}\right)dy = \left[y-\frac{3y^2}{4\delta}+\frac{y^4}{8\delta^3}\right]_o^\delta = \frac{3\delta}{8}.$$

Drag per unit width, $D = \rho\int_o^\delta u(U-u)dy = \rho\, U^2\int_o^\delta\left[\frac{u}{U}-\frac{u^2}{U^2}\right]dy$

$$D = \rho\, U^2\int_o^\delta\left[\frac{3}{2}\times\frac{y}{\delta}-\frac{1}{2}\times\frac{y^3}{\delta^3}-\frac{9}{4}\times\frac{y^2}{\delta^2}+\frac{3}{2}\times\frac{y^4}{\delta^4}-\frac{1}{4}\times\frac{y^6}{\delta^6}\right]dy$$

$$D=\rho U^2\times\left[\frac{3y^3}{4\delta}-\frac{y^4}{8\delta^3}-\frac{9y^3}{12\delta^2}+\frac{3y^5}{10\delta^4}-\frac{y^7}{28\delta^6}\right]_o^\delta$$

$$=\frac{39}{280}\times\rho U^2\delta\,.$$

$$\tau=\mu\times\frac{du}{dy}=\mu U\times\left[\frac{3}{2}\times\frac{1}{\delta}-\frac{3}{2}\times\frac{y^2}{\delta^3}\right]=\frac{3}{2}\mu U\times\left[\frac{1}{\delta}-\frac{y^2}{\delta^3}\right]$$

At the surface of plate, $\tau_o=\dfrac{3\mu U}{2\delta}$.

Drag force, $D=\int_o^x\tau_o\,dx=\dfrac{39}{280}\times\rho U^2\delta$

$$\frac{3}{2}\times\frac{\mu U}{\delta}=\frac{39}{280}\times\rho U^2\times\frac{d\delta}{dx}$$

$$\int_o^X dx=\int_o^\delta\left(\frac{13}{140}\times\frac{\rho U\delta}{\mu}\right)\times d\delta$$

$$X=\frac{13\rho U\delta^2}{280\,\mu}\,,\quad\therefore\ \frac{\delta}{X}=\frac{4.64}{\sqrt{\rho UX/\mu}}=\frac{4.64}{\sqrt{R_x}}$$

Skin friction coefficient,

$$C_f=\frac{39}{280}\times\frac{4.64}{\sqrt{R_x}}\times\frac{1}{0.5\rho U^2x}=\frac{1.292}{\sqrt{R_x}}$$

Drag on both sides of plate,

$$D=2\times\frac{39}{280}\times1.2\times16^2\times\frac{40}{1000}=3.42N\,.$$

Shear stress, $\tau_o=\dfrac{3}{2}\times\dfrac{1.8\times10^{-5}\times16}{4\times10^{-3}}=1.08\times10^{-2}\ N/m^2$.

Displacement thickness, $\delta_*=\dfrac{3}{8}\times40=15mm$.

Drag on a Bridge Pier

Downstream of a bridge pier in a wide river 5m deep, the velocity defect is proportional to $[1-(y/b)^{3/2}]^2$ and the breadth $2b$ of the wake is 6m. The river speed is 4m/s and the least speed in the wake is 1.2m/s. Determine the drag on the pier.

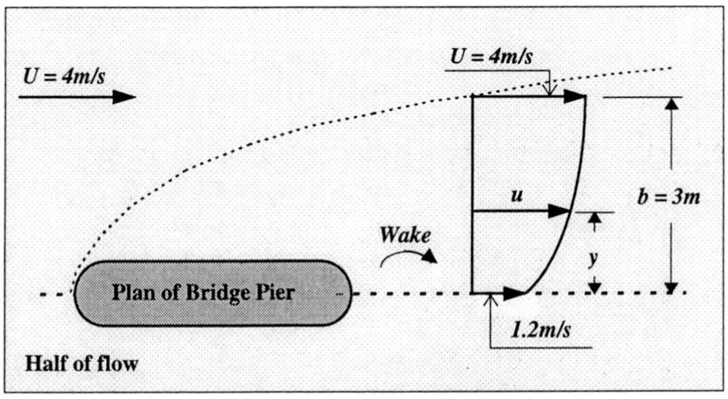

Velocity defect in the wake of the bridge pier

$$U-u=K\left[1-\left(\frac{y}{b}\right)^{3/2}\right]^2$$

When $y=0$, $u=1.2m/s$. $U-u=4-1.2=2.8=K\times[1-0]$

$$U-u=2.8\times\left[1-\left(\frac{y}{b}\right)^{3/2}\right]^2.$$

Rearranging and expanding,

$$u=U-2.8\left[1-2\left(\frac{y}{b}\right)^{3/2}+\left(\frac{y}{b}\right)^3\right]=1.2+5.6\left(\frac{y}{b}\right)^{3/2}\times2.8\left(\frac{y}{b}\right)^3$$

Put $U=4m/s$.

$$\frac{u}{U}=0.30+1.40\times\left(\frac{y}{b}\right)^{3/2}-0.70\times\left(\frac{y}{b}\right)^3.$$

$$\left(\frac{u}{U}\right)^2=0.09+1.96\times\left(\frac{y}{b}\right)^3+0.49\times\left(\frac{y}{b}\right)^6+0.84\times\left(\frac{y}{b}\right)^{3/2}$$

$$-0.42\left(\frac{y}{b}\right)^3-1.96\left(\frac{y}{b}\right)^{9/2}$$

Drag on pier per metre depth per side, $D=\int\rho u\times(U-u)dy$.

$$=5\times2\,\rho U^2\int\left[\frac{u}{U}-\left(\frac{u}{U}\right)^2\right]dy=10\,\rho U^2\times$$

$$\int_o^b\left[0.21+0.58\left(\frac{y}{b}\right)^{\frac{3}{2}}-2.24\left(\frac{y}{b}\right)^3+1.96\left(\frac{y}{b}\right)^{\frac{9}{2}}-0.49\left(\frac{y}{b}\right)^6\right]dy$$

$$=10\rho\ U^2\times\left[0.21+\frac{0.58\times2b}{5}-\frac{2.24b}{4}+\frac{1.96\times2b}{11}-\frac{0.49b}{7}\right]$$

$$=10\ \rho\ U^2\ b\ \times(0.21+0.23-0.56+0.37-0.07)$$

$$=10\times10^3\times4^2\times3\times0.18=8.64\times10^4\ N=86.4kN\,.$$

Total drag on pier, = 86.4kN.

Power to Move a Plate Sideways

Define, with a sketch, the term boundary layer thickness. A smooth flat plate, 2.5m long and 0.8m wide, moves lengthways at 3m/s through still water. The plate is assumed to be completely covered by a turbulent boundary layer in which the velocity distribution is given by: $[1-(u/U)]=(y/\delta)^{1/7}$ and the shear stress by, $\tau_o=0.023\times\rho U^2\times(\nu/U\delta)^{1/4}$, where U is the steady velocity of the plate, u is the velocity in the boundary layer at a distance y from the surface of the plate, δ is the thickness of the boundary layer, and ν and ρ are the kinematic viscosity and density of the water respectively. Calculate the total drag on the plate and the power required to move it. Derive any formulae you use.

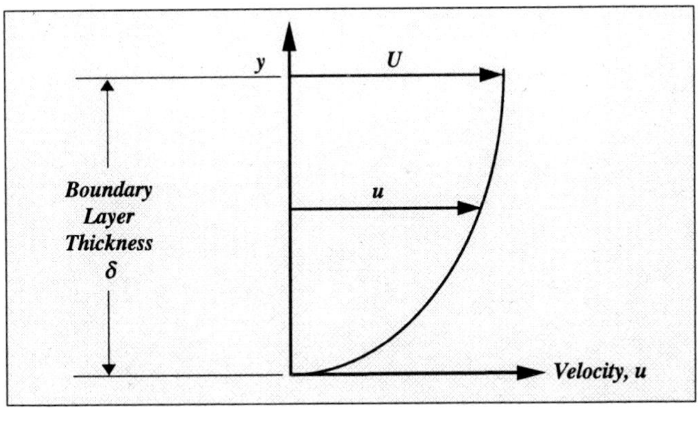

For engineering purpose, the thickness of the boundary layer is defined as the normal distance y at which the velocity is within one percent of the undisturbed velocity U.

$$\textbf{\textit{Drag force,}}\ D = b\times\int_0^X \tau_o\,dx = \rho b\times\int_0^\delta u\times(U-u)dy$$

$$D = \rho bU^2\delta\times\int_0^1\left[\frac{u}{U}-\left(\frac{u}{U}\right)^2\right]d\left(\frac{y}{\delta}\right)$$

$$= \rho bU^2\delta\times\int_0^1\left[\left(\frac{y}{\delta}\right)^{1/7}-\left(\frac{y}{\delta}\right)^{2/7}\right]d\left(\frac{y}{\delta}\right)$$

$$= \rho bU^2\delta\times\left[\frac{7}{8}\times\left(\frac{y}{\delta}\right)^{8/7}-\frac{7}{9}\times\left(\frac{y}{\delta}\right)^{9/7}\right]_0^1.$$

Also, $D = b\times\int_0^X 0.023\times\rho U^2\times\left(\frac{\upsilon}{U\delta}\right)^{1/4}dx$

$$\int_0^X 0.023\times\rho U^2\times\left(\frac{\upsilon}{U\delta}\right)^{1/4}\times bdx = \frac{7}{72}\times\rho U^2\delta$$

$$\int_0^X dx = \int_0^\delta\left[\frac{7}{72\times0.023}\times\left(\frac{U}{\upsilon}\right)^{1/4}\times\delta^{1/4}\right]d\delta$$

$$X = \frac{28}{72\times0.023\times5}\times\left(\frac{U}{\nu}\right)^{1/4}\times\delta^{5/4}$$

$$\therefore\ \delta = 0.377\times X\times\left(\frac{UX}{\nu}\right)^{-1/5}$$

$$\delta = 0.377\times2.5\times\left(\frac{3\times2.5}{9.5\times10^{-7}}\right)^{-1/5} = 0.039m.$$

Displacement thickness, $\delta = 0.039m = 39mm.$

$$\text{Drag, } D = \frac{7\times1000\times0.8\times3^3\times0.039\times2}{72} = 27.5\times2 = 55N.$$

Power, $P = Drag\times Velocity = 55\times3 = 165W.$

Drag of a Plate Moving in Water

Sketch the flow along a flat plate and any possible separation. Develop an equation for the growth of the turbulent boundary layer which is assumed to cover completely a flat plate moving lengthways with relative velocity U in a fluid of kinematic viscosity ν and density ρ. The velocity u, relative to the plate, at a distance y from the plate is given by: $u/U = (y/\delta)^{1/9}$, where δ is the boundary layer thickness. The local shear stress on the plate is given by: $\tau_o = 0.023\times\rho U^2\times(\nu/U\delta)^{1/5}$. Calculate the total drag on a plate, length $X = 2m$ and breadth $b = 0.4m$, moving in water with a velocity $U = 8m/s$. Assume zero pressure gradient along the plate.

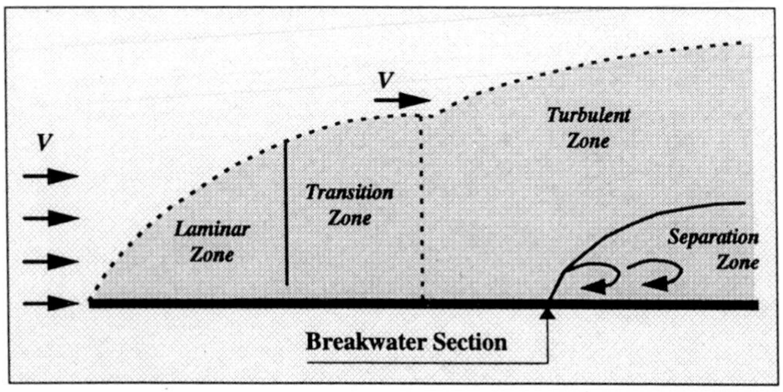

Drag per unit width of plate is:

$$\rho\times\int_0^\delta(U-u)\,u\,dy = \rho\times\int_0^\delta\left[U-U\left(\frac{y}{\delta}\right)^{1/9}\right]\times U\times\left(\frac{y}{\delta}\right)^{1/9}dy$$

$$= \rho U^2\delta\times\int_0^1\left[\left(\frac{y}{\delta}\right)^{1/9}-\left(\frac{y}{\delta}\right)^{2/9}\right]\times d\left(\frac{y}{\delta}\right)$$

$$= \rho U^2\delta\times\left[\frac{9}{10}\times\left(\frac{y}{\delta}\right)^{10/9}-\frac{9}{11}\times\left(\frac{y}{\delta}\right)^{11/9}\right]_0^1$$

Drag per unit width, $D = \frac{9}{110}\times\rho U^2\delta$

$$\frac{9}{110}\times\rho U^2\times\frac{d\delta}{dx} = \tau = 0.023\times\rho U^2\times\left(\frac{\upsilon}{U\delta}\right)^{1/5}$$

$$3.557\times\frac{d\delta}{\delta x} = \left(\frac{\upsilon}{U\delta}\right)^{1/5},\ \text{and}\ 3.557\times\delta^{1/5}\times d\delta = \left(\frac{\upsilon}{U}\right)^{1/5}dx$$

Integrating, $\frac{5}{6}\times3.557\ \delta^{6/5} = \left(\frac{\upsilon}{U}\right)^{1/5}\times x + const = 0$

$$\delta^{6/5} = 0.3373\times\left(\frac{\upsilon}{U}\right)^{1/5}\times x$$

$$\delta = 0.3373^{5/6}\times\left(\frac{\upsilon}{U}\right)^{1/6}\times x^{5/6} = 0.404\times R_x^{-1/6}\times x$$

$$\textbf{\textit{Drag,}}\ D = \frac{0.4\times9\times10^3\times64\times0.404\times2}{110}\times\left(\frac{9.5\times10^{-7}}{2\times8}\right)^{1/6}$$

$$= \frac{169.3}{10}\times\left(\frac{0.95}{16}\right)^{1/6} = 169.3\times0.0594^{1/6} = 10.57N$$

D = 10.57N.

The total drag for two sides of the plate $= 21.14N.$

Problems on Boundary Layer Theory

[1] The turbulent boundary layer at the rear end of a plate, 1.25m wide, 3m long, past which water flows at 2.5m/s is 125mm thick and the velocity distribution in it is of the form $u/U = (y/\delta)^{1/4}$. What is the drag on the plate and how far outwards has the main stream been displaced? (251N, 25mm)

[2] Water of kinematic viscosity $\nu = 0.93mm^2/s$ flows over a flat plate 3m long and 1m wide. The plate is assumed to be completely covered by a turbulent boundary layer with a thickness at the end of the plate of 49mm. The velocity distribution in the boundary layer is given by $u/U = (y/\delta)^{1/7}$ and the shear stress by $\tau_o = 0.023\times\rho U^2\times(\nu/U_\delta)^{1/4}$. Calculate the Reynolds Number at the end of the plate, the free stream velocity and total drag on one side of the plate, and the value of the displacement thickness.

(6.6×10^6, 2.05m/s, 20N, 6.13mm

[3] Laminar flow takes place between two horizontal parallel flat plates of lateral extent, separated by a distance t. Derive an expression for the velocity distribution between the parallel plates and show that the mean kinetic energy/mass is $0.772u^{-2}$ where u is the mean velocity of the flow.

Laminar Flow Between Parallel Plates

Flow Equations for Parallel Plates

If the flow is assumed to be one-dimensional as shown below, the velocity V varies at each boundary from zero to a maximum V_{max} in the centre. The velocity gradient and hence the shear stress τ is a maximum at the boundaries and zero at the centre.

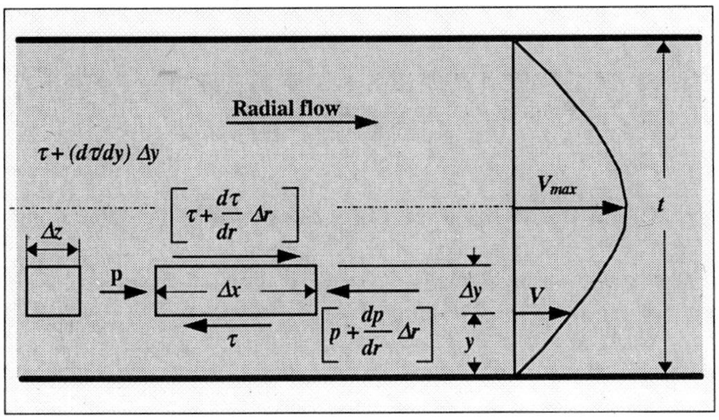

Fig.9.7- Flow between parallel plates.

By considering a small body of fluid, the forces can be equated in the direction of flow to give,

$$p \times \Delta y \Delta z - \left(p + \frac{dp}{dr} \Delta r \right) \times \Delta y \Delta z - \tau \Delta r \Delta z + \left(\tau + \frac{d\tau}{dy} \Delta y \right) \times \Delta x \Delta z$$

which reduces to

$$\frac{dp}{dr} = \frac{d\tau}{dy} \qquad (9.21)$$

This equation shows that in the absence of inertia forces, the pressure variation between parallel plates is equal to the variation of shear in the direction perpendicular to the flow.

Integrating with respect to y, $\tau = \frac{dp}{dr} \times (y + C_1)$.

When $y = t/2$, $\tau = 0$, $C_1 = -t/2$, $\tau = -\frac{dp}{dx} \left(\frac{t}{2} - y \right)$.

But, $\tau = \mu \frac{dV}{dy}$, and thus $\mu \frac{dV}{dy} = -\frac{dp}{dx} \times \left(\frac{t}{2} - y \right)$.

Integrating, $V = -\frac{1}{2\mu} \times \frac{dp}{dx} \times (ty - y^2) + C_2$.

When $y = 0$, $V = 0$, $C_2 = 0$, $V = -\frac{1}{2\mu} \times \frac{dp}{dx} \times (ty - y^2)$.

This is the velocity distribution equation and it is parabolic. The maximum velocity is at the centre at $y = t/2$.

Maximum velocity, $V_{max} = -\frac{t^2}{8\mu} \times \frac{dp}{dx}$ (9.22)

For a parabola, the mean velocity is $2/3$ of the maximum value,

Mean velocity, $V = -\frac{2}{3} \times V_{max} = -\frac{t^2}{12\mu} \times \frac{dp}{dx}$ (9.23)

Pressure gradient, $\frac{dp}{dx} = -\frac{12\mu V}{t^2}$ (9.24)

which shows that when t and μ are constant, the pressure gradient remains constant along the direction of flow.

If the plates are inclined, gravity forces affect the pressure gradient dp/dx. This can be accounted for by replacing dp/dx with the gradient of piezometric head,

$$\frac{dh}{dx} = \frac{dz}{dx} + \left(\frac{1}{\rho g} \times \frac{dp}{dx} \right) \qquad (9.25)$$

in which the x-direction is taken parallel to the plates and the z-direction is vertically upwards.

Radial Flow Between Circular Plates

Consider the radial outward flow between two parallel circular plates, Fig.9.8.

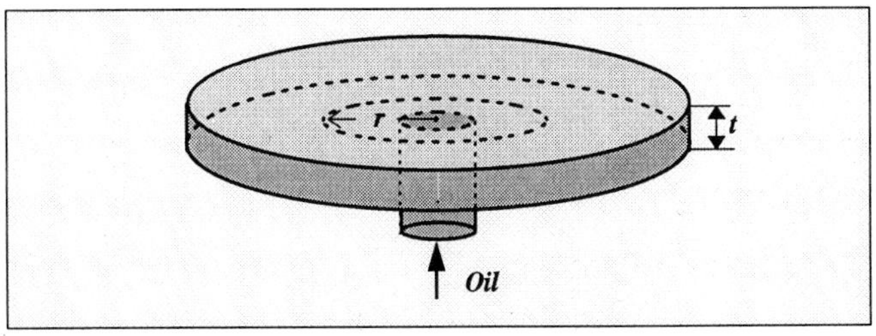

Fig.9.8- Radial flow between circular plates.

At any radius r, $dQ = 2\pi r \times V dy$.

$$Q = \frac{2\pi}{2\mu} \times \int_0^t -\frac{dp}{dr} \times (ty - y^2)\, dy = -\frac{dp}{dr} \times \frac{\pi}{\mu} \times \left[\frac{t\,y^2}{2} - \frac{y^3}{3} \right]_0^t$$

$Q = -\frac{dp}{dr} \times \frac{\pi r t^3}{6\mu}$. Therefore, $-\frac{dp}{dr} = -\frac{6\mu Q}{\pi t^3} \times \frac{1}{r}$, and

$$\int_{p_1}^{p_2} dp = \frac{6\mu Q}{\pi t^3} \times \int_{r_1}^{r_2} \frac{1}{r} dr .$$

$$\therefore\ (p_1 - p_2) = \frac{6\mu Q}{\pi t^3} \times \log_e \left(\frac{r_2}{r_1} \right) \qquad (9.26)$$

The discharge, $Q = \frac{\pi t^3 \times (p_1 - p_2)}{6\mu \times \log_e (r_2 / r_1)}$ (9.27)

Flow Between Circular Plates

Two horizontal circular flat plates, with centres on the same vertical line, are each 100mm diameter and separated by an oil film 0.5mm thick. The oil is supplied at a pressure of 200kN/m^2 through a pipe 10mm diameter placed centrally in the lower plate from where it flows radially outwards and discharges into the atmosphere at the periphery. The dynamic viscosity of the oil is 0.3Ns/m^2. Determine the volume flow rate. Neglect end effects.

The discharge, $Q = \dfrac{\pi t^3 \times (p_1 - p_2)}{6\mu \times \log_e (r_2 / r_1)}$

$$Q = 3.14 \times \left(\frac{0.5}{1000}\right)^3 \times \frac{200 \times 10^3}{6 \times 0.3} \times \frac{1}{2.305 \times \log_{10}(100/10)}$$

Flow rate, $Q = 1.89 \times 10^{-5}$ m^3/s.

Piston Moving in a Concentric Dashpot

Establish a relationship between volume flow rate and pressure gradient for the laminar flow of a fluid between two parallel stationary plates and use it to find an expression for the velocity of a piston moving in a concentric dashpot when a force is applied to the piston. A dashpot consists of a piston, 100mm in diameter and 50mm long, which moves axially in a cylinder with a uniform radial clearance of 0.75mm. The cylinder contains glycerine of viscosity 1.2Ns/m^2. Calculate the time taken for the piston to move a distance of 50mm under a force of 400N.

A dashpot is a device for damping out vibration; it consists of a piston attached to the part to be damped, fitting loosely in a cylinder of oil. Vibrational energy is absorbed in fluid friction. The flow of oil between the piston and the cylinder is similar to the flow between parallel surfaces.

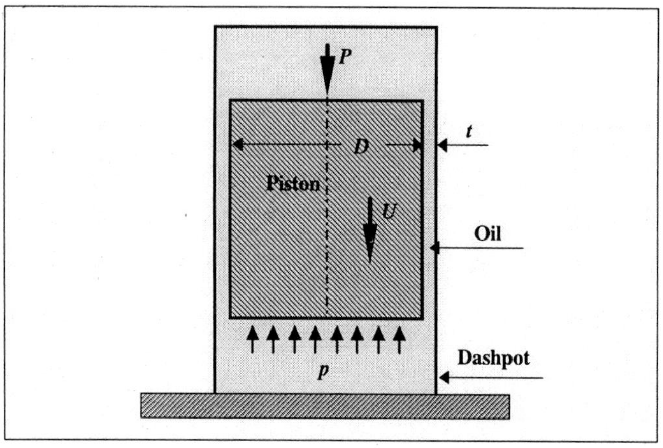

Fig.9.9- A piston moves in an oil dashpot.

Mean velocity, $V = \dfrac{2}{3} \times V_{max} = \dfrac{t^2}{12\mu} \times \dfrac{dp}{dx}$. Therefore,

Pressure gradient, $-\dfrac{dp}{dx} = \dfrac{12\mu V}{t^2} = \dfrac{12\mu Q}{\pi t^3 D}$

For the dashpot, the drop in pressure is due to the force P on the piston.

Pressure $= \dfrac{P}{\pi D^2/4}$. Therefore,

$$\frac{P}{\pi D^2/4} = \frac{12\mu Vl}{t^2}$$

Hence, $V = \dfrac{Pt^2}{3\pi \mu D^2 l}$.

This is the upward velocity of the oil through the clearance space. If U is the downstream velocity of piston, then by continuity principle,

$$U \times \frac{\pi D^2}{4} = V \times \pi Dt = \frac{Pt^2}{3\pi \mu D^2 l} \times \pi Dt$$

$$U = \frac{4Pt^3}{3\pi \mu D^3 l} = \frac{4 \times 400 \times \left(\frac{0.75}{1000}\right)^3 \times 1000}{3 \times 1.2 \times 3.14 \times \left(\frac{100}{1000}\right)^3 \times 50} = 1.19 mm/s.$$

Time $= \dfrac{x}{U} = \dfrac{50}{1.19} = 42s$.

Problems on Lubrication

[1] Two plane surfaces, one being fixed and the other moving with velocity V, are separated by a convergent film of lubricant drawn between them by the moving surface. Assuming two-dimensional viscous flow and the oil filament is very thin, show that the rate of change of pressure in the film in the direction of flow is:

$$\frac{dp}{dx} = \frac{6\mu V}{h^3} \times (h - h_o)$$

where h is the film thickness at the point considered, h_o is the thickness where the pressure p has maximum value and μ is the viscosity of the lubricant. If L is the length of the fixed surface, also show that the tractive force per unit transverse width required to maintain the steady motion of the moving surface is: Force $= \int_o^L \left(\dfrac{dp}{dx} \times \dfrac{h}{2} + \dfrac{\mu V}{h}\right) dx$

[2] A piston 75mm diameter and 100mm long moves vertically in an oil dashpot, the uniform clearance between the piston and dashpot wall being 1.2mm. Under its own weight the piston falls with uniform speed through 25mm in 50 seconds. With an extra weight of 1.33N on top of the piston it falls through 25mm with uniform speed in 43 seconds. Find the value of the coefficient of viscosity of the oil. (2.75 Ns/m^2)

[3] The thrust at the lower end of a vertical shaft is taken by a flat disc 100mm diameter, separated from a flat housing by an oil film 0.25mm thick. The dynamic viscosity of the oil is 1.3Ns/m^2. If the shaft rotates at 1000 rev/min, calculate the power absorbed by fluid friction. (58.9W)

CHAPTER TEN

TURBULENT FLOW IN PIPES

Introduction

An engineer tackling the design of a conduit for carrying fluid, whether a hydro-electric tunnel, a water-main, an oil pipeline, a sewer or an irrigation channel, is faced with the choice of a formula on which to base the calculations. Most formulae have been based on a range of data and extrapolation beyond those limits may lead to appreciable error. They generally contain empirical factors which are intended to take account of the various classes of construction, and these coefficients have to be assigned values based on experience. The purpose of this chapter is to present the advances in knowledge, by methods of calculation based on the theory of turbulence.

Establishment of Flow

As fluid enters the pipe the fluid at the boundaries is at rest and a large velocity gradient develops near the walls. At low Reynolds number $(R < 2000)$ the flow in a pipe leading from a reservoir, Fig.10.1a, is laminar and the boundary layer which develops at the inlet length of the pipe is illustrated in Fig.10.1b.

At the inlet of the pipe, the boundary layer develops along the curved entrance in much the same manner as it does for a plane boundary. At the inlet section of the horizontal pipe, the velocity distribution is essentially constant from wall to wall, gradually expanding until the layers from opposite sides meet at the centre approximately at the section:

$$x/D = 0.07 \times (UD/\nu) = 0.07 \times R \qquad (10.1)$$

Only from this section on is the flow truly uniform, having the parabolic velocity curve of established laminar flow. When the Reynolds number is sufficiently high, however, the laminar flow in the boundary layer will be unstable before this section is reached (Fig.10.1c). Under such conditions the ultimately uniform flow will be turbulent beyond

$$x / D = 0.07 \times \sqrt[4]{R} \qquad (10.2)$$

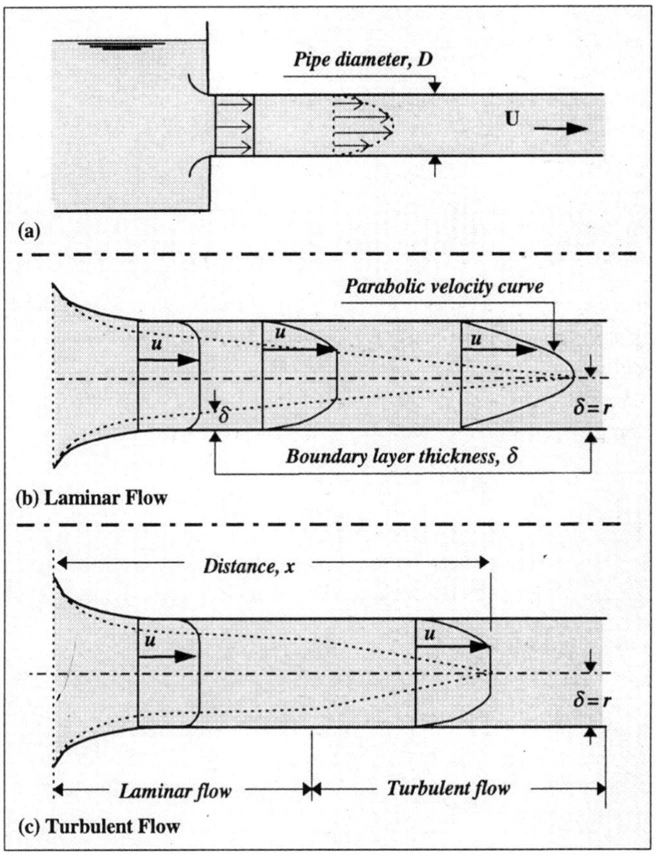

Fig.10.1- Boundary layer development in a circular pipe.

Velocity Variation

For the laminar flow near a plane boundary, it was found that an expression for the velocity distribution could be obtained by integration of Newton's formula for the shear stress in the form

$$du/dy = \tau/\mu \qquad (10.3)$$

From the parallel relationship for turbulent flow,

$$du/dy = \tau/\varepsilon \qquad (10.4)$$

one might therefore seek to obtain a corresponding relationship for the velocity distribution in the case of turbulence. During the integration however, the molecular viscosity μ could be considered constant for a given state of flow, while the eddy viscosity is known to vary with distance from the boundary. The variation of τ and ε together is such that the turbulent counter part of the laminar velocity gradient can, with good approximation, be written simply:

$$\frac{du}{dy} \times \frac{\tau}{\varepsilon} = \frac{\sqrt{\tau_o/\rho}}{K} \times \frac{1}{y} \qquad (10.5)$$

Herein ρ is the fluid density and K is known as the Karman "universal" constant which has been found experimentally to be 0.4. Integration of this expression leads to the general logarithmic distribution function,

$$u = 2.5\times\sqrt{\frac{\tau_o}{\rho}}\times\log_e(y)+C \qquad (10.6)$$

which states that in turbulent flow the velocity varies directly with the logarithm of the distance from the boundary, Fig.10.2.

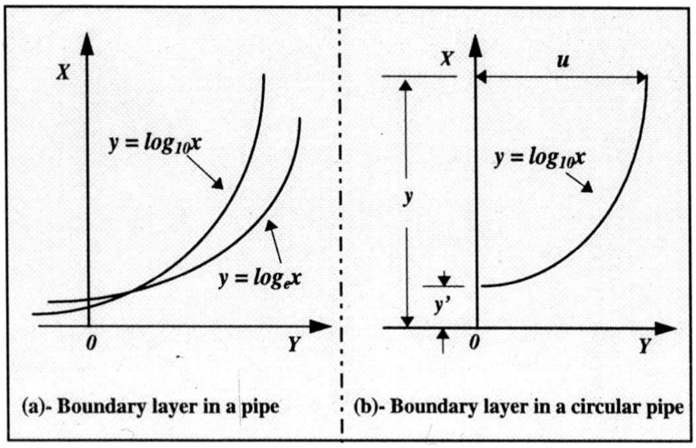

Fig.10.2- Development of the boundary layer in a pipe.

With reference to Figure 10.2 it will be seen that the constant of integration may be evaluated from the condition that $y = y'$ when $u = 0$. Hence,

$$C = -2.5\times\sqrt{\frac{\tau_o}{\rho}}\times\log_e(y') \qquad (10.7)$$

Introducing this value and dividing by τ_o/ρ the ratio of the local velocity of flow to the shear velocity will be found to depend only upon the ratio y/y'.

$$\frac{u}{\sqrt{\tau_o/\rho}} = 2.5\times\log_e\left(\frac{y}{y'}\right) = 5.75\times\log_{10}\left(\frac{y}{y'}\right) \qquad (10.8)$$

where, $V_* = \sqrt{\tau_o/\rho}$ is the shear velocity.

Derivation of Karman-Prandtl Velocity Equation

At first glance, the inherent tendency of the logarithmic curve to indicate a zero velocity from the boundary would appear to be in disagreement with physical fact. It must be realised, however, that the flow in the immediate vicinity of a smooth boundary is invariably laminar.

Inspection of Fig.10.3 will show however, that this zone of laminar motion must extend well beyond the distance y'; if a smooth transition is to exist between the velocity curves for the laminar and turbulent zones. Indeed, if one arbitrarily selects the intersection of the parabolic and the logarithmic curves as the nominal borderline, $y = \delta'$ between the two types of motion *(δ' representing the thickness of the laminar sublayer)* the parameters y' and δ' may reasonably be expected to be interdependent.

Since the distance $y = \delta'$ marks that stability limit of the laminar sublayer, it should, according to the stability theory be represented by a constant magnitude of the stability parameter,

$$\varepsilon = \frac{y^2}{\nu}\times\frac{du}{dy} \qquad (10.9)$$

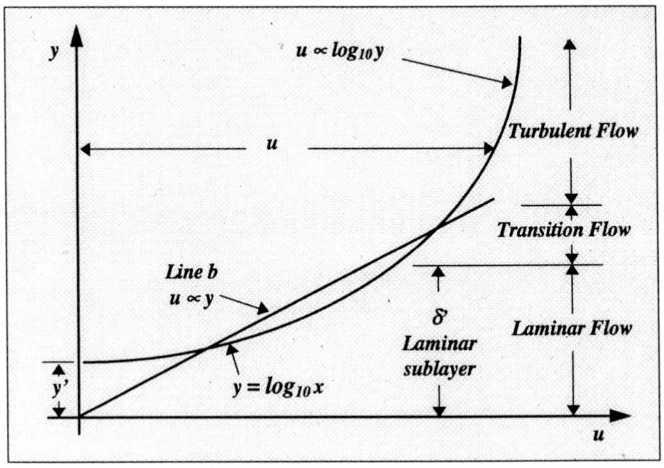

Fig.10.3- Velocity distribution near a smooth boundary.

Replacing, for simplicity, the parabolic segment as in Fig.10.2b by the straight line *b,* which it very closely approximates in this zone, equation 10.3 takes the form,

$$\frac{du}{dy} = \frac{\tau_o}{\mu} \qquad (10.10)$$

$$\varepsilon = \frac{y^2}{\nu}\times\frac{du}{dy} = \frac{(\delta')^2\times\tau_o}{\nu\mu} = C \text{ , or} \qquad (10.11)$$

$$\delta' = \frac{\sqrt{\varepsilon}\times\nu}{\sqrt{\tau_o/\rho}} = c'\,y' \qquad (10.12)$$

That this hypothesis is correct has been demonstrated by various experimental studies, in particular those of Prandtl's student Nikuradse on closed conduits. The latter yield, for the constants C and c', the values 135 and 107 where upon

$$\delta' = \frac{11.6\nu}{\sqrt{\tau_o/\rho}} \qquad (10.13)$$

$$y' = \frac{\delta'}{107} = \frac{0.108\nu}{\sqrt{\tau_o/\rho}} = \frac{1.11\nu}{V_*} \qquad (10.14)$$

Introduction of the latter expression for y' then results in what is known as the Karman-Prandtl equation for the velocity distribution in turbulent flow near smooth boundaries,

$$\frac{u}{\sqrt{\tau_o/\rho}} = \frac{u}{V_*} = 5.75\times\log_{10}\left(\frac{\sqrt{\tau_o/\rho}\times y}{\nu}\right)+5.5 \qquad (10.15)$$

while in the laminar sublayer

$$\frac{u}{\sqrt{\tau_o/\rho}} = \frac{u}{V_*} = \frac{\sqrt{\tau_o/\rho}\times y}{\nu} \qquad (10.16)$$

These equations are plotted in Fig.10.3 the semi-logarithmic form being used to show the nature of the equation and to give comparable emphasis to all zones of flow.

The experimental data of Nikuradse, which include measurements from the boundary layer to the centreline of a series of circular pipes at various Reynolds numbers are seen to follow closely the trend of the two equations. In the case of boundary roughness (Fig.10.4) it is to be presumed that a laminar sublayer will exist at the boundary if the roughness magnitude k is actually greater than the value of δ'. On the other hand one might expect the parameter y' to be directly proportional to *k.* As a matter of fact, experiments by Nikuradse and others, using pipes artificially roughened by cemented coatings of sand grains of diameter *k,* indicate that if $k > 10\delta'$, then $y' = k/30$.

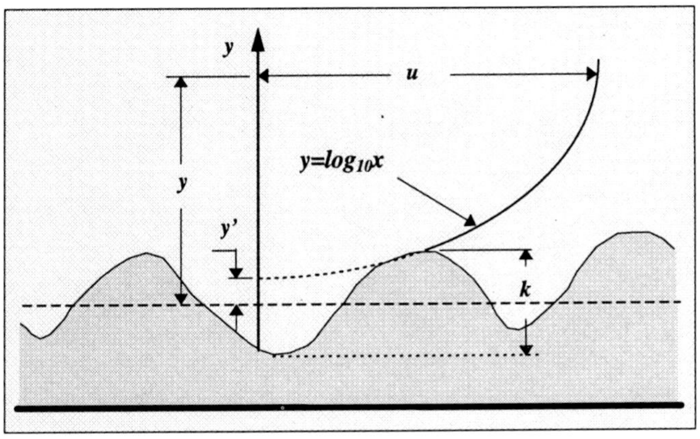

Fig.10.4- Definition sketch for evaluating the relative magnitude of boundary roughness.

Introduction of this value in equation (10.14) then leads to the following counterpart of equation (10.15) - the Karman-Prandtl equation for the velocity distribution in turbulent flow near rough boundaries.

$$\frac{u}{\sqrt{\tau_o/\rho}} = 5.75\ \log_{10}\left(\frac{y}{k}\right) + 8.5 \qquad (10.17)$$

which is plotted in Fig.10.5 together with Nikuradse's test data. It is again to be noted that the experimental points represent many series of measurements extending from very near the boundary to the centreline of the pipe.

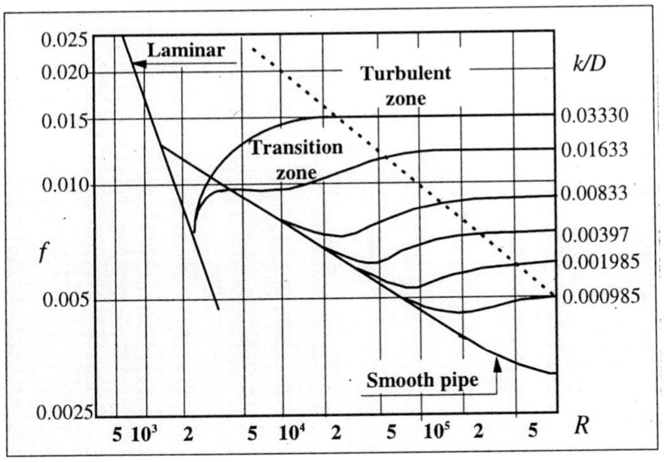

Fig.10.5- Variation of f with R for artificially roughned pipes.

The Mean Velocity

Although the logarithmic curve has an infinite slope at the limit $y = 0$ and continues to have a finite slope for all values of y, however great, such lack of agreement with actual conditions both at the boundary and very far away will introduce relatively little error when equations are integrated across a normal section to determine the corresponding rate of flow. Thus, from the equation of a circular tube

$$Q = \int_0^{r_o} 2\pi rudr = 2\pi \times V_* \int_0^{r_o}\left(5.5r + 2.5r \times \log_{10}\left(\frac{V_*}{\nu}\right)(r_o - r)\right)dr$$

Integrating by parts one finally has:

$$Q = \pi\ r_o V_* \left(5.75 \times \log_{10}\left(\frac{V_*}{\nu} r_o\right) + 1.75\right) \qquad (10.18)$$

Since $Q = \pi r_o U$ then the above equation becomes

$$\frac{U}{V_*} = 5.75 \times \log_{10}\left(\frac{V_*}{\nu} \times r_o\right) + 1.75 \qquad (10.19)$$

A similar procedure for the case of rough pipes will be found to yield the relationship

$$\frac{U}{V_*} = 5.75 \times \log_{10}\left(\frac{V_o}{k}\right) + 4.75 \qquad (10.20)$$

If, now one equation is subtracted from the other equation there will result identical expression have the form

$$\frac{u - U}{V_*} = 5.75\ \times \log_{10}\left(\frac{y}{r_o}\right) + 3.75 \qquad (10.21)$$

In other words, when referred to the mean velocity the Karman-Prandtl expressions for the velocity distribution near smooth and rough boundaries become identical.

Darcy-Weisbach Resistance Coefficient

For steady flow in a horizontal pipe the boundary shear is necessarily in equilibrium with the force due to the pressure gradient, i.e.,

$$\tau_o \times \pi D \times L = (p_1 - p_2) \times \frac{\pi D^2}{4}, \text{ or } \tau_o = (p_1 - p_2) \times \frac{D}{4L}.$$

Division of both sides of this equation by $1/2\rho\ U^2$, results in

$$\frac{\tau_o}{0.5 \times \rho U^2} = \left(\frac{p_1 - p_2}{L}\right) \times \frac{D}{2\rho U^2} \qquad (10.22)$$

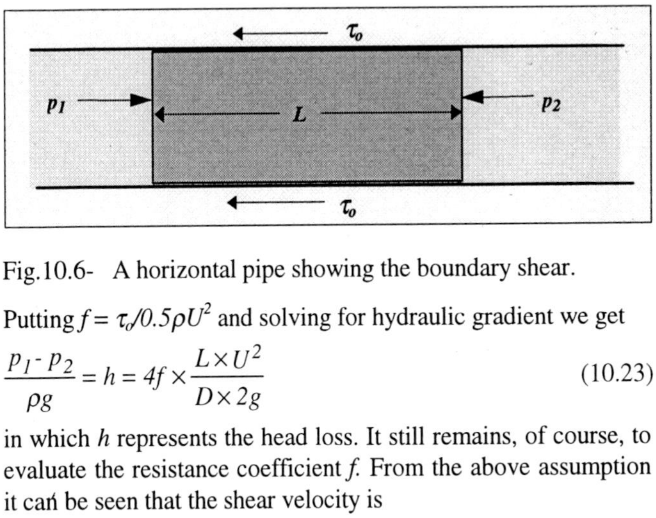

Fig.10.6- A horizontal pipe showing the boundary shear.

Putting $f = \tau_o/0.5\rho U^2$ and solving for hydraulic gradient we get

$$\frac{p_1 - p_2}{\rho g} = h = 4f \times \frac{L \times U^2}{D \times 2g} \qquad (10.23)$$

in which h represents the head loss. It still remains, of course, to evaluate the resistance coefficient f. From the above assumption it can be seen that the shear velocity is

$$V_* = \sqrt{\tau_o/\rho} = U \times \sqrt{4f/8} \qquad (10.24)$$

$$\frac{U}{U\sqrt{4f}} = \frac{1}{\sqrt{8}}\left(5.75\ \times \log_{10}\left(\frac{U\sqrt{4f} \times r_o}{\nu}\right) + 1.75\right), \text{ whence}$$

$$\frac{1}{\sqrt{4f}} = 2.03 \times \log_{10}\left(\frac{U \times D}{\nu} \times \sqrt{4f}\right) - 0.91 \qquad (10.25)$$

with a slight modification of numerical factors to confirm with experimental measurements, this then becomes the resistance equation for turbulent flow through smooth pipes.

$$1/\sqrt{4f} = 2 \times \log_{10} R\sqrt{4f} - 0.8, \text{ or}$$

$$1/\sqrt{f} = 4 \times \log_{10}\left(R\sqrt{4f}\right) - 1.6 \qquad (10.26)$$

An expression for the resistance coefficient of rough pipes may be obtained through the elimination of the shear velocity. Thus

$$\frac{U}{U\sqrt{4f}} = \frac{1}{\sqrt{8}} \times \left[5.75 \times \log_{10}\left(\frac{r_o}{k}\right) + 4.75\right]$$

$$1/\sqrt{4f} = 2.03 \times \log_{10}\left(\frac{r_o}{k}\right) + 1.68 \qquad (10.27)$$

With a slight modification of numerical values, this relationship will be found to indicate the limiting magnitude of the friction factor f for each of the roughness curves of Fig.10.5. The resistance equation for turbulent in rough pipes becomes,

$$1/\sqrt{4f} = 2\times\log_{10}(r_o/k)+1.74 \qquad (10.28)$$

$$1/\sqrt{f} = 4\times\log_{10}(r_o/k)+3.48 \qquad (10.29)$$

The above equation is plotted on Fig.10.5. together with Nikuradse's results of experiments on artificially roughened pipes. It is seen that the agreement between theory and experiments is satisfactory. It must be pointed out that some variation in the transition function from smooth to rough must be expected with other pipe roughness types. This was demonstrated by Colebrooke and White using non-uniform grain mixtures of mean diameter k and after investigating the transition curves for various commercial pipes they proposed the general transition formula:

$$\frac{1}{\sqrt{4f}} = -2\times\log_{10}\left(\frac{k}{7.4\times r_o}+\frac{2.51}{R\sqrt{4f}}\right) \qquad (10.30)$$

$$\frac{1}{\sqrt{f}} = -4\times\log_{10}\left(\frac{k}{7.4\times r_o}+\frac{2.51}{R\sqrt{4f}}\right) \qquad (10.31)$$

This equation is inconvenient to solve algebraically and a solution is considerably expedited by plotting the friction factor as a function R, with relative roughness k/D as parameters, yielding a family of curves rather than a single curve. These curves are shown in Fig.10.7.

Ageing of Pipes

The capacity of a pipe may deteriorate in time because of:

(a) an accumulation of deposits, especially at low places

(b) erosion generally (due to turbulence) and scour at bends

(c) surface roughness owing to decomposition of the concrete through the acidic action of water, and

(d) an accumulation of slime and interior growths of spongilla.

By suitable design of the intake works and avoidance of sudden changes in direction causing cavitation, it is possible to reduce the accumulation of deposits and also reduce to a minimum.

For water in steel pipes, the increase in roughness is approximately linear, so that the following equation applies $k = k_o + \alpha t$, in which k is the roughness at age t, k_o the initial roughness, t the time pipe has been in use in years, and α a coefficient to be determined by *experiment (typically from 0.002 to 0.007).*

An empirical expression depending on the pH (the hydrogen - ion concentration in water) value of the water carried has been derived:

$$\log_{10}(12\alpha) = 0.5\times(3.8+pH) \qquad (10.32)$$

It has been observed that α also depends on the velocity of flow; the higher the velocity the less is the growth.

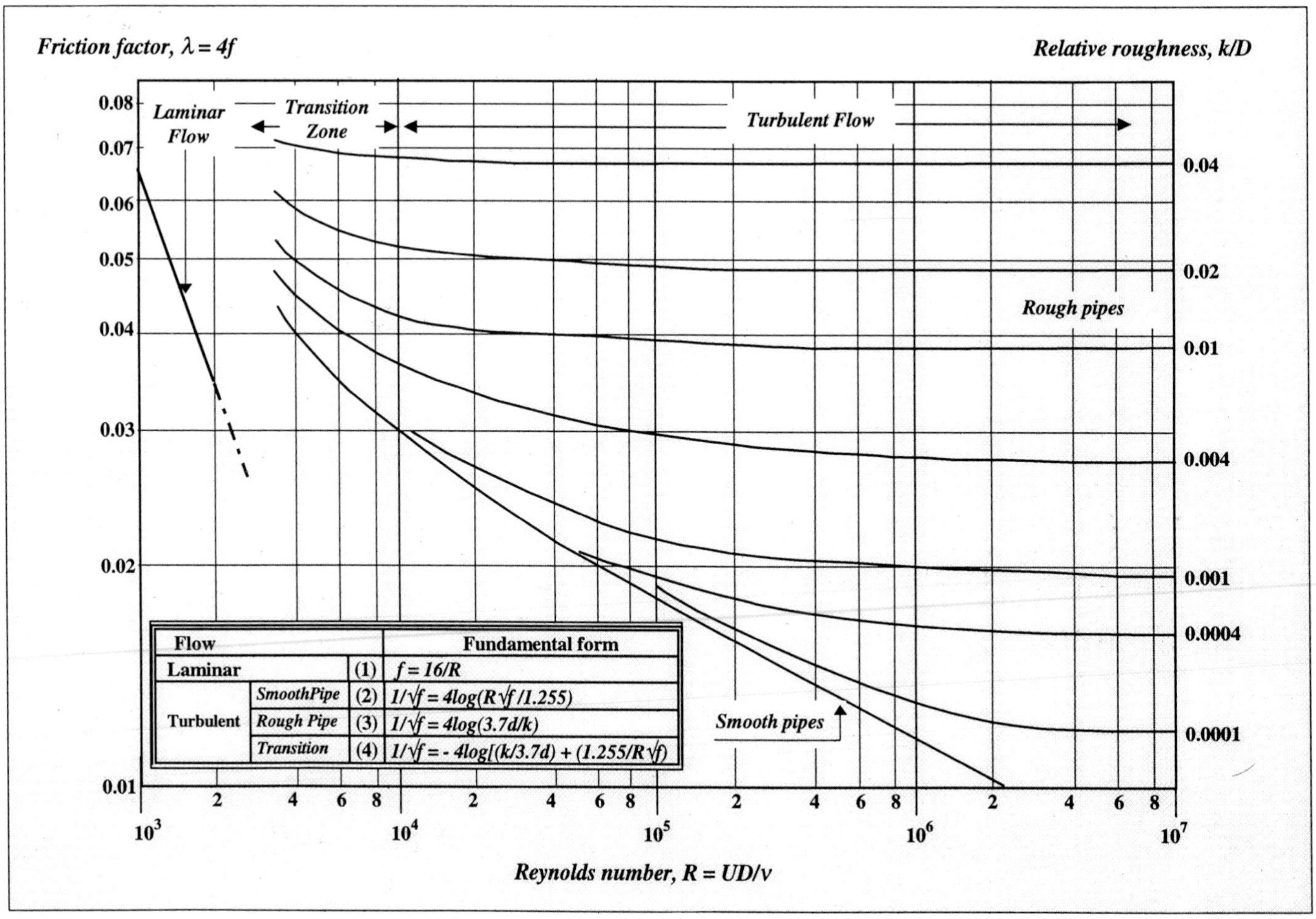

Fig.10.7- Relationship of friction factor f with Reynolds number R with relative roughness as a parameter for flow in pipes.

Examples on Pipe Lines

Pumped Storage Tank

Petrol, specific gravity 0.82 and kinematic viscosity 2.3 mm^2/s, is to be pumped through 250m of galvanised steel pipe at 90 litre/s into a storage tank. The pressure at the inlet end of the pipe is 345 kN/m^2 and the liquid level in the storage tank is 40m above that of the pump. Neglecting losses other than pipe friction determine the size of the pipe necessary.

Pressure $= \rho g \; Head$

$$\textbf{Head at pump} = \frac{345\times 10^3}{0.82\times 10^3 \times 9.81} = 42.88m.$$

Head loss limited to $42.888 - 40 = 2.88m = 4flV^2/2gd$

$$2.88 = 4\times f\times 250\times\left(\frac{0.09}{\pi d^2/4}\right)^2 \Big/ 2gd$$

$$d^5 = 0.2317\times f, \quad \frac{k}{d} = \frac{0.00015}{d}, \quad V = \frac{0.09}{\pi d^2/4}, \quad R = \frac{Vd}{\nu}.$$

Guess	d	V (m/s)	R	k/d
f = 0.004	0.247	1.872	201060	0.0006
f = 0.0045	0.253	1.786	196452	0.00059
f =0.005	0.259	1.713	192926.2	0.000579

Flow in a Pipe

For rough pipes the friction coefficient, f, is given by

$1/\sqrt{4f} = 2\log_{10}(d/2k) + 1.74$

Water flows through a pipe 0.75m diameter, 1200m long and with roughness size k = 0.24mm. The pressure head lost in friction in the full length of the pipe is 36m of water. Calculate the rate of discharge.

$$\frac{1}{\sqrt{4f}} = 2\log_{10}\left(\frac{0.75}{2\times 0.24\times 10^{-3}}\right) + 1.74,$$

$f = 0.00378, \; h_f = 4flV^2/2gd.$

$$36 = \frac{4\times 0.00378\times 1200\times V^2}{2\times 9.81\times 0.75}, \quad \therefore V = 5.4 \; m/s.$$

$$q = VA = 5.4\times(\pi/4)\times 0.75^2 = 2.385 \; m^3/s.$$

Pipeline Between Two Reservoirs

Two reservoirs containing water are connected by a concrete pipe which is 300mm diameter and 4km long. The dynamic viscosity of water is 1.12×10^{-3} Ns/m^2 and for concrete pipes the roughness k = 0.3mm. The flow rate through the pipe between the reservoirs is measured 0.1m^3/s. Calculate their difference in surface levels using the Moody diagram. A second concrete pipe 500mm diameter is laid parallel to the first pipe. Estimate the new total flow rate between the reservoirs.

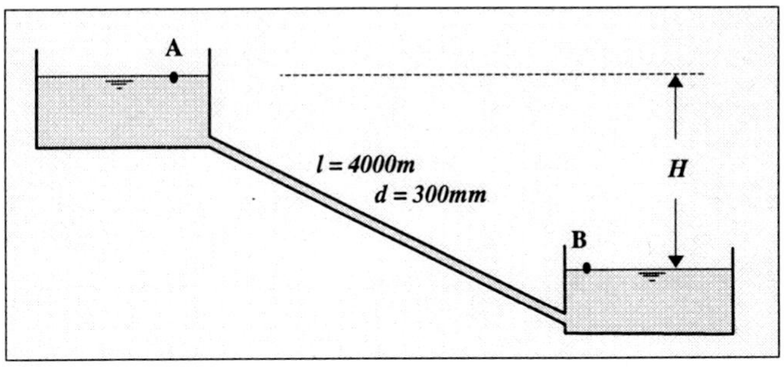

Apply total head between A and B:

$$\frac{p_A}{\rho g} + \frac{V_A^2}{2g} + Z_A = \frac{p_B}{\rho g}\times\frac{V_B^2}{2g} + Z_B + losses.$$

But $p_A = p_B = atmospheric \; pressure, \qquad V_A = V_B = 0.$

$$\therefore Z_A - Z_B = H = losses = \frac{4fl\times V^2}{2gd}$$

$$\textbf{Velocity, } V = \frac{0.1}{\pi/4\times 0.3^2} = 1.415 \; m/s.$$

$$\textbf{Reynolds number: } R = \frac{\rho Vd}{\mu} = \frac{1000\times 1.415\times 0.3}{1.12\times 10^{-3}} = 379{,}000.$$

$$\textbf{Roughness ratio, } \frac{k}{d} = \frac{0.3}{300} = 0.001.$$

From Moody diagram (Fig.10.7), $f = 0.0051$.

$$\text{Substituting, } H = \frac{4\times 0.0051\times 4000\times 1.415^2}{2\times 9.81\times 0.3} = 27.76m.$$

Difference in level, $H = 27.76m.$

$$\textbf{For 500mm pipe: } 27.76 = \frac{4\times f\times 4000\times V^2}{2\times 9.81\times 0.5}$$

$27.76 = 1631\times f\times V^2 \qquad \therefore V = 0.13/\sqrt{f}$

$$R = \frac{1000\times V\times 0.5}{1.12\times 10^{-3}} = 446{,}000\times V, \quad \frac{k}{d} = \frac{0.3}{500} = 0.0006.$$

Guess $f = 0.0045.$

$\therefore V = 0.13/\sqrt{0.0045} = 1.938 m/s.$

$R = 446{,}000\times 1.938 = 864348.$

From Moody diagram for three values of $R_e \propto k/d$, $f = 0.0044$ is approximately correct guess.

$\therefore Q = 1.938\times(\pi/4)\times 0.5^2 = 0.38 m^3/s.,$

Total flow, $Q_T = 0.38 + 0.01 = 0.48 m^3/s.$

Channel Discharge

The mean velocity in rectangular channel can be expressed by:

$$u_m = 5.75 \times \sqrt{\frac{\tau}{\rho}} \times \log_{10}\left(\frac{13.2d}{k}\right),$$

where τ is the mean shear stress, d the depth of flow and k the mean roughness size. Show that this is reasonably compatible with the relationship:

$$\frac{1}{\sqrt{4f}} = 2.03 \times \log_{10}\left(\frac{13.2d}{k}\right)$$

where f is the friction coefficient. Calculate the mean shear stress, Chezy's C, and the rate of discharge per metre width for a wide channel having 6mm roughness on a long slope of 1 in 800 when the uniform depth of flow 0.6m.

Since, $f = \dfrac{\tau}{0.5 \times \rho \times u_m^2}$ and $\sqrt{\dfrac{\tau}{\rho}} = u_m \sqrt{\dfrac{4f}{8}}$.

Substituting, $\dfrac{u_m}{u_m \cdot \sqrt{4f}} = \dfrac{5.75}{\sqrt{8}} \times \log_{10}\left(\dfrac{13.2d}{k}\right)$, or

$$\frac{1}{\sqrt{4f}} = 2.03 \times \log_{10}\left(\frac{13.2d}{k}\right)$$

From Darcy's formula, $i = \dfrac{f\,u_m^2}{2gy}$. $\therefore\ u_m^2 = \dfrac{2gyi}{f}$

From Chezy's formula, $u_m^2 = C^2\,yi$

Equating expressions for $u_m{}^2$ and simplifying, $C = \sqrt{2g/f}$.

The unit discharge, $q = Cy\sqrt{yi}$,

$$q = 101.5 \times 0.6 \times \sqrt{\frac{0.6}{800}} = 1.66 m^3/s \text{ per metre.}$$

Flow Between Reservoirs

Two reservoirs whose surface levels differ by 50m are connected by a 20km long pipeline which has a roughness of 0.06mm. Calculate the diameter of pipe required to give a flow rate of $0.6m^3/s$ from the upper reservoir to the lower reservoir. Assume the kinematic viscosity of water is $1.1410^{-6}m^2/s$ and the Colebrook-White equation is:

$$\frac{1}{\sqrt{\lambda}} = -2\ \log\left(\frac{k}{3.7d} + \frac{2.51}{R_e\ \sqrt{\lambda}}\right),\quad \lambda = 4f\ .$$

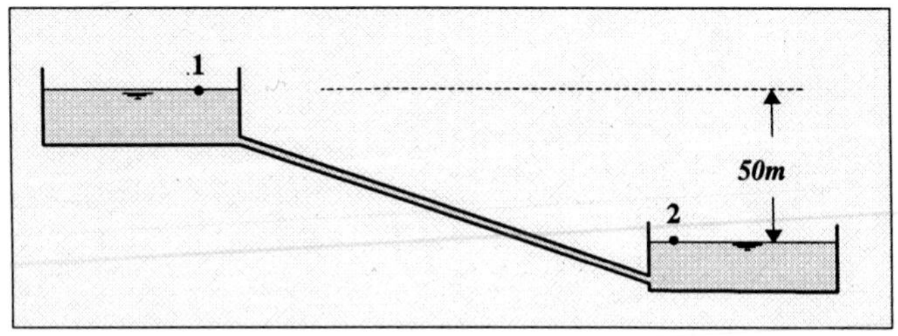

Apply Bernoulli between 1 and 2,

$$\frac{p_1}{\rho g} + \frac{V_1^2}{2g} + Z_1 = \frac{p_2}{\rho g} + \frac{V_2^2}{2g} + Z_2 + losses$$

$p_1 = p_2 =$ *atmospheric pressure,* $V_1^2/2g$ *and* $V_2^2/2g$ *negligible*

i.e. $Z_1 - Z_2 = losses.$

$$50 = \frac{\lambda l V^2}{2gd} = \frac{\lambda \times 20 \times 10^3 \times V^2}{2gd} = \frac{1019 \times \lambda\, V^2}{d}$$

Guess d = 1m. $\therefore\ V = \dfrac{0.6}{(\pi/4) \times 1^2} = 0.764 m/s.$

$$R = \frac{0.764 \times 1.0}{1.14 \times 10^{-6}} = 6.7 \times 10^5 .$$

$$\frac{1}{\sqrt{\lambda}} = -2\ \log_{10}\left(\frac{0.06 \times 10^{-3}}{3.7 \times 1} + \frac{2.51}{6.7\ \times 10^5 \times \sqrt{\lambda}}\right)$$

Try	$\lambda = 0.02$,	in LHS.	RHS gives $\lambda = 0.0130$.
Try	$\lambda = 0.013$,	in LHS.	RHS gives $\lambda = 0.0135$.
Try	$\lambda = 0.0135$,	in LHS.	RHS gives $\lambda = 0.0134$.

i.e., $\dfrac{1019 \times \lambda V^2}{d} = \dfrac{1019 \times 0.0134 \times 0.764^2}{1} = 7.97 \neq 50$

but $h_f \propto \dfrac{1}{d^5}$, *i.e.* $\dfrac{7.97}{50} \approx \dfrac{d^5}{1^5}$.

$$V = \frac{0.6}{(\pi/4) \times 0.692^2} = 1.6 m/s,$$

$$R = \frac{1.6 \times 0.692}{1.14 \times 10^{-6}} = 9.71 \times 10^5$$

$$\frac{1}{\sqrt{\lambda}} = -2 \log_{10}\left(\frac{0.06 \times 10^{-3}}{3.7 \times 1} + \frac{2.51}{9.71 \times 10^5 \times \sqrt{\lambda}}\right)$$

This gives, $\lambda = 0.0133$.

$$50 = \frac{1019 \times \lambda\, V^2}{d_{req}} = \frac{1019 \times 0.0133 \times 1.6^2}{0.692} = 50.13m.$$

Pipe diameter required = 0.692 say 0.7m.

Equation for Discharge

The logarithmic law for the flow in smooth pipes is given by:
$1/\sqrt{4f} = 2\log_{10}(R\sqrt{4f}) - 0.8$

where f = pipe friction factor and R = Reynolds number. Using this formula, and working from first principles show that for pipes of circular section, the rate of discharge can be written as:

$$Q = A\, d^{5/2} \times i^{1/2} \times \log_{10}\left(\frac{Bd^{3/2} \times i^{1/2}}{\nu}\right)$$

where i = slope of hydraulic gradient line, d is pipe diameter ν is the kinematic viscosity of the fluid and A and B are constants.

$$h_f = \frac{4\, flV^2}{2gd}.\quad 4f = \frac{2gd}{V^2} \times \frac{h_f}{l} = \frac{2gd}{V^2} \times i$$

For steady flow, $\left(\dfrac{h_f}{l} = i\right)$: $V = \sqrt{\dfrac{2gd}{4f} \times \dfrac{h_f}{l}} = \sqrt{\dfrac{2gd}{4f} \times i}$.

$$Q = a \times V = \frac{\pi}{4} \times d^2 \times \sqrt{2gdi} \times 2 \times \left[\log_{10}(R \times \sqrt{4f}) - 0.4\right]$$

$$= \frac{\pi}{4}\sqrt{2g} \times d^{5/2} \times 2 \times \left[\log_{10}\left(\frac{Vd}{\nu} \times \sqrt{\frac{2gdi}{V^2}}\right) - 0.4\right]$$

$$= \left(\frac{\pi\sqrt{2g} \times d^{5/2} \times i^{1/2}}{2}\right)\left[\log_{10}\left(\frac{d^{3/2} \times i^{1/2}}{\nu}\right)\sqrt{2g} - \log_{10} 2.51\right]$$

$$Q = \frac{\pi}{2}\sqrt{2g} \times d^{5/2} \times i^{1/2} \times \log_{10}\left(\frac{\sqrt{2g}}{2.51} \times \frac{d^{3/2} \times i^{1/2}}{\nu}\right)$$

$$= A \times d^{5/2} \times i^{1/2} \times \log_{10}\left(B \times \frac{d^{3/2} \times i^{1/2}}{\nu}\right).$$

where $A = \frac{\pi}{2} \times \sqrt{2g}$ and $B = \frac{\sqrt{2g}}{2.51}$ (which are constants).

Shear stress, $\tau_o = \frac{\rho \times V^2 \times f}{2} = 4.42\ N/m^2$.

Flow in a Rough Pipe

For the flow of water in a circular pipe, the friction factor f is related to the pipe dia. d and wall roughness size k under certain flow conditions by the equation:

$$\frac{1}{\sqrt{f}} = 4\log_{10}\left(\frac{d}{2k}\right) + 3.48.$$

Under such conditions show that the Chezy coefficient C is given by: $C = 18 \times \log_{10}(3.7d/k)$. It is sometimes found that the roughness elements of a pipe grow approximately linearly with time i.e., $k = k_o + \alpha t$, where k_o is the initial roughness of the pipe when first laid $(t = 0)$. Estimate the value of the constant α for a 900mm diameter pipe which when first laid conveyed $1m^3/s$ under a hydraulic gradient to $f = 0.0025$ but which after $t = 10$ years was found to convey only $0.875m^3/s$ under that gradient. A second 500mm diameter pipe of the same material is to be laid alongside the first and will operate under the same hydraulic gradient. Estimate the discharge in the 2nd pipe when first laid.

Head loss, $h_f = \frac{flV^2}{2gR}$, $V = \sqrt{\frac{2g}{f} \times R\,i}$

As for steady flow $h_f/l = i$ and the Chezy equation gives $V = C\sqrt{R\,i}$.

Comparing these:

$$C = \sqrt{\frac{2g}{f}} = \sqrt{2g} \times \left(4\log_{10}\frac{d}{2k} + 3.48\right)$$

$$= \sqrt{2g} \times 4\left(\log_{10}\frac{d}{2k} + 0.87\right) = 4\sqrt{2g}\left(\log_{10}\frac{d}{2k} + \log_{10}7.4\right)$$

$$= 4\sqrt{19.6} \times \log_{10}\left(\frac{7.4d}{2k}\right) \approx 18 \times \log_{10}\left(\frac{3.7d}{k}\right).$$

$$Q = AC\sqrt{Ri}.$$

$$Q_o = 0.637 \times 18 \times \log_{10}\left(\frac{3.7d}{k}\right) \times \sqrt{\frac{d}{4} \times 0.0025}$$

$$1.0 = 0.637 \times 18 \times \log_{10}\left(\frac{3.7 \times 0.9}{k_o}\right) \times \frac{0.05 \times \sqrt{0.9}}{2}$$

$$= 0.272 \times \log_{10}\left(\frac{3.3}{k_o}\right)$$

$$\log_{10}\left(\frac{3.3}{k_o}\right) = \frac{1.0}{0.272} = 3.68\ \therefore \frac{3.3}{k_o} = 4786 \text{ or } k_o = \frac{3.3}{4786}$$

Similarly, $\log_{10}\left(\frac{3.3}{k_1}\right) = \frac{0.875}{0.272} = 3.22\ .\ \therefore\ k_1 = \frac{3.3}{1659}$.

$k_o = k_1 + \alpha t$, or, $k_o = 3.3/4786 = (3.3/1659) + 10\alpha$. Hence,

$$\alpha = \frac{3.3}{10} \times \frac{4786 - 1659}{4786 \times 1659} = 0.13 \times 10^{-3}\ m/y = 0.13mm/year.$$

$k_o = 3.3/4786 = 0.691 \times 10^{-3}$.

For the 500mm of pipe:

$$Q = 0.196 \times 18\log_{10}\left(\frac{3.7 \times 0.5}{0.691 \times 10^{-3}}\right) \times \sqrt{\frac{0.5}{4} \times 0.0025}$$

$$= 0.196 \times 18\log_{10}(2680) \times \frac{0.05}{2} \times 0.707$$

Discharge, $Q = 0.196 \times 18 \times 3.428 \times 0.05 \times 0.353 = 0.213m^3/s$.

Flow in Two Parallel Pipes

Water flows through two pipes operating in parallel. Both are 1m in diameter and have a gradient of 1 percent. One pipe is smooth but the other has roughness elements of average size 4.5mm on its wall. Calculate the total flow through the pipes and the ratio of the flow, using the following formulae:

For smooth pipe, $\frac{1}{\sqrt{f}} = 4\log_{10}\left(\frac{R\sqrt{4f}}{2.5}\right)$

For rough pipe, $\frac{1}{\sqrt{f}} = 4\log_{10}\left(\frac{d}{2k}\right) + 3.48$

in which f is the friction factor, d the pipe diameter, and R the Reynolds number. Take the kinematic viscosity for water as $1mm^2/s$.

$\frac{h_f}{l} = i = \left(\frac{4fV^2}{2gd}\right)$, $V = \sqrt{\frac{2gdi}{4f}}$, $\sqrt{f} = \sqrt{\frac{2gdi}{V^2}}$, and $Q = Va$.

Smooth Pipe: $\frac{1}{\sqrt{f}} = 4\log_{10}\left(\frac{Vd}{\nu} \times \frac{1}{2.5}\sqrt{\frac{2gdi}{V^2}}\right)$

$$= 4\log_{10}\left(\frac{\sqrt{2g}}{2.5}\right) \times \frac{1}{\nu} \times d^{3/2} \times i^{1/2} \quad = 4 \times 5.25 = 21$$

$i = 1/100;\ 1/f = 21^2 = 441.\ \therefore\ f = 1/441 = 0.00227.$

$$V = \sqrt{\frac{2gd}{4 \times 0.00227} \times \frac{1}{100}} = \sqrt{21.6} = 4.65\ m/s.$$

$Q_S = V a = 4.65 \times 0.784 = 3.65m^3/s.$

Rough Pipe:

$$\frac{1}{\sqrt{f}} = 4\log_{10}\left(\frac{1000}{2 \times 4.5}\right) + 3.48 = 4\log_{10}(111.1) + 3.48$$

$= 4 \times 2.046 + 3.48 = 8.184 + 3.48 = 11.664.$

$1/f = 11.664^2 = 136\ ,\ \therefore\ f = 1/136 = 0.00735.$

$$V = \sqrt{\frac{2gd}{4 \times 0.00735} \times \frac{1}{100}} = \sqrt{6.67} = 2.58m/s.$$

$Q_R = V \times a = 2.58 \times 0.784 = 2.02\ m^3/s.$

$Q_{total} = 3.65 + 2.02 = 5.67m^3/s.$

Ratio of flow, $Q_S/Q_R = 3.65/2.02 = 1.65$.

Partial Flow in a Sewer

A circular sewer is required to convey $2260\ m^3/h$ when the depth of flow is one quarter of the diameter. The slope is 1:2000 and the average radius of the roughness projections on the side of the sewer is 0.1mm. Determine the diameter of the sewer to the nearest 10 mm.

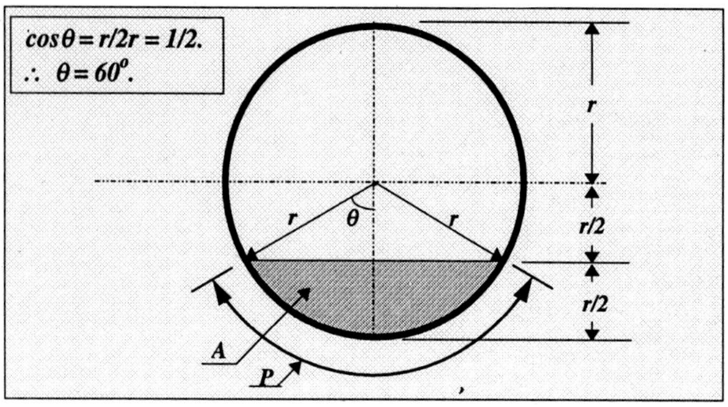

$$A = \frac{\pi r^2}{3} - \frac{r}{2} \times \sqrt{r^2 - \frac{r^2}{4}} = \frac{\pi r^2}{3} - \frac{r^2}{2} \times \sqrt{\frac{3}{4}} = 0.62 \times r^2$$

$$P = 2\pi r \times \frac{120}{360} = 0.67 \times 3.14 \times r = 2.1 \times r$$

$$R = \frac{A}{P} = \frac{0.62 \times r^2}{2.1 \times r} = 0.295 \times r$$

$$Q = \frac{2260}{3600} = AC\sqrt{RI} = 0.62 r^2 \times C\sqrt{\frac{0.295 \times r}{2000}} = 0.628 .$$

But $C = 18 \times \log_{10}(6R/a)$, where a = roughness radius.

$$C = 18 \times \log_{10}\left(\frac{6 \times 0.295\, r}{0.0001}\right) = 18 \times \log_{10}(17700 \times r)$$

$$0.628 \times r^2 \times 18 \times \log_{10}(17700 \times r) \times \sqrt{\frac{0.295\, r}{2000}} = 0.628$$

$$r^2 \times 18 \times \log_{10}(17700 \times r) \times 0.012 \times \sqrt{r} = 1$$

Try r = 1.0m:

$18 \times \log_{10}(17700) \times 0.012 = 18 \times 4.248 \times 0.012 = 0.92$

Try r = 1.1m:

$1.21 \times 18 \times 4.29 \times 0.012 \times 1.05 = 1.17 \;\therefore\; r = 1.05\text{m}$

Diameter of sewer = 2.1m.

Ageing of Pipes

Sketch the variation of the friction factor *f* with Reynolds number and the ratio of wall roughness to pipe diameter *k/d*, for laminar and turbulent flow in pipes. Specify the conditions for which the following equation applies:

$$\frac{1}{\sqrt{f}} = 4\log_{10}\left(\frac{d}{2k}\right) + 3.48$$

The difference in level between the catchment reservoir and service reservoir of a town water supply is 75m. The reservoirs were originally connected by a pipe, 1m in diameter and 30km long, designed to convey 0.9 m^3/s. At the end of 10 years service it was found to convey 0.8 m^3/s. Assuming the roughness to increase linearly with time t in accordance with $k = k_o + \alpha t$, determine the roughness k_o of the unused pipe and the growth per year α.

At high Reynolds numbers, the curves become horizontal indicating the flow to be independent of viscous effects (and R) and presumably the thickness of the laminar sublayer is negligible compared to the wall roughness. The flow is referred to as rough turbulent for which the following applies.

$$\frac{1}{\sqrt{f}} = 4\log_{10}\left(\frac{d}{2k}\right) + 3.48$$

$$V_1 = \frac{Q}{A} = \frac{0.9}{(\pi/4) \times 1^2} = 1.142 m/s. \quad h_f = \frac{4flV^2}{2gd}.$$

$$75 = \frac{4 \times f_1 \times 30 \times 10^3 \times 1.142^2}{1 \times 2 \times 9.81}. \quad \therefore\; f_1 = 0.0094.$$

$$\frac{1}{\sqrt{0.0094}} = 4\log_{10}\left(\frac{d}{2k_1}\right) + 3.48$$

$4\log_{10}\left(\frac{d}{2k_1}\right) = 1.71$. ∴ ***Roughness coefficient,*** k_1 ***=0.0058m.***

$$V_2 = \frac{Q}{A} = \frac{0.8}{(\pi/4) \times 1^2} = 1.02 m/s.$$

$$f_2 = \left(\frac{1.142}{1.0}\right)^2 \times 0.0094 = 0.0118.$$

$$\frac{1}{\sqrt{0.0118}} = 4\log_{10}\left(\frac{d}{2k_2}\right) + 3.48$$

$4\log_{10}\left(\frac{d}{2k_2}\right) = 1.43$. ∴ ***Roughness coefficient,*** k_2 ***= 0.0185m.***

∴ ***Growth rate,*** α ***= 0.0185 - 0.00979 = 0.0087m/year.***

Asphalt Lining of Pipes

Define the pipe friction factor f and explain its variation with Reynolds number and the ratio of wall roughness to pipe diameter, k/d, for different types of flow. Specify the conditions under which the following equation applies:

$$\frac{1}{\sqrt{f}} = 4\log_{10}\left(\frac{d}{2k}\right) + 3.48$$

Water is pumped with a mean velocity of 1.5m/s through a pipe 2m in diameter and roughness k = 30mm. It is proposed to line the pipe with asphalt 15mm thick which would reduce the roughness to 0.12mm. The pump efficiency is 75% and power costs 1 penny per kilowatt hour. What is the saving in running cost per year per kilometre of pipeline?

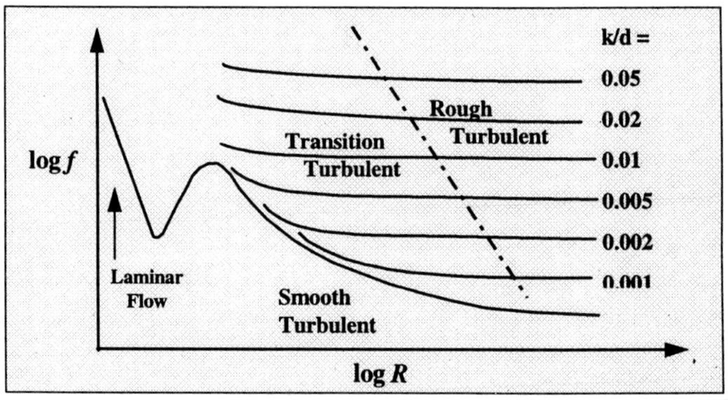

At very low Reynolds numbers, the flow is laminar with $f = 16/R$, the wall roughness has no effect. At Reynolds numbers above the critical value of 2300, the curve for any particular roughness seems to start from the line for flow in smooth pipes and then falls until the laminar sublayer is disrupted by the wall roughness. At higher Reynolds numbers, the curve becomes horizontal, indicating the flow to be independent of viscous effects (and hence *R*) and presumably means the thickness of the sublayer is negligible compared to the wall roughness. The flow is known as rough turbulent for which the following equation applies:

$$\frac{1}{\sqrt{f}} = 4\log_{10}\left(\frac{d}{2k}\right) + 3.48.$$

For the old pipe:

$$\frac{1}{\sqrt{f_1}} = 4\log_{10}\left(\frac{2\times 1000}{2\times 30}\right) + 3.48 = 4\times 1.523 + 3.48 .$$

$$f_1 = \frac{1}{9.58^2} = 0.010913 .$$

For the asphalted pipe:

$$\frac{1}{\sqrt{f_2}} = 4\log_{10}\left(\frac{1.97\times 1000}{2\times 0.12}\right) + 3.48 = 4\times 3.914 + 3.48$$

$$f_2 = \frac{1}{19.13^2} = 0.0027 .$$

Head losses:

$$h_1 = \frac{4flV^2}{2gd_1} = 4\times 0.01091\times\frac{1000}{2}\times\frac{2.25}{2\times 9.81} = 2.5m$$

$$h_2 = \frac{4flV^2}{2gd_2} = 4\times 0.00273\times\frac{1000}{1.97}\times\frac{2.25}{2\times 9.81} = 0.635m$$

Discharges:

$$Q_1 = \frac{\pi\times d_1^2}{4}\times V = \frac{\pi\times 2^2}{4}\times 1.5 = 4.71m^3/s .$$

$$Q_2 = \frac{\pi\times d_2^2}{4}\times V = \frac{\pi\times 1.96^2}{4}\times 1.5 = 4.56m^3/s .$$

Difference in power, $\Delta p = P_1 - P_2 = \frac{\rho g}{\eta}\times(Q_1 h_1 - Q_2 h_2) .$

$$\Delta P = \frac{1000\times 9.81}{0.75}\times(4.71\times 2.5 - 2.56\times 0.635) = 116\times 10^3 W .$$

Saving per year $= \frac{116\times 10^3\times 365\times 24\times 3600\times 1.0}{10^3\times 3600\times 100}$ **= £10,180.**

Costs of Alternative Schemes

A 1m diameter pipeline is 35km long and connects two water supply reservoirs having a difference of surface level of 60m. After several years service the pipeline was found to convey $0.8m^3/s$. It is desired to increase the flow by 50 per cent either by installing a new pipe of the same diameter and $f = 0.005$ alongside the original pipe meeting it at an appropriate point, or by installing an electric pump with an overall efficiency of 80%. Using the information given below, determine which of the two alternative schemes would give the lower annual expenditure.

Pipe costs £10 per metre laid.
Pump costs £100 per kW installed.
Electric power costs 0.2p per kWh.
Interest rates are 12% per annum on capital cost.

(i) New Parallel Pipe (Length x)

$V = Q/A = 0.8/(\pi/4)\times 1 = 1.02m/s$

$h_f = 4flV^2/2gd$ *(neglect outlet loss).*

$60 = 4f\times 35\times 1.02^2\times 10^3)/(1\times 2\times 9.81)$. $\therefore$ $\mathbf{f_1 = 0.008.}$

$1/\sqrt{0.008} = 4\log_{10}(1/2k_1) + 3.48 .$ $\therefore$ $\mathbf{k_1 = 0.0058m.}$

New flow, $\mathbf{1.5\times 0.8 = 1.2m^3/s.}$

$h_f = KQ^2 = 4flQ^2/2gA^2$. $K_e = K_d + K_s$.

$K_e = 60/1.02^2 = 41.67m.$

$$K_s = \frac{4\times 0.008\times(35{,}000 - x)}{1\times 2\times 9.81\times 0.785^2} = \frac{(35{,}000 - x)}{377.82} .$$

$$\frac{1}{\sqrt{K_d}} = \frac{1}{\sqrt{K_1}} = \frac{1}{\sqrt{K_2}} .$$

$$K_1 = \frac{4\times 0.008\times x}{2\times 9.81\times 0.785^2} = \frac{x}{377.82} .$$

$$K_2 = \frac{4\times 0.005\times x}{2\times 9.81\times 0.785^2} = \frac{x}{604.52} .$$

$$\frac{1}{\sqrt{K_d}} = \frac{1}{\sqrt{x}}\times(19.43 - 24.586) = \frac{x}{1937.4} .$$

$K_e = K_d + K_s$, $41.67 = \frac{35{,}000 - x}{377.82} + \frac{x}{1937.4}$. $\therefore$ $\mathbf{x = 23{,}922m.}$

Annual cost in repayment of interest,

$$= \frac{23{,}922\times 10\times 12}{100} = £28{,}705 .$$

(ii) Pump in Pipeline

Head to obtain a flow of $\mathbf{1.2m^3/s}$ ***in original pipe is:***

Head, $h_f = \frac{35{,}000}{377.82}\times 1.2^2 = 133.4m.$

Power = $\frac{\rho gQH}{\eta} = \frac{1{,}000\times 9.81\times 1.2\times 73.4}{0.8} = 1080kW.$

Capital cost of pump = £108,000.

Annual consumption of electric power,

$$= \frac{9810\times 1.2\times 73.4\times 24\times 365}{0.8} = 9.46\times 10^6\ kWh.$$

Total annual cost,

$$= \frac{108\times 10^3\times 12}{100} + \frac{9.46\times 10^6\times 0.2}{100} = £31{,}880.$$

First scheme gives lower annual expenditure.

Pumped Reservoir

Water is being pumped at a rate of $0.15m^3/s$ from one reservoir into a reservoir whose surface level is 20m higher. The combined length of suction and delivery pipes is 100m and both pipes are 0.2m in diameter with an internal roughness of 0.03mm. Calculate the power supplied to the pump if it has an efficiency of 75%. If the pump is located with its suction inlet 2.5m above the surface of the lower reservoir and the length of the suction pipe is 10m, calculate the pressure at the suction inlet to the pump. The Colebrook-White equation is:

$$\frac{1}{\sqrt{f}} = -4\log_{10}\left(\frac{k}{3.7d} + \frac{2.51}{R\sqrt{4f}}\right)$$

and the kinematic viscosity of water may be assumed to be $1.0\times 10^{-6}\ m^2/s$.

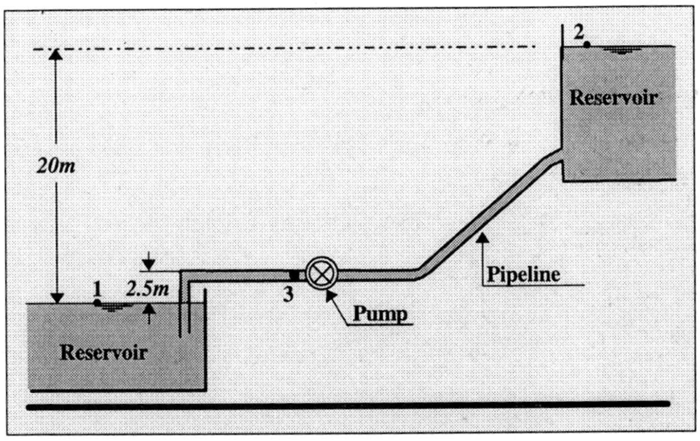

Apply Bernoulli's equation points 1 and 2

$$\frac{p_1}{\rho g}+\frac{V_1^2}{2g}+z_1+head\ from\ pump=\frac{p_2}{\rho g}+\frac{V_2^2}{2g}+z_2+losses$$

$p_1 = p_2$ atmospheric pressure = 0 gauge.

$(V_1^2/2g)+(V_2^2/2g)$ negligible at surface of reservoirs, i.e.

Head from pump, $=(z_2-z_1)+losses=20+\dfrac{4flV^2}{2gd}$.

To find f use Colebrook-White equation.

$$V=\frac{Q}{A}=\frac{0.15}{(\pi/4)\times 0.2^2}=4.77m/s.$$

$$R=\frac{Vd}{\nu}=\frac{4.77\times 0.2}{1\times 10^{-6}}=9.55\times 10^5$$

$$\frac{1}{\sqrt{f}}=4\log_{10}\left(\frac{0.03\times 10^{-3}}{37\times 0.2}+\frac{2.51}{9.55\times 10^5\times\sqrt{4f}}\right).$$

Solve by iteration.

Try, $f=0.005$. Calculate RHS and LHS = 0.00349.
Try, $f=0.0399$. Calculate RHS, and LHS = 0.00354.
Try, $f=0.00359$. Calculate RHS, and LHS = 0.0354.
i.e. $f=0.00354$.

Head for pump $=20+\dfrac{4\times 0.00354\times 100\times 4.77^2}{2g\times 0.2}=28.2m.$

Power Input $=\dfrac{\rho QgH}{Efficiency}=\dfrac{\rho\times 0.15\times g\times 28.2}{0.75}=55.3KW.$

Apply Bernoulli's equation between points 1 and 3 to find pressure at suction inlet.

$$\frac{p_1}{\rho g}+\frac{V_1^2}{2g}+z_1=\frac{p_3}{\rho g}+\frac{V_3^2}{2g}+z_3+losses$$

$p_1=0$, $\dfrac{V_1^2}{2g}$ is negligible.

$$\frac{p_3}{\rho g}=(z_1-z_3)-\frac{V_3^2}{2g}-\frac{4flV_3^2}{2gd}=$$

$$=-2.5-\frac{4.77^2}{2g}-\frac{4\times 0.00354\times 10\times 4.77^2}{2\times 9.81\times 0.2}$$

$p_3/\rho g=-2.5-1.16-0.82=-4.48.$

Pressure at the suction, $p_3=\rho g\times 4.48=-43.9\ kN/m^2$.

Pipe Discharge and Shear Stress

Equation below applies to the flow of water in a circular pipe of constant cross section:

$$\frac{1}{\sqrt{f}}=4\log_{10}\left(\frac{d}{2k}\right)+3.48$$

Using this relationship and working from first principles show that the rate of discharge can be expressed as:

$$Q=Ad^{5/2}\times\left(\frac{p}{l}\right)^{1/2}\times\log_{10}\left(\frac{Bd}{k}\right)$$

where p is the loss of pressure due to friction in a length l of pipe, d is the diameter, k is the mean height of the pipe roughness, f is the friction factor and A and B are constants. To what type of flow does this formula apply? Water flows through a pipe 75mm in diameter and 1200m long with a mean roughness height of 0.2mm. The pressure head lost to friction over the total length of the pipe is 30m of water. Calculate the rate of discharge and the shear stress at the wall of the pipe.

$$\frac{1}{\sqrt{f}}=4\log_{10}\left(\frac{d}{2k}\right)+3.48=4\times\left[\log_{10}\left(\frac{d}{2k}\right)+0.87\right],\text{ i.e.}$$

$$\frac{1}{\sqrt{f}}=4\log_{10}\left(\frac{3.797\times d}{k}\right).$$

$$Q=\frac{\pi d^2V}{4}=\frac{\pi d^2}{4}\times\left(\frac{2gdh_f}{4fl}\right)^{1/2}=\frac{\pi d^{5/2}}{4}\times\left(\frac{p}{2\rho l}\right)^{1/2}\times\frac{1}{\sqrt{f}}$$

$$=\frac{\pi d^{5/2}}{4}\times\left(\frac{p}{2\rho l}\right)^{1/2}\times 4\log_{10}\left(\frac{3.707\times d}{k}\right)$$

$$=Ad^{5/2}\times\left(\frac{p}{l}\right)^{1/2}\times\log_{10}\left(\frac{3.707\times d}{k}\right),\quad\text{where }A=\frac{\pi}{\sqrt{2\rho}}.$$

For rough turbulent flow:

$$=\frac{\pi}{\sqrt{2\rho}}\times\left(\frac{75}{1000}\right)^{5/2}\times\left(\frac{9810\times 30}{1200}\right)^{1/2}\times\log_{10}\left(\frac{3.707\times 75}{0.2}\right)$$

$$=\frac{\pi}{\sqrt{2000}}\times\frac{154}{10^5}\times 15.66\times\log_{10}(1390)=\frac{0.1683}{\sqrt{1000}}$$

Discharge, $Q=\dfrac{\pi d^{5/2}}{\sqrt{2\rho}}\times\left(\dfrac{\rho gh}{l}\right)^{1/2}\times\log_{10}\left(\dfrac{3.707\times d}{k}\right)$

$$Q=\frac{\pi d^{5/2}}{\sqrt{2}}\times\left(\frac{gh}{l}\right)^{1/2}\times\log_{10}\left(\frac{3.707\times d}{k}\right)=0.00532m^3/s.$$

$1/\sqrt{f}=4\times 3.143=12.572.\ \therefore\ f=1/12.572^2=0.00632.$

$$\tau_o=p\times\frac{\pi d^2}{4}\Big/\pi dl=\frac{pd}{4l}=\frac{9810\times 30\times 0.075}{4\times 1200}=4.6\ N/m^2.$$

Shear stress, $\tau_o=4.6\ N/m^2$.

Problems on Turbulent Flow in Pipes

[1] Derive an expression for the discharge Q in a pipe in terms of diameter d, roughness k and hydraulic gradient i, when $1/\sqrt{f}=4\log_{10}(d/2k)+3.48$

[2] Water is pumped through a smooth pipe, 250mm diameter with a pressure drop of 90mm of water per kilometre of pipe. Determine the flow rate and the shear stress at the wall of the pipe. $1/4\sqrt{f}=4\log_{10}(R\sqrt{4f})$, $\nu=1.15mm^2/s$.

($0.0067m^3/s$, $0.055N/m^2$)

[3] Two reservoirs, whose surface levels differ by 35m, are connected by a 1km long pipeline of 300mm diameter and roughness 1.1mm, both inlet and outlet being submerged. Calculate the rate of flow in the pipe and the average shear stress at the wall of the pipe. If the flow in the pipeline were reversed, calculate the power which must be supplied to a centrifugal pump, efficiency 78%, if the flow is to be increased by 25%. $1/\sqrt{f}=4\log_{10}(d/2k)+3.48$.

($0.19m^3/s$, $26N/m^2$, 271KW)

CHAPTER ELEVEN

OPEN CHANNEL FLOW

Development of Water Resources

The development of water projects begins with the assessment of the water resource potential in river and ground water basins and takes into account the various factors and characteristics interacting in the system. Plans are then made by integrating the resources with the current and future demand estimates, bearing in mind the physical and financial aspects involved. The development plans produced could include water supply, irrigation, drainage and reclamation, flood protection, hydropower etc. Open channel flow plays an important part in all these projects.

Types of Open Channel Flow

The term open channel includes rivers, canals, aqueducts, and conduits and in addition sewers and pipes which run partially full and do not present a solid boundary to every side of the contained liquid, i.e. the presence of a free surface of flow. The force producing flow is provided by gravity due to the slope or gradient of the channel.

Open channel flow occurs in a number of forms, from the flow of water in mountain streams to the flow at a constant depth through a prismatic channel. It may be classified as steady or unsteady, uniform or non-uniform. Steady flow occurs in channels of constant cross-section A and slope S with no obstruction or control structure placed in them. The depth for a steady uniform flow is called the normal depth, Fig.11.1. In steady uniform flow the discharge Q is the same and the depth everywhere is constant along the length of the channel.

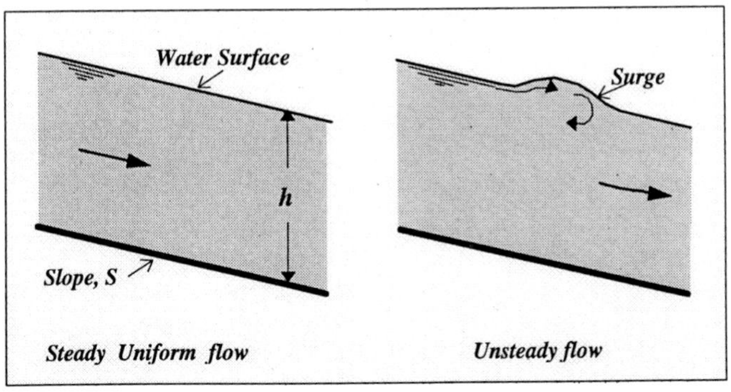

Fig.11.1- Steady uniform and unsteady flows in channels.

Steady non-uniform flow occurs in any irregular channel in which the discharge does not change with time; it also occurs in regular channels when the flow depth and hence, the average velocity changes from one section to another. Both types of flow are called varied flow, Fig.11.2.

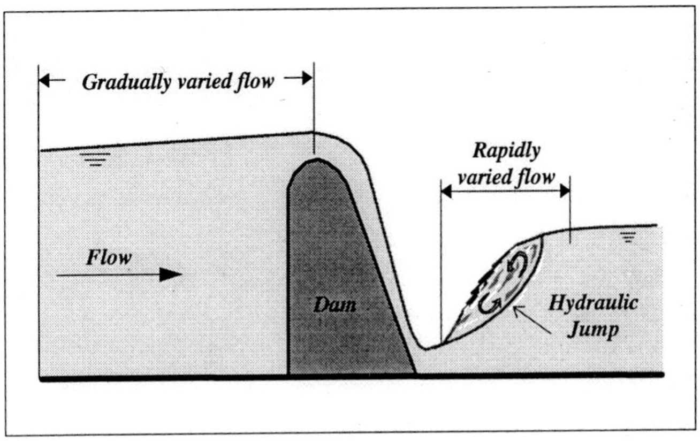

Fig.11.2- Gradually and rapidly varied flows.

When the change in depth of flow or section is gradual it is called gradually varied flow and methods are available by numerical integration or graphical means, for computing flow depth for a known discharge and channel dimensions and roughness and the conditions at one section.

When the change in depth of section occurs in a short distance or suddenly, the flow is termed rapidly varied flow and an abrupt expansion. The hydraulic jump downstream of a dam spillway or a sluice gate is an example of rapidly varied flow or steady non-uniform flow.

Unsteady uniform flow rarely occurs in channel flow, it is quite difficult to observe. Channel surges and wave motion are examples of this type.

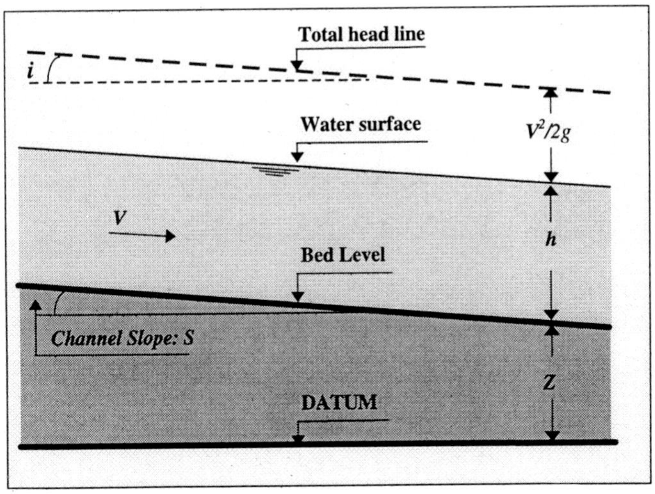

Fig.11.3- Uniform flow in open channels.

Uniform Flow in Open Channels

Several equations are used to calculate the rate of flow in an open channel when the flow is uniform. The main equation is the Chezy equation, which can be derived by use of basic principles of fluid mechanics and is given by:

$$V = C\sqrt{R \times S} \qquad (11.1)$$

where V is the average velocity of flow in m/s, C is a coefficient depending on the roughness and cross-sectional area of the channel, A, R is the hydraulic radius *(cross-sectional area divided by the wetted perimeter A/P)*, and S is the slope of the total head line *(the slope of the water surface or bed of the channel S when the flow is uniform)*.

The Chezy coefficient is most frequently determined by the Manning expression

$$C = \frac{1}{n} \times \sqrt[6]{R} \qquad (11.2)$$

where n is the Manning roughness coefficient of the channel.

Combining equations we get the Manning formula:

Velocity, $$V = \frac{1}{n} R^{2/3} \times S^{1/2} \qquad (11.3)$$

Discharge, $$Q = \frac{A}{n} R^{2/3} \times S^{1/2} \qquad (11.4)$$

Experimental values of n (Manning's Roughness Coefficient) are given below in Table 11.1.

Material	n
Plastic, glass, drawn tubing	0.009
Neat cement, smooth metal	0.010
Planed timber	0.011
Wrought iron, welded steel	0.012
Concrete, asphalted cast iron	0.013
Un-planed timber, vitrified clay	0.014
Cast iron pipe	0.015
Riveted steel, brick	0.016
Rubble masonry	0.017
Smooth earth	0.018
Firm gravel	0.020
Corrugated metal pipe	0.022
Channels in good condition	0.025
Channels with stones and weeds	0.035

Table 11.1- Values of Manning coefficient n.

Total and Specific Heads

The design of discharge channels and waterways under bridges calls for the knowledge of the water level so that retaining walls and other structures may be constructed to the appropriate height. A useful first approximation to some changes in depth may be made by assuming that the water is an ideal fluid, without friction. It is only if the changes in depth occur over a long length of channel that frictional forces become important (Fig.11.4).

Consider the longitudinal section of a small portion of an open channel, with its bed inclined downstream. As the fluid is assumed to be ideal, the total head will be constant at all sections of the flow.

$$\textit{Total Head } H_1 = \textit{Total Head } H_2$$

$$\frac{V_1^2}{2g} + h_1 + z_1 = \frac{V_2^2}{2g} + h_2 + z_2 \qquad (11.5)$$

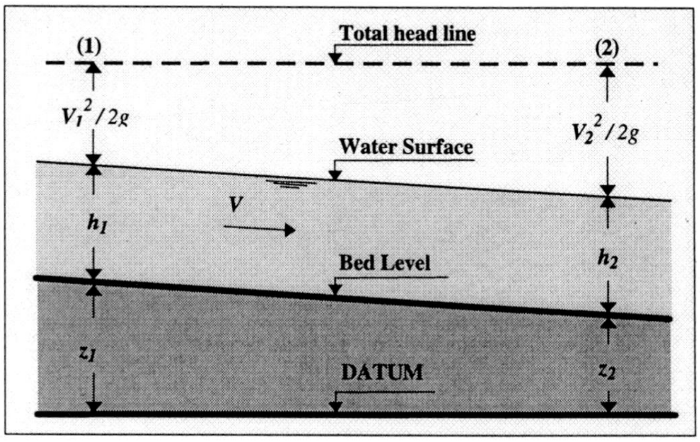

Fig.11.4- Ideal flow of fluids without friction.

A line can therefore be drawn at a height H_T above the datum and its height above this datum represents the total head of the fluid at any cross-section of the channel. This line is called the Total Head Line.

The total head, as above, is given relative to an arbitrary datum, but it proves convenient for many purposes to measure it relative to the bed level of the stream at the cross-section concerned. It is then called the specific head, H, of the stream. That is in general terms:

$$\textit{Specific Head} = H = \frac{V^2}{2g} + h \qquad (11.6)$$

so that a particular value of H can be made up of varying proportions of velocity head $V^2/2g$ and depth head h. A certain flow Q could take place at a high speed but a small depth or vice versa if H is fixed, the only provision being that the flow per unit width q must also be the same for the two conditions. Thus for any section of flow, $q = Vh$ and substituting for V in the specific head equation,

$$H = \frac{q^2}{2gh^2} + h \qquad (11.7)$$

This equation may be plotted, Fig.11.5 as a graph of H against h for a constant value of q, forming a curve with a maximum value of H.,

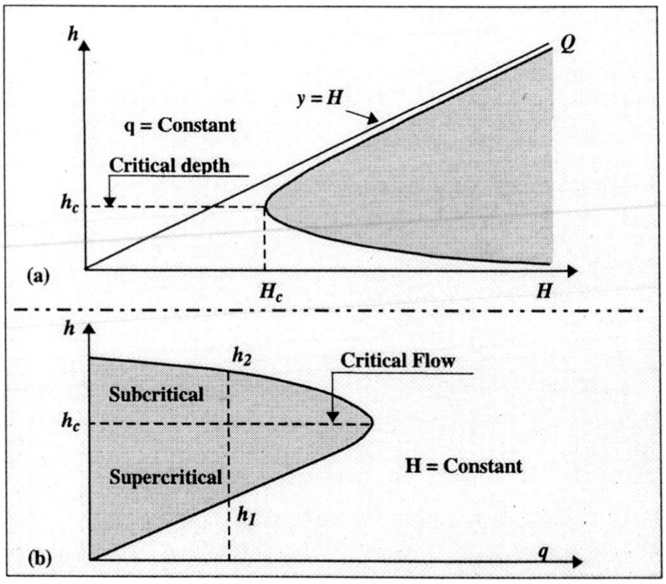

Fig.11.5- A plot of equation (11.5) for H and q constant.

In general if a given flow q has a definite specific energy per unit weight of fluid H_1 it can occur at two possible depths h_1 and h_2 one above and one below at which H would be a minimum for that flow. If the flow is at the larger depth h_2, the velocity $V=q/h_2$ is small, and the condition is called slow or tranquil, or sub-critical flow; when the flow is at the smaller depth h_1, then V is large and the condition is called fast or shooting or super-critical flow.

Critical Depth of Flow

The depth at which the minimum value of H occurs for a given unit discharge q may be simply obtained by differentiating equation (11.7) with respect to h, thus,

$$\frac{dH}{dh} = \frac{q^2}{2g}(-2h^{-3}) + 1 = 0 \,.$$

For minimum value of H, that is:

$$\frac{q^2}{gh^3} = 1 \qquad \text{or} \qquad h_c = \sqrt[3]{\frac{q^2}{g}} \qquad (11.8)$$

where h_c is called the critical depth. The corresponding velocity is then the critical velocity V_c which is given by

$$q = V_c\, h_c \qquad (11.9)$$

Substituting for q in equation 11.8 gives,

$$h_c = \sqrt[3]{\frac{V_c^2 \times h_c^2}{g}} \quad \text{or} \quad h_c = \frac{V_c^2}{g} = 2\times\left(\frac{V_c^2}{2g}\right)$$

Thus when the flow is critical, that is travelling so as to have the minimum head for its unit discharge q, the depth is twice the velocity head. Under this critical condition also the specific head H_c is:

$$H_c = \frac{V_c^2}{2g} + h_c = \frac{h_c}{2} + h_c = 1.5\, h_c \quad or \quad h_c = \frac{2}{3} H_c \qquad (11.10)$$

Now consider the condition when H is constant, then q will be a maximum when the depth is critical. Fig.11.5 shows a curve of q against h for a fixed value of H, again using the equation 11.7 for the plotting. This curve shows a maximum at $h = h_c = 2/3\ H$. Thus if the flow in a channel is the maximum possible with the particular boundaries concerned, then somewhere along it the depth must be h_c and the velocity V_c. If the position of the critical depth is known, then a single measurement of the depth there will determine the velocity, for $h_c = V_c^2/g$ and also the discharge for $h_c = \sqrt[3]{q^2/g}$.

The principle of critical flow can be used for designing metering devices for discharge measurements in an open channel. Two such devices are the broad crested weir and the venturi flume.

Broad Crested Weir for Flow Measurement

Consider the longitudinal section of the channel shown in Fig.11.6. A flow of q per unit width approaches the weir. With sufficient length and height, it is found that the surface is drawn down to a new depth h, and remains there, parallel to the raised bed. Since there are no restricting forces on the fluid, the discharge will be a maximum possible with the head content of the fluid. In fact conditions will be critical on the straight length of weir, with $h_2 = h_c$.

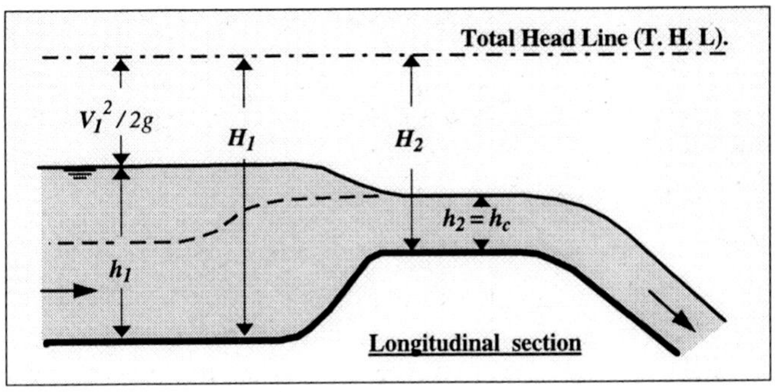

Fig.11.6- Channel with a broad crested weir.

Since $\quad h_2 = h_c = \sqrt[3]{q^2/g} \qquad (11.11)$

then, $\quad q = \sqrt{g}\,(h_c)^{3/2} \qquad (11.12)$

A single measurement of h_c will enable q to be found. This method of measurement is not much used in practice for the surface of the fast moving water over the weir is difficult to determine accurately; there is a tendency for ripples and waves to appear which obscure the mean surface.

It is more common to express q in terms of the specific head H_2 of the fluid, which at the place where the flow is critical, is 1.5 times the depth. That is, $H = 1.5\, q^{2/3}/g^{1/3}$ or using $g = 9.81 m/s^2$, $q = 1.7\, H^{3/2}$, the total discharge (where b is the width of the weir),

$$Q = 1.7\, b \times (H)^{3/2} \qquad (11.13)$$

Venturi Flume

The quantity of fluid flowing along a channel can be measured by restricting the width as shown in Fig.11.7. This is known as a Venturi flume and corresponds to the throat of a Venturi meter used for the measurement of discharge in pipes.

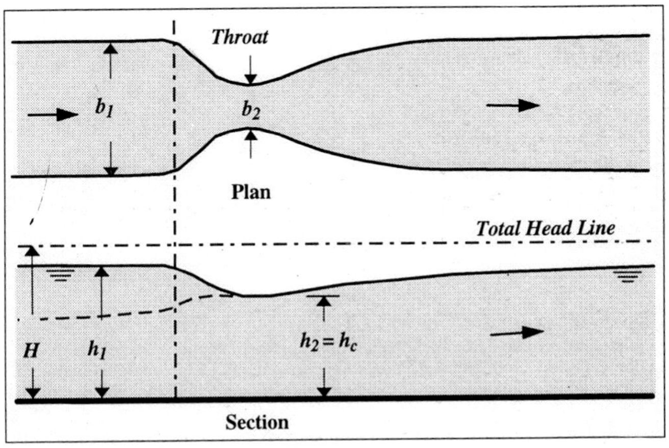

Fig.11.7- Venturi flume for flow measurement in a channel.

By exactly the same reasoning as for a broad-crested weir, the discharge is given by:

$$Q = 1.7\, b_2 \times (H)^{3/2} \qquad (11.14)$$

where b_2 is the width of the throat. If there is no assurance that the flow is critical at the throat, because of a high down-stream level, then an additional water level gauge must be placed at the throat to measure h_2 there. In this case, the flow equation of a drowned weir is used,

$$Q = C_d \times b_2 \times h_2 \sqrt{2g\,(h_1 - h_2)} \qquad (11.15)$$

where h_1 and h_2 are measured above the channel bed and C_d is the coefficient of discharge found experimentally.

One way of ensuring critical depth at the throat is by putting a rise in the channel bed at the throat, thus combining a weir and a venturi flume as shown in Figure 11.8.

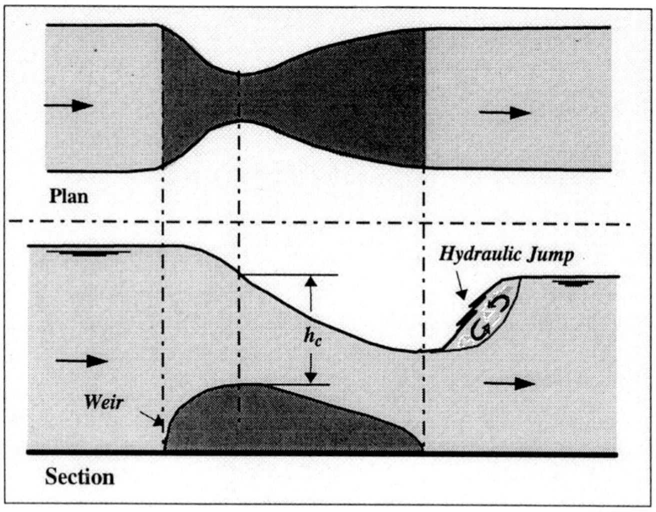

Fig.11.8- Venturi Flume with a hump.

Hydraulic Jump

The hydraulic jump is commonly made to form at a gate or spillway for a two-fold reason; the appreciable conversion of kinetic head of the mean flow into energy or turbulence that reduces the total head; and the resulting increase in depth and reduction in velocity reduces the tendency of the flow to erode the bed of the down-stream channel. The phenomenon can be described as follows (Fig.11.9).

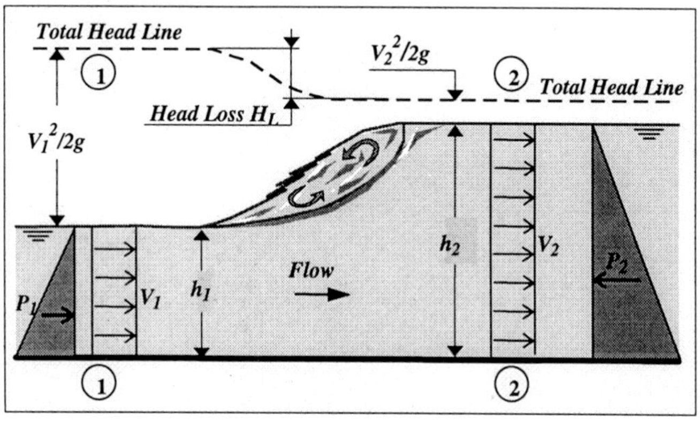

Fig.11.9- Hydraulic jump, showing the parameters to apply Newton's second law of motion.

According to Newton's second law of motion, the rate of loss of momentum must be equal to the unbalanced hydrostatic force acting on the moving mass to retard its motion.

$P_2 - P_1 = \text{Rate of change of momentum}$

$$\frac{1}{2}\rho g\,(h_2^2 - h_1^2) = \rho q\,(V_1 - V_2) \qquad (11.16)$$

But, $V_1 = q/h_1$ and $V_2 = q/h_2$.

Hence substituting: $h_2^2 + h_2 h_1 - 2q^2/gh_1 = 0$

Solving this quadratic for h_2 and h_1, respectively:

$$h_2 = -h_1/2 + \sqrt{2q^2/gh_1 + h_1^2/4} \qquad (11.17)$$

$$h_1 = -h_2/2 + \sqrt{2q^2/gh_2 + h_2^2/4} \qquad (11.18)$$

The loss of head in the jump is,

$$H_L = \left(\frac{V_1^2}{2g} + h_1\right) - \left(\frac{V_2^2}{2g} + h_2\right) \qquad (11.19)$$

The height of the jump is defined as $h_j = h_2 - h_1$.

Substitution of the Froude number,

$$F = V/\sqrt{gh} \qquad (11.20)$$

$$F_1 = \frac{V_1}{\sqrt{gh_1}} = \frac{q}{h_1 \times \sqrt{gh_1}}$$

$$F_2 = \frac{V_2}{\sqrt{gh_2}} = \frac{q}{h_2 \times \sqrt{gh_2}}$$

and rearranging, we get,

$$\frac{h_2}{h_1} = \frac{1}{2} \times \left(\sqrt{1 + 8F_1^2} - 1\right) \qquad (11.21)$$

$$\frac{h_1}{h_2} = \frac{1}{2} \times \left(\sqrt{1 + 8F_2^2} - 1\right) \qquad (11.22)$$

The length of the jump is found experimentally to be approximately six times its height, i.e. $6 \times (h_2 - h_1)$.

Calculation of Surface Profile

As it is rare that uniform flow can be maintained throughout the whole of the length of a channel, the effects of local variations can be considered, on the assumption that the discharge is in no way affected. The causes that result in an increase in depth for example as points downstream are compared include an obstruction across the channel such as a weir or barrage. The amount by which the depth is increased or the water headed up by an obstruction is known as afflux. We shall concern ourselves with the methods whereby the profile water surface is calculated.

There are a number of methods of calculating surface profiles; analytical, graphical and numerical methods, the latter which is often used in the design office is discussed in this Chapter.

Consider a short length of rectangular cross-sectional channel in Figure 11.10. The bed has a slope S and the frictional forces on the bed have resulted in the total head line being sloped at gradient i. The slope of i is connected to the velocity and depth by Chezy's and Manning's equations.

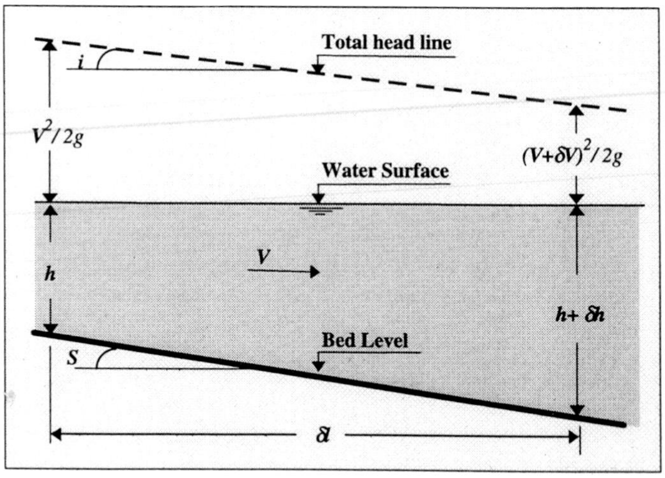

Fig.11.10- Flow in small length of channel.

The velocity and depth of the stream have both changed as the fluid traverses this length of channel, the former from V to $V+\delta V$, the latter from h to $h+\delta h$. The specific head changes from H to $H+dH$, since all the variables are assumed to increase in the direction of motion. Equating the enclosed within horizontal parallels.

$H + S\,\delta l = (H+\delta H) + i\,\delta l$, but $H = h + (V^2/2g)$ and

$$H + \delta H = \frac{(V+\delta V)^2}{2g} + h + \delta h$$. Substitution gives,

$$\frac{V^2}{2g} + h + S\delta l = \frac{(V+\delta V)^2}{2g} + (h+\delta h) + i\delta l \text{ , or}$$

$(S-i)\times\delta l = \delta h + (V\times\delta V/g)$ *(ignoring second order terms), or*

$$(S-i)\times\frac{\delta l}{\delta h} = 1 + \frac{V\times\delta V}{g\delta h} \qquad (11.23)$$

As the discharge per unit width q, is constant at both cross-sections, we have, $q = Vh = (V+\delta V)\times(h+\delta h)$. On multiplying out and ignoring terms of the second order $V/h = \delta V/\delta h$.
Substituting in the slope equation, gives

$$(S-i)\times\frac{\delta l}{\delta h} = 1 - \frac{V^2}{gh} \text{ , or } \frac{\delta h}{\delta l} = \frac{S-i}{1-(V^2/gh)} \text{ , and in the limit,}$$

$$\boxed{\frac{dh}{dl} = \left[S-i \middle/ 1-\left(\frac{V^2}{gh}\right)\right]} \qquad (11.24)$$

This differential equation for the rate of change of depth in a channel due to both friction and gravity effects has only one major assumption; that the discharge per unit width is constant. It can only be solved by numerical methods. Further simplification may be made by writing $V_2 = q_2/h_2$. Then,

$$\frac{V^2}{gh} = \frac{q^2}{gh^3} = \left(\frac{h_c}{h}\right)^3 \text{ and so } \frac{dh}{dl} = \frac{S-i}{1-(h_c/h)^3}.$$

The connection between S and i is often expressed by the Manning formula. At normal depth the equation

$$q = \frac{1}{n}\times h_n \times R^{2/3} \times S^{1/2}.$$

For a wide channel or river $R=h_n$, then $q = \frac{1}{n}\times h_n^{5/3}\times S^{1/2}$.

and for any other depth, $q = \frac{1}{n}\times h^{5/3}\times i^{1/2}$.

Equating the right hand sides of these two equations and re-arranging,

$$\frac{i}{S} = \left(\frac{h_n}{h}\right)^{10/3} \text{ and } S - i = S\left(1-\frac{i}{S}\right) = S\left[1-\left(\frac{h_n}{h}\right)^{10/3}\right].$$

The differential equation for increment of depth becomes

$$\boxed{\frac{dh}{dl} = S \times \frac{1-(h_n/h)^{10/3}}{1-(h_c/h)^3}} \qquad (11.25)$$

A third equation for the surface profile can be deduced as follows. Consider the retarded flow shown in Figure 11.10. The total head of any section is $H_T = (V^2/2g) + h + z$. Differentiating and putting $V = Q/A$,

$$\frac{dH_T}{dl} = -\frac{Q^2}{gA^3}\times\frac{dA}{dl} + \frac{dh}{dl} + \frac{dz}{dl} \qquad (11.26)$$

In most practical problems, it is possible to simplify the above sufficiently to permit direct integration of the equation for l. Assume a wide rectangular channel with unit discharge (q), $A = bh$, $q = Q/b$, $R = A/P = h$.

From Chezy's formula $q = C\times(hS)^{1/2}$,
$dH_T/dl = i$ *(slope of total head line)*$= q^2/C^2 h^3$
$dz/dl = S$ *(slope of channel bed)* $= q^2/C^2 h_n^3$
(i.e. for uniform flow of depth h_n*).*

Substituting in above equation:

$$-\frac{q^2}{C^2 h^3} = -\frac{q^2}{g h^3}\times\frac{dh}{dl} + \frac{dh}{dl} - \frac{q^2}{C^2 h_n^3}$$

Putting $q^2/g = h_n^3$ and slope of channel $S = \frac{q^2}{C^2 \times h_n^3}$, we obtain,

$$\boxed{\frac{dh}{dl} = S\left[\frac{1-(h_n/h)^3}{1-(h_c/h)^3}\right]} \qquad (11.27)$$

Any of the equations (11.24), (11.25) or (11.27) may be integrated by an approximate numerical method to calculate a surface profile. The possible range of h is divided into a number of increments Δh, the greater the number the better the accuracy. The mean gradient for each increment is then calculated assuming mean height h is constant over the whole of the increment. The integration is best carried out in a tabular form working from the control structure.

Classification of Surface Profiles

Of initial interest in qualitative analysis of the surface profile is the sign of the dh/dl, for if it is positive the depth will increase and if it is negative the depth will decrease, in the direction of flow. Evidently this sign will depend on whether S is positive or negative and whether h_n/h and h_c/h are greater or less than 1. Six important profiles are described below which can be computed by using above equation.

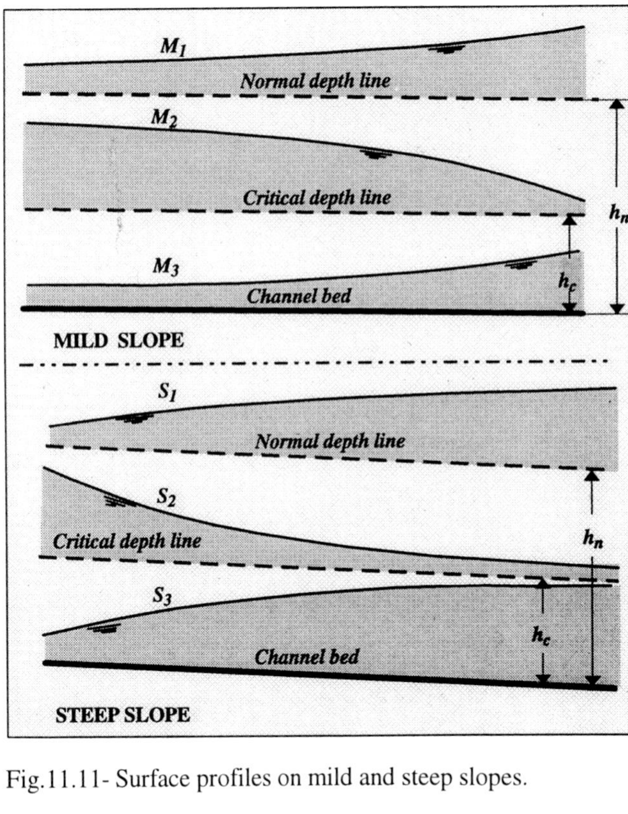

Fig.11.11- Surface profiles on mild and steep slopes.

Practical Examples on Surface Profiles

(a) Slow river entering a lake or approaching a weir.
(b) Slow river approaching a waterfall or other step down.
(c) Discharge from a sluiceway into a mild slope bed.
(d) Follows a hydraulic jump profile on a steep slope.
(e) Change in channel slope to steep.
(f) Flow from a spillway into a steep bed.

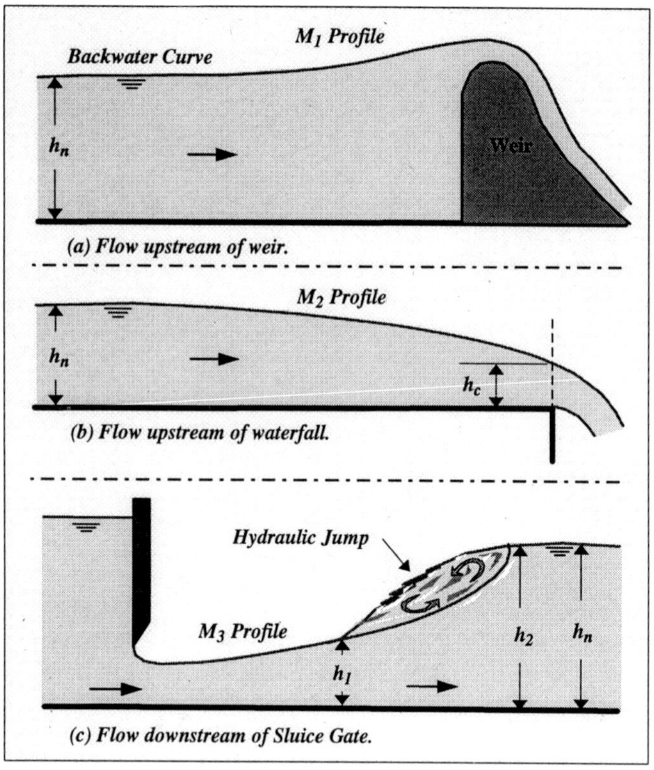

Fig.11.12- Surface profile on mild slopes.

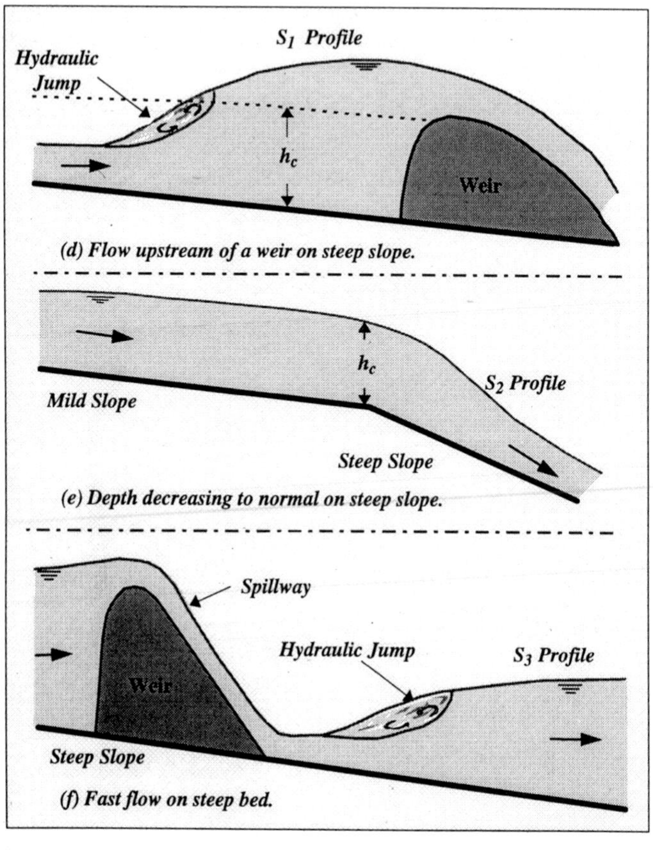

Fig.11.13- Surface profiles on steep slopes.

Sediment Transport in Rivers and Channels

Sediments in streams may be transported either by rolling or sliding along the bed (**bed load**), by bouncing along the bed (**siltation load**), or in suspension in the turbulently moving water (**suspended load).** Currently the approach used in sediment estimation is based on a separate analysis of bed load, in terms of tractive force at the bed, and of suspended load, in terms of turbulent fluctuation mechanism, with those two increments added then to give the total load.

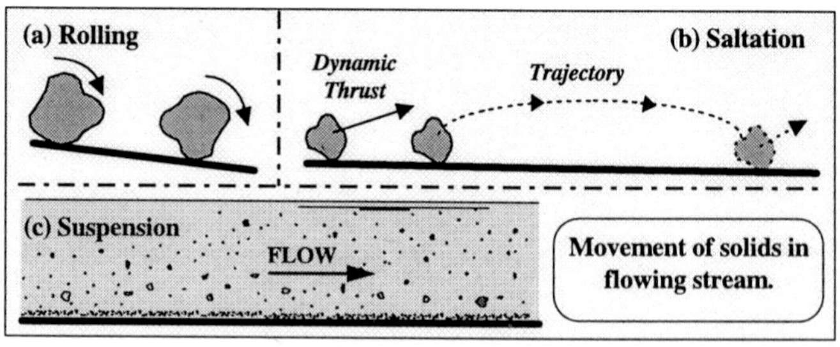

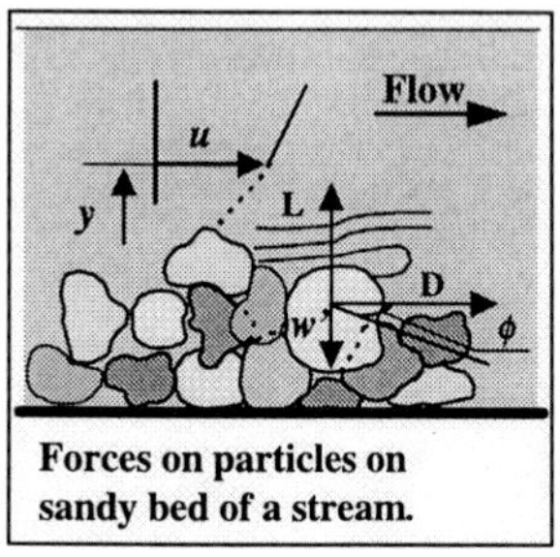

Flow
u
y
L
D
W
ϕ
Forces on particles on sandy bed of a stream.

A mechanism for the movement of sediment particles on the bed of a stream is shown in the diagram. As the flow passes over the particles the streamlines are deflected upward and around the particles thus forming a wake downstream. As a result forces are generated on the particle which may be divided into a drag force in the direction of the mean velocity and a lift force perpendicular to it. The force resisting the motion of the particles is the submerged weight of the particle plus any forces caused by contact with other particles in the bed.

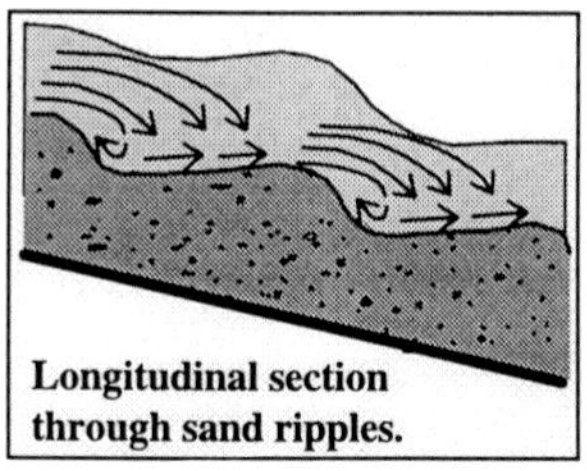

Longitudinal section through sand ripples.

In addition to the transport of individual particles, complexity arises in the interaction of particles with each other and its effect on the flow. This interaction manifests itself by the formation of sediment waves or bars on the channel bed.

One of the earliest formulae to relate the bed transport rate g_s to the flow conditions was that of DuBoys in 1879.

$$g_s = \psi(\rho g)^2 \times S^{1.4} \times (nq)^{1.2}$$

where ψ is an experimental function, S is the channel slope, n is Manning's coefficient and q is the unit discharge (see Chapter 20 of Book 2).

The particles in the suspended load tend continually to fall by gravity to the bed; conversely the turbulence of the water tends to throw the bed particles into the flow area and to maintain them there. As mean velocities V in the vertical depth h are commonly obtained by averaging the velocities at 0.2 and 0.8 of the depth, it is convenient to use these locations also for measurements of sediment concentration C. Straub found the following formula for the suspended load per unit width of flow:

$$g_s = \left(\frac{3}{8} \times C_{0.8h} + \frac{5}{8} \times C_{0.2h}\right)\left[\left(\frac{1}{2} \times U_{0.8} \times h\right) + \left(\frac{1}{2} \times U_{0.2} \times h\right)\right]$$

For accurate estimates, integrating sediment samplers are used for measurements in channels and rivers.

Examples on Uniform Flow

Critical and Normal Depths

A rectangular channel 6m wide, Manning coefficient $n = 0.02$, is carrying a flow of $12 m^3/s$ (Fig.11.14). Calculate (a) the normal depth for a slope of 0.0015, (b) the critical depth, (c) the critical velocity, (d) the critical slope.

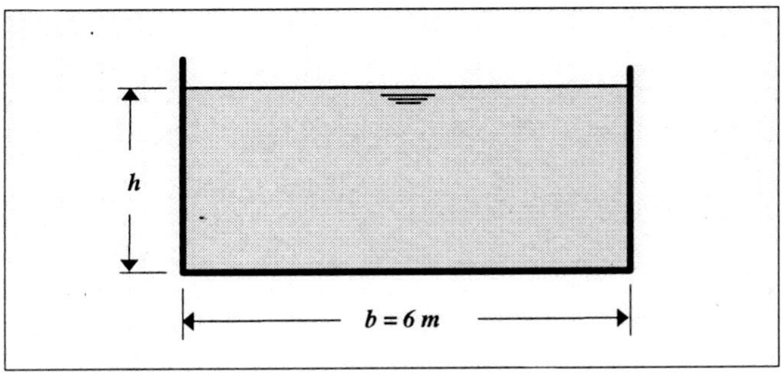

Fig.11.14- Cross-section of a rectangular channel.

(a) Normal Depth, h_n. $V = (1/n) \times R^{2/3} S^{1/2}$

$$R = \frac{6h}{2h+6}, \quad \left[\frac{6h}{2h+6}\right]^{2/3} = \frac{12 \times 0.02}{6h \times \sqrt{0.0015}} = \frac{1.033}{h}$$

Since $Q = \frac{A}{n} \times R^{2/3} \times S^{1/2}$, then,

$$12 = \frac{6h}{0.02} \times \left[\frac{6h}{2h+6}\right]^{2/3} \times \sqrt{0.0015}$$

$$6h^{2.5} = 2.1\,h + 6.3 \quad \text{or} \quad 6h^{2.5} - 2.1h - 6.3 = 0.$$

Try	h =1.15	1.2	1.16
get	- 0.206	+ 0.64	- 0.04

Normal Depth, h_n. $= 1.16m.$

(b) Critical Depth, h_c.

$$h_c = \sqrt[3]{\frac{Q^2}{gb^2}} = \sqrt[3]{\frac{12^2}{9.81 \times 36}} = 0.74m.$$

(c) Critical Velocity, V_c.

$$V_c = \frac{12}{6 \times 0.74} = 2.703m/s.$$

(d) Critical Slope, S_c.

$$R = \frac{6 \times 0.74}{1.48 + 6} = 0.594$$

$$\sqrt{S_c} = \frac{V_c\, n}{R^{2/3}} = \frac{2.703 \times 0.02}{0.594^{2/3}} = 7.651 \times 10^{-2}.$$

Critical Slope, S_c $= 0.0059.$

Supercritical Flow in a Rectangular Channel

The discharge in a rectangular concrete channel 4.5m wide (see Fig.11.14), $n=0.012$, is $12 m^3/s$ when the bed slope is 1 in 100. Find the normal depth of flow and determine whether the flow is subcritical or supercritical.

$$\text{Discharge, } Q = \frac{A}{n} \times R^{2/3} \times S^{1/2}$$

$$12 = \frac{4.5h}{0.012} \times \left[\frac{4.5h}{2h+4.5}\right]^{2/3} \times \frac{1}{10}.$$

Solve by trial and error.

try $h = 0.55$m $\quad 12 = 0.58 \times 20.854 = 12.1.$

Normal Depth is h_n $= 0.55m.$

$$\textit{Critical depth, } h_c = \sqrt[3]{\frac{Q^2}{gb^2}} = \sqrt[3]{\frac{144}{9.81 \times 4.5^2}} = 0.898m.$$

Since $h < h_c$, therefore, **flow is supercritical**.

Critical flow in a Triangular Channel

For constant slope channels of prismatic but non-rectangular cross-section under critical flow conditions the cross-section area of flow, A, the water surface width, b, and the channel discharge, Q, are related by $Q^2 = g\,A^3/b$, where g is the acceleration due to gravity (Fig. 11.15). A channel of Vee-shaped section has side slopes at 30° to the horizontal. It is required to carry a discharge of $10 m^3/s$. Calculate the centreline depth for critical flow conditions.

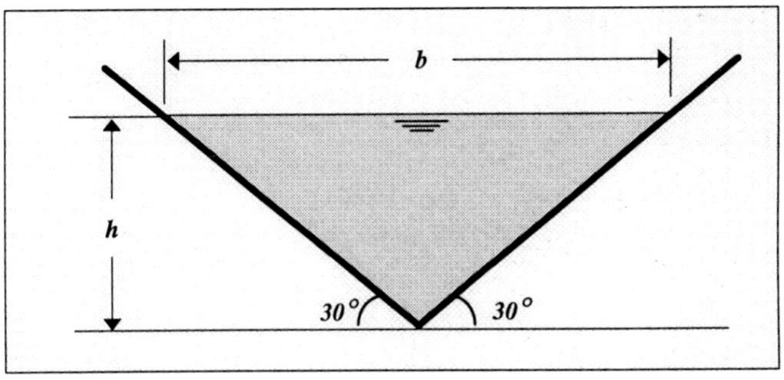

Fig.11.15- Cross-section of a triangular concrete channel.

$Q^2\, b / g\, A^3 = 1$, $Q = 10 m^3/s$.

$$\frac{100\,b}{9.81 \times (bh/2)^3} = 1 \text{ , where } b = 2h/\tan 30° = 3.464h.$$

$$100 \times 3.464h = 9.81 \times \left(\frac{3.464h^2}{2}\right)^3 = 9.81 \times \left(\frac{3.464^3}{8}\right) \times h^6$$

$h^5 = 6.796$, $\quad \therefore$ ***Depth*** $h = 1.467m.$

Critical Flow in a Rectangular Channel

A flow rate of $15 m^3/s$ in a rectangular concrete channel 12m wide has a depth of 1.5m (Fig.11.16). Calculate its specific head and determine the flow is subcritical or supercritical. If $n=0.017$ what is the critical slope of this channel for this flow rate. What channel slope should be provided to produce uniform flow at a depth of 1.5m.

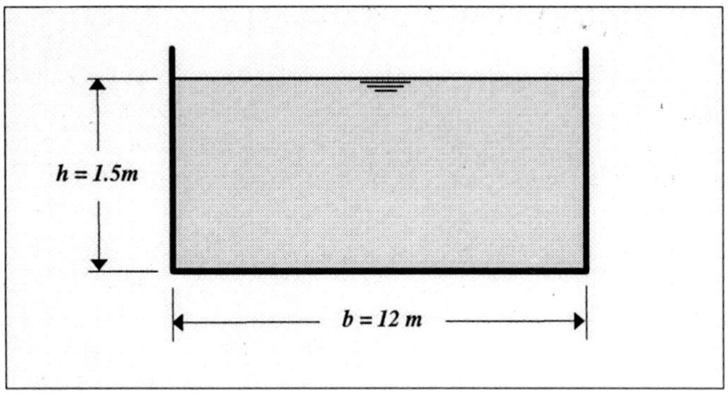

Fig.11.16- Cross-section of a rectangular concrete channel.

Critical Depth, h_c.

$$H = h + \frac{V^2}{2g} = 1.5 + \left(\frac{15}{18}\right)^2 \frac{1}{2 \times 9.81} = 1.535m .$$

$$h_c = \sqrt[3]{\frac{Q^2}{gb^2}} = \sqrt[3]{\frac{225}{9.81 \times 144}} = 0.542m .$$

Since $h > h_c$, therefore, the **flow is subcritical.**

Critical Slope, S_c.

$$V_c = \frac{1}{n} \times R_c^{2/3} \times S_c^{1/2} \text{ , and}$$

$$V_c = \frac{15}{12 \times 0.542} = 2.306 \text{ m/s.}$$

$$R_c = \frac{A}{P} = \frac{12 \times 0.542}{12 + 1.084} = 0.497 .$$

$$\sqrt{S_c} = \frac{2.306 \times 0.017}{0.497^{2/3}} = 6.248 \times 10^{-2} .$$

$S_c = 3.9036\ 10^{-3} = 1{:}256.$

Slope for uniform flow, S.

$$V = \frac{1}{n} \times R^{2/3} \times S^{1/2} \text{, and}$$

$$V = \frac{15}{18} = 0.8333 \text{ m/s.}$$

$$R = \frac{18}{12+3} = \frac{18}{15} = 1.2 .$$

$$\sqrt{S} = \frac{V \times n}{R^{2/3}} = \frac{0.8333 \times 0.017}{1.2^{2/3}} = 1.2545 \times 10^{-2} .$$

Slope, $S = 1.5739\ 10^{-4} = 1{:}6353.$

Trapezoidal Channel of Minimum Section

A trapezoidal channel is to be designed to convey $5 m^3/s$ of water at normal depth, and to have a bed-slope 1:1600 and sides inclined at 45° to horizontal (Fig.11.17). Determine the minimum cross-sectional area for the channel.
Assume Chezy's $C=50\ m^{1/2}/s$.

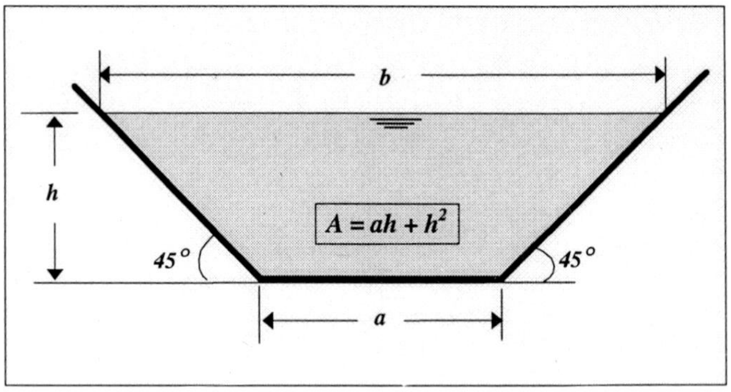

Fig.11.17- Cross-section of a trapezoidal channel.

Chezy's equation for velocity:

$$V = C\sqrt{RS} \text{ and } Mean\ velocity,\ V = \frac{Q}{A} = \frac{5}{ah+h^2}$$

$$R = \frac{A}{P} = \frac{ah+h^2}{a+2\sqrt{2}\,h}, \quad A^2 h = 16A + 29.2h^2 ,$$

Substituting,

$$\frac{5}{ah+h^2} = 50 \times \sqrt{\frac{ah+h^2}{a+2\sqrt{2}h} \times \frac{1}{1600}}, \quad or$$

$$\frac{1}{(ah+h^2)^2} = \frac{100 \times (ah+h^2)}{1600 \times (a+2\sqrt{2}h)} .$$

This can also be written as $(ah+h^2)^3 = 16 \times (a+2\sqrt{2}h)$, which gives

$$A^3 = 16\left(\frac{A}{h} - h + 2.83h\right) = \frac{16A}{h} + 29.2h$$

Differentiate,

$3A^2\, dA \times h + A^3\, dh = 16\, dA + 2 \times 29.2 \times h\, dh.$

$dA\ (3A^2h - 16) = dh\ (-A^3 + 58.4\ h).$

$$\frac{dA}{dh} = \frac{-A^3 + 58.4h}{3A^2 \times h - 16} = 0 \quad (for\ minimum\ area).$$

Hence $A^3 = 58.4h$.

Substituting into equation for A^3 above, gives

$58.4h = 16a + 16 \times 2.83h = 16a + 45.3\ h \quad or\ 13.1h = 16a.$

Bed width $a = 0.82\ h$, and $A = 1.82h^2$.

$1.82^3 \times h^6 = 58.4h, \quad or\ h^5 = \frac{58.4}{1.82^3} = 9.68 .$

Depth, $h = 1.675$ *m and*

Bed width $a = 1.292$ *m.*

Examples on Spillways and Weirs

Overflow Spillway Chute

Figure 11.18 shows a spillway chute of rectangular cross-section throughout, discharging water from a large reservoir to a horizontal channel. Calculate the discharge from the reservoir when its level is 2m above the spillway crest. Sketch the water surface profile and critical depth line throughout, inserting values for these in the crest region and at the point where the 4m channel becomes horizontal. If a hydraulic jump occurs on the horizontal bed a short distance downstream from the start of the 4m channel, what is the total rate of energy loss in the jump? Neglect friction.

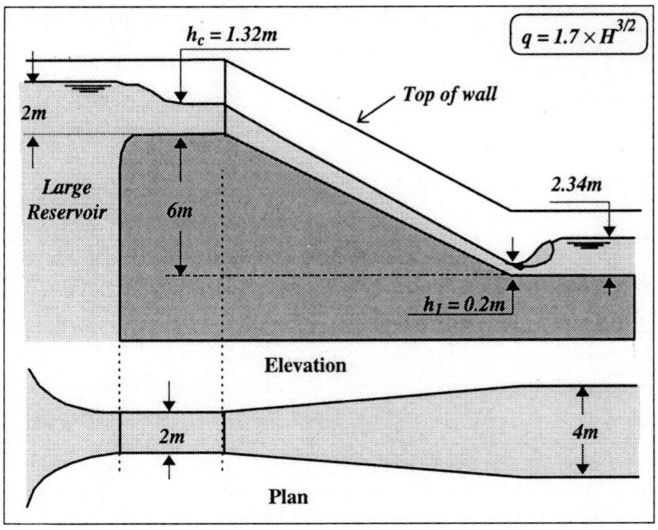

Fig.11.18- A spillway chute of rectangular cross-section.

$$Q = 1.7 \times 2 \times 2^{3/2} = 9.5 m^3/s, \quad q = \frac{9.5}{2} = 4.75 m^3/s/m.$$

Critical depth: $= h_c = \sqrt[3]{\frac{q^2}{g}} = \sqrt[3]{\frac{4.75^2}{9.81}} = 1.32m.$

$$H = h_1 + \frac{V_1^2}{2g}, \qquad 8 = h_1 + \frac{(4.75/2)^2}{2 \times 9.81 \times h_1}$$

By trial and error, $h_1 = 0.2m$.

$$h_2 = -\frac{h_1}{2} + \sqrt{\frac{2 \times q_1^2}{g h_1} + \frac{h_1^2}{4}}$$

$$= -0.1 + \sqrt{\frac{2 \times 2.4^2}{9.81 \times 0.2} + \frac{0.2^2}{4}} = 2.34m$$

$$H_2 = h_2 + \frac{V^2}{2g} = 2.34 + \frac{(4.75/4)^2}{2 \times 9.81 \times 2.34} = 2.39m.$$

$$H = H_1 - H_2 = 8 - 2.39 = 5.61m.$$

Energy loss $= \rho g \times Q \times H = 1000 \times 9.81 \times 9.5 \times 5.61 = 524$ **kW.**

Reservoir Spillway and Conduit

The hydraulic structure shown in the Figure 11.19 has a constant upstream water level and passes 10 m^3/s through the top spillway channel which is rectangular in section. The partially closed gate in the circular conduit restricts the conduit flow area by one half. Calculate the depth of flow, where it is constant, in the spillway channel at the 2m width and at the 4m width. Calculate also the rate of discharge from the conduit. Neglect friction in the spillway and bend losses in the conduit.

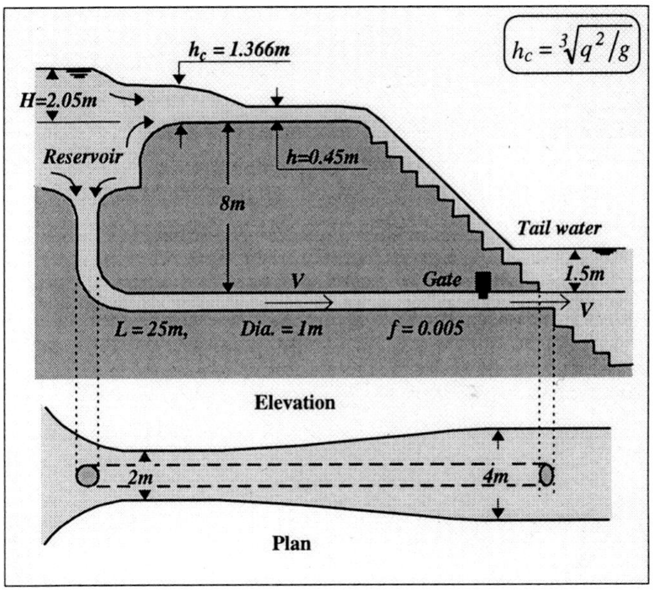

Fig.11.19- Reservoir spillway and conduit.

$q = 5 m^3/s$ *per m.*

$$h_c = \sqrt[3]{q^2/g} = \sqrt[3]{5^2/9.81} = 1.366m.$$

Specific head, $H = 1.5\,h_c = 1.5 \times 1.366 = 2.05m.$

$$H = h + \frac{V_1^2}{2g}, \qquad \text{i.e. } 2.05 = h + \frac{(2.5)^2}{2 \times 9.81 \times h^2}$$

$$h^3 - 2.05\,h^2 + 0.318 = 0.$$

By trial $h = 0.45m$.

Head difference $= 2.05 + 8 - 1.5 = 8.55m.$

Head loss, $8.55 = \frac{4flV^2}{2gd} + \frac{V^2}{2g} = \frac{V^2}{2g} \times \left[\frac{4 \times 005 \times 25}{1} + 1\right]$

Solve equation for *velocity in pipe,* $V = 6.1 m/s$.

Discharge: $Q = \frac{\pi}{4} \times 1^2 \times 6.1 = 4.8\, m^3/s.$

Bifurcated Channel

A horizontal 11m wide rectangular canal is bifurcated as shown in the Figure 11.20 into a 6m wide and 5m wide rectangular channel. In one arm of the bifurcation, the flow is controlled by a 5m wide vertical sluice gate, in the other arm, by a 6m wide streamlined broad crested weir whose crest is 0.5m above the canal bed. The flow over the weir is gauged by measuring the water level just upstream at A. For the depth of flow at A of 1.31m, calculate:

(a) the flow over the weir:
(b) the flow through the sluice gate if it is 0.2m open:
(c) the total flow in the upstream canal.

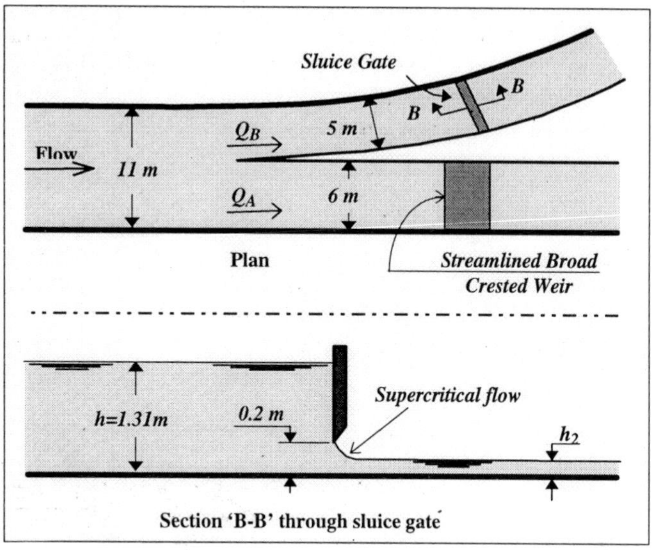

Fig.11.20- Bifurcated channel.

For channel with sluice gate.

Assume coefficient of contraction under gate = 0.62. Therefore, $h_2 = 0.2 \times 0.62 = 0.124m$.

Since flows downstream of gate and weir are supercritical, this flow cannot influence the upstream conditions, therefore the depth in the approach channel must be 1.31m, as in the weir channel; hence h_B is also 1.31m.

Apply specific head equation across gate:

$$1.31+\frac{V_B^2}{2g} = 0.124 + \frac{V_2^2}{2g}, \quad \therefore\ 1.31\ V_B = 0.124\ V_2.$$

$$1.31+\frac{V_B^2}{2g} = 0.124+\frac{1.31^2 V_B}{0.124^2 \times 2g}$$

$$1.186 = \frac{V_B^2}{19.62} \times 110.61 = 5.638 \times V_B^2$$

Hence, $V_B = 0.459m/s$ and $Q_B = 5 \times 0.459 \times 1.31 = 3.01m^3/s$.

For channel with weir.

Critical conditions over weir: $h_c = \sqrt[3]{Q_A^2/g\, b_A^2}$

$$1.31+\frac{V_A^2}{2g} = h_c+\frac{V_c^2}{2g}+0.5$$

or $1.31\ V_A = h_c\, V_c$.

Velocity upstream of weir: $V_A = \dfrac{h_c V_c}{1.31}$.

Hence, after substitution we have

$$1.31 + \frac{h_c^2 V_c^2}{1.31^2 \times 2g} = h_c + \frac{V_c^2}{2g} + 0.5$$

$$h_c = \frac{h_c \times V_c^2 \times b_A}{g \times b_A}, \qquad \therefore\ h_c = \frac{V_c^2}{g}$$

$$1.31 + \frac{h_c^3}{1.31^2 \times 2} = h_c + \frac{h_c}{2} + 0.5$$

$$\frac{h_c^3}{3.43} - 1.5\,h_c + 0.81 = 0$$

$$h_c^3 - 5.15\,h_c + 2.78 = 0$$

Solve by trial and error.

try $h_c = 0.8m$ $\quad f(h) = 0.51 - 4.12 + 2.78 = -0.83$
try $h_c = 0.5m$ $\quad f(h) = 0.13 - 2.57 + 2.78 = +0.34$
try $h_c = 0.6m$ $\quad f(h) = 0.22 - 3.09 + 2.78 = -0.09$

Critical depth $h_c = 0.58m$ and ***Critical velocity,*** $V_c = 2.385m/s$.
The discharge is then $Q_A = 0.58 \times 2.385 \times 6 = 8.30\ m^3/s$.
Total discharge is $Q_T = Q_A + Q_B = 8.30 + 3.01 = 11.31\ m^3/s$.

Flow Downstream of Dam Spillway

Describe the three possible tailwater conditions which can occur at the foot of a spillway. The maximum discharge over the spillway of a dam is $3m^3/s$ per metre width. The depth of flow at the foot of the spillway at this discharge is 0.234m and the bed of the tailwater channel is horizontal (Fig.11.21). A broad crested weir is to be built into the tailwater channel in order to make a hydraulic jump occur at this discharge. Calculate the height of the weir required.

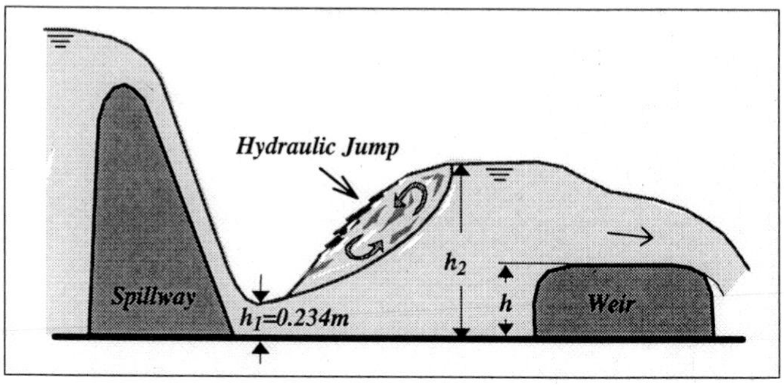

Fig.11.21- Flow downstream spillway.

Possible tailwater conditions:
- free flow with M3 surface profile
- free flow with hydraulic jump
- submerged flow conditions.

Velocity at base of spillway = $q/h_1 = 3/0.234 = 12.82m/s$.
$(Froude\ Number)^2$, $(F)^2 = 12.82^2 / (9.81 \times 0.234) = 71.6$.

Conjugate depth for hydraulic jump is given by:

$$\frac{h_2}{h_1} = \frac{1}{2}\times\left(\sqrt{1+8F^2} - 1\right), \quad \frac{h_2}{0.234} = \frac{1}{2}\times\left(\sqrt{1+(8\times 71.6)} - 1\right)$$

$\therefore\ h_2 = 2.686m.$

Corresponding velocity $= 3 / 2.686 = 1.117m/s$.

Specific head of flow $= 2.686 + (1.117^2/2g) = 2.75m$.

Critical depth of flow at 3m³/s $= \sqrt[3]{\dfrac{q^2}{g}} = \sqrt[3]{\dfrac{3^2}{9.81}} = 0.972m$.

Critical velocity $Vc = 3 / 0.972 = 3.09$ *m/s.*

Specific head at critical depth $= 0.972 + \dfrac{3.09^2}{2g} = 1.458m$.

Apply specific head equation between points upstream of weir and critical section at weir. Neglect head losses.

Specific head upstream = Specific head at critical section + h

Height of Weir: h = 2.75 - 1.458 = 1.292m.

Broad-Crested Weir

The flow in a rectangular channel is to be measured using a broad-crested weir of height d. Starting with an expression for critical depth show that the flow rate Q is given by:

$$Q = 1.7b\left(h_1 + \frac{V_1^2}{2g} - d\right)^{3/2}$$

A 3m wide rectangular channel has a bed slope of 1 in 1500 and a Manning's n of 0.016. A measuring weir in the form of a streamlined hump 0.8m high spans the channel (Fig.11.22). Determine the afflux caused by the weir when the flow rate is 7.5 m³/s. One correction for velocity of approach will suffice.

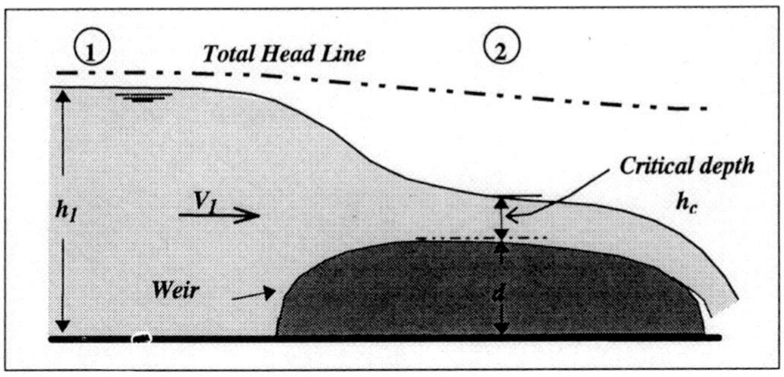

Fig.11.22- A broad crested weir.

For rectangular channel, critical depth $h_c = \sqrt[3]{Q^2/g\,b^2}$,

Specific head $H = 1.5 \times h_c = \dfrac{3}{2} \times \sqrt[3]{Q^2/g\,b^2}$.

Applying specific head between 1 and 2: $H_1 = H_2 + h$.

$$h_1 + \frac{V_1^2}{2g} = \frac{3}{2} \times \sqrt[3]{Q^2/g\,b^2} + d$$

$$\frac{Q^2}{g\,b^2} = \left(\frac{2}{3}\right)^3 \times \left(h_1 + \frac{V_1^2}{2g} - d\right)^3$$

$$Q = \sqrt{g} \times b \times \sqrt{\left(\frac{2}{3}\right)^3 \times \left(h_1 + \frac{V_1^2}{2g} - d\right)^3}$$

$$Q = 1.7b \times \left(h_1 + \frac{V_1^2}{2g} - d\right)^{3/2}.$$

For $Q = 7.5\ m^3/s$, applying Manning's equation:

$$Q = \frac{A}{n} \times R^{2/3} \times S^{1/2},$$

$$7.5 = 3h \times \frac{1}{0.016} \times \left(\frac{3h_n}{3 + 2h_n}\right)^{2/3} \times \left(\frac{1}{1500}\right)^{1/2}$$

$$1.55 = h_n\left(\frac{3\,h_n}{3 + 2\,h_n}\right)^{2/3}$$

Solving, ***normal depth***, $h_n = 1.78m.$

For Weir: $7.5 = 1.7 \times 3 \times \left(h_1 + \dfrac{V_1^2}{2g} - 0.8\right)^{3/2}$

$$h_1 + \frac{V_1^2}{2g} = \left(\frac{7.5}{1.7 \times 3}\right)^{2/3} + 0.8.$$

Assume $\dfrac{V_1^2}{2g} = 0$, $\therefore$ ***Depth,*** $h_1 = 2.09m.$

i.e. $V_1 = \dfrac{7.5}{2.09 \times 3} = 1.19 m/s$,

$$\frac{V_1^2}{2g} = \frac{1.19^2}{2g} = 0.07m.$$

Substituting, $h_1 = 2.09 - 0.07 = 2.02m.$

Afflux = 2.02 - 1.78 = 0.24m.

Flow Measuring Weir

A rectangular channel, 3m wide and bed slope 1 in 150, carries a discharge of 7.5 m³/s (Fig.11.23). A measuring weir in the form of a streamlined hump, 0.5m high, spans the channel. Determine the depth just upstream of the weir. Deduce whether a hydraulic jump will form upstream of the weir and, if so, determine approximately its distance from the weir. Take Chezy's C for the channel to be 55 $m^{1/2}/s$.

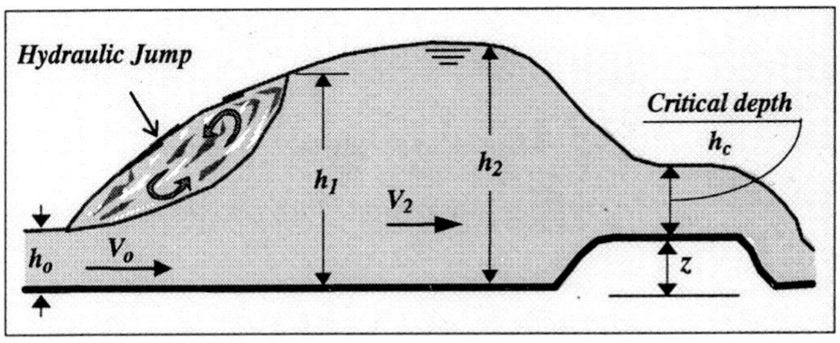

Fig.11.23- A rectangular channel with measuring weir.

Critical depth: $h_c = \sqrt[3]{\dfrac{Q^2}{gb^2}} = \sqrt[3]{\dfrac{7.5^2}{9.81 \times 3^2}} = 0.86m.$

$V_o = \dfrac{Q}{3\,h_o} = C\sqrt{R_o S_o}$, where $R_o = \dfrac{3\,h_o}{3 + 2h_o}$

$$\frac{7.5}{3\,h_o} = 55 \times \sqrt{\frac{3h_o}{3 + 2\,h_o} \times \frac{1}{150}}$$

Hence by trial and error $h_o = 0.78m,$ $V_o = 3.2m/s.$

Since $h_o < h_c$, **flow is supercritical.**

Specific head upstream: $H_o = h_o + \dfrac{V_o^2}{2g} = 1.3m$.

Assuming no friction losses ***the minimum value of specific head over the hump is:*** $H = H_o - z = 1.3 - 0.5 = 0.8m.$

Now the minimum value of specific head possible is,

$H_c = (3/2) \times h_c = 1.29m.$

Since $H_c > H$ supercritical flow is not possible just upstream of the hump. A hydraulic jump forms and flow is subcritical.

Total head upstream of weir: $H_c + Z = 1.79m.$

$$1.79 = h_2 + \frac{V_2^2}{2g} = h_2 + \left(\frac{Q_2}{h_2^3}\right)^2 \times \frac{1}{2g} \qquad \therefore\ h_2 = 1.79m.$$

For the hydraulic jump:

$$\frac{h_1}{h_o} = \frac{1}{2} \times \left(\sqrt{1 + 8 \times F^2} - 1\right), \qquad \therefore\ h_1 = 0.945m.$$

Approximate distance of jump from weir assuming horizontal water level = (1.79 - 0.945) × 150 = 125m.

Weir Control Structure

The weir shown in Figure 11.24 is used as a control structure for a sluice, the downstream bed level of which is 0.6m lower than the upstream level. If a standing hydraulic jump is formed just downstream of the weir, its conjugate depths being 0.25m and 1.8m, determine the depth and velocity at section 1 upstream of the weir. Calculate the force on the weir per metre width.

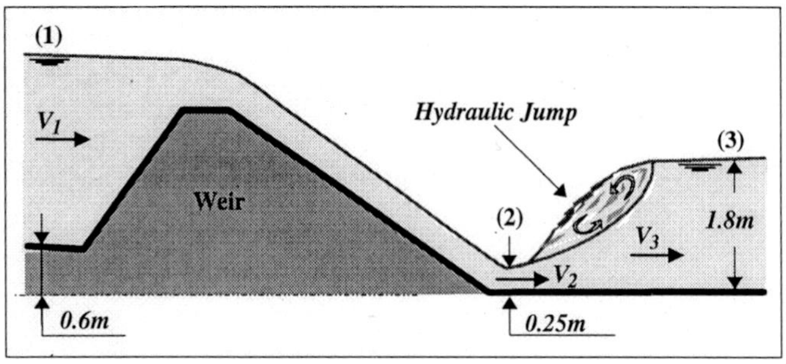

Fig.11.24- Cross-section of a weir with a hydraulic jump.

Applying momentum equation for jump:

Rate of change of momentum = Applied hydrostatic force

$$1.8V_3^2\rho - 0.25V_2^2\rho = \rho g \times \frac{0.25^2}{2} - \rho g \times \frac{1.8^2}{2} = -15.7\rho .$$

$1.8\ V_3^2 - 0.25\ V_2^2 = -15.7.$

Applying Continuity equation: $h_1 V_1 = h_2 V_2 = h_3 V_3$.

$\therefore\ 0.25\ V_2 = 1.8\ V_3,\ or\ \ V_2 = 7.2\ V_3$.

Substitute into above equations:

$1.8\ V_3^2 - 0.25\ (7.2\ V_3)^2 = -15.7,\ or\ 1.8\ V_3^2 - 13\ V_3^2 = -15.7$

$V_3^2 = 15.7/11.2 = 1.4 m/s.\ \therefore V_3 = 1.18\ m/s\ and\ V_2 = 8.5 m/s.$

$h_1 \times V_1 = h_2 \times V_2 = 0.25 \times 8.5 = 2.12.\ \ \therefore\ h_1 = 2.12/V_1$.

Applying Bernoulli equation between 1 and 2:

$$h_1 + 0.6 + \frac{V_1^2}{2g} = h_2 + \frac{V_2^2}{2g}$$

$$\frac{2.12}{V_1} + 0.6 + \frac{V_1^2}{2g} = 0.25 + 3.69 = 3.94 .$$

$V_1^3/19.62 - 3.34\ V_1 + 2.12 = 0,\ \ or\ V_1^3 - 65.4\ V_1 + 41.6 = 0.$

$\therefore$ ***Velocity***, $V_1 = 0.64 m/s$ and ***Depth***, $h_1 = 3.31m$.

Applying momentum equation for weir:

Rate of change of momentum = Applied hydrostatic force

$\rho h_2 V_2^2 - \rho h_1 V_1^2 = (\rho g h_1^2/2) - F - (\rho g h_2^2/2)$

$$10^3 \times \left(\frac{8.5^2}{4} - 3.31 \times 0.64^2\right) = \frac{10^3 \times 9.81 \times (3.31^2 - 0.25^2)}{2} - F$$

$F = [(1000 \times 9.81/2) \times (10.96 - 0.06)] - [1000 \times (18.06 - 1.36)]$

Force on weir, $\boldsymbol{F = 53464 - 16700 = 36760N = 36.76kN/metre\ width.}$

Flow Through a Venturi Flume

A venturi flume 2m wide at the entrance and 1m at the throat has a horizontal base. Neglecting hydraulic losses in the flume, calculate the flow if the depths at entrance and throat are 0.8m and 0.7m respectively. A hump is now installed at the throat of height 0.5m so that a standing wave is formed beyond the throat. Assuming the same flow as before, calculate the increase in upstream depth.

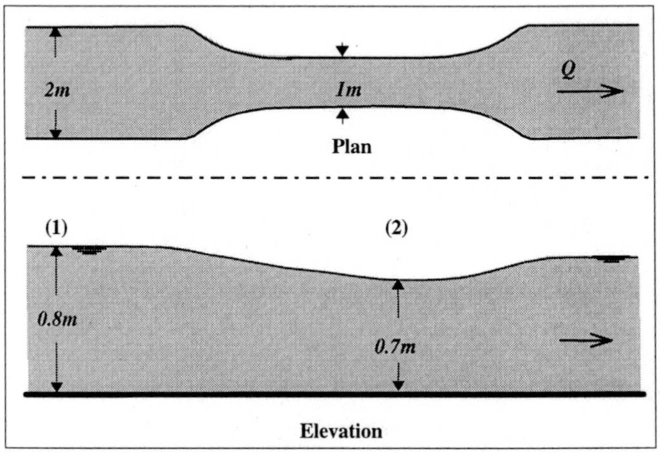

Channel with measuring flume.

(i) Applying specific head between points 1 and 2:

$h_1 + (V_1^2/2g) = h_2 + (V_2^2/2g)$

Applying continuity equation: $Q = V_1 A_1 = V_2 A_2$.

$\therefore\ 0.1 \times 2g = V_2^2 - V_1^2 = 1.962.$

$V_1 = (1 \times 0.7)/(2 \times 0.8) \times V_2 = 0.4375\ V_2.\ \therefore\ V_2^2 = 5.224\ V_1^2.$

$V_1 = 0.682 m/s$ and $Q = 0.682 \times 0.8 \times 2 = 1.09 m^3/s.$

$(ii)\ Q = V_c \times A_c.\ \ \therefore\ 1.09 = V_c \times 1 \times h_c$.

Also, $V_c^2 = g h_c\ (F = 1).$

$h_c = V_c^2/g = 1.09/V_c$.

$\therefore\ V_c = 2.2 m/s\ and\ h_c = 0.495m.$

$$h + \frac{V^2}{2g} = 0.5 + h_c + \frac{V_c^2}{2g} = 1.242 .$$

$$h + \frac{1.09^2}{2^2 \times h^2 \times 2g} = 1.242 = h + \frac{0.15}{h^2}$$

$f(h) = h^3 - 1.242\ h^2 + 0.015 = 0.$

$f(1) = 0.257;$ $\quad f(1.5) = 0.596;$ $\quad f(1.2) = 0.045;$

$f(1.22) = 0.0177;$ $\quad f(1.23) = -0.003.$ $\quad \therefore\ \boldsymbol{h = 1.23m.}$

Increase in upstream depth = 1.23 - 0.8 = 0.43m.

Examples on Venturi Flumes

Flow Through Venturi Flume

It is proposed to install a "critical depth" Venturi flume in a long rectangular channel 4m wide with a constant bed slope of 1 in 169, a Chezy coefficient of 60 $m^{1/2}s^{-1}$ and a normal depth of flow of 0.82m. Cross sections are everywhere rectangular and the flume is to have a hump, 0.50m high in its throat section. The depth of flow at entry to the flume is required to be 3m (Fig.11.25). Investigate the feasibility of this proposal, particularly having regard to the possible formation of a hydraulic jump upstream of the flume. Calculate the required throat width for the flume. Without further calculations, sketch the surface profile between points upstream and downstream of the flume where the depth is normal.

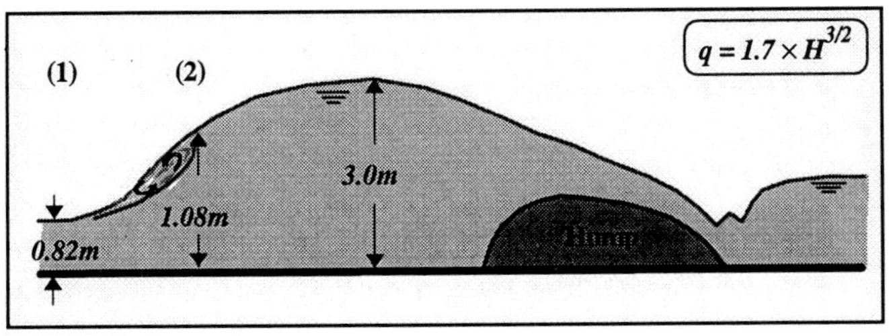

Fig.11.25- Venturi flume with a hump.

For normal flow the velocity is,

$$V_1 = C\sqrt{RS} = 60\sqrt{\frac{4\times 0.82}{5.64}\times\frac{1}{169}} = 3.52\ m/s.$$

The unit discharge, $q = 0.82 \times 3.52 = 2.89\ m^3/s$ *per metre.*

Total discharge, $Q = 4 \times 2.89 = 11.55\ m^3/s.$

Critical depth, $h_c = \sqrt[3]{\frac{2.89^2}{9.81}} = 0.95m,\ (h_1 < h_c).$

The slope is steep and the flow is supercritical.

For a depth of 3m just upstream of the flume, the flow must change to subcritical condition through a hydraulic jump.

For $h_1 = 0.82$, the conjugate depth of the jump is,

$$h_2 = -0.41 + \sqrt{\frac{16.58}{8.04} + 0.168} = 1.08m.$$

$$Q = 1.7b \times H^{3/2}, \quad H = 2.5 + \frac{V_2^2}{2g}$$

with $V_2 = \frac{2.89}{3} = 0.96\ m/s$ and $\frac{V_2^2}{2g} = 0.047.$

Width of throat, $b = \frac{11.55}{1.7\times 2.547^{3/2}} = 1.68m.$

Sluice Gate with a Hump

A rectangular channel 6m wide is carrying a flow of $24 m^3/s$ at a depth of 3m (Fig.11.26). The flow is controlled by a partly raised sluice gate. Calculate the depth of the jet issuing under the gate. Just downstream of the gate the floor of the channel is raised by 0.5m by a streamlined hump. Calculate the depth of water over the hump.

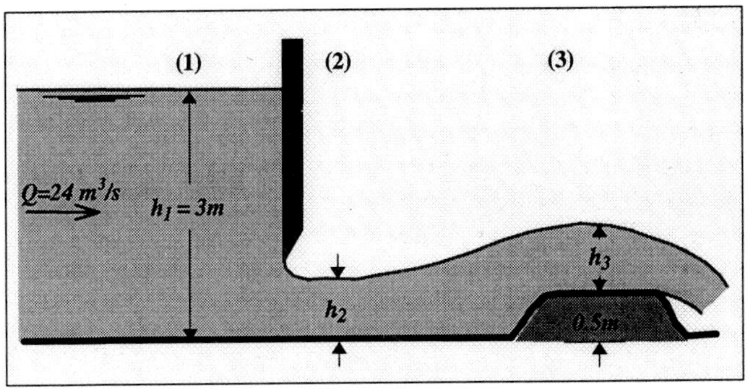

Fig.11.26- Flow downstream of sluice gate in a rectangular channel with a hump.

Specific head upstream of gate: $H = h_1 + \frac{V^2}{2g} = h_1 + \frac{Q^2}{2gA^2}.$

$$H = 3 + \frac{Q^2}{2g\times 36\times h_1^2} = h_2 + \frac{Q^2}{2g\times 36\times h_2^2}$$

$$3 + \frac{24^2}{2\times 9.81\times 36\times 9} = h_2 + \frac{24^2}{2g\times 36\times h_2^2} = 3.091.$$

$$h_2^3 - 3.091\ h_2^2 + 0.815 = 0.$$

Solve by trial and error

$h_2 = 1.2m, \quad f(h) = -1.908.$

$h_2 = 0.5m, \quad f(h) = 0.125 - 0.7727 + 0.815 = 0.167.$

$h_2 = 0.6m, \quad f(h) = 0.216 - 1.111 + 0.815 = -0.080.$

Therefore, $h_2 = 0.565m$ and $H = 3.091m.$

$$3.091 = 0.5 + h_3 + \frac{Q^2}{2g\times 36\ h_3^2},$$

$$h_3^3 + 0.815 - 2.591 h_3^2 = 0.$$

Solve by trial and error,

Try $h_2 = 0.6m, \quad f(h) = 0.098$

Try $h_2 = 0.7m, \quad f(h) = -0.111$

Therefore,

Depth $h_3 = 0.65m$ and

Critical depth, $\boldsymbol{h_c = 1.177m.}$

Channel Contraction

A horizontal channel is of rectangular cross section. It carries a stream which at one end is 2.75m wide and 1.85m deep (Fig.11.27). A little further downstream the width is 2.15m and the channel is 300mm higher but the water surface is 125mm lower. Calculate the rate of flow in the channel. What should be the difference in bed levels at the two sections if the water surface is to remain level for the same discharge?

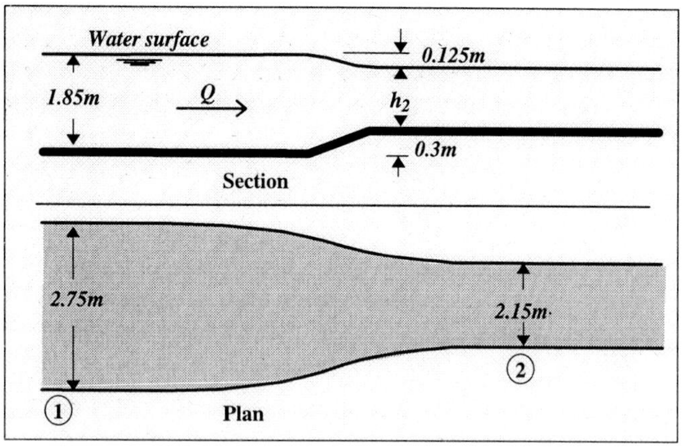

Fig.11.27- Channel flume contraction.

$$H = 1.85 + \frac{Q^2}{2g \times 1.85^2 \times 2.75^2} = 0.3 + h_2 + \frac{Q^2}{2g \times h_2^2 \times 2.15^2}$$

$1.85 + Q^2 \times 1.969 \times 10^{-3} = 0.3 + 1.425 + Q^2 \times 5.43 \times 10^{-3}$.

$3.46 \times 10^{-3} \times Q^2 = 0.125, \quad \therefore Q^2 = 36.127.$

Therefore, ***Total discharge*** $Q = 6.01\ m^3/s$.

$$1.85 + 6.01^2 \times 1.969 \times 10^{-3} =$$

$$z + 1.85 - z + \frac{6.01^2}{2g \times (1.85 - z)^2 \times 2.15^2}$$

$(1.85 - z)^2 \times 0.0711 = 0.398.$ *i.e.* $1.85 - z = 2.366.$

Therefore, ***Difference in bed levels***, $z = -0.516m$.

Measuring Flume with Raised Bed

In order to measure the flow rate of water in a rectangular channel 3.25m wide a section of the channel has its width reduced to 2.50m and the bed is raised by 0.35m. Calculate the flow rate in the channel if the depth of flow just upstream of the reduced section is 2.2m causing the water level in the reduced width section to fall by 0.2m (Fig.11.28). When the flow rate is reduced by 50% the depth of flow just upstream of the reduced width section is 1.4m. Calculate the depth of flow in the reduced width section.

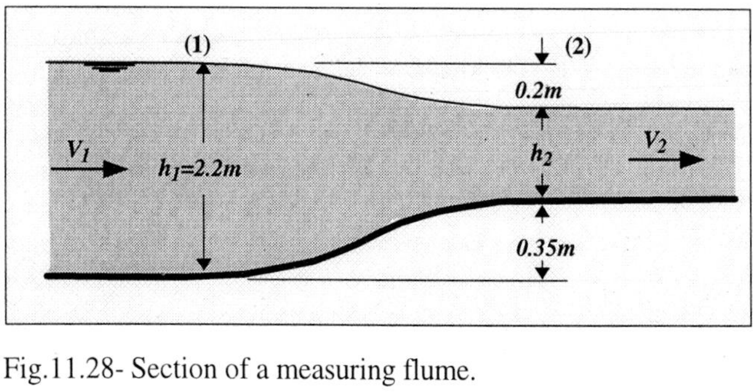

Fig.11.28- Section of a measuring flume.

$h_2 = 2.2 - 0.35 - 0.2 = 1.65m.$

Apply specific head between points 1 and 2, $H_1 = H_2 + z$.

$2.2 + (V_1^2 / 2g) = 1.65 + (V_2^2 / 2g) + 0.35$.

By continuity, $Q = A_1 V_1 = A_2 V_2$, *i.e.*

$V_1 = \frac{Q}{3.25 \times 2.2}$ and $V_2 = \frac{Q}{2.5 \times 1.65}$. Substituting,

$$2.2 + \frac{Q^2}{2g \times (3.25 \times 2.2)^2} = 1.65 + \frac{Q^2}{2g \times (2.5 \times 1.65)^2} + 0.35$$

$0.2 = 0.002\ Q^2, \ \therefore$ ***Total discharge,*** $Q = 10m^3/s$.

Q reduced by 50%, new discharge $Q = 5m^3/s$. $H_1 = H_2 + z$.

$$1.4 + \frac{5^2}{2g \times (1.4 \times 3.25)^2} = h_2 + \frac{5^2}{2g \times (h_2 \times 2.5)^2} + 0.35$$

$$1.46 = h_2 + \frac{0.204}{h_2^2} + 0.35.$$

Assume critical depth in reduced section, i.e. only 1 root at known point, i.e. $h / dh_2 = 3\ h_2^2 - 2.22\ h_2 = 0, \ \therefore h_2 = 0.74m$.

But substitution confirms that this a root of ***critical depth,*** h_c,

$h_c = \sqrt[3]{5^2 / (g \times 2.5^2)} = 0.741m.$

Measuring Flume

Figure 11.29 shows a measuring flume. The width of the channel is 2.5m and that at the throat is 1.2m. What is the discharge assuming ideal flow?

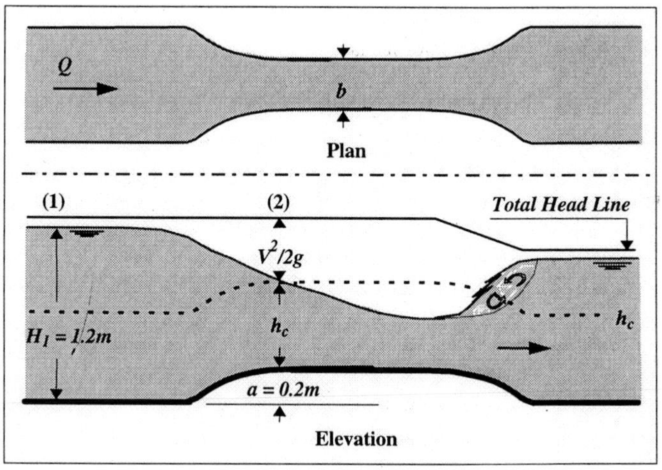

Fig.11.29- Channel with measuring flume.

Applying Bernoulli's equation between points 1 and 2 yields:

$$H_1 - a = h_c + \frac{V_c^2}{2g} = h_c + \frac{Q^2}{2g \times b^2 \times h_c^2}, \text{ with } h_c = \frac{2 \times (H_1 - a)}{3}.$$

$$\frac{H_1 - a}{3} = \frac{Q^2}{2\,gb^2 \times (2/3)^2 \times (H_1 - a)^2}.$$

$$Q^2 = \left(\frac{2}{3}\right)^3 \times gb^2 (H_1 - a)^3 \ \therefore Q = \left(\frac{2}{3}\right)^{3/2} \times g^{1/2} b (H_1 - a)^{3/2}$$

$Q = \sqrt{8/27} \times \sqrt{9.81} \times 1.2 \times 1.0 = 1.71 \times 1.2 = 2.05\ m^3/s.$

Upstream velocity, $V_1 = 2.05/(1.2 \times 2.5) = 0.68m/s$.

$V_1^2/2g = 0.024m$, $h_c \approx 0.67m$. Therefore,

Discharge, $Q = 1.71 \times 1.2 \times 1.024^{3/2} = 2.12m^3/s$.

Examples on Sluice Gates

Flow Downstream of a Sluice Gate

Figure 11.30 shows a large, deep reservoir discharging into a horizontal 5m wide rectangular channel. The flow in this channel is controlled by a sluice-gate. If the water surface in the reservoir is 10m above the channel bottom and the depth of water downstream of the gate at (2) is 1.0m, what is the water velocity at (2)? A short distance downstream, at (3), the channel is to be made narrower. What is the minimum width at (3) to maintain the same flow conditions at (2)? Describe with the aid of a sketch the flow conditions in the channel if the width at (3) were made still smaller. Assume the gate opening remains unchanged. Neglect friction.

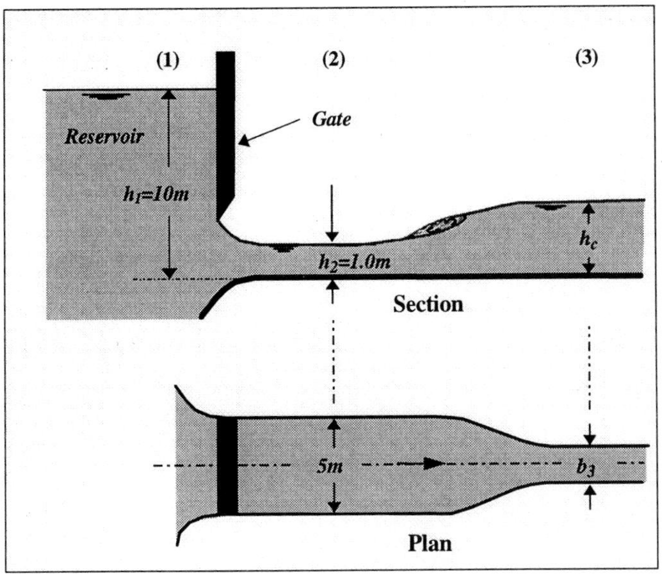

Fig.11.30- Large reservoir discharging into a rectangular channel.

Apply specific head across the sluice gate.

$$\frac{V_1^2}{2g}+h_1=\frac{V_2^2}{2g}+h_2 \text{ . Therefore, } 10=\frac{V_2^2}{2g}+1,$$

i.e. $V_2 = 13.3\ m/s$.

The discharge, $Q = 13.3\times5\times1 = 66.5m^3/s$,

and the depth $H = 1.5\times h_c$.

Critical depth: $h_c=\dfrac{10}{1.5}=6.67m$.

$$h_c=\sqrt[3]{\frac{q^2}{g}}, \qquad \therefore \frac{q^2}{g}=6.67^3.$$

The Unit discharge $q = 54m^3/s$ *per metre width*.

The Minimum Width $b_3=\dfrac{66.5}{54}=1.23m.$

Baffle blocks Downstream of a Sluice Gate

Water is discharged under a sluice gate at the rate of 75 m^3/s into a horizontal rectangular channel 6m wide. The depth just upstream of the sluice gate is 6m (Fig.11.31). In order to encourage the formation of a hydraulic jump concrete baffle blocks are placed across the channel just downstream of the sluice gate. If the force exerted on the blocks is *100kN,* calculate the depth just downstream of the hydraulic jump.

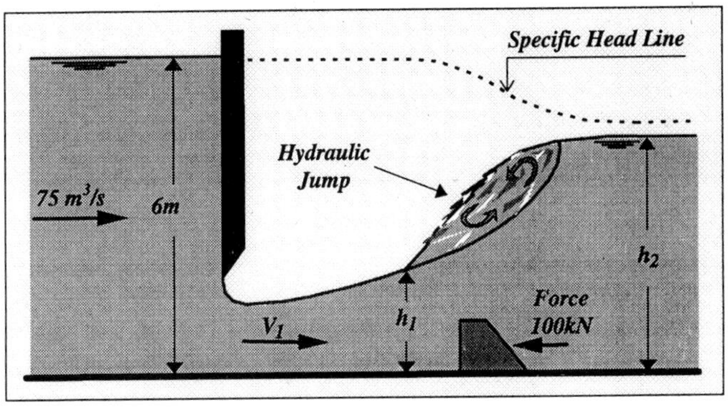

Fig.11.31- Discharge under a sluice gate.

Apply specific head across the sluice gate.

$$6+\left(\frac{75}{6\times6}\right)^2\times\frac{1}{2g}= h_1+\left(\frac{75}{6\times h_1}\right)^2\times\frac{1}{2g}$$

$h_1^3 - 6.22\,h_1^2 + 7.96 = 0$. By trial, $h_1 = 1.26m$.

Hence $V_1=\dfrac{75}{6\times1.26}=1.92m/s$.

Applying ***Momentum equation*** across the hydraulic jump:

$$\rho g\,(1.26\times6)\times\frac{1.26}{2}-\rho g\,(h_2\times6)\times\frac{h_2}{2}-100\times10^3 = \rho\times75\left(\frac{75}{6\times h_2}-9.92\right)$$

$$690.7-29.43\times h_2^2 = \frac{93.75}{h_2}, \text{ or}$$

$$29.43\times h_2^3 - 690.7\times h_2 + 93.75 = 0.$$

By trial and error, *the* ***downstream depth*** $h_2 = 3.92m$.

Force on a Sluice Gate

A 4m wide rectangular channel which has a bed slope *of 1 in 3000 and* a Manning's n of *0.02* carries a discharge at a normal depth of 1.2m. At one section the flow is controlled by an undershot sluice gate. The depth of water issuing from under the gate is such that a hydraulic jump forms immediately downstream of a gate. Calculate the depth of water issuing under the gate and the force on the gate.

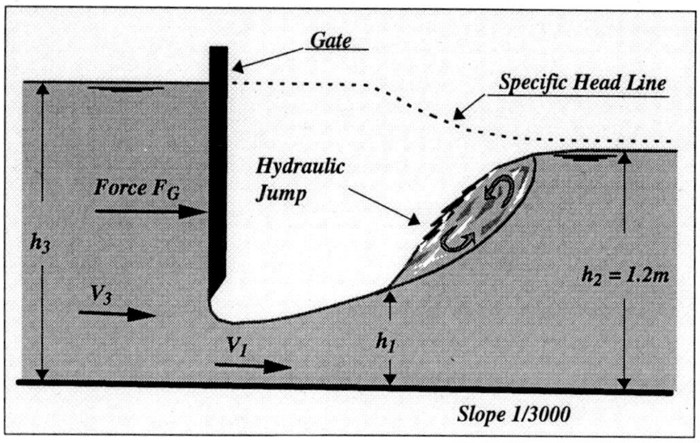

Fig.11.32- Flow downstream of a sluice gate.

Using Manning's equation, $Q = \frac{A}{n} \times R^{2/3} \times S^{1/2}$.

$$Q = 1.2 \times 4 \times \frac{1}{0.02} \times \left(\frac{1.2 \times 4}{4 + 2 \times 1.2}\right)^{2/3} \times \left(\frac{1}{3000}\right)^{1/2} = 3.6\ m^3/s.$$

$$\textbf{\textit{Velocity, }} V = \frac{3.6}{1.2 \times 4} = 0.75 m/s.$$

For hydraulic jump, the ratio of conjugate depths,

$$\frac{h_1}{1.2} = \frac{1}{2}\left(\sqrt{1 + \frac{8 \times 0.75^2}{g \times 1.2}} - 1\right).$$

Therefore, $h_1 = 0.105m$, and $V_1 = 8.57 m/s$.

Apply specific head across the sluice gate: $H_3 = H_1$.

$$h_3 + \frac{3.6^2}{2g \times (4 \times h_3)^2} = 0.105 + \frac{3.6^2}{2g \times (4 \times 0.105)^2}$$

$$h_3 + \frac{0.0413}{h_3^2} = 3.85, \quad h_3^3 - 3.85 h_3^2 + 0.0413 = 0.$$

Solve by trial and error, $h_3 = 3.85m$.

Therefore, $V_3 = \frac{3.6}{3.85 \times 4} = 0.233\ m/s.$

Apply momentum equation across gate:

$F_3 - F_1 - F_G = \rho Q (V_1 - V_3)$.

$$\frac{\rho g}{2} \times 4 \times 3.85^2 - \frac{\rho g}{2} \times 4 \times 0.105^2 - F_G = \rho \times 3.6 \times (8.57 - 0.233).$$

$$290 \times 10^3 - 0.216 \times 10^3 - F_G = 30 \times 10^3.$$

Force on sluice gate, $F_G = 259kN$.

Discharge Under a Sluice Gate with a Flume

A 5m wide sluice gate discharges 7.0m^3/s from a large reservoir into a channel whose width decreases gradually to 2.0m and whose bottom rises 0.5m. Determine the minimum reservoir level so that the gate is just not submerged, neglecting friction. Calculate the corresponding gate height for these conditions if the total discharge under the gate is given by $Q = d\,(32gH)^{1/2}$, where H is the level of water in the reservoir measured from the channel bed under the gate, and d is the height of the gate opening. Draw the profile of the water surface along the channel.

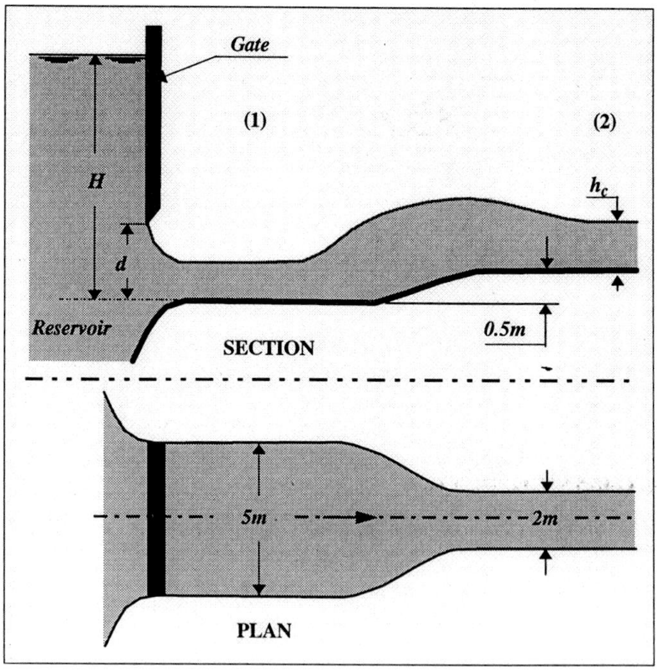

Fig.11.33- Channel contraction downstream of a gate.

$q_1 = \frac{7}{5} = 1.4\ m^3/s$ *per metre width of channel.*

$q_2 = \frac{7}{2} = 3.5\ m^3/s$ *per metre width of throat.*

Critical depth, $h_c = \sqrt[3]{\frac{q_2^2}{g}} = \sqrt[3]{\frac{3.5^2}{9.81}} = 1.075m.$

$h_{c2} = 1.075m.$

$Q = 1.7b \times \sqrt{H^3}$, $\therefore \sqrt{H^3} = \frac{7}{2 \times 1.7} = 2.06$, i.e. $H_2 = 1.62m$.

Water level upstream of a hump $= 1.62 + 0.5 = 2.12m.$

Discharge: $Q = d \times \sqrt{32g\,H}$

Height of gate opening, $d = \frac{Q}{\sqrt{32g\,H}}$

$$d = \frac{7}{\sqrt{32 \times 9.81 \times 2.12}} = 0.27m.$$

Supercritical Transitions

Channel contractions and expansions for subcritical flows are designed for minimum head losses by proper streamlining of the boundaries. If supercritical flow exists, as in the above example, the accent of design is shifted to the reduction of the standing wave patterns which appear as a result of such flows. Most designs have to be tested and evolved by physical model testing before construction (see Chapters 19 and 20).

Examples on Surface Profiles

M1 Surface Profile

A wide channel (in which the hydraulic radius closely approximates to the depth of flow) has a Chezy C equal to $45\ m^{1/2}/s$ and a constant bed slope such that a uniform flow of $1.5\ m^3/s$ *per metre width* occurs at the critical depth. With age the channel roughness changes to a Chezy C value of $30m^{1/2}/s$. For the same flow of $1.5m^3/s$ *per metre width* the depth at a measuring station on the channel is $1.25m$, and at another point further downstream the depth is $2m$. Using a single stage calculation, determine the approximate distance apart of the measuring stations.

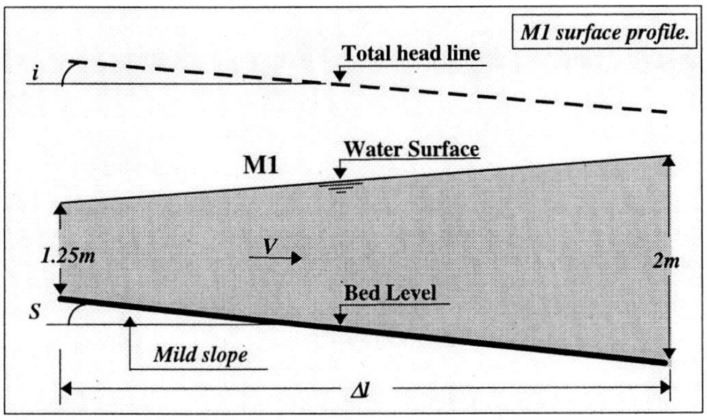

Fig.11.34- Backwater surface profile.

Uniform flow:

Chezy's equation, $V = C\sqrt{R\,S}$ and $q = Vh$.

For critical depth, $q = C \times h_c\sqrt{h_c \times S}$ and $h_c = \sqrt[3]{q^2 / g}$.

$$q^2 = C^2 h_c^2 \times h_c S = C^2 h_c^3 \times S .$$

Substitution for h_c, $q^2 = C^2 \times \dfrac{q^2}{g} \times S$, and $S = \dfrac{g}{C^2}$.

Slope of channel, $S = \dfrac{9.81}{45^2} = 0.0048$.

Non-uniform flow:

Mean depth, $h = \dfrac{1.25 + 2}{2} = 1.625m$.

$$q = C \times h \times \sqrt{R \times i} = 30 \times 1.625 \times \sqrt{1.625 \times i} .$$

Slope of total head line, $i = 0.00058$.

$$\frac{dh}{dl} = \frac{S - i}{1 - V^2 / gh},$$

$$\frac{2 - 1.25}{\Delta l} = \frac{0.0048 - 0.00058}{1 - (1.5 / 1.625)^2 / (9.81 \times 1.625)} .$$

Appropriate distance between measuring stations $\Delta L = 168m$.

M2 Surface Profile

At one section in a long wide rectangular channel, the bottom slope changes abruptly from 0.004 to 0.01. The rate of flow is $2m^3/s$ per metre width and Chezy's C is $65m^{1/2}\ s^{-1}$ throughout. Specify the water surface profile and estimate the position, relative to the break in the channel slope, at which the depth approaches the normal depth of flow.

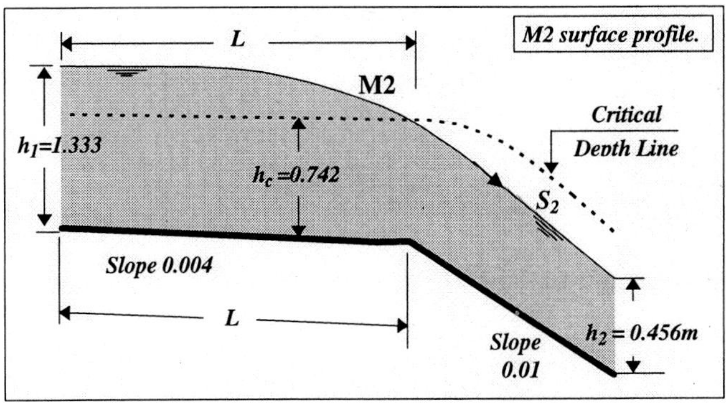

Fig.11.35- Change of channel slope.

Critical depth, $h_c = \sqrt[3]{\dfrac{Q^2}{gb^2}} = \sqrt[3]{\dfrac{4}{9.81 \times 1}} = 0.742m$.

First slope, $V_1 = C\sqrt{h_1 S_1}$, *(R = h for a wide channel).*

$(2/h_1)^2 = 65^2 \times h_1 \times 0.004 = 1.69h_1$, $\quad \therefore\ h_1 = 1.333m$.

Second slope, $V_2 = C\sqrt{h_2 S_2}$.

$(2/h_2)^2 = 65^2 \times h_2 \times 0.01 = 0.09467h_1$, $\quad \therefore\ h_2 = 0.456m$.

Length L of M2 curve on first slope:

For a wide river, $\dfrac{dh}{dl} = S\left[1 - \left(\dfrac{h_n}{h}\right)^3\right] \Big/ \left[1 - \left(\dfrac{h_c}{h}\right)^3\right]$.

where S = bed slope, h_m = normal depth and h_c = critical depth.

$$L = \int dl = \frac{1}{S} \times \int_{0.742}^{1.32} \left[1 - \left(\frac{h_c}{h}\right)^3 \Big/ 1 - \left(\frac{h_n}{h}\right)^3\right] dh$$

$$L = \frac{1}{S} \times \int_{0.742}^{1.32} \left[1 - \left(\frac{0.742}{h}\right)^3 \Big/ 1 - \left(\frac{1.333}{h}\right)^3\right] dh .$$

Tabulate 3 ordinates and find lengths using Simpson's rule.

h	1.320	1.031	0.742
$1\text{-}(0.742 / h)^3$	0.8224	0.6272	0
Δh		0.289	
$1\text{-}(1.333 / h)^3$	0.0298	-1.1613	-4.7980
$\dfrac{1\text{-}(0.742/h)^3}{1\text{-}(1.333/h)^3}$	-27.597	-0.540	0
Simpson's Products	-27.597	-2.160	0
The sum $\Sigma(\Delta L)$		**29.757m**	

Simpson's rule:

$$L = \frac{1}{S} \times \left[\frac{1}{3} \times \Delta h \times (\mathit{1st} + \mathit{last} + 4\sum \mathit{evens} + 2\sum \mathit{remaining\ odds}) \right]$$

$$L = \frac{1}{0.004} \times \left[\frac{1}{3} \times 0.289 \times 29.757 \right] = 718m .$$

Distance from change of slope to within 1% of upstream normal depth is about 0.72km.

M2 Surface Profile

A $4m$ wide rectangular channel, with a Manning's n of 0.012, carries a discharge of $12.5 m^3/s$. At one section the channel slope changes from $1/2000$ to $1/300$ with the $1/2000$ slope on the upstream side. Sketch the surface profile across the change of slope, indicating the types of surface curve involved. Determine the depth of flow at the intersection of the two slopes. Using an iterative method, with three slopes, calculate the distance upstream from the change of slope to a point where the depth of flow is 10% different from the normal depth.

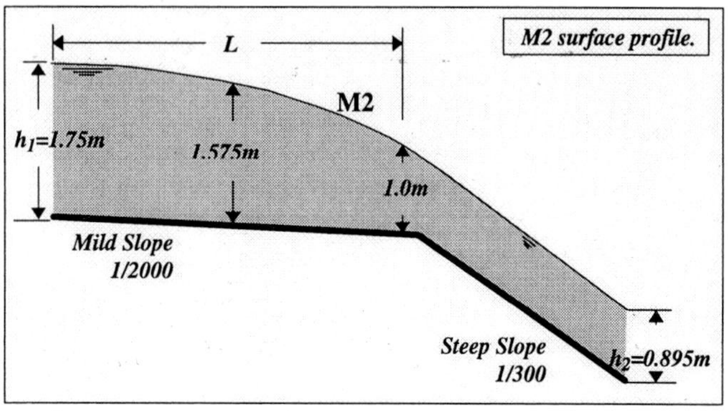

Fig.11.36- Break in channel slope.

The gradually varied flow equation is $\frac{dh}{dl} = S - i \Big/ 1 - \left(\frac{V^2}{gh} \right)$,

and Manning's equation, $Q = \frac{A}{n} \times R^{2/3} \times i^{1/2}$.

First slope, $12.5 = \frac{4h_1}{0.012} \times \left(\frac{4h_1}{4 + 2h_1} \right)^{2/3} \times \sqrt{\frac{1}{2000}}$

Normal depth, $h_2 = 1.75m.$

Second slope, $12.5 = \frac{4h_2}{0.012} \times \left(\frac{4h_2}{4 + 2h_2} \right)^{2/3} \times \sqrt{\frac{1}{300}}$

Normal depth, $h_2 = 0.895m.$

Critical depth, $h_c = \sqrt[3]{\frac{Q^2}{g \times b^2}} = \sqrt[3]{\frac{12.5^2}{g \times 4^2}} = 1m$.

1st slope: $h_1 > h_c$ $\therefore$ **Mild slope.**

2nd slope: $h_2 < h_c$ $\therefore$ **Steep slope.**

Depth at intersection: $h_c = 1m$

For first slope, 90% of normal depth = 1.575m, i.e. distance for change from 1m to 1.575m required.

Suggest 3 *steps* $= 0.575 / 3 = 0.19m$.

For each step assume mean depth h_m, area A_m, wetted perimeter P_m, velocity V_m and Froude No $F_m^2 = V_m^2 / gh_m$.

From Manning's equation

$$i = Q^2 \times n^2 \times \frac{P_m^{4/3}}{A_m^{10/3}} \quad \text{and} \quad S = \frac{1}{2000} = 0.0005 .$$

Use a numerical method to calculate the distance increment

$$\Delta l = \frac{(1 - F_m^2) \times \Delta h}{S - S_m} .$$

From the table below, the distance upstream to where the depth is 10% of normal depth = 633m.

h	1.575	1.383	1.192
h_m	1.479	1.287	1.096
A_m	5.916	5.151	4.384
P_m	6.958	6.575	6.192
V_m	2.110	2.430	2.850
$F_m^2 = V_m^2/gh_m$	0.308	0.466	0.756
$S_m = (Q^2 \times n^2 \times P^{4/3}/A^{10/3})$	0.00078	0.00117	0.00186
$dl = (1-F_m^2) \times dh/S - S_m$	- 475	- 152	- 35
$L = \Sigma(\Delta l)$ distance		**662m**	

The length of surface profile M2 to within 10% of the normal depth is 662m.

M3 Surface Profile

A wide sluice gate with a discharge coefficient of 0.95 discharges water into a horizontal channel. If the depth behind the sluice gate is 7.5m and the least depth of flow immediately downstream of the sluice is 0.65m, compute the water surface profile downstream of the gate to a point where the depth is 80% of the critical depth. The channel frictional characteristic may be represented at any point by the equation $V = 60 \times (h\, i)^{1/2}$, where h is the depth of flow in a wide channel and i is the water surface gradient. If the channel is long enough for a hydraulic jump to form, describe briefly, with the aid of a diagram, how the position of the jump may be determined.

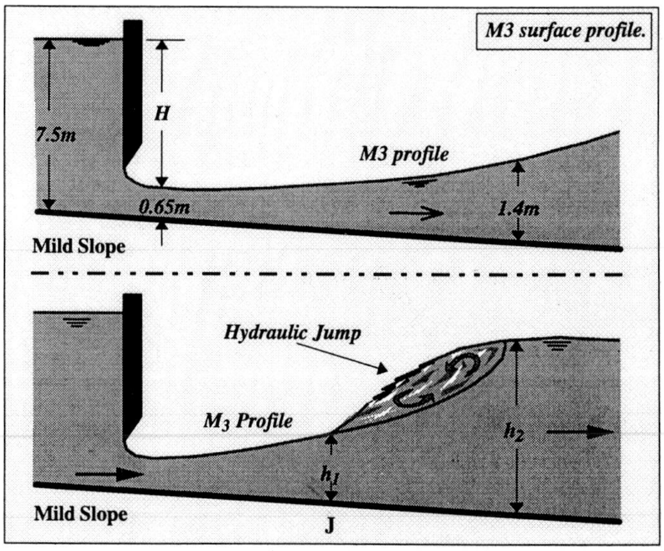

Fig.11.37- Surface profile downstream of a sluice gate.

Unit discharge under gate: $q = C_d \times h \times \sqrt{2gH}$.

$$q = 0.95 \times 0.65 \times \sqrt{2 \times 9.81 \times (7.5 - 0.65)} = 7.45\ m^3/s/\ metre.$$

Critical depth, $h_c = \sqrt[3]{\frac{q^2}{g}} = \sqrt[3]{\frac{7.45^2}{9.81}} = 1.74m$, $\therefore 0.8h_c = 1.4m.$

Length of M3 curve downstream of gate.

An appropriate method of calculating this length is by using $V = 60 \times \sqrt{h \times i}$ to calculate water surface gradient i by assuming the mean velocity depth for each reach $i = \Delta h/\Delta l$, hence find Δl for each reach, as shown below.

Increment	*Mean depth*	*Mean velocity*	*S*	*Δh*	*Δl*
0.65 - 0.90	0.775	9.62	0.0331	0.25	7.55
0.90 - 1.15	1.025	7.26	0.0152	0.25	16.45
1.15 - 1.40	1.275	5.85	0.0074	0.25	33.60

The length of surface profile M3 = ΣΔl =57.6m.

The position of the jump is determined along the M3 curve by calculating the conjugate h_1 for a known downstream depth h_2,

$$h_1 = -\frac{h_2}{2} + \sqrt{\frac{2q^2}{gh_2} + \frac{h_2^2}{4}}$$. ***Jump occurs where height = h_1.***

S1 Surface Profile

At a station along a wide rectangular channel a weir raises the water depth to 2.0m. The rate of flow is $1m^3/s$ per metre width and Chezy's C is $70m^{1/2}s^{-1}$. Sketch the surface profile in the channel and calculate the length of the backwater curve upstream of the weir, the bottom slope is 0.003.

$$\frac{\Delta h}{\Delta l} = S\left[1-\left(\frac{h_n}{h}\right)^3 \Big/ 1-\left(\frac{h_c}{h}\right)^3\right]$$

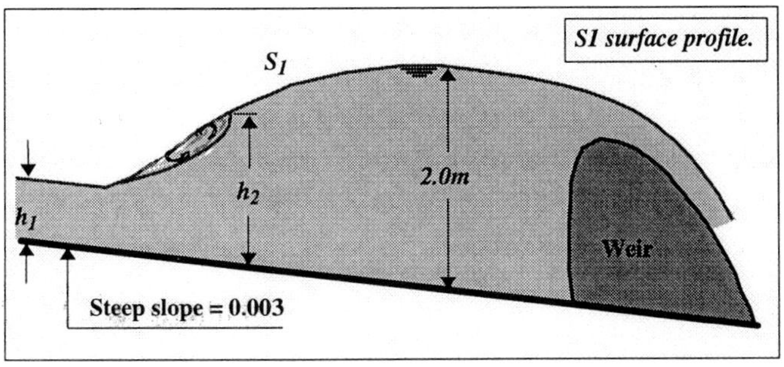

Fig.11.38- Surface profile upstream of a weir.

Normal depth, $h_1 = \sqrt[3]{\frac{q^2}{C^2 \times S_1}} = \sqrt[3]{\frac{1^2 \times 333}{70^2}} = 0.404m.$

Critical depth, $h_c = \sqrt[3]{\frac{q^2}{g}} = \sqrt[3]{\frac{1^2}{9.81}} = 0.467m$.

Since $h < h_c$, therefore, steep slope and S1 curve is formed downstream of hydraulic jump.

Conjugate depth of hydraulic jump:

$$h_2 = -\frac{h_1}{2} + \sqrt{\frac{2q^2}{gh_1} + \frac{h_1^2}{4}} .$$

$$h_2 = -0.202 + \sqrt{\frac{2 \times 1}{9.81 \times 0.404} + \frac{0.404^2}{4}} = 0.537m .$$

Divide into four increments and consider mean depth h_m for each reach Δl.

Depth Increment	2.0 - 1.6	1.6 - 1.2	1.2 - 0.8	0.8 - 0.537
Mean depth (h_m)	1.8	1.4	1.0	0.669
$(h_m/h)^3$	0.-0176	0.037	0.102	0.340
$(h_c/h)^3$	0.0112	0.024	0.066	0.22
Δh	0.40	0.40	0.40	0.263
Δl	129	127	125	72
L = ΣΔl	453m			

Length of backwater curve upstream of weir is L = 453m.

S2 Surface Profile

At one section in a long wide rectangular channel, the bottom slope changes abruptly from *0.004 to 0.01*. The rate of flow is $2m^3/s$ per metre width and Chezy's C is $65\ m^{1/2}\ s^{-1}$ throughout. Specify the water surface profile and estimate the position, relative to the break in the channel slope, at which the depth approaches the normal depth of flow. Sketch without further calculation the surface profile if the sequence of bottom slopes were reversed. Include in this sketch the critical depth and normal depth lines.

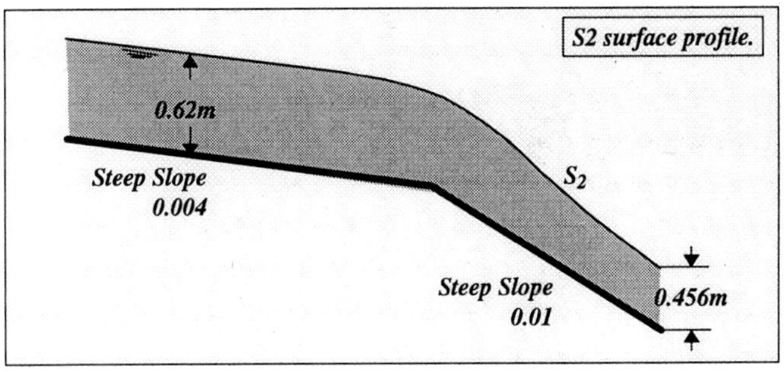

Fig.11.39- Abrupt change of slope.

Critical depth: $h_c = \sqrt[3]{\frac{q^2}{g}} = \sqrt[3]{\frac{2^2}{9.81}} = 0.741m$.

Normal depths:

$q = C \times h \times \sqrt{h \times S}$, for wide channel $R = h$.

$q^2 = C^2 h^2 \times h\,S$ and depth $h = \sqrt[3]{\frac{q^2}{C^2\,S}}$.

First slope, $h_1 = \sqrt[3]{\frac{q^2}{C^2\,S_1}} = \sqrt[3]{\frac{4 \times 250}{65^2}} = 0.62m$.

Second slope, $h_2 = \sqrt[3]{\frac{q^2}{C^2\,S_2}} = \sqrt[3]{\frac{4 \times 100}{65^2}} = 0.456m$.

Since h_1 and h_2 are less h_c, both slopes are steep and the flows are supercritical.

Length L of S2 curve on second slope:

For a wide river, $\frac{dh}{dl} = S\left[1-\left(\frac{h_m}{h}\right)^3\right] \Big/ \left[1-\left(\frac{h_c}{h}\right)^3\right]$.

Divide the curve on the lower slope into four increments Δh and calculate the corresponding value of Δl. Use the mean value of h for each reach.

Depth Increment	0.62-0.58	0.58-0.54	0.54-0.50	0.50-0.456
Mean depth (h_m)	0.600	0.560	0.520	0.478
$(h_m/h)^3$	0.441	0.541	0.672	0.870
$(h_m/h_c)^3$	1.880	2.310	2.900	3.720
$\dfrac{1-(h_m/h)^3}{1-(h_m/h_c)^3}$	-0.635	-0.350	-0.173	-0.048
Δh	- 0.040	- 0.040	- 0.040	- 0.044
Δl	6.30	11.40	23.10	91.73
$L = \Sigma \Delta l$	132.57m			

The length of surface profile S2 curve on the lower slope of channel is equal to 132.6m.

S3 Surface Profile

At one section in a very long wide rectangular channel the downhill bottom slope suddenly decreases from 1 in 100 to 1 in 225. The rate of flow is $2m^3/s$ per metre width and Chezy's *C is* $55m^{1/2}/s$ throughout. Estimate, relative to the break in the slope, the length of channel over which the flow is non-uniform. Give examples of six surface profiles.

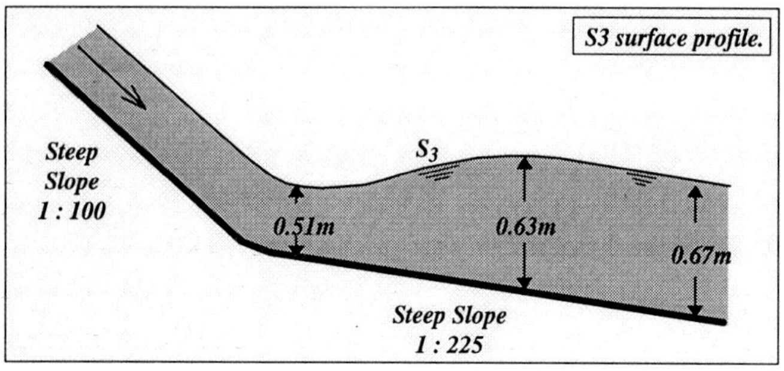

Fig.11.40- Channel with downhill bed slope.

Critical depth: $h_c = \sqrt[3]{\dfrac{q^2}{g}} = \sqrt[3]{\dfrac{2^2}{9.81}} = 0.741m$.

Normal depths: $q = C \times h \times \sqrt{h \times S}$, for wide channel $R = h$.

$q^2 = C^2 h^2 \times h\, S$, and the ***normal depth*** is, $h = \sqrt[3]{\dfrac{q^2}{C^2\, S}}$.

$$\textit{First slope depth},\ h_1 = \sqrt[3]{\frac{q^2}{C^2\, S_1}} = \sqrt[3]{\frac{4 \times 100}{55^2}} = 0.51m.$$

$$\textit{Second slope depth},\ h_2 = \sqrt[3]{\frac{q^2}{C^2\, S_2}} = \sqrt[3]{\frac{4 \times 225}{55^2}} = 0.67m.$$

Since h_1 and h_2 are less h_c, both flows are supercritical and S3 curve is formed on the lower slope.

0.95 × Normal depth = 0.95 × 0.67 = 0.636m.

Length L of S3 curve on second slope.

For a wide river, $\dfrac{dh}{dl} = S\left[1-\left(\dfrac{h_n}{h}\right)^3\right] \Big/ \left[1-\left(\dfrac{h_c}{h}\right)^3\right]$.

Approach normal depth to within 5%. Divide the curve on the downstream channel into four increments Δh = 0.03m, and solve in a tabular form the values of Δl, using the mean value of increment for each reach.

Depth Increment	0.51-0.54	0.54-0.57	0.57-0.60	0.60-0.63
Mean depth (h_m)	0.525	0.555	0.585	0.615
$1-(h_2/h)^3$	- 1.080	- 0.760	- 0.500	- 0.290
$1-(h_c/h)^3$	- 1.800	- 1.370	- 1.030	- 0.750
$\Delta h/ \Delta l$	2.670	2.460	2.160	1.720
Δl	11.25	12.20	14.56	17.45
$L = \Sigma(\Delta l)$	55.46m			

The length of surface profile S3 to within 5% of the normal depth on the bed slope is 56m.

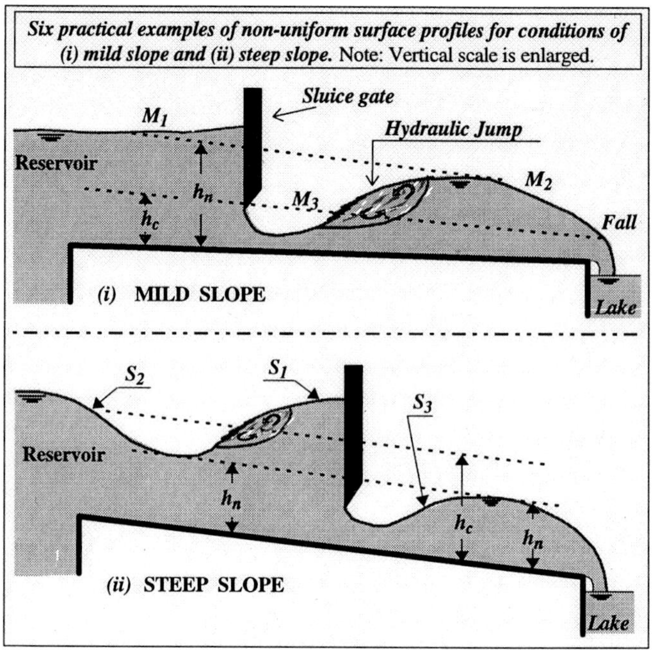

Fig.11.41- Six examples of surface profiles.

Permissible Velocity in Alluvial Channels

The maximum permissible velocity in an alluvial channel *V* is the maximum velocity which will not scour the bed and sides of the channel. A list of permissible velocities in various soil formations is shown in the table below. Using the permissible velocity as a criterion, the design procedure for stable channels is as follows:

1. Estimate the side slope, and *V* for the channel surface.
2. With known discharge *Q*, compute the area *A* = *Q/V*.
3. Calculate the hydraulic radius *R* from Manning's formula.
4. Calculate the wetted perimeter, *P* = *A/R*.
5. Using the expression for *A* and *P*, solve for the bed width of channel and depth of flow.

Channel Material	*n*	Velocity, *V (m/s)* Clear Water	Silty Water
Fine sand	0.020	0.45	0.76
Sandy loam	0.020	0.53	0.76
Silt loam	0.020	0.60	0.90
Alluvial sands	0.020	0.60	1.10
Firm loam	0.020	0.76	1.10
Volcanic Ash	0.020	0.76	1.10
Stiff Clay	0.025	1.14	1.50
Alluvial silts	0.025	1.14	1.50
Shales	0.025	0.80	1.80
Fine gravel	0.020	0.76	1.50
Graded loam	0.030	1.14	1.50
Graded silts to cobbles	0.030	1.2	1.67
Coarse gravel	0.025	1.2	1.80
Cobbles and shingles	0.035	1.5	1.67

Examples on Bridge Piers

Flow Around a Bridge Pier

Figure 11.42 shows a channel of rectangular cross section *3m* in width carries *8.57 m^3/s* of water at a normal depth of *1.5m.* Estimate the change in upstream depth which would result from the installation of a centrally located pier *0.9m* wide and *1.8m* long with well-rounded leading edge.

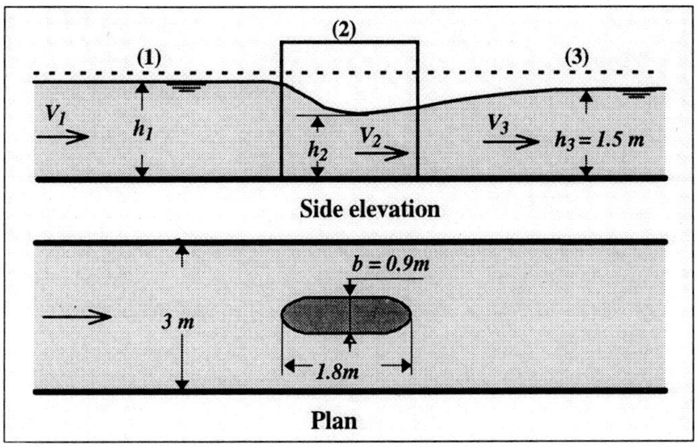

Fig.11.42- Flow around a bridge pier.

Through the use of the continuity and momentum equations, the depth and velocity at section *2* may be determined from known values at section 3. Thus $Q = h_2 \times V_2 \times (B-b) = h_3 \times V_3 \times B$, and, assuming the same pressure on the rear face of the pier as in the neighbouring flow, the momentum equation:

$$B\times\left(\rho g\times\frac{h_2^2}{2}-\rho g\times\frac{h_3^2}{2}\right)=Q\times\rho\times(V_3-V_2).$$

Substituting numerical values, $Q = 8.57 = 3\times 1.5\times V_3$

$\therefore\ V_3 = 1.9 m/s.$

$$V_2=\frac{Q}{h_2\times(B-b)}=\frac{8.57}{2.1\times h_2}=\frac{4.08}{h_2}.$$

$$3g\times\left(\frac{h_2^2}{2}-\frac{2.25}{2}\right)=8.57\times\left(1.9\times\frac{4.08}{h_2}\right).$$

By trial, ***depth*** $h_2 = 1.2m.$

$$\therefore\ V_2=\frac{4.08}{h_2}=3.4m/s \text{ and } H_2=\frac{3.4^2}{19.62}+1.2=1.79m.$$

$$H_2-H_1=1.79-1.5\times\frac{1.9}{19.62}=0.115m.$$

If it is assumed that the surface losses along the pier are negligible in comparison with the form losses in its wake, the equality of specific heads at sections 1 and 2 then permits calculation of the upstream depth: $(V_1^2/2g) + h_1 = 1.79m.$

Also, $h_1=\frac{8.57}{3V_1}$ or $V_1=\frac{2.856}{h_1}$, $\frac{2.856^2}{h_1}+h_1=1.79$

solution of which by trial yields:

Upstream depth, h_1 = 1.61m.

Drag Force on Bridge Piers

A straight uniform reach of a river *150m* wide is crossed by a bridge supported on three identical slender piers (Fig.11.43). Upstream of the bridge the river is *3m* deep and flows *2 m/s.* Downstream of the bridge, at a section where the drag of the piers has diffused throughout the whole stream, the depth is *2.9m.* Estimate the drag force on each pier. Estimate what the downstream depth would have been if only two such piers supported the bridge, the upstream conditions remaining constant.

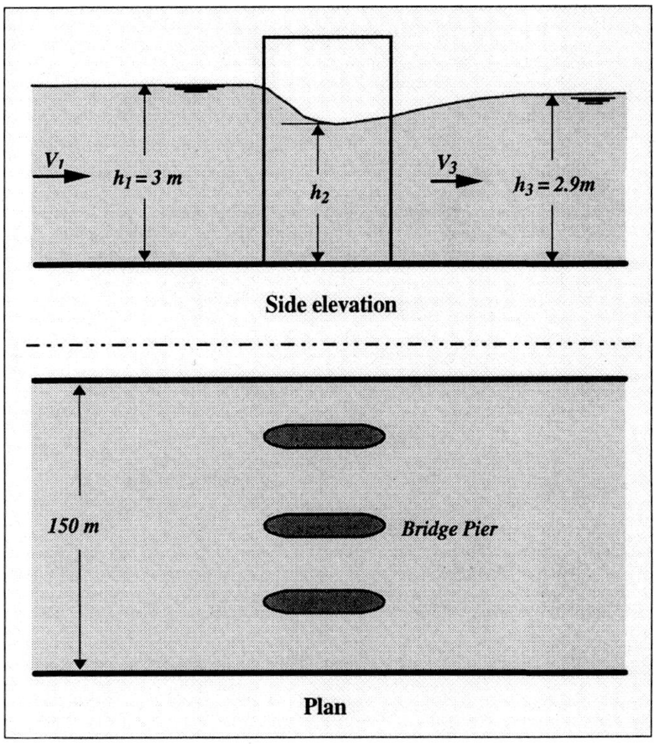

Fig.11.43- Drag on bridge piers.

Assume the drag on each pier is *D.*

Momentum equation.

$$\rho g\times A_1\times\overline{h_1}+\rho Q\times V_1=\rho g\times A_3\times\overline{h_3}+\rho Q\times V_3+3D$$

$$9.81\times(150\times3)\times\frac{3}{2}+(2\times3\times2)=$$

$$9.81\times(150\times2.9)\times\frac{2.9}{2}+(2\times3\times2)\times\frac{2.9}{2}+3D$$

Drag Force, *D = 127 kN.*

With two piers, use 2D = 254 kN in above momentum equation.

$$h_3^3-11.1\times h_3+7.35=0$$

Downstream depth, h_3 = *2.95m.*

Problems on Open Channels

Problems on Uniform Channel Flow

[1] A rectangular channel, 10m wide, carries a discharge $8m^3/s$ at a depth of 1m. Prove the flow is subcritical and find its specific head. (Subcritical)

[2] The discharge through a rectangular channel, 4.5m wide with n=0.012, is 12 m^3/s when the bed slope is 1 in 100. Is the flow subcritical or supercritical? (Supercritical)

[3] An open channel of rectangular section of breadth 1m and slope 2 in 1,000 conveys water at the rate of $3m^3/sec$. What is the depth of uniform flow when $C = 55$. (1.95m)

[4] Design of a stable channel - Calculate the bottom width and the depth of flow of a trapezoidal channel laid on a slope of 0.0016 and carrying a design discharge of 11.42 m^3/s. The channel is to be excavated in earth containing non-colloidal coarse gravels and pebbles. For the given conditions the following are estimated: n = 0.025, side slope 1:2, and maximum permissible velocity = 1.37m/s (Page. 112). Hints: Using Manning's formula,

$1.37 = (1/0.025) \times R^{2/3} \times \sqrt{0.0016}$, $R = 0.794m.$

$A = 11.42/1.37 = 8.36m^2$ and

$P = A/R = 8.36/0.794 = 10.53m.$

$A = (b + 2h) \times h = 8.36m^2.$

$P = (b + 2\sqrt{1+4} \times h) = (b + 2\sqrt{5} \times h) = 10.53m.$

Solving the above equations simultaneously,

Bottom width, b = 5.7m

Depth of flow, h = 1.05m.

Problems on Sluice Gates

[1] A sluice discharges a stream of 1.5m deep into a rectangular channel 6m wide. What will be the flow rate if the depth upstream of the gate is 6m? The conditions downstream cause a hydraulic jump to occur at a place where concrete block have been placed on the bed to dissipate energy and stabilise the jump. If the downstream depth is 3m, calculate the force on the blocks. ($87.3m^3/s$, 40.2kN)

[2] The flow from a reservoir into a rectangular channel 3m wide is controlled by a sluice gate. When the reservoir level is 3.5m above the bed of the channel the gate is raised to allow a jet 0.5m deep to flow into the channel. The coefficient of velocity of the jet may be taken as 0.98. Determine the necessary depth in the channel so that a hydraulic jump will form just downstream of the gate. Calculate the power dissipated in the jump. (3.3m, 118kW)

[3] Find the force on a sluice gate in a channel discharging $85m^3/s$ at 10m/s. The sluice and channel are 6m wide and the bed is horizontal. (425kN)

[4] A wide rectangular channel, bed slope 1 in 2000 carries a discharge of $2.5m^3/s$ per m width. Manning's formula for the channel is $v = 120\, h_n^{2/3}\, S^{1/2}$ where h_n is the normal depth of flow. Determine the depth of flow issuing under a sluice gate in the channel in such that a hydraulic jump forms just downstream of the sluice. The flow downstream of the jump is at normal depth. Determine also the depth on the upstream side of the sluice gate and the force on the gate. (0.77m, 0.975m, 15N/m)

Problems on Flumes and Weirs

[1] Calculate the discharge over a broad-crested weir 0.3m high which spans the bed of a horizontal channel 1.5m wide. The depth of water just upstream of the weir is 0.9m. Work to within an accuracy of about 3%. ($13.5m^3/s$)

[2] Derive the formula $Q = 1.7BH^{3/2}$ for the flow through a venturi meter flume. A venturi meter is to be constructed in a channel 5m wide. If the upstream depth is not to exceed 3m and the discharge $17m^3/s$, what would be the width at the throat for critical flow there? If it was desired to ensure critical flow by a streamlined hump 0.6m high, what should now be the width? (1.86m, 2.59m)

[3] A long rectangular channel, 10m wide, delivers water from a reservoir. A venturi flume is installed in the channel, having a streamlined hump 0.6m high and a throat width of 5m. The depth of water at the entrance to the flume is 2m. Calculate the discharge through the flume. ($14.6m^3/s$)

Problems on Non-uniform Surface Profiles

[1] In a rectangular channel, 2.5m wide with n = 0.013, there is a waterfall which draws down the water to the critical depth. The channel has a slope of 1 in 1000 and the normal depth of flow is 1.2m. Using a step by step method with depth increment of 0.15m, determine the distance back from the fall to the place where the depth is normal. (729m)

[2] A sluice spanning the entire width of a very long wide rectangular channel, bed slope = 1/900 and $C = 70m^{1/2}s^{-1}$ discharges $2m^3/s$ of water per metre width freely at 0.3m depth into the channel. Specify and evaluate the surface conditions downstream of the sluice.
(Length of curve from sluice to start of jump = 131.8m)

[3] Water runs down a 50m wide spillway at $280m^3/s$ on to a long concrete apron (n=0.015) which has uniform downward slope of 1 in 2500. At the foot of the spillway the depth of flow is 600mm. How far from the spillway will a hydraulic jump occur? For a wide channel taking $R = h$. (130m)

Examples on Computer Programs

Deviation of Equation for Surface Profile

Show that the rate of change of depth h at any point x along a rectangular open channel is given by:

$dh/dx = (S_o - i)/(1 - F^2)$

where S_o is the slope of the channel bed, i is the slope of the total head line and F is the Froude number.

$$\delta x S_o + h + \frac{V^2}{2g} = h + \delta h + \frac{(V+\delta V)^2}{2g} + \delta x i$$

$$(S_o - i)\times\delta x = \delta h + \frac{V\times\delta V}{g} + \frac{(\delta V)^2}{2g}$$

$$S_o - i = \frac{\delta h}{\delta x} + \left(\frac{V}{g}\times\frac{\delta V}{\delta x}\right) + \left(\frac{\delta V}{2g}\times\frac{\delta V}{\delta x}\right).$$

Limiting value, $S_o - i = \dfrac{\delta h}{\delta x} + \left(\dfrac{V}{g}\times\dfrac{\delta V}{\delta x}\right)$

$$S_o - i = \frac{dh}{dx} + \left(\frac{V}{g}\times\frac{dh}{dx}\right)\times\left(\frac{dV}{dh}\right) = \frac{dh}{dx}\times\left(1 + \frac{V}{g}\times\frac{dV}{dh}\right)$$

For a rectangular channel width B,

$V = Q/Bh$, $dV/dh = -Q/Bh^2 = -V/h$.

$S_o - i = \dfrac{dh}{dx}\times\left(1 - \dfrac{V^2}{gh}\right)$. Putting $F = \dfrac{V}{\sqrt{gh}}$, therefore,

$dh/dx = (S_o - i)/(1 - F^2)$

Use of Spreadsheets for Surface Profile

The computer is a powerful tool for the numerical calculations in solving engineering problems, particularly those which require many trials and iterations. Examples of procedures and a program for the solution of surface profiles are given.

The following procedure may be used:

1. Calculate the mean values of h, V, b etc.
2. Set up spreadsheet column headers for the mean variables including h_m, V_m, b_m, Froude number, dh/dx, dx and Σdx.
3. Calculate the normal depth h_n using Manning's formula.
4. Calculate the critical depth h_c.
5. Assume a depth interval Δh and key-in values of h.
6. Key-in formulae to calculate h_n, V_n etc.
7. Key-in formulae to calculate f, C etc.
8. Consider dh/dx equation.
9. Calculate the sum of values of dx.
10. When satisfied that the results are correct draw a chart showing the surface profile.

Computer Program for a Surface Profile

A rectangular channel, 1.5m wide, carries a discharge of 0.7m^3/s. The slope of the channel is 1 in 1600 and Manning's roughness coefficient n is 0.015. Write a computer program to calculate the length of channel over which the depth of flow changes from 0.65m to 0.75m.

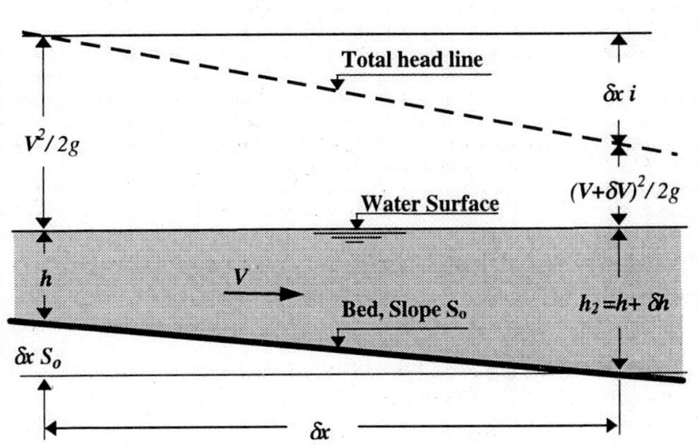

$$\frac{\Delta h}{\Delta x} = \frac{S_o - i}{1-(V^2/gh)}, \quad or \quad \frac{\Delta x}{\Delta h} = \frac{1-F^2}{S_o - i}$$

```
10   SI=100       ............  No. of Iterations
20   X=0
30   G=9.81
40   B=1.5        .................  Channel Width
50   S0=1/1600    .................  Bed slope
60   Q=0.7
70   N=0.015      ............  Manning's number
80   h1=0.65      ..............  Initial depth
90   h2=0.75      ................  Final depth
100  D2=(h2-h1)/SI   ..................  Δh
110  h=h1
120  A=B*h        .........................  Area
130  P=B+2*h      ...................  Perimeter
140  R=A/P        ...............  Hydraulic radius
150  U=Q/A        ......................  Velocity
160  F2=U*U/(G*h) ....................  F²
170  S=(Q*N/(A*R**0.6666))**2  ..  i = (nQ/AR^(2/3))²
180  D1=(1-F2)/(S0-S)*D2  .............  Δh
190  X=X+D1
200  h=h+D2
210  IF h<h2 GO TO 120
220  PRINT "REACH= ",X
230  END.
```

Computer Modelling Equations

Differential Equations

Computational methods in hydraulics for the calculation of flow variables such as depth, discharge, velocity or pressure involves the solution of a number of partial deferential equations. These equations are grouped into three types and are referred to as elliptic, parabolic and hyperbolic equations. The **elliptic** equations are those of the Laplacian kind:

$$\frac{\partial^2 \psi}{\partial x^2}+\frac{\partial^2 \psi}{\partial y^2}=0 \tag{11.28}$$

This equation describes a flow system which is in equilibrium. These may include the flow of groundwater (see Chapter 22). It represents steady conditions with no time variation.

The parabolic equations describe a system which is in transition from one steady state to another through either heat changes or turbulence characteristics. They are used in thermodynamics analysis for heat transfer and are of the following type:

$$\frac{\partial \psi}{\partial t}-\sigma \times \frac{\partial^2 \psi}{\partial x^2}=0 \tag{11.29}$$

The equation may also be applied to the drawdown in groundwater as a result of a pumping test or the diffusion of density currents in an estuary and also the erosion and movement of beach deposits.

The hyperbolic equations are represented as follows:

$$\frac{\partial^2 \psi}{\partial t^2}-c^2 \times \frac{\partial^2 \psi}{\partial x^2}=0 \tag{11.30}$$

They describe a fluid system in which a propagation of state takes place. Examples include the propagation of channel surges and sea waves as well as unsteady flow and shock waves in pipes and closed conduits.

The independent variable t in equations (11.29) and (11.30) above, can be substituted by a symbol y and the three equations can then be combined into the generalise partial differential equation of the second order.

$$A\times\frac{\partial^2 \psi}{\partial y^2}+B\times\frac{\partial^2 \psi}{\partial x \partial y}+C\times\frac{\partial^2 \psi}{\partial x^2}=D \tag{11.31}$$

where A, B, C and D are functions of the variables x, y, $d\psi/dx$ and $d\psi/dy$. In this equation there are dependant variables and independent variables x and y whose variations can be expressed as:

$$\frac{\partial}{\partial x}\left(\frac{\partial \psi}{\partial x}\right)dx+\frac{\partial}{\partial y}\left(\frac{\partial \psi}{\partial x}\right)dy=d\left(\frac{\partial \psi}{\partial x}\right) \tag{11.32}$$

$$\frac{\partial}{\partial x}\left(\frac{\partial \psi}{\partial y}\right)dx+\frac{\partial}{\partial y}\left(\frac{\partial \psi}{\partial y}\right)dy=d\left(\frac{\partial \psi}{\partial y}\right) \tag{11.33}$$

Equations (11.30), (11.31), (11.32) and (11.33) can be arranged in a matrix form as follows:

$$\begin{bmatrix} C & B & A \\ dx & dy & 0 \\ 0 & dx & dy \end{bmatrix}\begin{bmatrix} \dfrac{\partial^2 \psi}{\partial x^2} \\ \dfrac{\partial^2 \psi}{\partial x \partial y} \\ \dfrac{\partial^2 \psi}{\partial y^2} \end{bmatrix}=\begin{bmatrix} D \\ d\left(\dfrac{\partial \psi}{\partial x}\right) \\ d\left(\dfrac{\partial \psi}{\partial y}\right) \end{bmatrix} \tag{11.34}$$

The characteristic directions can be found by equating the determinant of the left hand side matrix to zero:

$$C\,dy^2 - B\,dxdy + A\,dx^2 = 0. \ \therefore\ A\times\left(\frac{dx}{dy}\right)^2 - B\times\left(\frac{dx}{dy}\right)+C=0$$

$$\frac{dx}{dy}=\frac{B\pm\sqrt{B^2-4AC}}{2A} \tag{11.35}$$

The three different types of partial differential equations are recognised by the characteristics associated with them. For an elliptic equation there are no real characteristics and the solution can be obtained analytically. Parabolic equations effectively have one real root and again a solution can generally be obtained analytically. For hyperbolic equations, which have two different real roots, analytical solutions are not possible. Non-analytical techniques such as finite difference, finite element or the method of characteristics are used. Examples of the hyperbolic equations include those for calculation of surface profiles and discharges in rivers, estuaries and coastal waters. The equation used to compute density currents along an estuary is known as the transport diffusion equation which is rather complicated and in general needs a non-analytical solution.

Methods of Solution

Generally there are three methods of solutions used in mathematical modelling and computational hydraulics, namely: **Characteristics**, **Finite Difference** and **Finite Element Methods**. The **method of characteristics** can be adapted on the computer in a similar way to the manual graphical method, and the characteristic lines are drawn on a connected plotter.

Finite difference method is more suitable for solving on a digital computer than the characteristics method. There are two broad methods of solution which are called **explicit** and **implicit schemes**. The explicit solution progresses from one boundary to the other, grid point by grid point, using known values to make a calculation. The implicit solution utilises recurrence relationships between the unknown variables and the time level under calculation, in order to sweep into the calculation known boundary values at both ends of the model. **Finite element method** is not extensively used but it is suited to approximate irregular boundaries but which produces difficulty in the approximation of the differential equations.

CHAPTER TWELVE

DYNAMICAL SIMILARITY

Introduction

In the investigation of a problem in a fluid dynamics, we begin by putting down the variables, influencing the problem. The next step is to pick out the principal unknown and to determine the form of the relation between this and the remaining quantities. Dimensional analysis, is of great value in reducing this relation to its simplest general form, stripped of irrelevant or nonessential features.

When measurements are used to determine the unknowns in a flow phenomenon, special techniques are used to ensure that any experiment is a faithful reproduction of the true phenomenon. The technique of reproducing of the behaviour of a flow on a different scale is known as **modelling**. In fluid dynamics, modelling is always aimed at scaling down. The conditions that a model reproduces the aspects of the actual flow include **geometrical and dynamical similarities**. Geometrical similitude requires that the configuration of the model is a scaled down reproduction of the prototype. Dynamic similarity requires that, at corresponding points in the model and prototype, the physical behaviour be identical apart from a change in scale.

The basic principle of the dimensional method is that all the terms in any equation connecting a number of physical quantities must be of the same dimensions in Mass (M) in Length (L) and in Time (T), or what is the same effect, the relationship must be one between groups of quantities, each of which is dimensionless, i.e. is a pure number. There are two methods of treatment in the analysis: (i) Rayleigh Method or singular method which is dealt with in Chapter Six, and (ii) Buckingham Method or the Π Theorem which is described below.

Buckingham Method (Π-Theorem)

The principal tool of dimensional analysis, was first brought before the engineering world by Buckingham in 1915. The essence of this theorem is as follows:

"In a physical problem including n quantities in which there are m dimensions, the quantities may be arranged into (n-m) independent dimensionless parameters".

Let A_1, A_2, A_3 ---- A_n be the quantities involved, such as pressure, viscosity, velocity, etc. If the first variable A_1 depends upon the independent variables A_2, A_3 ----- A_n and upon no others, the general functional relationship may be written in the form:

$$A_1 = f(A_2, A_3, A_4, \text{ - - - - - } A_n) \qquad (12.1)$$

Owing to the mathematical equilibrium between the dependent and the independent variables, these may be grouped in another functional relationship equal to zero:

$$f(A_2, A_3, \text{ - - - - - - - - - } A_n) = 0 \qquad (12.2)$$

If π_1, π_2, etc., represent dimensionless groupings of the quantities A_1, A_2, A_3 etc., they may be grouped into (n-m) dimensionless terms:

$$A_1 = \phi(\pi_1, \pi_2, \pi_3, \text{ - - - - - - - - - } \pi_{n-m}) = 0 \qquad (12.3)$$

In each term there will be (m + 1) variables, only one of which need be changed from term to term.

Proof of the Π-theorem may be found in Buckingham's paper. The method of determining the Π-parameters is to select n of the A-quantities with different dimensions, that contain among them the m dimensions and to use them as repeating variables together with one of the other A-quantities for each Π. For example, let A_1, A_2, A_3, contain M, L and T not necessarily in each one, but collectively. Then the first Π-parameter is made up as

$$\Pi_1 = A_1^{x1} A_2^{y1} A_3^{z1} A_4 \qquad (12.4)$$

the second one as

$$\Pi_2 = A_1^{x2} A_2^{y2} A_3^{z2} A_4 \qquad (12.5)$$

and so on until

$$\Pi_{n-m} = A_1^{xn-m} A_2^{yn-m} A_3^{zn-m} A_n \qquad (12.6)$$

In these equations the exponents are to be determined so that each Π is dimensionless. The dimensions of the A-quantities are substituted and the exponents M, L and T are set equal to zero respectively. These produce three unknowns for each Π- parameter, so that the x, y, z exponents can be dertermined, and hence the Π - parameter.

If only two dimensions are involved, then two of the A-quantities are selected as repeating variables, and two equations in the two unknown exponents are obtained for each Π term. In many cases the grouping of A-terms is such that the dimensionless arrangement is evident by inspection. The simplest case is that when two quantities have the same dimensions, e.g. length, then the ratio of these two terms is the Π- parameter. The procedure is best illustrated by the following examples.

Model Experiments and Dynamical Similarity

In many engineering problems it is not possible, or not economical, to make full size experiments, so that experiments on small scale models must be substituted. These models must be designed and the test results interpreted in accordance with the principles of similitude.

The principles of similitude require that there be geometric, kinematic and dynamic similarity between model and prototype. Geometric similarity is provided by constructing the model so that all linear dimensions of the model have some predetermined ratio to the corresponding dimensions of the prototype. Kinematic similarity requires that corresponding particles of fluid traverse homologous paths in the proper time ratios in model and prototype. Kinematic similarity can be obtained if the model is geometrically similar to the prototype and if the ratio of resisting to impelling forces is the same at all points in the fluid. The latter condition is called dynamic similarity. The impelling force is the inertial force resulting from the velocity and mass of the fluid. The resisting forces which tend to retard or change the direction of the fluid velocity may be viscous forces, gravity forces, surface tension forces or elastic forces. Only the first two are ordinarily of importance in hydraulic model studies.

In most problems of flow, the force of inertia is involved and, consequently, certain standard ratios of forces have been described by dimensional analysis, each of which involves the inertia force, as follows:

Reynolds number, R $= \dfrac{\text{Inertia force per unit area}}{\text{Viscous force per unit area}} = \dfrac{\rho VL}{\mu}$

Froude number, F $= \dfrac{\text{Inertia force per unit area}}{\text{Gravity force per unit area}} = \dfrac{V}{\sqrt{gL}}$

Mach number, M $= \dfrac{\text{Inertia force per unit area}}{\text{Elastic force per unit area}} = \dfrac{V}{\sqrt{K/\rho}}$

Weber number, W $= \dfrac{\text{Inertia force per unit area}}{\text{Surface tension force per unit area}} = \dfrac{\rho V^2 L}{\sigma}$

Application to Notches and Weirs

For measuring the discharge of liquids in open channels, notches and sharp-crested weirs are extensively employed. It is usual to make them with sharp edges of thin rustless metal plates. The nappe is the sheet of falling liquid which must spring clear of the downstream face. The head over the weir is the difference of level of the crest of the notch or weir and the surface of the liquid upstream before the surface begins to curve downwards towards the weir.

For flow over a triangular weir, Fig.12.1, the seven quantities involved are Q the discharge, the head h, θ the angle of the notch, g the acceleration of gravity, the density ρ, μ the viscosity and σ the surface tension of the liquid.

The functional relationship is:

$$f(Q, \upsilon, \sigma, \theta, \rho, g, h) = 0 \qquad (12.7)$$

Therefore there must be four dimensionless parameters. Angle θ is dimensionless, hence it is one π - parameter. The other dimensionless groups are:

$$f(Q\rho^a g^b h^c, \mu\rho^d g^e h^f, \sigma\rho^x g^y h^z, \theta) = 0 \qquad (12.8)$$

where $\rho, g, h,$ are the repeating variables.

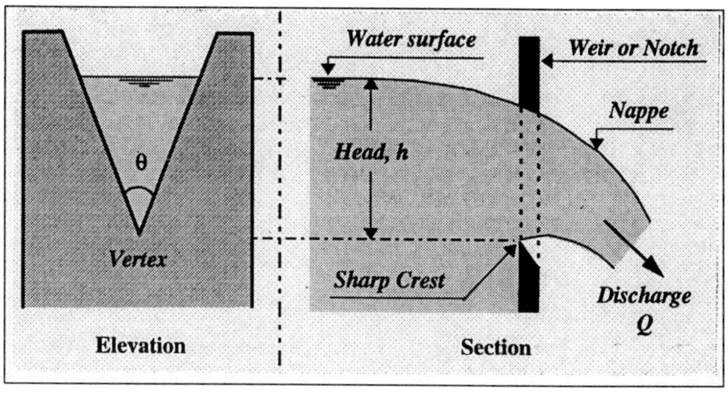

Fig.12.1- Flow over V-notch.

For the first product: $\pi_1 = Q\,\rho^a g^b h^c$ (12.9)

$$L^3 T^{-1} M^a L^{-3a} L^b T^{-2b} L^c = M^o L^o T^o$$

Equating power indices:

$a = 0$ $\quad 3 - 3a + b + c = 0$ $\quad \therefore\ -1 - 2b = 0$

$a = 0$ $\quad b = -1/2$ $\quad \therefore\ c = -5/2$

$$\pi_1 = Q/g^{1/2} h^{5/2} \qquad (12.10)$$

For the second product: $\pi_2 = \rho^d g^e h^f \mu$ (12.11)

$$ML^{-1} T^{-1} M^d L^{-3d} L^e T^{-2e} L^f = M^o L^o T^o$$

$1 + d = 0$ $\quad -1 - 2e = 0$ $\quad \therefore\ -1 - 3d + e + f = 0$

$d = -1$ $\quad e = -1/2$ $\quad \therefore\ f = -3/2$

$$\pi_2 = \mu/\rho\, g^{1/2} h^{3/2} \qquad (12.12)$$

For the third product: $\pi_3 = \sigma\,\rho^x g^y h^z$ (12.13)

$$MT^{-2} M^x L^{-3x} L^y T^{-2Y} L^z = M^o L^o T^o$$

$1 + x = 0$ $\quad -2 - 2y = 0$ $\quad \therefore\ -3x + y + z = 0$

$x = -1$ $\quad y = -1$ $\quad \therefore\ x = -2$

$$\pi_2 = \sigma/\rho\, g\, h^2 \qquad (12.14)$$

$$f\left(\frac{Q}{g^{1/2}h^{5/2}}, \frac{\mu}{\rho\, g^{1/2}h^{3/2}}, \frac{\sigma}{\rho g h^2}, \theta\right) = 0 \qquad (12.15)$$

Solving,

$$Q = g^{1/2} h^{5/2} \phi\left(\frac{g^{1/2}h^{3/2}}{\upsilon}, \frac{\rho g h^2}{\sigma}, \theta\right) \qquad (12.16)$$

This can be written for $\theta = 90^o$,

$$Q = Ch^{5/2} \qquad (12.17)$$

C is a function of Reynolds number $(g^{1/2}\ h^{3/2}/\ v)$ and the Weber number $(\rho g\ h^2/\sigma)$. When the angle θ is greater than or less than 90°, the coefficient C varies approximately as $\tan\theta/2$, this being unity for $\theta = 90^o$, and C is approximately 2.5.

The variation of discharge with head may be obtained by differentiating, the equation $Q = Ch^{5/2}$. Therefore,

$$\frac{dQ}{dh} = 2.5 \times Ch^{3/2} \qquad (12.18)$$

It follows that a small change or error in estimating h produces 2.5 times the percentage change or error in Q.

Application to Ship Models

When a body is partially submerged, that surface waves are produced and part of the resistance to motion is due to this wave formation. Hence the water is lifted against gravity by the water pressure; thus the influence of gravity must be taken into account by the inclusion of g. Then the resistance is given by:

$$R = \phi(\mu, g, \rho, V, d) \text{ or } f(R, \mu, g, \rho, V, d) = 0 \qquad (12.19)$$

Since there are six quantities and three fundamental units there must be 6 - 3 = 3 dimensionless products in the reduced equation.

$$\therefore\ f(R\,\rho^a V^b d^c,\ \mu\,\rho^d V^e d^f,\ g\,\rho^x V^y d^z) = 0$$

As before for the first two groups,

$$\Pi_1 = \frac{R}{\rho V^2 d^2},\ \Pi_2 = \frac{\rho V d}{\mu} \text{ and } \Pi_3 = \frac{gd}{V^2} \text{ or } \frac{V^2}{gd} \qquad (12.20)$$

$$f\left(\frac{R}{\rho V^2 d^2}, \frac{\rho V d}{\mu}, \frac{V^2}{gd}\right) = 0 \qquad (12.21)$$

$$R = \rho V^2 d^2 \times f\left(\frac{\rho V d}{\mu}, \frac{V^2}{gd}\right) \qquad (12.22)$$

The problem of ship resistance R is a different one, for here, it has been shown in Chapter 6 that:

$$R = \rho V^2 d^2 \phi\left(\frac{Vd}{\upsilon}, \frac{V}{(gd)^{1/2}}\right) \qquad (12.23)$$

For true dynamic similarity both the Reynolds number Vd/v and Froude number $V/(gd)^{1/2}$ must be the same for the model and the prototype ship.

Suppose first that $\dfrac{V_m}{(gd_m)^{1/2}} = \dfrac{V_p}{(gd_p)^{1/2}}$, or $\dfrac{V_m}{V_p} = \left(\dfrac{d_m}{d_p}\right)^{1/2}$.

This gives the speed at which the model must be towed. Now suppose that $\dfrac{V_m \times d_m}{\upsilon_m} = \dfrac{V_p \times d_p}{\upsilon_p}$, or $\dfrac{\upsilon_m}{\upsilon_p} = \left(\dfrac{d_m}{d_p}\right) \times \dfrac{V_m}{V_p}$.

It will therefore be seen that the requirement of Vm/Vp for waves to be similar is not the same for friction to be similar. Equating the right-hand sides of the equations, the values of v_m/v_p will be found which ensures that both eddies and waves are similar, i.e.,

$$\left(\frac{d_m}{d_p}\right)^{1/2} = \left(\frac{d_p}{d_m}\right) \times \frac{\upsilon_m}{\upsilon_p} \text{ and } \frac{\upsilon_m}{\upsilon_p} = \left(\frac{d_m}{d_p}\right)^{3/2} \qquad (12.24)$$

Thus if true similarity is to be achieved for both friction and waves the fluid in which a small scale model is to be tested must be less viscous than the water in which the prototype will float. For a 1:20 scale model (and this would be an unusually large one for the merchant ship). We find,

$$\frac{\upsilon_m}{\upsilon_p} = \left(\frac{1}{20}\right)^{3/2} = \frac{1}{89}. \text{ When } \frac{V_m}{V_p} = \left(\frac{1}{20}\right)^{1/2} = \frac{1}{4.47}.$$

There are, in fact, no cheap, safe fluids of so small a viscosity that complete similarity can be obtained in this matter.

The method of overcoming this difficulty was devised by Froude during the last century. The total resistance to motion is divided into two portions (a) the frictional resistance R_1 and (b) the wave-making resistance R_2.

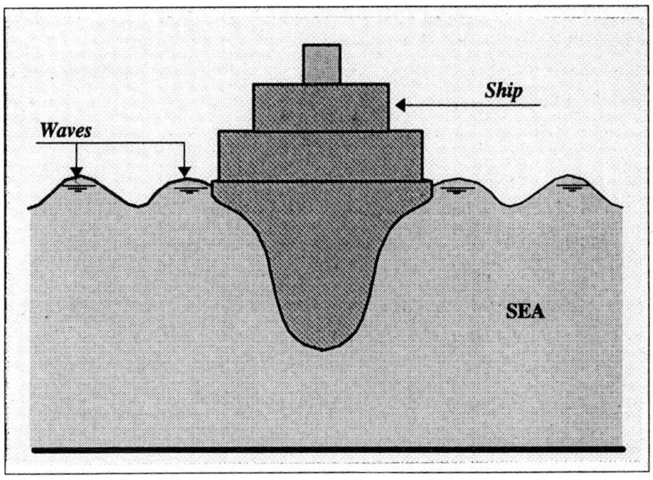

Fig.12.2- Resistance to a ship.

Thus for prototype $R_p = R_{p1} - R_{p2}$

and for model $R_m = R_{m1} - R_{m2}$

The frictional resistance can be computed from an empirical formula derived by Froude from the results of his celebrated experiments on skin friction, namely $R_1 = KAV^n$, where K is a constant, A is the surface area, and V is the velocity of the model or prototype.

The values of K and n can be found by towing long thin boards through water. Under these conditions, the surface area being large, the frictional drag is very large compared with the wave-making resistance. The values of K and n thus determined, R_{p1}, and R_{m1} can be calculated.

A model, geometrically similar to the ship is then towed through water at the "corresponding speed" as given by:

$$V_m = V_p \times \left(\frac{d_m}{d_p}\right)^{1/2}$$

This experiment gives the total resistance R_m of the model. Hence $R_{m2} = R_m - R_{m1}$

But for truly dynamically similar conditions,

$$\frac{R_{p2}}{\rho_p V_p^2 d_m^2} = \frac{R_{m2}}{\rho_m V_m^2 d_m^2}.$$

Hence, $R_{p2} = \dfrac{\rho_p V_p^2 d_p^2}{\rho_m V_m^2 d_m^2} \times R_{m2}$, But $\dfrac{V_p}{V_m} = \left(\dfrac{d_p}{d_m}\right)^{1/2}$

$$R_{p2} = \frac{\rho_p}{\rho_m} \times \left(\frac{d_p}{d_m}\right)^3 \times R_{m2}$$

Hence the total resistance of the prototype ship may be found from $R_p = R_{p1} - R_{p2}$.

Drag Force $= \rho V^2 A \phi(R)$

If we put $C_D = \rho V^2 A\ \phi(R)$, $D = 0.5 \times C_D = \rho V^2 A$

where C_D is known as the drag coefficient, which depends on the surface area and shape of the body.

Total Drag = Form Drag + Friction Drag.

Examples on Dynamical Similarity

Thrust of a Ship's Propeller

Assuming that the thrust T of a ship's propeller depends on the propeller diameter D and rotational speed n, the speed of the ship V, the density of ρ and the dynamic viscosity μ of the fluid, use dimensional analysis to derive a functional similarity usually assumed for propellers. The performance of a propeller 5m in diameter is studied by means of a geometrically similar model 0.25m in diameter. When the model is tested in a fresh-water tunnel at a rotational speed of 30 rev/s and a water velocity of 2.0m/s the thrust and torque are 180Nm respectively. Determine the corresponding speed of rotation, thrust and power of the ship's propeller when the speed of the ship is 6 m/s in sea water of density 1026 kg/m^3.

(a) Dimensional analysis: $T = f(\rho, D, V, n, \mu)$

$$\pi_1 = \frac{T}{\rho D^2 V^2}, \quad \pi_2 = \frac{\mu}{\rho V D}, \quad \pi_3 = \frac{nD}{V}$$

$$\therefore\ T = \rho\, D^2 V^2\, \phi\left[\frac{\mu}{\rho V D}, \frac{nD}{V}\right]$$

Since it is impossible to satisfy that $\mu/\rho VD$ and nD/V be the same for model and prototype propellers, it is usual to neglect the effect of viscosity and arrange nD/V to be the same.

(b) Model analysis:

$$\frac{n_m D_m}{V_m} = \frac{n_p D_p}{V_p}, \text{ i.e. } \frac{30\times 0.25}{2} = \frac{n_p \times 5}{6}$$

Speed of rotation, $n_p = \dfrac{6\times 30\times 0.25}{2\times 5} = 4.5 \text{ rev/s.}$

$$\frac{T_m}{\rho_m D_m^2 V_m^2} = \frac{T_p}{\rho_p D_p^2 V_p^2}, \text{ i.e.}$$

$$\frac{180}{1000\times 0.25^2 \times 2^2} = \frac{T_p}{1026\times 5^2 \times 6^2}$$

Thrust, $T_p = \dfrac{180\times 1026\times 25\times 36}{1000\times 0.0625\times 4} = 665kN$

$$\text{Power, P} = T\times V = \rho\, V^3 D^2 \times \phi\left(\frac{\mu}{\rho V D}, \frac{nD}{V}\right)$$

P_m = Torque $\times\ \omega = 4.9\times 2\pi \times 30 = 923W$

$$\frac{P_m}{\rho_m D_m^2 V_m^3} = \frac{P_p}{\rho_p D_p^2 V_p^3}$$

$$P_p = \left(\frac{1026}{1000}\right)\times\left(\frac{6}{2}\right)^2 \times\left(\frac{5}{0.25}\right)^2 \times 923 = 10.2\times 10^6\, W$$

Dynamic Similarity For Pipes

Show by dimensional analysis that:

$$\frac{\Delta p}{L} = \frac{\rho V^2}{d}\times\phi\left(\frac{\rho V d}{\mu}\right)$$

where $\Delta p/L$ is the pressure drop unit length in a pipe diameter, d, carrying fluid of dynamic viscosity, μ, and density, ρ, at a velocity V. An air duct, 1.5m diameter, is to be designed to carry air at a velocity of 5m/s. The pressure losses in the air duct are to be investigated using a model, 200mm diameter, which has water as the fluid. Calculate the velocity of the water if there is to be dynamic similarity between the air duct and the model. If the pressure loss per unit length in the model at this velocity is 500N/m^2, calculate the pressure loss per unit length in the air duct. Assume ρ_{air} = 1.23kg/m^3, μ_{air} = 1.8 × 10^{-5} Ns/m^2, and μ_{water} = 1.14 × 10^{-3} Ns/m^2.

$$\frac{\Delta p}{L} = \frac{\rho V^2}{d}\times\phi\left(\frac{\rho V d}{\mu}\right)$$

For dynamic similarity: $\left(\dfrac{\rho V d}{\mu}\right)_{air} = \left(\dfrac{\rho V d}{\mu}\right)_{water},$

$$\frac{1.23\times 5\times 1.5}{1.8\times 10^{-5}} = \frac{1000\times V\times 0.2}{\mu_{water}}$$

$$\left(\frac{(\Delta p/L)\times d}{\rho V^2}\right)_{air} = \left(\frac{(\Delta p/L)\times d}{\rho V^2}\right)_{water},$$

$$\frac{(\Delta p/L)\times d}{1.23\times 5^2} = \frac{500\times 0.2}{1000\times 2.92^2}$$

Pressure drop per unit length air duct = 0.24N/m^2.

Force on a Bridge Pier

Assuming that the force, F, exerted on the outside of a solid cylinder by a fluid flowing past it, is dependent on the diameter of the cylinder, D, the density, ρ, kinematic viscosity, ν, and velocity of the fluid, u, determine by the method of dimensional analysis, a relationship between dimensionless numbers involving these quantities. Tests performed on a cylinder of diameter 0.25m in air gave the following forces per metre length of the cylinder.

Speed of air (m/s)	23	36	46	57
Force (N)	23.7	78	152	248

Calculate the force that will be exerted on a bridge pier of diameter 0.3m situated in 3.3m depth of water flowing with velocity 4m/s. Assume, ρ_{air} = 1.23kg/m^3, ν_{air} = 1.48 × 10^{-5}m^2/s, and ν_{water} = 1.31 × 10^{-6}m^2/s.

Force, $F = \phi(D^a, \rho^b v^c u^d)$

$MLT^{-2} = K\,[L^a (ML^{-3})^b (L^2 T^{-1})^c (LT^{-1})^d]$

(M) $1 = b$ $\therefore b = 1$

(L) $1 = a - 3b + 2c + d$ $\therefore c = 2 - d$

(T) $-2 = -c - d$ $a = 1 + 3 - s(2 - d) - d$ $\therefore$ a = d

$F = K[D^a \rho^1 v^{2-d} u^a]$

$$\therefore\ F = \rho v^2\, \phi\left(\frac{uD}{v}\right)$$

For dynamic similarity: $\left(\frac{uD}{v}\right)_{air} = \left(\frac{uD}{v}\right)_{water} = \frac{4\times 0.3}{1.31\times 10^{-6}}$

Velocity of air: $u_{air} = \frac{4\times 0.3}{1.31\times 10^{-6}}\times\frac{1.48\times 10^{-5}}{0.25} = 54.2m/s$.

Force in air per metre length of cylinder is estimated:

$$F_{air} = 152 + \frac{248-152}{57-46}\times(54.2-46) = 152+71.6 = 223.6N$$

$$\therefore\ \frac{F_{air}}{F_w} = \frac{\rho_{air}\upsilon_{air}^2}{\rho_w \upsilon_w^2}$$

Force in water per metre length of cylinder is estimated:

$$F_w = \frac{1000\times 1.31^2\times 10^{-12}\times 223.6}{1.23\times 1.48^2\times 10^{-10}} = 1430N.$$

Force on bridge pier = 3.3 × 1430 = 47190 N = 4.71 kN.

Power for Rotating Disc

A disc diameter D which is immersed in a fluid of density ρ and coefficient of viscosity μ has a constant rotational speed N. Under these conditions the necessary power to drive the disc is P. Show by dimensional analysis that

$$P = \rho N^3 D^5 \times \phi\left(\frac{\rho N D^2}{\mu}\right) = \theta(\rho, N, D, \mu)$$

A disc rotating in water at a given temperature absorbs 895 Watt when revolving at 1600rev/min and 2014 Watt when rotating at 2000rev/min. Estimate what would be the corresponding power if the disc were revolving at 1800rev/min in a fluid of viscosity ten times larger than that of the water and of density 0.9 of the density of the water.

Expressed as a power series: $P = K(\rho^a N^b D^c \mu^d)$

and in dimensions $ML^2 T^{-3} = K\,[(ML^{-3})^a T^{-b} L^c (ML^{-1} T^{-1})^d]$.

Equating power indices:

(M) $1 = a + d$ $a = 1 - d$

(L) $2 = -3a + c - d$ $b = 3 - d$

(T) $-3 = -b - d$ $c = 2 + d + 3 - 3d = 5 - 2d$

$P = k\,(\rho^{1-d} N^{3-d} D^{5-2d} \mu^d)$

$$P = \rho N^3 D^5 \times \phi\left(\frac{\rho N D^2}{\mu}\right)$$

General solution: $P = A\times\left(\frac{\rho N D^2}{\mu}\right)^n \times \rho N^3 D^5$

$$895 = A\left(\frac{\rho_w\, 1600\, D^2}{\mu_w}\right)^n \rho_w\, 1600^3 D^5$$

$$2014 = A\left(\frac{\rho_w\, 2000\, D^2}{\mu_w}\right)^n \rho_w\, 2000^3 D^5$$

Dividing the two equations:

$$\frac{895}{2014} = \left(\frac{1600}{2000}\right)^n \times \left(\frac{1600}{2000}\right)^3 = \left(\frac{4}{5}\right)^{n+3},\ \therefore\ 0.444 = 0.8^{n+3}.$$

$\log_{10}(0.444) = (n+3)\log_{10}(0.8)$. $\therefore\ n = 0.632$.

To find the power in water P_w at 1800 rpm: $\frac{1.2}{P_w} = \left(\frac{1600}{2000}\right)^{3.632}$.

Power in water P_w ***at 1800 rpm = 1372.8W***

Since in fluid at 1800 rpm and in water at 1800 rpm the diameter d is constant then:

$$\frac{P_w}{P_f} = \left(\frac{\rho_w}{\rho_f}\right)^{1.632} \times \left(\frac{\mu_f}{\mu_w}\right)^{0.632},\ \text{i.e.}$$

$$\frac{1372.8}{P_f} = \left(\frac{1}{0.9}\right)^{0.632} = 5.089$$

Power in fluid P_f ***at 1800 rpm = 270W***

Similarity of Pipe Flow

If the resistance force per unit length, R, in a pipe is dependent upon the flow velocity, V, the pipe diameter, d, and the dynamic viscosity, μ, and density, ρ, of the fluid flowing, it can be shown by dimensional analysis that:

$$R = \rho d V^2 \times \phi\left(\frac{\rho V d}{\mu}\right)$$

A pipe 50mm in diameter carries air at an average velocity of 25m/s. The density of air is 1.23kg/m^3 and dynamic viscosity is 1.8×10^{-5}Ns/m^2. Calculate the flow velocity of water through the same pipe which would correspond to the same friction factor, f, if the viscosity of water is 1.12×10^{-3}Ns/m^2. What is the ratio of the drop in pressure per unit length for the two cases?

$$\frac{\rho_a V_a d_a}{\mu_a} = \frac{\rho_w V_w d_w}{\mu_w},\ d_a = d_w.$$

Velocity of flow, $V_w = \frac{V_a\times\rho_a\times\mu_w}{\mu_a\times\rho_w}$

$$V_w = \frac{25\times 1.23\times 1.12\times 10^{-3}}{1.8\times 10^{-5}\times 1000} = 1.913m/s.$$

Ratio of drop in pressure, $\frac{R_a}{\rho_a d_a V_a^2} = \frac{R_w}{\rho_w d_w V_w^2}$

Ratio, $\frac{R_a}{R_w} = \frac{\rho_a\times V_a^2}{\rho_w\times V_w^2} = \frac{1.23\times 25^2}{1000\times 1.913^2} = 0.21$.

Flow Measurements by V-Notch

It can be shown that by the method of dimensions, it can be deduced that a rational formula for the flow over a vee notch is:

$$Q = g^{1/2} h^{5/2} \phi\left(\frac{g^{1/2} h^{3/2}}{v}, \frac{\rho g h^2}{\sigma}, \theta\right)$$

where Q is the flow, h is the head above vertex, ρ is the density, v is the kinematic viscosity, σ is the surface tension, θ is the angle of the notch, and g the gravity. Experiments with water on a 90° vee notch show that a practical formula for the flow is given by: $Q = 1.35h^{2.48}$, Q and h being in SI units. Neglecting surface tension, estimate the percentage error involved if this formula is used for measuring the flow of oil whose kinematic viscosity is ten times that of water.

The discharge, $Q = hv \times \phi\left[\left(\frac{gh^3}{\upsilon^2}\right)\left(\frac{\rho\upsilon^2}{\sigma h}\right)\theta\right]$

giving, $Q = g^{1/2} h^{5/2} \phi\left[\left(\frac{g^{1/2} h^{3/2}}{\upsilon}\right)\left(\frac{\rho g h^2}{\sigma}\right)\theta\right]$.

General solution can be written as: $Q = A \times \left(\frac{h^{1.5}}{\upsilon}\right)^n \times h^{2.5}$

where A and n are unknown.

Practical formula is: $Q = K\, h^{2.48}$.

Equating equations for Q, $A \times \left(\frac{h^{1.5}}{\upsilon}\right)^n \times h^{2.5} = K\, h^{2.48}$.

Comparing powers of h: $1.5n + 2.5 = 2.48$, $\therefore$ ***n = - 0.0133.***

For water, $K_w = A \times v_w^{0.0133}$.

For oil, $K_{oil} = A \times v_{oil}^{0.0133}$.

$$Q_{estimated} = Q_{act}\left(\frac{\upsilon_w}{\upsilon_{oil}}\right)^{0.0133} = Q_{act}\left(\frac{1}{10}\right)^{0.0133} = \frac{Q_{act}}{1.0312}.$$

Therefore, flow is underestimated by 3.12%.

Model of a Ship Propeller

The thrust, T, of a ship is given by:

$$T = \rho D^2 V^2 \phi\left(\frac{\mu}{\rho V D}, \frac{nD}{V}\right)$$

where D is the propeller diameter, n the rotational speed of the propeller, V the speed of the ship, ρ the density, μ dynamic viscosity. The performance of a propeller 5m diameter is studied by means of a geometrically similar model 0.25m diameter. When the model is tested in fresh water at a rotational speed of 30 rev/s and a water velocity of 2m/s the thrust and torque are 180N and 4.9Nm respectively. Determine the corresponding speed of rotation, thrust, and power of the ships propeller when the speed of the ship is 6m/s in sea water of density 1026kg/m³.

For dynamic similarity: $\left(\frac{nD}{V}\right)_m = \left(\frac{nD}{V}\right)_{ship}$

$$\frac{30 \times 0.25}{2} = \frac{n \times 5}{6}.$$

Speed of ship propeller, n = 4.5rev/s.

$$\left(\frac{T}{\rho D^2 V^2}\right)_m = \left(\frac{T}{\rho D^2 V^2}\right)_{ship}, \text{ i.e.}$$

$$\frac{180}{1000 \times 0.25^2 \times 2^2} = \frac{T}{1026 \times 5^2 \times 6^2}$$

Thrust of ship propeller, T = 664.8kN.

$$\left(\frac{Torque}{Thrust \times D}\right)_m = \left(\frac{Torque}{Thrust \times D}\right)_{ship}, \quad \frac{4.9}{180 \times 0.25} = \frac{x}{664800 \times 5}$$

Torque of ship propeller = 3,619,46.66.

Power = 3.619 × 10⁵ × 2π × 4.5 = 10.233MW.

Resistance of a Ship

A ship has a length of 100m and a wetted area of 1200m². A model of this ship of length 4m is towed through fresh water at 1.5m/s and has a total resistance of 15.5N. The model has a skin resistance/wetted area of 14.5N/m² at 3m/s and the skin resistance is proportional to *(velocity)*$^{1.9}$. The prototype ship in sea water has a skin resistance of 43N/m² at 3m/s and a velocity index of 1.85. Calculate the speed and total resistance of the prototype ship at conditions corresponding to the model speed of 1.5m/s. The relative density of sea water is 1.026.

From dimensional analysis, an expression for the force on a body placed in a moving fluid is of the form:

Resistance, $S = \rho V^2 l^2 \phi(R, F, ..)$.

where R is the Reynolds number and F is the Froude number. But in model testing, complete dynamic similarity is impossible as it is difficult to achieve equality for both R and F for both model and prototype for normal fluids used for testing. Fluids of vastly differing viscosities would be called for to obtain equal R and F simultaneously.

Total Resistance = Skin friction resistance + wave resistance

The skin resistance is a function of R and is obtained by towing flat plates through water. Wave resistance is a function of F. It is obtained by (*total resistance - skin resistance).* Thus obtain total resistance of model by towing and obtain skin resistance and then calculate wave resistance of model. Scale up for wave resistance of prototype by making F equal and add to skin resistance by scaling up model test results giving total resistance of prototype.

$F_m = F_p$, $(V^2/gl)_m = (V^2/gl)_p$ giving same wave pattern.

$$V_p = V_m \times \left(\frac{l_p}{l_m}\right)^{1/2} = 1.5 \times \left(\frac{100}{4}\right)^{1/2} = 7.5 m/s.$$

Also, $\frac{Area\ of\ model,\ A_m}{Area\ of\ prototype,\ A_p} = \left(\frac{l_p}{l_m}\right)^2$.

$$A_m = 1200 \times \left(\frac{4}{100}\right)^2 = 1.92 m^2.$$

Skin resistance for model at 3m/s speed, $S_m = K_m \times V_m^{1.9}$.

$$1.92 \times 14.5 = K_m \times 3^{1.9}. \therefore K_m = \frac{14.5 \times 1.92}{3^{1.9}} = 3.45.$$

Skin resistance at 1.5m/s $= K_m \times V_m^{1.9}$.

$$= \frac{14.5}{3^{1.9}} \times 1.92 \times 1.5^{1.9} = \frac{14.5 \times 1.92}{3.74} = 7.45 .$$

Wave resistance, $W_m = 15.5 - 7.45 = 8.05N$.

From the dimensional analysis expression: $\frac{W_p}{W_m} = \frac{\rho_p l_p^2 V_p^2}{\rho_m l_m^2 V_m^2}$

$$W_p = 8.05 \times 1.026 \left(\frac{100}{4}\right)^2 \times \left(\frac{7.5}{1.5}\right)^2 = 1.29 \times 10^5 \; N .$$

Total resistance of prototype at 3m/s speed, $S_p = K_p \times V_p^{1.85}$.

$$K_p = \frac{43}{3.85} \times \frac{N \times s^{1.85}}{m^{3.85}} .$$

At 7.5m/s speed, $S_p = 43 \times \left(\frac{7.5}{3.5}\right)^{1.85} \times 1200$

$K_p = 43 \times 5.46 \times 1200 = 2.82 \times 10^5 N.$

Total resistance of prototype, $S_p = (1.29 + 2.82) \times 10^5 N.$

$\boldsymbol{S_p = 4.11 \times 10^5 N = 411kN.}$

Model of Atomised Liquid

A liquid is atomised by being ejected from an orifice into still air. The average diameter b of the droplets produced depends on the mean velocity V of the liquid in the orifice, the orifice diameter B and the liquid properties; density ρ, dynamic viscosity μ and surface tension σ. Using dimensional analysis, deduce a functional relationship to describe this system. State the physical significance of the dimensionless groups you obtain and suggest a rational basis for the presentation of experimental data obtained from such atomises. A fuel oil has a relative density of 0.85, a kinematic viscosity of 1.5×10^{-6} m^2/s and a surface tension of 2.5×10^{-2} N/m. It is to be atomised with an orifice of diameter 0.225mm and a mean velocity of 80m/s. Determine the orifice diameter and the velocity required for a model using water.

From data of question: $b = \phi\,[B, V, \rho, \mu, \sigma]$

$[L]\;[L]\;[LT^{-1}]\;[ML^{-3}]\;[ML^{-1}T^{-1}]\;[MT^{-2}]$

[M] = mass; [L] = length; [T] = time.

Take for example, B, V, ρ as remaining variables and deduces:

$$\frac{b}{B} = \phi\left\{\rho\frac{BV}{\mu},\; \rho\frac{V^2 B}{\sigma}\right\},\; R = \frac{Inertia\ force}{Tension\ force}, \text{ and}$$

$$W = \frac{Inertia\ force}{Surface\ tension\ force} .$$

Reorganise for plotting so that: $\frac{b}{B} = \psi\left\{\rho\frac{BV}{\mu},\; \frac{\mu^2}{\rho B \sigma}\right\}$.

Now U can be varied by increasing back pressure and for constant fluid properties and a given nozzle, $b/B = f(R)$ for a given W/R^2. Therefore plot as shown:

For dynamic similarity: $\left[\rho\frac{BV}{\mu}\right]_m = \left[\rho\frac{BV}{\mu}\right]_p$

m = model and p = prototype.

$$\left[\frac{\rho V^2 B}{\sigma}\right]_m = \left[\rho\frac{V^2 B}{\sigma}\right]_p \frac{\mu}{\rho} = D$$

$$B_m = \frac{D_m}{D_p} \times \frac{V_p}{V_m} \times B_p = \frac{0.95}{1.5} \times \frac{V_p}{V_m} \times B_p$$

$$B_m = \frac{\sigma_m}{\sigma_p} \times \frac{\rho_p}{\rho_m} \times \frac{V_p^2}{V_m^2} = \frac{7.35}{2.5} \times 0.85 \times \frac{V_p^2}{V_m^2} \times D_p$$

$\frac{V_p}{V_m} = \frac{0.633 \times 2.5}{7.35 \times 0.85} = 0.253$ and hence, $V_m = \frac{80}{0.253} = 316 m/s$.

$\therefore\ \boldsymbol{B_m = 0.633 \times 0.253 \times 0.225 = 0.036mm.}$

Calibration of a Compensation Water Pipe

A cast iron horizontal pipe, 1.2m diameter D, and 22m long, leads from the side of a tunnel to the river, downstream of the dam. The pipe entrance has rounded edges. A sluice gate is fitted at the downstream end. This sluice discharges under a head of 6m into a pool excavated in the rock bed of the river. Briefly, explain the steps required for calibration of the water pipe using a small scale model.

Expected maximum discharge through the pipe is given by:

$$Q_{max} = C_D \times A \times \sqrt{2gH} .$$

where A is the area of the pipe, C_D is the coefficient of discharge and H is the head.

Using $C_D = 0.8$,

$$Q_{max} = 0.8 \times \frac{\pi \times 1.2^2}{4} \times \sqrt{2 \times 9.81 \times 6} = 9.817 m^3/s .$$

Choice of Scale - the following factors apply:

(a) the largest laboratory pump readily available has a maximum discharge of 0.025 m^3/s;

(b) the model should be compact and easy to construct using material available at low cost;

(c) the results should be accurate, without scale effects over the range of compensation flows.

Choose a **scale ratio 1 in 12** and assume the Froude law. Equating Froude numbers for model and prototpye, we get:

$$\frac{V_m}{\sqrt{gD_m}} = \frac{V_p}{\sqrt{gD_p}}$$

$$\frac{V_m}{V_p} = \sqrt{\frac{D_m}{D_p}}$$

Since $Q = Velocity \times Area = VA$, then

$$\frac{Q_m}{Q_p} = \sqrt{\frac{D_m}{D_p}} \times \left(\frac{D_m}{D_p}\right)^2 = \left(\frac{1}{12}\right)^{5/2} .$$

Model discharge, $Q_m = 9.808 \times (1/12)^{5/2} = 0.0196\ m^3/s$.

The available pump is therefore satisfactory.

Pressure Drop in a Pipe

The pressure drop, Δp, in a pipe is assumed to depend on the pipe diameter, d, its roughness, k, the velocity of flow, V, and the density, ρ, and dynamic viscosity, μ, of the fluid flowing. Using Buckingham's method of dimensional analysis, with ρ, V and d as the common variables, derive a functional relationship between Δp and the other variables. The pressure drop in a 500mm diameter pipe with a roughness of 0.3mm carrying water is $4.5kN/m^2$ over a length of 10m. Calculate the pressure drop over a 30m length of pipe carrying a fluid whose viscosity is 10 times that of water and whose density is 0.9 that of water. The pipe has the same roughness as the water pipe and is tested under dynamically similar conditions.

Variables: $\Delta p, d, k, V, \rho, \mu$.

Dimensions: $(ML^{-1}T^{-2})$, L, L, (LT^{-3}), $ML^{-1}T^{-1}$

Number of groups 6 - 3 = 3 groups.

Let π_1 comprise ρ, V, d and Δp. Variables must be combined in dimensionless manner, *i.e.* $\rho^a V^b d^c \Delta p$.

$(ML^{-3})^a (LT^{-1})^b (L)^c ML^{-1}T^{-2} = M^oL^oT^o$.

Equating power indices:

M	$a + 1 = 0$	$a = -1$	
T	$-b - 2 = 0$	$b = -2$	
L	$-3a + b + c - 1 = 0$	$c = 0$	$\therefore \pi_1 = \Delta p/\rho V^2$

Similarity: $\pi_2 = \rho^a V^b d^c \mu$.

$(ML^{-3})^a (LT^{-1})^b (L)^c ML^{-1}T^{-1} = M^oL^oT^o$.

Equating power indices:

M	$a + 1 = 0$	$a = -1$	
T	$-1 - b = 0$	$b = -1$	
L	$-3a + b + c - 1 = 0$	$c = -1$	$\therefore \pi_2 = \mu/\rho Vd$

and $\pi_3 = \rho^a V^b d^c k$, $(ML^{-3})^a (LT^{-1})^b (L)^c L = M^oL^oT^o$.

Equating power indices:

M	$a + 0 = 0$	$a = 0$	
T	$-b + 0 = 0$	$b = 0$	
L	$-3a + b + c + 1 = 0$	$c = -1$	$\therefore \pi_3 = k/d$

i.e. equation: $\pi_1 = \phi(\pi_2\, \pi_3)$, $\dfrac{\Delta p}{\rho V^2} = \phi\left(\dfrac{\mu}{\rho V d}, \dfrac{k}{d}\right)$

For dynamic similarity: $\left(\dfrac{k}{d}\right)_{fluid} = \left(\dfrac{k}{d}\right)_{water}$

same k, $\dfrac{k}{d_f} = \dfrac{k}{0.5}$ also $\left(\dfrac{\mu}{\rho V d}\right)_{air} = \left(\dfrac{\mu}{\rho V d}\right)_{water}$.

$$\frac{10\,\mu_w}{0.9\,\rho_w V_f \times 0.5} = \frac{\mu_w}{\rho_w V_w \times 0.5}. \quad \therefore \ \boldsymbol{V_f = 11.1\, V_w}.$$

$$\left(\frac{\Delta p}{\rho V^2}\right)_{fluid} = \left(\frac{\Delta p}{\rho V^2}\right)_{water}, \quad \frac{\Delta p_f}{0.9\rho_f\,(1.11 V_w)^2} = \frac{4.5}{\rho_w V_w^2}.$$

$\therefore$ $\Delta p_f = 500kN/m^2$. But this will be over a 10m length, i.e. 30m.

$\therefore$ ***Pressure drop,*** $\boldsymbol{\Delta p_f = 3 \times 500 = 1500kN/m^2}$.

Problems on Dynamical Similarity

[1] The power, P, required to drive a disc, diameter D, at a constant rotational speed N, when immersed in a fluid density ρ, viscosity μ, is given by: $P = [\rho N^3 D^5\, f(\rho N D^2/\mu)]$. A disc rotating in water at a given temperature absorbs 900W when revolving at 27rev/s and 2kW at 37rev/s. Estimate the corresponding power if the disc were revolving at 30rev/s in a fluid of viscosity 10 times that of water and density 0.99 that of water. (3255.55W)

[2] A ship of length 130m has a wetted area of $2325m^2$. A model of this ship 4m long has a total resistance of 17.5N when towed through fresh water at 1.5m/s. The ship in sea water has a skin resistance/wetted area of $43N/m^2$ at 3m/s and the model in fresh water has a skin resistance/wetted area of $16N/m^2$ at 3m/s. The skin resistance F_s is given by $F_s = KAV^n$, where K is a constant, V is the velocity, A is the wetted area, $n = 1.9$ for the model and $n = 1.85$ for the ship. Calculate (a) the corresponding speed of the ship and (b) the shaft power required to propel the ship at this speed through sea water of density $1025kg/m^3$, assuming a propeller efficiency of 75%. (8.55m/s, 11150kW)

Fluid Mechanics Laboratory Work

As a part of University degree courses students are normally required to perform experiments selected from the following:

Part I Laboratory Experiments

1. Viscosity Determination
2. Verification of Bernoulli's Theorem
3. Flow Through a Venturimeter
4. Impact of Jets
5. Sudden Pipe Enlargement
6. Pressure Distribution Around a Cylinder
7. Lift and Drag of an Aerofoil
8. Pitot-static Tube Traverse
9. Pipe Friction
10. Flow Patterns
11. Flow over Notches.

Part II Laboratory Experiments

1. Stability of a Floating Body
2. Free Vortex Flow in a Bend Meter
3. Forced Vortex Motion with Paddles
4. Flow under Sluice Gate and Hydraulic Jump
5. Flow over Weirs and through Venturi Flume
6. Boundary Layer Development in a Wind Tunnel
7. Velocity Distributions along an Air Duct
8. Performance of a Pelton Wheel
9. Performance of a Centrifugal Pump
10. Performance of a Francis Turbine
11. Water Hammer Analysis.

In the first year of a course, the experiments should be short and simple to observe natural laws and to compliment the lectures and tutorials. In the second year the work should train students in standard testing methods and presentation of results in terms of dimensionless quantities.

A number of experiments should be written up as formal reports. A report should include: (1) title and date, (2) statement of objectives of experiment, (3) theory, (4) description and sketches of equipment, (5) test procedure and readings, (6) specimen set of calculations, (7) graphs, (8) discussion of results, (9) conclusions and (10) list of references.

CHAPTER THIRTEEN

UNSTEADY FLOW IN PIPES

Introduction

Whenever the rate of flow of a fluid in a pipe is varied, pressure changes arise due to the inertia of the fluid. It is a matter of everyday observation that when a valve in a pipe conveying water is rather suddenly closed a hammering noise is produced. This is a manifestation of a sudden and large increase of pressure and is the origin of the name **'water hammer'.** Sometime the hammering persists with regular periodicity unless action is taken to damp out the periodic motion. Especially in long pipe lines, water hammer is potentially destructive and arrangements must be made to limit the pressure rise, as by the provision of pressure regulators or surge tanks (see Chapter 17).

Slow Valve Closure

In order to obtain the physical laws of water hammer, the effect of changes in flow are first considered for a pipeline of cross-sectional area A and length L as shown in Fig.13.1. The pipeline is connected to a reservoir at its upper end and has a control valve at the lower end for regulating the discharge of water into the atmosphere. When the rate of change of velocity of flow in the pipe conveying liquid is small, it may be adequate to treat the liquid as **incompressible** and the pipe as **rigid**. If the flow at the control gate (Fig.13.1) is closed slowly unbalanced pressure head H_d will act at the gate on the mass of the water column. H_d is found by using Newton's second law of motion. The resultant hydrostatic force is equal to the rate of change of momentum within the pipe.

$$p_2\, A - p_1\, A - (\rho g \times AL \sin\alpha) = -\rho g\, AL \times (dV/dT) \qquad (13.1)$$

But, $p_2 = \rho g \times (H_o + H_d)$ and $p_1 = \rho g \times (H_o - Z_1)$.

$\therefore$ ***Rise in pressure head,*** $H_d = -(L/g) \times (dV/dT)$ (13.2)

If the valve is made to move in such a way that the deceleration is uniform with time T, then,

$$H_d = -\frac{LV}{gT} \qquad (13.3)$$

Rapid Valve Closure

Fundamental water hammer equations may be derived for a more general case of unsteady flow by taking into account the elasticity of the pipe wall and the compressibility of the fluid. Consider a long pipe from a reservoir to a consumer's valve. Suppose the valve is shut instantaneously, thus completely stopping the fluid near it. Further away upstream, the fluid is still moving so that the near fluid is compressed, increasing its pressure by Δp and density by $\Delta \rho$. In the piece of pipe shown in Fig.13.2, the fluid near the valve is stopped, and its pressure being Δp above the pressure in the moving fluid. A surge is formed between the two fluids which moves with a velocity C. To analyse the water hammer action, it is first necessary to create apparently steady flow conditions by looking at the situation through the eyes of an observer moving along the wave of changing conditions.

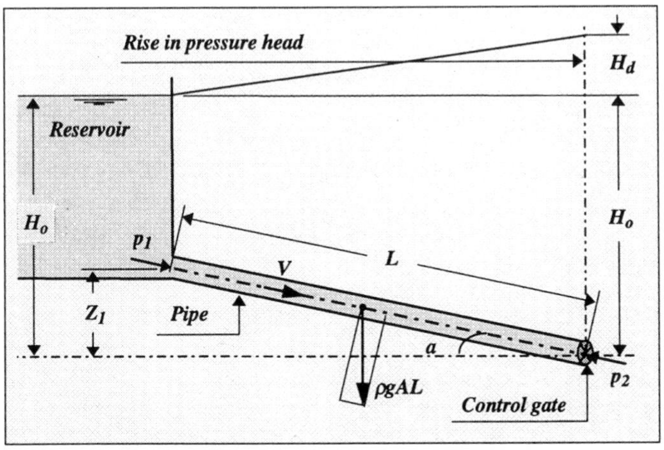

Fig.13.1.- Analysis of unsteady flow for slow valve closure.

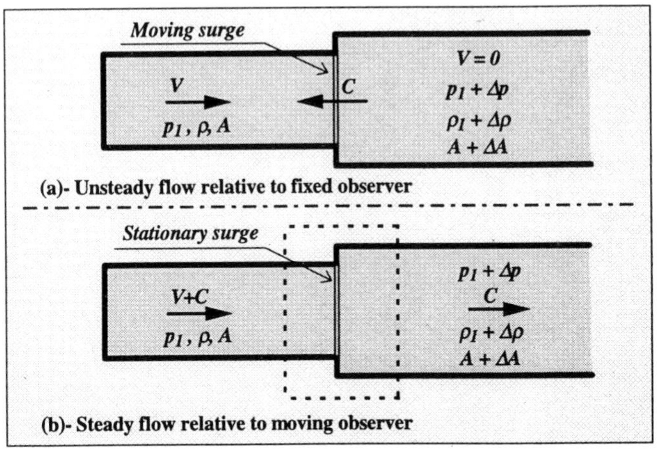

Fig.13.2- A junction between moving and stationary fluids.

By giving the whole system an equal and opposite velocity C, the motion becomes steady as in Fig.13.2b. Applying the continuity equation to the steady quasi-steady condition, applied in the control volume shown by the dotted lines in Figure 13.2b., the continuity of mass is:

$$\rho \times (C+V) \times A = (\rho + d\rho) \times C \times (A + dA) \tag{13.4}$$

$$\rho CA + \rho VA = \rho CA + \rho CdA + d\rho CA + d\rho CdA \tag{13.5}$$

$$\frac{d\rho}{\rho} = \frac{AV - CdA}{C \times (A + dA)} = \left(V - C \times \frac{dA}{A}\right) \Big/ C \times \left(1 + \frac{dA}{A}\right) \tag{13.6}$$

Since dA/A is small, $(1 + dA/A) \approx 1$. Therefore,

$$\frac{d\rho}{\rho} = \left(V - C \times \frac{dA}{A}\right) \Big/ C \tag{13.7}$$

If the equilibrium of half the pipe is considered, the increase in pressure, Δp, is acting across the diameter must be balanced by an increase in hoop shear, σ, in the pipe walls.

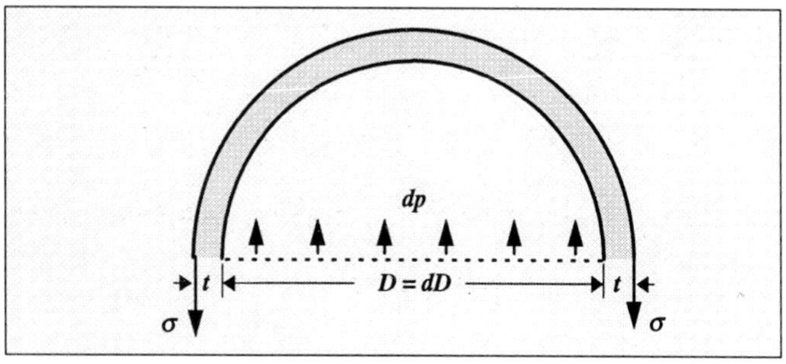

Fig.13.3- Pressure in a pipe.

$$2 \times \sigma \times t = dp \times (D + dD)$$

When dD is very small compared to the diameter of pipe D,

$$\sigma = \frac{dp \times D}{2 \times t} \tag{13.8}$$

Also **Young Modulus** $E = \dfrac{Stress}{Strain} = \sigma \Big/ \left(\dfrac{dD}{D}\right)$ (13.9)

$$\therefore \quad \frac{dD}{D} = \frac{\sigma}{E} = \frac{dp \times D}{2 \times t \times E} \tag{13.10}$$

$$\frac{dA}{A} = \left(\frac{\pi}{4} \times (D + dD)^2\right) - \left(\frac{\pi}{4} \times D^2\right) \Big/ \left(\frac{\pi}{4} \times D^2\right)$$

$$= \frac{\left(\frac{\pi}{4} \times D^2\right) + \left(\frac{2\pi}{4} \times D \times dD\right) + \left(\frac{\pi}{4} \times dD^2\right) - \left(\frac{\pi}{4} \times D^2\right)}{\left(\frac{\pi}{4} \times D^2\right)}$$

Since is $(\pi \times dD^2/4)$ negligible,

$$\frac{dA}{A} = \frac{2D \times dD}{D^2} = \frac{2 \times dD}{D} = 2 \times \frac{dp \times D}{2 \times t \times E}$$. Therefore,

$$\frac{dA}{A} = \frac{dp \times D}{t \times E} \tag{13.11}$$

By definition the **Bulk Modulus, K** is

$$K = \frac{Change\ in\ pressure}{Volumetric\ strain} = dp \Big/ \left(\frac{d\rho}{\rho}\right) \tag{13.12}$$

$$\therefore \quad \frac{d\rho}{\rho} = \frac{AV - CdA}{C \times (A + dA)} = \left(V - C \times \frac{dA}{A}\right) \Big/ C \times \left(1 + \frac{dA}{A}\right), \text{ or}$$

$$dp = V \Big/ \left[C \times \left(\frac{1}{K} + \frac{D}{t \times E}\right)\right] \tag{13.13}$$

in which V is the velocity of liquid subjected to pressure dp. Applying the momentum equation to the control volume shown by the dotted in Figure 13.2b:

$$pA - (p + dp) \times (A + dA) = \rho \times (C + V) \times A \times [C - (C + V)], \text{ or}$$

$$pA - (p + dp) \times A \times \left(1 + \frac{dA}{A}\right) = \rho \times (C + V) \times (-V) \times A \tag{13.14}$$

Putting $(1 + dA/A) \approx 1$.

$$-dp = \rho \times (C + V) \times (-V) \tag{13.15}$$

In most problems $C >> V$ and we can put $(C+V) \approx C$. Therefore,

$$dp = \rho CV \tag{13.16}$$

Substituting in equation (13.13)

Pressure rise, $dp = \rho CV = V \Big/ \left[C \times \left(\dfrac{1}{K} + \dfrac{D}{t \times E}\right)\right]$ (13.17)

Surge velocity, $C = \sqrt{1 \Big/ \left[\rho \times \left(\dfrac{1}{K} + \dfrac{D}{t \times E}\right)\right]}$ (13.18)

Pressure Variation for Instantaneous Value Closure

Figure 13.4 shows the conditions in the pipe at various times during the cycle and Figure 13.5 shows the variations of pressure with time (a) at the valve and (b) at the mid-point of the pipeline.

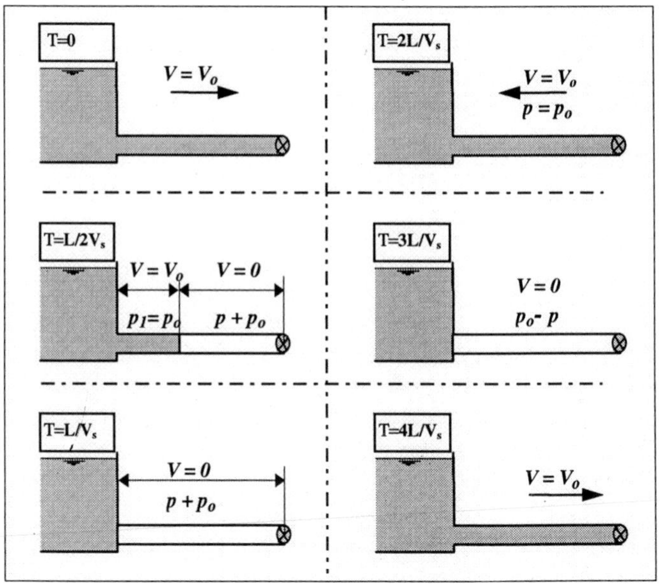

Fig.13.4- Conditions in the pipe during various cyclic times.

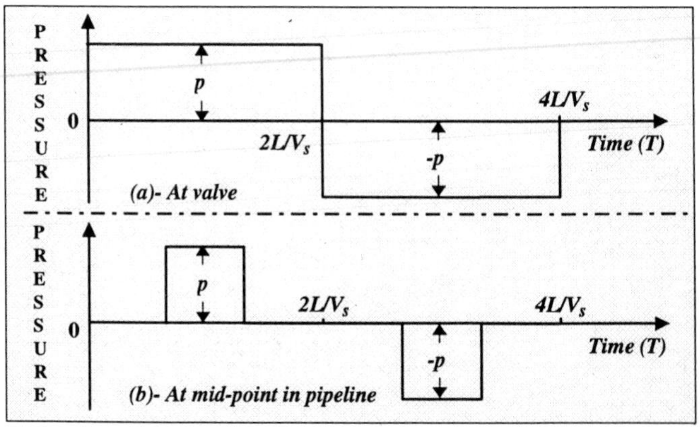

Fig.13.5- Variation of pressure with time.

Examples on Unsteady Flow in Pipes

Valve Closure in a Pipeline

Show that the pressure rise due to a sudden and complete closure of valve at the end of a pipeline carrying fluid is given by, $\Delta p = V\,(\rho K)^{1/2}$, where V is the initial mean velocity, ρ is the density and K is the Bulk Modulus of the fluid. Neglect pipe elasticity effects. A steel pipe having 600mm diameter and 8mm wall thickness conveys water at a mean velocity of 1.5m/s. Find the increase in pressure head produced by the sudden closure of a valve. Take K for water as 2×10^6 kN/m^2.

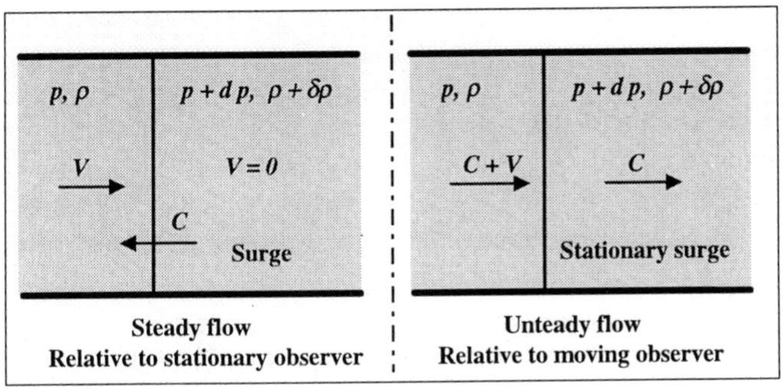

For the condition of quasi-steady flow (b), according to the momentum equation,

Resultant force = Rate of change in momentum.

$(p + dp) \times A - pA = (\rho + d\rho) \times AC \times C - \rho A \times (C + V)^2.$

Since C >> V, we can write $C + V = C$. $\therefore\ dp = d\rho \times C^2$.

But, Bulk modulus, $K = dp \Big/ \left(\dfrac{d\rho}{\rho}\right)$. Thus, $d\rho = \dfrac{dp}{K} \times \rho$.

Consequently, $d\rho = \dfrac{d\rho}{K} \times \rho \times C^2$ and $C = \sqrt{\dfrac{K}{\rho}}$

Applying the continuity equation,

$\rho A \times (C+V) = (\rho + d\rho) \times A \times C.$

$\therefore\ \rho V = \rho \times A \times C$

$$d\rho = \frac{dp}{K} \times \rho = \frac{d\rho \times V}{C} \text{ and}$$

$$dp = \frac{K \times V}{C} = K \times V \times \sqrt{\frac{\rho}{K}}$$

$$\therefore\ dp = V \times \sqrt{\rho \times K}$$

Pressure rise, $dp = 1.5 \times \sqrt{1000 \times 2 \times 10^6 \times 1000}$

$= 2.12 \times 10^6 N/m^2.$

Head rise, $\Delta h = 216.2$*metre head of water.*

Water Hammer in Elastic Pipe

The valve at the end of a 400mm diameter pipe 2km long is closed in 12 seconds in such a way that the retardation of the water is proportional to $T^{4/3}$, where T is the time in second that has elapsed since the start of closure. If the initial discharge is 0.15m^3/s calculate the rise in pressure. Compare this pressure with the pressure rise that would take place if the valve were closed instantaneously taking the bulk modulus of water, modified to allow for elasticity of pipe as 1.9×10^9 N/m^2.

$\dfrac{dV}{dT} = KT^{4/3}$. Integrating, $V = \dfrac{3}{7} \times KT^{7/3} + constant.$

Where $T = 0$, $V = 0.15 \Big/ \dfrac{\pi \times 0.42}{4} = 1.194 m/s$, $constant = 1.194.$

When $T = 12s$, $V = 0$, $K = -0.00845$

$dV/dT = -0.00845 \times T^{4/3}$.

For a rigid pipe, $H_d = -\dfrac{L}{g} \times \dfrac{dV}{dT}$

$$H_d = -\frac{2000}{9.81} \times 0.00845 \times 12^{4/3} = 47.33m.$$

Pressure, $P = \dfrac{1000 \times 9.81 \times 47.33}{1000} = 464.2 kN/m^2$.

Surge velocity, $C = \sqrt{\dfrac{1.9 \times 10^4}{1000}} = 1378.4$.

Pressure rise, $\Delta p = \rho CV = 1645.81 kN/m^2$.

Water Hammer in Rigid Pipe

A pipe 2 km long carries water, $K = 2 \times 10^9 N/m^2$, with a velocity of 1.2m/s. If a valve at the end of the pipeline stops the flow instantaneously, describe how the pressure in the pipeline varies and draw graphs showing how the pressure varies with time at the valve and at a point 500m from the valve. Calculate the magnitude of the pressure rise and the maximum time of closure for the valve for this full pressure rise to be developed. Neglect pipe friction and elasticity of the pipe.

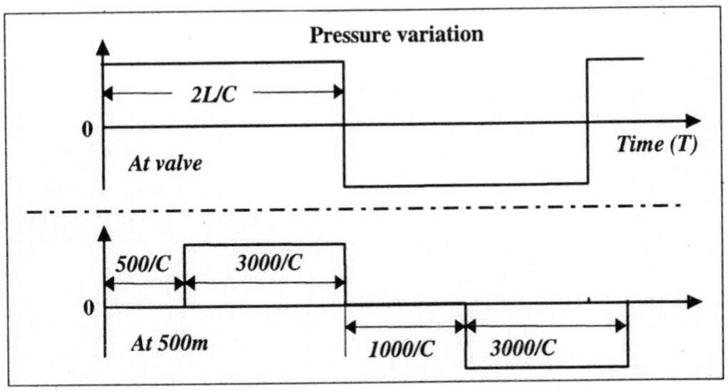

Surge velocity, $C = \sqrt{\frac{K}{\rho}} = \sqrt{\frac{2\times 10^9}{1000}} = 1414.21\ m/s.$

Pressure rise, $\Delta p = \rho CV = 1000 \times 1414.21 \times 11.2$
$= 1697056 N/m^2 = 1697 kN/m^2.$

Time for rapid closure, $T = \frac{2L}{C} = \frac{2\times 2000}{1414.21} = 2.288s.$

Water-hammer

Describe the phenomenon of water-hammer such as occurs in a pipe when the flow is suddenly stopped by closing a valve at the far end. A cast iron pipe 10cm internal diameter and 15mm wall thickness is conveying 0.1 m^3/s of water. Taking the modulus of elasticity E for cast iron as $1.0\times10^{11} N/m^2$ and the bulk modulus *K* for water as $2.0\times10^9 N/m^2$, calculate the maximum stress produced in the cast iron due to the instantaneous closure of a valve at the downstream end of the pipe. Neglect longitudinal stress in the pipe. The celerity, *C,* of the shock waves in the water is given by: $C = 1\Big/\sqrt{\rho\times\left(\frac{1}{K}+\frac{d}{t\times E}\right)}$

Celerity, $C = 1\Big/\sqrt{1000\times\left(\frac{1}{2\times 10^9}+\frac{0.10}{0.015\times 10^{11}}\right)} = 1330 m/s.$

Riemann invariants $R = Q \pm \frac{gAh}{C}$. $\therefore \frac{gA\Delta h}{C} = Q_o$.

$\rho g\Delta h = C\times\frac{Q}{A}\times\rho$, and $\Delta p = C\times\frac{Q}{A}\times\rho$.

$\Delta p = \frac{1330\times 0.1}{\pi d^2}\times 4\times 1000$

Force on pipe $= \Delta p \times d$

Stress in pipe $= \frac{\Delta p\times d}{2\times t} = \frac{1330\times 0.1\times 4\times 1000}{\pi\times 0.10^2\times 2\times 0.015} = 56.44 MN/m^2.$

(see Page 125 for a description of water hammer).

Water-Hammer in Steel Pipeline

A steel pipeline, 1.2km long, 150mm internal diameter, and 12.5 mm wall thickness carries 0.07 m^3/s of water. Calculate the pressure increase produced by a sudden closure of a valve at the downstream and of the pipeline, assuming the pipe to be longitudinally constrained. If the head of water at a point in the pipeline is 150m before closure, determine the stress in the steel at that point before and after closure. Calculate the maximum time in which the valve may be closed in order to produce the effects of an instantaneous closure.
For steel, Young's Modulus $E_s = 210\ GN/m^2$.
For water, Bulk Modulus $K = 2.1\ GN/m^2$.

For sudden closure, pressure head rise: $\Delta h = \frac{CQ_o}{gA}$

where t = pipe thickness and A = cross-sectional area of pipe.

Celerity of shock wave: $C = \sqrt{1\Big/\rho\left(\frac{1}{K}+\frac{2r}{t\times E}\right)}$

$$C = \sqrt{1\Big/\left(\frac{1000\times 1}{2.1\times 10^9}+\frac{1000\times 0.15}{210\times 10^9\times 0.0125}\right)} = 1369.3 m/s$$

Pressure rise due to valve closure, $\Delta p = \rho g \times \Delta h = C \times Q_p/A$

$$\Delta p = \frac{1369.3\times 0.07\times 4\times 10^3}{\pi\times 0.15^2} = 5.424\times 10^6\ N/m^2.$$

Pressure in pipe $= \rho g \times 150 = 1.472\times 10^6\ N/m^2.$

Stress in steel before closure due to p, $\sigma = 1.472\times 10^6\ N/m^2.$

Stress in steel after closure due to p, $\sigma = (1.472+5.424)\times 10^6.$
$\sigma = 6.896\ 10^6\ N/m^2.$

Hoop stress $\sigma = pr/t.$

1- Stress before closure $= \frac{1.472\times 10^6\times 0.075}{0.0125} = 8.83\times10^6 N/m^2$

2- Stress after closure $= \frac{6.896\times 10^6\times 0.075}{0.0125} = 41.37\times10^6 N/m^2$

Maximum time for valve closure, $T = \frac{2L}{C} = \frac{2\times 1200}{1369.3} = 1.753s.$

Unsteady Flow

Water, which may be assumed incompressible, is to pass from a large reservoir along a rigid pipe line 50m long and thence discharges through a valve to atmosphere. The pipe has a friction factor $f = 0.007$ and a uniform diameter of 100mm. The valve is initially closed and the gauge pressure in the pipe just upstream from the valve is then $20 kN/m^2$. Starting from first principles, and stating all your assumptions, determine the time taken after the valve is fully and instantaneously opened for the velocity of the water and in the pipe to reach 99% of the maximum possible velocity.

Note: $\int\left(\frac{1}{a^2-x^2}\right)dx = \frac{1}{2a}\ln\left(\frac{a+x}{a-x}\right) + constant$

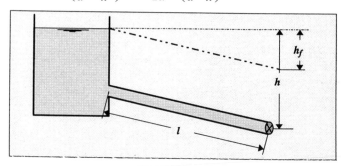

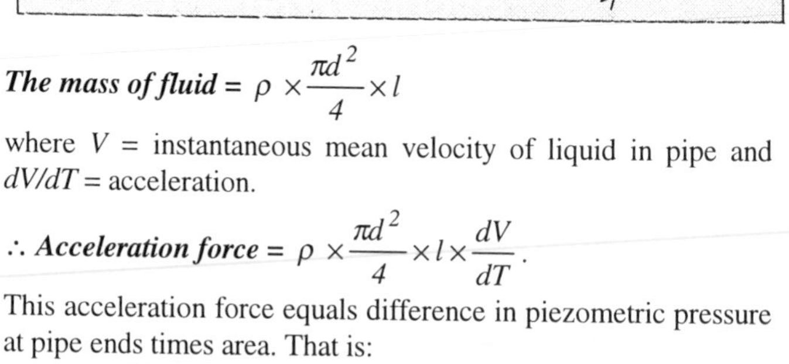

The mass of fluid $= \rho\times\frac{\pi d^2}{4}\times l$

where V = instantaneous mean velocity of liquid in pipe and dV/dT = acceleration.

$\therefore$ ***Acceleration force*** $= \rho\times\frac{\pi d^2}{4}\times l\times\frac{dV}{dT}.$

This acceleration force equals difference in piezometric pressure at pipe ends times area. That is:

$$\rho g\times(h-h_f)\times\frac{\pi d^2}{4} = \rho\times\frac{\pi d^2}{4}\times l\times\frac{dV}{dT}$$

We can assume the friction head loss is,

$h_f = \frac{4flV^2}{2gd} = \frac{k\times V^2}{2g}$, *(where f = friction factor).*

and that f is constant even for change in V. Also this form of h_f is assumed to hold for unsteady as it does for steady flow.

$$h - \frac{k\times V^2}{2g} = \frac{l}{g}\times\frac{dV}{dT}.\ \therefore\ dT = \frac{l}{g}\times\left[dV\Big/\left(h-\frac{k\times V^2}{2g}\right)\right]$$

h assumed constant for duration if acceleration for large reversion.

When $V = V_{max}$, $\frac{dV}{dT} = 0$. $h = h_{f_{max}} = \ln\left(\frac{k \times V^2}{2g}\right)$.

$$T = \frac{1}{g} \times \int_{o}^{V} \frac{2g}{k} \times \left(\frac{dV}{V_{max}^2 - V}\right) = \frac{1}{kV_{max}} \times \ln\left|\frac{V_{max}^2 + V}{V_{max}^2 - V}\right|$$

For $l = 50m$, $\therefore$ $T = \frac{4 \times 0.007 \times 50}{0.1} = 14 seconds$.

$V_{max}^2 = \frac{4 \times 10^3 \times 2}{10^3 \times 14} = 2.857$. Therefore,

Maximum possible velocity, $V_{max} = 1.69m/s$.

Time after valve is fully opened, $T = \frac{50}{14 \times 1.69} \times \ln(199)$

$T = 2.113 \times (90.688 + 4.6052) = 11.18 seconds.$

Rigid Pipe Line

A rigid pipe line joining a reservoir to a valve, which discharges to atmosphere, consists of numerous pipe lengths, $l_1, l_2, \ldots, l_n$, of cross-sectional area $A_1, A_2, \ldots A_n$, respectively joined in series. The corresponding slope angles are $\alpha_1, \alpha_2, \ldots, \alpha_n$ and at any instant of time the mean velocities in the pipes are $V_1, V_2, \ldots, V_n$ respectively. For valve closure derive a general expression for the relationship between the inertia head at the valve and the deceleration of the flow in the pipe adjacent to the valve. Neglect losses at pipe junctions and velocity heads and assume the fluid is incompressible. In a certain hydraulic turbine test the net pressure at the inlet valve to the turbine is 3MN/m^2 and the flow rate is 1.2m^3/s. The pipe line, of circular cross-section throughout consists of three lengths in series with the following dimensions:

Pipe	Length/(m)	Internal diameter/(m)
1 (joining valve)	150	0.6
2	250	0.75
3 (joining reservoir)	1200	0.9

For maintenance purposes the flow to the turbine is completely stopped by closing the valve in 8 seconds. The deceleration of the flow is proportional to $T^{1.3}$ where T is the time elapsed from the start of closure. Calculate the resultant pressure at the valve once closure is completed.

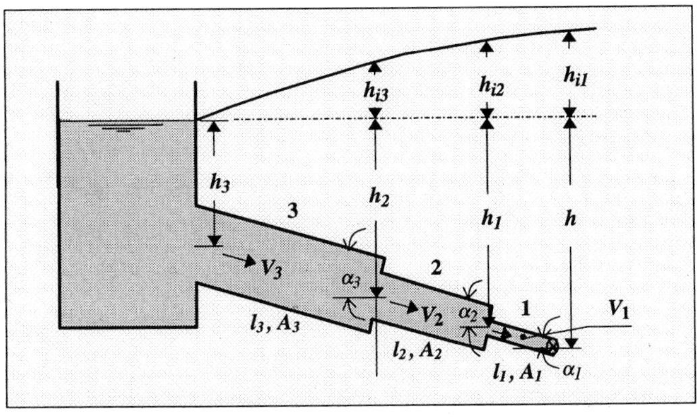

Applying the continuity equation: $A_1 V_1 = A_2 V_2 = A_3 V_3$

Deceleration force on column of liquid in **Pipe 1** is,

$$(h_f - h_1) + (h_{i_1} - h_{i_2}) - l_1 \times \sin\alpha_1 = \frac{l_1}{g} \times \frac{dV_1}{dT}$$

For pipe 2: $h_{i_1} - h_{i_2} = \frac{l_1}{g} \times \frac{dV_1}{dT}$ and $h_{i_2} - h_{i_3} = \frac{l_2}{g} \times \frac{dV_2}{dT}$.

For Pipe 3: $\rho g A_3[(h_2 + h_{i_3}) - h_3 - l_3 \sin\alpha_3] = \rho A_3 l_3 \times \frac{dV_3}{dT}$.

$$(h_2 - h_3) + h_{i_3} - l_3 \sin\alpha_3 = \frac{l_3}{g} \times \frac{dV_3}{dT}, \quad h_{i_3} = \frac{l_3}{g} \times \frac{dV_3}{dT}.$$

Applying continuity equation for pipes 1, 2 and 3 gives:

$$h_{i_1} = \frac{1}{g} \times \left[\left(l_1 \times \frac{dV_1}{dT}\right) + \left(l_2 \times \frac{dV_2}{dT}\right) + \left(l_3 \times \frac{dV_3}{dT}\right)\right], \text{ or,}$$

$$h_{i_1} = \frac{1}{g} \times \left[l_1 + \left(l_2 \times \frac{A_1}{A_2}\right) + \left(l_3 \times \frac{A_1}{A_3}\right)\right]$$

where in general, $l = l_1 + (l_2 \times A_1/A_2) \ldots\ldots + (l_n \times A_1/A_n)$.

$\therefore$ $h_{i_1} = \frac{l}{g} \times \frac{dV_1}{dT}$. $V_1 = \frac{1.2}{(\pi/4) \times 0.6^2} = 4.245 m/s$.

$\frac{dV_1}{dT} = -KT^{1.3}$. $\therefore$ $V_1 = \frac{i \times KT^{2.3}}{2.3} + constant$. This leads to,

$K = \frac{4.245 \times 2.3}{8^{2.3}} = 0.0821$, since $V_1 = 0$ at $T = 8s$.

$$l = 150 + 250 \times \left(\frac{0.6}{0.75}\right)^2 + 1200 \times \left(\frac{0.6}{0.75}\right)^2 = 843m.$$

$$H_i = -\frac{l}{g} \times \frac{dV_1}{dT} = \frac{843}{9.81} \times 0.0821 \times T^{1.3} = 7.06 \times 8^{1.3} = 105.3m.$$

After closure of the valve,

$H = (3 \times 10^6) + (9810 \times 105.3) = 3 + 1.033 \times 10^6 = 4.033kN/m.$

$\frac{d}{T} = \frac{2 \pm \sqrt{4 + 800}}{2}$. ***Say d/T =15.***

Water Hammer in Turbine Pipeline

Air admission valves are fitted along a rigid horizontal water pipeline 1000m long leading from a reservoir. Instantaneous closure of a valve at the outlet end causes an elastic water hammer wave to travel up and down along the pipeline in 1.3 seconds. If the initial steady velocity of flow is 0.6m/s, calculate the minimum initial pressure head in the pipeline for the air admission valves not to come into action. Why are Pelton wheels commonly controlled by the combined action of a needle or spear in the nozzle and a jet deflector?

As the pipeline is assumed to be rigid, there are no strains developed in the pipe material. The time of travel is:

$1.3 = (2 \times 1000)/C$. $\therefore$ $C = 1538.46m/s$.

Pressure, $dp = \rho VC = 1000 \times 0.6 \times 1538.46 = 923.07\ kN/m^2$

When the load is suddenly removed from the Pelton Wheel, the turbine wheel would race under the action of the impinging jet. This develops large centrifugal stresses in the material and overheats the bearings etc. The jet deflector can immediately be brought into play, deflects the jet and gradually stops the wheel. The needle valve can then be used to gradually start up the wheel again. See diagram for a Pelton wheel in a hydro-electric scheme on next page.

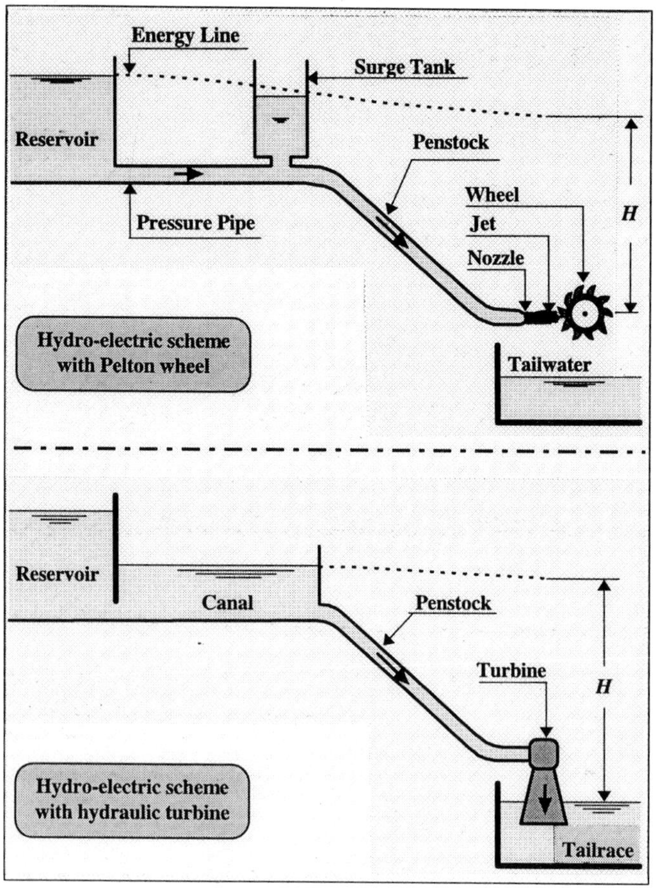

Valve Closure in a Pipeline

Describe the phenomenon of water hammer such as occurs in a pipe when the flow of fluid is stopped by suddenly closing a valve. A longitudinally constrained steel pipeline 0.6m in diameter, is 2500m long and has a wall thickness 10mm. The pipe delivers water to an impulse turbine through a horizontal nozzle of diameter 100mm and a coefficient of velocity 0.98. The velocity of afflux from the nozzle is 65m/s. A valve controlling the flow through the nozzle is instantaneously closed from the fully open position. Calculate the pressure head at the valve prior to closure and the maximum and minimum heads after closure. Neglect pipe friction. Sketch one cycle of variation of pressure head with time after valve closure. Indicate how this diagram would be modified by the inclusion of pipe friction.
For steel, modulus of elasticity, $E = 21\times10^7$ kN/m^2.
For water, bulk modulus, $K = 21\times10^5$ kN/m^2.

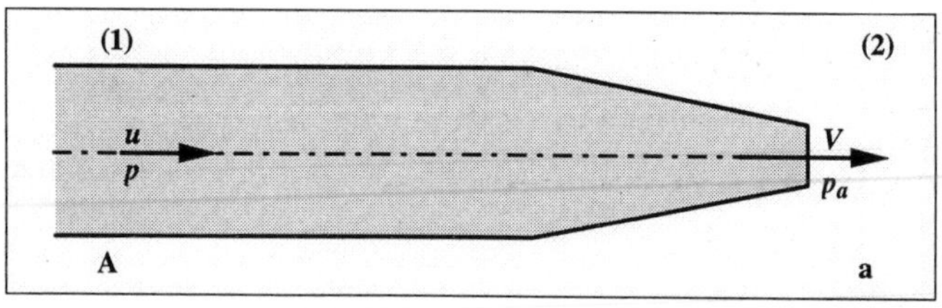

(a) Fluid stops, increase in pressure, compression of fluid and expansion of pipe. (b) Wave of changing condition moves from valve to reservoir all fluid in pipe at rest at increased pressure. (c) Equalising pressure moves from reservoir to valve. Fluid flowing out of pipe into reservoir, pressure restored to normal. (d) As fluid begins to move away from closed valve, reduction in pressure generated. Now wave of changing conditions moves from valve to reservoir. All fluid in pipe at rest, reduced pressure. (e) Fluid flows into pipe from reservoir to equalise pressure, wave of changing conditions moves from reservoir to valve. Valve still closed, cycle repeats from (b), gradually damped out.

$C_v = V_{act}/V$. $\therefore$ $V = V_{act}/C = 65/0.98 = 66.3 m/s$.

Discharge, $A\times u = a\times V$.

Velocity, $u = 66.3\times(1/6)^2 = 1.81 m/s$.

Applying Bernoulli's equation between 1 and 2:

$$\frac{p}{\rho g}+\frac{u^2}{2g}=\frac{p_a}{\rho g}+\frac{V^2}{2g}+\left(\frac{1}{C_v^2}-1\right)\times\frac{V^2}{2g}$$

Pressure head prior to closure,

$$\frac{p}{\rho g}=\frac{V^2}{2g\times C_v^2}-\frac{u^2}{2g}=\frac{66.3^2}{2\times9.81\times0.98^2}-\frac{1.81^2}{2\times9.81}=224\,m.$$

$$dp = V\Big/C\times\left(\frac{1}{K}+\frac{D}{tE}\right)$$

$$dp = 1.81\Big/C\times\left(\frac{1}{21\times10^8}+\frac{0.6}{(10/1000)\times21\times10^{10}}\right)$$

$=2.07\times10^6 N/m^2$, or $dh = 221m$.

Celerity of shock wave, $C=\sqrt{1\Big/\rho\times\left(\frac{1}{K}+\frac{D}{tE}\right)}$

$$C=\sqrt{1\Big/10^3\times\left(\frac{1}{21\times10^8}+\frac{0.6}{(10/1000)\times21\times10^{10}}\right)}=1145 m/s.$$

Time between extreme pressure, $T=\frac{2L}{C}=\frac{5000}{1145}=4.37s.$

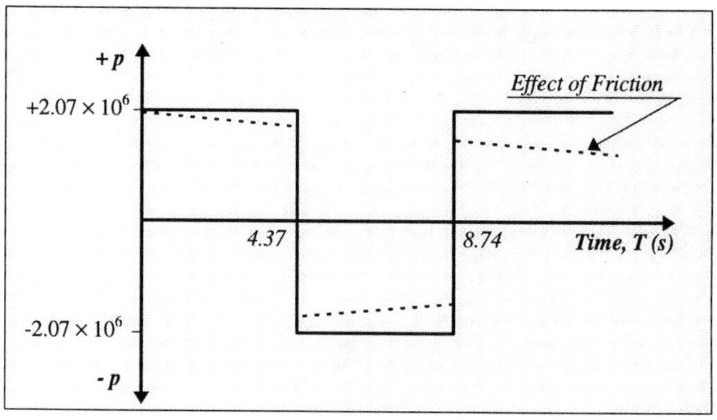

Problems on Unsteady Flow in Pipes

[1] A pipe line 730m long conveys 0.425m^3/s to a power plant which develops 485kW, the static head available being 150m. When the regulator valve was closed in 6s the rise in pressure behind the valve was found to be 325kN/m^2. If the velocity in the pipeline was retarded at a uniform rate, deduce the diameter of the pipe, the overall efficiency of the system, and the efficiency of the power plant just before the valve closure was begun ($f = 0.008$). (450mm, 78%, 84%)

[2] A steel pipe 600mm diameter, 3000mm long ends in a nozzle which gives a 100mm diameter jet. The static head available is 450m. If the pipe wall is 16mm thick and the friction coefficient $f = 0.0055$, determine the pressure behind the nozzle and the increase in circumferential stress in the pipe walls if the valve is closed in four seconds. For steel, the modulus of elasticity, $E = 210GPa$, and for water, the bulk modulus, $K = 2.1GPa$. (7.2MN/m^2, 58MN/m^2)

CHAPTER FOURTEEN

HYDRAULIC PUMPS AND TURBINES

Hydraulic Pumps and Turbines

A pump is a device for raising the liquid pressure. There are three principal types of pumps: (i) the centrifugal or radial flow pump, in which the water leaves the impeller in a radial direction; (ii) the screw or mixed flow pump, in which the water leaves the impeller in a direction having both an axial and a radial component; (iii) the propeller or axial flow pump, in which the water leaves the impeller in an axial direction. In addition to these three main pipes there are others such as the reciprocating pump and the Archimedean screw pump.

Turbines have the function of converting potential head into useful work at a rotating shaft. The first step is to convert potential head into pressure head in the approach pipes. In the turbine itself some or all of this head is converted into kinetic energy with only a very small loss. If all the energy at entry to the moving parts is kinetic energy then the turbine is an impulse type turbine, all other types are reaction turbines.

Centrifugal Pumps

A centrifugal pump is a device that raises a liquid by centrifugal force created by a wheel, called the impeller, revolving in a watertight casing. In operation the liquid enters the pump at the centre of the impeller, enters in a direction normal to the plane in which the impeller revolves and is thrown to the periphery by the centrifugal force resulting from the revolution of the impeller. The fluid passes through the channel between the rim of the impeller and the casing and issues at the discharge under pressure. A section through the pump is shown in Fig.14.1.

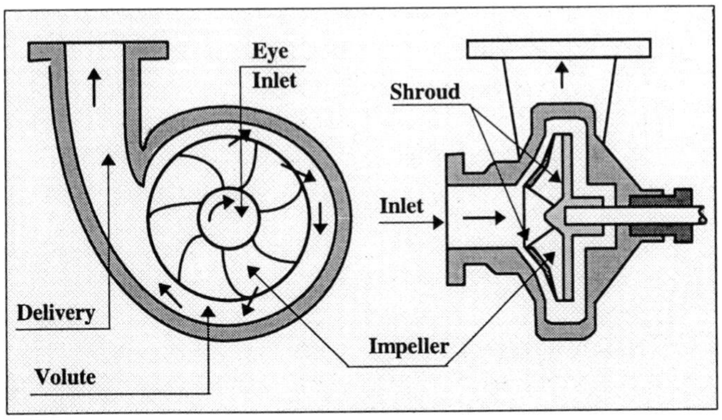

Fig.14.1- Volute type centrifugal pump.

Application of Euler's Equation for Pumps

In passing through the impeller the tangential component of the absolute velocity of the fluid is changed and there is a change of moment of momentum. The torque applied to the pump impeller is the difference between the moment of momentum at the inlet to and outlet from the impeller.

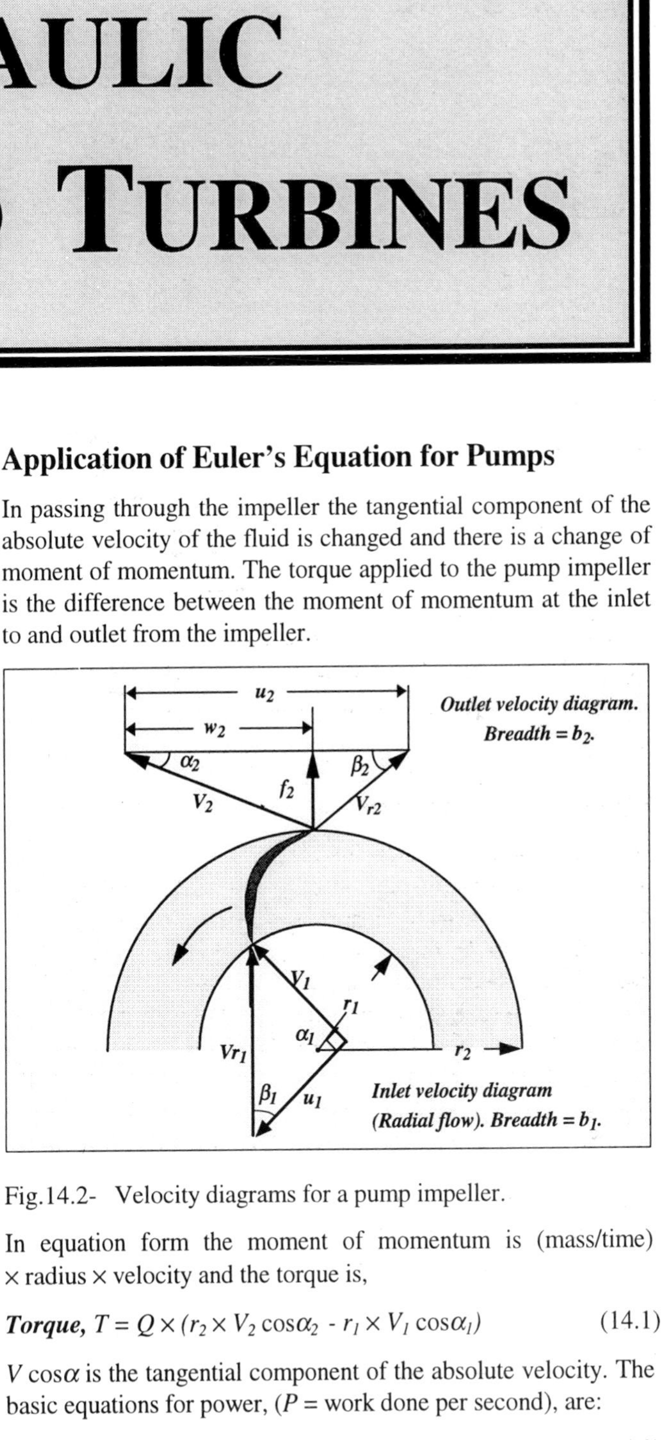

Fig.14.2- Velocity diagrams for a pump impeller.

In equation form the moment of momentum is (mass/time) × radius × velocity and the torque is,

$$\textit{Torque, } T = Q \times (r_2 \times V_2 \cos\alpha_2 - r_1 \times V_1 \cos\alpha_1) \qquad (14.1)$$

$V \cos\alpha$ is the tangential component of the absolute velocity. The basic equations for power, (P = work done per second), are:

$$P = \textbf{Torque} \times \textbf{angular velocity} = T \times \omega \qquad (14.2)$$

$$P = \rho Q \times w \times (r_2 \times V_2 \cos\alpha_2 - r_1 \times V_1 \cos\alpha_1) \qquad (14.3)$$

$$P = \rho Q \times (u_2 \times V_2 \cos\alpha_2 - u_1 \times V1 \cos\alpha_1) \qquad (14.4)$$

$$P = \rho g \times Q\, H_r \qquad (14.5)$$

Equations (14.2) and (14.4) relates the power exchange between the runner, operating at the angular velocity ω, and the head fluid, and define the quantity called the runner head H_r. Through substitution of equation (14.1),

$$H_r = (u_2 \times V_2 \cos\alpha_2 - u_1 \times V_1 \cos\alpha_1) / g \qquad (14.6)$$

since $u_2 = \omega \times r_2$ and $u_1 = \omega \times r_1$.

This equation of Euler gives the total head that would be developed (or absorbed) by a runner without losses. For a pump, it is commonly called head input; for a turbine head utilised. Since $w_1 = V_1 \cos\alpha_1$ and $w_2 = V_2 \cos\alpha_2$, equation (14.6) may be written as:

$$H_r = (u_2 \times w_2 - u_1 \times w_1)/g \qquad (14.7)$$

If the fluid enters the impeller radially ($\alpha_1 = 90^o$) the $\cos\alpha_1 = 0$ and the fluid has no moment of whirl at this point. Hence,

$u_1 \times V_1 \cos\alpha = 0$, and

$$P = \rho Q \times u_2 \times V_2 \cos\alpha_2 \qquad (14.8)$$

$$H_r = (u_2 \times V_2 \cos\alpha_2)/g \qquad (14.9)$$

Putting $u_2 = V_2 \cos\alpha_2$ and considering only a unit weight of fluid flowing per second, equation (14.9) is then reduced to,

$$H_r = \text{Work done per unit weight} = (u_2 \times w_2)/g \qquad (14.10)$$

Centrifugal Pump-Efficiencies

If there are no losses the pressure rise, or head generated in the pump, will be equal to the energy given to the fluid by the impeller. Energy given to the fluid = $(u_2 \times w_2)/g$, provided the fluid enters the impeller radially. If losses occur, then

Manometric head, H_m = Total energy of fluid at inlet of pump - Total energy at outlet of pump, or

Manometric head, $H_m = (u_2 \times w_2)/g$ - *losses* (14.11)

If pressure gauges are placed on the suction and discharge pipes, the energy at inlet and energy at exit are respectively,

Energy at inlet $= (p_s/\rho g) + (v_s^2/2g)$ (14.12)

Energy at exit $= (p_d/\rho g) + (v_d^2/2g) + h$ (14.13)

where h is the difference in elevation of the pressure gauges. If the suction and delivery pipes are of the same diameter, $v_s = v_d$. Furthermore, if the gauges are on the same level (*i.e.* $h = 0$), the manometer pressure head, ***H_m = pressure rise in impeller + the pressure rise in the diffuser - losses,*** or,

Manometer pressure head, $H_m = (p_d/\rho g) - (p_s/\rho g)$ (14.14)

$H_m = (1/2g) \times (f_1^2 + u_1^2 - f_1^2 \operatorname{cosec}^2\beta)$ - *losses* (14.15)

Manometer efficiency $= H_m/(u_2 \times w_2 / g)$ (14.16)

Mechanical efficiency $= \rho g \times H_m \times Q / (T \times \omega)$ (14.17)

Performance of Machines

Pumps: The flow rate, $Q = \phi\,(\rho, N, D, p)$, where ρ = density of water, N = speed (rev/min), D = impeller diameter, and p = pressure difference

Expressed as a power series: $Q = K \rho^a N^b D^c p^d$

and for dimensional homogeneity:

$(L^3T^{-1}) = (ML^{-3})^a (T^{-1})^b L^c (ML^{-1} T^{-2})^d$

Equating power indices:

(M) $0 = a + d$	$a = -d$
(L) $3 = -3a + c - d$	$b = 1 - 2d$
(T) $-1 = -b - 2d$	$c = 3 - 2d$

$$Q = K \rho^{-d} N^{1-2d} D^{3-2d} p^d \qquad (14.18)$$

$Q = ND^3 \times K \times (p/\rho N^2 D^2)^d = ND^3 \times \phi(p/\rho N^2 D^2)$

Since $p = \rho gH$, therefore $p/\rho = gH$, and

$Q/ND^3 = \phi(gH/N^2 D^2)$.

Hence for two dynamically similar systems a and b, if we make

$$\frac{H_a}{N_a^2 D_a^2} = \frac{H_b}{N_b^2 D_b^2}, \text{ then } \frac{Q_a}{N_a D_a^3} = \frac{Q_b}{N_b D_b^3} \qquad (14.19)$$

Turbines: ***Power,*** $P = \rho gQH$. i.e.

$$P = \rho gHND^3 \times \phi\left(\frac{gH}{N^2 D^2}\right) \qquad (14.20)$$

$$P = \rho gH \times \left(\frac{N^2 D^2}{gH}\right) \times ND^3 \times \phi\left(\frac{gH}{N^2 D^2}\right)$$

$= \rho N^3 D^5 \times \phi(gH/N^2 D^2)$.

So for turbines: $P = \rho N^3 D^5 \times \phi(gH/N^2 D^2)$ (14.21)

Hence for two dynamically similar systems a and b, if we make

$$\frac{H_a}{N_a^2 D_a^2} = \frac{H_b}{N_b^2 D_b^2}, \text{ then } \frac{P_a}{\rho_a N_a^3 D_a^5} = \frac{P_b}{\rho_b N_b^3 D_b^5} \qquad (14.22)$$

The specific turbine is a theoretical machine geometrically similar to the actual turbine considered but of such a size that working conditions dynamically similar to those in the actual turbine it develops 1kW under 1 metre head. The speed at which specific turbine runs is specific speed N_s and diameter the specific diameter D_s.

Actual turbines	P	H	N	D
Specific turbines	1	1	N_s	D_s

$$\frac{P}{\rho N^3 D^5} = \phi\left(\frac{gH}{N^2 D^2}\right), \text{ and } N_s = \frac{N\sqrt{P}}{H^{5/4}}. \text{ Since,}$$

$$\frac{H}{N^2 D^2} = \frac{1}{N_s^2 D_s^2} \text{ and } \frac{P}{N^3 D^5} = \frac{1}{N_s^3 D_s^5} \qquad (14.23)$$

$$\therefore \frac{D}{D_s} = \left(\frac{N_s}{N}\right) \times H^{1/2}, \text{ and } \frac{D}{D_s} = \left(\frac{N_s}{N}\right)^{3/5} \times P^{1/5}.$$

$$\left(\frac{N_s}{N}\right) \times H^{1/2} = \left(\frac{N_s}{N}\right)^{3/5} \times P^{1/5}. \text{ Therefore,}$$

$$\left(\frac{N_s}{N}\right) = \frac{P^{1/2}}{H^{5/4}} \qquad (14.24)$$

Pumps

The specific pump is a theoretical machine geometrically similar to the actual pump under consideration, but of such a size that working under conditions dynamically similar to those on the actual pump it pumps $1m^3/s$ against 1m head. The speed at which the specific pump then runs is the specific speed N_s and its diameter the specific diameter D_s.

$$Q/(ND^3) = \phi(gH/N^2 D^2) \qquad (14.25)$$

Actual Pump	H	N	D	Q
Specific Pump	1	N_s	D_s	1

Therefore, $H/N^2 D^2 = 1/(N_s^2 D_s^2)$, and also $Q/ND^3 = 1/(N_s D_s^3)$.

$$(D/D_s) = (N_s/N) \times H^{1/2} \qquad (14.26)$$

$$(D/D_s) = (N_s/N)^{1/3} \times Q^{1/3} \qquad (14.27)$$

$\therefore (N_s/N) \times H^{1/2} = (N_s/N)^{1/3} \times Q^{1/3}$, or

$$(N_s/N)^{2/3} = Q^{1/3}/H^{1/2} \qquad (14.28)$$

$$\therefore N_s = (N \times Q^{1/2})/H^{3/4} \qquad (14.29)$$

Impulse Turbines

The Pelton Wheel

Turbines are devices for converting the potential head of water into electrical energy. They may be classified as impulse or reaction turbines. The type of impulse turbine used is the Pelton Wheel. It normally operates under high heads of water such as mountain reservoirs The wheel consists of a number of nozzles at the end of a pipe from which jets of fluid strike a series of buckets or cups on the periphery of a wheel.

Consider the single-jet Pelton wheel of Fig.14.3. Losses occur in flow from the reservoir through the pressure pipe and penstock to the base of the nozzle, which may be computed from pipe friction formula.

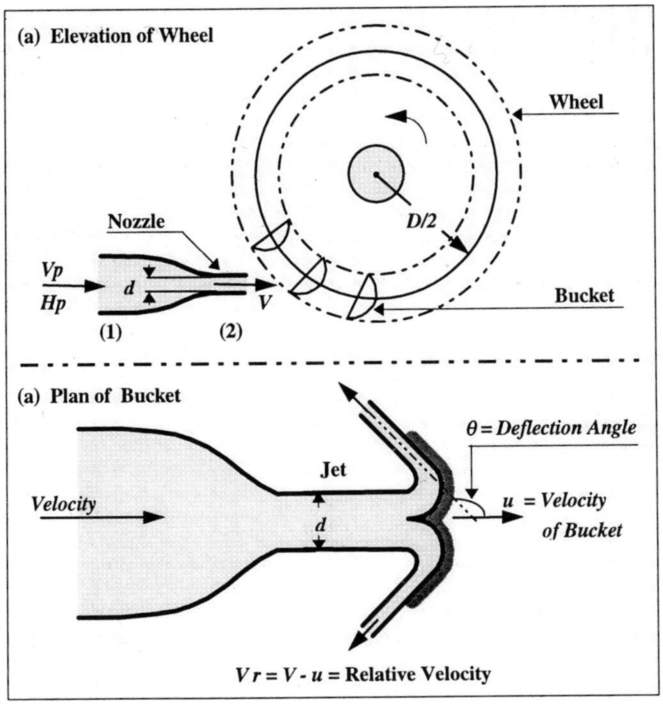

Fig.14.3- Pelton wheel bucket and velocity diagram.

At the base of the nozzle the **net total head** is:

$$H = \frac{p_p}{\rho g} + \frac{V_p^2}{2g} \qquad (14.30)$$

With C_v the nozzle coefficient of velocity, the jet velocity V is,

$$V = C_v \times \sqrt{2gH} = C_v \times \sqrt{2g} \times \left(\frac{p_p}{\rho g} + \frac{V_p^2}{2g}\right)^{1/2} \qquad (14.31)$$

The head lost in the nozzle is

$$H - \frac{V^2}{2g} = H - C_v^2\ H = H \times (1 - C_v^2) \qquad (14.32)$$

and the nozzle efficiency $\frac{V^2}{2gH} = \frac{C_v^2 H}{H} = C_v^2$ (14.33)

For a well-designed streamlined nozzle $C_v = 1.0$, $V = \sqrt{2g\,H}$.

The jet is applied tangentially to the wheel, and the velocity V is therefore a whirl velocity. On striking the bucket the jet is divided and turned through an angle θ, (Fig.14.3); the fluid velocity relative to the bucket is $(V\text{-}u)$ where u is the circumferential speed of the bucket, and this relative velocity is unchanged as the fluid passes over the bucket. Relative velocity leaving the bucket in the original direction of the jet is:

$$V_r \times \cos\theta = (V\text{-}u) \times \cos\theta \qquad (14.34)$$

The change of fluid momentum/s = $\rho Q \times$ *(change of velocity)*

in x-direction

$$\rho Q \times [(V\text{-}u) - (V\text{-}u)\times\cos\theta] = \rho Q \times (V\text{-}u)\,(1 - \cos\theta) \qquad (14.35)$$

where $Q = V \times (\pi \times d^2/4)$ is the discharge through the nozzle.

By the momentum principle the rate of change of momentum in any direction is equal to the resultant force in that direction. That is force in x-direction

$$F_x = \rho\, Q \times (V\text{-}u) \times (1 - \cos\theta) \qquad (14.36)$$

and this is the force exerted by the jet on the buckets. The torque applied to the wheel is:

$$T = F_x \times \frac{D}{2} = \rho\, Q\,(V - u)\,(1 - \cos\theta) \times \frac{D}{2} \qquad (14.37)$$

The power or rate of doing work on the buckets is simply the product of the force and the bucket speed, i.e.

$$Power = Force \times velocity = \rho\, Q \times u \times (V\text{-}u) \times (1 - \cos\theta) \qquad (14.38)$$

Since $Q = V \times a = \sqrt{2gH} \times a$, then H is constant (a usual case when water is supplied from a high level reservoir), V is a constant and $P \propto u \times (V - u)$ (14.39)

$$P = K \times (uV - u^2) \text{ (with K = a constant)} \qquad (14.40)$$

This relationship is plotted in Fig.14.4, and it is seen that there is a parabolic relationship between P and u. The maximum value of P_{max} occurs at a certain value of u of bucket speed, found by differentiation (see example on Page 135).

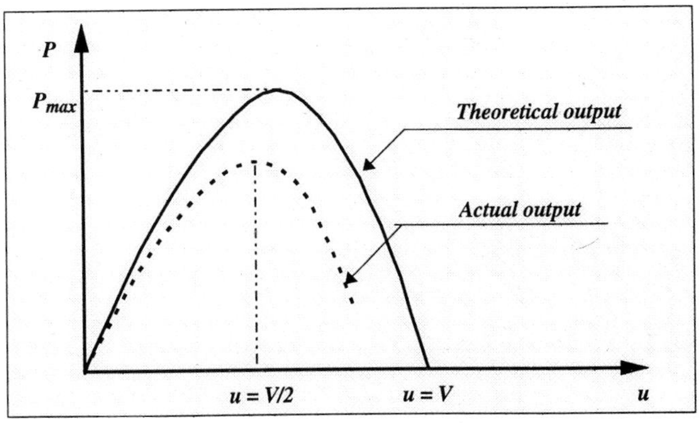

Fig.14.4- Theoretical and actual output power curves.

Radial Flow of Turbines

Francis or Reaction Turbines

For heads much below 150 metres, Pelton wheels become so slow and unwieldy that they are unsuitable for ordinary use. We therefore have recourse to the relatively faster running and more compact radial flow turbines sometimes referred to as Francis or reaction turbines.

The essential parts of an inward flow Francis turbine are: (1) an outer ring of stationary guide blades and (2) an inner ring of rotating blades which constitutes the impeller or runner. The fluid is fed to the runner all round the circumference from a volute casing through a ring of the stationary guide vanes, which produce a velocity of whirl. The turbine shown in Fig.14.5 is an inward radial flow machine known as a Francis turbine. For outward radial flow the guide vanes are inside the runner.

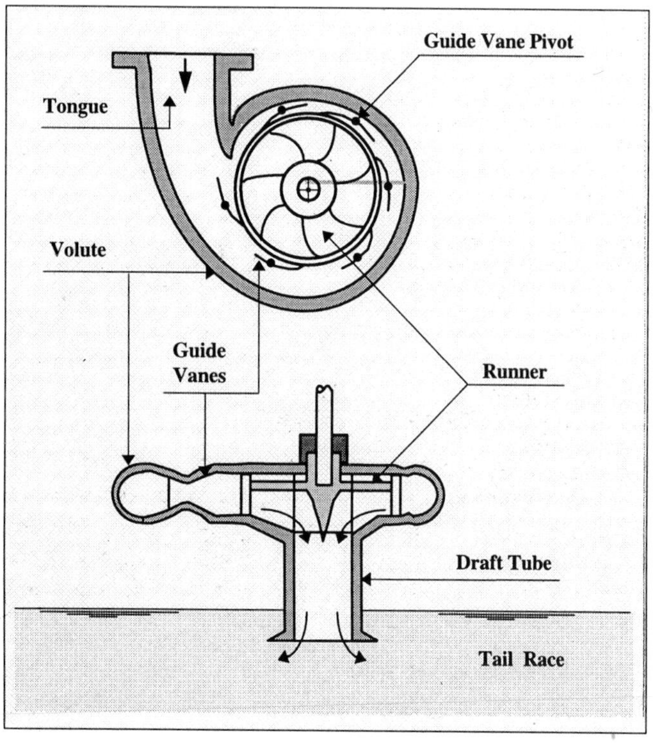

Fig.14.5- Radial flow turbine.

Power Developed by Radial Flow Turbines

The power developed by a turbine may be found by consideration of fluid velocities involved in Fig.14.6. Let,

V be the absolute velocity of fluid,

u be the tangential speed of impeller,

V_r be the relative velocity of the fluid,

w be the tangential component of absolute velocity of the fluid,

f be the radial component of absolute velocity of the fluid,

α be the guide vane angle,

β be the inlet angle of runner, exit angle of runner vane.

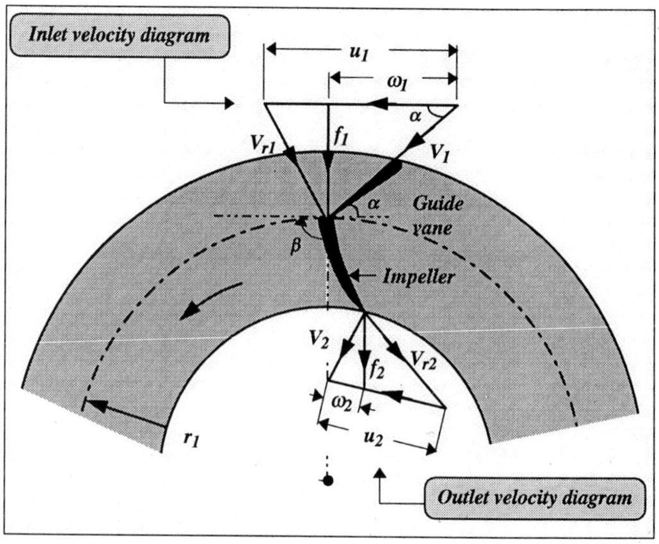

Fig.14.6- Flow through a Francis turbine.

The power equation derived for centrifugal pumps is applicable to reaction turbines if the subscripts are exchanged. That is, for turbines,

$$P = T \times \omega = \rho Q \times (u_1 \times V_1 \cos\alpha_1 - u_2 \times V_2 \cos\alpha_2) \qquad (14.41)$$

or equation (14.41) can be derived as the corresponding equation was for pumps, by utilising the turbine velocity diagram of Fig.14.6 in which $V_1^2 = u_1^2 + V_1^2 - 2\,u_1 \times V_1 \cos\beta_1$, and

$V_2^2 = u_2^2 + V_2^2 - 2\,u_2 \times V_2 \cos\beta_2$, that is,

$P = \rho g Q \times H_r = \rho Q \times (u_1 \times V_1 \cos\alpha_1 - u_2 \cos\alpha_2)$, from which,

$H_r = (1/g) \times (u_1 \times V_1 \cos\alpha_1 - u_2 \times V_2 \cos\alpha_2)$, or

$$H_r = (1/g) \times (u_1 w_1 - u_2 w_2) \qquad (14.42)$$

The angle α_2 is most commonly close to 90°, hence $u_2 \times V_2 \cos\alpha_2$ is small and for purely radial outflow from the runner $\alpha_2 = 90^o$. Then,

$H_r = (1/g) \times (u_1 \times V_1 \cos\alpha_1 - u_2 \times V_2 \cos\alpha_2)$, or

$$H_r = (u_1 \times V_1 \cos\alpha_1)/g = (u_1 \times w_1)/g \qquad (14.43)$$

The power delivered by the turbine is:

$$P = \eta_t \times \rho g \times QH \qquad (14.44)$$

in which η_t is the turbine efficiency. The power output from the generator is:

$$P = \eta_m \times \eta_t \times \rho g \times QH = \eta \times \rho g \times QH \qquad (14.45)$$

in which η_m is the mechanical efficiency of the generator and $\eta = \eta_m \times \eta_t$ is the overall efficiency of the turbine.

Examples on Hydraulic Turbines

Maximum Efficiency of a Pelton Wheel

Derive an expression for the maximum theoretical efficiency of a single jet Pelton Wheel in terms of the deflection angle of the buckets. Comment on the final results

From equation (14.40), ***Power***, $P = K\,(uV - u^2)$.

$$\frac{dP}{du} = K \times \frac{d}{du} \times (uV - u^2) = K \times (V - 2u\,) \;=\; 0$$

$V - 2u = 0$ *(P being maximum).*

Thus for a given input head H and discharge Q, the theoretical maximum output power of a Pelton wheel is developed when the bucket speed is half the jet (whirl) speed and is,

$$P_{max} = \rho Qu \times (V - u) \times (1 - \cos\theta) = \rho\, QV^2 \times (1 - \cos\theta)/4$$

The input power to the nozzles given by H and Q is $P_E = \rho gQH$ so that the maximum efficiency of the machine at the maximum output power = Output/Input = P_{max} / P_E.

$$\eta_{max} = \frac{\rho\, Q\, \times V^2 \times (1 - \cos\theta)/\,4}{\rho g\, Q\, H} = \frac{V^2 \times (1 - \cos\theta)}{4gH}$$

on inserting $V = \sqrt{2g\,H}$, we get $\eta_{max} = \dfrac{1 - \cos\theta}{2}$.

It is not possible to make $\theta = 180^o$ and therefore $\eta_{max} = 100\%$, as the jet leaving such a bucket would strike other buckets, giving a retarding force on the wheel and less efficiency. With $\theta = 165^o$, a typical value $\eta_m = 98.3\%$. This is the efficiency of the wheel itself in converting fluid to mechanical energy.

Vertical Shaft Radial Flow Turbine

The geometry of a blade in the runner of a vertical-shaft radial flow turbine is shown below. The width of the flow passage at the runner inlet is 85mm and the flow area at the runner inlet equals that at outlet. The water level in the supply reservoir is 130m above the centre of the runner and the surface of the water in the tail race is 2.5m below it. The head loss due to friction in the supply pipe is given by the relation $h_f(m) = 0.35 \times Q^2$ where Q is the volume flow rate (m^3/s). Assuming operating conditions in the turbine correspond to minimum outlet kinetic energy, determine: (a) the outlet angle of the upstream guide vanes, (b) the hydraulic efficiency of the turbine, and (c) the dimensionless specific speed when the mechanical efficiency is 96% and the runner rotates at 8 rev/s.

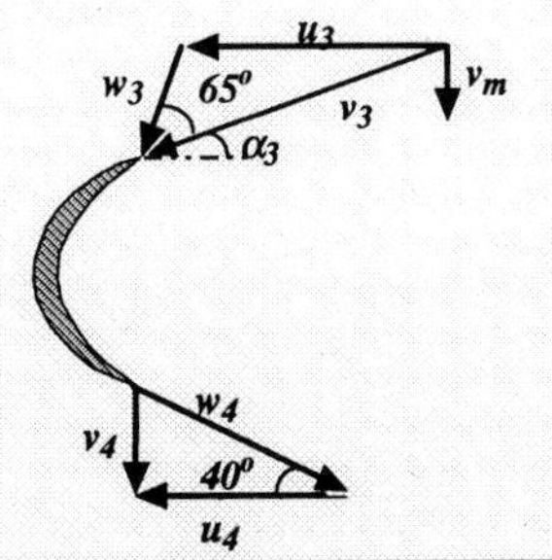

Outlet triangle right-angled so that v is a minimum in exit K.E. at minimum. Therefore, friction losses in draft tube and K.E. to tail race both at minimum.

Constant flow area $v_m = constant.\ u_4 = 2\pi \times 0.35 \times 8 = 17.6 m/s.$

$u_3 = 2\pi \times 0.60 \times 8 = 30.16 m/s.\ \ v_m = 17.6 \times \tan 40^o = 14.77 m/s.$

$Q = 10.17 \times 2\pi \times 0.60 \times 0.085 = 3.255 m^3/s.$

$v_m \times \cot\alpha_3 = u_3 \times \cot 40^o = 30.16 + 14.77 \times 0.4663 = 37.05 m/s.$

$\therefore \cot\alpha_3 = 37.05/14.77 = 2.51.$

Outlet angle of upstream guide vanes, $\alpha_3 = 21^o 42'$.

Neglect $v_2^2/2g$ at different outlet, new head H is:

$H = 130 + 2.5 - h_f(pipe) = 132.5 - 0.35 \times 3.255^2 = 128.79m.$

Hydraulic efficiency of turbine, $\eta_h = u_3 \times v_{m3} / H.$

$$\eta_h = \frac{30.16 \times 14.77 \times 2.51}{9.81 \times 128.79} = 88.5\%\ .$$

$P = \eta_h \times \eta_m \times \rho g \times QH = 0.885 \times 0.96 \times 9810 \times 3.255 \times 128.79$

$= 3.495MW.$

$$K_n = \frac{n \times (P/\rho)^{1/2}}{(gH)^{5/4}} = \frac{8 \times 10 \times 34.95^{1/2}}{1263^{5/4}} = \frac{80 \times 5.9119}{7529}$$

Dimensionless specific speed, $K_n = 0.0626$ rev.

Inward Flow Reaction Turbine

The head at the inlet to an inward flow reaction turbine is 85m and the available flow rate is 18m/s. The outer radius of the turbine runner is 1.5m, the runner width at inlet is 0.3m, its speed of rotation is 200 rev/min and the hydraulic efficiency of the runner is 90%. Calculate the angles of the guide vanes and runner vanes at inlet for maximum efficiency.

Consider inlet velocity triangle.

Flow rate, Q = flow velocity × inlet area $= 18 \times v_f\ (2\pi \times 1.5 \times 0.3)$

$v_f = 6.37 m/s.\ \ u = (200/60) \times 2\pi \times 1.5 = 31.42 m/s.$

Power development $= \rho Q \times (v_{w1} \times u_1 - v_{w2})$

For maximum efficiency $v_{w2} \times u_2 = 0$

Power $= 1000 \times 18 \times (v_{w1} \times 31.42) = 565560\ v_{w1}.$

But efficiency = 90%. Therefore,

Power $= 0.9 \times \rho gQH = 0.9 \times 1000 \times 18 \times 9.81 \times 85 = 13508370W.$

Thus, 13508370 = 565560 v_{w1}. Therefore, $v_{w1} = 23.88 m/s.$

Guide one angle $= \tan^{-1}\left(\dfrac{v_f}{v_w}\right) = \tan^{-1}\left(\dfrac{6.37}{23.88}\right) = 15^o$.

We can calculate angle $\theta = \tan^{-1}\left(\dfrac{31.42 - 23.88}{6.37}\right) = 49.8^o$.

Runner inlet angle, $\beta = 90^o + \theta = 90^o + 49.8^o = 139.8^o.$

Output Power of a Pelton Wheel

A Pelton wheel 2m diameter is supplied with water by a nozzle which is 0.2m diameter and has $C_v = 0.97$. The head at the nozzle is 250m and the buckets are so shaped that if stationary they would deflect the jet through 165°. Calculate the speed, in revolutions per minute, at which the wheel should rotate in order to work at maximum overall efficiency. If the overall efficiency of the wheel at this speed is 88%, calculate the output power of the wheel.

Maximum overall efficiency when $u = 0.46 \times V$.

$$V = C_V\sqrt{2g \times H} = 0.97 \times \sqrt{2 \times 9.81 \times 250} = 67.93 m/s.$$

$$\therefore\ V = 0.46 \times 67.93 = 31.25 m/s.$$

$$V\ (in\ r.p.m) = (31.25) \times (1/2\pi) \times 60 = 298.8\ r.p.m.$$

Flow rate, $Q = 67.93 \times (\pi/4) \times 0.25^2 = 3.334 m^3/s.$

Output power $= 0.88 \times \rho Q g h = 0.88 \times 1000 \times 3.334 \times 9.81 \times 250$

$\mathbf{= 7196531.02\ W = 7196.6 kW.}$

Design of Pelton Wheel Jets

A Pelton wheel 1.5m diameter is supplied with water by two nozzles, $C_v = 0.97$. The head at the nozzles is 200m and the buckets are so shaped that when stationary they would deflect the jets through 170°. At a speed of 375 r.p.m the hydraulic power generated is 3800kW. If the relative velocity of the jets is reduced by 10% by friction in passing over the buckets, calculate from first principles the hydraulic efficiency and calculate the diameter of the jets.

Force $= \rho Q \times [v - u - (0.9\,(v - u) \times \cos 10^o)]$

$= \rho Q \times (v - u) \times (1 + 0.9 \times \cos 10^o)$

Torque $= (Force \times r) = \rho Q \times (v - u) \times (1 + 0.9 \times \cos 10^o) \times r$

Power $= T \times \omega = \rho Q \times u \times (v - u) \times (1 + 0.9 \times \cos 10^o)$

$\omega = (375/60) \times 2\pi\ (rad/s)$, and $u = \omega \times r = 29.45 m/s.$

$$v = C_V\sqrt{2gh} = 0.97 \times \sqrt{2 \times 9.81 \times 200} = 60.76\ m/s.$$

Hydraulic efficiency, η***, is therefore,***

$$\eta = \frac{\rho Q \times 29.45 \times (60.76 - 29.45)(1 + 0.9\ \cos 10^o)}{\rho Q \times 9.81 \times 200} = \mathbf{88.65\%.}$$

$$3800 \times 1000 = 1000Q \times 29.45\ (60.76 - 29.45)\ (1 + 0.9 \cos 10^o)$$

$\therefore$ ***Flow rate,*** $Q = 2.184\ m^3/s.$

To find the diameter of jet: $2.184 = 2 \times (\pi/4) \times d^2 \times 60.76$

Diameter of jet, $d = 0.1513 m.$

Hydraulic Efficiency of a Pelton Wheel

A Pelton wheel 1.6m diameter develops an output power of 8000kW at a speed of 400 r.p.m. under a net head of 300m. If overall efficiency is 90% the coefficient of velocity of the nozzle is 0.97, and the blade angle 165°, calculate the quantity of flow and the hydraulic efficiency.

Available power $= 8000 \times 10^3/0.9 = 8888.8 \times 10^3 W.$

Also, $8888.8 \times 10^3 = 1000 \times 9.81 \times 300 \times Q$. Hence,

Quantity of flow, $Q = 3.02\ m^3/s.$

Hydraulic power $= \rho Q \times (v - u) \times (1 + \cos\theta) \times u$

$u = (400/60) \times 2\pi \times 0.8 = 33.51 m/s.\ \theta = 15^o$

$$v = C_V\sqrt{2gh} = 0.97 \times \sqrt{2 \times 9.81 \times 300} = 74.42\ m/s.$$

$= 1000 \times 3.02 \times (74.42 - 33.51) \times (1 + \cos 10^o) \times 33.51 =$

Hydraulic power $= 8130.12 kW.$

Hydraulic efficiency $= \dfrac{8139.12}{8888.88} \times 1000 = 91.56\%$.

Problems on Turbines

[1] It is required to design a Pelton wheel, which is to develop a brake power of 9.5 MW under a net head of 245m, at a speed of 6 rev/s, assuming the jet diameter is 1.9 of the wheel diameter. Calculate (a) the number and diameter of jets required, (b) the diameter of the wheel, and (c) the flow rate. Assume the speed ratio is 0.45, the overall efficiency 86% and the nozzle coefficient $C_v = 0.98$.
(5, 135mm, 1218mm, 4.6m^3/s)

[2] The buckets of a Pelton wheel deflect the jet through 170° and the relative velocity is reduced by 12% by bucket friction. Calculate the hydraulic efficiency for a speed ratio of 0.47, ignoring nozzle losses. The diameter of the wheel is 1.0m and there are two jets for which $C_v = 0.98$. The overall efficiency is 90%. Under a gross head of 615m the wheel develops 1250kW when the friction loss in the pipe is 49m. Calculate the speed of rotation of the wheel and the nozzles' diameter. (91%, 926 rev/min, 39mm)

Cavitation in Turbines

Consider the flow through a turbine with a draft tube, as shown below, and apply the total head equation between sections (2) and (3): $H_2 + H_s + (V_2^2/2g) = H_a + (V_3^2/2g) + H_L$,
where H_a is the atmospheric pressure head and H_L is the head loss. The head representing the kinetic energy of the flow entering the draft tube is $V_2^2/2g$. The purpose of the draft tube is to convert as much as possible of this velocity head into pressure head to increase the generation of power. As H_s is increased the pressure is reduced reaching the vapour pressure of the water. The formation and collapse of air bubbles, known as cavitation, cause vibration, loss of efficiency and damage to machinery.

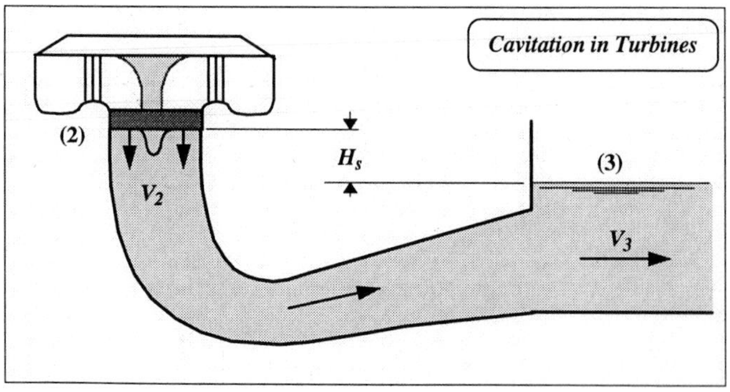

Examples on Pumps

Performance of a Centrifugal Pump

A centrifugal pump has a "dimensionless specific speed" of 0.08 rev and runs at a constant speed of 24 rev/s. When operating at a maximum overall efficiency of 81% the total pressure produced by the pump is $400kN/m^2$. The pump is to supply water through a pipe 55m long, the static lift being 15m. For a flow rate Q m^3/s, the total losses in pressure between the supply sump and the inlet flange of the pump amount to $1.5Q^2$ MN/m^2. Available delivery pipes have diameters of 100mm, 150mm and 200mm. For each pipe, $f = 0.0085$. Justify a choice of delivery pipe and for this pipe calculate the power required to drive the pump. For the pump it may be assumed that the efficiency-flow rate curve is a parabola and that the pressure developed varies linearly with flow rate.

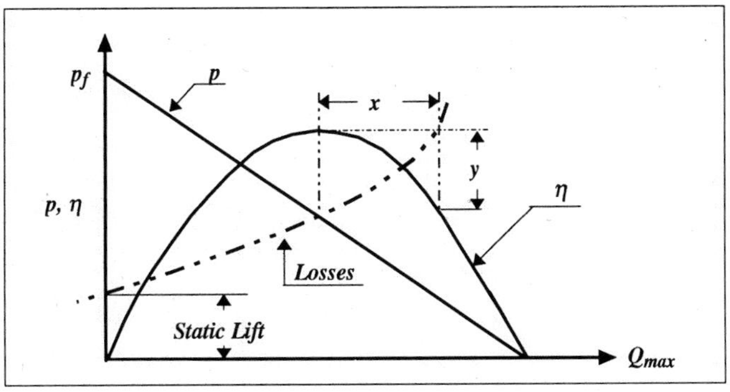

$$K_p = \frac{n\sqrt{Q}}{(gH)^{3/4}} = \frac{n\,Q^{1/2}}{(p/\rho)^{3/4}}$$ at maximum efficiency η_{max}.

$$\therefore\ Q_{\eta max} = \frac{0.08^2}{24^2} \times \left(\frac{400 \times 1000}{1000}\right)^{3/2} = 0.0889\ m^3/s.$$

When $Q = 0$, $p_f = 800\ kN/m^2$. When $p = 0$, $Q = 0.1778m^3/s$.

$$\therefore\ p = p_f - \frac{p_f}{0.1778} \times Q = 800 \times 10^3 - \frac{800 \times 10^3}{0.1778} \times Q$$
$$= (8 - 45Q) \times 10^5\ N/m^2.$$

For maximum efficiency, the frictional head loss in the pipe is:

$$p_f = \frac{400 \times 10^3}{1000 \times 9.81} - 15 - \frac{1.5 \times 10^6 \times 0.0889^2}{1000 \times 9.81} = 2.409 \times 10 N/m^2.$$

$$p_f = \rho g h_f = \frac{1000 \times 9.81 \times 4 \times 0.085 \times 55 \times 0.0889^2}{2 \times 9.81 \times (\pi/4)^2 \times d^5}$$

$d^5 = 4.975 \times 10^{-5}$ $\therefore$ $d = 137.8mm$. ***Choose 150mm diameter pipe.***

$$p = 10^3 \times 9.81 \times 15 + 1.5Q^2 \times 10^6 + \frac{4 \times 0.0085 \times 55Q^2 \times 10^3}{2 \times (\pi/4)^2 \times 0.15^2}$$

$= (8 - 45Q)$.

$\therefore$ $Q^2 + 0.2094Q - 0.03038 = 0$.

This gives a ***flow rate*** $\boldsymbol{Q = 0.0987m^3/s}$.

$p = [8 - (45 \times 0.0987)] \times 105 = 3.56 \times 10^5\ N/m^2$.

From η curve, $y = kX^2$. $\therefore \eta = y = 81\%$.

$$k = \frac{81}{0.0889^2},\quad y = \frac{81}{0.0889^2} \times (0.0889 - 0.0987)^2 = 0.984\%.$$

$\therefore \eta = 81 - 0.984 = 80\%$.

$$\textbf{Power, } P = \frac{pQ}{\eta} = \frac{3.56 \times 10^5 \times 0.0987}{0.80} = \mathbf{43.3kW}.$$

Design of a Centrifugal Pump

A centrifugal pump has an impeller, inner radius 75mm outer radius 150mm and breadth at inlet 50mm. The inlet blade angle is 30° and the outlet blade angle is 30° backward-facing. If the water flow rate is $0.06m^3/s$ and there is no change of flow velocity through the pump, calculate: (a) the impeller speed for shockless entry, (b) the pressure head at outlet assuming 50% of the velocity head at outlet is converted and (c) the input power required to run the pump at this speed if the mechanical efficiency is 70%.

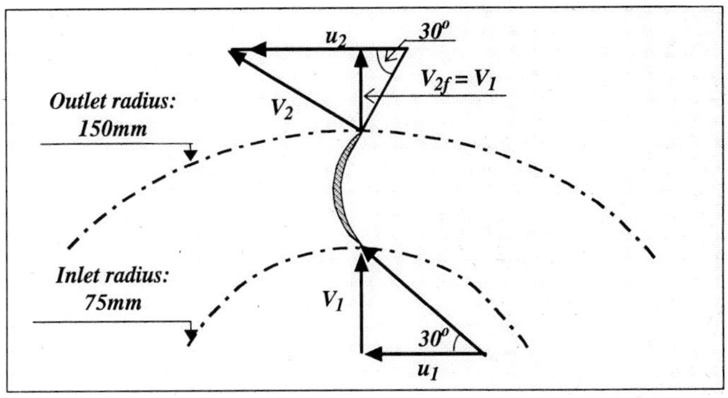

$$V_1 = \left(\frac{\text{flow rate, } Q}{\text{Inlet flow area, } A}\right) = \frac{0.06}{2\pi \times 0.75 \times 0.05} = 2.546m/s$$

For shockless entry, $V_1/u_1 = \tan 30^o$.

$u_1 = V_1/\tan\alpha = 2.546/\tan 30^o = 4.411m/s$.

$\therefore$ ***Speed = 4.411/ (2π × 0.075) × 60 = 562rev/min.***

Total head at exit $= (V_{w2} \times u_2)/g$.

$u_2 = (562/60) \times 2\pi \times 0.15 = 8.822m/s$.

$V_{w2} = u_2 - (u_{2t}/\tan\alpha) = 8.822 - (2.546/\tan 30^o) = 4.412m/s$.

$(u_2 \times V_w)/g = (8.822 \times 4.412)/9.81 = 3.968$.

$V_{w2} = V_2 \times \cos\alpha = 4.412m/s$, and $V_{f2} = V_2 \times \sin\alpha = 2.596m/s$

$\tan\alpha = 2.546/4.412 = 0.577$. $\therefore$ $\alpha = 29.99^o$.

$V_2 = V_w/\cos\alpha = 2.546/\cos 29.99^o = 5.094m/s$.

Pressure head = 3.968 - [(0.5 × 5.094²) / 2 × 9.81] = 3.307m.

Power required, P = (ρQ × V_w2 × u_2)/0.7 = 3336.22W.

Selection of Most Suitable Pump

Water is to be pumped through a vertical distance H, of 30m at a flow rate Q, of 50 litres/s. Both the suction and the delivery pipes are 0.16m diameter and have a friction factor f, of 0.0064. The total length of the pipes is 40m and losses at valves, bends etc., amount to 2.5 times the velocity head in the pipes. The pump is directly driven at a speed n, equal to $48/y$ rev/s, where y is an integer. The following single-sides, single-entry centrifugal pumps are available:

-	1	2	3	4
K_n/ (rev)	0.068	0.073	0.085	0.090
D/ (mm)	250	295	310	285

where $K_n = nQ^{1/2}/(gH)^{3/4}$, is the dimensionless specific speed, and D is the outer diameter of the impeller. In each case the outlet blade angle is 25° measured relative to the backward facing tangent, and the width of the impeller passages at outlet equals $D/8$. Neglecting blade thickness and whirl slip, and assuming an overall efficiency of 72% and a mechanical efficiency of 96%, justify your selection of the most suitable pump.

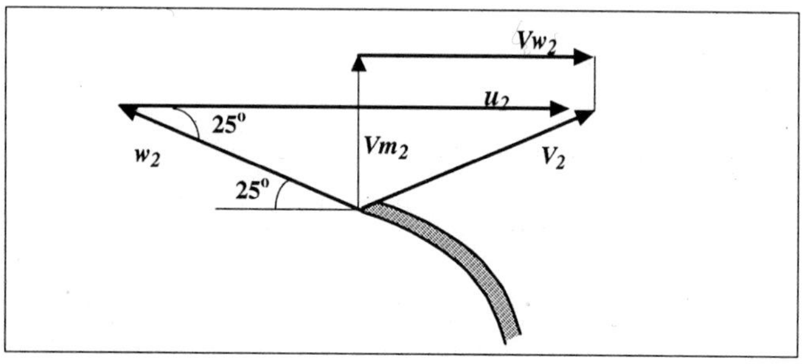

Velocity in pipe, $V = \dfrac{0.05}{(\pi/4)\times 0.16^2} =$ ***2.49m/s.***

Head losses, $h_l = 2.5\times\dfrac{V^2}{2g} + \dfrac{4fl}{d}\times\dfrac{V^2}{2g} = \left(2.5+\dfrac{4fl}{d}\right)\times\dfrac{V^2}{2g}$.

$$h_l = \left(2.5+\frac{4\times 0.0064\times 40}{0.16}\right)\times\frac{2.49^2}{19.62} = 2.81m.$$

Head losses, $\boldsymbol{H = H_g + h_l = 30 + 2.81 = 32.81m}$.

$$K_n = \frac{nQ^{1/2}}{(gH)^{3/4}} = \frac{48}{y}\times\frac{0.05^{1/2}}{(9.81\times 32.81)^{3/4}} = \frac{48\times 0.223}{76y} = \frac{0.141}{y}$$

If $y = 2$, $K_n = 0.0705 rev/s$. This suggests pump 1 or 2. Therefore, $n = 24 rev/s$ and diameter D in metres.

Outlet flow area $= \pi D \times D/8 = \pi \times D^2/8$.

$$V_{m2} = \frac{0.05}{\pi D^2/8} = \frac{0.1274}{D^2}\ m/s.$$

$u_2 = \pi \times n \times D = 24 \times \pi \times D = 75.4 \times D\ (m/s)$.

$$\frac{gH}{u_2 V_{w2}} = \frac{0.72}{0.96} = 0.75,\quad u_{w2} = \frac{9.81\times 32.81}{75.4D\times 0.75} = \frac{5.69}{D}\ m/s.$$

$$\tan 25^o = \frac{V_{m2}}{u_2 - V_{w2}} = \frac{(0.1274/D_2)}{(75.4\times D)-(5.69/D)}.$$

$75.4 \times D^3 - 5.69 \times D = 0.1274 \times \cot 25^o = 0.2736$.

Solve by trial and error.

Neglect first the RHS of 0.2736:

$D^2 = 5.69/75.4 = 0.0754$.

$\therefore D = 0.2746m$.

Next, substitute for $D = 0.2746m$:

$D^3 = 1/[75.4\times(0.2736+5.69\times 0.2746)] = 0.2437$. $\therefore D = 0.29m$.

Substitute for $D = 0.29m$:

$D^3 = 1/[75.4\times(0.2736+5.69\times 0.29)] = 0.255$.

$\therefore$ **D = 0.2943m.**

This is near enough so choose Pump 2.

Problems on Hydraulic Pumps

[1] A centrifugal pump running at 1000 r.p.m. is supplying 0.1m^3/s against a head of 25m. The blade angle at outlet is 35° backward pumping and the velocity of flow is constant at 1.5m/s. Calculate the impeller diameter if 50% of the velocity head at exit is converted into pressure head. (0.18m)

[2] Discuss the importance of the concept of specific speed for a rotodynamic pump. Define the quantity and outline how the definition is arrived at. A rotodynamic pump is to be used to supply a liquid of relative density 0.88 at the rate of 10 litre/s against a pressure of 5 MPa. Designs of pumps are available with dimensionless specific speeds of *0.036, 0.08, 0.16, 0.30 and 0.6 rev.* The pump is to be driven by a synchronous electric motor with a speed *(50/n) rev/s,* where n is an integer. Which design of pump and what speed should be used? (Multi stage pump, $K_n = 0.036$ rev at 50 rev/s)

[3] The pump is being used to deliver water against a static head of 8m through a pipeline in which the head loss is related to the flow rate by the equation $h_f = 2500\ Q^2$. Calculate the flow rate produced by the pump and the input power required. (0.03m^3/s, 3.79kW)

[4] Two identical pumps connected in parallel, are used to lift water over a vertical distance of 15m by means of a pipeline 100m long 0.1m diameter for which the friction factor $f = 0.005$. Estimate the total volumetric flow rate and the power supplied to each pump. The characteristics of each pump are as follows:

Q (m^3/s)	0	0.01	0.02	0.03	0.04	0.05
H (m)	29.5	28.0	25.5	21.5	15.5	3.5
η (%)	0	56	73	68	49	11

Hints: Plot H and η against Q.

$$H_T = H_s + h_f = H_s + \left(4flQ^2/gdA^2\right) = 15 + 16{,}500Q^2.$$

Calculate and plot H_T for values of $Q = 0, 0.01, 0.02, 0.03, 0.04$ and 0.05. From graph,

Total volumetric flow rate $= 0.0275m^3/s$ for both pumps.

Power for a head of 27.2m and efficiency of 0.635 is:

$P = \rho gQH/\eta = (1000 \times 9.81 \times (0.0275/2) \times 27.2)/0.635)$

$= 5.78\ kW$ *per pump.*

Examples on Pump Operation

Axial Flow Pump Discharge

The characteristics of an axial flow pump delivering water are as follows:

Q (m^3/s)	0.0	0.04	0.069	0.115	0.138	0.180
H (m)	5.6	4.20	4.35	3.380	2.420	0.0

When two such pumps are connected in parallel, the flow rate through the system is the same as if they are connected in series. Determine the flow rate that a single pump would deliver when connected to the same system. Assume the system characteristic to be purely resistive (no static lift).

When pumps in parallel the discharge is doubled.

Q_{pv} (m^3/s)	0.0	0.08	0.138	0.230	0.276	0.360

When pumps in series the head is doubled.

H (m)	11.20	8.40	8.70	6.76	4.84	0.00

Since the flow rate is the same for both series and parallel connections of the two pumps, the system resistance must pass through point A.

A parabola representing the system characteristic is drawn through this point and through the origin as there is no static lift. It crosses the single pump characteristic at B, which would be the operation point for the single pump.

System characteristic:

The head loss due to friction, $H = KQ^2$

Substituting at point A, $4.4 = K \times 0.142^2$. $\therefore K = 218$.

When the flow rate $Q\ (m^3/s) =$ 0.04, 0.08, 0.12
the operating point $H\ (m)$ 0.35, 1.40, 3.14.

$\therefore$ ***Operating point for single pump,*** $H = 3.15m$, *and*

Flow rate delivered from a single pump, $Q = 0.12\ m^3/s$.

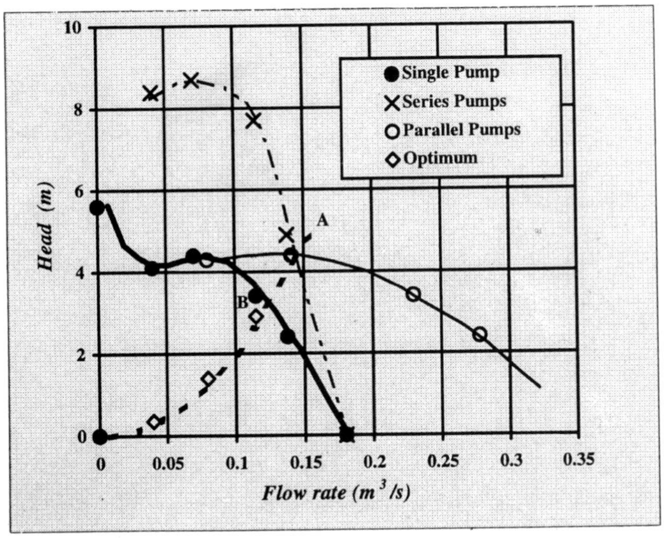

Centrifugal Pump Speed

A pump has the following characteristics when running at 1450 rev/min speed:

Q (m^3/s)	0.00	0.225	0.325	0.425	0 545	0.65	0.75	0.80
H (m)	20.0	17.0	15.0	13.0	10.0	7.00	3.00	0.0

A system is designed where the static lift is 5m and the operating point is H = 11.1m and Q = 0.5m^3/s using the pump as above. The system is redesigned, the static lift being 5m as before but the frictional and other losses increase by 40%. Find the new pump speed such that the flow rate of 0.5m^3/s can be maintained.

The pump characteristic has an equation $H = KQ^2 + 5$.

For initial conditions: $K = \dfrac{11.1 - 5}{0.5^2} = 24.4$

For external characteristic add 40% to K, i.e. $K_1 = 34\%$.

New operating point has a head of $H_1 = 13.54m$.

At a speed of *1450rev/min* operating point on new curve = $12.2m$.

For a pump, $\dfrac{Q}{ND^3} = \phi\left(\dfrac{gH}{N^2 D^2}\right)$

For a constant D, $\dfrac{Q}{N}$ *and* $\dfrac{H}{N^2}$ must be the same for both pumps.

(i) New speed, $N = \dfrac{0.5}{0.46} \times 1450 = 1576$ *rev/min.*

(ii) New speed, $N = \sqrt{\dfrac{13.54}{12.2}} \times 1450 = 1528$ *rev/min.*

Average speed, $N_{ave} = \dfrac{1528 + 1576}{2} = 1552$ *rev/min.*

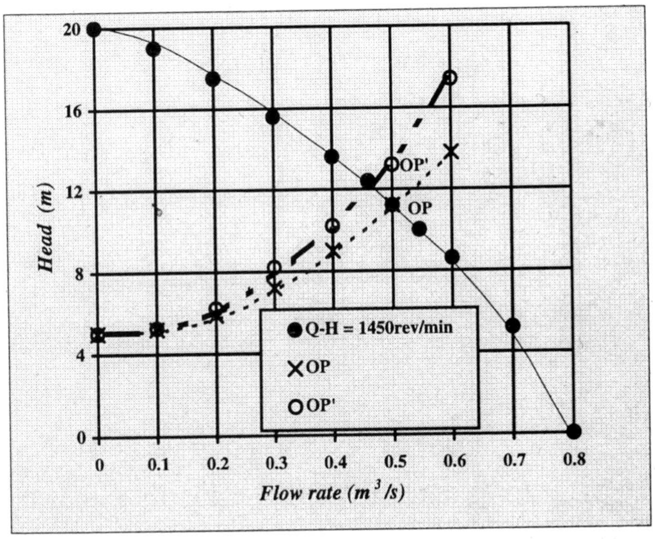

Centrifugal Pumps in Parallel

The characteristics of a centrifugal pump at constant speed are as follows:

Q (m^3/s)	0.0	0.012	0.018	0.024	0.030	0.036	0.042
H (m)	22.6	21.3	19.4	16.2	11.6	6.50	0.60
η (%)	0.0	74	86	85	70	46	8.0

The pump is used to lift water over a vertical distance of 6.5m by means of a 10cm diameter pipe, 65m long, for which the friction coefficient $f = 0.005$. (a) Determine the rate of flow and the power supplied to the pump. (b) If it is required to increase the rate of flow, and this may be achieved only be an addition of a second, identical pump (running at the same speed), investigate whether it should be connected in series or in parallel with the original pump. Justify your answer by determining the increased rate of flow and power consumed by both pumps.

To find system characteristic:

Head loss due to friction, $h_f = \dfrac{4 flV^2}{2gd} = \dfrac{32 fl\, Q^2}{\pi^2 g\, d^5}$

Total head required, $H = 6.5 + h_f$

$$h_f = \frac{32\times 0.005\times 65\times Q^2}{\pi^2\times 9.81\times 0.1^5} = 10741\times Q^2$$

Q (m^3/s)	0.01	0.02	0.03	0.04
H (m)	7.57	10.80	16.17	23.69

(a) *From operating point, $Q = 0.0267 m^3/s$, $H = 14.2m$, $\eta = 78.57$.*

Power $= \dfrac{\rho g\times QH}{\eta} = \dfrac{1000\times 9.81\times 0.0267\times 14.2}{0.785} = 4.74\,kW.$

(b) With two identical pumps running at the same speed in series the head is doubled, and in parallel the discharge is doubled.

Pumps in series: $Q = 0.033 m^3/s$, $H = 18.2m$, $\eta = 59\%$.
Pumps in parallel: $Q = 0.035\ m^3/s$, $H = 19.6m$, $\eta = 86\%$.

Power for pumps in series, P_S:

$P_S = \rho g\times QH/\eta = 10^3\times 9.81\times 0.033\times 18.2/0.59 = 10\,kW.$

Power for pumps in parallel, P_P:

$P_P = \rho g\times QH/\eta = 10^3\times 9.81\times 0.035\times 19.6/0.86 = 7.8\,kW.$

Connecting pumps in parallel is more efficient giving higher discharge at lower power.

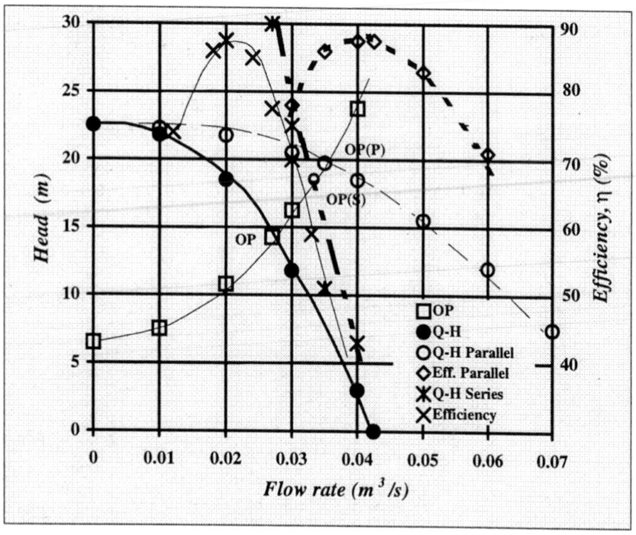

Large and Small Pumps

A centrifugal pump has an impeller diameter of 0.5m and its characteristics are as follows:

Q (m^3/s)	0.00	0.10	0.15	0.20	0.25	0.30
H (m)	40.0	37.5	33.0	27.5	20.0	12.0
η (%)	0.0	73	82	81	71	48

Draw the characteristics of a geometrically similar pump having impeller diameter of 0.562m and running at the same speed. If the two pumps operate against a system which includes a static lift of 10m and is such that the smaller pump delivers $0.22 m^3 s^{-1}$, establish the operating point of the larger pump and the operating efficiencies of both pumps. Show on your graph some lines connecting the corresponding points on the two characteristics.

Since pumps are running at the same speed, from the dimensional analysis, $Q/ND^3 = \phi\,(gH/N^2 D^2)$. Hence for dynamically similar pumps running at the same speed $Q\ \alpha\ D^3$ and $H\ \alpha\ D^2$.

The pump characteristics for $D_1 = 0.5m$ is drawn and to obtain the pump characteristic for $D_2 = 0.562m$, points A, B, C and D are selected and the similarity laws are applied as follows:

$$Q_2 = Q_1\times\left(\frac{0.562}{0.5}\right)^3 = 1.420\times Q_1$$

$$H_2 = H_1\times\left(\frac{0.562}{0.5}\right)^2 = 1.263\times H_1$$

Using these relationships points A^1, B^1, C^1 and D^1 are obtained, and through them is drawn the new characteristics for $D_2 = 0.562m$.

Operating point of smaller pump is at $Q = 0.22 m^3/s$, $H = 24m$ *and* $\eta = 77\%$.

Since the static head = 10m the system characteristic has an equation $H = KQ^2 + 10$, where $K = (24-10)/0.22^2 = 289$.

When the flow rate $Q\ (m^3/s)$ 0.1, 0.2, 0.25, 0.3, 0.35.
the operating point $H\ (m)$ 12.9, 21.6, 28.1, 36,0 45.4.

∴ ***Operating point for the larger pump is at OP^1,*** $H = 34m$.

Flow rate delivered, $Q = 0.29 m^3/s$ and $\eta = 81\%$.

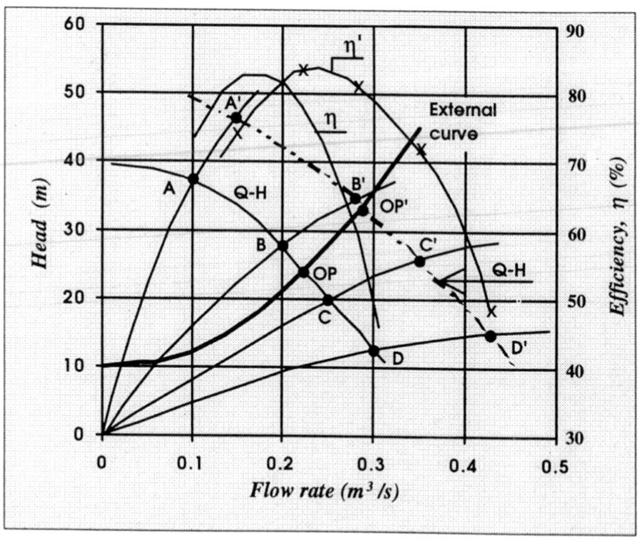

Hydraulic Machinery

Reciprocating Pumps

A pump is a machine driven by a motor to increase the pressure head of a fluid. They are be broadly divided into two general types: displacement and centrifugal. The displacement type includes the reciprocating type in which a piston or plunger alternately draws water into a cylinder on the intake stroke and then forces it out on the discharge stroke; and the rotary type, in which two rotating pistons interlock and draw water into the chamber and force it practically continuously into the discharge pipe. As the crank is rotated at uniform speed by the driving engine or motor, the plunger moves to and fro in the cylinder. On the outward stroke the partial vacuum behind the plunger enables the atmospheric pressure acting on the surface of the water in the well to force water up the suction pipe and past the suction value into the cylinder. On the inward stroke the suction value closes, the delivery value opens and the water is forced up the delivery pipe.

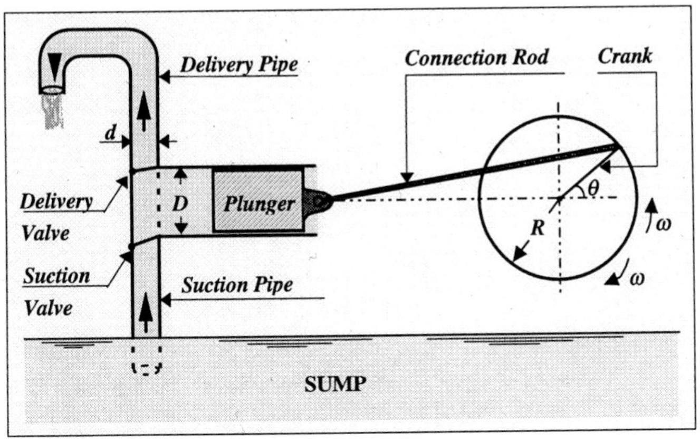

Fig.14.7- Reciprocating pump.

Let D = diameter of plunger, R = radius of crank or throw, and n = speed of crank shaft in rev/s.

Volume of water swept per stroke is $= \dfrac{\pi D^2}{4} \times 2R$

Under ideal conditions the rate of discharge per second is

$$Q = \frac{\pi D^2}{4} \times 2R_n$$

Owing to leakage past the valves and plunger and to lag in the closure of the valves, the actual discharge Q_a is always less than Q. The ratio between them is expressed in the form of a percentage slip which has the value

$$\textbf{Percentage Slip} = \frac{Volume\ Swept - Volume\ Discharge}{Volume\ Swept} \times 100$$

$$\textbf{Percentage Slip} = \left(\frac{Q - Q_a}{Q}\right) 100$$

$$\textbf{Actual Discharge} = Q_a = \frac{\pi D^2}{4} \times 2R_n \times \left(\frac{100 - Slip}{100}\right)$$

In pumps maintained in good condition the percentage slip is of the order of 2 percent or even less.

Flow Variation with Air Vessels

An air vessel is a closed chamber communicating with the delivery pipe at a point as close to the pump as possible, the upper part of the chamber being charged with compressed air, Fig.14.8. During the delivery stroke nearly all the water that the pump delivers in excess of the mean discharge is diverted into the air vessel and there stored. During the ensuing suction stroke, the pump discharge is zero and the flow in the delivery pipe is maintained by the stored water yielded up by the air vessel.

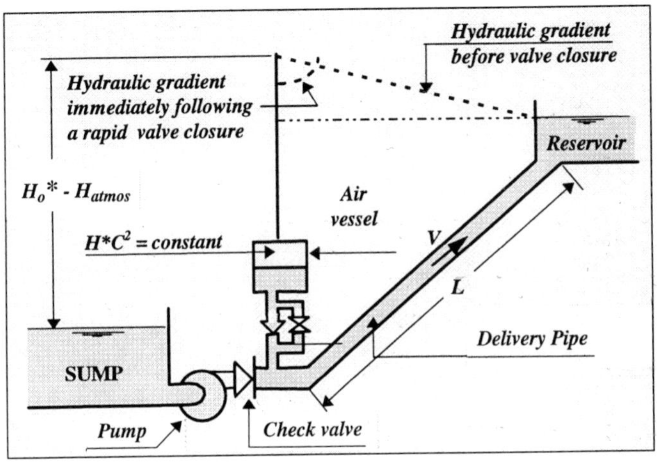

Fig.14.8- Air vessel for reciprocating pump.

The Hydraulic Press

When a pressure is applied to the surface of a fluid, it is transmitted equally to all parts of the fluid. This property is taken advantage of in many hydraulic machines, notably in the Bramah's Press. The press is a machine by which large weights may be lifted by the application of a much smaller force. A diagrammatic view of a hydraulic press is shown in Fig.14.9. The weight W is lifted by the large ram which is subjected to the high pressure of fluid. This is produced by the force (F) acting on the plunger P. The intensity of pressure is the same throughout the chamber. Therefore

$W = pA$ *and* $F = pa$. $\therefore$ $W = (A/a) \times F$

Thus the mechanical advantage obtained by means of this press is equal to the ratio of the areas of the ram and plunger.

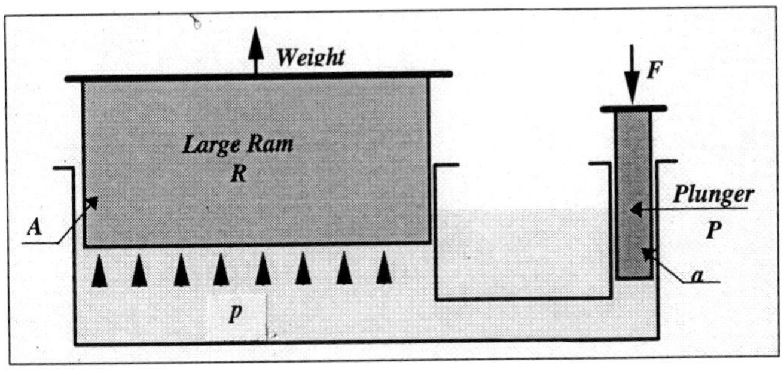

Fig.14.9- Bramah hydraulic press.

Hydraulic Accumulators

Since the delivery from a reciprocating pump is not uniform and since it is necessary to have some reserve of energy to meet a sudden or abnormal demand, some means of storing pressure energy is a necessary adjunct to the hydraulic power press. With the high pressure in common use the elevated storage tank is out of the question and the accumulator takes its place. Pressure water from the pump, is not led directly into the supply mains, but first into an accumulator from which it is taken to feed the pipeline.

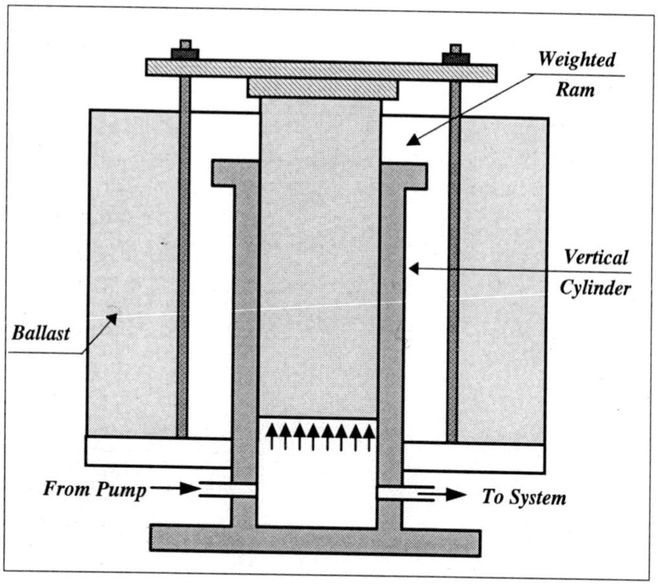

Fig.14.10- Weight-loaded hydraulic accumulator.

Usually a hydraulic accumulator, Fig.14.10, works in conjunction with the press: it permits high-pressure water to be stored in the accumulator cylinder while the press is at rest, while during the working stroke of the press it releases a supply of water which augments the supply from the pump.

An accumulator consists of a vertical cylinder fitted with a weighted ram, whose weight and area is adjusted so as to give the required pressure in the mains. As shown in the diagram, the dead load on the accumulator ram is provided by ballast contained within a plate-work shell. When the ram reaches the top of its stroke, the pump is automatically tripped out. Sealing of the rams, both of the press and of the accumulator, is ensured by the U-shaped packing rings.

Reciprocating Water Pump

A horizontal, double-acting, reciprocating water pump, with a bore and stroke of 160mm and 320mm respectively, runs at 0.4rev/s. The suction pipe is 100mm diameter, 8m long and the suction lift is 4m. There is no air vessel connected to the suction pipe. The discharge pipe is 100mm diameter, 400m long and the outlet *(at atmospheric pressure)* is 30m above the pump. A large air vessel is connected to the delivery pipe at a point 20m from the pump. The motion of the piston is simple harmonic and the friction factor f for both pipes is constant at 0.009.

Leakage of the valves reduces the theoretical volume flow rate by 2%. Assuming dynamic pressures, and inlet and outlet losses for each pipe are negligible, calculate the absolute pressure in the cylinder on each side of the piston at the beginning, middle and end of each stroke. *(Atmospheric pressure = 101 kN/m²).*

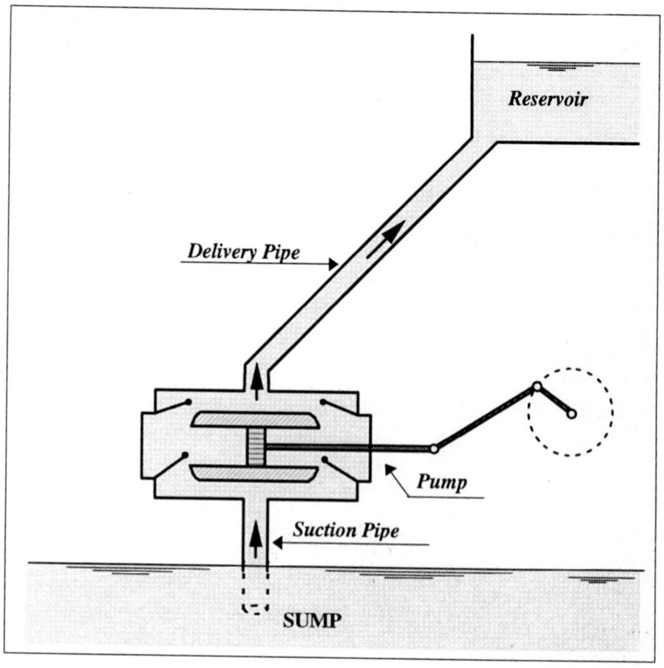

Fig.14.11- Double acting pump.

Maximum speed of water in pipe:

$$V_{max} = 0.402 \times \left(\frac{160}{100}\right)^2 = 1.028 m/s.$$

Maximum acceleration of piston $= \frac{V_\omega^2}{r} = \frac{0.402^2}{0.160} = 1.010\ m/s^2.$

Maximum acceleration of water in pipe $= 1.01 \times 1.6^2 = 2.585 m/s^2.$

$$\textbf{Flows} = 2 \times 0.98 \times \frac{\pi}{4} \times 0.160^2 \times 0.320 \times 0.4$$

$$= 5.05 \times 10^{-3} m^3/s = 5.05 l/s.$$

Mean velocity of water in pipe $= \frac{5.05 \times 10^{-3}}{\pi \times 0.1^2/4} = \frac{20.2}{10 \times \pi}$

$= 0.643 m/s.$

Static pressure, $p_{static} = 4 \times 9.81 \times 10^3 = 39.24\ kN/m^2$

Delivered pressure, $p_{deliv} = 30 \times 9.81 \times 10^3 = 294.30\ kN/m^2$

Suction, p_f *at mid stroke* $= h_f \times \rho g.$

$$h_f \times \rho g = \frac{10^3 \times 4 \times 0.009 \times 8 \times 1.028^2}{2 \times 0.100} = 1.525 kN/m^2.$$

Acceleration pressure at ends of stroke,

$$p = l_\rho \times \frac{dV_{max}}{dt} = \frac{8}{9.81} \times 2.585 \times 10^3 \times 9.81 = 20.67 kN/m^2.$$

Discharge, p_f***, in 20m of pipe to air cylinder at mid stroke,***

$$p_f = \frac{1.525 \times 20}{8} = 3.81 kN/m^2.$$

Steady: p_f ***in 400 - 20 = 380m of pipe at mid stroke,***

$$p_f = \frac{4 \times 0.009 \times 380 \times 10^3 \times 0.643^2}{2 \times 0.100} = 28.25 kN/m^2.$$

Acceleration pressure in 20m of pipe,

$$= 20 \times 10^3 \times 2.585 = 51.7 kN/m^2.$$

Ideal Fluid Theory

Flow of an Ideal Fluid

The ideal fluid theory gives solutions for flow patterns that are of value in real fluids of low viscosity when large volumes of fluid are considered. The resulting pressure and velocity distributions are valid except near the boundary walls and in the wakes of submerged bodies. In all cases the fluid is assumed ideal and two-dimensional. It has no viscosity and it is incompressible.

The paths of fluid particles can be shown by drawing streamlines (Fig.1a) such that the velocity vector is tangential to the straight or curved streamline. Thus there is no flow across a streamline and the portion of fluid lying between any two streamlines can be considered separately In two-dimensional flow the lines of motion is in one plane, usually the *x-y* plane, and the streamlines are identical in all planes parallel to this plane.

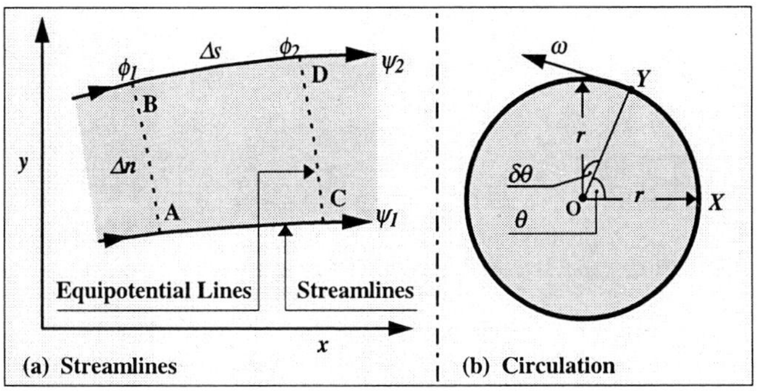

Fig.1- Flow between two streamlines and circulation.

Stream Function - Consider the flow between two streamlines shown in Fig.1a. The flux (mass per unit time) across any line *AB* in the fluid is,

$$\psi = \int_A^B v_n dn \tag{1}$$

where dn = element of line, v_n is the normal velocity component and ψ is the stream function.

Velocity Potential - If v_s is the velocity at point *B* and *ds* is a short distance along the streamline from that point then the velocity potential at point *D* is: $\phi = \int_B^D v_s ds$ (2)

Circulation and Vorticity - Consider a small circuit with radius *r* round any point *O* (Fig.1b). The component of the relative velocity of *YO* along the circuit is ωr where ω is the angular velocity at *Y*. The small distance $ds = rd\theta$. The **circulation** for this circle is: $\int_o^{2\pi} \omega r \times rd\theta = r^2 \times \int_o^{2\pi} \omega d\theta = 2\pi r^2 \omega_a$ (3)

where ω_a is the average angular velocity of particles on the circle. The **vorticity** at any point is defined as the circulation per unit area round a small circuit and is equal to $(2r^2\omega_a)/r^2 = 2\omega_a$. When the vorticity at all points in the fluid is zero, the motion is said to be **irrotational.**

Theoretical Combination of Streamlines

Uniform Flow: For velocity *U* parallel to positive direction of *x*-axis (Fig.2a), $\psi = Uy$. For velocity *V* parallel to positive direction of *y*-axis, $\psi = -Vx$. The numbering and sign conventions are shown in Fig.2.

Source and Sink - For two-dimensional flow, a source is a point from which the fluid flows radially out in all directions (Fig.2c) For an output or strength of the source *m*, the stream function can be shown to be $\psi = m\theta/2\pi$; where θ = angular polar co-ordinate. The velocity at any radius *r* is $\omega = m/2\pi$; radially outwards. A *sink* is a point to which the fluid flows radially from all directions (Fig.2) It is the exact converse of a source, and $\psi = -m\theta/2\pi$.

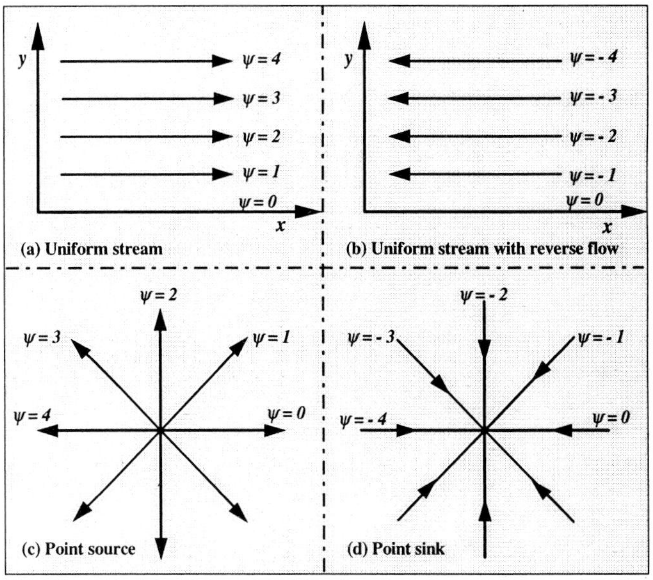

Fig.2- Graphical plotting of streamlines for uniform stream, source and sink.

If source and sink are of equal strengths the streamlines are a system of co-axial circles passing through positions of source and sink as shown in Fig.3a.

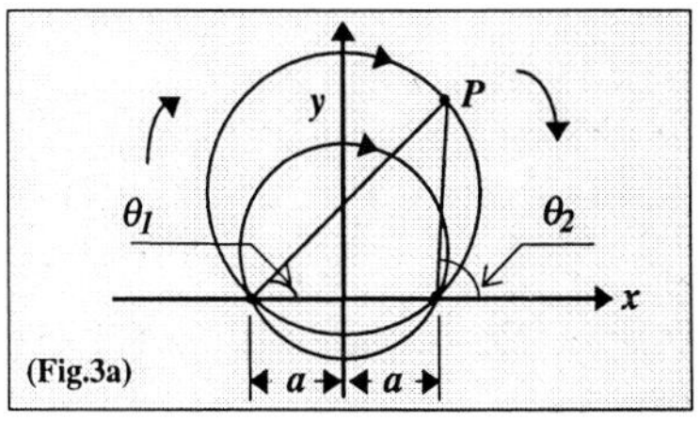

(Fig.3a)

$$\psi = \frac{m}{2\pi} \times (\theta_1 - \theta_2) = \frac{m}{2\pi} \times \tan^{-1}\left(\frac{2ay}{x^2 + y^2 - a^2}\right) \tag{4}$$

Source in uniform flow
The dividing streamline (Fig.3b) is a 'half-body' shape, the size of which is determined by the strength of the source and the velocity of uniform flow.

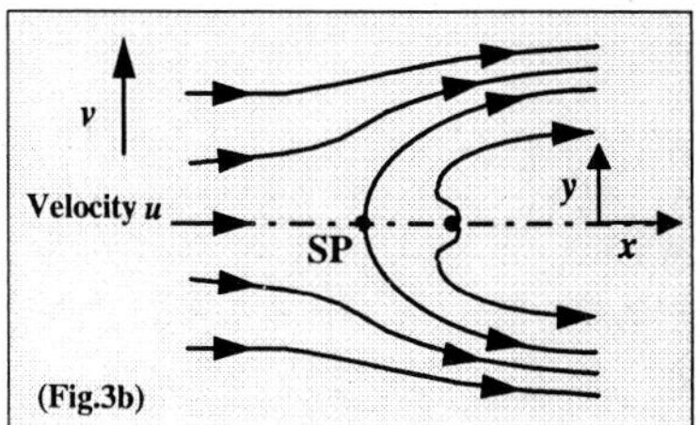

(Fig.3b)

The stream function $\psi = Uy - \frac{m\theta}{2\pi} = Uy - \frac{m}{2\pi} \times \tan^{-1}\left(\frac{y}{x}\right)$ (5)

The horizontal and vertical components of velocities are:

$$u = U - \frac{m}{2\pi} \times \left(\frac{x}{x^2 + y^2}\right) \quad \text{and} \quad v = \frac{m}{2\pi} \times \left(\frac{y}{x^2 + y^2}\right) \qquad (6)$$

The stagnation point *SP* is on the x-axis where $y = 0$ and $v = 0$. Therefore, $u = U - (m/2\pi x)$. Thus on the boundary where $u = 0$, the position of the source from the stagnation point is $m/2\pi U$.

Graphical Combination of Streamlines

Fundamental streamline patterns are usually compounded to form a single set of streamlines representing a practical flow problem. Suppose two such patterns are drawn (Fig.4a), each with its streamlines having the same interval of ψ and numbered consecutively. At the intersection of streamlines the total flux of the combined flow will be the algebraic sum of each individual flux. Thus, if all points having the same total flux are labelled, a smooth curve joining them will be a streamline for the resultant motion (Fig.4a).

Compounding Source and Sink

The fluid enters the space between two parallel plates by a small hole *A*, the source and leaves it by a small hole at *B*, the sink (Fig.4b). The strengths, i.e. the flux from *A* and to *B*, are equal but opposite in sign. At *A* fluid would flow radially in all directions. At *A* and *B* set off straight lines at equal angles 15° and number them *1, 2, 3*. Then draw smooth curves through the intersections where the numbering on the intersecting lines adds up to *2, 3, 4, 5, 6, 7, etc.*, these being the flux numbers of the curves $\psi_1 + \psi_2$ curves, the increment unit being $15^o/360^o$ or *1/24* of the strength of *A* or *B*.

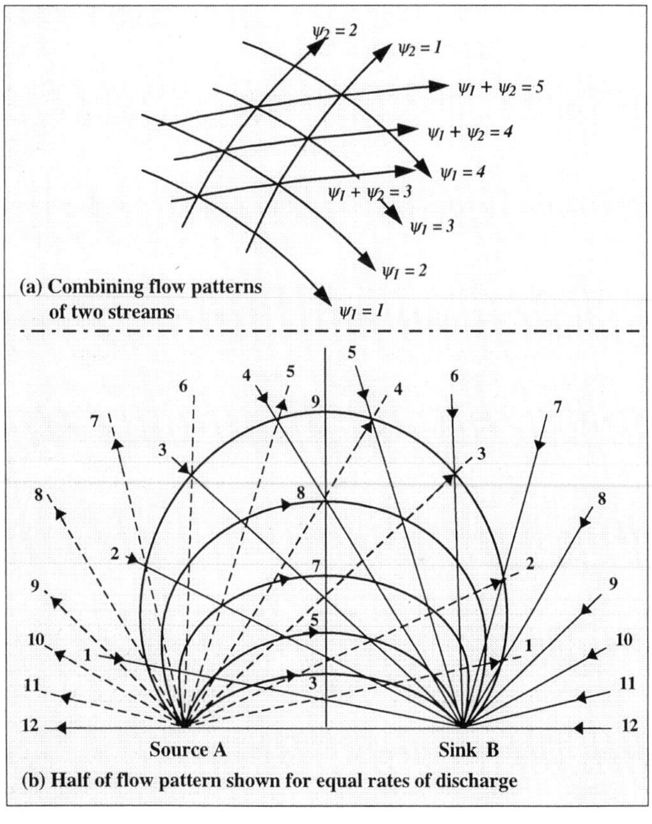

Fig.4- Graphical plotting of streamlines.

Combination of Sink in Uniform Stream

A sink is a point into which the fluid flows radially in all directions as shown in Fig.5. The total flux across any circle is equal to the strength of the sink *m*. For a circle of radius *r*,

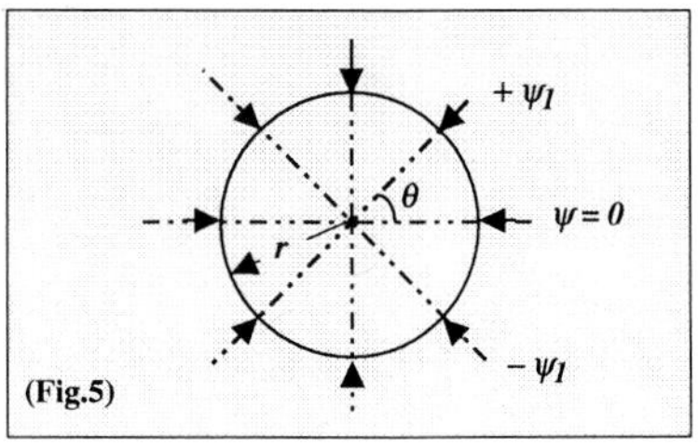

$m = -2\pi r\omega$. Over angle θ, from $\psi = 0$, the next streamline is given by the flux across the arc *XY* or $\psi_1 = -mr\theta/2\pi r = -m\theta/2\pi$; where θ lies between $+\pi$; and $-\pi$.

The streamlines resulting from a uniform stream flowing over a sink are shown in Fig.6. The scale for the uniform stream is 35mm = 10 units of flow. The sink has a strength of 16 units. Half of the flow pattern is shown from $\psi = 0$ to $\psi = -8$ by increment of $\psi = -1$. For the sink strength of 16 and intervals of $\psi = 1$, we have $-16\theta/2\pi; = 1$ or $\theta = -\pi/8 = 22.5^o$. The straight radial lines are drawn into the point sink at equal intervals of 22.5^o. These are combined with the uniform horizontal stream to produce the resultant flow pattern with intervals of $\psi = -1$. A practical example of such a pattern is in ground water for a well in a uniform stream in a confined aquifer or permeable stratum *(see Chapter 22 of Book Two)*.

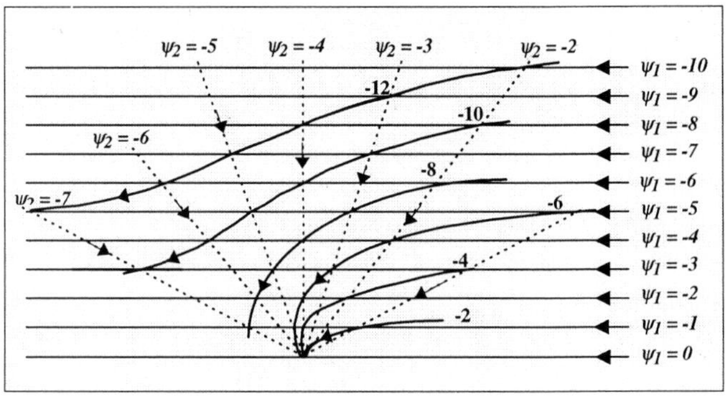

Fig.6- Streamlines for a sink in a uniform stream.

Flow Patterns Around Solid Objects

The above methods of drawing streamlines may be extended to plotting flow patterns around solid objects placed in a fluid flow. The patterns are all applicable to "perfect" fluids. Real fluids, however, can have appreciably different properties to ideal fluids. They are viscous, mostly turbulent and have friction against solid surfaces. It would then not be surprising to find the flow patterns in real fluids are somewhat different from the ideal fluid patterns around the same solid configuration and they are normally determined by laboratory experiments (Fig.7).

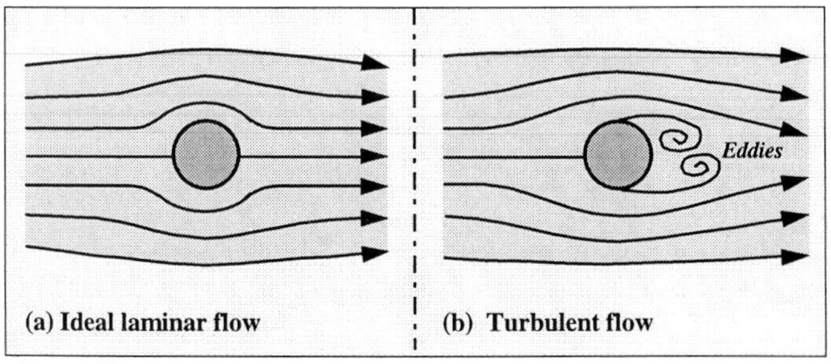

Fig.7- Flow past a cylinder.

History of Hydraulics

It is interesting and important to know about the development of the subject of hydraulics and the scientists and engineers whose names are associated with it. The term hydraulics is derived from a Greek word meaning water. The history of hydraulic projects dates back to the ancient civilisations. The Sumerians and Babylonians along the Euphrates and Tigris rivers created a network of irrigation canals dating from 4000BC. The greatest of the channels was the 400km long Nahrwan Canal which is still identifiable today.

Large irrigation works, including dams and canals, were built by the ancient Egyptians about 2500BC. Recently the irrigation systems of the Incas (2000 year old) in South America have been restored to working order to provide much needed progress in a rural economy. The Marib masonry dam in the Kingdom of Sheba, Yemen, supported an extensive irrigation system for nearly 1500 years until its failure in 550AD. The kanats of Persia, dating back 3000 years, were a system of tunnels and adits which served both as infiltration galleries and underground transmission tunnels without evaporation. There is evidence of irrigation works and earth dams built in Sri Lanka around 300BC. In India, the Bhojpur reservoir and dam were constructed around 1100AD creating a huge storage.

The contributions of the Greeks and Romans were extensive. Archimedes (287-212BC), first postulated the laws of hydrostatics and flotation and invented the screw pump which is still used today. From about 300BC to 150AD, the Romans built water works for the City of Rome, and there are remains of over 200 aqueducts and drainage systems in Europe credited to them. They first invented the hand pump with wide applications all over the globe.

During the 17th century, Galileo (1564-1642) using the Tower of Pisa, discovered the law of falling bodies. Around 1640 Torricelli applied it to the concept of the velocity head. Galileo also performed experiments on flow of water through an orifice at the bottom of a tank and observed that the rate of flow is proportional to the square root of the head.

In 1732, Henri Pitot (1695-1771), the French inventor, introduced the Pitot tube for measuring the velocity head. In 1738, the Swiss physicist, Daniel Bernoulli (1718-1798), derived the total head equation bearing his name. Leonhard Euler about 1755 founded the mathematical study of hydrodynamics for the flow of ideal frictionless fluids. The mathematics of classical hydrodynamics was later advanced by the British scientists Kelvin and Lamb. Other contributors included the French physicist J L Poiseuille (1799-1869) who worked on laminar flow in pipes.

The development of engineering hydraulics started during the 18th century with the increasing demands of the Industrial Revolution in Europe for generating power using the water wheel, pipes and channels. Antoine de Chezy (1718-1798), Chief Engineer of Paris Water Works, carried out tests on channels in 1775 and developed his equation. Later, the Italian engineer, Venturi (1746-1822), described and analysed the hydraulic jump using the momentum equation.

The Water Works at London Bridge for the supply of the City of London with water from the River Thames, showing the water wheel with lifting apparatus (1749).

The French engineer, Henry Darcy (1803 - 1858), developed his equations for flow in pipes and seepage through soils. Bazin (1829 - 1917), carried on the work of Darcy. Other engineers continued the development with the American Engineer, J B Francis inventing the Francis turbine; and Robert Manning, Chief Engineer of the Irish Public Works Department, publishing in 1889 his formula for flow in open channels.

In Great Britain, classical experiments by the naval architect William Froude about 1870 and by the physicist Osborne Reynolds about 1883, led to the laws of model testing as an important engineering tool. The recognition by Professor Reynolds (1842-1912), of a non-dimensional parameter, called the Reynolds number, constituted a major development for the criterion of the similarity of motion for all fluids. Lord Rayleigh extended Reynolds' work and developed the method of dimensions, which has provided a generalisation in the subject of fluid mechanics and hydraulics.

Experimental work on models towed in water tanks was developed by Froude (1810-1879) for the design of ships. Other factors contributing to the development of the subject included the increase in the use of hydraulic machinery and steam turbines for the conveyance of fluids and their actions within the prime movers themselves.

Early in the 20th century, Ludwig Prandtl (1875-1953), in Germany, made a great contribution to fluid mechanics in the development of the boundary layer theory and the fundamental laws of flow in pipes. His work was extended by CM White under whom the author received his research training at Imperial College, London.

Today much of the research work is organised in teams working mainly in universities and government departments all over the world. In this respect, the US Bureau of Reclamation, the UK Hydraulic Research Station at Wallingford, the Danish Hydraulic Institute, the Delft Hydraulics Laboratories in the Netherlands and Sogreah in Grenoble, France, have made substantial contributions in physical model testing and computer modelling for engineering design.

Bibliography and Notation

Bibliography

Fluid Mechanics
VL Streeter and EB Wylie, 1985.

Mechanics of Fluids
IH Shames, 1992.

Fluid Mechanics
FM White, 1993.

Open Channel Hydraulics
RH French, 1994.

Hydraulic Engineering
JA Roberson, JJ Cassidy and MH Chaudhry , 1994.

Notation and Symbols

The symbols used in this book are mainly standard notation. Since the number of variables exceed the number of symbols available, some symbols represent more than one meaning. However, these occur in different parts of the book. Suffixes 1,2,3, etc., are used to meet particular needs, e.g. at inlet and outlet of control sections or volumes. The symbols ln and log refer to natural logarithm to the base *e* and to the base 10 respectively. The symbols are clearly shown on the diagrams throughout the book.

STANDARD SYMBOLS

Symbol	Quantity
A	Cross-sectional area
C_D	Drag Coefficient
C_L	Lift Coefficient
C_c	Coefficient of Contraction
C_d	Coefficient of Discharge
C_v	Coefficient of Velocity
C	Chezy Coefficient
D	Drag Force
d	Diameter
E	Modulus of Elasticity
F	Force
F	Froude Number
f	Darcy's coefficient of friction, porosity
G	Velocity Gradient
g	Gravitational Acceleration
H	Total Head
h	Static Head
h_f	Friction Head Loss
i	Slope of Hydraulic Gradient
K	Bulk Modulus
k	Mean Height of Roughness Projection
l	Length
M	Mach Number
N	Revolutions per Minute
P	Power
P	Wetted Perimeter
p	Pressure
Q	Volumetric Flow Rate
q	Volumetric Flow Rate per Unit Width
R	Characteristic Gas Constant
R	Hydraulic Radius (Hydraulic Mean Depth)
R	Reynolds Number
r	Radius
S	Bed Slope
s	Volume
T	Time
t	Thickness, Time
u	Velocity
V	Mean Velocity
w	Specific Weight
z	Potential Head

GREEK SYMBOLS

Symbol	Name	Quantity
α	Alpha	Angle
β	Beta	Angle
δ	Delta	Boundary Layer Thickness
δ^*	Delta	Displacement Thickness
η	Eta	Efficiency
θ	Theta	Angle
μ	Mu	Dynamic Viscosity
ν	Nu	Kinematic Viscosity
π	Pi	Constant (3.14)
ρ	Rho	Density
σ	Sigma	Surface Tension
τ	Tau	Shear Stress
ϕ	Phi	Potential Function
ψ	Psi	Stream Function
ω	Omega	Angular Velocity

CONVERSION FACTORS

Imperial Units		SI Units
in =	25.4	*mm*
ft	305	*mm*
ft	0.305	*m*
yd	0.914	*m*
in^2	645	mm^2
in^2	6.452	cm^2
in^2	0.000645	m^2
ft^2	0.0929	m^2
yd^2	0.836	m^2
in^3	16400	mm^3
in^3	16.4	cm^3
in^3	0.0000164	m^3
ft^3	0.0283	m^3
yd^3	0.765	m^3
litre	0.001	m^3
in^3	0.0164	*litre*
gallon	4.55	*litre*
ft^3	28.3	*litre*
yd^3	765	*litre*
cm^3	0.0001	*litre*
oz	0.0283	*kg*
lb	0.454	*kg*
lb/ft^3	16.0	kg/m^3
lb/in^3	27.7	kg/m^3
lbf	4.45	*N*
kgf	9.81	*N*
tonf	9.96	*kN*
lbf/in^2	0.00689	N/mm^2 (MN/m^2)
$tonf/in^2$	15.4	N/mm^2
lbf/in^2	6896	N/m^2
lbf/ft^2	47.6	N/m^2
lbf/in^2	0.0703	kgf/cm^2
$tonf/in^2$	1.575	kgf/mm^2
Pa	0.0000101	kgf/cm^2
Pa	0.000145	lbf/in^2
ft/water	0.0305	kgf/cm^2
ft/water	2.99	kN/m^2
ft lb	1.36	*Nm*
^oF	$\frac{^oF - 32}{1.8}$	^oC
^oK	$^oK - 273$	^oC

Index to Book One

Acknowledgements and Information

It is a pleasure to express my gratitude to my institution, the University of East London, and to many individuals and organisations who assisted in the preparation of the books. I owe a tremendous debt to several colleagues who by personal kindness have proof read the manuscripts. In particular I should like to express my gratitude to Dr John Grubert who read the manuscripts thoroughly and checked all the calculations. They were carefully reviewed by and helpful suggestions received from Professor Reginald Schofield. Many of his and other colleagues' suggestions have been incorporated in the texts. I also wish to thank sincerely Dr Paul Smith for his constant encouragement and proof reading. To Professor Barry Gorham who proof read and commented constructively I express my deepest appreciation.

Special thanks are due to London University where I served as "Recognised Teacher" and Chairman of the Civil Engineering Sub-committee of Staff Examiners for the internal and external BSc(Eng) degrees.

I am of course much indebted to previous authors. The author of any text book depends largely upon their predecessors and I have gained much from the works of Addison, Rouse, Morris and many others. I am also very grateful to many individuals who have helped in the production of the books. Dr Kamel Hachouf assisted greatly in the preparation of the two books. For his help and understanding I am most grateful.

Many thanks are due to Mr Tom Juffs for his unstinting support and help throughout the project. Much typing and amendments were patiently made by Mrs Linda Day to whom I am most grateful. I would like to thank also, Mrs Joy O'Neill for her assistance and typing.

For the preparation of the excellent index I am grateful to Mr John Noble. I would like to express my thanks to Mr Terence O'Connell and Mr Tom Samson (Chorley & Handford) for their loyal support and assistance. For advice and assistance I am grateful to Mr Peter Clarke, Mr John Bell, Mr Paul Campfield and Mr Martin Snelling.

I acknowledge with many thanks the assistance I have received from past and present colleagues including Professor Brian Clayton, Dr John Douglas, Mr Robert Armstrong, Mr John Davies, Mr Geoffrey Faulkener, Mr Stephen Day, Dr Richard Jacob and Mr Frank Rendell. Appreciation is expressed to colleagues who gave general advice, including Mr Cliff Archer, Dr David Hardwick, Mr Bert Crookes, Professor W Jenkins, Professor Ben Barr, and others.

I wish to thank firms and research organisations for the useful information and photographs inserted in the books. These include Hydraulic Research at Wallingford, EPSRC, USBR, Anglian Water, Thames Water, Southwest Water, Northwest Water, Water Research (SA), Montgomery Watson, British Gas, WS Atkins, Binnie & Partners, Knight Piesold Taywood Engineering, Roger Prestons, Noble Denton, John Brown Engineering, British Rail Research, Kellogg Ltd, Wellpore Ltd, Proudman Oceanographic Laboratory etc. Thanks are also due to the Institution of Civil Engineers, Institution of Mechanical Engineers and the American Society of Civil Engineers.

I would like to express my sincere gratitude to my wife Irene for her patience and understanding far beyond the call of duty. To members of the public and students worldwide who have kindly supported my books, some of which are in their seventh and eighth editions, I express my deepest appreciation.

I have found the field of hydraulic engineering both interesting and challenging. I commend it to young engineers and hope that the books will generate interest and inspiration for the generations of engineers in the 21st century.

Hydraulic Book Series by Professor Naib

For Education, Scholarship and Professional Advancement

Book One: **Fluid Mechanics, Hydraulics and Environmental Engineering (ISBN 1 8745 36 066)**

- Basic Fluid Mechanics for all branches of engineering.
- User friendly concise text aimed at first and second year undergraduate and diploma students.
- Fundamental principles, analysis and application to solution of engineering problems and design.
- Topics spanning the interests of aeronautical, chemical, civil, and mechanical engineers.
- Self contained chapters to allow the lecturer flexibility in organising a course.
- Material for a two year fluid mechanics and hydraulics course.
- Large number of solved examples plus problems for students to practice.
- Excellent diagrams to make the understanding of the theory and problems easy.
- Concise theory is given without unnecessary details.
- Two companion books, one deals with basic topics and the second with advanced specific topics and design.
- Advantage of continuity with the second book when teachers are recommending course books.

Book Two: **Applied Hydraulics, Hydrology and Environmental Engineering (ISBN 1 8745 36 058)**

- Concise treatment with solved examples at an attractive price.
- User friendly handbook aimed at final year degree, diploma and masters levels.
- Comprehensive references for the practising engineer.
- Inclusion of design examples with a discussion of design principles.
- Class notes, solution manual and homework exercises for use by lecturers and course tutors.
- Self contained chapters for selection by the lecturer.
- Books 1 and 2 serve the needs of students for the full period of their studies. Each book substantially stands alone.
- Helps students to gain a broad overview of the subject and also provides detailed treatment of specialist topics.
- Provides students with an authoritative reference book which they can use after they leave university.

Book Three: **Jet Mechanics and Hydraulic Structures (ISBN 0 9019 87 832)**

- Manual of scholarly works for research engineers, masters students and practising engineers.
- Experimental and photographic techniques explained.
- Summary of research on free turbulent jets.
- Hydraulic design of control and transition structures.
- Research on rectangular and trapezoidal channel expansions.
- Research on surface plane jet, parallel wall and deflected jets.
- Research on jet dispersion in channels and dissipation in deep pools and chambers.
- Research on diffusion downstream of submerged sluice gates.
- Research and design of hydraulic energy dissipators, drop structures, conduit outfalls and supercritical diffusers.

Please Order through: Research Books, P. O. Box 82, Romford, Essex RM6 5BY, Great Britain.